By Eleanor Perényi

Liszt

Liszt by Devéria, 1832. Bibliothèque Nationale, Paris. Photo: Harlingue-Viollet

Liszt

The Artist
As Romantic Hero

ELEANOR PERÉNYI

AN ATLANTIC MONTHLY PRESS BOOK
Little, Brown and Company—Boston—Toronto

FIRST EDITION

T 11/74

The author wishes to thank Jacques Vier for his permission to quote in her translation, passages from his *La Comtesse d'Agoult et son temps,* Paris: Librairie Armand Colin, 6 vols., 1955–63, and Nouvelles Editions Latines for permission to quotes, in her translation, passages from *Les Romantiques et la musique,* by Thérèse Marix-Spire, Paris: 1954.

Passages from Balzac's *Béatrix,* translated by Rosamond and Simon Harcourt-Smith, are reprinted with permission of Elek Books Limited, London.

Quotations from *George Sand: Correspondance;* edited by Georges Lubin, 10 vols., Paris, 1967. © Editions Garnier Frères, Paris, Edition Georges Lubin, collection des Classiques Garnier. Reprinted by permission.

Where an English language edition is not cited, the translations are the author's own.

LIBRARY OF CONGRESS CATALOGING IN PUBLICATION DATA
Perényi, Eleanor Spencer (Stone), date
   Liszt: the artist as romantic hero.
   "An Atlantic Monthly Press book."
   Bibliography: p.
   1. Liszt, Franz, 1811–1886. I. Title.
ML410.L7P3   780'.92'4 [B]   74-8916
ISBN 0-316-69910-1

ATLANTIC–LITTLE, BROWN BOOKS
ARE PUBLISHED BY
LITTLE, BROWN AND COMPANY
IN ASSOCIATION WITH
THE ATLANTIC MONTHLY PRESS

Designed by Susan Windheim

*Published simultaneously in Canada
by Little, Brown & Company (Canada) Limited*

PRINTED IN THE UNITED STATES OF AMERICA

For William Abrahams

Contents

Illustrations

C'est un grand malheur de perdre, par notre caractère, les droits que nos talents nous donnent sur la société.

— Chamfort

PART ONE

Romantic Origins
(1811–1833)

Chapter 1

LISZT WAS the first musician to benefit from the Romantic cult of genius, to be an international celebrity lionized by society, fought over by women, decorated by kings and governments like a military hero. Like Byron, he invented a type that long outlasted him, surviving in popular mythology as the original long-hair, destroyer of grand pianos, the Don Juan of music.

All his life he was haunted by this self-created demon who even now blights his genius and obscures his stature as one of the innovators in nineteenth-century music. As composer, conductor, discoverer of talent, polemicist, he has yet to find his place. He comes down to us through his sins of personality in the guise of charlatan, the supreme poseur, when he was nothing so simple. He was the child of French Romanticism, and its prisoner. "The mad, handsome, ugly, enigmatic, terrible, often very childish child of his time," Heine called him, an epithet that implies his vices: virtuosity and *folie de grandeur.* "Being nobody, it is necessary for me to become somebody," he told his French mistress, and it was the battle cry of the post-Napoleonic age in which he grew up. Balzac had the same idea: "What do I want? I want ortolans; for I have only two passions, love and fame." Berlioz informed his parents: "I am voluntarily driven toward a magnificent career. . . ."

The Romantic ego is insufferable and Liszt is of all Romantics the most insufferable. He had to be. He had somehow to keep afloat in the era that replaced the diligence with the steam engine, invented the telegraph and the universal press. He was a witness at the birth of the philistine. The pitfalls are familiar now that we know about mass taste and the maw of fame that devours all but the most resistant of culture heroes, the blowing up of a personality until it bursts. He had no such examples to go by. He was born two years after Haydn's death; he died the year after Alban Berg's birth, and there is no comparable gap in artistic chronology. The risks he ran were new, and partly of his own making. Yet he stayed the course. He didn't die young like Chopin or go mad like Schumann. He outlived Balzac, his coeval, by forty years; he had a happier life than Berlioz. And in the end he paid his debts, balancing his accounts in the disappointments of old age.

It needed more than genius or professionalism to get through the nineteenth century and the birth-pangs of the modern world. "My son will write whatever kind of composition you consider most profitable." Thus Leopold Mozart to the Leipzig publishers, vouching for a journeyman's modesty inconceivable to Liszt and most of his contemporaries, who may not have been more embattled than their predecessors but thought they were, and the difference was crucial: a world of self-consciousness had intervened. Not only did they feel entitled to much higher rewards than had formerly accrued to the artist, they attached an altogether different significance to his metier. No longer was it a question of giving pleasure to the man or institution who could afford to pay for it. Romantic art was its own justification, its creator at once outside and superior to society's requirements. Above all, he was an innovator, an emphasis that was in itself a new thing, a kind of psychological symptom not unconnected with the ideal – derived from technology – of progress. Novelty, invention, were an obsession with a composer like Berlioz, who often seemed to rest his whole case on it – for example, this: "When Monteverdi tried to add the chord of the unprepared dominant seventh, criticism and denunciation . . . were heaped on him. . . . When melody came to prevail, the cry was that art was degraded and ruined, and the sanctity of the rules abolished – it was clear that all was lost. Next in turn came modulation. . . . The innovator would keep saying, 'Do but listen; see how . . . delightful it sounds.' 'That is not the point,' he was told. 'This modulation is prohibited. . . .'" [1]

Historically, this is moonshine. Monteverdi worked for musically sophisticated princes who made him rich and famous. Berlioz was projecting his own experience on a past to which it did not correspond. Novelty, in short, was not novel. The change was in the artist's situation. For El Greco one king of Spain was enough. It was his release from patronage that drove the artist and particularly the composer into the wilderness. Until the beginning of the nineteenth century, instrumental music was composed almost exclusively for a limited and for the most part knowledgeable élite – people who were themselves intelligent amateurs and practitioners. After 1800, the conditions altered and so did the type of the professional musician.

The big-scale personality is a rarity in music before Beethoven. Family men who love an off-color joke, the humdrum geniuses of the seventeenth and eighteenth centuries turn out their masterpieces by what seems like automatic writing. They don't read books or notice landscapes; they aren't recognizably men of culture or special sensibility. The interpretive yield from a study of their lives is close to zero, so large is the apparent rift between the commonplace little man and his glorious works. (The prevalence of the *Wunderkind* has of course always suggested that musical talent operates on some inaccessible circuitry, quite different from that of the other arts. We all know, more or less, how a picture is painted or a book written — but there are no Sunday composers, nor is it said that every man has at least one symphony in him.) Not until the advent of the Romantics do we begin to see a connection between a man's life and his music — and lives that are interesting in themselves: Liszt, Chopin, Berlioz, Wagner, are almost outlandishly individualized, and in their lives we can trace, or think we can, some of the sources for what they composed. The creative mystery is diminished but we are on a familiar road.

The composer took so long to reach this point because of the quirk in social history that made music the last of the arts to be democratized. Under the patronage system, unless like Gesualdo he was born a prince himself, the musician was somewhere between the cabinetmaker, say, and the animal trainer. He belonged to the lower orders, not only by birth (and a surprising number were the sons of domestic servants) but in the estimation of society. The famous story of Mozart being made to sit with the valets in Colloredo's household has point not because the fact was unusual — Haydn lived over the stables at Eszterháza — but because he put up a fuss and was pitched into the street for doing so. The episode in fact gives a wrong idea of how the system worked, which on the whole was very well. The Colloredos were rare, the climate generally benign. Over the centuries it produced unprecedented storehouses of talent in families like the Bachs. That family tree had fifty-three names when Johann Sebastian compiled it in 1735 — an exceptional record; but there were six Scarlattis, seven Purcells, eight Couperins, twelve Webers.

In effect, there was a kind of trade union, European in scope, that in its heyday (say the middle of the eighteenth century) offered a number of benefits. Nobody, for instance, starved. The musician died in rags much less often than the poet, suicides were virtually unknown, and neglect of the kind that Schubert suffered exceedingly rare — neither he nor Mozart is typical, each in his way being a casualty of the interregnum. Since most of those who kept musical establishments did so because they loved music, patrons and patronized spoke a common language, a situation the modern composer might well envy. Haydn testified to how satisfactory it could be: "My prince was always satisfied with my works. I had not only the encouragement of constant approval, but as conductor of an orchestra, I could make experiments, observe what made an effect and what weakened it. . . . I was cut off from the world, there was no one to confuse or torment me, and I was forced to become *original*." [2] (It should be added that one of the richest families in Europe paid him seventy-eight pounds a year and kept him in a state amounting to captivity.)

What followed was a liberation of sorts as music was urbanized, conservatories founded, concert halls built. It has been pointed out that the modern symphony orchestra is about the same age as the steam engine, and its invention was concurrent with other changes. The old sources of talent began to dry up. There were no more musical dynasties after 1800. Most of the composers born after that date belonged to the same class as their future audiences: the bourgeoisie. They were the children of schoolmasters (Chopin), doctors (Berlioz), publishers (Schumann), bankers (Mendelssohn, Meyerbeer). Though scarcely treated as social equals by the aristocracy — Liszt was the first to crash that barrier — there was no question either of their dining in the servants' hall. They were educated men, who travelled for other purposes than to earn a living on the concert circuit; and they were prepared to assert themselves as artists, not merely craftsmen or furnishers of a commodity.

Had music been in the same stage of development that literature and painting approximately were, all might have been well. But the princely establishments had done their work too effectively. However arbitrarily administered, they had had a hothouse effect that enabled the composer (unless he wrote for the opera) to ignore popular taste and to pursue his discoveries pretty much as he chose. The consequence was that instrumental music by the time of Beethoven's death had outstripped the general public's capacity to understand it. It acquired a wide audience at the moment when it could least accommodate it, with the predictable result that it failed where a play like Victor Hugo's *Hernani*, touted as a revolutionary drama like no other before it — and very few since — had no difficulty scoring a popular success. By contrast, Berlioz's *Symphonie fantastique*, presented the same year and far more authentically revolutionary in form and content, depended on a knowledgeable group of insiders for its limited impact.

Hugo and his fellow writers, notably Gautier and Gérard de Nerval, were nevertheless the formulators of the dogma of modernity. They constructed the apparatus of the avant-garde as we know it and were the first to pronounce that art, like politics, is divided into parties: conservatives who elaborate on the past and a militant élite that pioneers the future. Artists have always belonged to one or the other category and sometimes both. But the reduction of these facts to doctrine *was* new and profoundly affected the two composers, Liszt and Berlioz, whose friendships among the Romantic writers exposed them to it. Berlioz, by nature a solitary and a less diversely gifted personality than Liszt, discarded this early influence. Liszt's education at the hands of the Romantics left marks on him that endured well into middle age and never entirely disappeared.

"It was this air he carried about with him . . . of knowing strange and far-off things, of having a horizon in which the Parisian horizon — so familiar, so wanting in mystery, so perpetually *exploité* — easily lost itself, that distinguished him. . . . He was not all there, as the phrase is; he had something behind, in reserve. . . ."[3]

This is Henry James, and the subject is Turgenev, who arrived in Paris forty years after Liszt. It will do just as well for the young Magyar who conquered Paris in the 1830's. He was fortunate. The French had not always welcomed exotics, who in previous centuries had passed for barbarians as well. But to the generation reared on Byron's bandit heroes, Chateaubriand's Gallicized redskins and Fenimore Cooper's wooden ones, strangeness was an advantage. Within a year of each other (1831–1832), Victor Hugo introduced the gypsy into literature and Delacroix went off to Morocco to paint the Moors. Liszt was not quite a noble savage but in these contexts he was at least a kind of white Mohican.

Had he chanced to be small and hideous, his exotic origins would no doubt have gone unnoticed. He was, however, a beautiful young man, tall and fair with candid blue eyes, eminently suited to play a leading part in a society that set a high value on physical allure. The Romantics were indifferent to the charms of old age, personified in the wizened countenances of the *philosophes*. To be "beautiful, free and young" was in Gautier's phrase the ideal, and a gnome like Sainte-Beuve endured agonies in consequence. Equally desirable was it to have genius, or if not what is often an acceptable substitute — temperament. Liszt had both.

Paris had its *émigré* artists even then: Heine, self-exiled in 1831, the year of the Polish insurrection whose failure also brought Adam Mickiewicz and many other Poles. A high proportion of the salons where artists were cultivated belonged to women who preferred not to live under Russian or Austrian rule: Cristina Belgiojoso, Marie Kalergis, Marcelline Czartoryska, Delphine Potocka. But Liszt was not part of an emigration, political or otherwise. He was brought to Paris as a child prodigy and for largely accidental reasons remained there. Nor did Hungarians then enjoy the glamorous reputation, the sorrowful prestige attached to dissident Poles, Piedmontese and others. He represented himself; but in the witness box of French life, even this must be explained: prophet art thou, bird or devil? One must know the answer or think up a good story.

He thought one up. He let it be surmised that he was part gypsy and descended from a noble family fallen on hard times. Neither was remotely true, which made no difference because no one knew anything about

Magyars anyway. (Nor did Liszt.) Ethnology didn't exist as a science and the times were infected with Hegelian theorizing about "epic" races. Fanny Lewald, a minor German novelist who knew Liszt well in the 1850's, thought he looked Sarmatian, whatever that meant. Saint-Saëns wrote that his name was "sliced by the *z* of the Slavs as if by a furrow of lightning." His modern biographers haven't improved matters much. Ernest Newman dwells on the something "not German" in his character, as if there were a sinister conclusion to be drawn.

Once and for all: Hungarians or Magyars are not Slavs, Sarmatians, gypsies or failed Germans. They belong to the Finno-Ugric race and are related to Turks and Mongolians; they do not speak an Indo-European language. Liszt didn't know this because he left Hungary when he was ten years old and forgot whatever he had known of his country or its speech, which was probably very little. The friends he later made among the Magyar aristocracy didn't help either. They will have spoken Hungarian badly if at all: Austria frowned on the use of minority languages in the empire (Latin was official in the Magyar Diet until 1805); they were also unfashionable. Revolutionary patriots like István Szechényi and József Eötvös were handicapped by linguistic deficiencies in 1849. So it wasn't Liszt's fault that he couldn't speak, and when in old age he wanted to repatriate himself, couldn't learn his native language. But it was a pity. Had he been able to read untranslated sources he could have avoided the worst blunders in his book on gypsy music, which confuses gypsy techniques with Hungarian folk music. And he could have saved himself the embarrassment of pretending to be a nobleman in disguise. Hungarian family names are easily placed. If noble, they end in *y* or *yi*, which is like *von* or *de* and refers to a place. Occasionally, an ancient name like Bornemisza, meaning "doesn't-drink-wine," stands for a trait. Liszt is a plebeian name; it means *flour* and is as common as Smith.*

Cut off from his history, he therefore became in a manner French. He neither spoke nor wrote any other language well. His German, such as it was, was flavored with a strong Viennese accent and the English quotes in his letters are comically off the mark; his Italian was better but conversational only. His manners too were school of Paris, down to the absurdities: a little phrase like *comme il faut* he used with a world of meaning. But for all that no Frenchman for a moment mistook him for anything but a naturalized alien. Dim as always about foreign orthography, his closest

---

* There is also a distinct possibility that the name was Hungarianized by the addition of the *z* (which in Magyar is silent and merely makes the *s* that comes before it sound like *s* rather than *sh*) and was really List, which is German. Western Hungary, where Liszt was born, is more German, or properly Austrian, than Hungarian and it is certain that such of his ancestors' other names that are known are exclusively German. Thus, since his mother was indubitably Austrian, there is a good chance that he had little if any Hungarian blood.

French friends couldn't spell his name correctly. He was Litz or Lits, it always came out wrong, and it added to the mystery of who and what he was.

Among the Romantics one dressed one's part. They were the first aesthetic rebels to capitalize on the symbolism of clothes and hair styles. "Yes," said Gautier, "they had hair, these chevaliers of the future — one isn't born with a wig — and they had a lot, which fell in soft, shining curls, because it was well-combed. . . . These brigands of thought didn't look like perfect notaries, one must admit, but their costume, ruled by individual fantasy and a just feeling for color, borrowed to advantage from painting. . . ." [4] The conversation pieces of the 1830's look like over-dressed feasts of the gods and wholly allegorical until one recollects that these were real parties, where George Sand in Turkish trousers, Berlioz with his topiary coif, Gautier and Musset *en dandy*, really did group themselves like statuary around the piano while Liszt, in velvet or his gorgeous Hungarian pelisse, trailed the famous hands over the keyboard. In that world the uncolorful personality hadn't a chance, and Liszt wasn't the only one to fudge the facts a bit: Balzac too felt the need to touch up his ancestry and add a *de* to his name.

Liszt's origins were, however, more than humble. He was born, October 22, 1811, in a village called Raiding in German. (Its Hungarian name is Doborján, just as his name is properly Liszt Ferencz, the Hungarians like other Orientals putting the family name first.) His father, Adám Liszt, was a steward to the Eszterházy princes, his mother Anna, née Läger, was a draper's daughter from lower Austria. Like himself, his biographers have found these details distressingly commonplace and to compensate usually add that 1811 was The Year of the Comet. *"Elle paraissait de bon augure,"* says Guy de Pourtalès of a typically Lisztian stage property. [5]

The Viennese, pointing east from the heights above Vienna, like to tell you that Asia begins where the Danube disappears into a smoky plain. Liszt's village is just over the horizon, invisible in the haze, and though so close to the capital, it is true enough that Europe comes to an end somewhere this side of it. The Austro-Hungarian frontier is a real one. Beyond it, the well-sweeps are bent like lateen sails and the geese in their glassy ponds shriek at passersby like fierce heraldic birds. The villages, stranded in a vast alluvium, look Turkish — a straggle of stucco houses set endwise to the street, their wooden porches hung with squash and peppers. But only in operettas was the daily life in such a place rich in romance. The gypsy bands did not play every day and the Hungarian peasant was among the wretchedest anywhere. Agriculture is not delightful to those who don't own the land, and Adám Liszt was chained to its restrictive routines: in summer the work never ends; in winter there is little to do but keep warm. Adám in fact hated it, especially as his job was a comedown for him. Himself the son of an Eszterházy employee, he had grown up at Eisenstadt, the family's principal residence, where he had come in contact with Haydn and Hummel and acquired some knowledge of music. The move to the Raiding estate deprived him of what little society he had known and professionally was a demotion. When therefore he detected signs of unusual talent in his son, something more than paternal pride was involved. He saw the possibility of escape from his prison. It should have been easy. Given his almost feudal relation to a family equally celebrated for its wealth and its love of music, he needed only to call attention to the existence of his gifted child.

The Eszterházys occupy a position like the comet's in Lisztian annals, imparting an air of splendor and significance which if not entirely spurious is close to it. One of their princes did employ Haydn (it is less often remembered that his successor, the head of the house in Liszt's time, fired the old man), patronized Hummel, and that a cadet branch hired Schubert for one unhappy summer. These associations apart, they were not unlike Texans, disgustingly rich and, as in the case of the Eszterházy who turned up at George IV's coronation in a diamond-studded suit, frequently vulgar beyond words. Like Texans, they imported their architects, their furniture and landscape gardeners. They spent most of the eighteenth century constructing vast, unsuitable replicas of European palaces in the swamps of western Hungary. These great houses were solely for display. Since the Eszterházy were not kings, they served no purpose. Eszterháza, the most famous, was like a glass bell, sealed off from the crowds that at Versailles could walk in the park and watch the Sun King eat his dinner. Nor were the owners beloved, either as landlords or patriots. Reactionary since the founding of the dynasty in 1687, the family was on the wrong side of every Hungarian revolt against Austrian rule, every attempt at reform. Their reward was the hundreds of thousands of hectares they possessed until the first World War — and even after it.

It really isn't surprising that they took so little interest in Liszt — they never had been concerned with developing native talent. The oddity is the credit they get for launching him when if the story as we have it is correct they did nothing of the sort. The little Liszt was taken once to play before the prince, praised and dismissed. Nothing was said about getting him an education, musical or otherwise. He was ten years old. Something had to be done. Adám asked for and was graciously granted the use of an Eszterházy palace in Pressburg (Pozsóny in Hungarian; now, under Czech rule, Bratislava) for a concert at which the boy was to raise money by subscription. The affair cost the Eszterházys nothing and did net him a fund of six hundred gulden a year. The committee set up to handle it was headed by the Counts Apponyi, Erdödy and Szapáry and it is they and not the family on whose estates he was born whom Lisztians ought to honor.

One might expect that such a beginning would make a republican of the child subjected to it. Not a bit of it. Liszt was one of the snobs of history. For all he said to the contrary, and he said a great deal, he didn't want the order of things destroyed, only rearranged like the seating at a grand dinner, with himself at the head of the table. Carl Alexander, Duke of Saxe-Weimar, once observed that Liszt was what a prince should be; and as he interpreted princely conduct, that was what he tried to be. Far from resenting the furred and feathered magnates decked in brocade and precious stones, whose hands he had kissed in childhood, he desired to emulate what he imagined to be their virtues, and only erred, as upstarts do, in having rather better manners.

The Liszt family moved to Vienna when he was ten years old, and he didn't see his country again for twenty years. It was an imaginary place to him, just as he was for practical purposes an imaginary Hungarian. Hungary stood in his memory as a piece of earth with, in the distance, a gaudy palace — not such an inaccurate picture at that. And if ever there was a convincing argument for heredity over environment, he was it. If not really a Magyar, he was a marvelous facsimile, and this was at once an advantage and his undoing, for many of the characteristics that damned him in Europe would have passed unnoticed in his native land — his passion for women, above all, and his terrible conceit. This weakness of outnumbered peoples was mentioned by Miklós Zrinyi, a western-minded poet and general, as early as the seventeenth century; and the theme was reiterated by Szechényi in the nineteenth. Vanity, he said, was the principal obstacle to Magyar progress, and he cited Hungarian vintners who were deaf to suggestions for improving their product because unable to believe there could be a better. *Extra Hungarium non est vita* was a popular saw when the country was a half-derelict feudal state — to which it can be added that the verb *to explain* in Hungarian is literally *to Magyarize*. Backward agrarians until after the second World War, the Hungarians had the familiar failings of such societies. Liszt's critics tirelessly accused him of being overdressed, oversexed and vain as a peacock. All true, and just as true of the Pole, the Sicilian, and the Southern cavalier. Male swagger is the agrarian's answer to the bureaucrats and city slickers who in spite of repeated whippings in battle have somehow settled on his back: it is Priapus's last stand.

Chapter 2

PSYCHOLOGY, supposed to do some of the biographer's legwork for him, falls flat when it comes to the child prodigy. Nobody knows why musical talent in particular should so often manifest itself in the very young — or why it should strike in certain places at specific times: why were so many musical prodigies born to Jewish parents in the Russian Pale beginning at about the middle of the nineteenth century? (How, on the other hand, did it happen that four of the composers known as the Russian Five did not begin as musicians at all?) Again, most but by no means all composers have been virtuosi on some instrument. (But Wagner could barely manage a piano and Berlioz's only instrument was the guitar.) Liszt anyhow was the real thing, a golden-haired cherub whose little fingers skipping over the keyboard sent audiences into raptures; and he suffered the consequences.

The type has disappeared from concert stages, presumably because the unadmitted sadism that took pleasure in his exploitation has found other outlets. The upgrading of childhood has rendered the prodigy obsolete and the parent who tried to foist one on the public would probably wind up explaining himself to the authorities. Not without reason: the suspicion that an unscrupulous parent lurks behind the baby performer has been warranted as often as not, from Leopold Mozart on down. It was in Liszt's case — though Adám Liszt has somehow escaped censure.

He wasn't exactly a monster. Far less resourceful and intelligent than the senior Mozart, he was in worldly affairs simply a fool, one of nature's bunglers. Hard evidence that he actually mistreated his son is wanting outside a rather doubtful source. Unpublished parts of Marie d'Agoult's memoirs do state that Adám brutalized the little Liszt — information Liszt may or may not have given her. Her horror, amounting to a pathological manifestation, of Liszt's performing self, makes her unreliable, and he certainly told no one else that his father was actually cruel to him. He tried to remember him kindly. Adám nevertheless did extensive damage, some of it irreparable. Liszt was five or six, rather late as prodigies go, when he first climbed a piano stool and demonstrated unmistakable signs of a musical gift. Adám was admittedly in a spot unless the Eszterházys chose to subsidize many years of training. His management was nevertheless deplorable. From first to last, he assumed it was his job to push and shove and secure introductions to important people, and that the rest was up to the child. It was of course essential to move to Vienna or some other musical capital, but there Adám's reasoning stopped. It never entered his head that he might himself go to work to support his little tribe — though he knew bookkeeping and he had a younger half-brother in the Austrian civil service who might have had some ideas.* Quite simply, a boy of ten or eleven was to maintain himself and two adults while simultaneously getting his lessons, and even these Adám was not prepared to pay for.

There was another cause, one might suppose, for disquiet. Liszt was not strong. Sudden and frightening illnesses punctuated his childhood, fevers and what may have been a mild form of epilepsy. In reality of course he had an iron constitution or he wouldn't have survived the abuses he and others inflicted on it. But he was high-strung and delicate and unless I misread a strange sentence in one of his letters to Marie d'Agoult, had lost a brother to tuberculosis. The line is: "*Si je n'avais pas perdu un frère de la poitrine, il fût un temps ou j'aurais été ravi qu'un peu de froid m'eut débarrassé de la vie.*" ("If I hadn't lost a brother from lung disease, there would have been a time when I would have been delighted if a little cold had relieved me of life.") [1] This would seem to mean that although an only child in every biography, he at some time witnessed a death scene; and since his son Daniel died at twenty *de la poitrine*, it looks as though consumption "ran in the family." If so, the killing regime imposed by Adám becomes the more irresponsible. What with lessons, practice, and his public performances, Liszt for years can scarcely have seen the light of day.

Some of this was unavoidable. There is no way out of the hours at his instrument the performing musician must go through. Either he has mastered its technical demands by adolescence or it is too late. Fresh air and alternative mental stimuli are necessary antidotes but Liszt had to do with-

---

* This relative, Edouard Liszt — the only one Liszt had, or at least knew about — was always referred to as a cousin. Though nothing of interest is known about him, he became a prominent jurist and was invaluable to his nephew as long as he lived, handling his investments and performing many quasi-legal services. Liszt, hopeless about money, depended on him absolutely.

out them. He had no schooling. The village priest at Raiding probably taught him to read and write and that was all. He read everything he could get his hands on but the absence of intellectual discipline together with uncertainty over what language he could rightly call his own constituted a handicap not to be overcome, and an especially serious one to a would-be theorist and man of ideas. He worked hard to remedy his deficiencies but was never able to forge a critical tool equal to Schumann's or Berlioz's. Even his handwriting was a source of shame to him. The result was an often misplaced respect for people he believed to be more cultivated than himself, in particular the two pretentious women who undertook to get his thoughts on paper.

It was natural that he would invent or skip large portions of such a childhood, less so that the standard texts of his life should incorporate so many incomprehensible muddles. They do, however, and one can only pick one's way. We are told, for example, that in Vienna Adám first applied to Hummel to teach his son, and on learning that the fee was a guinea a lesson, turned to Carl Czerny — who was interested enough to offer instruction for nothing. But it happens that Hummel was not living in Vienna in 1821; he was then *Kapellmeister* at Weimar and can only have been interviewed during a leave of absence. And what of the six hundred gulden subscribed to pay for lessons? At best, Adám must have been guilty of mismanagement that Liszt in later life tried to conceal — a supposition that the flighty man's subsequent conduct more than bears out.

Nor was Czerny the best choice in the world, though he might have been worse. Adám had been Liszt's only teacher, and according to Czerny, a bad one. The child's playing was "completely irregular, careless and confused, and he had so little knowledge of correct fingering that he threw his fingers all over the keyboard in an altogether arbitrary fashion. Nevertheless, I was amazed by the talent with which Nature had equipped him. I gave him a few things to sight-read, which he did, purely by instinct, but for that very reason in a manner which revealed that Nature herself had here created a pianist. . . . Never before had I so eager, talented or industrious a student." [2]

If the object was to equip Liszt to be an old-fashioned virtuoso, Czerny did his work well; but he had no insight into his pupil's temperament and his point of view was dated. He was a formalist who thought in mechanistic terms. Bravura, glitter, sonority, all repelled him. "Rather wild and confused" was his verdict when he heard Liszt sixteen years later in Paris. He was a good man, an honest musician, and Liszt was devoted to him. He did not really understand the kind of material he had to work with.

Sadly, the two men who would have were just around the corner, so to speak, and the biographer's hand itches to unite him with them. The first was Schubert and Liszt was introduced to him. But Schubert's poverty and his rowdy life among the plebs did not recommend him to Adám and the misty encounter (which may be apocryphal) passed. With Beethoven, the ground is more solid. He received the Liszts; he was also by then almost totally deaf, worried to savagery by personal affairs and he loathed child prodigies. Adám's cringing approach will also have been repulsive.

Beethoven's visitors wrote their remarks in the conversation books, dreadful reminders of his affliction, and that for April, 1823, contains this, written either by or for the boy: "I have often expressed the wish to Herr von Schindler to make your lofty acquaintance, and am rejoiced now to be able to do so. As I will give a concert on Sunday the 13th I most humbly beg you to grant me your exalted presence." Further on, Schindler elaborated:

Little Liszt has urgently requested me humbly to beg you for a theme on which he wishes to improvise at his concert tomorrow. He will not break the seal until the times comes. The little fellow's improvisations do not seriously signify. The lad is a fine pianist but, so far as his fancy is concerned, it is far from the truth to say he really improvises. Carl Czerny is his teacher. Just eleven years old. Do come. . . . It is unfortunate that the lad is in Czerny's hands. You will make good the rather unfriendly reception of recent date by coming to little Liszt's concert. It will encourage the boy. Do promise me to come.[3]

This is a puzzle. Why was it unfortunate that Czerny was Liszt's teacher when Czerny was Beethoven's friend? What was the unfriendly reception? A previous snub from Beethoven, or an unsuccessful concert of Liszt's? There is, anyway, no indication that Beethoven granted the request to appear at the Sunday performance – the same where he is supposed to have climbed the platform and bestowed the succession on the child with a kiss. Liszt himself was the sole source for this story, widely disbelieved in his lifetime. Beethoven did not go to concerts, which he was too deaf to hear. What perhaps did happen was an encounter at one of the informal concerts given regularly by Czerny's pupils, sometimes attended by Beethoven. There the little boy, pretty as a picture, may have charmed the old bear into giving him a hug.

There is still the unfriendly reception. If it refers to a falling-off of interest in the wonder child, now familiar to the Viennese, it may clear up another puzzle. Adám Liszt suddenly packed up his family in the autumn of 1823 and departed, via several German cities, for Paris. We are told that the twelve-year-old Liszt was now ready for the Paris Conservatoire. But in the opinion of Czerny, a better judge than Adám, he was not. And there was the further fact, surely ascertainable even to the flighty Adám, that the Conservatoire was closed to foreigners. (Or is this another canard? César Franck, a Belgian, was admitted in 1837, which either means that the rule could be relaxed or had been rescinded.) So the real motive looks like simple greed coupled with the realization that the Viennese public had been pumped dry.

Father and son got the bad news the morning after they arrived, when they called on Cherubini, the terrible-tempered old Florentine who ran his institution like clockwork and liked nothing better than to enforce its rules. The little Liszt fell on his knees and kissed Cherubini's hand, terrified that this might not be the custom in France – and indeed it was not. Nor did it help when Adám presented a letter of recommendation from Metternich, anything but an open sesame to a Tuscan. Unmoved by his petitioners, who were behaving like barbarians, the old composer would not budge.

With this refusal, any pretense that Liszt was in search of a musical education was abandoned. He took a few lessons in theory from Reicha but his full-time and candid exploitation had begun. For the next five years he was worked without letup. *Le petit Lits* was adopted by the Faubourg Saint-Germain and the giddier lights of the Bourbon restoration. Soon he was getting two thousand francs for a salon appearance. He toured the French provinces and went three times to England, where he was set before George IV like a little blackbird baked in a pie. He was made ridiculous as only a clever child or a trained animal can be. Gall, the "phrenologist," interrupted a concert to take a cast of his skull, bumpy with genius of course. The tragedian Talma, a figure of fun in a toga, clasped him to his breast onstage.

He more or less guessed what was being done to him. Spasms of self-contempt were followed by sulks and fits of religious mania that were particularly worrying to his mother. Anna Liszt is a robust but shadowy figure. Ordinary and not well educated, she seldom appears as an active influence but may have had more than we know. Liszt respected her all his life. It is doubtful if he loved her. She was too sensible and realistic, whether prescribing for her grandchildren or denouncing Liszt for calling their Paris apartment a rathole. Nothing of the kind, she said, "It costs two hundred francs a month and there aren't any rats." Liszt's religious leanings received no encouragement from her. She was strongly anticlerical and when he announced his desire to study for the priesthood she threw up her hands. (Forty years later when she heard he had taken minor orders she burst into tears.) She must have blamed Adám too for the state of affairs because she took the unusual step of returning to her native Austria. Left alone, Adám told his distracted son, "You belong to music and not the church" – a stupid thing to say. The two were not incompatible, while Liszt's stunts at the piano – improvisations on *Zitti, zitti* and the like – bore about the same relation to music that Carême's sugar palaces did to architecture.

Adám did not know the chances he was taking. In later life Liszt railed against this period of his youth: "There came over me a bitter disgust against art," he wrote. ". . . Vilified and degraded to the level of a more or less profitable handicraft . . . a source of amusement for distinguished society. I felt I would sooner be anything in the world than a musician in the pay of the exalted, patronized and salaried by them like a conjuror, or the learned dog Munito. . . ."[4] With such feelings he might have turned his back on music forever. But Adám, out of avarice or witlessness or both, kept up the pressure. He was even prepared to push the boy into the ultimate absurdity, the composition of an opera, for which at age fourteen he was not remotely equipped. But opera was then (and for another thirty years or so) the only certified route to fame and fortune, and he had to write one. Its title was *Don Sanche, ou Le Château d'amour* and on the musical side he was helped, maybe more than helped, by Paer, one of those composers of Italian opera whose works could not have vanished more completely if they had been inscribed in Hittite or Maya.* Two mediocre poets supplied the libretto and the whole thing went up like a Montgolfier balloon (October 17, 1825), only to descend as rapidly. There was no disguising the thinness and immaturity of a work whose title alone would give it away, and it was withdrawn after four performances. Fashionable audiences were not enough.

Adám was haunted by Mozart's career and tried vainly to make Liszt's conform to it. Prodigy into composer: it seemed easy and needed only a happier ending. But the beginning too was wrong. Liszt was in the first place rather a slow starter, and if he had shown half Mozart's precocity, it was too late in history. The France of Charles X was not that of Marie Antoinette and art as well as society was in ferment, which Liszt, young as he was, must have felt. He was unusually sensitive to cultural atmospheres and he read books. He had moreover made at least one important contact: the singer Adolphe Nourrit starred in *Don Sanche* and he was a musician of the new school, a cultivated man who frequented writers and was aware of musical spheres beyond those of Italian opera. He and Liszt were to introduce Schubert songs to private audiences in the early 1830's. How well they knew each other before Adám's death is a question but such a man was in a position to alert an intelligent adolescent to dramatic changes in the weather. The Romantic cloudburst was about to descend on Paris and it is inconceivable that Liszt was blind to the lightning in the summer sky.

Meanwhile tour followed tour until his health gave way. Doctors advised the seaside, and in August 1827 he travelled with Adám to Boulogne. There, with great suddenness, Adám died, of a "gastric fever" that was probably typhoid. His last words were of a prescience he hadn't often shown in life: "My child," he is supposed to have said, "I leave you very

---

* E. Haraszti, a well-known Liszt scholar, flatly says that *Don Sanche* was entirely composed by Paer. (*Le Problème Liszt, Acta Musicologica*, p. 131)

much alone, but your talent will protect you. Your heart is good and you don't lack intelligence. All the same, I fear for you on account of women. They will trouble and dominate your life." [5] One wonders how he knew. Liszt later said that at sixteen he was so ignorant about sex that the sixth and tenth commandments had to be explained to him. If that was true, Adám had second sight.

Neither then nor later did Liszt utter a complaint against this parent who had used him, if not with cruelty, with striking inefficiency, for he left no money and a load of debt. A money-maker since he was ten years old, Liszt was so poor that he had to sell his beautiful Érard piano, a gift from the manufacturer. That may also have been a gesture. Poverty-stricken though he was, he was determined to give no more concerts. At sixteen, he went into retirement, supporting himself and his mother, whom he recalled from Austria, by giving music lessons. It was the first of his clean sweeps, that no one knew better than he how to execute. The curtain descends with a crash and the principal retires. When he returns, months – or in this case years – later, it is against a new mise-en-scène, wearing a new costume. *Le petit Lits* was seen no more in the antechambers of the Faubourg. He lived quietly in the rue Montholon, in a little flat full of books he had bound in dove-colored paper. He sent up a flare or two, compositions of interest mostly for what they foretold.* But it is a shadowy time, of which, except for a single episode, he rarely spoke.

He fell in love. She was Caroline de Saint-Cricq, the daughter of Charles X's minister of commerce, and of course a pupil. The Saint-Cricqs, one feels, must have been mad. The tutor was a danger well known, and not only to carefully reared virgins inclined to lose their heads in the democracy of love. He was also a carrier of subversive thoughts on art, philosophy and politics – as were Kant, Hegel and Hölderlin, for example, all at one time or another hired to teach in aristocratic families. A music instructor might have appeared less of a danger than these – had he been anyone but Liszt, who was a maiden's dream of good looks and alight with ideas. An otherwise unsentimental Swiss lady who was wise enough to chaperon *her* daughter to his atelier a few years later babbled to her journal that she wished she could record his every word: "It was all luminous, daring, striking, powerful and full of truth, profound like everything else that emerges from that logical and original head. . . . He said he was incompetent; he burned with genius and despaired because he couldn't attain his ideal. . . ." [6]

Given the circumstances, nothing much can have happened beyond a stolen kiss or two but Liszt took it as a tragedy when the Count de Saint-

---

* Humphrey Searle (*The Music of Liszt*, 1966) singles out *In Memory*, his first essay in the Hungarian style, the title probably meant for Adám, and the *Étude en 48 exercises*, which is the earliest sketch for the *Transcendental* Études.

Cricq behaved in the classic manner and showed him the door. His bitterness, in which injured pride was the solvent for thwarted passion, endured for several years, and in a sense forever. He didn't forget Caroline. On his way to Spain in 1844 he made a considerable detour to visit her — she had long since married — at her home near Pau. He left her a ring in his will. She obviously had a permanent effect on his relations with women. Not again did he risk a rejection, least of all from a woman of aristocratic birth — not that there was much danger: titled women threw themselves at his head all his life, while he eschewed permanent alliances.* But she left a sore spot.

Still, lost love cannot have been the only reason for the prostration that followed the Saint-Cricq affair. He sank so low that one Paris paper printed his obituary. The stresses preceding Adám's death, the death itself, must have contributed. Adám's crime was to have poisoned (if temporarily) the well of music for him; but the death of a tyrant is only worse for having been secretly desired. It is also possible that he was suffering from *mal de René,* a recognized ailment among the young who read Chateaubriand and came down with it like mononucleosis. (Joseph Delorme, Sainte-Beuve's hero, is made to die of it, along with t.b. and a "fatal" temperament.) Akin to Wertherism, *mal de René* plunged its victims into a melancholia that threatened to be terminal but may have been mildly beneficial to nerves like Liszt's that were in need of a rest.

Relief came with the revolution of 1830. His mother is credited with saying that the cannon cured him and was quite likely right. One of the functions of revolution is to make us aware of other people. We rejoin, however briefly, the human race. *Les trois glorieux,* as those three days were called, when Paris broiled under a July sun, were in many respects a catastrophe for France. With Charles X, a royal dinosaur, driven from the throne, a vote would probably have created a republic. So thought old Lafayette. Acting as front man for the bankers and landlords, he intervened and delivered the kingdom to Louis-Philippe — a lesson to those who put their faith in senile military men. Louis, the bourgeois monarch, wasn't a bad man, or altogether a bad king. He ruled in peace for eighteen years, a period of business expansion at home and thriving colonialism abroad, stamped by fat-cat complacency. But the redress of grievances was indefinitely postponed, making inevitable the explosion of 1848.

Liszt can have had only the haziest idea of what the uproar in the streets was about. He only knew that he must be on the side of the rebels, and he at once began to compose a "revolutionary symphony." Like the revolution

---

* Newman (*The Man Liszt,* 1935) says that in 1845 Liszt sought the hand of the Countess Valentine Cessiat, who was Lamartine's niece, and that she turned him down (p. 157). If so, it was the only honorable proposal of his life. But I know of no hard evidence that he did anything so out of character.

itself, this fizzled out, to be rekindled in 1848–1849, and ultimately abandoned with only the first movement completed. A chaotic sketch is all that
survives of the original, and musically it doesn't tell us much. It is in the
margin, scribbled at white heat and barely legible, that the emotions of a
very young man spill over. Dated "27, 28, 29 July — Paris," the words read
like jottings made on the spot: "Indignation, vengeance, terror, liberty!
disorder, confused cries (wave, strangeness) fury . . . refusal, march of
the royal guard, doubt, uncertainty, parties at cross-purposes . . . attack,
battle . . . march of the national guard — enthusiasm, enthusiasm, enthusiasm . . ."

He was to change his mind about revolutions, like most of his contemporaries. (Among his elders there was already a general adjustment and
rush for jobs: Hugo published an "Ode to Young France" that welcomed
the new regime; Dumas *père* became a royal librarian; Balzac considered
standing for parliament.) The July days were beneficial to him because
they roused him up and introduced him, as it were, to his time. New men
in every field were elbowing their way to the fore. He determined to be one
of them. Whatever the demerits of the July monarchy, it was benevolent to
the arts and, having quelled a political upheaval, it allowed an aesthetic
one to take place under its nose. The dullest of kings unwittingly presided
over the great decade of French Romanticism. One could say they took
office at the same moment.

Chapter 3

"FRANCE IS the heart of Europe. As one proceeds from its borders, social life dies slowly away; one can judge the distance from Paris by the degree of animation or languor of the country to which one retires." The *grande nation* has not changed much. That passage from the *Mémoires d'outre-tombe* was accurate when Chateaubriand wrote it, and one could argue that it still is. The French revolution and the Napoleonic wars were the creators of modern Europe, which is inconceivable if they are left out. They struck with the force of a tidal wave and, in recession, exposed the chaos and hopes of a new age. Intelligent men everywhere understood that nothing would be the same again. Sainte-Beuve (born in 1804) said of his youth that he was sick from the end of the old world, sick from the beginning of the new — and it was this sickness, which resembles the efflorescence of certain wines, that produced the movement called Romanticism.

The name is a rock for the historian, who must either navigate around it or try to define it, and neither course is satisfactory. The very midwives who helped bring it into the world, like Goethe, seem to be wrong. "The classical I call healthy," he said to Eckermann, "the romantic the sick. Thus the *Nibelungenlied* is as classical as Homer, for they are both healthy and vigorous. Most modern literature is not romantic because it is modern but because it is sick, morbid and weakly; and ancient literature is not classical because it is ancient but because it is strong and fresh and happy and healthy. If we distinguish between classical and romantic by these criteria, we shall soon get this matter clear." [1]

We shall soon do nothing of the sort. Aside from the impossibility of arbitrating between sick and well — where does Oedipus go? Hamlet? What counts, subject or treatment? — Goethe's definition is sown with thistles because it is not making a valid distinction between classic and romantic: he is talking about vitality. Where it is present, he argues for health and ignores the staggering maladjustments of the Nibelungs; and where he sees the flame waver, opts for romantic. But what about his own Werthers and Wilhelm Meisters, robustly handled neurotics? In fact, the *Nibelungenlied* with its multiple perversions, murders, substitutions and ultimate apocalypse was fertile ground for romantics. Which isn't to say that it is a Romantic work.

Classic and romantic are modern terms whose usefulness when applied to the remoter past is dubious at best. Romantic antecedents can be traced to Euripides and *The Bacchae,* if not earlier. (The Dionysian movement in the sixth century has been called "the Romanticism of antiquity.") The heretical poetry of the *trouvères* (whose name, from the Provençal meaning *to find* or *to invent,* rings a Faustian change) is essentially romantic. So are Tasso's laments. But to point this out is only to name the pantheon that exerted magisterial power over the nineteenth-century artists who spelled romantic with a capital *R:* Dante, Cellini, Tasso, Ronsard, Shakespeare — in music, Monteverdi, Gluck. A glance is enough to show that a common denominator was imposed by a particular point of view, not by historical fact. The pasting of modern labels on the past erases the authenticity conferred by time and context. Dante isn't a romantic because Liszt read him with Victor Hugo's spectacles; nor is Gluck transformed because Berlioz heard a modern sound in his clashing cymbals.* Misrepresentation is inevitable when the classic-romantic antithesis is invoked to enforce artificial categories. Stretched to infinity, the terms become useless — as, for example, when romantic comes to stand for the chaotic and undefined, while classic means discipline and clarity: Art of whatever category can be achieved only by the successful conquest of one by the other — which is why Valéry is also wrong when he says that "the essence of classicism is to come afterward," that "composition, which is artifice, succeeds to a certain primitive chaos of intuition and natural development." [2] Of course it does; but this is not the difference between classicism and romanticism. It is a

---

* Mario Praz, whose *Romantic Agony* is far and away the finest study of this untidy subject, has this to say of history versus the subjective interpretation of it: "With a little imagination it might be . . . possible to discover 'exotic Romanticism' in Marco Polo, by interpreting the passage about the palace of Cublai Can in the light of Coleridge's *Kubla Khan.* Except that at the time of Marco Polo this type of exoticism had not yet come into being; besides, who would be bold enough to represent Marco Polo as a Romantic *ante litteram?*" (*Romantic Agony,* p. 5). Nor will he allow, and very rightly, Dante to be a Romantic on account of such lines as: *Quale ne' plenilunii sereni/ Trivia ride tra le ninfe eterne/ Che dipingon lo ciel per tutti i seni.* That they moved a Romantic like Liszt to tears is beside the point.

process familiar to anyone who has tried to reduce an image to canvas or paper.

Nevertheless, there is a distinction to be made—and it does begin with the birth pangs which the classical artist tries to conceal, while the romantic summons us to the accouchement. The classicist stifles his cries in the sheets, making his work look "easier." The romantic does the opposite. When Delacroix writes, "I have no love for reasonable painting. There is in me an old leaven, some black depth that must be appeased. If I am not quivering and excited like a serpent in the hands of a soothsayer I am uninspired," [3] he is calling attention to a mediumistic state peculiar, in that it is emphasized, to the romantic artist. Like certain children marked for distinction in primitive societies, he assumes he is unique, with something unique to say — one reason why in art he often seems an upstart with delusions of grandeur. He does not follow the rules. The bad taste that often afflicts him can be defined as genius without the limitations of what we call style. Berlioz in *Les Troyens,* a masterpiece of Romanticism though he himself would not have acknowledged it, wished for nothing less than to endow music with "a new means of action" — and the definition will do for the movement he disavowed. Delacroix's huge, iridescent compositions like the *Massacre at Scio,* Stendhal's fictions with their "Spanish" endings, Hugo's passionate meditations on exotic themes, Liszt's symphonic poems — all, like *Les Troyens,* belong to Romanticism by virtue of their defects. They are like buildings under construction, for which the plans, received in a dream, have been mislaid. With the so-called unities dissolved, the artist is on his own, working without a net, and the suspense this creates is one of the identifying marks of a romantic presence.

It remains to try to define historical Romanticism. Goethe's lifetime conveniently spans its development from a semi-disreputable cult of the picturesque (ruins, storms, Salvator Rosa effects) to the subtler conception of *das Kranke* and thence to what Goethe was so sure it wasn't, the life-force behind nineteenth-century art. The word itself of course appears much earlier, in English in the sixteen hundreds, when Pepys, using the French spelling, applied it in the literal sense: like the old romances, *Tristan* and the *Morte d'Arthur.* For all its Latin origin it has always conveyed a mood more associated with northern twilight than with Mediterranean sun — at least in the sense that it is assumed that Mediterranean man cuts up his thoughts and his landscapes into clear manageable shapes, while Nordic man, the forest dweller, feeds on dreams: in Novalis's definition, "distant mountains, distant men, distant happenings, all are romantic." And certainly Romanticism is, in its dwelling on the remote, the unknown, and what Jean Paul called *Sehnsucht,* a longing for what is not there, an Anglo-Germanic phenomenon. (It would be impossible to render *Sehnsucht* into Italian, for example — the sentiment itself would be alien, so there is no word for it.) But Romanticism was more than a literary or pictorial conceit. It could be called the taproot to the European unconscious after 1750, the *id* of its art.

This puts it in apparent opposition to the movement toward scepticism and orderly inquiry called the Enlightenment; but a complex mind like Rousseau's cautions against a facile dualism. A romantic in his mythologizing of the self and nature, he was the tough-minded pragmatist in his proposals for reform of the state, education, and the individual's relation to society. He was the true founder of Romanticism, the delineator of its future character as a movement of protest against the tragedy of the modern world.

The loss of individuality under the combined pressures of governmental authority and the industrial age, the wreck of nature, are such overriding concerns today that we forget how long ago the panic started. Yet there is scarcely an issue, from the crisis in education to the ruin of the environment, that Rousseau would view with astonishment. He foresaw everything. He and Baudelaire — who is technically a post-Romantic — stand at opposite edges of the same lunar landscape but their reactions are hardly to be distinguished except by Baudelaire's greater pessimism. It was Baudelaire but could have been either who wrote in his journal:

The world is about to end. Its sole reason for continuance is that it exists. . . . I do not say that the world will be reduced to the clownish shifts and disorders of a South American republic, or even that we shall perhaps return to a state of nature and roam the grassy ruins of our civilization, gun in hand, seeking our food. No; for these adventures would require a certain remnant of vital energy, echo of earlier ages. As a new example, as fresh victims of the inexorable moral laws, we shall perish by that which we have believed to be our means of existence. So far will machinery have Americanized us, so far will Progress have atrophied in us all that is spiritual, that no dream of the Utopians, however bloody, sacrilegious or unnatural, will be comparable to the result.[4]

Rousseau's generation looked to revolution to effect a cure: Baudelaire's did not, and that was the difference. The French revolution proved the possibility of action but not its efficacy. Napoleon, child of the upheaval, embarked France on a mission of vainglorious reform that stunted her growth for a century. Yet all the *soi-disant* Romantics were Bonapartists by temperament — even Chateaubriand, who loathed Napoleon and devoted his finest writing to his downfall. Napoleonic Europe was a kind of lost paradise for those who were children in its heyday — Hugo, Berlioz and the rest — a might-have-been whose disappearance hurt them more than they knew. There the self-made hero, the outsider, had triumphed. After the cutting down to size of the Corsican brigand, the victor in any contest seemed always to be the same: a stout fellow in a frock coat, coining money. While for the writer, the artist, the early nineteenth century proved a false dawn. If anything, he lost influence. No subsequent group of intellectuals achieved the power or the prestige of the Encyclopedists before 1789.

The Romantic hero was a response to this fundamental conviction of impotence, reflecting the search for dominion and uniqueness at the moment when these were uniquely threatened. Master of his fate since the Renaissance, European man by 1800 was taking in the fact that he might be done for. In literature his answer was a return to a world ruled by condottieri, redskins, corsairs — types either extinct or on the brink of a final solution. Byron's Giaours and Laras, Chateaubriand's insupportable René — "to love and to suffer was the double fatality he imposed on whoever approached his person" — Hugo's Olympio, "a demigod born in the mingled murmurings of nature, pride and love," are well-known *Doppelgängers* for their creators, male daydreams of Arcadia.*

On the face of it, the Romantic hero was a lost cause. Absorbed in the colonization of the globe and in material progress, Europe could have no use for the species. Yet he proved to have more than a literary substance. With minor alterations he survived as one type of revolutionary: in Russia and elsewhere, he was the idealist born to affluence, who casts it all away, a nationalist who wears the peasant's dress and quotes the native poetry. Which isn't to say that Romanticism was ever a political movement in the strict sense of the word.

The common ground where the Romantic and the revolutionary met was emotional and cultural. It had nothing to do with practical politics. In youth the Romantic often fancied himself an anarchist; by the time he was thirty-five, he was in nine cases out of ten a staunch conservative. Apart from the instinctive sympathy of rebel for rebel, what they shared was their assessment of culture — no longer the exclusive province of the ruling class. Thus, folklore and the world beyond Europe were explored not primarily as adjuncts to decoration (*chinoiserie*, Dresden shepherdesses, etc.), but on the novel assumption that art was no less art for being indigenous, composed in a native idiom. For two hundred years, the canons of European taste had been simply those of the French court. Peasant art was contemptible unless elevated and refined to an aristocratic parody of the simple life (and for that matter even the perfection of a Chinese bowl was considered to be enhanced by the addition of a *bronze doré* cage). Roman-

---

* Byron and Chateaubriand make fascinating twin histories, since both were allowed by the accident of birth to play out their fantasies. Both were Celts, born on the peripheries of their respective countries, and both suffered from this to some degree, but since they were also noblemen were allowed to capitalize on a glamorous-outsider status. And each in his way had to capitulate, Byron by expiring in the Greek war, Chateaubriand by taking up reactionary politics and becoming an ambassador — a fate not impossible for Byron had England not rejected him.

ticism, avowedly hostile to science, actually approached the scientific point of view when it undertook to throw out the standards of the academy and to judge "inferior" and "superior" in the terms imposed by the work itself; but it did so for social rather than scientific reasons: the old world was finished and art must remove its wig. It was not by accident that in countries like Russia, where it went without saying that native architecture, native music, even the native language, were relics of barbarism, the arrival of Romanticism invariably portended the discovery and revaluation of the national heritage.

A book like Liszt's on gypsy music must be judged in this context. It is a bad book; even the title is a misnomer; that isn't the point: he was a pioneer in his decision to write about the subject at all. Of course there was much that was meretricious in his attitude, as in that of many of his contemporaries — a sentimental patronage toward *le peuple* from which the professional revolutionary was not free. It has also become increasingly difficult to draw the line between the kind of nationalism fostered by the Romantic movement and sheer jingoism. But for that Liszt's generation cannot be held responsible. As artists, they regarded themselves as citizens of a universal state, not of a particular country. In the same sense, they were also genuinely humanitarian, for once it is accepted that artists everywhere labor in the same vineyard, certain arbitrary distinctions fall away.

By 1830, the artist could see as clearly as any other worker that the industrial revolution was being engineered for the benefit of a class that ignored his needs while exploiting his talents as ruthlessly as if he stood at a loom. Liszt's years as a musical drudge opened his eyes to the analogy — making him, in 1834, the passionate partisan of the striking silk workers at Lyon. But he wasn't the only or even the first of his group to adopt the vocabulary of protest. The poet Alfred de Vigny was probably the earliest to voice the position, and the more powerfully since he was born to privilege. His essay is immensely long, in form a preface to his play *Chatterton,* which it ends by overshadowing; the gist is this:

It is in his first youth that [the poet] feels his strength and foresees the future of his genius, that he lovingly embraces life and nature, that he arouses mistrust and suffers rebuff. He cries to the people: "It is to you that I speak," and the multitude answers justly enough: "We do not understand." He cries to the state: "Heed me and help me live." But the state replies that it is set up to protect positive interests. "Of what use are you?" Everybody against him is in the right. Is he then in the wrong? What can he do? [5]

Liszt and Vigny were meeting nearly every day when this was written, and there is no doubt that Liszt's essays *On the Situation of Artists* were modelled on it. (They appeared a year later, May–October, 1835, in the

Gazette Musicale.) They were, however, more violent, and more extraordinary because no musician had ever said such things before. Much of them is rant, yet a sample needs quoting if his life is to be understood:

For the artist — sufferings, debasement, persecution. For art — shackles, exploitation, economic reforms, institutions, the Opera, the schools, and so on, that are either imperfect or baneful, gags and handcuffs. Everywhere, among all classes of executant musicians, professors, composers, we hear complaints, recantations, expressions of discontent or rage, vows of change or reform, aspirations towards a future that will be broader and more satisfactory . . . that witness to the fermentation of the new leaven. More or less openly, more or less profoundly, all are suffering. Whether it be in their contact with the public or with society; the theatre directors, the critics, the government clerks, the music sellers; whether it be, in a word, in their civil, their political or their religious relations . . . no matter; *all suffer.* . . .[6]

If there is something childish in this wholesale condemnation of everything and everybody, Liszt's point was still the same as Vigny's; and it was this active sensation of being one with the insulted and injured at whatever level rather than any political doctrine that drove the Romantic to interest himself in what Berlioz quaintly called "the social question." The proto-Marxist ring is in fact deceptive. But it is worth noting how Liszt's fury (and Vigny's cooler indignation) differ from the black resignation of Baudelaire almost a generation later. Unlike his successors, the Romantic wasn't ready to call it quits. Reserves of rage kept him afloat long after it could be proved that the case was hopeless. Berlioz's *envoi* to his enemies was a model of defiance: "And as for you madmen, more stupid than dogs or bulls, my Guildensterns, my Rosencrantzes, my Iagos, my precious Osrics, farewell . . . my friends; I despise you all, and trust to have forgotten you before I die." [7]

He despaired because he had hoped so much. Because the Romantic had traits in common with the modern dropout — clothes and hair as well as the deeper attributes of alienation — it would be easy, and very wrong, to confuse them. The spirit is altogether different. For all its pessimism, the movement swarmed with life like a spring sea and was rich with genius. When Balzac wrote that he trusted for Louis-Philippe's sake, "posterity will say, 'under Victor Hugo's reign, under Lamartine, under Béranger, there was a king who took the name of Louis-Philippe'" it was but one more example of the arrogance of men who, whatever else they suffered, did not doubt themselves for one moment. They were great big people, and full of effrontery. Hugo's motto was *Ego Hugo,* no less; Liszt's *Génie oblige.*

Life couldn't altogether incapacitate such people (Gérard de Nerval was their only suicide), nor should they be thought of as steeped in perpetual gloom, often as they referred to their tears. The energy they poured out in

a cornucopia of novels, poetry, treatises, letters, symphonies, vast pano-
ramas in paint and sound, was formidable. It is a great thing to have
shared a youthful faith. When it was all over, Gautier could still write that
"today's generation have difficulty imagining the effervescence of spirits
in that epoch; it was a movement like the Renaissance. The sap of life
circulated. Everything germinated, burgeoned, burst out at once. Dizzying
scents came from the flowers; the air intoxicated, and one was mad with
lyricism and art. One felt one was about to rediscover the lost secret, and
it was true, one had rediscovered poetry." [8]

Chapter 4

THE EPOCH Gautier describes was roughly the sixteen years between 1827 and 1843, or to choose a convenient parenthesis, between the publication of Hugo's *Cromwell* with a preface that undertook to define Romantic dogma — "Our era is above all dramatic and by this very fact lyric also" — and the failure of his *Les Burgraves*, embodying the same principles and as robustly dramatic as its predecessor, in 1843 received like champagne that has gone flat.

It will be said that this is much too restrictive, that it makes Romanticism exclusively French, and finally that a movement of such dimensions cannot begin with a preface and end with an unfavorable review. True of course. The force behind Romanticism was not confined to France and did not beach itself for another hundred years; every subsequent movement in the arts, to the Surrealists and beyond, owes something to its example. At its widest point it embraces most of what we mean by modern or avant-garde, terms not to be defined without reference to the Romantic precedent.* But it is precisely at this point that history returns us to Paris in the

---

* I am aware of the objections to this thesis, notably on the part of avant-garde artists and critics *soi-disant*, who dislike it because it is in conflict with their delusion of uniqueness, of having broken with the past — a delusion that however rather affirms than denies the relationship since the Romantics shared it, and were indeed the first to elevate it into a principle. Alternatively, the refusal to recognize an historical precedent may stem from confusion between spirit and form: because the Romantics invented the cult of innovation (as well as opening the door to primitivism, magic, dreams and other currents in modern art), it does not follow that they invented Symbolism, Cubism, Surrealism, etc., though these are, I think, demonstrably branches of the same

1830's. It was the French Romantics and not their English or German counterparts who were writing or painting romantically who named themselves in capitals. They were the first aesthetic rebels to form a militant coterie (Gautier speaks of the "army of Romanticism" and compares it to the youthful legions who followed Napoleon to Italy), a vanguard laying claim to an artistic radicalism appropriate to the post-revolutionary age, "art for our time." It was this sense of temporality, of possessing a sensibility distinctively modern, that they exploited in a series of confrontations like the first night of *Hernani* — providing the psychological format for all such confrontations since: the debut of the *Sacre du Printemps;* the New York Armory show; the Dadaist manifestoes. Hugo's elaborately staged charade was the prototypical avant-garde event, employing all the riot-inducing techniques of publicity and polemic that were to become standard; just as it was Hugo who more than anyone else gave the movement its self-consciousness — a further and essential element in avant-gardism that is likewise a Romantic discovery. In the simplest terms, art is modern when it thinks it is, when it sees itself from the historical point of view, and defines its own position in relation to it. (It is we and not the practitioners of the style called Mannerism who have given it its name.)

Such a development presupposes a metropolitan setting. It requires opera houses, theatres, newspapers, and a public; it must be at or near the seat of power, because it is only in relation to power and its appurtenances that a group like the Romantics can make itself felt. (One reason why the Lake Poets were romantic but not *the* Romantics.) To lay siege to the artistic or political establishment, one must be where it is. Paris had all this and something more. Thanks to the salons, no other European capital was so prepared to welcome and civilize the new men. In the best of them, wit and talent far outweighed mere birth, making "the aristocracy of genius," a favorite Romantic conception, more nearly realizable than elsewhere. The Romantic poet did not moulder in attics. As it happened, several of them — Musset, Vigny, Nerval — belonged to the upper class by birth, but that wasn't the source of their power; in other societies they might well have lost caste when they took up poetry and associated with bohemians.*

---

tree. Renato Poggioli (*The Theory of the Avant-Garde,* 1968) rightly observes that successive generations have congratulated themselves on the liquidation of the Romantic heritage when in fact what took place was the trashing of false and decadent elements mistakenly assumed to be the real thing, "something become conventional, a pathetic mode, a taste for the sensational" (p. 49). (For a just comparison, look at Delacroix's *Massacre at Scio* and Picasso's *Guernica,* both outraged depictions of a current event, both execrated by the classicists of their day — the Delacroix was called "a massacre of paint" — having in common a dramatic passion that transcends their physical dissimilarity.)

* I use the word though it did not yet exist. Bohemianism came later and was a decadent version of the Romantic style. It stands for the break with so-called good society which in the 1830's the artist did not contemplate.

In Paris that didn't happen. An out-and-out parvenu like Balzac had no difficulty making his way into aristocratic circles — and aristocratic beds. Nor did Liszt. Chopin spent the latter part of his life (after the break with Sand) being cosseted by princesses, in such exquisite settings as the Hôtel Lambert on the Île Saint-Louis. Berlioz, a rarity among Romantics in that he wasn't a snob, didn't happen to care for high society but when he chose to frequent it encountered no obstacles either.*

The Romantic in short was dramatizing himself when he assumed the outsider's guise and when he inveighed against society meant something other than the fashionable world he found it so easy to penetrate. The difficulty was indeed all the other way. For someone like Liszt, who adored high life, the problem was to evade the blandishments of a society that, apart from everything else, has been more attracted to novelty, which is the essence of fashion, than any other. It isn't by accident that Paris, the world's capital of fashion, should also have been the center of modern art for more than a century. Little as the comparison may please, the avant-garde artist and the creator of fashion are alike in their worship of original-ity and contempt for the outmoded — nor does the comparison shock the French, who decorate their great dressmakers with the Legion of Honor and elect Cocteau to the Academy though he did draw for *Vogue*. (One is reminded that French Symbolism's most beautiful review was also called *La Vogue*.) That is the danger. For what is fashionable soon enters the public domain, to descend finally into commercialized *Kitsch* or camp, what-ever word we choose to describe the ultimate fate of debased styles — thus pushing the artist always closer to nihilism or the incommunicable. The pressure to produce what cannot be reproduced becomes a scourge.

If the Romantics largely avoided this hazard it was because their influ-ence didn't extend into the decorative arts, the surest route to populariza-tion. (Because Delacroix was a painter and not a decorator or an illustrator like Moreau and Félicien Rops, he did not father a style like *art nouveau*, which has proved so adaptable at the department-store level.) Even so, they did not escape popularity. More exactly, Hugo, Balzac and George Sand did not — though Sand's fame partly derived from her dressing like a man, her lovers, etc. Liszt's celebrity too was colossal, but only as a per-former. The others had mostly to be satisfied with recognition by the

---

* Marie d'Agoult's memoirs contradict this with regard to musicians, who she in-forms us "still had their place apart; in spite of the eagerness to have them, they ap-peared in the salons only on the footing of inferiors" — even Rossini, who for a fee of 1500 francs would arrange private concerts with himself at the piano, and singers to round out. They arrived in a body, remained together behind a rope, and departed by a side door. But as we shall see, Mme d'Agoult was inordinately conscious of class distinctions and not really to be trusted in these matters. Nor did she make Liszt's acquaintance behind a rope. They met at the house of a mutual friend. No doubt what she says was true of musicians at an earlier date but not in 1830.

"happy few" to whom Stendhal dedicated the *Roman Journal,* or like Vigny with retreat to an ivory tower. (I use the phrase advisedly — it was first coined to fit his situation.)

Either way, there was a deep ambivalence in the Romantic's attitude to success. On the one hand, he longed for fame and glory, which meant communicating with the greatest possible number of people. Berlioz dreamed of municipal concerts attended by thousands; such was the quality of his music that only a few hundred people understood or liked it, driving him to the opposite position: that art was a holy calling whose secrets could be divulged only to certain initiates. This paradox, central to Romanticism, was new, since the artist under the *ancien régime* was not obliged to worry about his stance vis-à-vis the public. It was also unresolvable, and still is. Romanticism may have been, in Ortega's phrase, "the first-born son of democracy." It was not, as he also says, "par excellence, the popular style." * Romanticism did not survive by virtue of having created artifacts acceptable to the masses (which would have destroyed it) but because it didn't: what was truly advanced in its content kept its virtue and became the fertilizing agent for future advances. And this is why the Romantic attitude toward the public has likewise proved to be a lasting model. With the demise of high art, the avant-garde has lost its function; but those of an age to remember how it worked will, in the presence of the Romantics, be haunted with a sense of *déjà vu.* We feel we have been there before and indeed we have.

Even the cast of characters is familiar. We recognize the charismatic leader, swollen with power (Hugo), and his satellite critic, eaten with envy and secret disapprobation (Sainte-Beuve); the young bravos (Vigny, Liszt, Gautier, Nerval); the mistress-mother with her newest lover (George Sand, Musset). We seem to know the aloof ones who yet always turn up (Delacroix, Chopin), and to have seen the actress they all fall in love with (Marie Dorval). We have met the house-critics and the publishers (Jules Janin, Émile de Girardin, the Bertins) and been asked, perhaps, to the Thursdays of the beautiful eccentric who receives in black velvet and keeps a little Moor to guard her door (Cristina Belgiojoso), or to the Fridays of the other one, the enchantress whose editor husband everyone is rather afraid of (Delphine Girardin). We have stood on the fringes of the crowd making

---

* These statements are the basis for his contention (in *The Dehumanization of Art*) that Romanticism was not the antecedent of modern avant-gardes. It is disconcerting that the illustrious Ortega should have felt this, and I can only account for it (as does Poggioli) by supposing that he confused the Romantic idealization of "the people" with public acceptance of Romantic art and poetry, which was minimal — as noted, mostly confined to novels. One wonders what this popular style was that conquered the people who hadn't been able to "stomach" the older, classical art. It is anyway the fact that the public that couldn't stomach one couldn't stomach the other either and was about equally indifferent to both.)

small talk with the extras (Charles Didier, Jules Sandeau, Victor Pavie, in-numerable others). And we almost know what the small talk was about: the last ill-attended concert, the *vernissage* that provoked such dense comment from a critic outside the pale. If nothing else, we identify the tone, the interior, highbrow smugness that pervades even the gossip.

The smugness is of course justified. To have been on the inside track, an original investor so to speak, is the earned reward for snubs and failure. The tone should nevertheless be marked for what it is, a form of hubris that had not existed before:

About two hundred persons were in the hall, listening religiously. After a few minutes, the audience grew restless; people began to talk, each telling his neighbor of his increasing discomfort and boredom. Finally . . . nine-tenths of the audience got up and left, complaining aloud that the music was unbearable, incomprehensible, ridiculous. . . . Yet in one corner of the room there was a small group . . . whose thoughts were very different. . . . This tiny fraction . . . suspecting what was going to happen, had huddled together so as not to be bothered in their contemplation. After a few bars . . . I did indeed fear I might be bored, though I kept listening. Shortly the chaos seemed to unwind, and just when the public's patience gave out, mine revived, and I fell under the spell of the composer's genius.[1]

Here are all the hallmarks of the avant-garde point of view: the bourgeois sheep rigorously divided from the informed goats, of whom the author is one. He is in fact Berlioz. The year is 1829 and the small group those who had come to hear Beethoven's quartets (in this case, the C-sharp Minor) for the first time in France. He doesn't say who they were but we don't need to be told because with minor variations they were always the same. If musicians: Adolphe Nourrit, Chrétien Urhan, Chopin, Liszt, Ferdinand Hiller, and Berlioz himself. If writers: Mérimée, Heine (though not in 1829), Sainte-Beuve, Vigny, Dumas *père,* and so on. Who was at the first reading of Hugo's *Marion de Lorme?* Sainte-Beuve, Vigny, Mérimée. . . . And who described it? Balzac. It was his debut into the *cénacle* and he was scared to death: "Miserable newcomer admitted for the first time to that social mystery, what manner are you to adopt? . . . There is only one safe course for you, an attitude of suffocated silence because your rapture is so great that the words stick in your throat." [2] (Irony that would, incidentally, have been lost on Hugo.) Who crowded the Odéon when Kemble's troupe brought Shakespeare to France for the first time in living memory? It hardly pays to research the lists. Only illness or a trip abroad can cause an absence. The Romantics took for granted that they must publicize with their presence those events deemed peculiarly their own, and neither personal animosities nor divergent opinions were allowed to interfere. Thus Delacroix studiously dissociated himself from

Hugo's leadership and thought the Romantic designation absurd. Berlioz had no use for Chopin. Sainte-Beuve and Heine had grave reservations about Liszt. The permutations were endless. They did not affect the determination to unite in the face of critics and a public presumed to be hostile, ignorant — above all, old.

To be old has always been an aesthetic sin; to the Romantics it was also synonymous with fogeyism, and implied a heart and brain hardened like the arteries. They were not the last to confound gray hairs with bourgeois values without explaining why they must go together; they were assuredly the first. To emphasize this was the whole purpose of the so-called battle of *Hernani,* conceived and announced as a challenge offered by youth to decrepitude, enthusiasm to stuffy middle age.

It is important to understand that this capital event (February 25, 1830) was not spontaneous. Had the *perruques* (literally wigs, hence figuratively, bald old men) in the audience merely hissed their disapprobation of lines that did not pause in the middle or the unseemly realism of the opening, "It will soon be midnight," Hugo might have left with nothing worse than a mild failure. He intended to go down with guns blazing if not actually to ensure a *succès de scandale.* It was to this end that he recruited his legions of bearded, long-haired students, armed them with scarlet tickets bearing the password *Hierro* — from a Spanish battle cry — and installed them in their places hours before the curtain went up. His lieutenants too were provocatively clothed, Gautier in his famous *gilet rose* and Nile-green trousers, and nothing omitted that might give offense. The long-hairs stared insolently at the bald pates: "Off with their wigs!" was the cry. Signs of restiveness were howled down. The result was entirely satisfactory. The play became the talk of the town and had an unusual run of forty-five nights.

Hugo's more perceptive contemporaries were not taken in by this performance, or by the play — which the majority of them disliked intensely. Balzac and Stendhal detested it; Sainte-Beuve got out of writing a review, knowing it would have to condemn the ranting and the fustian however much it praised the poetry. Berlioz was cool: the innovations, "these runover lines and broken half-lines which enrage the classicists leave me quite indifferent." Still, he had to admit that "Hugo has destroyed the unities of time and place and for that I take an interest in him as a daredevil who risks death to set a mine under an old barrier." Hugo had in fact overturned certain classic principles, and it is surprising that Stendhal at least did not see this. Or perhaps he did see it, and as an innovator himself, wasn't particularly impressed. The truth was that *Hernani,* simply as a play, was pure melodrama and its bombast not without appeal to the taste it was supposed to affront. (Stendhal said that the "tirades" reminded him of classical tragedy.)

Hernani was all the same a milestone in art history, and a lesson to Liszt, among others, in the techniques of propaganda. (He was later to stage a similar confrontation between the old and the new styles in his "duel" with Thalberg.) It showed him how the bourgeoisie might be flogged into submission with a good show — a dangerous practice that he justified on the ground that the public was thus educated in spite of itself. This too is an idea we will encounter again.

Chapter 5

WE DON'T KNOW how or when Liszt joined the *cénacle,* the Romantic inner circle that as its name indicates was like a club. There are several reasons for this and the first is his habit of treating his life like an episodic novel, written straight off without corrections. Except for a brief moment when he and Marie d'Agoult shared a notebook, he didn't keep journals and almost alone in a confessional age he left no *histoire de ma vie* — possibly because a halfway honest one would have rocked Europe.*

---

* He has also been unlucky in his biographers. The semi-official life, *Franz Liszt als Künstler und Mensch* (Leipzig, 1880–94) is by Lina Ramann. It was written largely at the dictation of his mistress Carolyne Wittgenstein and although he corrected it here and there, it is unreliable — as well as being abominably written. Peter Raabe's *Franz Liszt* (Stuttgart, 1931) is accurate as far as it goes. It is also dull and in German, a hindrance to those weak in that language. Guy de Pourtalès's *La Vie de Franz Liszt* (Paris, 1927) ought to be better than it is. The author had connections with Cosima Liszt and claims "oral sources" but as he doesn't specify what they were, he can't be relied on either, and his tone is maudlin. Sacheverell Sitwell's *Liszt* (London, 1934) is perhaps best described as amusing, if you enjoy the mandarin style. He has a feeling for Liszt's music, and no respect whatever for facts; it is truly astounding to find so many mistakes in a book long looked on as the standard biography in English. Finally, there is Ernest Newman's *The Man Liszt* (New York, 1935, reissued in 1970), a strange study, written out of uncontrollable hatred for its subject. Having grossly misrepresented Liszt in his *Life of Richard Wagner* (London and New York, 1933) Newman apparently felt he hadn't gone far enough and produced this.

All of the above are particularly weak on Liszt's Paris background and the Romantic movement. That has been left to French scholarship in rather recent years, and admirably thorough it has been. I am especially and heavily indebted to Jacques Vier's *La Comtesse d'Agoult et son temps* in five volumes (Paris, 1955); to Thérèse Marix-

Because he was all his life such a conspicuous figure, there are innumerable contemporary mentions of him, and after his death a flood of reminiscence that must have quickly become a drug on the market — even his barber wrote one. For all that he was an oddly secretive man, not given to discussing his personal life. There was a great deal his closest friends didn't know: he never, for example, talked about his love affairs; he left that to his mistresses — two of whom wrote books about him — and to the gossip columnists. Money and health were two subjects he avoided whenever possible. Nor was he particularly anxious to go into detail about work in progress. He liked impersonal conversations about philosophy, politics or literature — or pointless ones where nothing serious was said. In either case, he gave little away: anecdote and reminiscence were not his strong point.

The letters: like everybody else he wrote a staggering number. (Wherever did they find the time? Toward the end, he was answering more than two thousand letters a year and he did rebel.) But they are irregularly spaced according to whether he was travelling or settled and there were naturally many more saved when he was old and famous than when he was younger. Few have survived from his Paris years, and what has is mostly trivial, notes that today would be the stuff of a telephone call. Occasionally these are useful. A scribble that invited Heine to meet him at a certain café establishes that it was Liszt who introduced Heine to George Sand — it tells us nothing about a friendship that to judge from Heine's published articles on Liszt must have been touchy and ambiguous. Another jotting to Marie d'Agoult announces the arrival of George Sand in Paris in August of 1834: "Alfred de Musset talked a lot about her the other day. He will present me to her if he sees her again." [1] *If he sees her again* is a footnote full of melancholy interest to students of the Sand-Musset affair, then in its last gasp. It doesn't tell us how Liszt met Musset, why Musset considered introducing such a potential rival to a mistress he was already losing — or if he did.

With Alfred de Vigny, with Balzac and Victor Hugo and half a dozen others we are similarly in the dark about times and places. According to d'Ortigue, it was Liszt's custom to call on the writers he admired without bothering to secure introductions. He mentions Lamartine, Abbé de Lamennais, Victor Hugo, Vigny, Sainte-Beuve, Étienne de Senancour, George Sand and Pierre Ballanche as those he got to know in this way — it isn't a bad way; writers who say they can't be disturbed are usually lying. Still, d'Ortigue must be wrong about some of his names. Another source has Liszt at a literary party in 1829, where he met Mérimée, Hugo, and prob-

Spire's *Les Romantiques et la musique* (Paris, 1954), containing research it would take years to reproduce; and to the new edition of George Sand's letters (Éditions Garnier Frères, 1966).

ably Sainte-Beuve. Lamennais he is thought to have been introduced to by d'Ortigue himself; while for Senancour, author of *Obermann*, the pessimistic novel that toured Switzerland in Liszt's pocket and was part of the libretto for the first *Année de pèlerinage*, a likely intermediary was Sainte-Beuve, whose advocacy had raised *Obermann* from obscurity. (Senancour was sixty in 1830 and not a member of the *cénacle*. Liszt however often visited him "to talk Christianity, our habitual subject.")

Vigny moved in several worlds but Liszt may have met him through Berlioz. It is anyway Berlioz who paints a vivid little landscape with figures that puts Liszt and Vigny together. Berlioz, lately married, was living in Montmartre, then a garden suburb and rather out of the way. He depended on the visits of his friends. "I can't tell you how much this springtime scene moves and saddens me," he wrote Liszt in the spring of 1834, praying him to bring Vigny and others. "Why aren't you both here now? Perhaps tomorrow I will feel differently. Are we really playthings of the air? . . . and is Moore right when he says . . . 'There's nothing bright but Heaven!' . . . But my heaven is the poetic world and there is a slug in every blossom. . . . Look here, come and bring Vigny with you. I need you both." [2] This characteristic plea was successful. They came, sat in Berlioz's garden and "discussed art, poetry, philosophy, music and drama – in a word all that constitutes life – in the presence of this beauty of nature and Italian sunshine that has favored us these past days."

But what was *said* about art, music, drama? We are too seldom told, though here we can perhaps guess. In May 1834, Berlioz, who was finishing *Harold in Italy* on time stolen from his everlasting journalism, was "dead tired and bored from scribbling . . . for those rascally papers," aching from "wounds to my artistic affections." Liszt had just met Abbé de Lamennais, a cataclysmic event that introduced him to "humanitarian art." Vigny was embarking on his *Chatterton* preface. Is it not imaginable that some portion of the contents was inspired by Berlioz's passionate laments (Vigny had no direct experience of poverty or the sufferings he protested except as he apprehended them through his friends), and that it may have been this same conversation that suggested to Liszt his parallel essay?

That reconstruction may be faulty but such cross-fertilizations did constantly occur. More than the natural desire to ease loneliness and foregather with comrades is involved when Berlioz cries, "I need you both." Such calls abound. "It is quite impossible that you shouldn't dine with me next Saturday . . . along with Lamartine and Alfred," writes Deschamps to Hugo in 1828. "I have *got* to consult you about the whole of my poem . . . and fully intend to give you a reading of it. . . . Lamartine had not seen your wonderful preface to *Cromwell*, so I lent it to him. Needless to say, he is madly enthusiastic. . . ." [3] Hugo writes to Vigny: "I feel a strong need to give you *Les Orientales* and the *Condamné;* I feel a strong need that you shouldn't be angry with me; I feel a strong need that you shall not say 'Victor is neglecting me'; because I admire you and love you with more than most men have of love and admiration." [4] The unhappiest hour of Sainte-Beuve's life may have been when he had to tell Hugo he could no longer visit him: "When one is in such a state . . . it is better to hide, to try to achieve peace of mind, to let the gall drip away, to do one's best not to stir up too much mud, to accuse oneself at the bar of one's own conscience, at the judgment-seat of a friend like you. . . . Do not answer this, dear friend; do not ask me to come and see you; I could not do it." [5] Sainte-Beuve was in love with Madame Hugo and jealous of the master. It was nevertheless true that Hugo's loss was more shattering than hers. The Romantic movement was founded on the interaction of personalities incessantly in touch, on the asking and giving of opinion (since that of outsiders hardly mattered), somebody's brief to be filed: "Come on, Magnin, *plump* for it!" they shouted when a dispute arose in the *Globe* office over whether to go all out for *Hernani.*

That is why the urban setting was vital. The Romantic sincerely believed that he hated cities. When Hugo rented an apartment in the rue Notre-Dame-des-Champs, he described it as "a place of monastic calm, suited to a poet, hidden away at the far end of a shady avenue," and luxuriated in this communion with "nature." But no Englishman would have thought that the gardens, dovecotes, windmills and rustic bridges of the neighborhood had much to do with nature; while the unsentimental Sainte-Beuve called the apartment itself "a battlefield" tramped over by Hugo's legions, where one wasn't for a moment alone. The Romantic might stroll in the meadows at the head of his troupe (Hugo did this often, and half a lifetime later in Germany, so did Liszt) but evening usually found him safe in a gaslit café, at a theatre or a noisy party.

Liszt never recovered from this early training in personal and professional conviviality. Like Hugo and everybody else he knew in his youth, he paid lip service to the joys of solitude, and avoided it. Try as he would, he couldn't convince himself that social life was an evil — or, given Hugo's example, that it interfered with the artist's output. On the contrary: had he not, by the fluke of circumstance and his own burning desire, been able to insinuate himself into precisely this group of talkative, gregarious and exhaustingly creative people, to see them day after day and night after night, he might never have been a composer worth bothering about, and assuredly not the one we know.

From the *cénacle*'s earliest days, all eyes were on Victor Hugo, "the one man to whom everybody turned for the watchword of the day," said Baudelaire. "Never was royalty more legitimate, more natural, more wholeheartedly acclaimed, more confirmed in its occupancy of the throne by the powerlessness of rebellion." [6] He looked in 1830 like the young Napoleon — dark thyroidal eyes under a towering brow, sulky, conceited mouth; at twenty-eight he was the most exciting younger poet in Europe and intensely aware of his position. He had everything: genius, a beautiful wife, a growing family, and had never known an hour of obscurity. He was a natural conqueror and there were many who found his vaingloriousness unendurable. It was a losing fight. To the majority of young men seeking their fortune in the arts, he was irresistible and they flocked to his standard. They were received with a cordiality that — one of them remembered — "was enough to make a man go nearly out of his mind." Wherever the Hugos lived was the nerve-center of Romanticism.

The monastic retreat in rue Notre-Dame-des-Champs didn't last long. The landlord objected to the racket, forcing a move to rue Jean-Goujon. In 1832 they moved again, to the exquisite Hôtel de Guéméné in the Place Royale and a set of rooms splendid enough even for Hugo — though of course hideously furnished. Hugo, like Balzac, wasn't happy unless surrounded with bric-a-brac, with phoney Gothic and Renaissance pieces, with red damask and Venetian chandeliers. This is the setting of the Romantic conversation pieces and everybody was there. Hugo's guests complained of starvation. There were no refreshments served and you had to leave your stomach in the cloakroom, according to Houssaye — your critical sense too. The poet's vanity was hard to swallow. Nevertheless his rooms were jammed with disciples and by 1833 Liszt was among them. "I saw our friend Hugo and Dumas again this week," he wrote Marie d'Agoult. "Decidedly it's the only world, the only society I will frequent in future; the rest seems so empty to me, so boringly pointless." [7] The poet basking in his glory was a powerful object lesson. He had challenged his epoch in the preface to *Marion de Lorme:* "The nineteenth century, while still in its early years, produced an Empire and an Emperor. Why should a poet not now appear who would be to Shakespeare what Napoleon was to Charlemagne?" And everybody knew exactly whom he had in mind. Liszt was twenty-three, an age when that sort of thing is catching. "When I've spent a few hours with V. H. I feel a crowd of hidden ambitions stirring in my heart," he wrote — a telling confession.[8]

Liszt could admire Hugo wholeheartedly because he was outside the rivalries that rent the literary community.* He was also humble — all gratitude for the brilliance lavished on him by these remarkable older men. Hugo's remark that Beethoven was the "greatest thinker in this visionary

---

* Whether from prudence or by accident he also kept his hands off its women, thus avoiding endless trouble. Even then, it seems he preferred the aristocracy. He spent the winter of 1832 in the Alpine château of the Countess Adèle Laprunarède, later the Duchess de Fleury.

art [of music]" he considered a dazzling *aperçu;* Lamartine's advice that he "look well at nature . . . whose inspirations are worth more than those of the salons" he reverently treasured. So great was their prestige that it didn't occur to him to challenge them when they ventured on ground he knew more about than they did. Instead, he embarked on a course of self-education that must be unique for a musician.

Nos ancêtres les gaulois was for ages the French schoolboy's introduction to history. If we are what we read, then Liszt was French and not the descendant of Hunnish warriors. D'Ortigue records that on a typical day he read dictionaries for four consecutive hours. "He studied Boiste and Lamartine with the same ardor." He would buttonhole people with questions as touching as they were foolish. "Teach me the history of France," he said to Mignet. But that was just what Mignet could not do. No amount of digging in dictionaries and parsing of Diderot could give him the tradition that Berlioz took in with his milk. Since both belonged to the first generation of composers to be directly influenced (they would have said inspired) by literature, this difference was critical. Some of Berlioz's literary discoveries were earthshaking to him. Shakespeare revealed in a lightning flash "the whole heaven of art." His inner balance, rooted in family, country, language, habits of intellectual restraint, was not seriously disturbed. Liszt had no such equilibrium and what his hectic comings and goings amounted to was the well-known search for identity, for the parent that Adám was not. He couldn't construct a racial memory of Descartes, Racine, Voltaire — symbols of rationalism to which Romanticism was in part a reaction. Many of his recorded speeches sound like translations from some idiom profoundly un-French — very much, in fact, like the ramblings of Chekhov's half-educated provincials when they begin to philosophize:

> Don't doubt that the future of the world is in everything. . . . What do the mistakes, the weaknesses and dissentions of the champions of truth matter? . . . This breathless generation will pass and lose itself like a winter torrent. . . . After it, new warriors, better disciplined and instructed by our reverses, will gather up our scattered arms from the battlefield and discover the magic virtues of Hercules' arrows.[9]

That speech was delivered to George Sand on a Swiss mountainside. "Embrace me, my poor Franz," she replied tenderly, "and may God hear you. You think and talk not badly for a musician."

That was the truth and must have hurt. His culture was impressive *pour un musicien,* a race that Rousseau said read little and yet was so in need of reading and reflection (a thought surely familiar to Liszt, who revered the *Dictionnaire de musique*). When the smoke is cleared from his literary references, they are seen to be limited and they were never revised. His taste was formed when he was in his twenties and he read more or less the same books for the rest of his life. He failed to discover Flaubert, and although he knew Baudelaire and is supposed to have admired him, there is no reason to think he was at all familiar with the poetry. (Both men were after his time in Paris.) Odder still is his apparent indifference to the great Russian writers. He had special and intimate ties with Russia through various mistresses and the Russian school of composers; he was acquainted with Turgenev, who was the lover of his lifelong friend Pauline Viardot-García, but if he read him or any other Russian novelist we don't hear of it. Those who try to make an intellectual out of Liszt are under a misapprehension.*

But if literature and his associations with writers did not turn him into an original thinker, let alone the metaphysician he sometimes tried to be, they did help to create the artist, who is unimaginable without his halo of European culture and the lustre it lent to his music. Reading transformed the illiterate little *enfant prodige* into a cosmopolitan composer — gave him his vocation and his destiny. Without it, he might have been content to be what many have mistakenly thought he was, the rival of a pianist like Thalberg or the successor to Paganini. His ambition went far beyond either. In his own mind he belonged to the heroic few, doomed to glory and misfortune, in whom art and life are one. In one of his open letters to George Sand (1837) he defended the use of the explanatory preface on just that ground:

The work of certain artists is their life. . . . The musician above all, who is inspired by nature but without copying it, exhales in sound his life's most intimate mysteries. He thinks, he feels, he speaks in music; but because his language, more arbitrary and less definite than all others, lends itself to a multitude of diverse interpretations . . . it is not unprofitable for the composer to give in a few lines the psychic sketch of his work . . . to explain the fundamental idea of his composition. The critic is then free to praise or blame the manifestation of his thought. . . .

Few books appear today without prefaces, a sort of second book about the book. Often superfluous when it is a question of a book written in everyday language, does not this precaution become absolutely necessary . . . not for instrumental music as conceived up till now (Beethoven and Weber excepted), music squarely ordered on a symmetrical plan . . . but for the compositions of the modern school, which generally aspire to be the expression of *a tormented individuality?* [My italics.] [10]

* T. Marix-Spire, like many French scholars, I think overestimates this side of Liszt. To prove her point, she supplies many quotes like the one given above. I still feel that Sand had the last word. But neither is it true (as Haraszti and others have it) that his culture was entirely a superficial salon product. To certain works — *The Divine Comedy* for instance — he was committed with his whole being.

The analogies, we see, are with literature throughout, even when not explicitly stated. The composer of the modern school, like the Romantic poet, is preoccupied with the revelation of his tormented self. (There is even an implied borrowing from poetry in the mention of music ordered after a symmetrical plan. We don't quite see why this should be easier to grasp than some other kind unless we recall the arguments over Hugo's "formless" rhyme schemes, in which the meaning overruns the end of the line. Asymmetry is thus equated with modernity in both cases.) He seems to be saying that modern music is primarily confessional; and his symphonic music undoubtedly was. The prefaces that following his own prescription he supplied to his "readers" snap before us like the slides in a magic lantern, each an illumination of his self-image. That to *Tasso* explains that "it has been our aim to embody in the music the great antithesis; the genius who is misjudged by his contemporaries and surrounded with a radiant halo by posterity." [11] There follows the plot-line, "to illustrate three moments inseparable from his immortal fame." Even if we didn't know from other sources that he strongly identified himself with Tasso, these preliminaries would give it away. The introduction to the symphonic poem *Hamlet* is yet more bare-faced: "Hamlet, like every exceptional person, imperiously demands the wine of life. . . . He wishes to be understood by [Ophelia] without the obligation to explain himself to her. . . . She collapses under her mission, because she is incapable of loving him in the way he must be loved, and her madness is only the decrescendo of a feeling, whose lack of sureness has not allowed her to remain on Hamlet's level." [12] This was an original hypothesis: it would be incomprehensible if we were unaware of his relations with Marie d'Agoult.

Whether instrumental music can or should be made to bear these burdens belongs elsewhere. The issue here is that they were often (though not always) artificially imposed after the fact. *Tasso* was not conceived in three parts as the preface implies. The middle came to him long after the rest and the whole was revised over many years. *Les Préludes,* which has a complicated genesis out of poems by Joseph Autran, wound up with a title from one of Lamartine's meditations with which it has nothing to do. Such jugglings are common, and prejudicial to his argument that a psychic sketch of the composer's intentions is useful to the listener. They make us ask whether the whole literary apparatus was not a mere conceit, or worse, a form of public relations.

The same question can be asked about all so-called programmatic music, and answered in various ways. But although a number of Liszt's claims are easily disproved, it remains, I believe, the fact that an enormous amount of his music *was* confessional — in a way, the autobiography he didn't write. It all seems to be there: landscapes observed, airs overheard; erotic and religious experience; poetry and history; treasures and trash. It wouldn't be difficult to draw a picture of his life from the music alone. In this one respect, his approach to his music did not change — or better to say, he did not realize that it had, even when the disparity between his ostensible subject matter and his treatment of it approached totality: a late work titled *From the Cradle to the Grave* after a dismally bad and sentimental painting by his friend Count Michael Zichy is an extreme example. The name informs us that he never got over his passion for the Hungarian aristocracy or improved his taste in pictures. But in 1881–1882, when this last of the symphonic poems was composed, his music had long since taken leave of even the most tenuous link with inspiration of this sort: *From the Cradle to the Grave* is sober, refined, strange — anything but what the title might call to mind. But the habit stuck. To the end, when his pieces were becoming as abstract as Mondrian's, he gave them names to intimate they were "about" something. (In his defense, *From the Cradle to the Grave* was not typical either. He had in general a genius for titles and invented a number of brilliantly descriptive terms: transcendant execution, rhapsody, symphonic poem.) He did not notice the disparity because his whole theory of art had been founded on Romantic syncretism, a theory he didn't re-examine after it had ceased to have any real application to his music.

The metaphysical union of the arts was one of several Germanic conceptions (see Schlegel's "Architecture is frozen music") to be celebrated by poets like Vigny: "*Musique, poésie, art pur de Raphaël, vous deviendrez un seul Dieu.*" It became a kind of secular monotheism and was part of the basis for that religion of art, so-called, that dominated Romantic thought. Its intention, denied by rationalism, was to blur the distinction between one form and another. Thus Hugo's *Orientales* intoxicated with its lush word-pictures, at about the same time that Delacroix was reminding himself of certain passages in Byron, ". . . the end of the *Bride of Abydos;* the *Death of Selim,* his body tossed about by the waves and that hand — especially that hand. . . . I feel these things as they can be rendered in painting." [13]

There was only one trouble with this from the composer's point of view. It presupposed that the arts are synchronized like clocks and advance at the same pace, and this was not true in the first half of the nineteenth century — which saw technical innovations in music not matched by what was happening in the other arts, whose break with the past was more emotional than technical, a revolution of feeling rather than of form. For all the shock they caused to establishment critics, neither Delacroix's brushwork nor Hugo's broken lines were in themselves all that radical. In painting the real break came only with the Impressionists, when the camera began to refocus the painter's eye and aniline dyes (mauve, for instance, so important to Monet) to alter his palette. We must wait for the Symbolists before we can say for certain that modern poetry has been invented — though it in no way denigrates Hugo that this should be so. When Valéry writes that to get a clear view of his stature "one has to realize what the poets born within the climate of his influence have had to invent in order to . . . compete with him at all," [14] he is telling us what every Frenchman knows, that Hugo is the greatest of French poets ("Alas!" said Gide) but also that his very size forced on his successors the innovations that he did not make.

That these eventually were made by poets who related verse to music doesn't undermine the point: the Symbolist theory of "instrumental poetry," Mallarmé's idea that word-chains can be modulated into major and minor keys like a musical phrase, shaky stuff if taken too literally, are proof that poets had sensed the time-lag between the art of music and their own — a lag which the Romantics in their heyday did not grasp. (It would have astonished Hugo to be told that he had something to learn from Berlioz or Liszt — and astonished them as well.) Balzac like Hugo was a juggernaut who devoured everything in sight, a titan, but his narrative methods were conventional. He invented no new way to *write* a novel, and it is the more to his credit that he recognized and saluted his unsuccessful contemporary who did: Stendhal. (But Stendhal, through the accident of circumstance, was not a member of the *cénacle*.)

The clocks in short were set at different hours, with instrumental music in advance of the others. Partly this was due to technological developments in the instruments themselves — music was the first of the arts to feel directly the effects of the industrial revolution — but these developments had been spurred in turn by the increasingly complex demands of composers; and public taste, clinging tenaciously to opera, had long since lost touch with a form never very familiar to it. Thus the supposed difficulties of mastering Hugo's new-fangled verse were as nothing to those experienced by the average opera-lover confronted with the last Beethoven quartets.

This fundamental flaw in Romantic "unity" wasn't understood by the men of letters who dominated the movement, whose knowledge of the other arts was surprisingly scanty. Hugo's favorite painter, for example, was not Delacroix but Louis Boulanger or the Devéria brothers. About music he and his friends knew least of all. George Sand was the exception. Through Liszt, she acquired a real interest in "the modern school," which led her eventually to Chopin. (Delacroix was also devoted to Chopin but chiefly for his playing and what Delacroix terms his seraphic personality, not his originality as a composer.) The rest, when they could endure to listen, were either (like Stendhal) in love with Rossini and Cimarosa, or (like Gautier and Mérimée) attracted to *chansons populaires*. On the whole, the level of Romantic music appreciation was below that of the previous century. They produced no Diderots, d'Alemberts or Rousseaus, and no novel in the same class with *Le Neveu de Rameau*, that mysterious farce that is at the same time a musical treatise.

Someone is now going to mention Balzac, and to point out the many representations of musicians in Romantic fiction. It is true that Balzac wrote *Gambara*, about a Berlioz-like figure, and *Béatrix*, which features Gennaro Conti, a simulacrum of Liszt. Sand put Chopin into *Lucrezia Floriani*, where he appears as Prince Karol. Both were fascinated with the possibilities of these types, who were new to fiction as they were to art and society, and both failed to create more than a pasteboard figure tacked to a musical background. Prince Karol has actually shed his musical attributes altogether and is a portrait of Chopin as weakling and prig. Gennaro Conti is an Italian opera singer with one or two Lisztian traits unconvincingly thrown in. Only for *Gambara* did Balzac go to the trouble of a little research: he hired one Jakob Strunz, a German hack, to work up the technical stuffing. What he actually knew about music may be deduced from his confession elsewhere that an orchestra is "an ill-assorted and bizarre assembly . . . wherein inexplicable movements take place, where they all seem to be blowing their noses more or less in time." [15]

This jolly philistinism was common. There was Gautier's *mot:* "Music is the most disagreeable and expensive of all noises." That was part pose; but it was rare to find music spoken of intelligently. It was an aphrodisiac: "To listen to it is to love better what one loves. It is to think of voluptuous secrets" (Balzac). An off-stage accompaniment to serious business: "I perceive that a piece of music is good when it throws me into brilliant ideas about the object that actually occupies me" (Stendhal). "Music is the vapor of art. It is to poetry what reverie is to thought" (Hugo).

Nonsense of that sort infuriated Berlioz, who did not hesitate to say that the writers either had no feeling for music or were moved only by the most trivial melodies. He lambasted Stendhal: "M. Beyle, who has written a *Life of Rossini* and the most irritating stupidities on music, for which he thinks he has a feeling . . ." [16] Such harsh judgments came less easily to Liszt in youth. (Though he may have agreed with Berlioz, he only ventured that the *Life of Rossini* was "fairly interesting.") In awe of the poets as Berlioz was not, he was disposed to accept their standards and overlook their limitations. And that path did not lead to the composer's lonely atelier. It led straight to that "somebody who would afterwards do something," a personality out of a book. He did what the *cénacle* with its musical innocence and simultaneous worship of expressionism expected of him. Consciously or not, he was egged on to cultivate the bravura self that came all too easily to him, and to play down the serious composer whose existence it did not suspect.

The distinction he made between public and private performance has often been remarked on: for the public, the big glittering pieces, operatic fantasies, or the works of Beethoven, Weber and Hummel performed, as he admitted himself, "with a hundred insolent alterations" that would make them more palatable to "a public always slow to apprehend beautiful things in their august simplicity." That was in 1837, and he assured his correspondent [Sand] that he had disengaged himself from this "false path." It wasn't true. Mendelssohn was complaining of the same "lamentable misdemeanors" in 1842. Private occasions were different. When his fellow musicians were present we have their word for it that he was as meticulous as he was unforgettable. Berlioz recalled one of their intimate evenings: ". . . and the [Beethoven] sonata in C sharp minor, and the light dimmed, and the five listeners lying on the rug in the dark, and our magnetization, and Legouvé's tears and mine, and the respectful silence of Schoelcher . . . my God, my God, you were sublime that evening." [17]

A curious fact remains: why should there be no record, public or private, of his playing any of those early works that now interest us most, the sketches perfected in the first *Année de pèlerinage*, the first version of the *Harmonies poétiques et religieuses* (1834), the *Apparitions?* For larger audiences, perhaps not — though the temptation to insert a little masterpiece like the first *Apparition*, so admired by Busoni, one would have thought irresistible. But why not have taken advantage of his position within the *cénacle* to introduce himself as a composer and to educate thereby some of those in need of it?

The *Harmonies* is a particularly curious omission. Its "source" was Lamartine: the title is from a collection of his poems and the piece prefaced by a long crib from the master that is an early example of Liszt clutching at the robes of poets. "There are hearts broken with grief, rebuffed by the world, who seek refuge . . . in their thoughts, in the loneliness of their souls, to weep, to wait or to worship; may they be visited by a Muse solitary like themselves, find sympathy in her harmonies, and sometimes say while listening to her: we pray with thy words, we weep with thy tears, we invoke thy songs!" [18] As so often with Liszt, the epigraph is misleading. The piano does not weep or wail. The piece that follows is a bold experiment, mostly without time or key signatures, and full of chromatic harmonies. Which may be why it was never, as far as I can discover, played to Lamartine, with whom Liszt was well acquainted. Or was Lamartine simply not interested? Hugo apparently knew nothing of the songs Liszt set to his words, or of *Ce qu'on entend sur la montagne,* the symphonic poem based on his *Feuilles d'automne.*

The sketchiness of our knowledge speaks for itself. We know little about what Liszt played to his friends in the 1830's because they knew too little to tell us. We are repeatedly informed that "his genius astonished me," that "it has been well said that he is the apocalypse," hardly ever given the name of the composition. Music to this audience was evanescent as fireworks. Musset said no art was so perishable. Hugo found Mozart's *Requiem* "already full of wrinkles" (*déjà ridée*); to Gautier, any musical masterpiece out of the past was "dead." The problem would seem to be how he got these men to listen to him at all.

I believe he may have done it by a kind of trick. Improvisation appealed to the Romantic because it gratified his craving for personal theatre, for magic and the spontaneous. To listen to an improvisation was to catch the artist in the act. Eavesdropping on Liszt one day in her country house, Sand wrote: "I adore the broken phrases he strikes from his piano so that they seem to stay suspended, one foot in the air, dancing in space like limping will-o'-the-wisps. The leaves on the lime trees take on themselves the duty of completing the melody in a hushed, mysterious whisper, as though they were murmuring nature's secrets to one another." [19] She wanted to believe what her professional experience contradicted, that he was composing by accident, taking his cue from "nature." In this way, improvisation was also thought to communicate secrets, like blurted speech, and so to reveal the heart. Marie d'Agoult wrote of "a great and beautiful evening" that "he played the piano — improvised — as he sometimes talks to me."

He may have been improvising on that occasion. There must have been many others, when he was actually playing a composed work and his audience didn't realize it. Searle has an interesting comment on the *Harmonies poétiques et religieuses*, "a kind of free improvisation." In it, he says, "we can see Liszt trying to reproduce the effect of his own playing in a more minute way than had ever been attempted before." [20] How to tell, then, whether one was hearing a spontaneous invention or a composed piece? Liszt with his inborn instinct for dramatic necessity was the last man to enlighten an audience that didn't want to know. We imagine him surrounded, as in the pictures, with the wits and thunderers, men who if they couldn't be talking would just as soon have gone home or to a brothel — and wonder how they were silenced. Even the *Hammerklavier* would hardly have done it (too long for one thing), and how much less one of his own novelties, unless it could be presented as an impromptu. He was adept at creating the necessary atmosphere of suspense and mystery. Would he play or would he not? Would lightning strike? One disgruntled guest observed his method with scepticism: "Hair to the winds, his glance fixed on the ceiling as if looking for inspiration, he lets his hands fall casually on the keyboard, which makes dissonant sounds, and is feeling his way to a prelude when suddenly he gets up, closes the piano with a bang and announces that the bear won't dance tonight."

When "the Liszt problem" (a favorite title for monographs) is discussed, what one critic calls "the tragedy of his life and the reason for his not becoming the savior of nineteenth-century music, and with it of modern music" is invariably ascribed to his years on the concert stage — 1840–1847 — and the bad habits he then acquired. But it wasn't the everlastingly guilty public that made a virtuoso of him, that taught him to attitudinize like a second Byron and subordinate one of the century's finest musical intelligences to sheer effect. It was the demands made on him by Romantic society — or call it his inability to resist those demands. The public was not more indifferent to accuracy and quality, or more intent on the Lisztian personality at the expense of all else, than the non-musical heroes of his youth. Of course Balzac made him an opera singer: he had to be a performer of some kind, if not a singer then "the Paganini of the piano" or another stereotype.

Liszt invented the solo recital. Writing from Italy in 1839, he invited Cristina Belgiojoso to "imagine that, wearied with warfare, not being able to compose a program that would make sense, I have ventured to give a series of concerts all by myself, affecting the Louis XIV style and saying cavalierly to the public, 'The concert is — myself.'" [21] It is doubtful if anybody else would have dared make that statement, especially to Italian audiences, considered the most frivolous in Europe. At the opera they chattered unceasingly, pausing only for the arias, and could hardly be persuaded to attend concerts at all unless offered a variety of diversions, singers and monologists as well as the star turn. This was what Liszt meant by composing a program, not the choosing of his pieces, and it was pretty much the custom everywhere but in the most serious German cities. Other virtuosi took the situation for granted. Knowing the attention span of the average audience to be about that of a ten-year-old at the circus, they played an operatic fantasy, half a sonata, and were probably glad not to do more. Not so Liszt, brought up in a tougher school, and with an ego twice the size of theirs.

It would be going too far to say that his character was exclusively shaped by his early contacts with writers. He was nevertheless the first performer in musical history consciously to relate his life to literature and to see himself in the light of a fictive (one is tempted to say legendary) hero, a musical version of the mysterious stranger, the *poète maudit*. It was this extra dimension that made him unique. The age was rich in pianists, a few of whom may have been his equals, or in the classical style his superiors. None had his emotional range, his power to compel eye and ear to his person. Is this simply saying that he had genius? Not quite. Of course he did, and it is also true that a riveting presence cannot be acquired. Something happened when Liszt appeared before a crowd that if not unrelated was extraneous to his music-making. Sex was part of it, and it worked on men as well as women. But many a forgotten actor could have made the same claim. Aside from his enormous gift and his sex-appeal, what moved people about Liszt was his representation of a type familiar in literature but not in music, and this was to a very great extent a conscious creation, arrived at through the absorption of literary images. If Byron and Victor Hugo had never lived, there would have been no Liszt.

Chapter 6

LISZT'S MUSICAL INFLUENCES are ostensibly better documented than his literary ones. It is more accurate to say that repetition has turned them to stone. Three events are agreed to have been decisive in the years 1830 to 1833: Paganini's Paris debut; the meeting with Berlioz; Chopin's arrival from Warsaw with his portfolio of masterpieces under his arm. Enshrined in nineteenth-century theory about genius, these are adduced like so many revelations. So the whole art of the virtuoso is said to have been opened to him by Paganini in a flash of brimstone straight out of the *Tales of Hoffmann*, while Chopin taught him the poetry of the piano — and much more.

Like most clichés, these have some substance. Liszt was more open to received impressions than nearly any musician one can think of. Eclectic is the dismissive word, and the wrong one because it implies lack of originality and he was almost always original. But his forms were diverse as a tropical jungle's growth, and to many people as repellent. Bartók, who devoted a lot of attention to Liszt for obvious reasons, says this:

> Every composer, even the greatest, must start from something that already exists. . . . From this point, one composer, the innovator, gradually reaches new points; another — the great traditionist — develops what already exists to a stage never foreseen. . . . Liszt, however, did not start from any one point, nor fuse together in his works several related things; he submitted himself to the influence of the most diverse, contradictory, almost irreconcilable elements.[1]

Bartók lists these, beginning with "Berlioz's rather commonplace melody," "Chopin's sentimentality" and going on to bel canto, gypsy rhythms, Gre-

51

gorian chants, Spanish and Italian folk music. To which one could add that he was exposed to a greater diversity of materials than many of his contemporaries because he travelled more. But his willingness to absorb them reflected in the first place the Romantic interest in the exotic, while his researches into Gregorian chant will have had a similarly Romantic origin — in the cult for the Middle Ages and the revised attitude to the "primitive" that in the plastic arts did away with the idea that Gothic sculpture, for example, was but a botched attempt at classical perfection. He wasn't, in other words, floundering around as Bartók half implies, grasping at anything and everything that might serve his purpose. Still, if so many elements can be discovered in his music, the question of influences cannot be simple.

Let us begin with Paganini. That Liszt was "the Paganini of the piano" is a legend I despair of laying to rest but it is worth a try. Meaningless comparisons — Beethoven is the Michelangelo of music, Copenhagen is the Paris of the North — save trouble; and where they have been in use for generations die hard. "Liszt consciously set out to outdo Paganini" is only the latest contribution to the litany, no matter what the evidence to the contrary. Would it be any use to point out that while the Paganini *Capricci* are a convenient starting point for Liszt's bravura style, he had actually begun to develop what he called transcendental execution as early as 1826, in the *Études en douze exercices?*

Paganini made his Paris debut on March 9, 1831, and he was all that the Romantic imagination could desire: a tiny body yellowing like wax, mortuary clothing, the whole alarming aspect of an animated puppet captured in Delacroix's portrait. His playing, to us, would be horrible. The Paganini violin crowed like a cock, sobbed like a woman. Virtuosity at his level has something of the monstrous, akin to the *castrato*'s feats with the voice and the spatial ambiguities of the Mannerists. He belonged, in short, to the Italian past and rather signalled the end of a tradition than the beginning of a new one. He was also forty-nine years old and riddled with disease, making it the more curious that he should be an idol for the young Liszt, ardent advocate of the new age.

The premise is that there was also something diabolic about Liszt, what Sitwell calls his Mephistophelian side, for which we are referred to *Mephisto* Waltzes, and — of all things — the *Faust* Symphony (a wonderful instance of confusing author with subject, because if everybody who used the Faust story was Mephistophelian, we must attach hoofs to Goethe, Berlioz and poor old Gounod as well) and the *Dante* Sonata. (Because of the *Inferno?* But the title of this piece is actually *Sonata d'après une lecture de Dante* from a poem by Victor Hugo — a characteristic piece of Lisztian word-play.) As proofs of a hellish personality, these are bootless; everybody used these themes.

Yet there is a reason for the attribution and it has to do with Liszt's life.

As Paganini was suspected of unspeakable practices, so Liszt was endowed with every vice. It is common to quote Gregorovius's description of him: Mephistopheles disguised as an abbé. Gregorovius was only reflecting a universal disapproval. Liszt, he thought, was a burnt-out case, ruined by wine and women; and he was abetted by appearances. The abbé's cassock, donned when Liszt was fifty-four, was the last straw to moralists. How dared he dress up like a man of God? And the glaring old boy in the last photographs does have a devilish cast — very like that of the aged Tolstoy, who faces the camera with the same green-eyed defiance. There is only one hitch: unless one happens to think fornication between consenting adults a sin, there was nothing wicked about Liszt, who was generosity itself and never betrayed a friend. The sexual adventures they made such a fuss about were perfectly straightforward. Corrupted beauty, the purging properties of degradation were unknown to him: he never plucked the flowers of evil.

Yet one disregards a century of tradition at one's peril. Not only did Liszt inspire comparisons with Paganini, it has been said over and over again that he felt a kind of spiritual kinship with him. What is the basis? First, that on hearing Paganini he suffered one of those seismic shocks he was subject to in his youth and at once set about composing the *Grande Fantaisie de bravoure sur la Clochette de Paganini,* which was followed by the six *Études d'exécution transcendante d'après Paganini.* These explosive pieces, horrendously difficult and requiring a technique that only Liszt himself commanded at that time, reproduce the Paganinian *diablerie* exactly — something Liszt was extraordinarily good at: he could translate almost anything for the piano and get a startling likeness to the original. He did the same for Berlioz, Beethoven, Schubert and a dozen other composers in his transcriptions of symphonic and operatic scores, and even songs. So it was unexceptional that he captured the essence of Paganini. His studies, moreover, actually form a rather small part of the extensive musical literature "on a theme of Paganini." Schumann transcribed a larger number of the caprices than Liszt did and isn't considered to have been in thrall to Paganini for that reason, any more than were Brahms, Busoni, Rachmaninoff and a host of others who worked on the same material. By themselves, Liszt's Paganini studies do not point to a fixation.

Then there is his letter to a pupil in 1832, reprinted in every biography:

For this fortnight, my spirit and my fingers are working like the damned; Homer, the Bible, Plato, Locke, Byron, Hugo, Lamartine, Chateaubriand, Beethoven, Bach, Hummel, Mozart, Weber, are all around me. I study them, think about them, devour them with fury; furthermore, I practice four or five hours (thirds, sixths, octaves, tremolos, repeated notes, cadenzas, etc.). Ah, if only I don't go mad you will find an artist in me. Yes, such an artist as you demand, such as is needed today. "And I too am a painter," cried Michelangelo the first time he saw a masterpiece. . . . Though small and poor, your friend has been repeating those words of a great man ever since Paganini's last concert.[2]

A tribute to Paganini certainly, but of what kind? Nowhere does he say that he wants to be an artist *like Paganini,* and if he had meant that, the rest of the letter would be a gibberish, for what had Homer and the Bible, let alone Locke, to do with an art like Paganini's? The operative line is "an artist . . . such as is needed today." Paganini wasn't that. He flew on one distorted wing and his outlook was old-fashioned — evidenced among other things in his rejection of the concerto he commissioned from Berlioz: "I am not given enough to do." (Berlioz turned it into *Harold in Italy.*) Liszt was fully aware of these limitations. He recognized in Paganini a "genius that knew neither master nor equal," the words he used in a necrology written in 1840, but he did not want to resemble him and was careful to explain why not: "Let the artist of the future renounce, then, and with all his heart, the vain and egotistical role of which Paganini was, we think, a last and illustrious example; let him fix his goal not in himself but outside himself; let virtuosity be to him a *means,* not the *end;* let him always remember that . . . *Genius obliges."* [3] That Liszt's own ego was quite as overwhelming as Paganini's is here beside the point, which is that he was at no time out to beat Paganini at the game of virtuosity but determined to be a very different kind of artist.

There may be a generic likeness between extremes of a type. Paganini with his fiddle, Liszt with his piano were exaggerated personages who performed the "impossible." But there was a further distinction, less obvious than it sounds: a piano isn't a violin. Liszt's piano was virtually a new instrument, whose range and power were still being explored. Paganini's violin was an old one, one of the few to have survived into the nineteenth century with only minor alterations. Liszt in 1832 was making discoveries in a new medium; Paganini had taken an old one about as far as it could go. There is all the difference in the world.

Music is the only art to depend on a subsidiary race of craftsmen and a complex manufactory, which is why old and new are appropriate terms, almost as if one were speaking of machines. All but a few of the instruments we know today were dependent on industrial techniques for their invention or the developments that make them playable in a modern orchestra. The brasses, the woodwinds, the tympani are nineteenth-century products and were a drastic improvement over their predecessors. But the most spectacular changes of all occurred in the instrument called the pianoforte — from the name given it by its inventor Bartolommeo Cristofori, *gravicembalo col piano e forte,* in 1709. The gravicembalo took more than a hundred years to develop into the grand piano and to displace its rivals, the harpsichord and the clavichord. It did so eventually because of its superior dynamics (unlike the members of the spinet family, which work on the plectrum principle, it had hammers — hence *Hammerklavier*), not of interest to the majority of eighteenth-century composers, by 1800 more and more important. On the clavichord a fugue could be rendered with exquisite precision, but its frail voice could be heard only in tiny rooms. The harpsichord's tone could be brilliant as a diamond, but the fingers couldn't control it — all dynamic changes had to be made, as on an organ, with a mechanical device, the swell pedal — and it too was created for drawing rooms.

It was the desire to escape these limitations that led composers and pianists (Clementi, Cramer, Hummel, Ries, Field, and of course Beethoven himself) to the pianoforte. But as late as 1820 it still was not a satisfactory instrument because made of wood. Struck with any force, its wires gave way; thicker wire put an intolerable strain on the wooden casing. The iron frame, introduced by Broadwood, Érard and others (some Scotch and some American), solved this problem and was probably the single most important contribution, for without its metal skeleton the piano could not have resisted the onslaughts of nineteenth-century pianists, including Liszt. The other problem was the action — a word that anybody who has ever struck a piano (or a typewriter) key understands in principle. How it works and how it evolved from Cristofori's relatively simple mechanism to the sophisticated one in use today requires pages of diagrams in any well-founded encyclopedia. On its construction depends what happens when the key is hit, whether it must be lightly or heavily depressed, how rapidly it rebounds, and whether the tone lingers or not. In the early nineteenth century two kinds of action were in vogue, giving rise to two different schools of execution, the German or Viennese and the English. Here we see, perhaps for the first time, an art-form in submission to technology: the construction of the piano dictated the pianists' style. The German instrument, said Hummel, "may be played upon with ease by the weakest hand. It allows the performer to impart to his execution every possible degree of light and shade, speaks clearly and promptly, has a round, flute-like tone. . . ." [4] The English was heavier, "the keys sink much deeper, and consequently, the return of the hammer on the repetition of the note cannot take place so quickly." A counterpoise to this was the greater sonority.

Generally speaking, the English piano prevailed, because it produced the richer, *chiaroscuro* tonalities required by Beethoven — who more than anyone else fathered the modern pianoforte, although the power and flexibility he demanded were not achieved until too late to be any use to him. He harried and chivvied the manufacturers all his life but by the time his magnificent Broadwood was delivered to him he was too deaf to play it, and striking wildly at the keys soon reduced it to a heap of wire. (It was later acquired and lovingly preserved by Liszt.) It lacked, of course, iron framing, first patented in 1820 and not by Broadwood. Nor did it have repetition action, invented and patented by Sebastien Érard in 1821. This device overcame the last of the piano's serious defects, the sluggish action that prevented the player from regaining control over the hammer before the key had returned to its equilibrium. In effect, it speeded up the response and was vital to "touch," the cantabile or singing tone and the pearly *glissandi* that were Liszt's specialties.

This is vastly to oversimplify the modifications and inventions that produced the modern piano. The significance is that all the major ones had been made in Liszt's boyhood; by 1830 he was playing an instrument substantially the same as ours. They came to maturity together — and through another hazard, in intimate association. The Liszts made the acquaintance of the Érard family soon after they arrived in Paris. The Érards seem to have made a pet of the little foreign prodigy and thereafter always saw to it that he had a first-class piano at his disposal. It worked both ways. He in turn did much to publicize their new product, and adopted the repetition action well before its advantages were widely recognized. When he went to London in 1824, handbills announced that he would "display his inimitable powers on the New Grand Piano Forte invented by Sebastian Érard," rather as if a racing driver had been introducing a new kind of car.

It was always recounted of Liszt that he would play on any piano and preferably a bad one in need of tuning so as to demonstrate his superhuman control over it — and that was only half a joke. He also collected a number of historic instruments besides the Beethoven Broadwood, including a spinet that had belonged to Mozart. But by and large, he stuck to Érards. In the years when he toured Europe from one end to the other, they went with him, dragged somehow over Spanish and Russian roads, across the Black Sea to Constantinople, perpetually delayed and out of tune when they arrived, yet somehow in place when the moment came. "Liszt pianos" litter the civilized world like fragments of the Parthenon and he may have played on any or all of them; the piano now enshrined in the Hofgärtnerei, the house where he spent his last years in Weimar, is a Bechstein. But in the years of his pianistic fame, he associated himself with the pioneering Érards, and it would be interesting to know (documentation is wanting) the influence this fact alone may have exerted on his obsession with the technical possibilities of the instrument — a good deal more, I would guess, than exposure to Paganini, though that undoubtedly pushed him in the same direction. We know he had an unusual interest in the mechanics of sound production: as late as the 1850's, he commissioned from Alexandre, the inventor of the harmonium, a fantastical construction with a triple keyboard, sixteen registers and stops to reproduce the winds, the whole after his own design. This monster had no progeny but seems to show a continuation of that spirit which in youth led him to flights not unlike those of pioneer aviators who looped-the-loop or flew upside down.

The comparison isn't inapt. There was a daredevil, barnstorming quality to his early tours that recalls the days when flying machines performed at carnivals. Which isn't to say that he was a super-mechanic, the fault of the old school and not of Liszt, who regarded the instrument as an extension of his being, who once wrote:

You see my piano is for me what his frigate is to a sailor or his horse to an Arab — more indeed: it is my very self, my mother tongue, my life. Within its seven octaves it encloses the whole range of an orchestra, and a man's ten fingers have the power to reproduce the harmonies which are created by hundreds of performers.[5]

One can't imagine a Hummel or a Czerny with those feelings, which show us too why Liszt's virtuosity was of another order than Paganini's, why he didn't invent his transcendental technique in order to outdo the Italian wizard. The *Études d'execution transcendante,* his masterpieces in this vein, are not mere gymnastics, intended "to do for the piano what Paganini had done for the violin." * They are a direct personal expression and as auto-biographical as anything he wrote. Their story is his discovery and conquest of the piano, his relation to it in early life.

The originals were composed when he was fifteen and ambitiously titled *Études en 48 exercices.* Only twelve were actually written and they were expectably Czernyesque. Between 1835 and 1839, he recast them into an edifice of heroic size and difficulty. Schumann studied the two versions in 1839, before he had met Liszt or heard him play. Yet he immediately saw the point:

. . . we cannot fail to observe that the original simplicity, which is natural to the first flow of youthful talent, is almost entirely suppressed in its present form. In addition, the new version provides a criterion for the artist's present more in-tense way of thinking and feeling; indeed it affords us a glimpse into his secret

---

* I quote Alan Walker's essay on "Liszt's Musical Background" in a recent anthology, *Franz Liszt: The Man and His Music* (New York, 1970). In search of reasons "to ex-plain the extraordinary hold Paganini had over the young Liszt's imagination," Walker supplies the following: Liszt, he writes, was "ill" when he first encountered Paganini, suffering from the "severe psychological depression" following the Saint-Cricq affair, and spending all his time indoors, reported dead, etc. "Among his few friends" in whose company he sought consolation was Abbé Lamennais, who "had a somewhat morbid influence over him." It seems, says Walker, "essential to sketch in this much of Liszt's background because it helps to explain why he was so receptive to Paganini. . . ." (*Franz Liszt: The Man and His Music,* p. 46.) Mr. Walker is a musicologist, Doctor of Music at the University of Durham and a composer. It hardly seems possible that not a single fact he adduces is correct. Liszt was not ill in 1831, having long since re-covered from the illness that caused his death to be reported in 1828. He had a host of friends but the Abbé Lamennais was not among them: they did not meet until 1834.

intellectual life with the result that we often remain undecided whether not to envy the boy more than the man, who appears unable to find peace. . . . There can be no doubt . . . that we have here to deal with an extraordinary, multiply moved mind as well as with a mind influencing others. His own life is to be found in his music.[6]

Schumann, it should be said, didn't mean that altogether as a compliment. He disapproved of the life — hectic, urbane, in a word, French — and of the music it produced, which would never suit German taste: "What may yet be expected from him is a matter of conjecture. To win the favor of his fatherland [sic], he would, above all things, have to return to serenity and simplicity. . . ." Yet he concluded that it was "useless labor" to apply ordinary criteria to the remodeled études:

Such compositions must be *heard;* they were wrung from the instrument with the hands; and hands alone can make them resound. And one ought also to see their composer play them; for just as the sight of any virtuosity elevates and strengthens, so much more does the immediate sight of the composer himself, struggling with his instrument, taming it, making it obey. . . . These are true storm and terror études — études for at most ten or twelve people in the whole world.[7]

So they were; they still are. Yet here was perhaps the ultimate difference between Liszt and Paganini. The Italian hoarded the secrets of his trade like some tiresome old alchemist, refusing even to rehearse with an orchestra for fear someone would "catch on." (One can fancy the result in performance.) At its most taxing, Liszt's piano music wasn't intended to be a magician's trick. He worried that the *Transcendental* Études *would* be unplayable by anyone but himself and over the years worked steadily to simplify them. In 1852, the whole set was republished in revised form, from which abnormal difficulties were excised. To Paganini, such a proceeding would have been shocking, for if not a classicist he was of the old school that abhorred any demonstration of art in progress, anything less than a perfectly turned product. Liszt on the other hand was an interminable reviser. It was a rare piece of material that lost its viability for him, and anyone with the curiosity to do so was at liberty to study, through successive publications, the evolution of his musical thought.

Yet when all is said, and little as I think him to have been moved by Paganini's musical example, Liszt certainly did take note of one aspect of Paganini's art — his stagecraft. Many writers have stated (on what basis I don't know) that he actually adopted many of the Italian's platform mannerisms. Since I can find no contemporary confirmation of this, I doubt that he did anything so childish. *His* mannerisms — the wearing of gloves which were melodramatically removed and dropped to the floor before he began to play; the tossed mane of hair; the turning of the "Dantesque" profile to the audience — were obviously his own, dependent on physical attributes that Paganini did not possess. But the notion that a performer could also be an actor, could create suspense by his manner of appearing on a platform, by pregnant pauses, etc., he may easily have developed from his observation of a master of such devices. On the other hand, the most prominent feature of what came to be called Lisztomania did not derive from Paganini. Women did not faint or show the symptoms of orgasm at Paganini's concerts, and at Liszt's they did. In this area too he must be allowed to have made his own discoveries.

Chapter 7

IF LISZT was so mesmerized by Paganini, it is curious that he shouldn't have followed his usual custom of introducing himself — and would not an accolade from Paganini have been as effective propaganda as Beethoven's kiss? It wasn't bestowed and I can't discover that they ever made one another's acquaintance. The real-life Paganini, who lived in Paris and although reclusive was in touch with the musical world, doesn't enter into the real life of Liszt.

Very different were his flesh-and-blood relations with Berlioz and Chopin, flawed with rivalries and misunderstandings. He was unlucky in most of his men friends, who were ambivalent toward him and, notoriously, each other. These two were good examples. He met Berlioz in 1830 and in the familiar way. Excited by the rehearsals of the *Fantastique*, he rushed around to present himself to the composer. He encountered Chopin in 1831, immediately after Chopin's arrival in Paris. Thereafter he saw both constantly until he left France in 1835. But not, if it could be helped, together. Chopin cordially disliked Berlioz and his music. Berlioz's atrocious quip at Chopin's death, *"Il se mourait toute sa vie"* (He has been dying all his life), marks his contempt — and his cruel streak. Liszt, the wholehearted admirer of each, was caught in the middle.

Berlioz did at least love Liszt, though not his music and not after Wagner came on the scene — generosity wasn't one of his virtues, and he couldn't forgive Liszt the variety of his musical sympathies. Chopin's feelings are more mysterious. On intimate terms with Liszt for years, he displayed little warmth for him and may have harbored under his fastidious exterior an active animus. The only compliment he is known to have paid him on paper, and it has been done to death because it *is* the only one, is on examination a divided tribute:

I write you without knowing what I am scribbling, because Liszt is playing my studies and transporting me out of my respectable thoughts. I should like to steal from him his way of playing my own études.[1]

A corollary would be this aside about his good friend:

He may one day become a deputy or even a king, in Abyssinia or the Congo. But his compositions will be buried in souvenir albums, together with volumes of German poetry.[2]

Chopin may have persuaded himself that he had a case against Liszt, one of whose offenses was to introduce him to George Sand — and how often must he have asked himself whether Liszt had been his forerunner in her affections and her bed. (There were of course a score of others but Liszt was surely the most irksome to contemplate.) Sand apart, and their mutual admiration for Chopin's music, they had little in common. Liszt, the very childish child of his time, embroiling himself in Saint-Simonism, in "humanitarian art" and the Catholic revival, was to Chopin an object for ridicule. Insofar as he thought of politics at all, he was a reactionary and he despised the hullabaloo of controversy that was the very air Liszt breathed in those days. Given these dissimilarities of temperament and outlook, it would have been something of a miracle if they *had* arrived at a real understanding of each other's strengths and weaknesses; but that cannot excuse the underhandedness of Chopin's conduct, his sneers behind Liszt's back and the emptiness of gestures like the dedication of Opus 25 to Marie d'Agoult, which she and Liszt took for a vote of confidence when it was nothing of the sort.

There is still a grave disservice of Liszt to Chopin, his biography of him, published after Chopin's death. It is an abominable book, whose turgid writing, essays on the Polish nobility and other digressions brand it as coming from the hand of Liszt's mistress Carolyne Wittgenstein, herself a Pole. Liszt ought never to have let it see the light; and it isn't as if he hadn't been told by the best authority that it wouldn't do. Sainte-Beuve was shown the manuscript. Politely but firmly he said it would have to be completely rewritten. Ignoring this, Liszt published it anyway, raising several questions: how could he, if he wanted to honor Chopin, have allowed such a piece of trash to be signed with his name? That he did so makes one think he cared less about Chopin than indulging Carolyne's urge to write.*

Superficially, he and Chopin were cut from the same cloth: both from eastern Europe, both pianists, and susceptible to the same female type. Hungary and Poland have always considered themselves cousin countries, alike in social structure and tragic history. But the Poles, oriented to France, were more civilized than the Hungarians; and Chopin (half French anyway) reflected this greater refinement. He was also better born than Liszt, better educated, and without Liszt's ambitions to improve himself. At sixteen, he was the darling of the Warsaw Conservatory, and at twenty-one, when he arrived in Paris, he was to all intents and purposes a finished artist. He was without a blemish, and he died too soon, leaving a body of work just right in size, whose quality has never been in serious dispute; whereas Liszt's long, disordered life is a parable of misspent gifts and his oeuvre like a half-excavated city in distracting disarray.

Chopin's weaknesses were his lungs and a chilly, anemic temperament. (It is sometimes said that he broke with Liszt because, having lent him his apartment, he discovered that Liszt had used it for an assignation. That wasn't the cause of the rupture though it could have been the last straw. There was an old-maidish side to Chopin.) Somehow with him, ennui is just around the corner. He was too polished, too incurious — and he misjudged or undervalued every one of his mighty contemporaries, including his friend Delacroix. Only George Sand brings this wraith to life. Warmed by her fires, he glows fitfully. After she casts him aside, the glow expires.

His refined and tenuous taste was appalled at the flamboyance of Liszt's virtuoso career. That he himself easily resolved the conflict between performer and composer that gave Liszt so many hours of anguish was however not entirely attributable to his more rarified nature. His glassy fragility — he weighed a bit over a hundred pounds — ruled out performances for more than a few dozen people. He was at his best in a salon. His pianissimi extended to infinity; tiny nuances were treated like butterfly wings under a microscope, and it all came out like a delicate moonlit *haiku*. "You listened, as it were, to the improvisation of a poem," said Charles Hallé. Even the famous rubato was under perfect control. (He kept a metronome on his piano and used it more than once to prove that he was playing in correct time.) †

---

* The research that went into it was minimal. A questionnaire was sent to Chopin's sister, who for some reason didn't fill it in herself but turned it over to Chopin's Scottish friend, Jane Stirling. A copy with her answers exists. But either it wasn't returned to Liszt or he and Carolyne decided not to bother with it.

† Unless a duplicated quote is involved, he and Liszt hit on the same metaphor to describe this slightly displaced beat. *Chopin:* "Fancy a moving tree with its branches swayed by the wind — the trunk is in steady time, the moving leaves are the melodic inflections." *Liszt:* "Do you see those trees? The wind plays in the leaves, life unfolds

These qualities, we are told, had an immense effect on Liszt. "Paganini had opened the door to transcendental bravura; Chopin opened it to style, poetry, finesse," says Harold Schonberg.[3] From Sitwell we learn that "the effect of Chopin upon him was to open new sources of poetry." [4] And from Humphrey Searle, that "what he chiefly showed Liszt was the poetical approach to music. Liszt had been reading intensively . . . and the effect of Chopin was to make him connect music more closely with the rest of his thought. Instead of writing music to fill the academic forms he had been taught in his youth, he now began to see every piece as the musical expression of a certain state of mind or idea, sometimes derived from literature or art, sometimes from experience." [5]

That is the received wisdom, and one would like to know who handed it down in the first place. Not Liszt's contemporaries, who failed to observe any Chopin-like transformation in his playing after 1832. Chopin's own comment, that he would like to steal Liszt's way with his études, indicates the reverse, that Liszt did *not* play them as he did. Those who heard them both saw no resemblance, and used quite different terms to describe them. Of Liszt, Hallé wrote:

[He] was all sunshine and dazzling splendor, subjugating his hearers with a power that none could withstand. For him there were no difficulties of execution, the most incredible seeming child's play under his fingers. One of the transcendent merits . . . was the crystal-like clearness which never failed him for a moment, even in the most complicated . . . passages; it was as if he had photographed them in the minutest detail upon the ear of his listener. The power he drew from his instrument was such as I have never heard since, but never harsh, never suggesting "thumping." His daring was as extraordinary as his talent. At . . . a concert given by him and conducted by Berlioz, the *Marche au supplice*, from the latter's *Symphonie fantastique*, that most gorgeously orchestrated piece, was performed, at the conclusion of which Liszt sat down and played his own arrangement, for the piano alone, of the same movement, with an effect even surpassing that of the full orchestra, and creating an indescribable furore.[6]

Surely a being so endowed can be called something more than a "unique synthesis" (Walker's phrase) of Paganini and Chopin? It is as if Liszt had had no gifts of his own but was a kind of collage, bits and pieces of other men skillfully combined. On the one hand, he revs up his technique à la Paganini; on the other he "translates" Chopin "into a language fit for the largest concert halls." (That according to J. A. Fuller Maitland in *Grove's Dictionary*.) The fact is that he did not even see Chopin as Chopin saw himself; for Chopin was a modernist *malgré lui* and when Liszt singled

---

and develops beneath them, but the tree remains the same — that is Chopin's rubato!" Liszt's less concise version sounds like a paraphrase of Chopin's, which is probably the case.

out his "bold dissonances and strange harmonies" for praise, he wasn't pleased. (Any more than he was gratified by Schumann's encomiums. Since to him *Carnaval* scarcely qualified as music, he suspected that Schumann was making a fool of him.) God knows what aspect of his music he did want emphasized — his melody perhaps. Or his "poetry." That is just what Liszt did not choose to do.

Estimates of Chopin's influence on Liszt's compositions are in general more cautious — possibly because it is difficult to show that a link existed. The assertion that Chopin taught him to see every piece as the musical expression of a state of mind derived from literature, art or experience, if taken literally, would mean that he owed the core of his art to Chopin. Only it happens that Chopin himself wasn't that kind of composer. Neither art nor literature plays any part in his music, and still less the philosophic and humanitarian concerns that fired Liszt. (The sorrows of Poland, yes — but that was all.) If anyone was free from the strain of trying to connect the struggles of his time with music, of forcing literary and pictorial themes into moulds that did not always fit them, it was Chopin. Not for him to depict everything under the sun, to tear canvases from the walls, invade Shakespeare's stage and Dante's hell. Not for him the wordy preface. His pieces have numbers, not names. They announce themselves simply as studies, dances, and nothing annoyed him more than attempts to interpret them in terms of actual experience. (George Sand did that once on Majorca, when he played for her the prelude known as the "Raindrop." Had it not, she inquired, come to him from the sound of the rain on the roof? And, she says, "He protested as strongly as he knew how — and rightly — against the childishness of such aural imitations." [7] Schumann on the other hand was delighted to describe the butterfly that inspired *Papillons,* and that was one of the differences.) *

There is still the possibility that individual works of Liszt will, if prodded sufficiently, expose some kind of relationship. Alan Walker is of interest

---

* Chopin's unwillingness to program his music was actually a bother to Liszt, who once undertook to supply an apocryphal story to explain the F Minor Fantasy: Chopin is alone in his rooms; he has quarrelled with Sand, and plays the piano to console himself. A knock (first two bars). Enter Liszt, Sand, Camille Pleyel and others (agitated triplets). George kneels and asks forgiveness. The visitors leave (final march). Liszt swore he got this rigmarole from Chopin himself. He was certainly lying. He never saw Chopin after the Sand affair was under way, even assuming that Chopin would have told him such an absurd tale. Worse was to come. Chopin interpretation reached its apogee in Hans von Bülow's edition of the preludes. He gave them names — *Suicide, Presentiment of Death,* and the like, and produced a set of solemn analyses that have to be read to be believed. (See Schonberg: *The Great Pianists,* pp. 127–29, for hilarious quotes.) But neither Bülow nor Liszt was going beyond nineteenth-century custom. Beethoven's *Sonata quasi una fantasia,* Op. 27, No. 2, spawned a whole literature under a title he never gave it — the "Moonlight." (See also E. F. Benson's Lucia novels for what this composition came to signify to middle-class taste in our own time.)

here. He postulates Liszt's envy of Chopin's études, which "had stolen his prerogatives." [8] The *Transcendental* Études were his answer. But can one have it both ways? Can these études be, at one and the same time, his response to Paganini and his challenge to Chopin? (One of them does have a Chopinesque theme, to be sure; but it was written first in 1826, before Liszt had heard of Chopin.) Walker does not lean on this point. He has more to say: he makes the astounding statement that from 1849 to 1855, Liszt succumbed to a Chopin mania, a spooky, "posthumous inspiration." This has the merit of being a unique theory as far as I know.* These were the years when Liszt was devoting himself to the orchestra, not the piano, which limits the field. Walker nevertheless pounces on *Funérailles, October 1849* and labels it a threnody for Chopin (who died in 1849), although it has long been known, and would be evident from the context, that it was actually a threnody for the Hungarian revolution, and that the Chopinesque echo in the middle section probably refers to his friend Felix Lichnowsky, who was assassinated in 1849 and who was a Pole — an associative "quote" that would be typical of Liszt. The composition as a whole does not resemble Chopin in the least.

Walker makes equally heavy weather of several pieces written in forms made famous by Chopin and not used by Liszt until after his death: two Polonaises, two Mazurkas, the Berceuse and the two Ballades. Walker ignores the coincidence that Liszt was living with a Polish woman of fierce national sympathies at the time and was therefore likely to compose occasionally in her native idiom; and he skates past the glaring dissimilarities between Chopin's Ballades and the better of Liszt's two, the B Minor, which is really a sonata, a big-scale work that breathes flame and has nothing in common with Chopin's treatment of the genre. And lastly, Walker cites Liszt's Berceuse, "almost a parody of Chopin's" — in the same key, and with configurations around a simple theme "not unlike Chopin's." If he means the first version, there is a shadowy resemblance, and again it was probably calculated. If he means the second, in which Liszt embellished the melodic line almost beyond recognition, Chopin's ghost fades further. Still, I would be willing to give Walker the Berceuse, feeble enough proof that Liszt was the victim of a post-mortem possession. As an illustration of the strange compulsion that drives even Liszt's admirers into trying to expose him as an imitator, in this case practically a scavenger, it does nicely. [9]

On a more reasonable level it would be just as wrong to pretend that

---

* I would propose to Mr. Walker that he ask Mrs. Rosemary Brown to verify it. She is the English housewife who claims to receive daily visits from Liszt, Chopin, Beethoven and others, and to take musical dictation from them. (A recording has been made of some of the works she has taken down.) When not so engaged they chat with her, supplying a certain amount of information not otherwise known.

Liszt got nothing from Chopin. On the contrary: He owed to Chopin his revelation of what a modern artist at the piano could be, and no one else could have given him that. The Hillers and Kalkbrenners and other pianists residing in Paris couldn't. Even Mendelssohn, who came to France concurrently with Chopin, was no use to him. Musically, they lived in opposing worlds. (Writers about Liszt forget that he knew Mendelssohn quite well in 1831–1832, and that if it was poetry he needed, Mendelssohn, who was a beautiful pianist, could as well have imparted it to him as Chopin.) Chopin's piano spoke a new language and one that Liszt instantly recognized — with the subordinate clause that Chopin was already a master while he was working his way out of the cocoon. I have said that it wasn't Chopin's *ars poetica* that he valued but his originality, his recklessness with harmonic structure and what old-fashioned pianists like Moscheles called his "hard, inartistic modulations." It isn't today very apparent that Chopin was a revolutionary, but that is how Liszt saw him: "One of those original beings . . . [who is] adrift from all bondage," he called him in one of the few passages in the Chopin biography that he must have written himself. (Chopin was not adrift, and if Liszt had put his mind to what he was writing, he would have tried to deal with the paradox of Chopin's classical bias, his exclusive love for Bach and Mozart and Bellini's liquid cantilena, instead of simply naming the quality that his own devotion to the modern spirit led him to regard more highly than any other.) When he first heard Chopin, a hundred flowers must have burst into bloom. Everything embryonic in him stirred to life under this stimulus, and most of all something that hasn't yet been mentioned, that responded uniquely to something in Chopin.

I can only call it Chopin's Polishness. Liszt in 1832 was thoroughly *dépaysé,* cut off from his roots. It is easy to say that Hungarian rhythms were in his blood. No doubt they were but he had found no way to utilize his Magyar heritage, not even the rubato that originating in the national dances of both their countries was as instinctive to him as to Chopin. It was Chopin with his melancholy exile's *Geist,* his sophisticated and entirely original incorporation of folk elements, who introduced him to his half-forgotten past, and in doing so, changed it, revealing in the desolate landscape of childhood possibilities undreamed of. Chopin's brand of gloomy patriotism, a sentiment that Liszt was later to express over and over again in a phrase that especially moved him — *"Oh, ma sauvage et lointaine patrie!"* — made a profound impression. In fact his Hungarian phase postdates his friendship with Chopin by many years; but it was Chopin who prepared him for it. (As perhaps also for his lifelong addiction to Poles.)

Chopin was in France *the* Pole. He arrived in Paris shortly after the fall of Warsaw and the collapse of the Polish rebellion in 1830–1831, having just composed the C Minor Étude in a fit of patriotic despair. *Salve Polonia!*

It was the cry in the salons presided over by the enchanting Polish women with whom Paris was already in love, and among liberals everywhere. Liszt did not fail to note it. Hungary's sorrows were in the future, but to one who had already contracted *mal de René* and come down with a bad case of Byronism, there was an affinity not to be overlooked. Chopin had risen from the mists beyond the Vistula. Might he not claim an origin as glamorous in the lands beyond the Danube?

Chapter 8

"THE DAY before the concert I received a visit from Liszt, whom I had never yet seen. I spoke to him of Goethe's *Faust*, which he was obliged to confess he had not read, but about which he soon became as enthusiastic as myself. We were strongly attracted to one another, and our friendship has increased in warmth and depth ever since. He was present at the concert and excited general attention by his applause and enthusiasm." [1] So Berlioz described his introduction to Liszt. The hint of condescension was probably unmeant, but in friendship as in love, the beginning foretells the end. Berlioz allows us to see that Liszt was the suppliant, not as well-read as he might have been, and that his admiration for Berlioz's music was his chief attraction. That evening he dragged Berlioz off to supper, and somehow we know who footed the bill. Berlioz's biographer calls this friendship "real, affectionate and serviceable." He neglects to add that the services were exclusively Liszt's for more than thirty years. [*]

To Liszt, that was natural enough. He felt he owed a great deal to Berlioz, and he would have been the first to admit that the concert (December

---

[*] Jacques Barzun's *Berlioz and the Romantic Century* (Atlantic–Little, Brown, 1950) is the definitive biography and we must all be grateful for its massive scholarship. It is no doubt natural too that Barzun should have adopted his subject's point of view toward his associates. It is nevertheless depressing to find Liszt fairly consistently downgraded throughout the book, even to a page of photographs labelled "Eminent Berliozians" that includes Flaubert and Sidney Lanier but omits Liszt. The reason must be that Barzun shares Berlioz's indifference to Liszt as a composer. He certainly believes as Berlioz did that Liszt betrayed him over "the Wagner question." But about that there can be two opinions, as we shall see.

5, 1830) was a landmark in his life. The *Symphonie fantastique* was the first piece of modern music he had ever heard. Overexposure has dimmed its lustre but not its historical importance, and we must grasp this in order to understand what Liszt felt.

The *Fantastique* was the first significant answer to the question of how the symphony would develop after Beethoven, and Berlioz was acutely, grandiloquently conscious of this. "I took up music where Beethoven left it," he is reported to have told Fétis. It was a statement to which he attached several meanings. The composer who aligned himself with Beethoven was committed to a masterpiece, a magnum opus — and that of a particular kind, which Berlioz defined as belonging to the *genre instrumental expressif,* "a poetic idea everywhere manifest, but with music wholly in command, with no help from words to give it precise expression." A unified musical gesture, in short, which meant the weakening though not the abandonment (as some thought) of the formalistic symphony plan divided into movements, each with its theme and development. On examination, Berlioz turns out not to have cast away the form but to have modified it by the invention of a device he called the *idée fixe,* a recurrent theme, which in differing contexts swells, diminishes, elaborates itself and in so doing binds the whole into a cohesive mass. Schumann in a celebrated review put it this way (and nobody, in the hundred and forty years since, has done better):

Neither significant in itself nor suited to contrapuntal development, the principal motif of the symphony grows on us more and more. . . . From the beginning of the second movement it gains interest and continues to do so until it winds through screaming chords into C major. In the second part it develops into a trio . . . with a new rhythm and new harmonies. . . . Towards the close it comes in again, but faintly and haltingly. In the third movement it appears as a recitative, interrupted by the orchestra where it takes on the expression of the most dreadful passion up to the shrill A flat, whereupon it seems to collapse into a swoon. . . . In the *Marche au supplice* it strives to speak again but is cut off by the *coup fatal.* In the vision, it appears upon a common C and E flat clarinet, withered, degraded and dirty. . . .[2]

Not the least interesting thing about this stunning piece of criticism is that it was written solely on the basis of Liszt's piano transcription of the *Fantastique,* produced in 1833 and the only score available to Schumann at the time. That he could rely on it for such a close reading testifies to Liszt's genius in this now lost division of music (lost because the invention of the phonograph killed its purpose, which was the dissemination of music not otherwise to be heard) as well as to his devotion. In all, he put in some three years of hard labor at transcribing Berlioz, including the whole of *Harold in Italy,* several overtures and the "melologue" *Lélio* (which he tried, unsuccessfully, to arrange for piano and orchestra). This concentration would seem at least as impressive evidence of an early revelation as the Paganini pieces or vague surmises about Chopin. Yet Berlioz has not figured as prominently as the other two in the mythology.

It is easy to see why. Transcriptions are now in disgrace, and besides it is well known that Liszt composed these mostly to help his friend get a hearing. His own orchestral works were twenty years in the future, and when he did turn to symphonic music his worst enemy couldn't accuse him of aping Berlioz. Their styles were utterly unlike: Liszt's interest was primarily in harmonics, Berlioz's gift for rhythm and melody, and so on. It is still true that many of Liszt's conceptions derived from Berlioz, with whom he had much more in common than, say, Wagner; and that the genesis of the symphonic poem has to be located in the *Fantastique*.

The *idée fixe* was self-evidently the ancestor of the leitmotif, Wagner's coarser, more literal application of the principle. In Wagner, Berlioz's subtle hint became a system clothed in full pedantic panoply. Liszt took a different path. The single thematic root that in the symphonic poems grows into a tree with many branches is still an evolution of the same idea. He might of course (so might Wagner) have arrived at it independently. That form is subordinate to expression was a Romantic premise he had as much right to as Berlioz, and indeed he carried it further than Berlioz did. But since the antecedent is there, why struggle to show that Liszt took no advantage of it? *

I have said that Liszt's music was autobiographic, allied in his mind to Romantic literature. But he wasn't the first to point the finger at himself or to supply the psychic sketch he spoke of as necessary. That too was Berlioz's contribution. When it came down to it, the *genre instrumental expressif* was not launched to sink or swim without benefit of words "to give it more precise expression." It arrived on the Paris scene fully equipped with a prospectus detailing what it was all about. Berlioz described it as a dramatic symphony. The drama, it turned out, was in five episodes and concerned "a young musician in love," whose anguish drives him to eat opium. Under its influence he dreams of a ball, a country excursion, an execution, a witches' Sabbath. This narrative caught the public fancy rather more than the music; it created in fact a scandal. Berlioz's passion for the Irish actress Harriet Smithson was anything but a secret and here he was, trumpeting his

---

* On the other hand, why omit it? Walker tells us that the Liszt-Berlioz friendship had "inestimable artistic consequences to both men," but the only one he mentions is Liszt's *Fantastique* transcription, "which shows how far [he] had advanced since his . . . studies with Czerny." (Is that all?) Berlioz is done with in a sentence. Paganini gets eight pages. More unaccountably, since he is an infinitely more careful and discriminating scholar and critic than Walker, the best, probably, that we have, Searle too passes over any detailed discussion of Berlioz's influence on Liszt. Perhaps he doesn't believe in it, but one would like to know why.

obsession to the world. The *idée fixe* was Harriet. The symphony was the first explicitly programmatic piece in modern history.

No, no, no, cries the eminent Berliozian. Only "common opinion" makes that mistake. The *Fantastique* was not programmatic, not autobiographical, and anyway it wasn't a new thing to attach a synopsis to a score. Berlioz was only conforming to custom — or alternately had thought up a rather original "promotional aid."[3] The internal contradictions in this argument are distracting: If he was only "obeying tradition," what was the scandal about? If the story wasn't literally true — Berlioz had never been to an execution with Harriet — what has that to do with it? The fact is that no previous program had gone beyond an evocative title and some notes on storms, natural upheavals and the like. No composer had said: This is *me;* these are my erotic projections. Of course they aren't to be taken literally, and they are rather more than less revealing for that reason.[*] Barzun by no means copes with these dilemmas. He doesn't really want to. The great thing is to absolve Berlioz from the curse of having written programmatic music — which he can't have done because he transmutes and does not depict experience, and always subordinates his story to the music.[†]

Yes: neither Berlioz, Liszt, Schumann nor any other composer of that generation for a moment intended it to be otherwise. Over and over they repeated the lesson: Our music isn't flatly representational, isn't imitative of the sounds and sights in the physical world.

Liszt: It is obvious that things which can appear only objectively to the perception can in no way furnish connecting points to music; the poorest of apprentice landscape painters could give with a few chalk strokes a much more faithful picture than a musician operating with all the resources of the best orchestra.[4]

Schumann (who, as Barzun does not mention, actually found the *Fantastique* libretto much too flat-footedly realistic but excused it on the ground that Berlioz wrote "for his own Frenchmen") approached the subject with great wariness: "People certainly err if they suppose that composers deliberately take pen and paper with the purpose of sketching, painting, expressing this or that."[5] Berlioz, subtler in theory than always in practice, called for *images ou comparaisons* — "which merely serve to awaken by sensations that are musical analogues of the original."

[*] In the midst of composing the *Fantastique,* Berlioz told a friend that he had just discovered "frightful truths, as to which there is no possibility of doubt" about Harriet. Presumably, they had to do with her morals. In any case, the shock to Berlioz is transmitted in passages like the arrival of the principal witch at the Sabbath, in which the *idée fixe* turns sour and vicious.

[†] This isn't quite clear either. On the one hand, we are told that the "musicodramatic fusion is automatic" (p. 157), elsewhere that the "action and musical ideas are interwoven quite carelessly" (p. 155). But see the whole argument in *Berlioz and the Romantic Century,* I, 152 ff.

Yet every one of these disclaimers is followed by a plea for the validity of music that transmits images, situations and ideas. Liszt's next sentence postulates the legitimacy of what happens when "these same things are subjected to dreaming or contemplation." "Have they not a peculiar kinship with music; and should not music be able to translate them into its mysterious language?" Schumann's follow-up is stronger still:

> . . . Yet we shouldn't too lightly estimate outward influence and impressions. . . . The greater the number of elements cognate in music, which the thought or picture created in tones contains, the more poetic and plastic the expression of the composition. And the more imaginatively or keenly the musician grasps these, the more his work will uplift and move us. Why should not the thought of immortality have seized Beethoven during his improvisations? Why could not the memory of bygone happy days have inspired another? Shall we be ungrateful to Shakespeare, who has inspired in a young tone poet a work not unworthy of himself — ungrateful to Nature, denying that we borrow of her beauty and nobility wherewith to grace our works? Italy, the Alps, the sight of the ocean, spring, twilight — has music indeed not told us anything of these? [6]

After which it can perhaps safely be stated that the *Fantastique* was a pioneer work of programmatic music in the sense that Berlioz and his friends interpreted the term. Obviously, the term itself ought to be trashed. It drives modern critics up the wall when it is applied to a composer they admire: others may have committed this aesthetic sin; not their man. (Or if, like Berlioz, he seemed to, he was only bluffing or meant something else.) We will still have to find another and better one to describe this particular art form, preeminently Romantic in all its complex derivatives. All that the hated program really signifies is the formal entry into music of the educated mind that has looked, travelled, thought, read.

Let Berlioz's original definition stand. Program music is the expression of an idea — literary, visual, philosophic, in Liszt's case, religious or humanitarian. The idea shouldn't be extraneous to the work ("a promotional aid"); neither should it be rendered at the expense of the musical structure, which it infuses and informs. (A reverse analogy from literature would be Proust's little phrase: it isn't scored for us, yet we "hear" it. No more does Berlioz, or Liszt, tell us the Faust story, but its penumbra can be sensed beyond their music on this theme.) In this way we will at least get clear what Berlioz *thought* he was doing, and Liszt after him.

Berlioz was one of the outstanding tributes to Liszt's powers of divination. He wasn't everybody's money. As with so many Romantics, his personality was written in his half-fabulous appearance. With his eagle's countenance and his hedge of hair he looked like a French-speaking bird of prey and was every bit as daunting as he looked. It took nerve to make friends with him, and more still to hang on. He combined intellect with bad judgment, wit with irrationality to a staggering degree and was unusually disaster-prone. Let everything hang on the fate of a certain concert and the heavens opened. Where women were concerned, he lacked elementary common sense. His love-life is summed up in the grimly comic heading to the forty-fifth chapter of his autobiography: I AM INTRODUCED TO MISS SMITHSON — SHE IS RUINED — BREAKS HER LEG — I MARRY HER.

Berlioz's relations with Harriet have echoes of Swann's with Odette. Ravishing in youth but a semi-imbecile (she couldn't learn French and when she tried to pursue her career in France was reduced to playing mutes on the stage), she felled Berlioz at a stroke when she appeared as Ophelia with Kemble's company. Unable to separate the actress from her part, he was incurable for several years and drove his friends mad. "Nothing was spared us," wrote Hiller, "neither the description of his sleepless nights, nor his nervous attacks, ending in tears, nor his prowlings in Paris and the neighboring country . . . nor his fugitive hopes, nor his hopeless resignation." [7] It was all quite unnecessary. Like Odette's, her object was matrimony. They *were* married and Liszt was their witness. The ill-fated knot was tied October 3, 1833. [*]

Berlioz's ambitions were as immoderate as his passions. Three bands and a chorus of five thousand was the sort of thing he envisioned for his works. (And why not, said the wags, a cannon or two thrown in?) But not all his defeats were self-inflicted. He needed what didn't exist in France, a well-endowed philharmonic establishment with enough imagination to take a chance on modern music. Lacking it, he had to resort to a hundred humiliating expedients. He had to hire halls and scrounge for musicians who could cope with his scores. His experience with the *Fantastique* was typical. For the first performance he got leave to use the concert room of the Conservatoire and the orchestra donated its services. But the rehearsal time was inadequate and the whole thing carried out in the teeth of old Cherubini's disapproval. He stalked the corridor outside muttering in his Italianated French, "*Ze n'ai pas besoin savoir comment il né faut pas faire!*" (I don't have to know how it shouldn't be done.)

A benefit arranged to pay off Harriet's debts was another catastrophe. It began an hour late, with Marie Dorval stealing the show in an extract from Dumas's *Anthony*. Harriet followed her in the fourth act of *Hamlet*, supported by some English amateurs, and fell flat. Liszt played Weber's

---

[*] Barzun mysteriously says that Liszt acted as witness partly to atone for "the evil gossip" he had helped spread about Harriet. Evil gossip there was, but I can find no shred of evidence that he helped to spread it, which would have been most unlike him. He never gossiped in that way or interfered in the love affairs of his friends. He may have warned Berlioz against her. Any friend would have done that. But if he calumniated her, it is unbelievable that Berlioz would have asked him to stand up with him, and thereafter made him *ami de la maison*.

Conzertstück to thunderous applause but by then it was getting late. Rattled, Berlioz miscued the opening to his cantata *Sardanapale* and his mixed bag of under-rehearsed performers made a hash of it. At midnight, half of them decided to go home. The other half were prepared to embark on the next number, the *Fantastique*, but poor Berlioz's nerves were shattered. He apologized to the public, now demanding to hear at least the *Marche au supplice*. "I cannot perform it with five violins. It isn't my fault," he cried. Whereupon, the audience rose and the concert terminated. "My enemies did not fail to turn the event into ridicule," he writes, "and to say that my music *drove musicians away*. . . . Ah cursed strummers! miserable wretches! Your names are protected by their obscurity; but I regret that I did not collect them." [8]

This awful evening says a great deal about the condition of instrumental music in France, the level of the performers' competence and the frivolousness, bordering on disrespect, of the public. (Habeneck's concerts at the Conservatoire were an exception but even he had no hesitation in substituting the Allegretto of Beethoven's Seventh Symphony for the Scherzo of the Fifth. Such liberties seemed quite all right to most people, though not to Berlioz or Liszt.) That was where Liszt came in. The public that had to be coaxed to a Berlioz symphonic program flocked to hear him play the same music on the piano, which he regularly did in the 1830's. His object was solely to be of use to Berlioz, but Berlioz wouldn't have been human if he hadn't somewhat resented this secondhand success. He wasn't writing for the piano after all, and the knowledge that he depended so heavily on Liszt's transcriptions must have been galling, especially when, as sometimes happened, they shared the same program and it was Liszt who carried off the laurels.

Harriet's debts and his own poverty forced Berlioz into journalism soon after his marriage, and this may well have influenced Liszt in the same direction, though heaven knows no group before or since has been more addicted to press-agentry than were the Romantics and the idea would probably have come to him anyway. Sainte-Beuve said of this period that one lived one's life through the newspapers: "A sheet with five thousand subscribers was practically a family of intimates." It is still possible to trace the rise and fall of reputations, the making and dissolving of alliances and love affairs, through the tidal action of criticism, travel reports, open letters, parodies, statements and restatements of faith that poured from the presses. Sainte-Beuve himself actually managed to betray his passion for Adèle Hugo through the unlikely medium of a book review about Diderot. ("When a man who has lost his youth but has not yet acquired the calm of old age is stricken with some deep and passionate love, it is bound to become surreptitious," etc.) George Sand's *Lettres d'un voyageur*, a semi-fictional form she more or less invented, Liszt's *Lettres d'un bachelier-ès-*

musique (modelled on hers), were mines of information to the initiated.*

Inevitably there was a certain amount of horn-blowing. Berlioz's "letters" from abroad recounted with relish his triumphs in Russia, Hungary and Germany — let the ungrateful French know what they were missing. Liszt went further. He deliberately used the press to build himself up as an intellectual and establish the difference between himself and a virtuoso like Thalberg, who didn't have opinions on the future of church music or show off his knowledge of Italian art. But not all his journalism was self-serving. As later with Wagner, he pushed Berlioz at every opportunity. When the Opera closed its doors to Berlioz, Liszt was ready with his denunciation: "Genius is grandeur in novelty . . . thought creating its own form. . . . Now, in what musical works do we find a higher degree of bold innovation, of profound thought and richness of form than in *Harold* . . . ?" [9] He urged Berlioz toward Germany with a famous phrase: "Germany is the country of Symphonies; it is therefore yours."

Berlioz's response to Liszt's ardent advocacy was in keeping with the disequilibrium of his nature. He frantically craved love and friendship, and up to a point returned them. His letters to Liszt would raise eyebrows if they hadn't been of a piece with a century that habitually overwrote itself. "I love you so, Liszt . . ." His core was cool and utterly self-centered. "You write me letters twelve pages long dealing with me and my affairs," he once admitted, "and I am naïve enough to answer you *on the same subject.*" He was — it is a minor virtue — honest enough not to feign the interest he didn't feel.

The bane of Liszt's life was the theory, subscribed to by his closest friends, that he was the greatest of living pianists, a composer of no special importance. Berlioz didn't say this in so many words; his every action proclaimed it. His memoirs are filled with praise for Liszt at the keyboard: "Never so powerful as when he has two thousand listeners to subdue . . ." "I so far forgot myself in my enthusiasm for Liszt as publicly to embrace him on the stage. . . ." You could read him from one end to the other without learning that Liszt was a composer to be reckoned with. His thirty-odd years of criticism included exactly two notices about Liszt's compositions.

In the 1830's, this was immaterial. Berlioz's eight years' seniority, his achievements, gave him the right to choose the terms of friendship. To pursue the same line twenty years later was another thing. Liszt wearied of Berlioz in the end. Berlioz had no right to number Liszt among his betrayers.

---

* T. Marix-Spire lists no fewer than seventeen periodicals, reviews and dailies to which Liszt and Berlioz, among others, contributed. Anyone wanting to keep abreast of artistic affairs in Paris at this period would have had to subscribe at least to the following: the *Revue des Deux Mondes,* the *Gazette Musicale, Le Monde, La Presse,* the *Journal des Débats, Le Globe.*

PART TWO

Grand and Literary Passions

(1833-1835)

Chapter 9

LISZT MET the Countess Marie d'Agoult toward the end of 1832, at the house of a mutual friend, the Marquise de Vayer.* Marie's autobiography makes it sound like the encounter of the century, and she wasn't far wrong. Their love affair could have been the blueprint for the Romantic grand passion: it had everything — including the social significance — missing from the Sand-Chopin story: *they* were both artists. Marie, as she never tires of telling us, was a great lady who sacrificed wealth and position for her humbly born lover, and openly bore him three children. That took courage. It also took an overpowering belief in certain ideals. La Rochefoucauld's maxim about love and books has seldom been more effectively proved. If Marie hadn't read Byron, Senancour, Goethe (and if Liszt had not), the drama of their story, from which the props are not detachable, wouldn't have existed.

Hear the trumpets sound when Liszt enters her life:

. . . I would say an apparition, lacking another word to describe the extraordinary sensation he gave me, altogether the most extraordinary person I had ever

---

* I accept Jacques Vier's date (*La Comtesse d'Agoult et son temps*, I, 139). Marie's memoirs say they met "at the end of the third year after the revolution of 1830," but she is contradicted by their correspondence. The dates vary from book to book. Barzun places their meeting in 1834, and unaccountably says that Berlioz introduced them. "Berlioz took Liszt, with the famous result that the pianist and the countess fell in love and eloped." (*Romantic Century*, I, 244). Berlioz, however, did not know the Countess d'Agoult until Liszt introduced them, nor did her salon in 1834 include any of the people mentioned by Barzun: Balzac, George Sand, Heine and Mickiewicz were all brought to her by Liszt and at a later date.

seen. A tall figure, thin to excess, a pale face with large sea-green eyes . . . an ailing and powerful expression, an indecisive walk that seemed rather to glide over than to touch the ground, a distracted air, unquiet and like that of a phantom about to be summoned back to the shades, this is how I saw the young genius before me. . . .[1]

Liszt, we can believe, was capable of a startling entrance even into the drawing room of a friend, but this is not he. It is Mrs. Radcliffe's Schedoni: "His figure was striking . . . it was tall, and though extremely thin, his limbs were large and uncouth, and, as he stalked along . . . there was something terrible in its air; something almost superhuman." It is Byron's Giaour — "But once I saw that face, yet then/ It was so mark'd with inward pain,/ I could not pass it by again. . . ." The citations could go on indefinitely. It is enough that we identify the hero whose fatal properties will make intelligible the action that follows.

The force of sexual passion (as distinct from the eighteenth-century idea of love as Delacroix's sombre eroticism is from the flowery licentiousness of a Fragonard) was the mainspring of Romanticism, perhaps its single greatest discovery. Romantic personalities bloomed in the complexity of their love affairs, which like their novels were on a grand scale and rich in detail. Rich, too, in a kind of emotional snobbery. Passion wasn't for everyman.

Victor Hugo to his fiancée: Love, for the world at large, is nothing but carnal appetite, or a vague tendency which possession extinguishes and absence destroys. That is why you have heard it said that *passion does not last.* Alas, Adèle, are you aware that *passion* means *suffering?* Do you really believe that there is any suffering experienced by the common run of mankind, so seemingly violent, in reality so feeble?[2]

Passion when taken for proof of superior sensitivity is always destructive, and this destructiveness too the Romantics valued for its own sake. Since passionate love is anti-social (unless accidentally harnessed to marriage), it can be counted on to lay waste to families and societies founded on the family, with their apparatus of inheritance and the passage of capital from one legitimately conceived generation to another. When Marie d'Agoult ran away with Liszt, she did more than desert a boring husband. Children and vast sums of money were at stake. Tossing those aside (temporarily, it turned out; her fortune came to her through her mother, and she managed to hang on to most of it), she struck a blow for female rights. She also tore up a social contract, and she understood that society would take its revenge.

Lovers like Liszt and Marie never tired of discussing the ideal life, by which they meant what most of us do: freedom from ties and convention, travel, and no money worries. The amazing thing is how often they actually achieved it, for a while. Proposing to live on love and art — the world's worst combination by the way, since they consume more or less the same resources — they plunged with reckless confidence, and a terrifying literal-ness. Others might dream of Italy or Spanish islands. The Romantics packed their books, manuscripts, grand pianos, mattresses, and such children as chanced to be on the scene — and struck out for ruined convents and crumbling villas. They were among the first to appreciate the advantages of impoverished countries where servants were cheap and *palazzi* without plumbing plentiful. Most of these honeymoons came to a bad end. Reality intervened in the form of intestinal fevers and acedia. They bore fruit all the same. Marie and Liszt were unlucky, and rather exceptional, in that they produced actual children. The more usual consequence of a grand passion was a book, several books if both sides contributed.

Never before or since (and that includes Bloomsbury) can so many *romans à clef,* pamphlets, and plays have accumulated around the emo-tional interchanges of a single group. Balzac said there would soon be "a whole tribe of authors ready to have their entrails pulped into paper so they can print the secrets of their lives on it. . . . The horrors of the liter-ary Colosseum are threatening." He knew what he was talking about. Con-sider the Sand-Musset affair, which spawned a novel each and his play *On ne badine pas avec l'amour,* plus the mass of material it supplied to other writers. Sand also cannibalized her affair with Chopin, wrote up Liszt and Marie, and was herself the heroine of an ex-lover's novel, Sandeau's *Mari-anna.* Marie's *Nélida* is about herself and Liszt. So is Balzac's *Béatrix.* And this by no means exhausts the cross-references or the minor characters like the young man Charles Didier, who had a gift for insinuating himself into novels.

How many scenes must have been enacted with a view to how they would transcribe themselves to paper — not to speak of the letters patently written with an eye on posterity:

Musset to Sand: I send you my final farewell, beloved. . . . I will not die until I have finished my book on me and you (on you especially). . . . I swear by my youth and my genius that on your grave shall grow only lilies without stain. With these hands I will inscribe your epitaph, cutting it deep in marble. . . . Posterity will speak our names as it does those of the immortal lovers who are forever linked — Romeo and Juliet, Héloise and Abélard. . . .[3]

This kind of thing is to be found interchangeably in Vigny, Hugo, Liszt, who was always swearing by his genius, and goes far toward explaining why the modern mind turns off Romantic love. It isn't only the rattle of the self that is distasteful. We know instinctively that Musset was nowhere near death, and still less was Sand, who was as strong as a horse and outlived him by nearly twenty years. The stainless lilies are also farcical, given her sexual history, and the dragging in of Héloïse and Abélard presumptuous. These shades — along with Dante and Beatrice, Paolo and Francesca — were summoned by Romantic lovers to sanctify and animate a present less glorious than the past they represented. Said Jules Sandeau: "We look upon ourselves as the accurst of destiny, as Fallen Angels . . . blood brothers of the *Giaour* and *Lara* . . . when heaven knows, we are just men deceived in love — of whom the world is full." [4]

Musset was too intelligent not to know this too. It is we who are likely to misunderstand. Soured on the forced imagery, we write off his sufferings as a fraud — and are wrong. Musset's anguish was real. It leaves us unmoved for stylistic reasons and because passion has lost its prestige. Like a famous work of art now exposed as a forgery, it depresses us because we once believed in it, and perhaps still do, while telling ourselves we ought to know better. Sex in plain language sounds more honest, as well as more democratic: everybody knows what the words mean. So did the Romantics and if we don't find them using them, it isn't because they feared the workings of the body; but they did look at them differently. Liszt slept with countless women; he passionately loved perhaps two or three. And when he writes to Marie d'Agoult, "Let us live, put your arm under mine, let me sleep peacefully on your heart, whose beatings have for me the mysterious rhythm of an ideal beauty, of eternal love," [5] he isn't just describing post-coital detumescence.

There is, I suppose, the chance that one day a batch of documents will turn up to show a Liszt as candidly pornographic in his interests as, say, the young Flaubert. Perhaps in his travels he too was more interested in whores than in ancient buildings, flirted with buggery, and reported his findings with the élan of a dirty-minded schoolboy. I doubt it. Unless somebody has done a massive job of suppression, the letters of Europe's most celebrated Lovelace wouldn't have raised a blush in Queen Victoria.

Whence, then, his frightful reputation? Look into it and it is strangely ill-founded. When he compared himself to Byron, he clearly knew nothing about Byron's sex-life, the moral sadism, the not-so-latent homosexuality. If it wouldn't start a laugh, one might hazard that he was something of an innocent. Compared to a Baudelaire or a Verlaine, he certainly was. He never debauched anyone. He told Arthur Friedheim he had "never brought shame to an innocent girl," and that was true: there were no Zerlinas in his life. In spite of his passing affairs with Marie Duplessis and Lola Montez, the courtesan had no special charm for him: "I have, as a rule no great liking for the Marion de Lormes or the Manon Lescauts of this world." His tastes, what one can learn of them, do not seem to have been even moderately perverse. Here is an extract from Marie d'Agoult's diary that appears to deal directly with the issue:

It is with a love full of respect and sadness that I contemplate his beauty. What nobility and purity in his features, what harmony in the beautiful lines of his face! His hair, vigorous and abundant as the mane of a young lion, seems to take part in the life of his brain; his rapid look burns and illuminates like an angel's sword, but even when he is most passionate, most altered by desire, one feels nothing gross in these desires, the most delicate modesty wouldn't be offended.[6]

As this indicates, he was fatally attractive to women — and that is the clue. The stories are everywhere the same. In Moscow, says Herzen bitterly, "the ladies flocked around him, as peasant-boys on country roads flock around a traveller while his horses are being harnessed, inquisitively examining himself, his carriage, his cap."[7] In Rome, at a reception at the Villa Medici, a bystander tells us "it was impossible to count the ravishing, celestial women who came to fall trembling, like poor little larks, at the feet of the terrible enchanter."[8] These are men speaking, and their scorn does not hide their envy. Liszt, I believe, has been very much the victim of masculine jealousy and of the Puritanic sour grapes that so often accompany it. That was true in his lifetime, and still is. Ernest Newman, beside himself at Liszt's concupiscence, devotes a long chapter in a rather short book to the only really disgraceful episode in his life — disgraceful because he allowed a cheap, half-crazed little publicity-seeker to make a fool of him. Olga Janina, who called herself "the Cossack Countess" though she was probably neither one nor the other, followed the sixty-year-old Liszt across Europe. Stupidly, he allowed her into his bed, and then couldn't get rid of her. After various attempts at poison, etc., she pulled a gun on him. Or so she said. Her book, *Souvenirs d'une cosaque,* is so patently the work of a deranged exhibitionist that no one need take it very seriously. It did Liszt enormous harm however.

Male resentment of Liszt focuses on two aspects of his amorous career: the number of his "conquests" and their quality. He did of course have a great many women. He also had three long liaisons that in other circumstances would count as marriages. Given the length of his life, and the temptations he was subjected to, particularly when he was a travelling virtuoso, the number does not seem excessive. The fact is that he was no more and no less a womanizer than Hugo, Balzac or Gautier. Or to choose at random, than Talleyrand, Wellington, Goya, and Chateaubriand. So why the furore? What seems to be at stake is quality.

Musicians as a whole haven't been distinguished in love — any more than they have been associated with war, alcoholism, drugs, politics or high society, all at one time or another pitfalls to the writer. Liszt was the exception. Prostitutes and drabs have figured often enough in the lives of composers — in those, that is, and they have been in the majority, that weren't quietly domestic. Liszt, in keeping with his social aspirations, was the first to have a spectacular career in love. Chateaubriand could claim as many duchesses. Why not? He was a *pair de France,* though he did, as Princess Lieven said, look like a hunchback without the hump. It was natural that he should capture France's most beautiful woman and keep her for forty years. Balzac had duchesses too — and again why not? With Liszt the rules changed. Somehow, he had no right to top-drawer women, and when they threw themselves at his head it was resented. Actresses and female novelists he could have been allowed; Lola Montez might have passed; and a *déclassée* baroness or two. Marie d'Agoult, Carolyne Wittgenstein, and Olga Meyendorff (his last official mistress) were not *déclassée;* and two of them staked position and fortune in order to live with him. Even his fellow Romantics found this intolerable.

His male biographers have discovered a way out. They describe Marie and Carolyne as masculine and God knows what they mean — nothing physical or sexual. The epithet (which is intended to be damning) refers to intelligence, "a mind like a man's," in turn based on the fact that they wrote books. But what books! Carolyne's twenty-four volumes on the *Causes intérieures de la faiblesse extérieure de l'Eglise?* The Chopin biography? Marie's *Nélida?* If these are the products of masculine intellects, male chauvinists are welcome. Carolyne Wittgenstein, strictly speaking, didn't have a mind. She was a sort of holy idiot with a European education. Marie d'Agoult had the makings of a brain, and its operation was marred by every "feminine" characteristic in the lexicon: she was vain, spiteful, self-pitying and inaccurate.

The other trait that defines them as masculine is more complicated. Each felt herself the prisoner of convention and a loveless, degrading marriage, and each desired to escape. But though they both had (or could get control of with a little ingenuity) independent fortunes, neither acted to achieve her independence until she met Liszt — not the approved route to female liberation. In effect, they exchanged one bondage for another, the involuntary for the voluntary; and it is here that Liszt's position becomes interesting, for it was he and not they who wanted it to be otherwise, he who urged them to think and act for themselves and to give up the old relation of slave to master. He didn't ask more of them than he could give himself, least of all the physical fidelity to which he attached little importance. He was in fact extremely advanced in his views on women's rights — and this too made for trouble, as it always will until women learn that they can't have it both ways, be free and yet not resent the man who offers them freedom.

When Liszt told Marie to do as she pleased ("Show them who you are"), even if it meant taking a new lover, she immediately knew what to think: he had ceased to care for her. It wasn't true, though her hysterical reaction eventually made it so. Though it may have been a happy coincidence (absolving him, Marie would have said, from responsibility), he had a basis for granting to women the freedom he claimed for himself. This was his Saint-Simonism, which struck him with full force when he was still in his early twenties, a critical age for the formation of sexual attitudes. For what it meant to young men of his generation, one can turn (as so often) to Herzen's *My Past and Thoughts,* the most invaluable of nineteenth-century memoirs. He describes the effect of Saint-Simonism on Moscow's youth with echoes (deliberate?) from Gautier.

These enthusiastic youths with their terry waistcoats and their budding beards made a triumphant and poetic appearance in the midst of the *petit bourgeois* world. They heralded a new faith; they had something to say; they had something in the name of which to summon the old order of things before their court of judgment. . . . On the one hand came the *emancipation of woman,* the call to her to join in common labour, the giving of her destiny into her own hands, alliance with her as an equal. On the other hand the justification, the *redemption of the flesh, réhabilitation de la chair!*

Grand words, involving a whole world of new relations between human beings; a world of health, a world of spirit, a world of beauty, the world of natural morality, and therefore of moral purity. Many scoffed at the emancipated woman and at the recognition of the rights of the flesh, giving to those words a filthy and vulgar meaning. . . . Sensible people grasped that the purifying *baptism of the flesh* is the death-knell of Christianity; the religion of life had come to replace the religion of death.[9]

Herzen, who despised the Liszt he saw in the 1840's, the idol of Russian drawing rooms, did not know it but this philosophy had been Liszt's since his early youth. I will speak later of the influence of Saint-Simonism on the rest of his thought. It is enough to say here that he fully accepted the Saint-Simonist doctrine that admitted women to the hierarchy of sexual pleasure, and with it the freedom of choice that is the first condition of emancipation. When Saint-Simon proclaimed that all privileges be abolished, he included that of being born male. So did Liszt. And it is this of course, and not the myth of a fabulous potency, let alone a Hindu-like proficiency, that explains his fascination for women, and why it lasted into his old age. He *liked* them — and what is too rarely suggested, respected them, or at least those that deserved respect. To paraphrase the cliché, some of his best friends were women, and that includes a number of past mistresses, the point being that these were superior women whom he treated in a superior way.* Marie

* The vile little Olga Janina describes his treatment of one of these at Weimar in 1870. She was Marie Mouchanoff-Kalergis, who had been a famous beauty but who was

d'Agoult was uncommon in her desperate resentment of their breakup. Because the women he chose were either independent in fortune, or had careers of their own (Camille Pleyel was a pianist, Charlotte Hagn an actress, Ungher-Sabatier an opera star), they did not feel "abandoned" when an affair reached its natural conclusion. They were for the most part women of the world and perfectly understood the rules of the game.

This isn't to try to rehabilitate him, a pointless exercise. I would only suggest that because he was without the bourgeois virtues of the Schumanns and the Mendelssohns, because he managed to shock an increasingly moralistic century, he wasn't for that reason a monster of depravity. To be besieged by women as he was and yet to do no lasting harm to any of them seems to me something of a triumph.

---

by then old and crippled. "What false graces, what false ideas, what false sentiments, what false hair, what a false posterior!" writes Janina. "There was nothing genuine about her but an issue in her leg, and her breath. This invalid . . . always walked with a crutch, but in Weimar X [Liszt], the most obliging of men, offered to do duty for this. Leaning on his arm, wearing a white wrap lined in pink, this ruin wandered along the shady paths in the park, cooing her whole repertory of recitatives, nocturnes, and cantilenas" (*Souvenirs d'une cosaque,* quoted in Newman, *The Man Liszt,* p. 261). It is characteristic of Newman that he thinks well of this passage, which proves Janina's veracity and clearsightedness into Liszt's "weaknesses, vanities and hypocrisies." It doesn't occur to him, or to Janina, that the picture of the old lovers wandering together in the Weimar park is a moving one.

Chapter 10

LISZT AND MARIE D'AGOULT attracted so much attention that there are many descriptions of them, and since they were an outstandingly handsome couple whom artists were always wanting to paint and sculpt, any number of oils, busts, sketches and medals. (Liszt alone must be the most copiously represented musician who has ever lived. He was "done" in every conceivable medium including wax — a statuette by Dantan — but except for an Ingres drawing made in Rome, never by a major artist. Nothing of him approaches Courbet's magnificent head of Berlioz, or Delacroix's of Chopin.) They had their admirers. Their detractors are naturally more interesting, and of these the most malicious and amusing is Balzac.

Béatrix, ou Les Amours forcés is the perfect example of how the Romantics fed on their private lives. Its history is complicated. George Sand, who had befriended Liszt and Marie in 1836, in 1838 had quarreled with Marie and wanted to do her in. Not daring to write the novel that was the regular instrument of revenge, she passed the idea along to Balzac instead. He was delighted. He had not met Marie and had therefore to depend on Sand to tell him what she was like. For the character of Liszt, whom he knew quite well, he depended on himself. What may have surprised and not altogether charmed Sand was her own appearance in the book. Letting nothing go to waste, Balzac made her a woman novelist Félicité des Touches who writes under a pseudonym, Camille Maupin. (Double and triple jokes here: Sand's real name was Aurore Dupin; Maupin is a reference to Gautier's ambiguously sexed Mlle de Maupin. As for Félicité des Touches, could one risk the translation "happy touches"?) It is Camille who describes Béatrix for us, word for bitchy word, no doubt, as the real George did:

[Béatrix] is straight and slender as a candle, white as the Host itself. She has a long, pointed face, a rather variable complexion . . . as if her blood had been sprinkled with dust in the night . . . the iris of her eyes is pale green . . . she often has rings under her eyes. Her nose, which describes a quarter circle, has nostrils close-set and delicate. . . . She has a Hapsburg mouth. . . . She has one of the most elegant waists . . . ever seen, her back is dazzling white . . . the bosom however is not as well shaped as the shoulders, and the arms have always remained on the thin side. For all that . . . nature has endowed her with the air of a princess that is impossible to acquire. . . . Without being strictly beautiful or even pretty, she can when she wants to produce an indescribable impression. She has only to put herself into cerise velvet with clusters of lace, tuck a few roses in her hair, and she looks divine.[1]

Enough, you might think (and I have cut heavily); but Balzac is too absorbed in the way one woman demolishes another to relinquish his victim:

For all her blondness, Béatrix lacks the true delicacy of her coloring . . . she has the face of a silver-point drawing . . . she is an angel who is on fire and drying up . . . she is best in full face; in profile her features look as if they had been caught between two doors.

And now for her character:

For three years, from 1828 to 1831, Béatrix, savoring the last parties of the Restoration, whisked through the drawing-rooms of Paris, appeared at Court, adorned the fancy-dress balls at the Elysée-Bourbon; she surveyed men, things, events and life from the eminence of her intellect. . . . The first moments of giddiness caused by the social whirl prevented her heart from waking up; it was in any case still numb from the horrors of those first days of marriage; the child, the delivery. . . .

During 1830 and 1831, Béatrix sheltered on her husband's estates from the political upheavals; she was as bored there as a saint in its niche. . . . When she got back to Paris, [she] decided that the revolution . . . would also turn into a revolution of manners. . . . M. Lainé's famous words, "The Kings are departing," had sunk deep . . . and now I fancy had come to influence her conduct. She toyed with new ideas, which during the three years following the events of July 1830 buzzed like midges in the sun . . . yet while enamored with these new principles, she remained like other aristocrats; she wanted to preserve aristocracy. She could, however, see no place in this new world for great names; the aristocracy were resuming that silent opposition they had once offered to Napoleon

. . . in a period like the present, a period of ideas, such a course was equivalent to abdication; she chose rather to look for happiness.

All this is flawlessly Marie, down to her circumstances, which are exact. One must remind oneself that Balzac was anticipating her memoirs by a quarter century. But when Béatrix meets "Liszt," there is a falling-off, a lapse into cliché: Gennaro Conti is "outwardly charming," "inwardly a fiend," and a "charlatan in matters of the heart."

He lacks the courage of his defects; he will smile at Meyerbeer, shower compliments on him, when he would really like to tear him to pieces. He is aware of his weakness, and affects a forceful demeanor. Moreover, his vanity is such that it makes him pretend to feelings that are utterly foreign to him. He affects to be an artist whose inspiration comes from on high. To hear him talk, art is something holy, sacred. He seems to be a fanatic, his contempt for worldly people is stupendous; his eloquence appears to be born of profound conviction. Here is a prophet, a demon, a god, an angel. In short, however your eyes may have been opened . . . he will take you in. . . . Listen to him talk. The artist, he declares, is a missionary; art is a religion with its priests and must have its martyrs. . . . You feel admiration for his convictions, but really he has none.

Here Balzac succumbed to the perils of the *roman à clef*. The references to art being sacred, and the artist a missionary, make it impossible that anyone but Liszt could be meant. At the same time, for plot purposes, he has to be a fake. "He affects to be an artist. . . ." Why "affects"? Why is he not in fact an artist? How do we know he has no convictions? We only have Balzac's word for it. No reason appears except that he is an Italian singer, which presumably rules out the possibility of honesty. How much more interesting if instead of a stage villain Balzac had produced a believable study of a complex personality. But that is not the course of the popular novelist. Balzac's artists in general conform to middle-class fantasies about them: they are weaklings who spout a lot of pretentious nonsense; sensible men give them a wide berth and only women are fooled by them. This comfortable philistinism helped to make *Béatrix* a best-seller.*

---

* It was serialized in 1839, rewritten and published as a novel in 1844. According to André Maurois (*Lélia:* p. 256) George in 1840 got cold feet and asked Balzac to prepare a cover for them in case Liszt or Marie took offense. He did so in a letter that denied any resemblance to persons living or dead. ". . . When it comes to the assumed original of Béatrix (on whom I have never set eyes), it really is a bit too much! My reasons for writing *Béatrix* are set forth in the preface, and I have nothing to add to what I have said there. I love Liszt as a man and an artist, and to assert that Gennaro has any points of resemblance with him is a double insult, for it strikes both at him and at me. . . ." If Maurois is right, the latter statement was a malignant lie. The mystery is then what purpose it could have served, for if he did *not* love Liszt, what did he care whether Liszt was offended or not? On the other hand, if the statement was true (and it sounds true), he had performed a really base action. What Liszt made of it, we will anyway never know. He ignored the whole thing.

In one respect Balzac's Marie was unfaithful to the original. He made her a pure-blooded French aristocrat. The real Marie was only half an aristocrat and only half French. Her father, the Vicomte de Flavigny, was an ultra who during the Revolution went into exile and fought with the Armée des Princes (which Chateaubriand, who fought in it too, called "a motley collection of grown men, old men, and children fresh from the dovecotes [which] made war at its own expense"). Its business carried him to Frankfort-on-Main where he entered into negotiations with the house of Bethmann, rich bankers who in due course provided him with a wife. Elizabeth Bethmann was a young widow of twenty-eight whose dowry went far toward repairing the ruin of the Flavigny family. They had a son, Maurice, and Marie, who was born at Frankfort in 1805.

Marie's *Souvenirs* dwell with pleasure on the age and grandeur of the Flavigny family, and on the financial and intellectual splendors of the Bethmanns. Their Frankfort mansion was the most considerable in the place, a center for balls and soirées attended by all the celebrities of the day: the Schlegels, the Humboldts, Metternich, Goethe. The house of Bethmann, she says, "exercised a sort of sovereignty, by its great wealth, by its good reputation, and also by a pure savor of Protestantism, which distinguished it in the eyes of the Lutheran, Catholic and above all Jewish population with which Frankfort was at that time encumbered." [2] (The ghetto was a blight on the city, which was only done away with in her childhood.) Her mother's generation, she implies, was free from anti-Semitism; but she relates at some length her grandmother's hysterics when Amschel Rothschild came to the house to congratulate a member of the family on the birth of a child, fearing that he brought contamination with him. This rampant Protestantism, we learn, went back to the Netherlands, where the family had its origin. Fleeing from there "at the time of the religious persecutions" (she doesn't specify which ones) they migrated to the Duchy of Nassau, and in the first half of the eighteenth century settled in Frankfort. Johann Philip and his brother Simon Moritz established the house of Bethmann in 1748.

The reader who detects something fishy here will be right. The story is full of obfuscations but the fact seems to be that the Bethmanns were converted Jews, descendants of the patriarch Schimsche Naphtali of Amsterdam. Not extraordinary in itself, except that Marie was at pains to conceal it — and cannot have succeeded, at least in Germany, where the origins of the Bethmanns were not a secret. (It is on record that when Maurice de Flavigny was attaché at the French Embassy in Berlin, he threatened people who mentioned his mother's Jewish ancestry.) So what were her motives? The question would be unimportant but that it has a certain bearing on history. Her daughter Cosima was a virulent anti-Semite whose marriage to Wagner was, among other things, a union of paranoids on the subject of Jews: at Bayreuth, they reared between them a monstrous cultural edifice that had for one of its foundations the need to eradicate Jewry from German life. Hitler's visits to their shrine were a kind of commemoration of this ideal, and it is terrifying to realize how close Cosima came to receiving him in person. She lived to be ninety-three, dying in 1930.

To know or suspect that one has Jewish blood is of course not to be inoculated against anti-Semitism. Cosima must have been familiar with her own background, and Wagner feared that he had a similar taint.* His panic is easier to explain than hers. Anti-Semitism was rife in the Germany he grew up in. Cosima was raised in Paris, another world. Nor can I discover that Marie transmitted anything resembling genuine anti-Semitism to her child. Her attitude toward Jews was that of most nineteenth-century liberals — that is, she seemed to be free from prejudice unless she ran against a Jew she happened to dislike, when he was seen to possess "Jewish" characteristics. This happened with Liszt's protégé Hermann Cohen, but was rare. She had her awful faults. Judging people on race wasn't one of them. And there is another odd facet. After her separation from Liszt, when she began to write, she took a decidedly Semitic pseudonym, calling herself Daniel Stern, and in her memoirs she gives the provenance of this name — Daniel, the judge, Stern, the star — without, however suggesting a Jewish antecedent.†

Marie's attempt to blot out this portion of her heritage must, I think, be different in kind from Cosima's. Marie was one of those women who, lacking the talent they long for, go through life in a daze of self-delusion. Her conceit was limitless. Every compliment ever paid to her is passed along in her autobiography: "You have a German glance, and the French smile." [3] "Six inches of snow on six feet of lava . . ." [4] It didn't suit her to be half a German-Jewish bourgeoise. Early on, she opted for her father's side of the family, which she embroidered like a medieval tapestry. As a girl, she hunted the stag, and on the property in Touraine her father purchased with his wife's money, played at being a *princesse lointaine*, Mélisande in a tower.

* In the consensus of modern scholarship, wrongly. He believed he was the son of Carl Friedrich Geyer, the charming painter his widowed mother later married, and there is good reason to think he was. He further believed that Geyer was a Jew, and about that was evidently mistaken. The Geyer family records, traced by Ernest Newman, show no Jewish antecedents.

† "Stern" is of course German, but Daniel is not; and on the whole I find it extraordinary that this, combined with easily ascertainable facts about the Bethmann family, is never noted by Liszt's or by her biographers, though it should be obvious that something she felt to be shady in her background had an effect on her character. But even Vier, who has gone into every conceivable aspect of her life, skips over it, tucking away in a footnote the remark that "it is possible the Bethmanns were of Israelite origin" (Vier: I, 326, n.). I myself owe the confirmation of a suspicion raised when I read her memoirs to Richard Gutman's fine new life of Wagner (*Richard Wagner*, Harcourt, Brace and World, 1968), which touches on this and many other neglected subjects.

Cosima's dislike of this mother, who bore her out of wedlock and neglected her throughout her youth in order to go on playing her role of injured enchantress, may after all have been the germ of her anti-Semitism — which significantly became allied to her hatred for all things French. If, as she must have, she thought of her mother as Jewish-French, much is explained.

Marie, at any rate, began when quite a young woman to build her legend. Tall and fair like the Flavignys, rich, and thanks to the traditions of the Bethmanns, much better educated than most girls of her class in France, she was strangely *triste*. Her father's death when she was fourteen helped to cast a spell of pessimism over her outlook, but it is clear she was a misfit from the start — moody and obstinate, and with a perverse streak that often caused her to cut off her nose to spite her face.

Her marriage was such an action. For no good reason, she threw herself away on Charles d'Agoult, the least desirable of her suitors. He was thirty-six to her twenty-two, a lame little veteran of the Napoleonic wars and not even rich; he had an undistinguished post at court. There was no hope that he might satisfy her, and he didn't. Nor did the birth of two daughters. Marie's dislike (which Sand thought unusually intense) for the physical process of childbirth was not compensated by any interest in the children after they arrived. (In this respect, her legitimate children fared as badly as the illegitimate and Claire de Charnacé, the only one to survive, not surprisingly turned out to be another neurotic.)

Unsuited either to marriage or to motherhood, Marie in another age would have known exactly what to do with her life. Her vanity required her to play a star part; Romantic literature suggested what the part should be. Her real gifts lay in quite another direction. Her passions were in her head; she had a horror of irregular situations and of people who weren't quite the thing. Bohemianism in any form offended her. Nature in short had designed her to be a society woman, a *salonnière*. Her elegance was one of the few genuine things about her. Everyone speaks of her beautiful clothes and from her memoirs it can be told that she had a genius for the choosing and arranging of interiors, for organizing perfect little dinners. In her own setting, where she was in control, she was a seductive woman. Out of it, she went to pieces, became querulous and demanding. Like a jewel in its box, she belonged to the fashionable life of Paris and never should have left it. But the destructive impulse that made her marry d'Agoult ruled out the not disagreeable life they might have had together. By 1832, she was languishing in melancholy half-seclusion at her exquisite château outside Paris, reading *Obermann*, and spoiling for trouble.

When years later Liszt was told she was writing her memoirs, he said he knew exactly what they would be: *poses et mensonges* (poses and lies). They are, and also so unclear in spots as to be indecipherable. Intent on

her self-image, she simply cannot tell a story straight. (Yet with typical il-
logic she saved most of Liszt's letters, knowing, surely, that they would
someday be read, and in several cases, flatly contradict her.) So she informs
us to begin with that when they met he was "in entire retreat," didn't play
in public, didn't go out. Whereas he described the winter of 1832–33 as
follows:

Liszt to Valérie Boissier, May 1833: Here, for four months, I've had neither sleep
nor rest. Aristocracy of birth, aristocracy of talent, aristocracy of fortune, elegant
coquetry of the boudoir, noxious atmosphere of diplomatic salons, stupid tumult
of the rout, yawns and applause at literary and artistic soirées . . . the ball, the
tea party . . . criticism and praise in every way exaggerated in the newspapers,
artistic disappointment, public success, I've had all that! . . . I've felt, seen, despised, cursed and wept.[5]

And in reply to one of Marie's own, frequent inquiries about how he spent
his time, he wrote carelessly: "You forget that I know thirty thousand
people in Paris, and willy-nilly, I have to endure some of them." [6]

The explanation for the discrepancy soon emerges. Marie wants us to
believe that her young genius was shy as a forest creature because it will
otherwise be obvious that she made the first approaches, enticing him to
her house with little notes, commissions and invitations, and that he was an
elusive prey. "There was between us something very young, very grave,
very profound and very naïve," she says, "that had no need to declare itself." More likely he was wary of a woman six years older than he, with a
husband and two children, dead serious and infinitely pleased with herself.
Marie could write without a suspicion of humor that she was free from
pedantry, as from all vanity, pretension and affectation; she had only a dislike for the commonplace, "fops and talkers." Was such perfection to be
resisted? Apparently it was.

Her autobiography, like many self-serving documents, discloses to the
cynical a number of things she didn't intend to reveal. This generally comes
about through her use of a device that might be called the baffling incident:
something happens for which there is no rational explanation; someone intimately known suddenly becomes a stranger, reacts mysteriously; his or her
appearance undergoes a change. It often happens that we aren't as puzzled
as we should be. Such an incident is Liszt's first visit to Croissy, her château
in the country.

Croissy was one of the loveliest places in France. Built for Colbert, it
stood in a park of forest trees where stag still barked, and among its rarities
were a gigantic rock-crystal lustre and alabaster commodes. Salons opening
one into the other revealed *boiseries* by Oudry; an octagonal library was
set with medallions illustrating La Fontaine's fables. To this fairy-tale castle
she invited Liszt, wanting, intending to impress him — poor penniless

musician that he was — and then was astonished when its grandeur daunted him.

He arrived in the evening and found her, for the first time in their acquaintance, with her two little girls, seated in one of the salons: "What happened suddenly in his mind?" she asks. "What thought struck him like an arrow? I don't know but his beautiful face changed, his features contracted. We couldn't speak. . . ." [7] To the reader, it is plain as daylight what happened, the sheer terror that must have struck him. Not to Marie, who goes on to relate that from that hour he avoided her, and when they did meet (on her insistence, as his letters, pleading illness, press of work, or simply the need to be alone, reveal) did what he could to deflect her pursuit:

He whom I had seen so full of enthusiasm, so eloquent about the good and the beautiful, so ambitious to elevate his life and devote it to great art . . . now made a parade of unbelief. . . . He praised worldly wisdom and the easy life; he amused himself in the defense of libertines. All at once and out of the blue, he made bizarre proposals to me, altogether unheard of from him; he praised what he called my beautiful existence, congratulated me on my position in the world; he admired, he said, my royal household, the opulence and elegance of everything around me. Was he serious? Or was it a kind of teasing? From his impassive manner, his gloomy air, I couldn't tell any more.[8]

He was in fact behaving boorishly enough to give a less determined woman second thoughts. "Without reproaches, Franz, to whom my presence brought neither joy nor peace, seemed to nourish I don't know what secret resentment against me. Once I even surprised in his glance a pale flash of hatred. . . . What was it? I didn't dare ask." We soon learn to recognize this situation, recurrent in her book, and perhaps though not certainly (it has the earmarks of feminine fantasy) in life. Presently he will be on his knees:

One day, under the cut of a stinging word . . . a complaint escaped me. . . . My tears flowed. Franz looked at me with consternation, torn by conflicting feelings that made his lips tremble. Suddenly, falling at my feet, clasping my knees, he begged in a voice I can still hear, with a profound and sorrowful look, to forgive him. This pardon, in the burning clasp of our hands, became an explosion of love, a vow, an oath to love each other wholly, without limit, without end, on earth as it is in heaven.[9]

It may have happened like that. Or it may not. The Liszt-d'Agoult correspondence is in bad need of editing and revision. As it stands, many undated letters hang in air, and some are undoubtedly in the wrong order, making it extremely difficult to establish times and sequences. On this

sketchy basis, it isn't until well into 1834 that he begins to sound like a
lover, about then that he starts to sign himself in German: "*Nicht
eines Engels, nicht Gottes, nur Dein.*" (Not an angel's, not God's, only
thine.) Here too are the first signs of her devouring jealousy — to which the
scene above may actually refer. He was at any rate forced into lengthy
justifications, not of his present but absurdly enough of his past, though at
twenty-three his conscience ought not to have weighed too heavily. It did,
however, as she discovered. Playing on this theme won her many a temporary victory that reversed itself in the end, without her ever noticing the
pattern. At first, he is contrite:

I was only a child, almost an imbecile with Caroline [de Saint-Cricq], a
cowardly and miserable poltroon with Adèle [de Laprunarède]. With you alone
do I feel young and a man. . . . I have often wept, and bitterly reflected in the
past year. . . . There is always in my heart an indefinable remorse that tortures
me secretly and when I'm idle — sometimes I tell myself that a thousand others
have had the same experience. At others, the storm breaks and then my sorrows
and hates break out furiously . . . then . . . dreams of love, ecstasy, hopes,
energy and the enthusiasm of youth return. . . .[10]

Still she hammers — surely there was more to it than that? — until he
bursts into a rage:

A man false and vulgar as you think me would not have said "I have no love
but what you give me." *I don't take back an iota* of my past life, however shameful
or bitter it may have been! . . . not an iota. I accept everything completely, and
if I were a hundred times more criminal, I would still accept everything, because
I want the woman I love to be *happy* to forgive me. It is only from her that I
would *accept* pardon.[11]

"False and vulgar" reveals that she was already treading on dangerous
ground. With her acute sensitivity to the nuances of their respective social
positions, one would have expected her to be more careful. Yet she was
always edging toward the ultimate offense: she "dreams" for example that
he might one day enter her world. He replies savagely. "Another time don't
talk to me about your dreams; *I could never* decide to take my place with
you in such a society. . . . I repeat for the hundredth time, it would be
impossible for me to take a new direction." [12] A little later, he warned her
again:

Society, the world, the family, have nothing to do with it. The question is and
remains religious — that is, between God and conscience. I weep at the burden I
have placed on you. Remorse freezes the marrow of my bones. . . . Your letters
kill me. Yes, there are words that never pronounce themselves in vain. That of

separation has been said and said again by me and by you. However miserable and cowardly the virtues of the *femme du monde* often seem to me, they are the only ones that will suit you henceforth. . . . Madame, you have two daughters and the future looks dark.[13]

Marie saw that if he wouldn't enter her world she had better try to enter his. To meet as strangers on neutral ground can be an advantage in the early stages of a love affair. It ceases to be one when sex ends and conversation begins. Stolen meetings in squalid rooms do not, or soon do not, add up to a shared experience. If love is to last, it must socialize itself, develop mutual friends — or better still, enemies. Marie did not know Liszt's friends. Alfred de Vigny, whom she lists (improbably) among her rejected suitors, was her only real contact with the Romantics apart from Liszt himself. (Delphine Girardin, born Delphine Gay, might have been another. They knew each other as girls but Marie, who didn't get on well with women, disliked Delphine and was envious of her brilliant salon.) Liszt was more than reluctant to unseal this entrance into his life: "As for my friend Chopin . . . it hasn't yet been at all possible to transmit your gracious message but tomorrow . . . I will wake him gently and tenderly with your prayers and invitations." [14] "It seems to me, Madame, that you asked me the other evening . . . to present to you our celebrated compatriot Heine." [15] Neither introduction appears to have come off. Sainte-Beuve, he acknowledged, asked after her "with much distinction," wondering if she were happy or sad. But the little critic had to wait for several years to be presented, until they were all in Rome together in 1839. Sainte-Beuve was indiscreet; Balzac was pushing — inquiring of Liszt whether he saw much of the countess. He was answered "more than coldly." *

Marie went so far as to give him an autograph album in which she asked him to collect famous signatures. He hated this chore — "this beastly album you've confided to me" — and flatly refused to approach celebrities like Chateaubriand. He would not be her errand boy. Nor would he, which is more pertinent, take advantage of his known connection with her. Tempting as it might be to display his magnificent mistress, to arrange for certain favored ones to visit her, he resisted the idea with all his strength and was undoubtedly right to do so. Marie was intelligent enough to know that these were the true luminaries in the post-revolutionary firmament. On the other hand, though she plumed herself on her republicanism, her belief in the aristocracy of intellect, she was still penetrated by notions of what was due the Countess d'Agoult; and artists, she found, were often slow on the uptake. When, but only after she went off with him, she did begin to

---

* Balzac ventured a clumsy witticism to the effect that to be complete a man needs seven women: the housewife, the mother, the wit, the hoyden, the elusive one, etc. Repeating this to Marie, Liszt noted, "You see that I am sadly incomplete." (Liszt-d'Agoult, I, 97.)

know Liszt's friends, this was a constant irritant. Chopin was *"grossier"* more than once; Félicien Mallefille was lacking in respect; George Sand's jokes were in terrible taste; Abbé de Lamennais looked like a village curate.

Eventually, she was obliged to master these prejudices, which were incompatible with the fate she had chosen. In the meantime, Liszt did not want the job of explaining his friends to her, or her to them; and there was no need to. In 1834 he didn't dream she would dominate his life for the next ten years. If anyone had asked him, he would have said that the great event of that period was his meeting with Lamennais.

Chapter 11

TO ASK whether Liszt was authentically religious is like wanting to know whether someone is really in love. There is no objective answer except that he thought he was. He was born a Roman Catholic and all his life maintained that he was a true believer, which isn't quite the same thing as a practicing Catholic. He was initiated into Freemasonry in the 1840's, for what that is worth, and notoriously lax in his observances. We hear of prayerful vigils but for years on end he avoided the formalities of Mass and the sacraments — with good reason. One cannot go on confessing the same old sin indefinitely. Yet he believed. In what exactly?

In what Chateaubriand called *Le Génie de Christianisme*. This book, published in 1802, was a lifeline to the Romantic whose incredulity kept him from the faith that his imagination craved. Chateaubriand, like Liszt a devout immoralist, anticipated the modern skeptic in his defense of the Church on aesthetic grounds. We can believe in Christianity, he said in effect, not because it is true but because of the artistic glories it has inspired. Cathedrals, the liturgy, the sound of bells, the drama and mystery of the Mass are beautiful and so command our credence in what they represent. The *Génie de Christianisme* was in other words a thinly disguised essay in paganism, in beauty worship that continually slid over into the voluptuous. Sainte-Beuve, seeing this, called Chateaubriand "the epicurean of the Catholic imagination." The same might be said of Liszt, and would go far toward identifying the quality of his character (and in his church music) that offended all those, often themselves irreligious, who interpreted Christian to mean pure, or respectable, or at least with a decent appearance of it.

This he was unable to provide. It is nevertheless true that the central struggle of his being was fought on religious lines. The cycle of good and evil, sin and repentance that evolved in him like a Faustian fable was entirely concentrated on his work. Thus the "good" Liszt fulfilled himself in serious music and despised the virtuoso's tricks; the "bad" one cheated by not doing his best and was punished in the withdrawal of his vocation. He was obsessed with the guilt of failed genius, gifts wrongly spent, and that was true I believe even when the subject seemed to be his sexual transgressions, as in the letters to Marie quoted above. At the deepest level, his remorse over his "miserable past" (a recurrent theme) really refers to time wasted in pleasure, the misdirection of energy.

No major composer can have suffered more acutely from vocational block — not the same as poverty of inspiration. Music was the oxygen he breathed. In Debussy's words, "the undeniable beauty of [his] work arises . . . from the fact that his love of music excluded every other kind of emotion." [1] Just so. But it leaves out the anguish. Eliot's condescending aphorism that "the more perfect the artist, the more completely separate in him will be the man who suffers and the mind which creates" demolishes Liszt at a stroke, and with him the majority of Romantic artists. In Liszt, there is no dividing the man from his music, which bears his features as unmistakably as a child, and was sometimes as indiscriminately begotten. There was a time (right up to Rossini, who rather than get out of bed to retrieve a dropped overture one cold morning, stayed where he was and wrote another) when fluency like his was accounted a blessing. That day was over for the Romantic artist, who travelled like a pilgrim with his mission strapped to his back, for whom no curse could be greater than to miss his goal; and in Liszt this not infrequently produced a kind of paralysis.

The journal he and Marie kept in common when they lived in Italy has many descriptions of the torture chamber he lived in when these moods were upon him:

She said to me today, "You ought to make better use of your time; work, learn, take exercise etc." She has often scolded me (in her way) for my laziness, my indifference; I am saddened by her words. I work, I use my time! And what have I to do with my time; what can I and what ought I to work at? I've thought and searched, and I feel no vocation in me, nor can I discover it outside myself. . . . I have all the *amour-propre* and all the pride of a high destiny; what I haven't is a calm and sustained conviction. . . . There is a storm in the air, my nerves are irritated, horribly irritated. I need a prey. I feel eagle's talons at my breast, my tongue is dry. Two contrary forces are at war in me; one pushes me to the immensity of infinite space, higher, always higher, beyond the suns . . . the other draws me toward the lowest, darkest regions of calm, of death, of nothingness. And I stay nailed to my chair, equally miserable in my strength and my weakness, not knowing what will become of me. . . . I am like the she-wolf in Dante: *Che di tutte brame, Sembiava carca nella sua magrezza.*[2]

Passages like this show that the frantic search for enlightenment was not a pose. Liszt's pursuit of intellectual and spiritual fashions, the autodidact's weakness, struck many people as ridiculous. Heine sneered at his propensity to "stick his nose into every pot where the good God cooks the future."[3] To Liszt there could be nothing more important than to know who and what the good God intended him to be. A great artist of course. But what kind? To find out, he investigated every movement in religious or philosophic thought available to him in the Paris of the 1830's.

He began with the Saint-Simonists. We know this because he was later at pains to deny it: "I never had the honor of being part of Saint-Simonism's religious and political family. In spite of my personal sympathy . . . my zeal wasn't at all greater than that shown at the same period by Heine, Börne and twenty others . . . who confined themselves to following the eloquent sermons of the Salle Taitbout."[4] Written to an enquiring editor in 1853, this dates his participation to the latter part of 1830, when the Salle Taitbout opened its doors.

Saint-Simonism was the most moving and coherent philosophy to appear in the wake of the French revolution. "It was at the foundation of our convictions and remained so unalterably," wrote Herzen, and had he been truthful Liszt would have said the same. Once or twice, very privately, he did. Thirty years afterward he wrote to a woman he trusted:

At the risk of seeming still very naïve to you, I will confess that I think more highly of the utility of certain ideas formerly preached by the disciples of Saint-Simon than it is expedient to say in the drawing rooms of *statesmen.* . . . "The moral, intellectual and physical amelioration of the poorest and most numerous class," "the pacific exploitation of the globe," "science associated with industry," "art joined to worship," and the famous apportionment "according to capacity" do not seem to me fantasies empty of sense.[5]

Saint-Simon's original emphasis was less on the arts than on science. Foreseeing the impact of technology, he wanted to humanize it, turn its energies toward projects of public utility. He proposed a socialist Utopia with a triumvirate of technicians to be the judges "of what is immediately practical in the projects . . . conceived and elaborated by savants and artists." His followers were to shift the balance in favor of the arts. "The useful is no longer enough," said Prosper Enfantin. "We want the beautiful." Only the artist, said Émile Barrault (who introduced Liszt to the inner circle), can reveal its direction to humanity:

The artist isn't a feeble bird in its cage that repeats the songs its master has taught it . . . he soars above the earth, and, a neighbor to heaven, it is from there that his inspired and often prophetic voice is heard. . . . Only the artist . . . by the power of that sympathy that embraces God and society, is fit to direct humanity.[6]

Barrault went further: The most powerful art was music, "that vague and mysterious language which speaks to every soul . . . and should be the only common language among men." Intoxicating words to a young music teacher recently dismissed by a petty minister for daring to make love to his daughter. From the Saint-Simonists Liszt learned that he belonged to the only aristocracy that ought to count, that of talent. Saint-Simon was not a democrat. A collateral relation of the great duke, he substituted for that egregious snob's elaborate hierarchy a hardly less elaborate one of his own, composed of savants, the propertied and the unpropertied. Power was to be confided to the first two. The "people" were given a largely passive role, like that of a patient being operated on for his own good. The principle corresponded to Liszt's motto: *Génie oblige.*

Saint-Simon was a crank of sorts — an inspired one, who retained a certain hold on reality. He saw that labor and the conditions under which it is performed were at the root of the social problem, an insight on which Marx and Engels were to draw heavily. He understood the dangers and possible benefits of science. His immediate successors were of another stamp, religious fanatics who degraded his philosophy to the status of a cult. He died in 1825. By 1830, Saint-Simonism was in the hands of Enfantin, a charlatan not without charm or intelligence, who either lost his wits temporarily or found it expedient to behave as if he had. Proclaiming himself the new Christ (*"Homo sum!"*) he founded a commune of a now familiar type, a "family" of free lovers and ungifted self-expressionists who wore fancy costumes and did their own work. Presently their "pope" was clapped into jail for disturbing the peace. Then something remarkable happened. Enfantin suddenly recollected that he was an engineer and a good one. Free, his "phalanstery" dismantled, he went to Egypt where he recommended that they cut a canal at Suez — some thirty years before it was begun. He wound up the respectable director of a French railway.

His attempt at apotheosis and subsequent disgrace finished the movement in France. They were also embarrassing to those who had attended his early séances at the Salle Taitbout and succumbed to his personality. After 1832, most of them hastened to say that they had never joined his commune, which was true, and never really taken him seriously, which was not. His departure left a vacuum to be filled.

When Enfantin grew a beard and put on the robes of a messiah, he wasn't altogether playing the fool. He recognized (as Saint-Simon himself did at the end of his life) that Saint-Simonism was too rational, that it lacked the evangelical fire to ignite the creation of a new society, and relied too heavily on simple good will, the feeblest of human impulses, for its success. Sainte-Beuve voiced more or less this objection when he remarked that no group had more of morality or less of divinity. Enfantin's subsequent bid for divinity was in part a response to this feeling that changes in the social order must somehow be harnessed to a vehicle of faith. That feeling survived in many of his followers, independent of the mockery he made of it. It led Sainte-Beuve, for one, to another revolutionary nucleus with aims very similar to those of Saint-Simonism but with a strong infusion of radical Catholicism. He probably took Liszt with him.

Sainte-Beuve's spiritual history, his struggles to find a viable premise on which to base his life, so closely parallel those of Liszt at this time that it would be desirable to know much more about their friendship than we do. It may have been at Sainte-Beuve's behest that Liszt first investigated Saint-Simonism. Sainte-Beuve almost certainly conducted him to the next stop on their common pilgrimage: the group revolving around the young Count de Montalembert and the much older Abbé de Lamennais, co-founders of the dissident *L'Avenir*, whose motto was *God and Liberty*.

Liszt was introduced, however it happened, to Montalembert at the beginning of 1833 (at about the same time that he met Marie d'Agoult). Montalembert was captivated:

Montalembert to Lamennais, March 1833: I can't remember ever having met a more sincere enthusiasm; this enthusiasm he has lately concentrated entirely on our religious and political doctrines; they have brought him to a real and practical faith.[7]

Faith was the operative word. It was the whole difference between the Mennaisiens (that is, the followers of Lamennais, whose name was alternatively spelled de la Mennais) and the Saint-Simonists. But it was crucial, and for Liszt the answer to his prayers — literally to his prayers because it allowed him to combine his instinctive piety with his revolutionary ardor. Lamennais was only one of many Catholics who sought to establish a new order within the matrix of the church; he was by far the most powerful, articulate and persuasive. Like Saint-Simon, he was a spiritual refugee from the bloodbath of the French revolution, which he blamed, in part, on the anti-clerical *philosophes*. But where Saint-Simon had spoken only of a "new Christianity" and wanted nothing to do with any existing church, Lamennais clung to the faith of his fathers. Divine law, he said, is the model for human law, the community of heaven (*société des anges*) which the faithful enter through the Eucharist can be the basis for a human society founded on "reason, calm and love." Paying no attention to the history of the Catholic Church here on earth, he called on it to deliver humanity from the wilderness — "Catholicism . . . far from having anything to fear from the changes taking place in the world . . . is itself the principal motor . . . it only can found and affirm the new social order. . . ." [8] It was as though Marxism had been conceived in the womb of the Middle Ages.

Félicité de Lamennais was born, like Chateaubriand, in Brittany, that primitive corner of Celtic France, and there was something in him of a fierce and shabby old Druid. He affected the coarse blue stockings and straw hat of the Breton peasant and steeped himself in Celtic pessimism: "Life is a gloomy mystery, the secret of which is faith." [9] "My heart absorbs sadness as a sponge takes up water." [10] He had a gift for aphorism (always admired in France) and for memorable sentences that have to be reread before it is realized that their rhythm is superior to their sense: "Art for art's sake is an absurdity. Its aim is the perfection of the being whose progress it discloses." [11] "Moved by a new spirit, led to science by faith and to liberty by order, the people will open their eyes and recognize that they are brothers because they have a common father." [12]

Sainte-Beuve was to turn on Lamennais: "Oh how I loathe the roles of agitator, tragedian and gladiator! . . . Is it that fundamentally [he] was neither a priest nor a philosopher? Was he nothing more than a fine but ambulating artist? It is all very well to possess a talent that can never grow stale; but it is a misfortune to have a mind that has never ripened." [13] There was more to the Abbé than that. He belongs to the long and honorable line of French mystics. His *Essai sur l'indifférence* is as original as anything since Pascal; his *Paroles d'un croyant* moved any number of writers who weren't really on his side. He *was* an artist. His reverence for Catholic tradition is really another, more humane and moving, version of Chateaubriand's. Unlike Chateaubriand, he had the courage to abandon it when he saw where it led. Hugo, Michelet, Vigny, Lamartine and many other writers came under his influence. All of them were obliged to follow Sainte-Beuve's example and give him up. His tragedy was to have been most dogmatic when he could least afford it, to have dealt out through his paper, *L'Avenir,* judgments that his own experience was shortly to prove fallacious.

L'Avenir was in principle an ally of the Romantics because it was against "weighting thought and genius with an iron yoke." Classicism stood for the despotic rule of kings, whose taste for order and repression it echoed:

L'Avenir cited Boileau and his emulators who dared to fix the rules of language and the arts like monarchs claiming divine rights. It wouldn't accept the conclusion, the freedom from arbitrary restraints that the Romantics demanded. "What we look for," said Montalembert in his review of *Notre-Dame de Paris*, ". . . is one thing only, the traces of that divine spirit, that celestial fire without which the world . . . would only be shadows." [14] And in Hugo's novel he did not find it. Here instead was "the culpable sacrifice offered by genius to the depraved taste of a degraded and dying literature," "lascivious images" the more inexcusable because in a book about a cathedral.

Balzac's *Peau de chagrin* got a warning: "We will examine your work with the religious conscience we apply to everything, and it won't be my fault if the moral object is too deeply *hidden* for these Catholic eyes to discover." [15] *L'Avenir* went about its editorial duties as narrow-mindedly as any Marxist critic on the watch for ideological slips.

The writers rebelled. Liszt did not. *L'Avenir's* dogmatism couldn't affect him in the same way. He was disposed to accept its rulings, which accorded with feelings he already had about the good and evil aspects of his work. Lamennais encouraged him to think that the impulse that periodically drove him toward the priesthood could as well be served at the altar of music. "God is the greatest artist," said Lamennais; "his work is the world," a maxim that could be taken to mean that the artist, more than most men, is formed in the image of his Creator. Saint-Simon had offered a social mission; Lamennais suggested the same thing but with religious overtones that made his teachings more congenial. And finally there was the man himself.

Liszt knew all about him through Montalembert, d'Eckstein and others associated with the Catholic revival, long before he met him. When he did at last set eyes on him, he fell in love. There is no other word. Lamennais had that effect on impressionable young idealists. Short, middle-aged and plain, he exerted a magnetism of which everyone speaks and no one can make quite intelligible. It was perhaps a Celtic charm and eloquence that got them. Liszt told George Sand that he had never met anyone (herself excepted) for whom he felt such "a mad and intense sympathy." The *Paroles d'un croyant*, published in the same month as their meeting, put him in a state verging on hysteria. He wrote to Lamennais:

> . . . Whatever the imprudence, almost the absurdity of paying you compliments, I can't resist telling you . . . how your pages have transported, overwhelmed, torn me to pieces with pain and hope! . . . My God, but they are sublime! . . . What genius, what charity! . . . From this date it is evident, not only to those chosen souls who have loved and followed you for a long time, but to the whole world, that Christianity in the nineteenth century, which is to say the whole religious and political future of humanity is in you! . . . Your vocation is

quite intolerably glorious. . . . Oh, you won't fail, will you, no matter what anguish and terrors assail your heart, you won't fail! . . .[16]

Lamennais had already failed. Having outraged the French clergy with his ultramontanism (absolute papal supremacy), he was now doing battle with the Pope himself. The immediate issue was the revolutionary movements in Ireland, Poland and Belgium. *L'Avenir* was the passionate partisan of these Catholic populations in revolt: "They are the avant-garde of humanity, marching to the conquest of the future." Gregory XVI did not see them in that light. He denounced in particular the Poles, who were Catholics, for rebelling against their Russian overlords, who were schismatics. A gulf opened before Lamennais and his adjutors. *L'Avenir* ceased publication and they journeyed to Rome to make their case. But Gregory seems to have understood sentences like "The liberty of the people has for its condition . . . the liberty of the church" better than they did themselves. Their theories were condemned in the encyclical *Mirari vos* of August 14, 1832. Lamennais returned to France completely disabused; the Vatican had acquired its most savage critic. He refused to eat his words. The *Paroles d'un croyant* reaffirmed his position — and sealed his fate. A second encyclical, *Singulari nos* of June 1834, pronounced it "detestable for its impiety and audacity," and for practical purposes he was excommunicated.

Here was a cause, a martyrdom, made to order for Liszt, who would not hear a word against his idol. When Marie ventured a criticism she was sharply reproved:

Neither *le grand V*[ictor] who sees in the *Paroles* . . . only a mediocre work . . . a pastiche full of useless redundancies . . . nor Lamartine, who advised our noble priest against publication . . . nor the vulgar articles in the *Constitutionel* . . . nor yet the palinodes and the fears of the noble Faubourg, have shaken my conviction. . . . You object slyly that the *Paroles* . . . are not evangelical; allow me to answer you with the Gospel: "The Kingdom of heaven suffereth violence, and the violent take it by force." [17]

The Abbé reciprocated. Liszt, he said, was *"bien plus qu'un artiste,"* the greatest pianist who had ever existed and full of soul. He must have been grateful for this sudden adherence from an unexpected source for he invited Liszt to visit him in Brittany. The invitation was accepted with "burning joy." La Chênaie, the manor house where Lamennais lived with a small group of disciples, has been called the Port-Royal of the Romantics. Its religious and scholarly routines were well known and it was considered an honor to be asked there, though it was a long way off — three days by diligence.

For Liszt, it was apart from all else an adventure. He seldom left Paris and he threw himself into this journey with a zeal that reminds us how young he was, writing of various Paris landmarks as if he never expected to see them again and thoroughly enjoying all the little delays and contretemps of travel. La Chênaie itself enchanted him:

Liszt to Marie d'Agoult: You imagine perhaps that La Chênaie is a little town or at least a small village with a curé, a mayor and an innkeeper. Not at all. We are obliged to hear Mass at a good half hour's distance . . . and if the desire for a drink overtakes us, we must cover the same distance to find a tavern. . . . We call La Chênaie, then . . . the house of the good and sublime Abbé, my host. [It] isn't very new, hardly notable, but fairly comfortably fitted up. The dining room and salon are on the ground floor; the Abbé's room and that of Thoughtful [sic: in English, a nickname for himself] on the first . . . and a library (as everything is covered with books here) which is inhabited by an extremely simple and distinguished young man, M. Boré, assistant to the professor of Armenian at the Library. On the second floor are various rooms under the roof, which look out . . . on a little flower-plot and vegetable garden . . . at the end of which there is a modest chapel bordered by the melancholy pines of the North. . . . All around are the woods which our good father makes us strike through every day prestissimo: Thoughtful even with his good legs has often a hard time keeping up. It's a nervous, abrupt, sustained way of walking – the march of a man of genius and special to Lamennais. Many of the alleys of trees he has planted himself. . . . He has also chosen his tomb under one of the rocks by the little lake. We sometimes sit on it, talking of God and the sorrows of humanity. All this countryside is extremely broken up, varied, full of charming views: it is almost a little Switzerland, and I think would delight you.

And now after the topography, the ethnography. Actually, our existence is fairly uniform. Thoughtful, who sleeps well, gets up at about the same time as his illustrious neighbor, who hardly sleeps at all. From seven to eight . . . he does the lazy, reading, putting on his tie, playing a little on the piano. At eight, they bring him his coffee. Ordinarily the Abbé comes to share this with him . . . which as you may imagine gives quite another intellectual tone to this already intellectual occasion. After which the good father usually starts to pace the room, talking with abandon: that's his habit. The conversation just begins to be animated, which happens in about two minutes, and he's off at the double, and this sometimes lasts for hours, without, I think, his noticing. He's a man in perpetual motion. I often think this kind of conversation would be insupportable to Mariotte [Marie] who can't stand people on their feet and has often reproached me for the same obsession. . . . From nine to midday, Th. works at his exercises in the salon and the Abbé stays in his room. At noon, he always takes a cup of chocolate and Thoughtful lunches alone. Shortly afterwards, we meet, and usually take a little walk together . . . dinner is served exactly at five. It's the only meal we eat together . . . it takes three-quarters of an hour, and though abundant in its simplicity (which however admits of partridges and excellent fowl), is simply an excuse for conversation . . . between Th. and the master of the house. Immediately after dessert, the Abbé (always dressed in a terrible old threadbare gray coat, always wearing the same blue socks like a coarse peasant and enormous shoes, rarely shined, perfectly at harmony with the rest), the Abbé, our good father, takes his straw hat, thoroughly used up and torn in various places, and says in a simpatico voice, "Let's go children, let's go for a walk," and we are launched into space for hours together. Really, he is a marvelous man, prodigious, absolutely extraordinary . . . loftiness, devotion, passionate ardor, an acute mind, profound judgment, the simplicity of a child, sublimity of thought. . . . I have yet to hear him say: I. Always Christ, always sacrifice for others and a voluntary acceptance of approbrium, of scorn, of misery and death! . . .[18]

The accounting for every hour of his day, the minutely observed particulars of the Abbé's house and person, are so untypical of Liszt (who could dispose of a city like St. Petersburg in a sentence and brush off an emperor with the remark that "he was nice to me") that they are alone enough to suggest an intense experience. Here for once is something like proof of an epiphany. "Our good father" had administered a spiritual shaking severe enough to open his eyes as well as loosen his tongue, and he was more affected than by any other encounter before or afterward. Not only did he adopt Lamennais's teachings root and branch, he clung to them more tenaciously than Lamennais did himself. Religiously and politically he was Lamennais's disciple long after his master had abandoned the Church and moved so far to the left that he was close to an out-and-out communist. All this may seem beside the point to a musician; to Liszt it was everything. At La Chênaie he received his vocation — or what he believed to be his vocation, which comes to the same thing — and it did not materially alter in his own mind for the rest of his life. That summer of 1834, when he was twenty-two, opened his career as an original composer. By the end of the year he had composed four remarkable works, two of them dedicated to Lamennais and all of them owing something of their inspiration to Lamennais's thought: De Profundis, an "instrumental psalm" for piano and orchestra, actually written at La Chênaie (and never finished); Lyon, a musical salute to the rebellious silk-workers in that city; the first Harmonies poétiques et religieuses and the Apparitions already referred to, whose source was ostensibly Lamartine but could equally be Lamennais because the poems for which they are named were written when Lamartine was very much under the Abbé's spell. (It may easily have been their Mennaisien echoes that drew Liszt in the first place.) *

Lamennais was also responsible for his first essay in journalism. The La Chênaie letter informs Marie, "I have made at your behest a little memo-

* The last of his compositions with an overt reference to Lamennais was written as late as 1860: Les Morts, "an oration for orchestra with male chorus," has a prose passage from Lamennais ("They too have lived on this earth; they have passed down the river of time . . .") interwoven with the score. According to Searle, the words were not intended to be declaimed, only to serve as a guide to the musical thought; but the work has been so performed in modern times "with very moving effect" (Searle: p. 102).

randum of our conversations" — and this memorandum (now lost) almost certainly emerged as the article on the future of church music. It cannot be supposed that Liszt on his own had given serious thought to a new form of sacred music "uniting on a colossal scale the theatre and the Church," dramatic poetry with liturgical simplicity. The chaotic style, the underlinings and exclamation points mark the essay as his own; the impulse behind it is unmistakably Lamennais's. "Come hour of deliverance when the poet and the musician will no longer speak of 'the public' but of GOD and the PEOPLE" [19] might have been lifted from *L'Avenir*'s pages.

Lamennais clearly saw in the malleable young man of genius a rare opportunity for putting his theories into practice. Disappointment awaited him — as he might have guessed had he been a musician, or a psychologist. The *De Profundis* composed in his house, brilliant as it was, showed Liszt's emotional and technical unreadiness for the task assigned. The orchestration is hardly more than a sketch and the piece as a whole an unresolved battle between religious and secular themes, spiritual and earthly passions.

Lamennais did not live to see his green fruit ripen. Liszt was himself middle-aged before he undertook the immense labor whose outlines he had drawn so long before at Lamennais's dictation. I have already remarked on his fidelity to the ideas received in his youth. Here is an uncanny example. Consciously or not, when he spoke of religious music in later life it was with Lamennais's Druidic voice: "The church composer is also preacher and priest," he wrote, "and where words cannot suffice to convey the feeling, music gives them wings and transfigures them." [20] Thus did Lamennais become the architect of his tragedy: years of devotion to the reform and enrichment of ecclesiastical music that ended in complete failure.

Liszt was probably the nineteenth century's greatest composer of religious music, alone in his blend of scholarship, originality and devotion. But who knows this? His more than sixty compositions in this field have suffered an almost total eclipse. In Protestant countries, his idiom was despised for its supposed showiness and sensuality. A critic as intelligent as Bernard Shaw lapsed into mindless ridicule when confronted with the *St. Elizabeth* Oratorio: "Liszt's devotion to serious composition seems as hopeless a struggle against natural incapacity as was Benjamin Haydon's determination to be a great painter." A Dannreuther, knowing nothing of the Mennaisien unity of the theatre and the Church, tells us pompously that "Liszt came to interpret Catholic ritual in a histrionic spirit. . . . The influence of Wagner's operatic method . . . is abundantly evident; but the result . . . is more curious than convincing" [21] — which is not even correct; Wagner's influence had nothing to do with it. That left the Catholic Church itself, and it rejected his offerings as vehemently as it had Lamennais's philosophy, for not dissimilar reasons. Too Catholic for Protestants, the music was too radical for Catholics, and instead of becoming, as had been his pious hope, part of a living tradition, it was allowed to die unheard.

The fault was of course his, for not realizing that it was too late for that kind of revival and that it was a hopeless business to pour so much talent and piety into a project at odds with history. Lamennais's mistake was to have confounded the course of Catholicism with that of the human race. He unlearned this fallacy. Liszt did not.

Chapter 12

"*Vous n'êtes pas la femme qu'il me faut, vous êtes celle que je veux.*" [1] (You aren't the woman I need, you are the one I want.) Liszt said that to Marie on July 30, 1833. She noted the date. What it augured for the future she was in a position to ask herself the following year, when Liszt met a woman of whom the reverse was true. On his return from La Chênaie he was introduced to George Sand, whom he did need and might have wanted had it not been for their respective situations.

As noted earlier, the Sand-Musset affair was in its terminal stage. They had recently returned from Venice, where Musset, lying delirious in the Danieli, had caught a wavering but accurate glimpse of Sand in the arms of his doctor. The doctor followed Sand to Paris. Scenes, illnesses, "last letters," fatal interviews, separations went on for months — and in the midst of it all, Musset (probably) took Liszt to call, a most injudicious move. Famously susceptible, she and Liszt might have been made for each other and all Paris waited to see them fall into bed together.

Aurore Dupin, Baroness Dudevant, whose literary alias was George Sand, was extremely attractive. Anglo-Saxons, associating her vaguely with George Eliot and remembering the men's clothing, are apt to think of her as large and horse-faced. She was on the contrary small and well-made, with big olivine eyes and beautiful hands. The celebrated trousers also give a wrong impression. They weren't male dress but a delicate burlesque of it and with them she wore pretty velvet jackets and frilled shirts. Jealous women like Marie d'Agoult noticed that the ensemble was alluring, not masculine at all. Her only male trait was her independence. An heiress and landowner in her own right, she was disposed to do as she liked, and what she liked best was to rough it at Nohant, her estate in the Berri. There she rode horseback, rising at dawn and ranging the countryside with a devouring gusto that recalls the young Colette; sweating, she would strip and bathe in the Indre, her native river. And day after day, in Paris or Nohant, Venice or Majorca, no matter what storms raged around her, she performed her writing stint, covering the pages with her large, confident, tranquil hand.

Liszt was half prepared to fall in love with her. "Can I allow myself to hope that . . . you would . . . be willing to count me among the five or six people whom you receive *more or less willingly* on rainy days?" he asked.[2] Soon they were exchanging miseries. "I stayed until two in the morning *en tête-à-tête* with Madame Sand; she suffers horribly," he wrote Marie.[3] Musset was still in the picture and in fact waking up to the danger of these evening visits, which Marie can't have liked either. The air was full of gossip, most of it hostile to Sand, who was felt to be treating Musset badly. Abruptly, she decided to remove herself to the country, and toward the end of January, Liszt received this:

Monsieur Listz [sic], you were good enough to interest yourself in my sorrows and talk to me of your own troubles. You demonstrated a very sweet and precious friendship for me. I don't know why but certain people around me thought this mutual sympathy was a livelier sentiment and even an intimate liaison. Others merely thought it curiosity and coquetry on my part. I call on you, my friend, and charge you with the task of justifying me to those with whom by some accident you may have had to exchange words on the subject. I am in a painful situation, a prey to such profound suffering and surrounded by such cruel suspicions, that I couldn't take advantage of any affection, no matter how innocent . . . it might be. . . . Allow me to beg you . . . not to come to see me, and to believe, in spite of that, that I won't allow you to drop the friendship you promised. I leave it on deposit in your heart and beg you . . . sometimes to address a prayer to God on my behalf, because I am very unhappy.[4]

Her *Journal intime* is more precise about what had happened:

What was it that Buloz said to me yesterday about M. Liszt? Can Alfred have spoken to him? Did he seriously think for one moment that I was about to fall in love with M. Liszt? Does he still think so? Ah my dear one, if you could be jealous of me, with what pleasure would I throw all these people out! . . . [But] to show Liszt the door now, what stupidity, dear Buloz! Why? For whom? I did think in the course of one or two interviews that he was in love with me, or disposed to be [and] perhaps that if I could I would have received him favorably, but I felt I must tell him . . . that he musn't think of it, when suddenly after the pretty reception I had given him . . . I became convinced that I was stupidly infatuated with a pointless virtue and that M. Liszt thought only of God and the Holy Virgin, who doesn't particularly resemble me. . . .[5]

In the country, Sand recovered her composure and wrote Liszt more favorably. The letter is lost but we have his answer:

Liszt to Sand, April 30, 1835: Monday in bed: . . . Your next to last letter hurt me very much. How often, passing your whitewashed house on the Quai Mala-quais, my heart was constricted with sadness and pain! . . . But as not the least vanity was ever involved in the pure and lively affection I felt for you, I didn't let it carry me away, I never blamed you. It seemed to me you were right to mistrust me, and anyway, isn't it your privilege to repulse, severely even, those of your friends who haven't sufficiently proved themselves? But I did suffer . . . because (as I think I told you one day), I have only once in my life felt (for the Abbé de Lamennais) anything like the mad and intense sympathy that made me want to be a little less ill-judged by you. Happily, your three lines . . . have done away with my pain. You wounded only to cure. . . .[6]

Sand replied from Nohant:

Do you take me for a conceited fool? I never thought you were in a state be-tween love and friendship for me. . . . I didn't suppose you could, in such circum-stances, feel anything but an *amitié* or an utter indifference that might allow you a sentimental pastime. . . . Let's drop it and never go back to it.[7]

They did drop it, and as far as can be determined never became lovers, though the possibility was always there. Sand must have known, by then, about Marie; Liszt may also have hesitated to betray his friend Musset. There were simply too many complications standing in the way of an affair. Friendship was another matter and although neither was believed capable of sustaining that cooler sentiment, they seem to have done it. Partly this was because Sand, in spite of appearances, had common sense, and was as free from conceit as a woman with her gifts could be. Rarer still, she really liked Liszt for himself — adored his genius without wanting to conquer it and treated him without affectation. She coddled and teased him, calling him Crétin and laughing at his foreign accent. Unlike Marie, who blushed at Anna's commonness, she was charming to his mother.

He responded with a kind of delighted bewilderment. He was, in the exact sense, crazy about her. Apart from everything else, she made life so enjoyable, so amusing. But that may also be why, in the end, he could re-sist her. All his great loves were humorless women who made heavy weather with their feelings. Sand could laugh at her sexual quandaries and worse — analyze them, as he knew from her novel *Lélia*. In its original version (published in 1833 and later purged of sections she feared were too revealing) this was a bold study of female frigidity, and the heroine, passing unfulfilled from man to man, was in many ways a self-portrait. Not entirely, and not enough in my opinion to have justified Maurois in calling his biography of her *Lélia* too. Like most women who experiment with sex, Sand got mixed results and her famous lovers were the least satisfactory from the technical point of view. But her letters to various men (particularly Michel de Bourges) and her journal do not describe an invariably frigid woman. Nevertheless Liszt, who had read and admired *Lélia* before he met her, might well have been chilled by its honesty and a detachment he liked no better than most men.

Sand came back to Paris in May 1835, and immediately became inseparable from Liszt and his circle. She had, it is true, her new lover Michel de Bourges, a militant republican lawyer, sinfully ugly. But he was too preoccupied with his defense of the Lyon insurgents * to give her much of his time or to care what she did with hers.

It will be recalled from his violent letter to her that Liszt had all but quarrelled with Marie d'Agoult over the *Paroles d'un croyant*. She did not admire Lamennais and wasn't clever enough to simulate interest in the subject that absorbed her lover. Sand at once succumbed to Liszt's enthusiasm, longed to meet the Abbé, going to the length of planning a pilgrimage of her own to Brittany. That was now unnecessary. Lamennais was in Paris for the trial and Liszt enchanted to act as go-between: "I will make a feast of putting you in *rapport*," he told her. "I will knock on your door on the 4th, 5th, 6th, 7th and 8th of May, and if you won't let me in, I will call a locksmith and force my way." [8]

The Abbé was perhaps less enthusiastic. He was prudish about women, didn't care for Sand's loose reputation, and expected little from her intelligence: he had never met a female who could follow an argument, he said. Sand, taking her cue from Liszt, was ready to find *him* flawless: "I want to kneel at his feet." His misogynism was unequal to this approach and he was soon toiling up her three flights of stairs every day. Her *Lettre d'un voyageur* to Liszt (August 1835) recalled those séances:

Now then, didn't we have some beautiful mornings and evenings in my attic with the blue curtains? . . . Weren't we the good children of God who blesses simple hearts? Didn't we watch the hours fly without wanting to hasten their course . . . ? You remember Puzzi at the feet of the Breton saint, who . . . spoke with the goodness and simplicity of an apostle? You remember d'Everard plunged into gloomy ravishment while you made music, raising his head suddenly to tell you in his deep voice, "Young man, you are great." [9]

* These were the leaders of the uprising eulogized by Liszt in *Lyon*. Their trial was the political event of the year — all the leaders of the republican party appearing for the defense — and was avidly followed by Liszt and his friends.

An obscure passage to the average reader, in fact an illustration of Sainte-Beuve's remark that a sheet with five thousand subscribers was a family. Everyone knew the location of the *mansarde bleue,* the identity of the Breton saint, and that d'Everard was a pseudonym for Michel de Bourges. The meetings in Sand's attic, at Liszt's apartment and in various restaurants had been news for months. The *Mercure de France* (Sand wrote for the *Revue des Deux Mondes*) had been given this glimpse as early as June:

Imagine an assembly of lions with M. de la Mennais for its king; M. de la Mennais transported all at once from the depths of his solitude at La Chênaie to the blaze of the lamps and candles in the rue de Provence, and surveying from his sofa a section of literary Paris, as he recently surveyed the Paris of the revolution. . . . The three rooms in which M. Liszt receives were, literally, encumbered. On one sofa, the author of *Indiana* [Sand] . . . listened charmingly to the author of the *Paroles d'un croyant.* In a dark corner, various gentlemen were given up to serious conversation. They were M. Ballanche, that philosopher of earlier ages . . . the illustrious editor of the *Catholique,* the baron d'Eichsten [sic — his name was d'Eckstein], and M. de Guerry, the eloquent preacher. . . . Elsewhere . . . Henry Heine opened a sparkling discussion . . . and leaning against a door, M. Barrault with his long Oriental beard, the Saint-Simonist not the deputy, recounted his souvenirs of Asia, aided perhaps by the beautiful black eyes of *La Juive,* mademoiselle Falcon [the star of Halévy's opera]. Ad. Nourrit sang, as he always does when the subject of his songs is religious — with the inspiration and voice of an angel.[10] *

With these notices we detect a change in Liszt's position. No longer the virtuoso extra at other people's gatherings, he is beginning to form his own group, something like a new school of socially conscious writers and musicians. Lamennais is their spiritual leader but it is Liszt who has placed him on his pedestal, Liszt who brings in the recruits to replace defectors like Sainte-Beuve. At the same time, the whiff of cultism emanating from the premises shows why, in the end, it won't work. Not only is Lamennais a doubtful proposition, at least two of the other characters are howling curiosities guaranteed to give any movement a shady name. The Baron d'Eckstein, a converted Jew, was a distinguished Orientalist who may or may not have found it expedient to join the Catholic revival in order to cloak his other activities: he was suspected, apparently correctly, of being

---

* This report, or another like it, threw Sainte-Beuve into spasms of irritation. Sand's *Histoire de ma vie* says he kept asking her what on earth she saw in such people: "A dinner to which Liszt invited M. de Lamennais, M. Ballanche, the singer Nourrit and me, seemed to [Sainte-Beuve] the most fantastic thing he could imagine. He demanded to know what could possibly have been talked about. . . . I answered that I hadn't an idea, that M. Lamennais must have talked to M. Ballanche, Listz [sic] to Nourrit, and I to the house cat" (Marix-Spire: fr. HV: IV, 333).

Metternich's chief spy in France. The Puzzi referred to by Sand was another bad hat. His real name was Hermann Cohen (he too was a convert) who at this time, aged fourteen, was thought to be as gifted a prodigy at the piano as Liszt had been, and Liszt had virtually adopted him. He toadied shamelessly to Lamennais, to Sand, and of course to Liszt, and was in return spoiled and petted until he became intolerable. Puzzi will appear again, sponging on Liszt. Qualities he must have had. His end was as remarkable as his beginning. After a career of debauchery he became a monk, founded religious establishments, and died nursing the French wounded in the Franco-Prussian war. In the meantime, he was not a reassuring presence.

The real difficulty was Lamennais, though Liszt would have died rather than admit it. The homespun pope lectured his followers endlessly on their mission. According to Sainte-Beuve, the rules of dialogue were unknown to him: he never paused for a reply. Liszt had already discovered how exhausting he could be at La Chênaie, where he felt the strain of "this continual feast of intelligence and soul." "Even here," he wrote Marie, "my heart is oppressed, my head full of anxieties and feverish passions. The presence of men tires me. . . ." [11] Lamennais did not consider that his artist friends had work to do; nor, given his ideological criteria, can we believe he would have been any judge of its quality. "Form," he wrote, "is the means and not the end; the end is the spiritual vision that it provokes, the thought it arouses, the emotion it produces; from which we see that form in Art can only occupy a subordinate position." [12] How noble, cried the followers — though neither Liszt nor Sand could have confirmed any such thing. He at his piano, she at her desk, were at the mercy of form and aware that it can never be subordinate. The Abbé's discourses, larded with le Beau, le Vrai, l'Idéal, in fact betray the natural philistine. That had been L'Avenir's weakness; it was his weakness still, though the good little children of God were too hypnotized to see it. Still, they couldn't help sharing a guilty secret: they were artists, he was a theologian; and when it came down to it, neither applied his preachments.

Sand indeed was bowled over by precisely that side of Liszt with which Lamennais had least to do. She was ravished by his performance, and her descriptions leave no doubt about the sensual nature of her response. "Because I have strong nerves and no instrument is ever too loud for me," she would creep under the piano when he played, like a little black cat who shivers with pleasure. At other times she would recline among her cushions in a physical stupor characteristic of her:

It is you above all, my dear Frantz [sic], whom I place in a picture flooded with light, magic apparition that rises from the shadows of my meditative evenings. In the candlelight, through the halo of admiration that surrounds you. . . . I

like, while your fingers impart new marvels to the marvels of Weber, to meet
your affectionate look . . . that seems to say, "My brother, do you understand
me? I speak to your soul." Yes, yes, inspired artist, I do understand that divine
language and cannot speak it.[13]

Where was Marie d'Agoult? The two women were obviously devoured
with curiosity about each other, and Liszt just as obviously reluctant to
bring them together. The details are indistinct. Sand's *Lettre d'un voyageur
sur Lavater* had this: "Do you remember the blonde peri in an azure robe
who descended one evening from heaven into a poet's attic, and seated herself between us, like the marvelous princesses who appeared to artists in
the joyous tales of Hoffmann?" [14] That is Marie, whose own memoirs supply
a less incandescent picture with a different locale: "Franz invited us to dinner at his mother's. Our interview was very singular. . . ." [15] She doesn't
say why but fixes a piercing feminine eye on Sand's tight velvet redingote,
her skinny flanks and heeled boots on tiny feet — the "glance that seemed
to see without looking." With her customary smugness she assures us that
Sand "took a great fancy to me and begged me to come and see her." Maybe; we are here in a twilight zone. Sand's attitude was ambiguous from the
first, grounded in the device of over-praise:

My beautiful countess with the golden hair, I don't know you personally, but I
have heard Franz speak of you and I have seen you. I think I can after that,
without foolishness or misplaced familiarity, tell you that I love you, that you
seem to me the only beautiful, estimable and really noble being I have observed
aglow in patrician circles. You must be a strong person to make me forget that
you were a countess. But now for me, you are the very type of fantastic princess,
artist, lover, noble in manners, language and appearance, like the daughters of
kings in legendary times. . . .[16]

So begins Sand's first letter to Liszt's mistress and it is full of irony. Sand,
albeit illegitimately, was the granddaughter of the Maréchal de Saxe, and
had she cared to boast of it, of royal blood. She was plainly jeering at
Marie's pretensions and the manner of her appearance in "the poet's attic"
— or Liszt's apartment as the case may be. A second letter confirms her
aggression:

I saw you, the first time, I found you pretty; but you were cold and I was too.
The second time, I told you that I detested the nobility, not knowing you were
of it. Instead of slapping my face, as I deserved, you talked to me about your
soul, as if you had known me for years. . . .[17] *

---

* French scholars have extended themselves over this incident, or incidents, the point
being to establish how well (if at all) Marie and Sand knew each other before Marie
went off with Liszt to Switzerland. The letter beginning "I don't know you personally"

There isn't, I think, much doubt that Sand thought Marie a fool, and that she was angered that Liszt should prefer "the princess" to herself. Marie's feelings, since her letters from this period are few (the pertinent ones may have been destroyed), must be a matter of speculation. I believe her jealousy of Sand to have been so extreme that she was ready to commit any folly if it would remove Liszt from Sand's vicinity.

---

used to be dated May 1835. It is now (in the new Lubin edition of Sand's letters) put forward to September and the phrase taken to mean something like "though we have met, I don't feel I really know you . . ." because it closes with the phrase "I nourish myself with the hope of going to see you" — which seems to mean "going to see you in Switzerland."

There are further complications. In Marie's unpublished journal, there is a terse notation, "Dîner de Mme. Sand," dated January 5, 1835, which is much earlier than they are known to have met. And finally, there is an unpublished letter from Marie to a friend (September 12, 1836), which states that "there was, before I left Paris, a dinner at a celebrated artist's that was most peculiar in the choice of guests. It made a lot of talk; I confine myself to mentioning a few of them: Abbé de Lamennais, Abbé Deguerry, Mme. George Sand, Barrault, Nourrit, the baron d'Eckstein, Ballanche, Berlioz etc." (Vier: I, 132) Except for Berlioz, this is clearly the dinner reported in the *Mercure de France* (see above), and Vier speculates that Marie may have been present. I don't think so. Aside from the malicious tone, which suggests she was excluded, and the possible mistake about Berlioz, she tells us elsewhere in her memoirs that she had never set eyes on Lamennais until he appeared in her salon a few days before she went off for Switzerland to meet Liszt — which rules out her attendance at any of the gatherings reported in the press that year.

Chapter 13

THE BIOGRAPHER CONFRONTED with a critical but poorly documented moment in his subject's life has an unsatisfactory choice before him. He can pretend to omnipotence, and run the risk that fresh evidence will someday make a hash of his story, or he can abdicate, tell the little he knows for certain and let the reader decide what it adds up to. The first six months of 1835 are such a period in Liszt's life. In June he went to Switzerland to join Marie, beginning an exile that permanently affected his future. We don't really know how it happened. Her account is full of inventions if not downright lies, and has significant gaps; his, as relayed years later to the biographer Lina Ramann through Carolyne Wittgenstein, can't be right either; and other sources are unhelpful. It nevertheless seems to me that a kind of truth *can* be pieced together from her tangled tale and the surviving letters and I therefore choose the know-it-all's part.

Marie's version is important, however mendacious, because it shows how her mind worked, hence what she was likely to do. After the burning avowals at Croissy, then, a hazy pastoral:

The hours, the days, the weeks that followed were pure enchantment. Without making any plan . . . or arranging anything, it happened that things went of themselves, always bringing us closer to one another. Franz, as he had promised, didn't seem to be the same man. Always tender, he brought a charming *douceur* to our relations. . . . But the storm was not far away.[1]

We are presumably in the summer of 1834. In October, her daughter Louise fell ill with one of those undiagnosable ailments, a "cerebral fever" caused by "autumn mists." She was removed to Paris, and in December she died. Marie gives pages to the gruesome details, the night sweats, the little figure starting up in bed, the final closing of the eyes. But as she has already confessed her indifference to these children, and we know her shocking record with the three to come, we follow her with reserve. The mourning veil slips when she lets out that the remaining daughter, little Claire, tried to comfort her and was so brutally repulsed that the grandmother had to intervene and put the child out to board.

Liszt's behavior now becomes, as so often with Marie, an enigma. He didn't come near her during Louise's illness and the first she heard from him was a note delivered with a pile of others after the funeral:

> I opened it at random, not noticing the handwriting. It was from Franz. He didn't hope to see me, he said, at such a moment. He didn't think his presence would console me. He was leaving for La Chênaie. [He] didn't say for how long. . . . There was a tone to the letter and in the decision it announced a coldness that should have hurt me. I felt, on the contrary, I don't know what bitter relief. Pain has its own selfishness. . . .[2]

Six months pass; his name is never mentioned in her presence; his image fades.

This is one of her more egregious falsehoods. Because of course he did not go to La Chênaie in December but the previous autumn. The letter she says she got after the funeral does not exist — how could it when the one he actually wrote at the time of Louise's illness and death (which does survive) is so different?

> Monday midnight. Be blessed, oh my God, blessed forever. She writes me this evening, as she leaves her child perhaps. Thank you, thank you! Now my heart overflows with joy and pride. Oh, I can't write to you. I don't even know if I can see you. . . . You tell me you thought of me constantly during those two days. You thought of me by the bed of Louise. . . . Forgive me, Marie, if I seem to forget at this moment your sorrows and our ills in order to speak to you of myself and those words, "I thought always of you. . . ." Forgive me, poor desolate mother, for this appeal to all that is most alive, close and forceful in our souls . . . in the presence of your daughter's deathbed. . . . You do understand me, don't you, you feel me in your flesh and bones? . . . You do understand, too, perhaps why (for a long while) I have tried to accustom your mind to unhappiness. There don't listen, don't read further. I think I am losing my mind, but I love you so much and in such an elevated way. Let me say one thing. Your maid told me . . . that you spoke of drowning yourself, of never seeing Claire [the other child] again, etc. This hurt me (in God's name, don't tax me again with egotism and insensibility! If only it were so . . .)[3]

So much for his callousness at the time of Louise's death. There are still aspects to this distraught letter that point to underlying truths in her story: something was wrong and had been for some time; she wrote a letter calculated to tear his heart and let him know she had thought of suicide. "Accustom your mind to unhappiness" is usually said by someone paving the way to a break — which her appeal rendered impossible at such a moment.

Her mention of La Chênaie, though chronologically wrong, may also be revealing. Lamennais decidedly opposed Liszt's connection with an older married woman and undoubtedly tried to talk him out of it during one or more of their rambles among the Breton rocks. Liszt may have tried to act on that advice when he got back to Paris in October — the month when little Louise fell ill, and also the month that introduced George Sand. Marie can't have missed the symptoms of infatuation that were so plain to others, and surely it would seem to her that George and the Abbé between them were a threat of the most dangerous kind. Unpleasant as the idea is, it isn't incompatible with her character or her habitual techniques that she should have capitalized on her loss in order to retrieve a lover more and more absent or distrait. It is even possible that her actual surrender, inevitably fussy and momentous, did not take place until despair made it necessary — that is, about January 1835; and in support there is a drastic change in Liszt's letters to her that spring. For the first time they scald the page. The hitch is that they are undated and perhaps incorrectly situated in the correspondence. If not, the question must then be whether we can accept a quasi-platonic relationship for more than two years. It is possible. Throughout her life, Marie was an imperious flirt who liked to keep men dangling. She smiled at their lusts, being herself rather cold. "I have always been susceptible to physical temptations, you to those of the heart and intellect," Liszt told her once. "You are as . . . hard as Alpine granite." She may therefore have stalled on the physical issue (which could also explain some of his sulky fits, his "*projets de soutane*") until driven by the fear of losing him — a hypothesis that may further be confirmed by the date of Blandine Liszt's conception, March 1835.

Marie doesn't breathe a word about her pregnancy, wanting us to think it didn't enter into the decision to go away together — hence her fiction that they didn't meet for six months — when in fact it was the whole point. But was it accidental or deliberate? If accidental, the likelihood is that she had only lately become his mistress. Either would indicate that she was in a panic and determined to bind him by physical means; and the likeliest source for that panic was Sand — or the baneful combination of Sand and Lamennais, the two beings that by his own account Liszt loved best in the world, neither of whom was or could be her friend.

One cannot blame her. Liszt's relations with Sand may have been as sexless as they both insisted they were. No woman in Marie's position was going to believe it. She forfeits the sympathies because her "confession" is without the one quality that makes such an exercise tolerable: it has not even the appearance of honesty. Having omitted Sand, Lamennais and her pregnancy, her narrative proceeds to another preposterous episode, this one also hinged on a letter — a mechanism she couldn't seem to get away from. It came out of a clear sky and announced Liszt's imminent departure from Europe; he wished to see her. "My blood, so long congealed in my veins, suddenly flew to my heart. Memory returned. . . ." [4] And their affecting interview takes place in the salon of his mother's apartment. "Poor mother," he cries at the sight of her. "What you have suffered! I have been concerned, perhaps not enough. Can you reassure me a little? Tell me about yourself. . . ."

He listened in complete withdrawal. When I came to describing the state I had fallen into after the death of my child, my injustices . . . my distress of spirit . . . then, at the sight of his name, how I had felt reborn, he seemed not to listen. . . . His face had taken on a calm I hadn't seen before. . . . "But you, Franz," I said . . . "What have you been doing all this time? What did you have to tell me? When do you leave?"

"*We* are leaving," said Franz . . . fixing me with a long look that seemed to tear consent from my heart. . . . "What are you saying, Franz?" . . . "I am saying that we cannot live like this any longer. Don't cry any more. I've already thought of everything you could say . . . I trembled for you. I decided to leave you . . . so that . . . if not happiness, you might have peace. And look what I accomplished! . . . what has become of you without me! No, no . . . Let us struggle and suffer, but let it be together. . . . We are young, brave, honorable, proud. We must have great faults or great virtues. We must confess to Heaven either the sanctity or the fatality of our love. . . ."

This splendid piece of Romantic *Kitsch* has the composite air of the daydream, in which real scenes mingle with might-have-beens and real sentences with those that were rehearsed but not uttered. It could be a reconstruction of a scene that occurred when she sprang it on him that she was with child — or it may be wholly imaginary. Liszt certainly never planned to quit Europe, though in May, when this interview is supposed to have taken place, he *was* thinking of another trip to Brittany. "When do you leave?" is perhaps an echo of that. Lamennais in any case now makes an entrance.

In the published memoirs, he calls on her without warning, having somehow divined the crisis and rushed from Brittany to intervene. She isn't impressed with him, a hideous little man with a shifty manner, and she finds him a poor advocate, "this apostle who had braved anathema to follow the inspiration of his heart." Was she not doing the same? Students of Marie's style know what will happen next. The Abbé falls on his knees:

"God forbid," he cries, "that I should dream of dividing two souls so made for each other. . . . [But] draw back, beautiful spirit, let me carry Franz away to solitude. . . . Talk to each other, but at a distance, until you are calmer, purified of passion that torments you. . . . Say you consent. . . . One word, one single word, and I will leave you the happiest of men." [5]

She will not utter the word and he rises, fixing her with a look of astonishment: "Goodbye, Madame, I ask nothing of you. I will pray God to enlighten you."

Lamennais was of course not in Brittany, and Marie's unpublished notes have a different, certainly truer version of what happened. In this, "a member of the d'Agoult family" (her husband?) asked Lamennais to tackle Liszt and beg him to use his influence "to dissuade Madame d'Agoult from a disastrous decision." Liszt replied that it would ill become him to take such a step and instead proposed that Lamennais do the talking. They went to her house together, Liszt remaining outside during the interview, which must have been harsher than Marie lets on. Lamennais felt strongly that she was ruining his young friend. "I augur no better than you do the future of this wretched Mme. d'A . . . ," he wrote to an intimate. "She is a soul consumed, extinguished to a frightening degree. It isn't probable I will have any future relations with her; but I must say that the person you mentioned to me [Liszt?] also used every effort to keep her from throwing herself into the abyss."

Finally, there is Liszt's (indirect) version in the Ramann biography. Incorrect in many minor details and reflective of Carolyne Wittgenstein's loathing for her predecessor, it nevertheless was printed with Liszt's sanction and must be to some degree true to the spirit if not the letter of what happened that spring. Says Ramann:

The illusory play in which his passion had entangled him now disgusted him; he felt the moment for separation had come. He would leave Paris; and as the concert season was drawing to a close . . . and he felt the need of rest . . . the moment seemed doubly favorable. . . . He hoped the Countess d'Agoult would agree with him. . . . But in this he deceived himself. She was so deeply ensnared in the web of her own spinning that she could indeed give up her husband and children, but not Liszt, could give up her illusion, but not her ideal at that time — to have a "great passion." Notwithstanding his representations, and against his wish, she left Paris: his reflection had come too late. [6]

Words like disgust are too strong, and here too the motive of her pregnancy is omitted. He loved Marie. If Ollivier's chronology is right, his last communication to her before she left France was this:

The day you can tell me with all your mind, all your heart, all your soul, "Franz, let us wipe out, forget, forgive whatever of the past was incomplete, afflicting, perhaps miserable; let us live for each other, because at this hour I understand and forgive as much as I love you," that day (and may it be soon) we will flee far from the world, we will live, love and die alone together.[7]

Second thoughts he must have had, attacks of the horrors when he thought of binding himself at the age of twenty-three. And at the last moment, I think we must accept that he would have got out of it if he could. Marie tries to give the impression that they left for Switzerland together. In reality, she travelled with her mother and brother-in-law, neither of whom was in the secret. She left a farewell letter to d'Agoult that warned him in vaguely ominous terms to expect the worst but did not mention Liszt: "I hide none of my sins and ask you to pardon me on the tomb of Louise; I ask you in her name what she asks of God for both of us; pardon and pity. . . ." She didn't ask for a divorce either. Because she was still unsure of Liszt? He had travelled ahead, with an agreement to meet her in Basel on the fourth or fifth of June. Was some further discussion envisioned?

Typographical accident is no substitute for knowledge but the following sequence of notes written from their respective hotels in Basel is to the eye the skeleton of a sad story:

Liszt to Marie: From six to eight, Herr Kopp takes me to the country. Before or afterward.
Marie to Liszt: Tell me the name of your hotel and your room number. Don't go out. My mother is here; my brother-in-law has gone. By the time you read this, I will have spoken to her, up till now I haven't dared say anything. It's a last and severe trial, but my love is my faith and I thirst for martyrdom. Wednesday. Three Kings.
Liszt to Marie: Here I am, since you summoned me. I shan't go out until I see you. My room is at the Hôtel de la Cigogne, number twenty on the first floor — go to the right. Yours. [Sic — in English.] [8]

We will probably never know what lay behind that chilling "Here I am, since you summoned me" (the word is *appelé:* called, summoned, sent for) or what passed between them in the course of the next four days. She didn't move to his hotel until June 10, and certain German sources say she burst in on him, unsuspecting as he was, followed by her trunks. If so, it can't really have been a surprise. But it is obvious that he behaved less than gallantly and that this had a permanent effect. She knew she had forced his hand, and that a large section of public opinion was against her for having done so. This spoiled her confidence, and explains her frights, her tendency to cry before she was hurt. She suffered, and was the first to say that she did. But he suffered too. He was too young to be tied to a demanding older woman (and thirty, then, was nearer middle age than it is now) and his career, it seemed, would be crippled as well. It can only be added that he didn't whine or try to assign blame where it didn't belong.

PART THREE

Years of Pilgrimage
(1835-1839)

Chapter 14

LISZT'S WAS THE FIRST generation of composers to roam abroad, dream among ruins, and to use their experience as source material. Berlioz lived off his two years in Italy for the rest of his life; Mendelssohn's *Wanderjahre* produced the Italian and Scotch symphonies, etc., but only Liszt kept an actual musical diary, the *Années de pèlerinage*, a collection of piano pieces that would alone make the years with Marie worthwhile. We can speculate on what he might have done if he had stayed in France. In fact, he had written little apart from the Lamennais-inspired pieces and had devoted far too much time to journalism and society. The passage to Switzerland opened a new era in his music.

The story of Mozart crossing the Alps without raising his eyes from the scores in his lap may be fantasy; it could have happened. To the hard-worked professional musician of an earlier age, travel meant business. He had no time to waste on sightseeing even if he had the inclination. (And anyway, the Alps weren't admired by the majority of eighteenth-century travellers. Addison called them "misshapen scenery"; Gibbon was amazed when it began to be the fashion to inspect glaciers.) The Romantic sensibility was among other things a luxury based on some degree of economic independence, nature worship being the artificial product of leisure and education. When Lamartine had advised Liszt to study *"la nature, notre livre à nous,"* he was not of course referring to the wilderness but to the European landscape as seen through the lens of poetry, painting and what was beginning to be known of folk history.

Liszt therefore travelled with a different set of baggage from his fore-runners, and thanks in part to Marie's money (soon, we will see, to be the cause of quarrels because he did not care to be a parasite), in a style un-known to them; and the result was a new kind of musical impressionism, at once sophisticated and personal. The *Années de pèlerinage* are in three volumes and extend, because of his habit of interminable revision, over a lifetime but were begun in Switzerland.* The titles in this first volume with their attendant quotations from Byron, Schiller and Senancour explain the subject matter: *Chapelle de Guillaume Tell; Au lac de Wallenstedt* (" . . . thy contrasted lake,/ With the wild world I dwell in, is a thing/ Which warns me, with its stillness, to forsake/ Earth's troubled waters for a purer spring"); *Pastorale; Au bord d'un source* ("In murmuring coolness the play of young nature begins"); *Orage; Vallée d'Obermann* ("Vast consciousness of Nature everywhere overwhelming and impenetrable, universal passion, indifference, advanced wisdom, voluptuous abandon, all the desires and all the profound torments that a human heart can hold, I have . . . suffered them all in this memorable night. . . ."); *Eclogue; Le Mal du pays;* and *Les Cloches de Genève* ("I live not in myself, but I become/ Portion of that around me.") These nine pieces are thus a Romantic traveller's itiner-ary of Swiss sights and sounds and their associations. Nothing quite like them had been attempted before and they remain extraordinarily fresh and original. They are of course the work of a very young man who is just be-ginning to explore a new branch of his art, and they have their weak spots. The best of them have a kind of pristine poetry eminently suitable to the folk material and evocations of the natural world — water effects, storms, Alpine horns and bells. (The use of folksong made Liszt a pioneer in this field later explored by Grieg, the Russians and others; but one is always being surprised by the earliness of Liszt's dates. Several of these pieces are harmonically startling as well. The *Vallée d'Obermann*, the most consider-able in the collection, shows him to have already mastered the technique of "thematic transformation" that is the mainspring of the symphonic poems composed twenty years later; the use of unrelated $\frac{6}{3}$ chords in *Eclogue* anticipates this device in the work of a whole generation of later com-posers.)

It probably goes without saying that Liszt's Switzerland was not ours. To the Romantic who crossed the Alps by diligence, it was an amphitheatre for

---

* I give the final title for simplicity's sake, though the first volume — *Suisse* — actually started out under another name and included pieces that had been published separately under different titles. It came out in 1842 and was called *Album d'un voyageur*. Be-tween 1848 and 1853, Liszt revised the whole collection, reissuing it under the present title (jettisoning some of the pieces that had been in the earlier volume), *Années de pèlerinage, Première Année, Suisse.* The second *Année* — *Italie* — has a similarly con-fusing history: it didn't appear in final form until 1858, though most of the pieces in it were composed, originally, in 1838–1839. The third *Année*, also *Italie*, belongs to his old age and includes the Villa d'Este pieces, masterpieces of that period.

the gods, nature in the raw, or almost. Marie, her latent German sentimentality aroused, described it:

Granite ramparts, inaccessible peaks reared between us and the world, as if to hide us from its view, hidden valleys, black pines that enveloped us in their shadow, murmur of lakes, dull rumblings of precipices, soft and catching rhythms of Alpine places that gave to our temporary ecstasy . . . the touch of eternal things, dear and dolorous fantoms of my youth, I evoke you in memory. . . .[1]

Though under obligation to construct a grandiose setting for her honeymoon with Liszt, she was expressing what most travellers felt, especially those who had read *Childe Harold* or *Obermann.* Voltaire at Ferney was forgotten, the thriving cities ignored. Switzerland to the imagination of the 1830's was all landscape, a hygienic Salvator Rosa, Italy without the bandits or the dirt.

For a holiday it would have been perfect, and for the month they spent roving the countryside (Marie makes it much longer) it offered all the delights of liberty and solitude. The trouble started when they had to settle down in Geneva to make a life together. With its Calvinist tradition, its stiff-necked intellectuals, it wasn't the ideal haven for illicit lovers, but Liszt was at least prepared to make the best of it. He rented an apartment, a whole floor with a view of the Jura and the Rhone. He found old friends — Pierre Wolff, Marie Potocka, the Belgiojosos, Eugène Boré who had been at La Chênaie — and through them was able to round up enough interesting men to give Marie the nucleus of a salon: Sismondi the historian; Adolphe Pictet, a retired officer and savant of great charm; the botanist with the delightful name of Pyrame de Candolle; James Fazy, owner of a liberal newspaper. He even provided her with one of those spaniel-like adorers who were to become a feature of all their households. These young men were sent on errands, made to play nursemaid on occasion to the neglected Liszt children, and must have had shoulders permanently damp from Marie's tears. Lacking women friends, it was to them she confided her "sufferings" at Liszt's hands, and one and all they naturally detested him; while he, though sometimes bored by them, was rather grateful than not for their existence. This Swiss one was Louis de Ronchaud, a young poet whom they referred to as "the daily," and unlike the others, he loved her for life.

Geneva had one or two other compensations. It had a Conservatory, where Liszt signed up to give lessons, an Academy, an excellent library. (Like all literate travellers, they were obsessed with the problem of getting books, so this was important. On a typical day, Liszt removed the following titles: "Mme. Necker, *Saint Augustine, Saint Teresa, Catechism of Trent,* Bossuet, Fénelon, Mme. Guizot, *On the Influence of Perfumes,* Phédon . . ."[2] A singularly eclectic selection, as Vier remarks.) It was a center for botanists and Marie was able to gratify her love of flowers with daily deliveries of alpines brought in baskets from the mountains. With the inevitable Érard sent for and installed, books to read, what Marie calls *tout un petit arrangement modest, mais agréable à l'oeil* ought to have been tolerable. It was not. Geneva was the first of many cities that Marie was to find unendurable. (Milan, Rome, Florence, even Venice was insupportable in the end.) She felt "like a carp on the grass," a fish out of water, an outcast. The truth was she was unprepared to live outside society. She despised the provincial Genevans but it is one thing to look down on the boors in the boondocks, another to discover that they look down on you; and Geneva was not kind to her. Local society, she found, was quite prepared to receive Liszt while excluding her. (But she also bit before she was bitten. Mme de Laprunarède, Liszt's old love, was living in the city and disposed to be friendly. Marie's response to her overtures was an insulting letter.)

Not that it approved of him. Among the old friends he found was a Mme Boissier, the Swiss lady who had been so taken with him in 1832. Time had sharpened her opinion, which we can assume was pretty much that of Geneva as a whole when he first arrived. It is diverting to watch it break down:

Liszt enters — his appearance has improved . . . his clothes aren't in the bad taste that distinguished them in Paris, and one sees he has had good feminine advice. He was friendly and is basically a good child. But the poor young man is horribly spoiled by the world and success. . . . He has had the ill-luck to live in a fashionable literary milieu that has fed him with its dangerous doctrines, its false ideas and its unbelief. . . . [He] is involved with a highly immoral system that is tied to the Saint-Simonians on the one hand and to Mme. Dudevant [Sand] on the other. The blessing of marriage and other trifles of that sort make him shrug his shoulders. He abandons himself to his passions with perfect frankness and freedom. If necessary he would present his countess to me without a blush. He has perhaps still a noble heart but he is mad. . . .[3]

On his third visit, she is weakening:

A singular young man, this Liszt: notable for his faculties, full of fire, of verve, of spirit, of genius. Then, a noble soul . . . disinterested, very generous. . . . Black and white in fact and yet lovable . . .

There was no such charity for Marie, Liszt's *belle dame* who has left her husband "and five or six children." She is "thirty at least, a faded blonde. Until her relation with Liszt, her reputation hadn't a blemish . . . but she was seized with a mad passion for him . . ." and this is followed by a spate of untrue gossip. Geneva was in short ready to forgive his sins but not hers, mostly because she was seen as a predatory woman, the instigator of the whole affair; which was of course the case.

They had barely arrived in Geneva when that traveller's curse, letters from home, caught up with them. They were from her mother and brother and to her dismay offered reinstatement. It was suggested that Mme de Flavigny fetch her at Basel and the two of them return to France with no one the wiser. (Whether the impending child was taken into account, Marie does not say.) Meanwhile, a formal separation would be arranged with d'Agoult. For once, Marie is truthful. She admits she didn't dare tell Liszt the contents of these letters for fear he would think the terms too generous to refuse. Yet as usual she wants her cake too. She paints a little picture of Liszt entering the room while she reads. He asks "like someone who doesn't want to hear anything disagreeable" whether she has good news from France. She turns her back, which he doesn't notice, and answers coldly — "Yes."

He guessed nothing where he wished to know nothing . . . from this moment, apparently totally insignificant, something changed. . . . I felt — as hadn't happened before — an empty space where our thoughts did not meet.[4]

Worse was to come. When Liszt left Paris, the little Puzzi Cohen, in floods of tears, had told him he would follow him to the end of the world, "on foot and begging my bread." He now, in mid-August, pleaded to be allowed to join them in Geneva and Liszt, with crashing want of tact, wrote his consent at once, not waiting to find out how Marie felt about it. Or better to say, he knew what the answer would be. She couldn't abide Puzzi. The "sacred intimacy" was ruined by this child whom Liszt took pains to educate, not only musically but — undoubtedly remembering his own illiterate youth — in history, art and philosophy, reading aloud to him with long commentaries.

A strange fact emerges as one follows Marie's travails. Over and over she repeats that she loved Liszt for his genius, and one would suppose that the great thing about their relationship, the redeeming feature that made it all worthwhile, was his music. Yet unless he was alone in a room with her, his playing was torture to her, and one could comb her writings almost without learning that he was a composer. Her letters never inquire about his work. Only once in her memoirs does she mention a composition by name: *Au lac de Wallenstedt,* "which Franz wrote for me . . . which I have never been able to hear without weeping" — and "wrote for me" seems the decisive term. Nowhere does she try to give an idea of the kind of music he composed, or how, or why. Were pieces like the *Dante* Sonata, the *Petrarch Sonnets* in the second *Année* not discussed? Her silence suggests more than the barrier between amateur and professional, especially as she wasn't quite an amateur. She had received an excellent musical education and played the piano acceptably. Yet ten years of intimate association with one of the century's most original composers and perhaps its greatest pianist failed to provide her with a single illumination to pass on to posterity. Only one conclusion is possible. For all her pretentious twaddle about his mission and his genius, she neither respected nor appreciated the kind of genius he was, and never overcame her innate disdain for musicians, who remained inferior to writers in her eyes. She did not love music, or not enough to make up for the (to her) degrading facts of the working musician's life.

Puzzi was such a fact. To Liszt it was natural and even necessary to teach; it was one of the things he did best and except for his years on the road he always had pupils. To Marie the boy was an intruder, his arrival a disaster. And that was nothing to how she felt about Liszt's playing in public. It was as if he were to expose himself in some indecent way and the fuss she made was pathological. The first occasion revealed the dimensions of her psychosis.

It was harmless enough. The Belgiojosos were having a charity concert to benefit the many political exiles living in Switzerland, mostly Poles and Italians. It was the sort of thing that Liszt was never known to refuse, yet Marie had for some reason decided he would find it unworthy. She had a rude awakening. He not only intended to play, he insisted she be there and arranged for a friend to take her — "to the theatre," she says, wanting it to appear that he had the bad taste to force her into a public place, though in fact the concert was in the Belgiojosos' apartments, which weakens her case. She made, anyway, a scene. Furiously he told her that although it was the last minute, he would go and remove his name from the program. She perceived that she had gone too far. She "took all the blame." She went, and the incident now takes on a nightmare intensity. In the blazing room where she sat with Puzzi, an "immense clapping broke out, dizzying, prolonged, twenty times repeated . . ."

Franz entered and saluted the public. My breathing stopped. I was for several moments . . . almost stifled. The applause ceased. In the deepest silence the first chords of the piano sounded. . . . By a peculiar accident or a secret magnetism, my glance crossed his. . . . How can I say what I felt? It was Franz I saw and it was not Franz. It was like someone impersonating him on the stage, with great art and verisimilitude, but who nevertheless had nothing in common with him beyond an empty appearance. His playing also troubled me; it was indeed his virtuosity, prodigious, dazzling, incomparable, yet it seemed strange. . . . Where was I? Where were we? . . . Who had brought me here? With what object? . . . It was indescribable anguish.[5]

What ailed her? Vier has spotted a pencilled note, never printed, in the margin of her manuscript dealing with this episode: "Aversion for the virtuoso beaten by his father, tortured since his childhood — depravity of the being who amuses for money." [6] An ugly and pitiless expression of feelings, more or less disguised while she lived with him, that were to surface in her novel *Nélida*. (And he wasn't, that evening, playing for money.) More or less but not entirely: Liszt, with a neurosis of his own on this subject, was aware of the depth if not the viciousness of her hatred for the virtuoso in him. And so, surely, were Sand and other friends close to them in those years. "How right you are not to speak of his *success*," she wrote Sand in 1838. "It is the *black spot* in my life," and she complained to Hiller of "the boobies who tell me I ought to be proud of his *triumphs!* Eh! I'm not proud at all. . . ." [7]

Sand, one gathers, was so conscious of Marie's sick attitude that she was inclined to overdo her own enthusiasm. She wrote incessantly to Geneva, cramming her letters with jokes, gossip — and praise. She knew all about the Belgiojoso concert (which Liszt, adding insult to injury, reported to the *Gazette Musicale* of December 6, 1835), and advertised her longing to have been present: *

> I ought to have been with you. . . . What would Puzzi-the-first [Liszt] have said if I had come in with my muddy gaiters and my suitcase and slapped him on the shoulder? . . . I would have had the greatest pleasure in the world in making you miss your entrance, [and] . . . in massacring your finale. I would have . . . pulled out a whistle, a pipe, a Jew's harp from my pocket and given the metaphysical public the teamster's hoot. . . . Jokes aside, dear children, if I had had a hundred *écus*, I would have come. . . . Why didn't you open a subscription to pay for my diligence? I declare to you that in six weeks or two months, if you are still there, I will come, no matter what storms rage in the heavens or what calm prevails over my finances.[8]

George's threats to visit the Swiss *ménage* were bandied back and forth for many months. She couldn't come because she was in the midst of a lawsuit to recover her property and the custody of her two children from her husband. Her inability to travel was a godsend to Marie. To Liszt and to Puzzi it was a grief. "Not a day passes," wrote the child, "when we don't speak of you with the extreme desire of having you near us. . . . Every day, M. Liszt and I make a long harangue to your medallion that everybody thinks looks so much like you and that recalls you so well." [9] To which Liszt added a postscript:

> I hope you won't always resist the ennui of our letters; because you ought to know that we have sworn to nag you until you do come and we can say, "Here is our second brother, the eldest of the family, who rejoices our days" . . . Goodbye. . . . Manage it somehow so that my affection won't be barren forever.

---

* This letter, formerly dated 1836, has in the new Lubin edition been put back to October 18, 1835, making it certain that the Belgiojoso concert was meant, though he gave a number of others in Lausanne and elsewhere in Switzerland during this time.

Chapter 15

EVERY LOVE AFFAIR reaches a point that in retrospect ought to have been the finish, and it is at this point that many lovers decide to marry. That usually mistaken solution wasn't open to Liszt and Marie and accordingly they ought to have parted in 1836, at a decent interval after Blandine's birth, when the adventure had run its course.

Blandine Liszt was born the week before Christmas 1835 and registered as follows with the Geneva authorities:

Blandine Rachel, natural daughter of François Liszt, professor of music aged 24 years and 1 month, born at Raiding in Hungary, and of Catherine-Adelaide Méran, *rentière* aged 24 years, born in Paris, both unmarried and domiciled at Geneva. Liszt has freely and voluntarily acknowledged that he is the father of the said child and has made the declaration in the presence of Pierre-Étienne Wolff, professor of music and of J. James Fazy aged 26 years. . . .[1]

Marie lied about her age, which Liszt may or may not have known. She doesn't trouble to conceal her complete lack of interest in the child, which is rather curious. It is true that she had no maternal instinct, so-called. Neither the births nor the early deaths of three out of the five children she bore had much effect on her. But simple feminine strategy might have served her here. "The mother of my children" is a cliché whose efficacy has repeatedly proved itself; and Liszt was not unpaternal by nature. Most young people found him a pushover. He adored Carolyne Wittgenstein's insipid daughter. He might have loved little Blandine, a ravishing baby, the *angiolin dal biondo crin* of one of his loveliest songs. His early letters about her are charming.

Liszt to Schumann, 1839: Her name is Blandine Rachel and her surname Moucheron [Gnat or Urchin]. It goes without saying that she has a complexion of milk and roses and her fair golden hair reaches to her feet like a savage's. She is, however, the most silent child, the most sweetly grave, the most philosophically gay in the world. . . . Well, my dear M. Schumann, two or three times a week . . . I play your *Kinderscenen* to her in the evening; this enchants her, and me still more, as you can imagine. . . .[2]

Unhappily, such fatherly upwellings were rare. Blandine was farmed out much of the time. Marie didn't want her around and Liszt was too distracted to care what he was missing. It was so with all three of the wretched, brilliant children, two girls and a boy, born to them. They were inexcusable parents and Romantic disdain for bourgeois values won't quite answer why they behaved as they did. George Sand doted on her two *"mioches"* who were carted everywhere with her. The little Liszts might as well have been orphans. Cosima, the only survivor, spoke poignantly of the effects of their isolation: "The extraordinary position created for us by our birth forged a bond between us three such as the majority of brothers and sisters can scarcely picture . . . and which I now drag about me like a heavy, cumbersome chain. . . . I often feel as though I had been torn up by the roots, for my heart is always seeking these two beings, who were so young, so original, so truly saintly, so completely mine." [3]

Marie, clinging to Liszt with all her strength, wasn't clever enough to see that their splendid children might also have forged a permanent bond between herself and him. She relied for that on the hopeless plan of living forever *in alta solitudine* (which she made her motto and had inscribed on a ring), away from the world, people, and the demands of Liszt's professional life. She had inklings that it wouldn't work. She speaks of "the cruel struggle between our natures, both sincere, noble and devoted, but both proud, insatiable; he, feeling and wanting love like a young man, unconquered, abounding with life; I, a woman distrustful of destiny, shattered by sorrow . . . turning aside from . . . reality to lose myself in an impossible ideal." [4]

After Blandine's birth the memoirs launch into another imaginary sequence in which, apologetic for the suffering Geneva has imposed, Liszt is inspired to say, "I've allowed myself to be invaded by mediocre people; I waste precious time. . . . You must forgive me. . . . We will leave all this . . . we will cross the Simplon and go to live in Italy." [5] She implies they left at once, and so jumps over the following eighteen months. They didn't go to Italy and it is unlikely that he made the proposal, having other things on his mind.

The first was money. It has been suggested that Liszt, having played few concerts between 1830 and 1834, was broke when he went off with Marie; and that she supported him until 1839. That wasn't true. He was active on the concert stage from 1833 on and he had always given lessons. During a representative period in their life together, April 1836 to December 1837, he gave twenty-one concerts with an average box-office of 1,200 francs apiece. With his other earnings (from publishers, lessons, etc.) this would have been adequate to maintain an ordinary family, and he did support his mother, pay for Blandine's upkeep, the rent, and so on. He certainly could not afford to clothe Marie, whose dresses reputedly cost 1,000 francs each, nor pay for her special soaps, perfumes, jewels, laces, books and botanicals. But since she was a woman of fortune, there was no reason why she shouldn't have purchased the luxuries she demanded. On the other hand, he would not and never did allow her to support *him*. Eager as she was to do so, he hated the very idea of it. Pride and generosity were among his outstanding characteristics. And that meant that he must work, travel, give concerts, keep his name before the public.

This seems elementary but was not comprehensible to Marie, and he learned early on not to tell her the whole truth about his plans or the precise length of any proposed absence. Accordingly, when he went to France in the spring of 1836 it was ostensibly to fulfill engagements in Lyon, where his friends the Montgolfiers (he was a piano manufacturer, his wife a music teacher) had arranged a series of concerts for him. In the biographies it is taken for granted that his real motive was to confront Sigismund Thalberg, touted that spring in Paris as his only living rival; and his ambition would indeed have required that he down an heir presumptive to his throne. With Marie working on him it wasn't that simple. He half agreed with her that his virtuoso career was a menace to those lofty intentions urged on him by Lamennais and others as well as herself. So it was rather in the mood of the drunkard returning to his bottle that he set off for France, and with something of the drunkard's imitation of relief that he discovered that the bar was closed. Arrived in Lyon, he learned that Thalberg had left Paris.

Liszt to Marie: Now that the temptation is over and for good, I will admit . . . that I was tormented beyond measure for two or three days by the immoderate desire to go to Paris and seat myself on the very day of my arrival in the orchestra of the Italiens, at Thalberg's concert. I sensed, I knew, that the spectator would get more attention than the principal actor. I would have been a sort of returnee from Elba. I would have wanted to applaud, to call out disdainfully: "Bravo," because I now feel something higher and stronger. . . .[6]

True, undoubtedly, as far as it went — and reassuring to Marie until she read on and discovered that he would go to Paris anyway, with or without

Thalberg. Her outburst at this is lost — Vier thinks she may have rushed to Lyon to stop him — but his reply survives, and is a declaration of his independence in every sense, though he stressed that his career at the piano was important to him as much for her sake as his own. "It is my only fortune," he wrote, "my only title, my unique possession that I don't want anyone whatever to touch. . . ." [7]

Paris to Marie was the enemy, but how could she have dreamed it would be that to Liszt? She hated Geneva because it wasn't a chalet beside an Alpine cascade. Liszt, the city man, was bored with it on other grounds. "There has been only one event here in the last six months," he wrote Sand, "and that event is myself." [8] He pined for the boulevards. Parroting the Romantic attitude to the capital, Balzac's beloved hell, the Gethsemane that Berlioz could never quit without a pang, he paid lip service to its horrors and thrived among them like a palm under gaslight. Like Baudelaire in a later day he experienced "the religious intoxication of great cities" and the "mysterious expression of sensual joy in the multiplication of Number" — that is, he loved crowds, and was perhaps most distinctively French in his inability to think alone. Pascal knew his countrymen when he said they could least endure to be by themselves, in a room. A French critic has called Liszt the great specialist of the mixed intellectual dinner in a public eating place (Les Frères Provenceaux, in his old neighborhood, was a favorite); he anticipated the Magny suppers organized by the Goncourts thirty years later. He had no sooner arrived in Paris than he laid on a brilliant evening. His guests were: Chopin, Meyerbeer, Montalembert, Delacroix, d'Eckstein, Ballanche, Barrault, Nourrit. After dinner they all went off to young Érard's flat where he regaled them with his *Soirées de Rossini* and a waltz "Mariotique." His report to Marie of his party could not repress his happiness: "*Grandissime succès de toute manière!*" he burst out. [9]

He had no difficulty reestablishing his musical reputation — if it had ever been in danger. Thalberg, however sensational he may have appeared at the time, wasn't in Liszt's class as a pianist and as a composer he didn't exist. His great stunt was to divide the melody between two hands in such a way that he seemed to be playing with three. Chopin had dismissed him long since, saying, "He plays excellently but he is not my man. Younger than I, pleases the ladies, makes potpourris from *La Muette*, gets his soft passages by the pedal not the hand, takes tenths as easily as I take octaves — has diamond shirt studs. . . ." [10] Wiser than he was later, Liszt didn't try to compete at that level. He hired the Salon Érard, a discreet setting, and allowed a select public to judge for itself how much his playing had improved. Berlioz, who covered his two concerts for the *Gazette Musicale*, was amazed. Gone was the tendency to exaggeration and rhythmic instability. He played the Beethoven *Hammerklavier*, "the Sphinx's enigma of every pianist . . . in a manner that, if the composer could have heard it in his grave, would have sent a thrill of joy and pride over him. Not a note was left out, not one added (I followed, score in hand), no inflection was effaced, no change of tempo permitted. . . . Liszt, in thus making comprehensible a work not yet comprehended, has proved that he is the pianist of the future." [11]

So much for Thalberg. Still Liszt did not return to Geneva. "*Quelle éternité que ce voyage!*" cried Marie, suspecting the worst. He had business to attend to, batches of new music to show his publisher; Lamennais was expected from Brittany. But she wasn't far wrong. Count Apponyi, the Austrian ambassador to France, calling one June morning on Cristina Belgiojoso, was shocked to find her *en negligée* with "M. Liszt, the pianist, in a black velvet jacket, long glossy hair falling to his shoulders, without a tie and with beret in hand." [12]

And what are we to make of his note to Sand of May 10?

I came to Paris *to hunt you down*. Can't we see each other again? In five weeks, I will be leaving Geneva to go to Naples. M. would very much have liked to offer you hospitality for at least ten days before we separate for such a long time. . . .[13]

Sand was in the country; they missed each other by a week. How was it that she wasn't in Paris to welcome him? Her lawsuit against her husband did make it necessary for her to be at Nohant and yet there is a curious tone in what I take to be her answer. "My good child and brother," it begins, and after details about the lawsuit, takes up the theme of her visit to Switzerland:

If you aren't leaving until the end of June, perhaps I could come to you and spend a few days. After which, you will fly to Italy, happy birds whose wings aren't clipped or cruelly torn, while I, lamer and more modest, I will sit down on the shores of a little lake to sleep and smoke away the rest of the season. . . .[14]

She then proceeds to a question put to her months earlier by Liszt and never answered: Was there anything to the rumor that young Charles Didier was her present lover?

What is it that people say? What they say of you and me. You know how true that is. Judge of the rest; many people in Paris and in the country say it isn't Mme. d'Agoult who is with you in Geneva but myself. Didier is in the same position. . . . In fact, I am not thinking of anybody in that way. . . . I have had enough of emotions on the grand scale. . . . I am one who likes to sleep peacefully. . . . And you? You're happy, you're young; a fine thing to love at twenty! If I were twenty I wouldn't be amusing myself writing you nonsense about what isn't love. That is all behind me. . . . I think you have a treasure in

Marie. Keep it always. God will call you to account if you haven't treated her well, you'll be deprived of the sound of harps for all eternity.*

I read this as a rebuff, in which she is saying, "If you love Marie, leave me alone." Sand was, after all, a complicated woman. She made up a tale about Liszt and his "princess," and may have half believed it. Earlier that year she dedicated her novel *Simon* to Marie with a mixture of incense and venom that may have deceived Liszt. Few women would have misinterpreted it: "Mysterious friend," began her preface, "be the patroness of this poor little tale. . . . Patrician, excuse the antipathies of the rustic teller. . . . Thrice noble heart, descend to her and make her proud. . . . Countess, be pardoned. . . . Hidden star, recognize yourself in these litanies." The irony would have pierced a thicker skin than Marie's (who, however, had to seem flattered). Liszt like most men wasn't bright about the battle his women were waging and couldn't understand Sand's feminine strategy toward Marie, or her irritation at his attentions to herself while he was still tied to his countess.

Sand was accustomed to getting the men she wanted. (Didier, by the way, *was* her lover.) She guessed rightly that Liszt's feelings for her were not entirely brotherly. Whatever the other motives, he went to Paris hoping to see her. His terms were unacceptable; and that may be all that saved Marie. Sand remained at Nohant.

There are other little mysteries about this voyage.

Liszt to Lamennais, May 20, 1836: Your letter, dear Father, only reached me the other day, a little before my departure from Lyon. . . . I bless you a hundred times over. . . . Though I had flattered myself that I perhaps deserved some such evidence of affection, I nevertheless didn't dare hope for it. . . . Various more or less delicate affairs which, thank God, have been arranged in an honorable and satisfactory way, called me to Paris. I expected to stay only four or five days. But yesterday Eugène [Boré] assured me positively that you would be here within a week. If that is your intention, will you be good enough to let me know *immediately* in a couple of words? I have such a very deep need to see you again. . . .[15]

What were the delicate affairs? At Marie's request, he had an interview with her brother. Money is a delicate affair, and it may have been about

---

* This letter used to be dated May 5, which would make it not an answer to Liszt's of May 10 and would mean — as Vier says (Vier: I, 213) that it was sent to Geneva and opened by Marie in Liszt's absence. The new edition of Sand's letters moves it forward to May 15 — which makes much better sense. It was in fact her first letter to either Marie or Liszt in two and a half months, which together with the contents would to me make it certain that it was a response to his from Paris, and was not sent to Switzerland as Vier assumes.

that. Maurice de Flavigny didn't hold Liszt responsible for his sister's conduct. He said later that Liszt had behaved in a gentlemanly manner throughout. The Flavignys were apparently ready to make the best of a bad job; there was no attempt to punish Marie by shortening her allowance, and no intimation from this quarter that Liszt was taking advantage of her wealth. The two men understood each other.

Lamennais arrived. Liszt waited two whole weeks for him, to Marie's intense displeasure. "To what a test have you put my love for Abbé de Lamennais!" she wrote. "If it were anyone else I should hate him." [16] Liszt treated this with reserve. They both knew that what he chiefly wanted from Lamennais was absolution for the events of the previous ten months. His answer was brief: "The Abbé de Lamennais has arrived, we have seen and understood one another, thank God, and my task is finished. Everything is better now. . . ." [17]

To defeat Thalberg, to see Sand again, to arrange Marie's financial affairs, to kneel before Lamennais — or simply to earn a few francs: any or all of these would have served to draw him back to France. The most telling of his various explanations was contained in the phrase, "It would have been a sort of return from Elba." Marie got him back this time. But sooner or later he meant to conquer Europe.

Chapter 16

HE REJOINED MARIE in early June. They rented a "hermitage" in the village of Monnetier. Her nerves calmed by his return and a revival of passion, she was able to endure his absences at Lausanne and Dijon, where he gave concerts in July. In Liszt desire and ambition fed each other. For her, it was enough that he wanted her. Actually that need went with others that were less easily satisfied. "Adorable letter from Vecchio," says her journal of this, written from Dijon:

> There are neither sun nor stars in my firmament. I must see you and begin in earnest a new life at last. I need rest. . . . I aspire to I don't know what odd and simple existence, at once ordinary and elevated. An existence completely ideal, completely solitary. . . . I am not healed of the past. My wounds ache on certain days. So put your kind hand on my heart, and let me sleep in your breast . . . there where I have buried all I have of sorrow, genius and tenderness. Oh, if you knew the things I have rendered up to you, time and again; what infinite aspirations, what sublime longings, what desires and dreams have been lost in you. . . .[1]

That put her in such a radiant mood that she could even put a good face on Sand's arrival, now definitely announced. "I am disposed to enjoy myself . . . [especially] as I know that afterward we will be alone together for a year," she wrote Liszt,[2] and with Sand went so far in camaraderie as to ask what she would be wearing so that she might procure the same and they be dressed alike, sister-fashion.

Ramifications to the rivalry over Liszt had built up between the two women in the year since they had met. Marie had literary ambitions of her own:

Marie to Sand, September 1835: You should know . . . that among the hundred and one bits of foolishness that make up the charm of our intimacy, one recurs more often than the rest; it is established that I burn to dispute the literary palm with you . . . and when I wake up after a leaden sleep . . . [he] doesn't fail to say that "The laurels of Miltiades keep Themistocles from sleeping," which is regularly followed by one of those idiotic bursts of laughter that do him so much good. . . .[3]

George replied: "You want to write, for heaven's sake write! When you want to bury the glory of Miltiades, it won't be difficult." And it was about this time that she began the back-handed courtship of Marie that verged, finally, on the improper. There was the dedication of the novel *Simon,* then this:

. . . If you want me to love you, you must begin by loving me; it's very simple. . . . A soft white hand encounters the . . . back of the porcupine, the charming animal knows the white hand won't harm it, but it knows it isn't very pretty . . . poor creature, and it waits before it responds until one gets used to its quills. Because if the hand it loves withdraws, there is no reason for it to return. . . . Let us see if you can give your heart to a porcupine. I am capable of anything. I will commit a thousand follies. I will step on your feet. I will answer you rudely for no reason, reproach you for faults you don't have. . . . I will turn my back on you, in a word, I will be insufferable until I am sure I can't anger or disgust you. Oh, then I will carry you on my back, I'll cook for you . . . wash your dishes, anything you say will seem divine to me. If you step into something filthy, I will find that it smells good. I will see you with the same eyes I see myself when I feel well and am in a good humor . . . that's to say when I consider myself perfection. . . .[4]

That was in January. In May, while Liszt was in Paris, Sand's tone turned disconcertingly Sapphic:

. . . Don't pity me, beautiful and good child of God. Each of us tastes happiness according to his nature. I long thought passion was my ideal. I was wrong, or else I chose badly. I believe in yours and am convinced that having known it so completely you couldn't survive its loss. If you had my past instead of your present, I think you would, like me, put peace of mind before everything. This peace isn't a *not-loving.* My heart is still young enough for disinterested affection. It can even rejoice in ardent devotions that are singular . . . enough, of which I will tell you the mystery one day when I'm chatting with you in Naples or Constantinople. I will explain something you don't know, a feeling with no name in actual language, which perhaps doesn't exist except in me and in the form I have given it: an emotion that is chaste, durable, peaceful, with an old man for its object, who has turned me into a young man in every accepted sense of the word (quite incapable in consequence of falling in love with any of the young people who are his brothers and friends). So *Madame!* Look out, or rather M. Franz had better be perfect, because this young man is presently at Marie's feet. But be reassured. The young man is entirely indifferent to the fair sex. *A baiser la femme,* as they say in the modern style, moves him as little as Puzzi or Maurice (my dear son). All I ask is to get through the world without umbrage. My happiness consists in not troubling that of others. . . .[5]

From the sentence beginning, "This peace . . ." this peculiar rigmarole was deleted from the old editions of Sand's letters. One sees why, but not quite what she meant by it. Who was the "old man"? Her new editors think it was Michel de Bourges and remark primly, "Let us not insist on the chastity of the sentiments he inspired." Indeed not. He was an intensely virile man of thirty-eight and in Sand created a violent sexual response. Of the rest, they remark that "George was not unaware that in the past three years she had acquired a certain reputation in this regard. . . . And to cap it, the other was also called Marie." [6] Anglo-Saxon readers will need to know that the other was Marie Dorval the actress, Alfred de Vigny's mistress, on whom Sand had developed a crush. "I have forbidden Marie to answer this Lesbian who is forever plaguing her," wrote Vigny in the margin of a letter.[7]

Whether George was or was not an occasional Lesbian is extraneous here. She was capable of pretending that she was. She had a gross sense of humor and often carried jokes too far. It delighted her to shock people, and Marie was easily shocked. I at any rate interpret the passage as an elaborate smoke screen and pride-saver. To Marie, she is saying in effect: Don't worry that I will try to take Liszt away from you, I'm not interested; while to Liszt she tosses the innuendo that Marie and not he is the attraction. Add to this her novelist's itch to tamper with a plot, stir it up and see what happens, and her motives are as intelligible as they can be at this distance. Nor do we know how Liszt and Marie took her insinuations. On the surface they were all delighted with each other, longing for the reunion.

Offhand, the auguries were poor. But in spite of the internal tensions, or it may be because of them, the expedition they made to Chamonix — which included Major Pictet, Puzzi, George's two children and her maid — was the greatest possible success, eight days of fun and happiness that none of them ever forgot. It was an essay in Romantic vagabondage and in a small way it made history. They saw to that. Sand's *Lettre d'un voyageur à Charles Didier* (*Revue des Deux Mondes,* November 1, 1836), Pictet's *Une Course à Chamounix,* subtitled *Fantaisie artistique pour servir de supplement aux lettres d'un voyageur,* were avidly read at the time and are still diverting.

The secret in such cases consists in establishing, as for a children's party, a distinction between the revelers and "the others" — the grownups or, here, the conventional tourists who are horrified by bizarre behavior. Every good party defies convention in some way. Both George and Pictet emphasized the dull-wittedness of the Swiss innkeepers and all those who, mistaking them for a troupe of gypsies or transvestites, *didn't know who they were.* That, with their defiance of middle-class mores, was the cream of the jest. The saving grace was that these attitudes hadn't yet hardened into contempt. George is herself a buffoon throughout, as we see from her description of her arrival in Geneva with Maurice and Solange, aged thirteen and eight. For some reason they were late (it was September 4 or 5), and the others had gone on to Chamonix, leaving word for her to join them. George was of course in men's clothes:

"Gentlemen, where you are stopping?"
It is the postillion speaking. — Answer: at M. Listz' [sic].
"Where does he live, that gentleman?"
"The same question I was going to ask you."
"What does he do?"
"Artist."
"Veterinarian?"
"He's a violin merchant," says a passerby, "I'll take you to him."
The lady at the indicated house tells us that Listz is in England.
"She's raving," says another passerby. "M. Listz is a musician at the theatre; you must ask after him from the manager. . . ." This person declares that Listz is in Paris. "Without a doubt," I tell him furiously, "he has gone to get a job playing the flute . . . right?"
"Why not?" says the manager.
"Here's the door to the public rooms," says I don't know who.
"All the young ladies who take music lessons know M. Listz."
"I'd like to speak to the one who is coming out just now with a copybook under her arm," says my companion.
"And why not, especially as she is pretty?"
. . . The young person blushes, lowers her eyes and with a stifled sigh replies that M. Listz is in Italy.
To hell with him! I'm going to sleep at the first inn I find; let him look for me. . . .[8]

At Chamonix, she is determined not to repeat the mistake of asking for Liszt by name. Instead she describes him to the innkeeper: "Short smock, long disordered hair, stove-in hat, tie rolled in a string, temporarily lame, usually humming the *Dies Irae* . . ."
" 'Certainly, sir,' replies the innkeeper. 'They are in N° 13.' "
She signs the register. Under *Place of birth*, Liszt had written Parnassus; his occupation he gave as musician-philosopher. To *Coming from* he an-

swered: Doubt; *Going to:* Truth. George filled in her own absurdities. *Names of travellers:* Family Piffoëls. (*Piff* is French slang for nose, a prominent feature in her and her children; Dr. Piffoëls was a nickname for herself often used in her journal.) *Home address:* Nature. *Coming from:* God. *Going to:* Heaven. *Place of birth:* Europe. *Occupation:* Loafers. *Date of Passport:* Eternity.

These jokes establish the air of truancy, a trifle heavy-handedly; they are also intended as declarations of a more serious kind. The dangers Liszt & Co. encounter are imaginary. There is no menace in a Swiss bureaucracy that requires to know one's passport number and ultimate destination. The questions are symbolic — so are the answers: nationality, they assert, is not important. Sand is European, not French, and Liszt a demigod with no residence. They are out of bounds, as even Pictet, the former major of artillery, understands and in his deadpan way enjoys.

He too presents himself at the desk. Scanning his upright appearance, the innkeeper asks, "Monsieur has come to arrest them?"

"Arrest whom?"

"That family with long hair and blouses that is making a witches' Sabbath upstairs . . ."

"How many are they?"

"Five, six, how should I know? . . . men, women . . . they come and they go and they change all the time." [9]

Pictet's aplomb was somewhat assumed. He was having, literally, the time of his life, but scholar and gentleman that he was he was more startled than he let on — at George's outfit, at Puzzi, in drag it seems, or looking so like a girl with his long locks and nightgowns that the servants at the inn couldn't tell the difference; * at Solange, George's fierce little daughter, a hamadryad, said Marie, dressed in boy's clothes like her mother. Only Marie, called in the private language Princess Arabella, or Mirabella, preserved her dignity with skirts and face-veils and parasols, riding sedately on her mule while the others scattered ahead of her in the Alpine valleys, helping the children to catch crickets — Liszt with a beret clapped to his mane, Sand puffing a cigar.

The ingredients somehow were right, different as the points of view were, the other three given to metaphysical ecstasies in the presence of nature, Sand puncturing the balloons as fast as they were released. "Is there any-

---

* The thought must occur that Puzzi was, among other things, a little queer, which of course would put Liszt's patronage of him in a different and sinister light. We are perhaps more alert to such possibilities than the nineteenth century was; but that particular accusation was never made. Puzzi's vice in later life was gambling, and he assisted Alfred de Musset in a downward path that in Musset's case had nothing homosexual about it.

thing duller than a mountain?" she asked, staring glumly at a view. When Liszt dutifully exclaimed at the Mer de Glace flowing from Mont Blanc — "beautiful . . . because nothing is missing from that tableau of death and silence" — she snapped, "Nothing but life." Romantic set-pieces, approved by the others, left her cold, from which Pictet concluded that she had no feeling for landscape. Briskly, she set him straight:

"Nature to you is a magic lantern you gaze into uttering cries of joy, like the children you are, which you forget when the show is over. I carry it in my heart and never stop looking at it. . . . Come on . . . let's climb that mountain and see if it knows you better than it does me. Major, I challenge you to a race! To whichever of us gets first to that grayish rock up there . . ." [10]

It was a salutary reminder that she, alone among them, was a country-woman. Pictet, for instance, and not unhumorously, would say that he had been searching for the principle of the universe.

"I," she announced, "am a pig merchant, who goes through life looking at how objects are colored, cut out and arranged, who doesn't know and doesn't want to know the cause of anything." This was what the others called her Piffoëls side, when she played the guttersnipe, talking rough, and prolonged contact with Marie tended to bring it to the fore. But she was no less preoccupied that the others with the journey's principal theme: what was the proper, right relation of art to nature? They discussed it daily, the major maintaining that art was a copy of the original. Absolutely not, said Liszt, and especially not in music. What connection could there be between Beethoven and a nightingale? A good question but Pictet was talking about the principle of imitation . . . "useful in that it gives a real-istic base to art, and prevents the artist from losing himself in the indefinite spaces of the ideal . . ."

George, smoking calmly, interrupted. "You are both wrong, my masters, art is creation."

"Agreed," said the major, "with the restriction . . ."

"With no restriction whatever. . . . Art creates as literally and totally as any power that brings forth something from nothing."

"You don't mean, however, that the products of art have the same reality as those of natural beings."

"I insist at least that art can create an illusion to the point where it is impossible to distinguish it from the real." [11]

The poignance of these conversations in Swiss inns lies, as they were conscious themselves, in the fact that their nature was already a myth. The essence of Romantic experience is to come too late to Arcadias that have lost their virtue, imposing a double vision on the beholder, the past in temporary coexistence with what will be. In fact Switzerland was fast becoming a tourist wonderland, and Pictet asked wistfully, "Do you think a country covered with hotels full of foreigners can possibly keep its national characteristics?" They knew the answer. George excoriates the English tourists — "The Englishman's aim in life is to return from a world tour without having dirtied his gloves or put a hole in his boot" — not only on account of their Englishness (though there was that) but because they were middle-class. She didn't say to herself that inspired by a race of nature-poets they too were in search of a vanishing Eden. She didn't know about the daffodils that came before the swallow dared.*

George and the major squabbled amiably as they traversed the Alpine landscape. She found him a stuffed shirt and because he was a scientist accused him of talking in hieroglyphics; he satirized her egalitarian lectures, saying that genius in future would have to be forbidden because confined to the few; science go by the board because simple people couldn't understand it; the fine arts be proscribed because they encouraged laziness. He tried, unsuccessfully, to pin her down, and told Liszt she was full of contradictions, "a mystery." Liszt laughed at the idea:

"George has nothing mysterious about her; on the contrary, she has the frankest nature, the freest from constraint, from all pretension, from all dissimulation, that I ever knew. She is crystal, Major, a crystal that certainly has its flaws, but who will never try to hide from you." [12]

The major saw further than Liszt, who was perhaps deceived by the high spirits. There were riotous evenings when Marie said they all seemed to have lost their minds: Liszt conducting a chorus of chairs and singing at the top of his voice, the major talking Sanskrit with unseen personages, George in fits of laughter. (It sounds as though they had drunk a good deal of the flaming punch that was one of George's specialties. It was always brewed at Nohant and no doubt the ingredients were procurable in Switzerland too.) She was a clever sketcher and left a charming souvenir of these goings-on, a drawing that shows the major declaiming, "The absolute is identical with itself." "What does that mean?" asks Liszt. "It's a bit vague," the major replies, and Marie, her head buried in sofa cushions, complains, "I've been at sea for ages."

---

* It is partly for this reason that I can't follow the scholarly T. Marix-Spire's argument that Liszt owed his *"sentiment de la nature"* to Sand, as if nature-worship had been anything but a universal phenomenon in industrialized countries. Moreover, as their dialogues show, there was a considerable difference between Liszt's bookish attitudes and Sand's down-to-earth love of country things — which he never acquired. According to Marix-Spire, "during the long Swiss days, [and] later at Nohant . . . [she] refined his sense of the concrete, restored to intuitive and spontaneous thought its proper value, reestablished the equilibrium between [his] artistic and intellectual faculties" (*Les Romantiques et la musique:* p. 491). Would that she had done anything of the sort — though given time, and without Marie's counter-balancing tendencies, she might have.

Dr. Piffoëls, however, if we can believe a letter to Michel de Bourges, was concealing urges the others didn't dream of.

> Except for Liszt, who is like a brother to me, whom I embrace night and morning in the presence of his mistress, I have not given or received a single masculine kiss from Bourges [the town] to Geneva and from Geneva to Bourges. . . . I suffered from my chastity, I don't hide it from you. I had exhausting dreams. The blood went to my head a hundred times and at high noon in the depths of beautiful mountains, listening to birdsong and breathing the sweet scents of forest and valley, I sat apart and alone with a heart full of love and my knees trembling with desire. . . . Still, I kept my serenity, which my dear friends Franz and Marie were themselves fooled by. They, to whom I tell almost everything, didn't know that I suffered sometimes to the point of crying out and fainting. . . . One night I was poisoned, as Marie was, by a dish at an inn. . . . [But] she at least was in the arms of her lover who looked after her devotedly. . . . I dragged myself from time to time to their room to see if they needed me, returning to throw myself shivering on my solitary bed, freezing, without so much as a dog to watch me suffer. . . .[13]

Michel de Bourges was sceptical that these torments were undergone on his account. She had already deceived him with Didier and it no doubt crossed his mind, as it does the reader's, that her frustration centered on Liszt. She may have been exaggerating, in tribute to the theory that nature was a potent aphrodisiac; but one can believe that she suffered when night after night the door closed on Liszt and Marie.

They were eight days on the road, ending at Fribourg where Liszt wanted to try out the cathedral organ, a celebrated instrument completed only two years earlier by Aloys Mooser. Mooser, together with the organist Jacques Vogt and one or two others, came in person to meet him and to demonstrate its powers — a circumstance that Sand immediately converted into a Romantic fable by representing it as a battle between Liszt and the dragons of tradition. Mooser and Vogt, she says, were only interested in the organ's technical marvels, while Liszt was penetrated "by mystical terrors and religious *tristesse*." She gives a sample of Vogt's detestable virtuosity — a "storm," in which could be heard "rain, wind, hail, distant cries, dogs in distress, travellers praying, disaster in the chalet, whimperings of frightened children, bells of lost cattle, crash of thunder, creakings of the fir trees, *finale*, devastation of the potato crop" — after which Liszt was allowed to seat himself and improvise on the *Dies Irae* from Mozart's *Requiem*. Lamennais's shadow clouds the prose:

> Ah yes! I say to myself as the divine wrath breaks over my head . . . there will be fear for those who haven't feared God . . . for those who have weighted their eyes with the shadows of ignorance . . . proclaimed the enslavement of

peoples as a divine institution . . . who have trafficked in humanity and sold its flesh to the dragon of the Apocalypse. . . .[14]

She was stumbling here, wrong even about what he was playing — her original version made it a *Dies Irae* of Liszt's own, which was later changed; Pictet, who knew music, says he improvised a fugue. Mooser's son was furious when he read her story. "One can't help but feel how alien to her were the emotions appropriate to music," he wrote, "and one glimpses all that must have been suffered in her company . . . by an artist like Chopin, whose soul was all music." [15] He further explained that the "storm" she despised had been a feature of organ concerts since time immemorial, a form of folk art. Here was a lamentable lapse in one of Lamennais's followers.

Liszt passed over these mistakes, calling her handling of the organ incident "worthy of her." He should have been ashamed. Mooser and Vogt were honorable craftsmen and musicians, undeserving of ridicule, and the truth was he had disappointed them. They said later that he had "wrestled with the great organ of St. Nicholas without bringing forth anything worthwhile," and as he had little or no experience of organs they were probably right. (Later in life he undertook to master the instrument, making expeditions with his friend the organist Winterberger to try out well-known ones, and he wrote several fine organ pieces.) Sand's account was good copy but he must have known how meretricious it was; he didn't often fool himself about music. On the other hand, he was regrettably willing to accept her buildup.

Chapter 17

BACK IN GENEVA, the little party continued to create a sensation. George had not been fabricating when she said that large numbers of people believed her to be the real heroine of Liszt's romance. Gossip to that effect was widespread and even appeared in the papers — it would be hard to say on what basis except that she was famous and Marie was not, and there was a satisfying fitness in the coupling of her amorous reputation with his. The public wanted them to be lovers and in the couple of weeks that George stayed in Geneva they did their best to forward that impression, appearing everywhere together, at concerts, restaurants, the theatre, strolling conspicuously in the streets. Geneva was transfixed.

Years later, Marie wrote to Pictet: "It must be admitted that you and I were a bit out of place in that illustrious Bohemia." They were so out of place that they became practically invisible. George and Liszt occupied stage center to the point that Jules Janin, giving the history of the little collaboration on which they presently embarked, made it appear that they were alone together. (Further piquance was added with the pretense that George was a man.) "George Sand has arrived!" he announced in the *Gazette Musicale* of January 1, 1837. "He comes back from the mountains with Liszt, his companion! They arrive arm in arm, the musician and the poet, and this time, by an unexpected revolution, it isn't the musician who makes music to the poet's words, it is the poet who makes words from the music. . . ." It is explained how this came about:

One autumn evening, at Geneva, a friend of Liszt was smoking his cigar in the gloaming while the artist was playing a recently composed piece; the listener, moved by the music, a little intoxicated by the smoke, by the murmur of [lake] Léman expiring on its shores, allowed his imagination to wander at will, even to clothing the sounds with human forms and dramatizing in his head a complete scene. He spoke of this at supper and tried to describe the vision he had had; they dared him to express the music in words and action . . . [and] . . . the composer having given him permission to abandon himself to his imagination, he laughingly took his pen and translated his dream into a form he called a lyric fantasy. . . .[1]

The piece was Liszt's *Rondeau fantastique sur un thème espagnol: El Contrabandista,* based on a popular song by Manuel García (father of the Malibran and Pauline Viardot-García); it is overlong and rather trivial. So are the couplets George concocted to go with it. Yet *El Contrabandista* made a great noise. Janin's article apart, Berlioz was moved to say it was "the most remarkable thing Liszt has written to date" and that "the best analysis of his work could not approach this beautiful translation into poetical prose."[2] * The furore was of course entirely due to the personalities involved, and to make it complete they presently descended together on Paris.

How this was arranged, in what must have been total opposition to Marie's wishes, is anything but clear. I think we can forget the usual explanation, which is the same as for his earlier trip — that he wanted to tackle Thalberg. The *Gazette Musicale* of October 2, 1836, carried a notice that Liszt would winter in the capital and Thalberg was nowhere on the horizon. He didn't appear until February 1837 and it is more probable that he came to Paris to challenge Liszt than the other way around. We further know that the whole plan of wintering in Paris was settled before Sand left Geneva, making it certain, in my opinion, that she was the deciding factor. The arrangement reeks of a collusion (which may have been unspoken) between her and Liszt. Daily intimacy would have revealed to her his restlessness in exile, his unwillingness to execute a further retreat into Italy — which Marie apparently still counted on — and dictated her solution to the principal problem. They all knew that a return to Paris, the scene of her former splendor and respectability, would be humiliating to Marie. There was no question of her bringing her bastard daughter with her (Blandine was left in Switzerland). She would still have to live in a common hotel,

---

* As one of Berlioz's very rare comments on Liszt's compositions, this deserves notice. He happened at the time to be trying to curry favor with Sand, whom he hoped to persuade into writing a libretto for him, or failing that, a play with a part for Harriet. But his praise is excessive to say the least — almost an insult, for if this bagatelle was the best thing Liszt had written, then he had written nothing worth discussion.

publicly branded an adulteress. It was hard to face, and Marie, who liked to see herself as a heroine, shrank from the day-to-day penalties. George accordingly offered the hospitality of Nohant for an indefinite period. She was prepared to redecorate the whole house to suit. "I see a thousand inconveniences that never struck me," she wrote. "I'm afraid the apartments will be cold and uncomfortable. I am having curtains made, a thing unknown till now. If I had time, I would have a wing built to my castle." [3] But though she was a kind woman and a born manager of situations that seemed to need it, she would never have gone to this trouble for Marie's sake alone.*

By this time, they all had nicknames. George was Piffoël; Liszt and Marie *les Fellows,* the English word. "Come soon, Fellows!" wrote George, "the Piffoëls count on you." But when Marie found that Liszt meant to stay in Paris and that the Nohant arrangements would be solely for herself, she balked. Urged to it, we can guess, by Liszt, she wrote from the Hôtel de France, rue Neuve-Laffitte, where they were stopping, and suggested instead that George come up from the country and join them. George was delighted:

I accept the proposal with joy. Engage me a room and we'll keep house as before and as afterward — *posteriori* as Franz says, which to me means Nohant. Get me a room with a big bed for Solange and me and a sofa or a cot for Maurice. We'll share your salon and our friends. . . .[4]

Sand's not always accurate *Histoire de ma vie* treats her two and a half months with the Fellows discreetly:

At the Hôtel de France, where Madame d'Agoult had decided me to live near her, the conditions were charming for a time. She received many writers, artists, and some intelligent men of the world. . . . There was admirable music, and in the intervals one could learn from listening to the conversation.[5]

That was giving more of the spotlight to Marie than she enjoyed at the time. A young Pole reports the results of a letter of introduction presented to Chopin:

Chopin received me very nicely and invited me to a soirée in honor of several illustrious persons. I therefore found myself in the presence of Mme. George Sand, a celebrated author, of a countess whose name I forget, M. [Eugène] Sue,

---

* To complicate matters further, Marie's memoirs — which treat the Nohant episode out of sequence and do not mention Paris (or Thalberg) at all — say that George invited her to Nohant because there was a cholera epidemic in Italy that made it necessary to postpone the Italian journey. Nowhere in the letters is such an epidemic mentioned; and though it may have existed, and come up in conversation, it can have had no bearing on the decision to go to Paris.

the Viscount Custine . . . Pixis, the Viennese pianist, Liszt and Nourrit. . . . Chopin played four hands with Liszt and the genius of Liszt much astonished me, but it was only a sample of his talent. Nourrit sang marvelously. . . .[6]

Ferdinand Denis, who knew Marie quite well, describes the same evening:

I went to Chopin's. . . . This time the little meeting took place because G. S. wanted to meet Custine and, I think, E. Sue. She was charming in her Turkish costume and she smoked enough, it seemed to me, to addle her brains. . . . Nourrit sang Schubert's Marguerite with less solemn ardor than the time he sang for M. de Lamennais. But still he was very fine and she seemed to feel it deeply.[7] *

The cast of characters tells the same story. Except for Eugène Sue, an old admirer of Marie, these were Liszt's friends, a reconstitution of the group he had assembled for George's benefit in 1835: Lamennais, Heine, Ballanche, Nourrit, Berlioz, etc., to whom he now added Chopin and perhaps Meyerbeer. Chopin brought in the Polish *émigrés,* of whom the poet Mickiewicz was the most appealing. Even the absentees were dictated by George: Musset, of course; Balzac, with whom she had temporarily quarrelled; Alfred de Vigny.

Of all Liszt's introductions to Sand, the most momentous was obviously Chopin; for the record (and fictional accounts of their meeting abound — even the year is usually given incorrectly) it didn't appear momentous then. Liszt had some trouble persuading Chopin that he would enjoy her company. Bluestockings made Chopin shy, but as Liszt later told the story, he happened one day to find his friend in a good mood and took advantage of it to bring around his ladies. All went well. Sand had a technique for disarming men who expected a flood of learned conversation. She fixed them with her big hazel eyes and smoked in silence, sometimes for hours. Chopin was relieved, charmed even; he didn't fall in love and neither did she, though he became an habitué of the salon in the Hôtel de France. At this period he will have shared the prevailing impression that Liszt and Sand were infatuated with each other.

Marie must have shared it too, and felt it the more because she had nothing overt to complain about. Open infidelity she might have coped with, the subtler treason of the mind and heart she might suspect but could not speak of. A simpler woman might even so have made a crashing scene

---

* This party (it was on December 13, 1836) is so thoroughly documented that we even have Sand's note of invitation to Heine: "Dear Cousin, if you can dispose of your evening from 9 to midnight, come and find us at Chopin's. . . . We are having there a little reunion, very intimate and well composed. Be one of us if you love us." (Sand, *Correspondance,* III, 596.)

— though she may have feared the results of that too. But she was miserable, as the perceptive Didier noticed. Still in love with George, who had lost interest in him, he attached himself to Marie. They were in the same boat and he admired her sad beauty. "I like her better than I do Liszt," he wrote in his diary. "She is a noble creature and very unhappy. . . . I find their present relationship puzzling, and rather think they are deliberately acting, that their affair is in its last gasp." [8]

The reader of the Liszt-d'Agoult correspondence regularly comes to the same conclusion — and must weigh the number of pages ahead of him to grasp how wrong he is. The affair is not going to end for years and years, and since neither of them, in the phrase we properly use to describe uncurable love or incurable illness, got over it, it lasted forever. Like a house that collapses stone by stone, it left a notable ruin. That Paris winter was for Marie certainly one of the stones.

There were others who were not enchanted with the prospect at the Hôtel de France, and one of them was Sainte-Beuve. This was the period that provided him with so many venomous notations in his poison-book. His disappointment in Lamennais, his envy of Liszt's beauty and virility, emptied themselves into that codex of frustration, *Mes poisons:*

The coterie of George Sand, Didier, Liszt, etc. (Lamennais, the naïve, apart), is a mass of affectations, of vanities, of pretension, of bombast and uproar of all kinds, a real *scourge* in fact, considering the importance of the talents.[9]

At other times, it is all Lamennais's fault:

. . . Lamennais has been odious for some while. His paper [*Le Monde,* successor to *L'Avenir*] is rabid. The good man cannot calm down. What sinks those people is the possession of a talent stronger than they are, that they can't govern. Lamennais is at the mercy of his pen; it can't but be violent and he can't but obey it. He makes me think of a naughty child with a gun larger than himself, loaded, that goes off in his hand. . . .[10]

Given his genital affliction, Sainte-Beuve's imagery is painfully apt. Men with ungovernable talent and guns or pens too powerful to control were symbols that made him cringe, that in the shape of Victor Hugo spoiled his life. But he was quite right. Romantic excess gets its deserts when he pulls the plug on it and there is no comparing his fine, astringent prose with their outpourings unless one happens to be an addict.

Here is Liszt's "Lettre d'un bachelier-ès-musique à un poète voyageur" of February 12, 1837, a "reply" to one of Sand's:

Oh, it would be a beautiful thing, my friend, to see the musical education of the people generally developed in France. The beautiful myth of Orpheus's lyre could once more, reduced to the scope of our bourgeois and prosaic century, partly be realized; music, though deprived of its ancient privileges could . . . become a beneficent and civilizing divinity and her children bind their brows with the noblest of crowns, that awarded by the people to him who becomes their liberator, friend and prophet.

The reader who imagines I am not doing justice to the originals (whether by Liszt, Sand, Vigny, or occasionally Lamennais) of the characteristic Romantic essay should be assured that he is getting the best of it. Never was prose more in need of the pruning knife and the excision of words like noble, sublime, magnificent. Stripped of their historical matrix, most of these writings, and that includes Hugo's prefaces, glaze the eye. What, after all, is Liszt saying? Apparently that the musical education of "the people" will result in the elevation of artists like himself. Here again is another central figure in his personal mythology — Orpheus, the artist-king who tamed the wild beasts with his lyre. And who are the beasts if not the *canaille*, the proles of the century? One sees his point but it was not perhaps the one he meant to make.

The inconsistencies were elaborated in his conduct. That winter, there was a movement to organize and train workingmen's choirs in some of the poorer districts of Paris. Nourrit promptly donated his services. Liszt was too busy to do more than attend a single rehearsal in a badly lighted hall and to advise *Le Monde*'s readers of his emotions:

. . . It was not without profound feeling that we heard these male voices, still a little rough, freshly intoning a simple song to Lamartine's words. . . . There is in these massed voices a sympathetic power that moves the vitals and vibrates the innermost chords of the heart. . . . "Vox populi, vox Dei!" [11]

They were all writing for *Le Monde*, the Abbé's new paper, which Sainte-Beuve was not alone in considering a disaster. Bérenger, devoted to Lamennais, nevertheless tried to stop him "from this folly." It was too late: "He has acquainted me more or less with his relations with Listz [sic] and G. Sand. But I am afraid that easy and good as he is, he will fall between Scylla and Charybdis." [12] How much influence either of them exercised on Lamennais's editorial policy is debatable but a good many people did look on *Le Monde* as little more than a house-organ for the Hôtel de France, "the humanitarian Olympus."

Humanitarian art was Lamennais's phrase and made to order for the lampooners. The *Gazette Musicale*, noting Liszt's appearance at a concert, inquired, "Is this a *humanitarian* hairdo? There is certainly nothing human about it." *Vert-Vert* published a long and wicked skit on the cavortings of the "gods" within the humanitarian Olympus on the third floor of the Hôtel de France.

. . . It isn't Saint Peter who opens the door . . . the gate of Heaven is opened by a redhead from Picardy. . . . You present yourself like an apostle, with recommendations from one or two saints, and you are admitted. The divinity who is blonde and very well brought up gives you a charming welcome. . . . All the gods are together . . . four old gods are playing boston in a corner. . . . Here is one who condescends to celebrity in our gangrened society; he is big and well nourished [Nourrit: a pun]. . . . Another god approaches him. What a contrast! This god is thin as a match: it is the god Franz. . . . If we were to have some music? Puzzi, open the piano! The god Puzzi dashes under the heads of three goddesses and opens the piano. The god Franz seats himself, his hair streaming to the floor. . . . Inspiration comes, the god's eye brightens, his hair vibrates, his fingers rattle and bang furiously on the keys. . . . Sublime, they cry. That will cost me twenty francs for repairs, says the divinity of the house. The god Puzzi says nothing, he vanishes. Franz! . . . thou art thou, says a grave male voice. Thank you, the god replies, thank you, George. The god thus addressed is in Turkish costume. He wears for a turban a shawl of glossy silk, he wears pantaloons . . . and leather slippers. He smokes cheap tobacco in a porcelain pipe . . . he is the center of the conversation. Some say to him, *Bonjour, George*, and others, How are you, Madame? Well, Major [Major Pictet], says the god George to another god: how do you like me in this outfit? You look like a camel merchant. This good major, always frank, always primitive! Then a little god with a ferret's face, spruce and hopping, unrolls a sheet of paper; they form a circle around him: it's a speech against the Pope, they say, you will see how the Abbé handled it! [Another pun, an awful one: *l'abbé l'a mené — Lamennais*] The Abbé reads; they applaud; midnight sounds, it is time to go. . . . They have talked, played cards, made music, smoked, drunk, read. The evening has been charming . . . you leave delighted with the humanitarian Olympus.[13]

George probably laughed heartily at this farrago of malice and inside jokes. Liszt, with no stomach for ridicule, and Marie, who never cracked a smile at herself, will have been less amused. And there were other attacks. Musset wrote a milder, more generalized one for the *Revue des Deux Mondes*. It just may have occurred to them that they were making a spectacle of themselves. There did at any rate begin to be symptoms of stress among the gods. Lamennais was troublesome. He still did not approve of Marie, for example; nor did he return George's adoration. Marie, delighted to point out his blunders to Liszt, later said that although George had come to him "in a mood of complete surrender, full of longing to devote herself blindly to the furthering of his views, and to make herself in some sort the handmaiden of his thought," [14] he had been "far from clever" in the way he treated her. Sand had in fact placed herself entirely at his disposal. "He is so good," she said, "and I am so fond of him, that I am prepared to give as much of my blood and ink as he may require." [15]

He required neither. It made no difference to him that she could name her own terms with any other editor in town. He was gruff and rude about the articles she submitted to *Le Monde*. His egalitarianism didn't extend to women's rights, and when she sent him her *Lettres à Marcie*, which deal with women's sexual and social indignities, the defier of popes recoiled in prudish dismay. He wanted to hear nothing about divorce; to her suggestion that one of the pieces be about "the role of passion in a woman's life" he replied by cancelling the series.

Liszt, an enthusiastic supporter of George's feminism, won't have liked this treatment — which may have had something to do with the disappearance of his own name from *Le Monde*'s contributors after February 1837. That, and the fact that the paper had also administered a public rebuke to him personally. The occasion was the Berlioz concert where he played his transcription of the *Fantastique* and according to Hallé outshone the orchestra. The *Gazette Musicale* agreed with Hallé that his triumph was complete. *Le Monde*'s reviewer told it a little differently. The crowd at first received him with less excitement than he was accustomed to, and he was unable to hide a scornful displeasure. This prompted a lecture:

To suppose that one has the right to disdain the masses, because they don't yet understand, is to falsify the mission of *gifted* men. To think that beauty exists only for a small number of the elect and to be concerned solely with their approval, isn't this to lower art from the great humanitarian role it is called upon to play and to abase it to the weak and sterile doctrine of art for art's sake? [16]

A strange comment for Lamennais to have authorized and doubly hard for Liszt to take because it underscored the intellectual flimsiness of his position. He couldn't disbelieve in art for art's sake and the concert in question perfectly illustrated the necessity for an elect if modern music was to make its way. Berlioz was not a popular composer, or Liszt would not have had to assist at performances of his work. Nor was it a tribute to public taste that his transcriptions generally were preferred to Berlioz's original. Audiences were inflamed first of all by his personality, and secondly by the trick of imitation, a piano doing the work of an orchestra. Marvelous! And not indicative of any mass instinct for originality.

Lamennais's dicta on music were as useless to the modern composer as his literary ones to the writer. Logically pursued, they would have led directly to social realism and the proscription of "degenerate" experiments — including, we can guess, Liszt's more unorthodox church music and all of the late piano works. (Though I am perhaps too hard on him. He was misplaced among the Romantics; he might have had a fruitful association with an artist like Courbet, whose burning social conscience produced authentic masterpieces like the *Funeral at Ornans*.)

It would be interesting to know how Liszt took his scolding from *Le Monde*, and still more whether he discussed it with Berlioz, older and wiser veteran of the avant-garde wars. Berlioz had his hour of interest in Lamennais: "What a man! Genius burns him, eats him away, desiccates him. He made me tingle with admiration." [17] He must soon have realized that the Abbé's preachments had no pertinence for him. (He knew his enemies and his vocation was in excellent order.) He was uncomfortable in the Hôtel de France. "One talked too much," he said afterward, "one didn't listen enough, one philosophized." [18]

Berlioz and Liszt saw — away from the Hôtel de France — a great deal of each other that winter. Berlioz was secretly engaged in a humiliating project, doctoring up the score of *Esmeralda,* an opera based on Hugo's *Notre-Dame de Paris.* The composer was Louise Bertin, the sister of his employers at the *Débats.* No more need be said. Liszt, for less cogent reasons, was also at work on *Esmeralda,* making a transcription of the vocal score that was pure waste of time from any angle because the opera, produced November 14, was deservedly a flop — howled down by an audience that knew all about the wire-pulling that had resulted in a costly catastrophe. It was for Berlioz a sickening experience. He had cheapened himself to no purpose — while his own opera *Benvenuto Cellini* languished for want of official favor.

Such were the realities that Lamennais sublimely ignored, that Berlioz and Liszt knew all about and surely discussed in language that did not include "humanitarian art." It is a fact that Lamennais's hold on Liszt loosened after that winter; and Berlioz may have contributed.

The irony remains: Liszt went on to become a popular performer on a scale never known before; and such were the contradictions in Lamennais's theory that it can easily be seen as justification for a phenomenon its author must have deplored. What did the Abbé make of the mob scenes, the fainting women who besieged his pupil in every European capital and in provincial towns from Spain to the Volga? Here was art for the masses with a vengeance. Or did Lamennais conceive that Liszt had failed in his mission by vulgarizing it? The distinction is a fine one, because as against the hysterical women there were the Hungarians turning out in their thousands in 1840 to crown their artist-king — a "humanitarian" event that may have hastened the Hungarian revolution, and at the very least was a landmark in a movement of national liberation.

We don't know what the Abbé thought of these developments. He and Liszt were by then on rather distant terms. It can be presumed — since his congratulations were not forthcoming — that he disapproved the éclat and the violence. Liszt's detractors, who have seen in him the vain and cynical exploiter of the piano, must still look to Lamennais for a reasonable interpretation of his *Glanzperiode* (time of glitter, glamour period — the name always given the years 1839–1847). Success like his simply cannot be had through deliberate fraud. The novel or the song that sells a million copies goes forth with its author's faith behind it, irrespective of its quality. Liszt could never have achieved his colossal celebrity if he hadn't believed — over and above the obvious appeals to his Napoleonic *amour propre* — that something larger than himself was involved. That is of course the common mistake of the power-mad personality. It won't quite do for Liszt, who differed from the type in knowing when to stop. When it dawned on him that Lamennais's prescription had expired, he shut the door forever on his career at the piano.

Chapter 18

IN JANUARY the ménage in the Hôtel de France broke up. George went back to Nohant with the expectation that Marie would be joining her shortly. But Marie was taken ill — "almost died" she told George, which was standard with her; she invariably depicted herself at death's door. Didier saw her in good health on January 20, when they had a cosy chat about George's faithless nature. Another friend reported, "She is leaving, then isn't leaving; she is staying, then isn't staying. . . . I think when she finally decides to take flight, she won't come back to sit under the same willow tree." [1] The willow was a coy metaphor for Liszt's hair, so the inference is that they were quarreling, probably about her being packed off to Nohant while he stayed in Paris. She didn't make up her mind to leave until early February.

George wrote smoothly to Liszt:

Good morning, dear Franz. Come and see us as soon as possible. Love, esteem and friendship claim you at Nohant. *Love* is a trifle ill at the moment. . . . *Friendship* is fat but well all the same. . . . Marie informs me there was some hope of Chopin. Tell him I beg and pray him to come with you; that Marie can't live without him, that I adore him. . . . I would like to surround Marie with all her friends. [2]

She had tried hard. She had redecorated the prettiest room in the house for Marie; it looked into lime trees and she filled it with camellias. Later a piano was shipped from Paris and placed by the windows. Her larder was stocked with game. She did her best to cheer Marie up. Marie had told her how she longed to make friends with the Nohant dogs and chickens. Her heart wasn't in it. Her cure boiled down to interminable conversations with George about Liszt — unwise revelations that eventually found their way into *Béatrix.*

Liszt's "Lettre d'un bachelier-ès-musique" of February 12 called Paris "a living chaos in which brutal passions, hypocritical vices, and shameless ambitions clash and struggle, wild to destroy each other." This perhaps meant that Thalberg was back in the city and Liszt wild to destroy him. His pose of proud superiority can have fooled nobody. Though he kept saying how strange it was that anyone should bother with such a mediocrity, an article in the *Gazette Musicale* of January 8 which he instigated and partly wrote was a savage attack on Thalberg. His compositions were pretentious, vain, boring. . . . "M. Thalberg is furthermore pianist to H. M. the Emperor of Austria and that means something to many people. For our part we have to admit we can't understand the artistic significance of these imperial distinctions. . . ." (Did those words ever return to smite him?) Next, he scheduled a set of concerts that far surpassed in seriousness, novelty and splendor anything Thalberg could have mustered and announced them aggressively as follows: "M. Liszt will give in the salons of M. Érard his first evening of instrumental music. The object of these sessions is to make known the works of the *grande école* of the piano, too often disfigured by incompetent executants."

He was as good as his word. The concerts (January 28 and February 4, 11 and 18) were unique in their time. His friends Urhan and Batta took respectively the violin and cello parts and the programs included five Beethoven trios never, it appears, heard before in Paris, sonatas for piano and violin, Chopin études, Schubert lieder (which must mean Liszt's transcriptions since Nourrit isn't mentioned). The critics were stunned. "An unheard-of thing," wrote Legouvé, "a trio, a simple trio that lasts forty-five minutes, was listened to . . . with no other interruption than the murmurs of enthusiasm repressed for fear of losing a single note. . . . The battle is won . . . the lesson has been learned! and if we use the word lesson, it is because it is the only one that can give the particular character of these performances." [3]

To hammer home the lesson Liszt wanted to do another notice, the terms of which he outlined to Marie — who regularly worked up his ideas in this way. (The extent of her contributions to the *Lettres d'un bachelier* has been much discussed and will be taken up later.) His shorthand went something like this: Attempt at musical education destined to fight the public taste for tinsel and mediocrity — Unhoped-for success — quick praise for Urhan and Batta — leave me out but say something about the Érard piano

— announce further concerts devoted to Beethoven, Schubert and Weber —
Conclusion: the business of "amusing the public" is finished.

She didn't answer and didn't write the notice. She wouldn't go to Paris
either, though he pleaded urgently: ". . . come and come soon; and understand and love me." She hated this combat with all her soul. Useless for
him to protest that "what makes me stay here is the need to fight against
the stupid mob, to conquer one by one the difficulties that hinder the
development of my personality." She didn't believe him, or rather she knew
that what held him was the same instinct that impels the matador to kill
his bull. He couldn't be satisfied with praise like Legouvé's, or with Thalberg's lack of stomach for the fight. When Thalberg avoided a dinner to
which they were both invited, he had to crow over it: "We laughed happily
at his absence . . ." and he treasured up a comment supposedly made by
Thalberg to mutual friends, that he would be incapable of playing four
bars of Liszt's *Réminiscences de la Juive.*

George was on Marie's side — or at least she understood that it would be
a mistake for Marie to go to Paris feeling as she did. It would only be adding to Liszt's problems.

Marie to Liszt: Need I tell you that the desire to see you devours me? Yet I
think I won't come yet. . . . I have been talking about it with George, who very
seriously advises me against it for many reasons . . . which have a certain
weight.[4]

And later:

I'm afraid of keeping you from your work, of irritating you, of being myself
very upset. . . .

He came to Nohant instead, a flying visit that did not comfort her. "I am
mortally sad," she wrote the faithful Ronchaud:

. . . My God, my God . . . could it be true that HE is condemned to an impossible task? Will my heart be a bottomless vessel into which he vainly casts all
the treasures of his genius and his love? . . . and that love and mine, is it
anything but the sublime lie of two beings who wanted to give each a happiness
neither believed in for himself? [5]

On March 12, Thalberg gave a concert at the Conservatoire. His big
numbers were his fantasy on Rossini's *Moses* and his variations on *God
Save the King* and he had a huge success with those who, as *Le Monde*
put it, prefer what is easy to what is beautiful. Even that was too much for
Liszt. The following Sunday he did the unprecedented, engaged the Opera,
which held ten times the number of people, and proceeded to demolish his

crusade against amusing the public with *his* fantasy on Pacini's *Niobe* and (a slight concession to quality) Weber's *Conzertstück*. Legouvé, again, was beside himself. To play all alone in that immense space still resounding from Meyerbeer's *Huguenots*, on a Sunday, with no advance notice, on a bad piano! Hearts constricted when he appeared on the stage, so tall, so thin, so pale. But the public was his after the fifth measure.

With that triumph in his pocket, he might have let the contest drop. The *Gazette Musicale* for March 26 announced a further duel, this time in person, between "the two talents whose rivalry is . . . agitating the musical world, and is like the indecisive balance between Rome and Carthage." Princess Belgiojoso had seen the chance of a lifetime to benefit her Italian refugees and simultaneously give the party of the year. Liszt and Thalberg were invited to meet face to face in her drawing room and *le tout Paris* to pay forty francs apiece to hear them.

Since no event from Romanticism's high noon has come down to us more resoundingly than this one (*Hernani*'s debut excepted), it is a pity we know so little about it.* Did the Belgiojoso pin water lilies in her hair as usual? Who exactly was there? Chopin? Berlioz? Curiously enough, though the affair is always written up as exclusively a battle between Liszt and Thalberg, no fewer than ten other musicians were on the program and two singers. Was the *Hexameron* played? This peculiar work, consisting of variations by Liszt, Thalberg, Pixis, Chopin, Czerny and Herz on a theme from *I Puritani*, was — according to Searle, who should know — composed especially for "a charity concert given at the house of Princess Belgiojoso" in 1837. I can't discover that there was *another* concert of the kind — but neither Searle nor anyone else says whether it was performed.

Marie would be helpful here — if only to supply a Gothic tale of how dreadful it was. She was so resolutely silent on the subject that she may not have been present, though she had been back in Paris for a week.† (A vision of her in collapse — "How could you do this to me?" — comes to mind, but perhaps does her an injustice — and anyway who can say that she wasn't, in this case, quite right?) Heine, however, was there, dripping acid: "The keys seemed to bleed. . . . Everywhere in the room were pale faces, palpitating breasts, and emotional breathing during the pauses. . . . The women are always intoxicated when Liszt plays." [6] Heine was one of

---

* There is even a muddle about the date, some authorities giving it as March 31, others April 5. I follow Marix-Spire who says it was March 31, and that he played his last concert in the Salon Érard on April 5. Altogether, and exclusive of the Urhan-Batta concerts and the Thalberg confrontation, she lists nine concerts that spring.

† Vier, so exhaustive and meticulous, is strangely hazy about this. Marie left Nohant March 22 or 23, yet Vier says she arrived in Paris "in time to attend the concert at the Opera and let her blond hair sparkle" — which is impossible since that concert took place on the nineteenth. He says nothing about her presence (or absence) at the Belgiojoso concert, which he dates April 5 (Vier: pp. 256, 249).

the first to notice the sexual side of Lisztomania, as he was also the first to speak of the political implications, and that was clever of him; but it had the effect of closing his mind to a phenomenon more complicated than that. He himself was overtaken with dizziness and pounding of the heart when Liszt played. He was furious but it happened, and one wishes he had devoted more study to it.

The *Gazette Musicale* had said that Liszt and Thalberg would "take turns at the piano." Thalberg played first. He repeated his *Moses* fantasia with all the pearly runs and arpeggios for which he was renowned. He was a handsome man of aristocratic presence — a hidden cause for Liszt's antagonism: Thalberg was the illegitimate son of a Count Moritz von Dietrichstein and a Baroness von Wetzlar. His style was cool, detached, if not really classic, and he was frantically applauded. But he hadn't a hope. He was in the wrong place at the wrong time and he wasn't a genius. Liszt's piece was as insignificant as Thalberg's (the *Niobe* again); it wouldn't have mattered if he had played "Chopsticks." * Their hostess gave the verdict now tarnished by repetition: Thalberg is the best pianist in the world; Liszt is the only one.

Neither was true. Half a dozen pianists were superior to Thalberg — Mendelssohn and Chopin to name two — and many more his equal. Liszt had slain a pygmy. His victory, like Hugo's in 1830, was symbolic. Thalberg's supporters were largely of the Faubourg Saint-Germain, antediluvians who admired him because he was, and played like, a gentleman and a royalist. Liszt belonged to the present, politically and emotionally. Said *Le Monde:* "We think M. Thalberg has got all that can be got from mechanical effort. Inspiration and feeling he is without and always will be; the poetic side of his art is hidden from him. . . ." Mechanical stood for the past, feeling for the future. Thalberg's epitaph was written, and Liszt was victorious from the same causes that were to make him supreme in Europe. Of course he was a greater pianist than Thalberg. There was no comparison and it was only another indication of the state of music that one was made. He didn't win on those terms. The palm awarded him in the Belgiojoso drawing room was given because he was the "child of his time," the *enfant du siècle* that Thalberg was not.

---

* Not as ridiculous as it sounds. He *did* write a variation on "Chopsticks," which it seems is a Russian nursery tune, for Borodin's children. Other contributors were Rimsky-Korsakov and Cui.

Chapter 19

THE FELLOWS WENT to Nohant in early May, intending to stay the summer. This time, Marie sang hymns to her release from Paris:

[At Nohant] it is a life of intimate feeling, religious reveries, of vague thoughts and abandoned conversations that can't be described. . . . How to paint the happiness one feels at being wrapped in a warm, perfumed, enlivening atmosphere, and the sacred affections that are to the heart what the air of May is to the senses? [1]

George expected everybody to be happy at Nohant because she was so happy there herself — and generally they were. It was a plain, handsome manor house without pretension: the main gates faced the village square and the garden, at that season scented with white lilac, was informal. Imperfectly standardized shrubs stood in tubs on the terrace; shaggy archways of vines bordered the lawn; an old tower housed the flock of noisy doves. A farm belonged also to the property, and woods abounding in wild strawberries; nearby flowed the Indre, one of those ravishing miniature rivers that bind the landscape of central France like so many ribbons.

Sand was a good if not an elegant housekeeper. She set an excellent table — though Sainte-Beuve complained of too much game and chicken on the menu. If you wanted something you had only to leave a note in a box for internal correspondence. (Sainte-Beuve once requested a comb and the following morning was given thirty to choose from.) The problem was too many people. George was madly hospitable. She invited everybody and those who weren't invited turned up anyway, sure of a welcome.

Liszt and Marie were urged to bring a houseparty, at the very least to include Chopin, Puzzi and Mickiewicz. The invitations probably were not delivered with much enthusiasm. Marie felt there was enough of a crowd already what with George's children, Maurice's tutor, Solange's governess, country neighbors of all shapes and sizes. "I bring you nobody," she wrote triumphantly, hoping no doubt for a quiet summer.

She had, as a matter of fact and in spite of her pleasure at being there, a number of faults to find with Nohant's manners and tone. The wretched tutor, whose name was Pelletan, causing him to be nicknamed the Pelican, was already in her bad books.

Marie to George, March 1837: Enclosed is a bit of paper which the Pelican thought it apropos to send me (without sealing it). . . . It is the first time in my life that I have received anything in this negligent and familiar style. Tell him that because I dispensed him completely from the respect he thought due me as a *countess*, that this is no reason for him to dispense with the deference he owes me as a woman. One can be in a hurry, a seal is quickly affixed and a Madame as quickly written. . . .[2]

George apologized for him; unfortunately he typified the roughness all too prevalent in that house. Rustic poetry had its counterpart in rustic humor. George writing to a friend in Berrichon dialect asked him to procure a straw saddle for Marie, "on which her ravishing and revered arse can pace the Elysian *allées* of the garden," and other of her cracks really were in ghastly taste. Another letter recounts: "Liszt made a fart this evening which he blamed on Solange. Miss Tempest [nickname for Solange's governess] praised the perfume. Mme d'A's stockings were found to be wet after an immoderate laugh."[3] The children too were allowed outrageous liberties: ghost walks and midnight serenades, horsehair cut up in the beds. Solange in later life remembered that Liszt was her ally in these goings-on, which he thoroughly enjoyed. Marie was appalled. Years afterward she told a friend that George's "want of deportment, her way of dressing, the gross farces of Nohant" were unpardonable. "Her lack of dignity compromises all women who write."[4] George's maternal feelings were an irritant too. "I can't admire this love of children, a blind sentiment in which the least of the animals is better than we," says her Nohant journal.

Still, it was a sort of Eden, with a charm that the stiffness of her prose cannot muffle: "A promenade along the Indre, the length of the woody path, across the meadows covered with forget-me-nots, nettles and English daisies, climbing many rustic fences, meeting with families of geese and herds of cattle majestically ruminating. . . ."[5] (Vier, her fervent admirer, concedes the defects of her writing, "which under a factitious romanticism preserves a sort of academic rigidity" leading her to prefer the formal to the idiomatic word. For example, *pavot* instead of *coquelicot* for "poppy.") She was actually persuaded to rise before dawn and ride horseback with George, which wasn't a success. Possibly because she now knew she was pregnant again, she was a timid horsewoman, needing help at every turn. It was gallantly given, George leaping from her mount to lead Marie's over bad spots. But we sense that the "young man" who had been at Marie's feet was beginning to tire of his part. (Or was just tired: during May and early June, George was riding half the night to rendezvous with Michel de Bourges at an inn, a program that with her active days would have finished a weaker woman. But in June it was all over. "Dawn," says the *Journal intime*, "my room . . . Friendly walls give me shelter. . . . How full the garden is of birds! There is a sprig of honeysuckle in my glass; how sweet it smells! Piffoël, how frightening is the calm in your breast! Is the flame really extinguished?" [6] And that was the end of de Bourges.)

Liszt, no sportsman, spent the mornings in his room. He brought with him the scores of the Beethoven symphonies and was transcribing Nos. 5, 6, and perhaps 7, as well as some of the Schubert lieder.[*] Another project was an article on Schumann, pressed by Berlioz through the summer. He sent scores, saying, "You're the only one, it seems to me, who can do it justice." Berlioz wanted the article but (to set straight his record with Liszt) he had other motives for keeping in touch with Nohant. He hoped that Sand would write a play for poor Harriet and he kept at this quite as persistently as at the Schumann article, entreating Liszt to use his influence. The women were against him. Marie did not like Berlioz and scorned Harriet. George, in principle the friend of any friend of Liszt, did not really like him either. Faithfully she reproduced what Liszt told her — that Berlioz was a hero, proud, courageous, locked in battle with Philistia — in an article published in 1835. She said nothing about his music because it was beyond her; and apart from Liszt, her other influences were in his disfavor. Musset, a dud about music, had no opinion of Berlioz; the Chopin-Delacroix circle, into which she presently passed, despised him.[†] In the interim, and at her most supine about opening Nohant to anyone that Liszt might desire, she couldn't discover a reason to include him.

[*] Searle says he "possibly" transcribed the Seventh in 1837, but it is uncertain — see George's note, "Here comes the Andante . . . ," etc. — that he got beyond the Sixth at Nohant and he did little composing the rest of that year. On the other hand, there are many mentions of Schubert songs in Paris and at Nohant, showing that he was at work on these well before the 1838 date given by Searle.

[†] Marix-Spire, who anxiously wishes it had not been so, goes to some length to create a fictitious presence for Berlioz at Nohant: "Though Berlioz is never named explicitly, it is certain that George met him . . ." (*Les Romantiques et la musique:* p. 529). "He would occupy more than once the guests at Nohant" (*ibid:* p. 550). This is working overtime. Sand's resistance was almost total and she would not write the play.

Her instinct was sound. Berlioz was incapable of play and at Nohant the deadly serious business of art was in the hands of talented actors who often could not distinguish their parts from the real thing. In its way, it was almost as much a stage as Paris itself, everyone eavesdropping on everyone else and keeping score in his journal. George's diary, June 5:

Magnificent weather, lots of breeze, majestic sound and movement in the lime leaves . . . Dull awakening . . . And that cursed piano won't wake up! What will I do with myself this morning? Bless God! . . . here comes the opening melody of the Andante of Beethoven's Pastoral symphony. Real music of summer . . .[7]

Nothing could be less like Marie than George's seizing of this chance to listen in on genius at work, and she made the most of it. Her windows were above theirs, whence issued "those sounds the whole world would give its soul to hear," that drove her to the pitch of Romantic speculation:

Is he perhaps trying out fragments of composition? . . . Beside him is his pipe, his ruled paper, his pens; each time he traces his thought on paper, he confides it to the voice of his instrument. . . . [But] I would rather believe he paces his room without composing, given up to tumult and uncertainty. It seems to me that in passing his piano he should toss out those capricious phrases without knowing what he is doing, obedient to an emotional instinct rather than a labor of the intelligence.[8]

Berlioz would have hooted at this, so typical of the literary Romantic's attitude to music, and assured her brusquely that composition was no less a labor of the intelligence than putting together a novel. Liszt indulged her fantasies because they flattered him, and at the same time bore out his thesis that the real artist is a sort of demigod. "What do we see?" inquires his "Lettre à George Sand." "Sculptors? No, makers of statues. Painters? No, picture makers. Musicians? No, manufacturers of music; everywhere *artisans* . . . nowhere *artists*." It would have been useless to point out to him that nearly all the great music of the past had come from men who called themselves artisans. He would simply have said this was evidence of a villainous system. By his definition, "the real children of art" exhibit pride and "a savage independence," hence are outside the laws including those that govern composition. He of course knew that this was ridiculous when literally applied — and that he did not compose "without knowing what he was doing," like a medium receiving messages from the beyond. He let the fallacy stand for ideological reasons.

If the mornings were like séances, the evenings were hallucinatory as

George brewed her flaming punch for the party assembled on the terrace. Now all nature enters the conspiracy, responding to music that seems not to come from human hands but from some distant cloud:

The moon went down behind the big limes. . . . A deep calm reigned among the plants, the breeze died exhausted on the long grass at the first chords of the sublime instrument. The nightingale still struggled, but in a fainting and timid voice. He had come close in the shadow of the foliage and like the excellent musician he is, pitched his ecstatic pauses to the tune and the measure. We were all sitting on the steps, listening to the sometimes charming, sometimes sorrowful phrases of the Erlkönig; burdened like nature itself with a mournful beatitude; unable to keep our gaze from the magnetic circle traced . . . by the mute sibyl in the white veil. Her steps slackened little by little as the artist passed into a series of strangely sad modulations on the tender melody. . . . Finally she came to sit on a branch that bent no more than if it had carried a phantom. Then the music stopped, as if a mysterious bond attached . . . its sounds to the life of this beautiful pale woman who seemed ready to fly to regions of inexhaustible harmony.[9] *

Liszt was at his best like this, surrounded with adoring women. When other guests arrived, he could be capricious and unpleasant. George warned a woman friend that "if he has promised to play, you can be sure he won't, and on the contrary when nobody is listening, the whim will take him to improvise." Some of the neighbors found him unbearable. "He has two manias that generate odious harassments," said one. "He likes to play cards and always wants to win, and though he understands nothing he likes to talk politics and will do anything to convince you that he is an accomplished diplomat." [10] (The neighbor was right on both counts. Liszt was a fiend at the whist table, and he did once say that he could have been "the first diplomat in Europe.")

Even George began to be annoyed with him. The house was filling up with her men friends. One of them was the actor Bocage, prodigiously handsome and prodigiously stupid. (Marie, earnestly trying to talk to him about Mickiewicz, received the query, "Miss who?") Liszt took the wrong line about him. George put a note into the box:

Dear Mirabella, have the goodness to make Crétin stop the jokes about me and Bocage. This bores me extremely and seriously irritates me. I *was* flirting a bit with Bocage, or rather he with me. It doesn't follow that I like to see him becoming impertinent, and there was a hint of that today. I don't know what Crétin

* Marie also described this evening — or one exactly like it; the dates don't quite tally — in her journal. The passage was reproduced in the third "Lettre d'un bachelier" but was nothing like as good as George's, being burdened with a tiresome imaginary dialogue about "the King of the Gnomes," a dead child, etc.

said to him. I'm sure nothing that wasn't proper . . . but does [Bocage] have the sense to understand? [11]

After Bocage came Félicien Mallefille, a young playwright, and rather suddenly Didier. In the confusion no one behaved well. George was annoyed with Didier. "She talks to me in that nasty, teasing way she has . . . my coming here was the worst of blunders," he wrote. Again he made Marie his confidante. Astoundingly, she told him that George "was ready to enter the world of gallantry," and was now incapable of either love or friendship. This calm betrayal of a woman who had sheltered her for many weeks cost Didier a sleepless night. He believed her, and left immediately.

Marie's feelings for George had curdled over the weeks. Her jealousy and spite knew no bounds, though they didn't reveal themselves until some eighteen months later when Sand went off with Chopin. These other men hanging about, the cult of the "Princess Mirabella," in no way undermined her conviction that she was the victim of a subtle plot. Her tormenting remarks to Didier upset the carefully constructed edifice of pretended friendship.

George in her journal of that summer said of Liszt that he was "sublime about great matters, and always superior even in the trivial. But, for all that, he is melancholy and bleeds from a secret wound." She didn't hazard the source of the wound, which may or may not refer to a passage between them. But if he was melancholy, Marie will have found that suspect too. As before, her pregnancy was singularly opportune. It prevented any idea Liszt may have had of a return to Paris and virtually guaranteed some form of exile for another year; it also showed George (and Liszt himself) where Liszt's allegiance lay.

The Fellows left Nohant July 24. George, who in March had pleaded with them to stay forever, "*à la mort*," made no protest. Whether Liszt ever spoke to her frankly or not, her mental album was full of snapshots, some of which were later passed on to Balzac while others were incorporated into her own novels.* She saw the road ahead with doomful clarity but there was nothing she could do. He belonged to Marie, whose farewell tears she likewise read accurately. There was no quarrel. She and Mallefille accompanied the party on horseback — as far as La Châtre, the nearest

---

* Marix-Spire cites *La Dernière Aldini* (published the following winter) and this piece of advice offered an artist contemplating marriage to an aristocrat: "The obstacles and the dangers exalt her love for you, but she is neither so strong in spirit nor so free from prejudice as she pretends . . . she has told me without realizing it . . . hundreds of things that prove to me that she thinks she is making an immense sacrifice for your sake . . . the day will come . . . when, even without regretting the world, she will accuse you of ingratitude, and it's a sad role for man to be the bankrupt in his wife's debt" (*Romantiques et la musique*: p. 560).

town. Liszt did not dream that this was the end. The two women probably understood each other better. Marie smoothed her ruffled plumage as follows:

I am convinced that there aren't such abysses between one person and another; that intelligences are not, after all, so disproportionate, and that certain qualities of the heart, certain superiorities of character often reestablish the balance between two people, one of whom seems to have dominated the other. . . . Can I say it in two words? It hasn't been useless to me to observe beside George the great poet, George the spoiled child . . . the weak woman, changeable in her feelings and opinions, illogical in a life always influenced by accident, rarely directed by reason or experience. I see how childish of me it was to think . . . that only she could give its full development to Franz's life, that I was the unhappy barrier between two destinies meant to merge and complete each other.[12]

Few would have agreed with her. A Liszt-Sand affair would not have lasted either but they would have been worthy of one another, and he been spared Marie's particular blend of smugness and self-pity. On the other hand, Marie was right that she was not the real obstacle. He distrusted George, her head-hunting and — yes — her casual morals. Years later he told Janka Wohl:

Madame Sand used to catch a butterfly and domesticate it in her box, feeding it on herbs and flowers — that was the period of love. Then she pricked it with her pin, while it still fluttered — that was the dismissal, which she was always the one to deliver. Afterward, she performed her dissection, impaling it for her collection of fictional heroes. It was this traffic in hearts given to her without reserve that finally disgusted me with her friendship.[13]

That wasn't quite true. It was Marie who ruined their friendship, which he tried vainly to patch up. But he had observed her at work on Musset, on Didier and others and the prospect was not encouraging even had he been — which was impossible — prepared to abandon Marie. It is still sad to think of the sympathy and the fun he missed.

Chapter 20

THE ITALIAN PROJECT was now to be realized but they went first to Switzerland where they inspected, briefly, their little girl. A serious child, said Marie, affectionate and rather nervous. Blandine can't have recognized them, which was just as well since there was no idea of taking her with them to *das Land*. They did not linger and in September crossed the Alps by the Simplon.

Air travel has destroyed the symbolism of that escape route from darkness into light, disorder into harmony. To Marie it promised a *vita nuova*. Paris, Geneva, Nohant receded into fog as they descended toward the lakes, where they found lemon and camphor trees, magnolias, aloes and jasmine in bloom. They thought they were in heaven; even Marie sounded happy, and it was many weeks before the litany began: the decadence of Italian music, the want of intellectual society, art works falling to pieces and so badly lighted you can't see them, rubbish in the shops. From the dawn of the grand tour it is the same old story. Yet bad as it was, the prospect of "improvements" was worse.

Marie to Pictet: One can still be in love at Bellagio, but no longer poetically alarmed by a storm, considering that every day at exactly eleven o'clock, one sees passing under the window the prosaic steamboat . . . tracing its invariable path from Como to Bellano. The picturesque is dying, dear Major, it is in its death agony. What will have become of sensitive souls in 1859 . . . where will you flee to? Already one takes a post chaise to the Grande Chartreuse, you'll see

172

that soon one will descend the falls of the Rhine in a steamboat, that a regular balloon service will be established to the Antipodes.[1]

Milan was their temporary goal and they were royally received there by the Ricordis, Liszt's publishers, who offered carriages, a box at the Scala, a country house. Presently Marie begins to sound like her old self. The cathedral was sublime of course, "a Te Deum in marble" (what *did* the nineteenth century see in this ugly building?), but the Scala was a bitter disappointment, an ark, and Donizetti's operas, much in vogue, miserable copies of Rossini. Milanese society was inane — partly, as she correctly observed, because the best of the young condemned themselves to idleness rather than serve their Austrian masters. Liaisons were openly discussed, she found, nobody cared what you did; and she foresaw that she would be bracketed with women like the Countess Samoyoff, separated from her husband on account of "adventures" and entertaining all and sundry. With such people Marie had no intention of associating. (Liszt however found the countess great fun and probably had a brief fling with her later on when he was alone in Milan.)

Another person she did not care to meet was Rossini, living openly with a Mlle Pelissier. There was a bad moment when it seemed that he would count on old friendship and try to introduce the unspeakable Pelissier. The crisis passed. He called alone, stayed ten minutes, and didn't come again. This was typical. Liszt doted on Rossini, many of whose operas he transcribed. With his black wig, this smiling monument to *pasta* was one of the delights of the age and Liszt wouldn't hear of dropping him. He saw him often and when Marie had retired to Como wrote her angrily, "The maestro is always charming. . . . He is supremely intelligent. I have never been and never could be deceived in him; he is just what I think he is."[2]

When Marie no longer cared to appear in public, they rented a villa on the lake, at Bellagio. She was happier here, *"in alta solitudine"* with Liszt. They played checkers, rowed on the lake, rambled in the hills — Marie on a donkey. She speaks of an especially beautiful and joyous day, his twenty-sixth birthday, when they picnicked under chestnuts and olives, returning to Bellagio in a sea of violet light. That evening they watched their boatman harpooning fish by torchlight. It was a sort of double celebration: Liszt had just finished his "twelve preludes — a worthy beginning to a series of original compositions." With this Marie lets us down again. What preludes? He didn't write any at this time. Does she mean the *Transcendental* Études (published in 1839)? The transcriptions of Rossini's *Soirées musicales*? But they aren't "original." Is it conceivable that she confused Liszt's études with Chopin's preludes, which he sent to Como with "a charming dedication" to her? * Not for the first time, one wishes she had either taxed her memory or paid closer attention to what the beloved was doing. But that was not really her point:

At the age when everything urges one to activity, when movement and change are almost a condition of life, he with his communicative spirit, whose occupations have always involved him in the world, in a word, the artist, that is to say the man of sensibility, of feeling and imagination, concentrates all his faculties in the narrow frame of a *tête-à-tête* existence. A bad piano, some books, the conversation of a serious woman are enough for him. He gives up all the pleasures of *amour-propre*, the excitement of the struggle, the amusements of social life, even the joy of . . . doing good; and he gives it all up without appearing to renounce anything.[3]

For a time he did. He wrote George that he was "the luckiest of mortals. Lake Como is very *bello. Mi piace* more than *lago di Genivra* . . . The princess is always the most adorable of creatures. We live alone and incredibly happy in each other. To distract myself sometimes from my happiness, I set to work. I think I have made some progress musically speaking, but what does it matter?"[4] One believes him — almost. Como is beautiful beyond words in October, and Marie's nerves were in better order than they ever were again. But the idyll didn't last; it was cut short by the birth of their second daughter.

Francesca Gaetana Cosima Liszt was born December 24, 1837 — the name Cosima recalling, in Vier's phrase, "for all her long life, the happiness of shared love." The origin of this universal fixation that she was named for the lake I cannot discover.† But only an incurable sentimentalist could see in Cosima — *"ma terrible fille"* as Liszt later called her — the memorial to an ideal passion. With her mother's will and her father's morals, she was a caution to careless begetters. Her parents learned to respect and even to fear her; at no time did they regard her in the light of a love-token. To Liszt her safe arrival meant he could proceed alone to Milan "without too

---

* Discussing Liszt's supposed envy of Chopin over these pieces (to which the *Transcendental* Études are imagined to be a "reply"), Alan Walker expresses amazement at the dedication to her "of all people!" (*Franz Liszt: The Man and His Music:* p. 59). But neither she nor Liszt found it extraordinary. Liszt was delighted, the preludes were "extremely remarkable," he told George — and in the same letter urged her when next she was in Paris to "see Chopin a little. He is absolutely my friend" (Marix-Spire: p. 619).

Maurois too is mixed up about Chopin's preludes. He thinks they were composed in 1838 at Nohant and dedicated to Marie because Chopin's "excessive sense of modesty had not allowed him to dedicate [them] to George" (*Lélia:* p. 266). But as they were composed months before his affair with George began, this is also much ado about nothing.

† It arises perhaps from the French spelling of Como — Côme — the circumflex denoting the presence of an *s*: Cosme.

much remorse," as he put it to Nourrit. To Marie it only meant weeks of hateful seclusion at Como.

From Milan came oysters, little combs, perfume, volumes of Balzac, and a stream of loving letters that did not quite conceal his pleasure at being in a town again. An astonishing dusk (*prima sera*) in Milan with a red-opal sky in the west, the moon and Venus shining with marvelous brilliance:

> My heart was filled with poetry. I dreamed of our sweet past, I felt more fully than ever . . . that we too have been saints, the elect, that we too have been crowned with immortal wreaths of love and poetry. . . . Then I remembered my old predilection for midday, and my walks in the sun, and the thousand sad and suffering melodies of my youth.[5]

But what, Marie always wondered, lay at the end of these promenades? A bachelor dinner with Rossini? Not very likely. A reception *chez* Samoyoff was more probable.

Marie took most of the credit for Liszt's aesthetic responses to Italy — "At the sight of a beautiful spot, or a magnificent monument, he told me he needed to see beauty through me; that I was for him like the word by which the beauty of things was revealed" — and with some justice, as his letters show:

> Here is a beautiful day. The light would be lovingly reflected on your Correggios . . . and your pale, beautiful head be lovelier still in front of these masterpieces.[6]

He compared her to Raphael's St. Cecilia, whom she did not resemble, and which mostly shows that like Charles Swann he found authentification for his love in his mistress's likeness to a painting. It was natural too to associate her with artifacts, for it was she who in her rather governessy way studied the guidebooks: the then standard Valéry (*Voyages historiques et littéraires en Italie*); Vitruvius; Chateaubriand's *Voyage en Italie;* probably Goethe. But to infer from this that Liszt would have been deaf, dumb and blind without her is to go a great deal too far. The second and third *Années de pèlerinage* are not the creations of an understanding working at second hand. Yet Vier, for one, devotes pages of analysis to Marie's *pensées* about Italy, managing to reduce Liszt to the status of companion to this interesting woman, whose progress as an art critic we are to take seriously.

The premise is that she was the real and exclusive author of the *Lettres d'un bachelier-ès-musique* — and it is a tricky one. Doubts about Liszt's authorship were current from the start, the earliest voiced in 1838 when the *Gazette Musicale* offered to show holographs proving them groundless. Unfortunately, there were no takers and the manuscripts were later lost or destroyed. Suspicions were not allayed either with the publication of the

Liszt-d'Agoult letters, which contain many references to material she is to work up — a number of which I have already quoted. Still other revelations (the most notable a savage and not always convincing attack by Emil Haraszti — *Franz Liszt: Author despite Himself*) that established the Chopin biography and the gypsy book as largely the work of Carolyne Wittgenstein, completed the destruction of his literary reputation. It then became the fashion to say that he hadn't written a line of his six-volume *Gesammelte Schriften.**

Undoubtedly she did a lot of the dirty work, organizing the material, looking things up, and so on — and much of the writing itself must be hers. The ideas are unlikely to have come from her and none of the sections relating to music, a subject she was incompetent to discuss. (Marix-Spire calls attention to the contrast between the bachelor's article on Meyerbeer's *Huguenots* published in 1837 and the feeble piece on Meyerbeer she produced unaided in 1842.) More important is the matter of vision. Though she plumed herself on her superior culture, she was not better informed than Liszt and still less had she his apocalyptic sense of art as revelation, and of its forms being essentially one. Consider this passage from the "Lettre" addressed to Berlioz:

> Each day, reflection gives me deeper insight into the hidden relation that links the creations of genius. Raphael and Michelangelo make me understand Mozart and Beethoven better. Giovanni de Pisa, Fra Beato . . . explain . . . Marcello and Palestrina to me. The Colosseum and the Campo Santo are not as far removed from the Eroica Symphony and the Requiem as one might think. Dante found his pictorial expression in Orcagna and Michelangelo; one day perhaps he will find his musical expression in the Beethoven of the future.[7]

One of Liszt's critics (Haraszti) finds it impossible that he could have written that. To me, it bears his signature as definitively as any piece of music. What did Marie know about Marcello or Palestrina? Beyond that, he is simply stating the Romantic thesis in terms of his Italian experience, and trying to say in words what the *Années de pèlerinage* try to say in music. The sentence about Dante is even more personal. Dante, we know, was to Liszt almost God — perhaps he *was* God in the way that the metaphysics of disbelief make possible. (Dante was divine, ergo there must be a God who could create Dante.) But these were reaches unknown to Marie.

On the face of it, it is preposterous that a society woman with literary pretensions and small talent should be given credit for writings that what-

---

* The German title is misleading: he never wrote in that language. Those articles that were written for German papers in the 1850's were translated from the French — many by Peter Cornelius — and the originals destroyed. When therefore they are quoted in French, it is the retranslation of a translation. What this boils down to is that no original manuscript of Liszt's writings exists to prove one way or the other who wrote it.

ever they lack in style * display a mind more curious, varied and eclectic than she possessed. It happens that a notebook has been found which outlines, in Liszt's own hand, the theories set forth in the bachelor's letters which of course are — avowedly, no disguise is intended — modelled on Sand's *Lettres d'un voyageur*. But if no such proof of original thought existed, there would still be the question of intent. Why were these articles written? And what were Marie's qualifications for writing them?

Even Vier must allow that her knowledge of the fine arts was as limited as Liszt's before they went to Italy, and that it was Liszt who gained them admission to many private collections, through Liszt that they met Ingres, then head of the French Academy in Rome, Bartolini, and many others who are called Marie's instructors. Why were they not also Liszt's? And how, if she was the superior observer, do away with the banality of her opinions outside the context of the *Lettres*? When Ingres conducted them through the Vatican collections, she reported to Pictet in language any tourist might have used:

We passed with respect the yellowed marbles and half-effaced paintings [Which? The Raphael frescoes?]. He talked as he walked and we listened like disciples . . . his eloquence transported us into bygone centuries; line and color came alive under our eyes; shapes altered by time and profane hands came to life . . . modern genius evoked the antique. . . .[8]

Surely Liszt could have done as well as that?

The truth is that neither of them was an informed judge of painting or architecture. They accepted for the most part the standards of their day. Marie preferred Murillo to Titian, didn't care for Palladio, closed her eyes to Baroque Rome; Liszt saw no material difference between Delacroix and Ary Sheffer and was enamoured of German painters like Schwind and Kaulbach. But whether their taste was good or bad, and every age has its received ideas, the works of art discussed in the *Lettres* are Liszt's and not Marie's choices. She, for example, disliked Raphael and in particular the *Marriage of the Virgin* in the Brera at Milan: "monotonous, effeminate" etc. This picture inspired the opening piece (*Sposalizio*) in the second *Année de pèlerinage*. Another Raphael, the *St. Cecilia*, was treated with parallel importance in a "Lettre" devoted to its symbolism: the saint's vision represents the mystery in the artist's experience, which he cannot communicate to men; it is the heavenly feast to which he alone is invited. Are we to suppose that this is Marie talking? Her memoirs in fact denigrate the picture — "not as admirable as I thought" — but we don't need to know that in order to recognize in the essay an interpretation that is wholly Lisztian.

---

* The deficiencies that mark Liszt's prose are for what it is worth equally present in his letters and quoted conversation. They seem to come from the same hand — or mind; which supposes a remarkable capacity for mimicry in both Marie and Carolyne.

Squabbles over who wrote which passages lose sight of the primary purpose of these articles which was to give expression to Liszt's ideas. (Marie was at liberty to express hers elsewhere and eventually did, with no interference from him or attempts to grab the credit.) Otherwise, they would make no sense. They don't make very much as it is unless they are seen for what they are — appendices to the *Années de pèlerinage*. He tried to explain this to his publisher Schlesinger:

> I have dared to name Titian and Veronese, and . . . allowed myself to speak of some of my personal impressions of the lagoons, the mauresque [sic] palaces etc. . . . But here you are, accusing me of becoming too *literary* (the last reproach I would ever think of deserving), you pretend that your subscribers only want and should only read about the *diminished seventh* and *the D sharp* . . . you sink my moonlit gondola and you ask me furiously what Giambellino, Donatello and Sansovino have to do with the editor of the *Gazette Musicale* . . .[9] *

What they have to do with music he has of course said many times before and will again: we can, like Schlesinger, reject the organic relation between the arts and assume that Liszt is toying with aesthetic furbelows. Do we need to know more than the musical construction of his Italian pieces? Does it matter what he thought he was doing? It goes against the modern grain to answer yes. (W. H. Auden, reviewing Gutman's life of Wagner, objects "on principle" to biographies of artists: "I do not believe that knowledge of their private lives sheds any significant light on their works." [10] Nor does he think one should write about music at all, because aside from purely technical analysis there is nothing to say except when it is bad: "When it is good, one can only listen and be grateful." It is interesting to note that his introduction to Baudelaire's *Journals* begins, "What kind of man wrote this book?" and that he tells us. There seem to be differing standards for music and for literature.) We no longer wish to hear the extra-musical echoes that Liszt wanted us to, and so his whole apparatus goes for nothing. But how are we to understand an artist if we omit the life of his mind — understand and not just be "grateful"?

I think we can't — which does, however, supply the last word on the *Lettres d'un bachelier*. If they weren't the more or less faithful transcript of Liszt's ideas on Italian art, life and musical customs, there would be no object in reading them. They are of interest solely for the insights they give into the composer of the second *Année de pèlerinage* — a collection of pieces unique for its attempt not to represent in any banal way various Italian masterpieces in poetry and the fine arts but to suspend them as it were in a musical medium that reflects Liszt's own psychology.

---

* Somebody must have slipped or couldn't read Liszt's handwriting. Giambellino I guess to be Giov. Bellini.

The titles in the collection are: *Sposalizio* (after Raphael's *Marriage*); *Il Penseroso* (the Michelangelo figure, prefaced with his quatrain that begins, "*Grato m'e il sonno*"); *Canzonetta del Salvator Rosa;* three *Petrarch Sonnets* (Numbers 47, 104 and 123); *Après une lecture du Dante.* A supplement of lighter pieces, *Venezia e Napoli,* was added later, making a delicious folkloric coda. The subjects therefore are a traditional if not quite conventional conspectus of Italian civilization. The treatment however is startling. It is as if one went to the theatre expecting to see a play by Victor Hugo and discovered it was by Pirandello instead. *Il Penseroso*'s novel harmonics anticipate *Tristan*'s by twenty years. *Sposalizio*'s Debussy-like texture gives it an astonishing resemblance to the first *Arabesque.* The time-sense gets a jolt.

This futurism (and I don't of course mean the movement so called in Italian painting) is continuously disconcerting in Liszt, and I believe accounts for the distaste he often arouses. With everything conspiring to make him a Romantic composer, and himself firmly anchored in the Romantic canon, we already see in these compositions evidence that he isn't a Romantic composer in the ordinary sense — doesn't, like Schumann or Chopin or Mendelssohn, pluck at the heartstrings with lyric Impromptus, Ballades, Songs without Words or any other ideal expression of small-scale Romantic sentiment. The pieces in the second *Année* are all so to speak in Romantic bindings; the bindings are about to burst: in the *Dante* Sonata, for instance, with its infernal chromatics, its chorale and love duet, one seems to hear the submerged sketch for a modern opera. The feeling throughout is of a subtle mismatch, a crisis brought on by the pressures of Romantic realism on a musical mind more iconoclastic than belongs to any of his contemporaries. And indeed they recognized the enemy in Liszt long before he was prepared to admit that he didn't belong in their company. Schumann's icy silence when Liszt played him the great B Minor Sonata, a work of terrifying anti-Romantic harshness that Liszt nevertheless dedicated to him, Brahms's comatose reception of the same piece, were early warnings of what would happen when he at length discarded even the pretense of a Romantic format. It was his fate to be rejected by his associates because he was too modern, and by modernists (in a later day) because he chose to fly Romantic colors — or so they thought until acquainted with the radical works of his old age, stark as buildings without a past.

It is now the fashion, beginning to verge on respectability, to admire these piano pieces, which are the summa of his achievement. They are no more and no less Liszt than the sometimes over-burdened experiments of his youth or middle age — only more accommodating to the contemporary ear. Suppose, then, that we listen to him in another way, as if his music, like his life, were a kind of *Bildungsroman,* a psychological novel of "progress." We might then observe that while he touches on a far wider range of European thought than any of his contemporaries, he isn't lost in the wilderness, unable to fix on a single "right" way to express himself, which toward the end he hits on largely by accident.

We would be ready enough to accept his method in a painter — say, especially, Picasso, whose early periods are classic or romantic just as Liszt's are, meaning that they are neither. The monumental women and attenuated clowns are sophisticated reconstructions that bear about the same resemblance to their originals as Liszt's *Penseroso* does to Michelangelo's statue, and they lead more and more explicitly to unorthodox visions, in Cubism and beyond. The parallel, though susceptible to strains, is fairly exact. Liszt too was essentially an explorer. He tried almost every form but opera, and having assayed it, marked out new possibilities, left it to others to develop. (I think this accounts for his insouciance about his failures, which didn't trouble him as much as his critics thought they should. Old branches died and fell from the tree; he forgot them — new ones would grow.) From composers in his day a steadier gaze was expected, a more consistent oeuvre: symphonies numbered from one to nine, each finer than the last. In Liszt we don't get them. Psychologically he is coherent, if we accept that he was on a perpetual voyage of discovery. Artistically, he presents a rocky road, since his discoveries weren't of equal importance.

At first glance, it is a paradox that Italy should have damped his ardent Romanticism. He went there a serious young ideologue, poor but honest, as befitted a disciple of Lamennais. Two years later he had not merely abandoned his ideals; as far as could be seen, the stigmata of the virtuoso were all over him. He was to the casual eye a fop and a show-off. Appearances were deceiving of course. His talents were what they always had been. It was the fact that Italy brought out a side of him that Paris had only glimpsed in the duel with Thalberg.

The trouble was the people. Buoyant as balloons, they soared above their griefs in happy decadence, showing no intellectual stamina. Their social structure was hopelessly corrupt, their art, which meant music, at its lowest ebb. The *Zeitgeist* didn't exist. Italian opera went its merry way, packing in a public that had never heard of the *grandeur sociale de l'art* and did not want to. Nobody read books and nobody fell in love: Werther and René had died in vain. So, anyway, thought the foreigner.

Marie to Pictet: The Italians want sweet sensations, not strong feelings, the melodies of Donizetti. . . . They know nothing of Beethoven but his name, of Schubert and Weber nothing at all. . . . Happy people! their sun is enough for them. . . .[11]

Pictet to Marie: Well, there you are, discontented too in Milan, the Italian capital of the arts. The chatter and noisy enthusiasm of the Italians seem as ridiculous to us, almost, as the Genevan impassivity. I'm not surprised, knowing you as I do; you have in you a *mésure* which applied to the things of this world will always make them appear dull and wretched to you. I predict it will be the same for Venice, Rome and Naples. . . .[12]

The failings were duly reported by the bachelor. "In no Italian town are there meetings of artists who could or would want to execute the symphonic works of the masters." Composers are on the same level with singers, if you please, and made to take the boos and cheers of the audience on stage: "One thinks of a waiter apologizing for breaking a pitcher rather than a proud victor coming to receive his laurels." Operas are concerts in costume, constantly interrupted with whistles and claps. Inevitably, there is the odious comparison: Italy is a circus, Germany the home of instrumental music, serious audiences, and — it is implied — the moral sense.

There was shock value in these reports, which Paris could hardly believe, though Berlioz had said the same and so had Mendelssohn. They still constituted news when printed over Liszt's signature. They were also true. But they did not really represent Liszt's ultimate judgment of Italy, which he dearly loved and easily forgave. He and Marie could never think alike about Italians, to him adorable, to her contemptible. Their notes are totally at variance: *She:* "The marquis . . . is a vain fool and *seccatura* of the first water. His daughter is frighteningly ugly and devoured with a disastrous passion for the piano." [13] *He:* "Rossini has just taken me to meet the Prince and Princess Hercolani, a charming young couple devoted to the *Gazette Musicale*. . . ." [14] She never made an Italian friend; he made dozens. She loathed Catholic Rome; he seems to have been at home there from the first. She laughed at Italian fashion; in the hands of Italian tailors he learned the art of dress and the delights of display. He wanted to order a carriage, to be driven by a Hungarian coachman in national costume, at a cost of 5,000 francs. "Crétin's tours have had a certain success in this country," he wrote Sand, "and with God's or the devil's help, he will little by little arrive at being completely polished, and no longer turn up soaked, grubby, badly groomed . . . at illustrious literary houses." [15] Marie agreed: "Crétin has become fantastically elegant . . . there is nothing good enough for him. Having expended so many words on his not wearing a hat with a hole in it . . . I see myself forced into harangues against luxury and *parure!*" [16] The Ingres drawing of a handsome young dandy, made in Rome in 1839, bears her out.

There is an Italian phrase for his behavior: *fare la figura,* roughly, put on a good show, with the implication that there may be little to back it up. In

Italy he picked up the habit of living beyond his means, throwing his money around in princely style. The Italians saw nothing wrong with this. It seemed natural to them as much else about him that in other countries, notably Germany and England, was thought lax or shocking.

He repaid their indulgence, up to a point, indulging them in turn. At one of his Milanese concerts the usual requests for themes on which he would improvise turned out to include "the railway," "the Cathedral," and "whether it is better to marry or remain a bachelor." Did the author of *De la situation des artistes* rise and leave the room? Not at all: ". . . I preferred to recall to the audience the words of a sage — whichever conclusion you may come to, whether to marry or remain single, you will always repent it." It was reprehensible, deplorable, but he couldn't even fault their behavior at the opera, where, said Stendhal, they "chattered rather more loudly than in the street." Stendhal forgave them on the ground that "the human soul needs four minutes of conversation . . . to refresh itself after a sublime duet, to be capable of taking pleasure in the air that will follow." [17] Liszt was lenient for the same reason: within their limitations, these were true lovers of music: "From the aristocrat to the least grocery boy," he. wrote, ". . . everybody takes sides for or against the prima donna. . . . The waiter who froths your chocolate tells you that Francilla Pixis sang the rondo in the *Cenerentola* very well; the man who shines your shoes isn't satisfied with the ornamentation of *Giuramento*." [18] Who could resist? "They have the look full of fire," he declared, "the enthusiastic disposition that makes artists!"

To Marie this seeming change of front meant a sellout. Her private notes are full of rage:

> Franz plays the Pacini piece and his waltz with great success: Paganini of the pianoforte, *il gran suonator di cimbalo,* etc., but really, never was success less flattering. The tour de force is all that strikes them, Donizetti's flattest melodies make them swoon, and all poetic work bores them profoundly.[19]

The papers, she says nastily, "continue to worship the *suonator* in the most grotesque way." A war of wills was shaping up that is reflected in the *Lettres d'un bachelier,* which praise and damn the Italian scene almost as if she and Liszt were writing alternate sentences.* The war is of course

---

* The reader should know that others see them differently. The *Lettres,* according to Vier, "united them more closely than the talisman of Tristan and Yseult. . . . Because in this association of genius with talent, the mastery of sound with the mastery of words . . . one must see the possibility, constantly offered to the Countess d'Agoult, of modeling, stylizing, and fashioning according to her dearest desires and most secret aspirations the face, spirit and heart of her lover . . ." (Vier: I, 296). That she was always trying to mould and teach Liszt, I would agree, and also that the letters played a part in the struggle. But as Tristan is about to flee Yseult, they hardly qualify as a "talisman." Rather obviously, they were one more bone of contention.

about something other than the state of music in Italy. A clue to its nature is an entry in their joint journal, dated August 1, 1838: "Rossini," he writes, "has injured and served the progress of art as Bonaparte injured and served the progress of societies. *He has perhaps too magnificently proved that art can do without conscience or truth.*" (Italics mine.) [20] A dark utterance from one on the brink of an international career.

Marie saw it coming. His ascendancy over Italian audiences fed his ambition at an alarming rate, and she was now in the position of lone critic, the unwelcome island in an ocean of praise. "I feel I lack the principle of life. . . . I'm not good for him; I throw sadness and discouragement over every day of his life," her diary said sadly. [21] Her desire was pathetic enough: "I wish I were a beautiful plant, a flower he loved, that his hand watered and cared for." A very feminine wish, seldom gratified. His, in its way was just as unreasonable. "Love me," he kept begging her, "and try above all to be a little pleased, a little gay, a little happy if that is possible." [22]

Chapter 21

THE BLOW FELL in Venice. They arrived at the end of March and Pictet's prophecy was promptly fulfilled. Venice was no better than Milan:

Marie's journal: I can't get accustomed to the Venetian water. I am getting thin and don't feel well. . . . A concert by candlelight at the Palazzo Mari; a fashionable audience. Franz plays *Les Puritains* and *L'Orgie*. Religious attention, amazement . . . While he plays *L'Orgie* a young girl of seventeen, Signorina Pallavicini, sits beside the piano. She looks first at his fingers, then at his face. . . . I imagined a whole dialogue between this young girl with a fresh complexion, ignorant of life, curious and disturbed at hearing the language of passion for the first time, and the musician, still young but pale and tired. . . . There happens to be a gardenia in my bouquet and its scent makes the Marquesa S. faint; her lover speaks to me about the Polish poet Mickiewicz. That night a bouquet on my bedroom table makes me feel ill; sometimes I think I am losing my mind, my brain is exhausted; I have wept too much. . . .[1]

In the midst of these *douleurs* Liszt found the one unanswerable reason for leaving her. News arrived of Danube floods, spreading devastation in Austria and Hungary. As she tells it, he entered her room rather brusquely one morning carrying a German newspaper. "It's horrible," he said. "I'd like to send all I possess. But all I have is my ten fingers and my name. What would you say if I were to fall unexpectedly on Vienna? The effect would be tremendous. The whole city would want to hear the little prodigy they knew as a child. They're enthusiastic and generous in Vienna. I'd make a fantastic sum. . . . This would take eight days. . . . What do you think?" [2]

She thought that "somebody else could help these poor people" and what about her — alone and ill? (Actually, she was not too ill to be sightseeing with a Venetian admirer, Count Emilio Malazonni, a replacement for Didier and Ronchaud called "Theodoro" in the memoirs.) She did not say so, knowing it was hopeless, and if anyone wondered about his sudden concern for a country he hadn't thought about for twenty years, he had the answer ready. An effusion in the *Gazette Musicale* of September 2, 1838, implied that he would have returned to Hungary long since but for her:

Oh, my wild and distant country, you unknown friends, my vast family! Your cries of pain recalled me to you. Moved to the depths by pity, I bowed my head, ashamed of having forgotten you for so long. . . . Why did harsh fate detain me? I was agitated by another cry of suffering, a weak voice but one all-powerful with me . . . a voice dear to me, the only one that never calls to me in vain. . . .*

The note struck here is false. One does not believe in *ma sauvage et loin-taine patrie*. Yet with Liszt it is never that simple. He was generous to the point of rashness and did give huge sums to the refugees. Some atavistic feeling for his country he probably had. But one knows, just the same, that he would have gone to Vienna no matter what. There was no resisting such an opportunity, which probably wasn't quite the bolt from the blue that Marie depicts. A letter to Princess Belgiojoso in 1839 says he had been thinking of a plunge for several years.

Treat this infantilism any way you like, it is no less true that I am obeying a sort of superstitious compulsion in throwing myself, as I am about to do . . . into an exterior life. It is more than time to think positively; reverie, passion and follies have had too large a place in my existence.[3]

To others, he wrote as of a fateful throw of dice that must be made: ". . . for me everything is the future [which] mustn't be indefinitely postponed. Within the next two or three years my game must be won or lost, so far as the piano is concerned. . . ."[4]

He left for Vienna April 7 and was away for the better part of two months. His timing was perfect. Vienna, already excited by a national disaster, was overwhelmed at the prodigal's return from the wicked, glamorous, republican circles that had claimed him since childhood. (He was accorded the prestige of a police investigation on account of his association with

---

* A baffling contribution to the problem of authorship. Marie did not believe in the least in his patriotic motives and would only have written such a thing under duress. On the other hand, if Liszt himself wrote it (and it certainly sounds like him), it was an insult since he had *not* heeded her weak voice.

Lamennais, Sand and others. The report was negative: "A vain and frivolous young man who affects the fantastic manners of the young Frenchmen of today." The d'Agoult connection however couldn't be overlooked at court, where he was pointedly not invited to play.) Great humanist, great lover, greatest pianist since Beethoven — it was a walkover. He was mobbed. His portrait and his autograph were hawked in the streets; the aristocracy fell over itself to entertain him. The concerts multiplied from two to six, then eight.

A modest man would have been hard put to it to convey the news to Marie in acceptable terms. He didn't try. His wonderful tale was poured out in letters swollen with newspaper clippings:

The post is leaving. Two lines only. Enormous success. Applause. Called back fifteen or eighteen times. Hall packed. Everyone astonished. Thalberg hardly exists for the Viennese. I am deeply moved by it all. I have never had anything like this success. You would have enjoyed it. . . . Without exaggeration no one since Paganini has had such a success. I am the man of the hour.[5]

His spirits at their highest pitch, he wanted her to join him and sent 200 florins to cover the journey: "I hunger and thirst to see you. How can I live without you. We'll go back to Italy together in three weeks or a month. But now I must show you my beautiful Danube, the forests . . ."

Marie says not a word of this letter or any like it. He wrote more and more rarely; the names of women appeared — one letter arrived with a "feminine seal," whatever that is, and she tore it up without reading it. (This is exquisitely Marie. No mortal woman has been known to tear up a letter with such suspicions in her mind; nor did Liszt, for obvious reasons, ever speak to her of women he was interested in unless she forced it out of him. The only woman he *did* mention on this occasion was Clara Wieck, Schumann's love, who had stayed over especially to hear him — and to Clara one did not make advances.) We recognize the approach of a lurid climax. "Theodoro," her Venetian beau, undertakes to write to Liszt, urging his immediate return: Marie is ill from "anxiety." The answer staggers them both. Liszt is grateful for Theodoro's care, but cannot leave Vienna. Why don't they both join him? Hearing this, Marie faints dead away. Reviving, she finds Theodoro at her feet: "Poor woman! Oh, if my life, my soul, my love could be anything to you. Parents, friends, fortune, career, all would be abandoned. . . ." After this, she lies "between life and death" for a week, then totters to her desk to write Liszt these lines:

You ask me to join you; it is two hundred leagues from here to Vienna. I can hardly get from my bed to my armchair. . . . You leave my wretched life to someone else's care. If I had died, you would, however, have had to come, or would you also have left to others the task of closing my eyes? [6] *

Her paranoia over the demands of his career reached its apogee with this episode. Further she could not go without throwing herself into the canal. But she did not give an inch in her conviction that "Franz had abandoned me from such petty motives. Not for a great work, or an act of devotion, or out of patriotism, it was for salon successes, gossip-column glory, invitations from princesses. . . ." [7] There was something in this, except that he hadn't abandoned her. He gave up a tempting extension of his tour because it would take too long — "And anyway, yes, I love you with all my strength. I belong only to you. Only you rule my whole being because only you know my life's secrets, my joys and my sorrows." [8]

He was back at the end of May. Marie sitting in Piazza San Marco receives a message that he is at the hotel. Rushing to their rooms, she flings herself in his arms: "Pray God I can love you again as I did." It wasn't quite the right note, and the situation hung fire for several days. Once again, they went through the unworthiness scene but this time he couldn't keep it up. He began to tell her about Vienna and it brought her down with a bump:

They had found a coat of arms for him (for him, a republican living with a great lady). He hoped I would be brave. Women had thrown themselves at his head; he was no longer ashamed of his faults. He saw them philosophically. He talked of necessities. . . . He was in the right against me; he was elegantly dressed; he talked only of princes; he was secretly pleased with his exploits.[9]

So she summons up her "womanhood, her *grande dame*'s pride" and utters the unutterable: She calls him a "Don Juan parvenu." After this, they get down to home truths. Vienna has shown him he can make a fortune in two years, enough to provide handsomely for the children. She meanwhile must go back to her old life, her own world. She has talent, she must use it, not subordinate herself to him, a position that has caused her nothing but suffering. "Don't play with me," he ended ominously, "because I will make you play too high." She should take on Theodoro: "He is what you need, a sad child, sweet, submissive, pure, patrician. . . ."

She saw she had gone too far and retreated, begging that they try again. Somehow, they patched it up, neither having accepted the other's position.

---

* This letter, not in the correspondence, is probably imaginary, though a surviving letter from Liszt does say, "I can't imagine what can have given you such pain in my letter to Emilio [that is, Theodoro]. It was proper and, I think, sincere." (Liszt-d'Agoult, I, 231.) Vier has his doubts about the incident. He notes that Liszt asked Marie to join him in the latter part of April, while her illness was in May. (Vier, I, 421, n. 226.)

The chapter closes with her passionate declaration that she had "never desired, wanted, asked but one thing; never suffered, never complained but of one thing; was never happy but from one cause . . . and he pretends not to understand! He did once. . . . When he confessed his first infidelity to me, he said: 'I could do it again, as I could break my head against a wall; in either case, you would see me no more.' "

Beneath this passage in their joint journal is Liszt's dry comment:

You remember my words, but those you said to me in various circumstances seem to have left no traces in your mind. For my part, I haven't forgotten them, though I have tried. When you can recollect them, they will explain many things you seem to find incomprehensible.[10]

That "Don Juan parvenu" was like a brand. He never forgave it.

Venice was now intolerable. No one, in those days before sea-bathing, thought of spending the summer months there. They moved to Genoa, where Liszt rented a magnificent villa, a carriage, horses; he was still spending recklessly because, it turned out, he was more than ever confident of earning large sums in the future. Opening the mail one day, Marie found a detailed outline for a German tour. He owned up to the negotiation, adding that since she couldn't possibly accompany him, she had best, as he had said earlier, return to Paris. What happened next can be judged from Daniel Liszt's birthdate the following May. He was the last of the unwanted children conceived in Marie's desperation. The German tour was cancelled and in July Marie was cooing fatuously to George:

The Fellows are more united than ever. . . . What can we do? We have the bad taste to find ourselves always more charming, incomparable, and when we try to separate to see the effect it would have on us, we turn gloomy. I begin to think we are condemned to love each other forever.[11]

She was lying. Liszt's state of mind had never been blacker. He couldn't work; he smoked too much and was living on coffee. When she tried to joke him out of the caffeine addiction, saying he must have picked it up in Venice, he turned on her: "What difference does it make? I'm killing myself. . . ," and he advised her not to speak of Venice. He wrote wildly to Ronchaud, "Look, if I ever fall in the water, let me sink to the bottom without trying to save me," [12] and talked of going to Constantinople and interesting the Sultan in "humanitarian music" — a letter to Nourrit treated this fantastic prospect with some seriousness.

He always returned to the piano, and his obsession now has the sound of a hero's task that must be accomplished before he can grasp the prize:

I know that at present I oughtn't to live in any one milieu because I am superior to any I could live in. I'm an intermediate being. I long to finish with the piano, I would then compose something beautiful that nobody could play, that I wouldn't play myself. Then would come somebody who would be to me what I have been to Weber, who would illumine me. . . .[13]

Again:

My place will be between Weber and Beethoven, or rather between Hummel and Onslow. I am perhaps a genius *manqué*, only time will show. I only know I am not a mediocrity. My mission will be to have introduced poetry into piano music with some brilliance. What I attach most importance to is my harmonics; that will be my serious work; I will sacrifice everything to it. When I've finished my tour as pianist, I will play only for my own public. I will shape and elevate it. Then in four or five years perhaps I'll try an opera.[14]

Liszt was the only major composer to have given years of his life to performance, and it has been generally agreed that this was his tragedy. There were times when he thought so too. These reflections show that he felt the decision to be inevitable, and we ought to remember that his contemporaries would have agreed with him, and not just because they thought he played better than he composed: simply, it would have been death to hide such a gift. Virtuosity was not itself a disgrace. Schumann had passionately desired to be a great pianist until he crippled his hand in the attempt; it was mostly his fragile health that deterred Chopin from a dazzling career. Only Marie held steadily to the conviction that Liszt was deserting a higher calling: "I see him accepting an inferior existence, abasing his ambitions. I suffer but I have nothing to say . . . and I sense . . . that if I can't associate myself with his plans I ought not to fight them." [15] She did fight them and later acknowledged that in "the cruel struggle we allowed to rise between us, I was often wrong; wrong above all in not having wanted or known how to suffer for your sake; the expression of my pain was often acid and vindictive." [16]

The quarrels were demoralizing to Liszt, whose entries in their notebook grow more and more distraught:

Why despair? Yet why hope? Why the why? The forces that dominate us obey laws we haven't determined. . . . In the torment of my anguished hours, when everything throbs, rips, is torn up in my heart, one thought, one remorse lingers — I ought to have made her happy! I could have! But can I still??? [17]

In reply she quotes Goethe: *Vermag die Liebe alles zu dulden, so vermag sie noch viel mehr Alles ersetzen.* (If love can endure everything, so much more can it replace everything.) Yet she returned a ring he had given her, a gesture that had an unexpected effect on him:

> I don't know why, but putting this ring back on my finger I suddenly felt cured of a long illness, and I allowed myself to be carried away by the confidence of my first youth, when we met. . . . Sometimes in the morning I voluntarily forget to put the ring on. I feel a curious pleasure in leaving to chance this sad and terrible sign of our union. Twenty times during the day I think of putting it on, and do nothing. . . .[18]

Meanwhile they were moving slowly down the peninsula and in the autumn found themselves in Florence. Here they made, as usual, a sensation. Princess Mathilde considered their arrival one of the events of the season:

> I've heard the famous Liszt, the celebrated pianist. He is a charming young man and he bears an astonishing resemblance to the Emperor [Napoleon] when he came to Italy in '96. He has given several concerts. . . . I'm delighted and enchanted with him. He is a man of vast genius and unexampled modesty; the other day he said to me quite seriously: "I promise you that I never sit down to the piano unless I'm told to, because I feel I must be very boring." But can I give you a greater idea of his talent than by telling you the Florentines have agreed to pay 15 pauls to hear him? Mme. Mouravieff said to me . . . "If I were young and pretty I'd go mad about him." There is a beautiful woman with him, she's left her husband and 5 children, she is the Countess d'Agoult, I met her at Bartolini's where she is having her bust done like I am and I found her very pleasant. She is tall and very thin, she looks like the figure of Hunger, but her face is very interesting and above all very noble; of course her conduct is inexcusable and yet when you see her you can't prevent yourself from being drawn to her. . . . She has done very wrong, there's no doubt of that, but at least she has been carried away by genius, not by self-interest; and that makes her guilty but not contemptible.[19]

It was bad enough to be censured by women like Mathilde, who hadn't a moral bone in her body but was cautious and conventional. The agony gnawing at Marie was that it had all been in vain, that as she said later, "The romance of my life was finished at thirty-two." (In reality, thirty-four.) Yet slowly she was, or pretended she was, becoming reconciled. She hit on a novel excuse for his future plans — or was it his? She began to tell people that it was for the children's sake he must relinquish their quiet life together: "It will take all we have of strength and reason to tear ourselves from the deep and serious happiness we find in each other. But every joy pays its tribute in sorrow . . . and the joy our children give us must be bought, for Franz, in the need to assure their independence." [20]

This was reasonable if rather sudden. He did worry about the support

of his children. The bit about the joy was humbug. In Florence, they had
to cope, for the first time, with little Blandine. (Cosima was left in Genoa.)
Her Swiss guardians had been worried about her — there is an unexplained
reference to a "crisis of separation" that upset her — and evidently thought
it best she be returned to her parents. Here is a tableau of how Marie handles her (she is three years old):

> I establish her on the cushions between her father and me and say absolutely
> nothing. She cries quietly for an hour and then goes to sleep. The rest of the day
> she is extremely serious and answers with a yes or no, but seems aware of feeling
> better and convinced of the uselessness of all resistance to me.[21]

She detected signs of aristocracy in the child's *hauteur* and noted with
pleasure that she paid no attention to her father's music — "She won't be a
musician, so much the better." He on the contrary thought "this personality
that won't give in to outside influence" came from him, and (as he told
Schumann) that she loved music.

In the interminable wrangles neither Blandine nor Cosima nor the unborn
son entered their calculations:

> Conversation with Franz about my winter in Paris. I must set myself up . . .
> form myself an entourage of distinguished people; and for that not worry about
> expense, dinners, presents. Go everywhere one should go; and only there: read-
> ings, lectures, first nights, receptions at the Academy. . . .[22]

What a cad! We are meant to feel this and would feel it if his estimate
of her needs hadn't been so accurate. He knew her better than she knew herself. (Nor, says Vier, was this the ultimatum she pretended. She had other
alternatives and considered them with some satisfaction. Unpublished portions of her memoirs indicate that d'Agoult was ready to take her back.)
She wasn't an adventuress by temperament and never would be, though one
can sympathize with the humiliation she felt at the prospect of that return.
To whom would it not seem that she had been sent back like an unwanted
package from its destination? In her obsession with this problem she never
thought of the children except as they constituted a further embarrassment.
Nor did he, though he was supposed to be sacrificing the best years of his
life to their welfare.

Chapter 22

FROM THE MOMENT she knew she would be returning to France, it was mandatory that Marie hang on to her one remaining female friendship there. George's good offices would have been invaluable to her reestablishment. Accordingly she proceeded to destroy whatever was left of Sand's tolerance and with it Liszt's most valued links with Paris. This gives to a classically feminine bust-up an importance it would not otherwise have.

For months after Nohant Marie tried to be cautious; but no matter how cordially her letters started out, claw-marks appeared. Overdone boasts of her blissful life with Liszt were mingled with gibes at Sand's various men and this sort of thing, apropos her social life in Paris:

I think you'll end by finding all sorts of people amusing. If one could retire with the elect on a mountain – good, but since the mountain is a molehill and the elect are never two together . . . it's better to stick to the plain and amuse oneself with grotesque types.[1]

George left an increasing number of these communications unanswered. Then came the affair with Chopin. Marie was beside herself, from no cause she could decently explain except that neither George nor Chopin chose to confide in their old friends. ("Probably," she told Pictet, "George was afraid neither Franz nor I would take the thing seriously.") The real source of her fury was of course that this story would eclipse the now rather tarnished one of herself and Liszt. "Decidedly, I pride myself on having made pianists the fashion," she wrote, still to Pictet. "George carries off Chopin, the

Princess Belgiojoso monopolizes Döhler. Agree that Marie has the best of it. It is true that these ladies were rather of my opinion, still . . ." [2]

Her informant was one Carlotta Marliani (formerly identified as an Italian or a Spaniard, now found to have been born, unglamorously, in Rouen — she was married to the Spanish consul), and she is the villainess of the piece. Neither wise nor witty, she had somehow endeared herself to Sand and through her come to be intimate with all the Hôtel de France set — which must be why Marie kept up a correspondence with her. Carlotta was a mine of information and it was she who posted the news (in October 1838) that George, the children, and Chopin were off to Majorca.

Marie to Carlotta Marliani: This trip to the Balearics amuses me. I'm sorry it didn't happen a year earlier, when G. was having herself bled. I always said: *In your place I'd rather have Chopin.* How many stabs of the lancet would have been spared her! Then she wouldn't have written the *Lettres à Marcie,* then she wouldn't have taken Bocage, and some good people think that would have been all the better. Will the Balearic establishment last long? Knowing them both as I do, they'll be at daggers drawn after a month. . . . Their temperaments are *antipodean,* but never mind, it's all too pretty for words, and you wouldn't believe how I rejoice for them both. What about Mallefille? How does he take it? . . . Was George perhaps right when she used to tell me . . . how stupid and absurd he was? . . . You do well to love Chopin's talent; it's the beautiful expression of an exquisite nature. He is the only pianist I can listen to not only without being bored, but with a deep sense of composure. . . . Really, I'm sorry not to be able to gossip about it all with you. I assure you it couldn't be funnier. . . . [3]

Marliani did the foreseeable. She wrote George in Majorca, warning her that Marie was a false friend and that it was best to have nothing more to do with her — advice that George was very ready to take. She asked for no explanations; she probably needed none, though she was eventually shown Marie's letter. This was on Lamennais's recommendation, for *he* now entered the fray and blinded by his antagonism to Marie did what he could to exacerbate the situation, not caring how it might injure Liszt. "I can assure you," he wrote George, "that . . . Mme M said nothing too much to you. . . . I had no idea of such corruption, of such a soul in fact, if soul there is, and this revelation of human nature . . . has profoundly saddened me." [4] George erased *les Fellows* from her life.

Incredibly, Marie displayed no uneasiness and less contrition. Carlotta's answer to her sarcasms — "I love George as she should be loved. . . . I hope . . . she arrives at the truth she certainly seeks" — elicited a stupefying lecture:

On what, if you please my pretty Consuless, from your height of a priori wisdom, do you base your judgment that I am incapable of loving and understanding my friends, and that apropos the easiest person in the world to understand, our poor Piffoël? Why do you want to take seriously something she couldn't take seriously herself, unless in these brief moments when the poetic genius seizes her and makes her mistake flints for diamonds and frogs for swans. I don't ask you to tell me anything at all about her, except if she is alive or dead. When I lived with her, I did all I could *not to know* certain details of her life. . . . The only serious thing for me, and I would say this to her face, is the falling-off of her talent. . . . It's obvious that the period of feeling (magnificently revealed in *Lélia* and the *Lettres d'un voyageur*) is ended. But it isn't B[ocage] or M[allefille] or Chopin who can help her. . . . She has now reached a point where she sees love as a purely physical need.[5]

So little did it occur to Marie that this too would make its way to George (or, seemingly, offend her if it did) that she attacked her directly. Learning from the newspapers in the spring of 1839 that George and Chopin would be briefly in Genoa, she wrote quite in the old spirit of Chamonix and suggested that they all spend the summer together, and when this dropped into a well of silence, concluded that there must be a conspiracy afoot. On August 20, she wrote again:

You will perhaps be astonished at my persistence in writing you, since your absolute silence of about eighteen months, the silence you seem to have *imposed* on Carlotta . . . and above all your *non-response* to my last letter, in which I begged you to come and spend the summer with us, say well enough that our relations have become inconvenient. . . . I have searched my conscience and can find *no shadow of guilt* on my side. Franz, too, is wondering how it is that your close connection with a man whom he feels he has a right to call his friend, should have the immediate result of severing all communication between us? . . . But I still refuse to accept such explanations as I might have found for this odd behavior. Frequent warnings, and the discouraging experience of so many broken relations in your past life seem to me . . . insufficient ground for such sad conclusions . . . and I still hope, I *sincerely desire* an explanation worthy of you. . . .[6]

This piece of effrontery (which I quote at length because it says more about Marie than almost any other document we have) was sent in Carlotta's care. She refused to forward it, saying it would have the opposite effect from that intended. Marie mailed it again, this time direct. It took George's breath away, and her first impulse was not to answer it. The objection, as she told Carlotta, was that Marie would wrongly blame Chopin for the rupture:

You saw how she accused him, the friend of Liszt (she says) of having detached me from her and him. . . . But the truth is . . . I don't even know how far, at the bottom of his heart, Chopin's friendship for Liszt goes. You know the excessive reserve of the former, his scrupulous delicacy. I only know that out of his friendship and devotion to me he would agree to carry the burden of any accusation to spare me painful explanations. His pride, too, would keep him from going ahead with an explanation on his own account . . . [and so] it is possible . . . that he would stay accused of Liszt's resentment and Madame d'Agoult's aversion. As I now know her, she would revive the upsets and rancors he doesn't need, so nervous, discreet and exquisite . . . as he is in everything. So I owe an answer to Madame d'Agoult, written or verbal. . . .[7]

When this was being written, Marie was in the midst of her farewell to Liszt and to Italy and too miserable to care what George or anyone else thought of her. Back in Paris she recovered her nerve, and demanded that Carlotta return the disastrous letters. Carlotta replied that she had given them to George — "a betrayal pure and simple," wrote Marie to Liszt.

She continued to press for an explanation and earlier biographers have always supposed she got it in a famous letter it now appears that George may not have mailed.[*] I give the gist of it: it deserves a high place in the annals of Amazonian warfare.

. . . I don't understand your appeal to our past. You know I threw myself into your . . . friendship with enthusiastic abandon. Infatuation is one of the things you laugh at in me, and not very charitably, at the moment when you are destroying what I had of it for you. You understand friendship differently. . . . You bring to it not the least illusion, the least indulgence. It follows that you should also bring to it an irreproachable loyalty and judge people as severely to their faces as you do behind their backs. One gets used to that . . . one can learn from it. . . . But you have only soft words, tender caresses, even gushingly sympathetic tears for those you love . . . [until] you talk, and above all, write about them. . . . [Then] you tear them down, slander them even, with charming grace. . . . It's a rude awakening for people who are treated this way, and they ought to be allowed to be a little pensive, silent and upset for a bit. [But] what you do then is outrageous. . . . You reproach them, with those reproaches that induce pride and pleasure in those who believe themselves loved but pain and pity in those who know they are hated. . . . Yes, hated, my poor Marie. Don't try to fool yourself. You hate me mortally. And as it is impossible that this could have happened with no motive and within a year, I can only explain you by recognizing that you have always hated me. Why? . . . I can't even guess. There are instinctive antipathies. . . . You have admitted to me often that you felt a certain animosity toward me before we met.

Devoted to Liszt as you are and with reason, and seeing that his friendship with

* The milder version, favored by the Lubin editors, simply says that, since Marie insists, George will meet her: "You will see that I have no resentment toward you. But I must tell you you have put one more pain in my life, and that it was I who received the wound for which you pity yourself." (Sand, *Correspondance*, IV, 804.) Marie quoted this more or less verbatim to Liszt, which is why she probably did not receive the other, longer one.

me was injured by your sarcasms, you wanted to give him . . . proof of your affection, and you made an immense effort to control yourself. You persuaded him that you loved me and perhaps persuaded yourself. Possibly too you were sometimes conquered by my friendliness. . . .

Now you're angry with me. . . . But calm yourself, Marie. I don't reproach you. You did what you could to substitute your heart for your intelligence as far as I was concerned. But intelligence won out. Beware of having too much, my poor friend. Too much kindness, as I have often found, leads . . . to finding oneself surrounded by the wrong people; an excess of insight leads to isolation and solitude. . . .

Here, then, is what is on my mind. Nobody turned me against you . . . and as long as I hadn't your handwriting before me, I abstained from judging your letters. . . .

Relax about all this, my poor Marie, forget me like a nightmare you had and are rid of at last. . . . Don't trouble yourself further with inventing strange stories to explain our mutual coldness to the people around you. I will no longer receive Liszt when he is here, in order not to give the least handle to the singular tale that places him between us like a *disputed* object. You know better than anyone that I never had a *single thought* of the kind. . . . (It's an idea that occurred only to Balzac.) It would therefore be unworthy of you to be afraid of it, or to say so, and still more, perhaps, to let it be said. I accept . . . all your mockery, but there are insinuations I will strongly resist.

Pull yourself together, Marie. This sad business is unworthy of you. I know you well. I know that in your spirit there is a need for grandeur — with which a little feminine uneasiness is perpetually at war. You aspire to chivalrous male conduct, but you can't give up being a beautiful and clever woman who gets the better of the rest of us. That is why you have no trouble praising me as a good fellow, while you can't find venom enough to smear my feminine self. In the end, you have two kinds of pride. Try to see that the latter wins out. You can, because God has richly endowed you and you will have to account to Him for the beauty, intelligence and seduction He has given you. This is the first and last sermon you will get from me. Please forgive me for it, as I forgive you the homilies you have preached to me without allowing me to hear them. . . .[8]

A false truce was declared but such breaches are never healed and Marie was soon up to her old tricks, defaming Sand, complaining of Chopin's inattention when she was ill. Within a few months a Siberian coldness set in that was broken only once — by Marie, some ten years later. It had no other result than an amplifying exchange of letters. Marie confessed the truth, that she *had* suspected George of double-dealing with Liszt: "Certain serious and clearly defined charges — to which public opinion and the attitude of *my* friends as well as some of yours, gave considerable weight — were the cause of those first outbursts of temper in Italy." [9] George too was conciliatory, but she did not apologize for her own base action, the dictation of *Béatrix* to Balzac. She was also bitchy enough to tell Marie what she knew would hurt her worst.

Liszt and Marie's final break-up took place in 1844 and after it he made several efforts to reopen his personal relations with Sand. She snubbed him relentlessly, leaving his letters from foreign parts unanswered or barely acknowledged. This could be interpreted as keeping her promise to Marie not to receive him; it could also mean that she took a certain pleasure in letting him sweat out the consequences of having preferred Marie to herself. Probably there was a little of both. There was no real necessity to inform Marie, and in these terms, of his efforts to see her:

From spite, I think, against you, he affected to *wish to seem* intimate with me as in the past. Did you not know that I refused these pretenses . . . that . . . I hardly saw your old friend from the moment when he ceased to belong to you, and that when I admitted to him that I no longer liked you, I made him understand that I would not make common cause with him against you? [10]

Since the row was almost exclusively about Liszt (not entirely, as the references to Chopin show), one asks how much did he know about Marie's actions? Surely he never saw the offending letters or he wouldn't have been surprised at George's silence — surprise he expressed on several occasions, though never to her directly. He left the correspondence in Marie's hands, which argues a kind of lethargy if not indifference. (And I would guess that it was just this failure to intervene, to discipline Marie, that put the icing on George's decision to see him no more.) This was perhaps the best measure of his state of mind in 1839. With his horizon suddenly become infinite, what did it matter if the woman he was going to leave quarrelled with another he was unlikely to see much of in future whatever happened? He was to see his mistake. "Forgive me," he wrote George in 1845, "for getting older and arriving at that point where noble memories are magnified in proportion as the meannesses of everyday life assume their true level. Though you might find me more *crétin* even than in the past, it is impossible for me not to put the highest value on your friendship. . . ." [11] It was too late. She did not answer.

Daniel Liszt was born in Rome in May 1839, an event shrouded in gloom and muteness. Neither parent had a word to say about him. Four months in Rome had done nothing to change Liszt's decision. On the contrary: "I feel a new era beginning for him," wrote Marie bitterly. "He is conscious of himself, of his future, he knows men and the world . . . He is stronger than strength itself." In the circumstances, Daniel's birth was the last straw. Her pregnancy, though it had kept Liszt in Italy for an extra year, had done little beyond damaging her looks. Henri Lehmann's portraits of them at this period are a cruel contrast. She is a ghost, gaunt and hollow-eyed and years older than Liszt, who gazes from his canvas with the proud and dreamy eye of the conqueror. (She recovered her beauty, as can be seen in the later Ingres drawing of her with her daughter Claire; but not immediately.)

There were one or two compensations. They were the center of attention as they always were, and Lehmann was enamored of her. Sainte-Beuve turned up, and was prepared to drop his aversion to humanitarian art, of which anyway there were few signs. He made himself delightful. "Went with Liszt and Madame d'Agoult to Tivoli and Hadrian's villa; great impression of the evening and the setting sun in those tall cypresses, near the rosy ruins; describe it . . . to L[iszt] in a big developed piece that will be my Poussin landscape," [12] says his journal for June 11 — which piece became a rather poor poem, dedicated to Liszt: *Vers la fin d'un beau jour, par vous-même embelli,/ Ami, nous descendions du divin Tivoli,"* etc. He later told Marie that he had tried to indicate the presence of a musical theme. He didn't succeed but Liszt may be said to have done it for him, some forty years later. This is the neighborhood of the third and last *Année de pèlerinage* and the wonderful pieces titled after the waters and cypresses of the Villa d'Este.

Liszt I think must always have been happy in Rome, the beloved city of his middle and old age, happy even in those miserable spring months of 1839. Bad as they were, they didn't poison the place for him, as later Paris was poisoned merely by Marie's inhabiting it. For her Rome was agony and so was the ravishing Villa Massimiliana near Lucca, where they spent July and August. Adorned with arcades and terraces, it was one of the loveliest of the many lovely places they lived in; to her it was hell.

My faculties are exhausted. I suffer horribly: I feel I can't live like this, that I must die soon or sink into imbecility and then what despair for him! His life would be shattered, his artistic future lost, his genius extinguished. . . . How I regret, at those moments when I see things clearly (and they are almost incessant) the blind and egotistical rapture that drove me to attach myself to him! [13]

In October he accompanied her to Livorno, gave her a bouquet, and left her in the midst of a violent storm. She had with her the two little girls. (Daniel was left at Palestrina with a nurse and the faithful Lehmann to keep an eye on him.) On October 19, she embarked with them for France, praying that the sea would swallow her. From Genoa where the ship touched, she sent him a moving farewell:

How to leave the soil of beloved Italy without a last adieu? How to watch these two, full, beautiful years detach themselves from my life without a regret? Oh my dear Franz! Let me tell you again . . . you have created a deep and unalterable emotion, one that will survive all the rest . . . a limitless gratitude. Be a thousand times blessed. . . . At the moment when I embarked at Livorno, the sun set in floods of gold and the melancholy moon rose among pale clouds; little by little she freed herself and lighted our crossing with a lovely light. I accepted this as a symbol of our beautiful, fleeing past, and of our future that begins so sadly but will be calm and pure.[14]

Love doesn't end like that, and it didn't for them. The fire, repeatedly stamped out, blazed up again at intervals for another four years and for poor Marie was never really extinguished — or for him either since the hatred he came to have for her can only be distilled from love. Her departure did not leave him untouched. He felt, and for many years, said, that she was the most important thing in his life. To Livorno he wrote as one distraught:

Good-bye, good-bye again. Don't ask me to tell you anything about anything whatever today. I only know that you were here, and now are not. Good-bye then, and let me always be yours and only yours. . . . To you, my love, my strength and my *vertu*. Good-bye, darling Marie. Think sometimes of how much I love you, and let that thought be sweet to you.[15]

PART FOUR

Annals of Furore
(1839-1848)

Chapter 23

THE *Glanzperiode* began with Liszt's return to Vienna in November 1839 and ended one September evening in 1847 at Elisabetgrad in southern Russia, when without announcements or fanfare he terminated his virtuoso career. The effect of his abrupt retirement at the age of thirty-six, at the height of his fame, was what he undoubtedly intended it to be. Far from plunging him into oblivion it fixed forever the Liszt legend in the public mind. His terrible ghost stalked the concert halls for another fifty years, impossible to ignore and dangerous to emulate — for who could say whether he had done more to ennoble or to debase the art of the piano, that, to paraphrase him on Rossini, he had not too magnificently proved it could do without conscience or truth?

Vienna could hardly wait to hear him again. "I will work like a madman . . . to keep up with this wave of enthusiasm, of which a good part, anyway, has to do with my personality. For the first time in my life, I find myself on real terms with a public." [1] So he told Marie and it was natural that it should be so. Vienna was the place to begin. It had a piano tradition that neither the French nor the Italians could boast, and in Beethoven the only pianist who could have prepared the way for Liszt. He had demolished the eighteenth-century style as early as 1790 and, a premature Romantic, was the first modern virtuoso. From him the Viennese had learned what that future of the piano would be; but he had no immediate successors. (Thalberg, for example, though Austrian, did not qualify.) In Liszt it was instantly recognized that one had been found.

"As a pianist I was always lucky," Liszt said once, and there did seem to be something in his stars. The *Zeitgeist* was on his side. The story is told that when he proposed to play the Weber *Conzertstück* in London somebody mentioned by way of discouragement that Moscheles had performed the same work earlier in the season. *"C'est une autre chose,"* said Liszt, meaning no disrespect to a fine executant. It was another thing, and not a question of technique alone, fingers that moved faster than other men's, or even of a memory that photographed a score at sight and kept it on file for a lifetime. These, though uncommon, are physical endowments. Friedheim says that in sheer technique he was surpassed by several later pianists; but he agrees with Anton Rubinstein's dictum: "In comparison with Liszt, the rest of us are children."

Friedheim believed that Liszt had mediumistic powers, and the ravings of otherwise rational people make one think he was right. A young Russian (Stassov) says, "We were like men in love, men obsessed. We had never heard anything like it before, never been confronted by such passionate, demonic genius." [2] More impressive is the cooler Kirchner's remark to Wagner after Liszt had played Beethoven's B-flat Major Sonata: "Now we can speak of having experienced the impossible, because it is impossible to believe what we have just heard."

These are differing ways to express what Berlioz found the best phrase for: Liszt's *sensibilité divinatoire*, which is akin to Delacroix's association of art with prophecy. It must have been this quality that gave so many people the sensation that he wasn't so much playing, in the ordinary meaning of the word, as projecting a mysterious utterance.

Siloti writes:

A pianist myself, I am yet unable to show how he played. . . . I cannot say he had a "big" tone; it was rather that when he played there was *no sound of the instrument*. [My italics.] He sat at the very piano which we young fellows used to break with our playing, an entirely unreliable instrument; but he could produce from it . . . music such as no one could form any idea of without hearing it.[3]

Amy Fay puts it even more strongly:

It does not seem as if it were music you were listening to, but as if he had called up a real living *form*, and you saw it breathing before your face and eyes. It gives me almost a ghostly feeling to hear him, and it seems as if the air were peopled with spirits.[4]

Heine is the most succinct of all: "The piano vanishes and — music appears."

The obverse was the tinkering with texts that Mendelssohn among others complained of — arbitrarily enough: the custom was universal. Mendelssohn himself was no stickler for accuracy and in his famous 1829 revival of Bach chopped and "modernized" the *St. Matthew Passion* at will. Not until much later was it deemed necessary to render scores as written, partly as a result of crusading efforts by Berlioz — and, surprisingly, Liszt. But that was instrumental music. The piano was different. When Liszt deplored the liberties taken with a Beethoven symphony, he somehow exempted himself. At the piano, it was allowable to be carried away by inspiration, to play, as it were, like one possessed.

It was repeatedly noticed that he played best when first confronted with a piece, and that after that he began to transpose simple passages into octaves and thirds, trills into sixths and to add phrases of his own until, in Borodin's words, what emerged "was not the same piece but an improvisation on it." Hiller, who objected to this inability to let well enough alone, offered an interesting explanation for it. He said that most compositions didn't, after the first try, give Liszt "enough to do," which sounds like a preposterous claim until we read Grieg's experience. Shown a Grieg violin sonata he had never seen before, Liszt sat down and played it through, "root and branch, violin and piano, nay more, for he played more fully and broadly. The violin part got its due right in the middle of the piano part. He was literally all over the piano at once, without missing a note, and how he played! With grandeur, beauty, genius, unique comprehension . . ." [5]

Such a gift, flourishing in a laxly interpretive age, must often have led him astray. It won't altogether dismiss the severity of the judgments passed on him by so many of his fellow musicians, especially in Germany, where Lisztomania properly began. Lisztomania was a complex phenomenon that Herzen attributed to German women's "idolatrous worship of geniuses and of great men," a religion proceeding from Weimar in the days of Wieland, Schiller and Goethe:

But since men of genius are rare and Heine lived in Paris, and Humboldt was too old and too much of a realist, they flung themselves, with a sort of hungry despair, on good musicians and passable painters. The image of Franz Liszt passed like an electric spark through the hearts of all the women of Germany, branding on them his high forehead and long hair. . . . [6]

Heine saw that it had a connection with politics: "This Lisztomania, I explained to myself, was a sign of the lack of political liberty beyond the Rhine," though his next sentence allows that it was just as effective in Paris, where Liszt produced "a delirium unparalleled in the annals of furore!" [7] But Heine was right about Germany and so was Herzen. Revolutionary students and women formed a large part of Liszt's constituency in central Europe. Unfortunately, his musical reputation was not in their hands and those whose business it was took a different view. The serious musical community never got over the unfavorable impression he made on it from 1840 to about 1844.

Germany in 1840 had experienced neither a social nor a cultural revolution. Outmoded as an antique engine, its musical establishment chugged along, fuelled by royal monies and staffed by intendants, *Kapellmeisters,* etc., who were graded and paid like civil servants, which they were. Audiences in many places were still subject to the caste system. As late as 1848 in enlightened Weimar, commoners sat on the left, nobles on the right in the royal theatre. The result was a degree of middle-class probity unmatched in any other artistic community. The typical German musician, and that includes Schumann, avoided scandal, private or public — one reason why Wagner, who courted scandal, earned a disproportionately stiff sentence for his part in the Dresden uprising.

Mendelssohn spoke for these good people when he denounced "Liszt's way in everything — a perpetual fluctuation between scandal and apotheosis. . . ." [8] Almost more damning was Schumann's verdict: "a French man of the world." The very word *French* was anathema, and has continued to be so to Liszt's German-oriented critics — beginning with Newman, who tells us that Liszt's "early Romanticism was of the French, not the German variety, a fact that made him alien to the ordinary German mind of the nineteenth century." And if you want to know how to interpret that, try the scholarly Arnold Schering:

> Liszt certainly aimed at the highest idealism and ardently strove to convert the ethical problems of his matter into the general-human. [This is Newman's translation, not mine.] But in few instances, apart from two symphonies, did he succeed in this. While in his idealism he was as German as any of the Weimar great ones, in his emotions he was never able . . . to shake himself quite free from French romanticism. . . . This is the reason why, of all these ethically so high-toned works, so few evoked a general response. The antipathy of the Brahms-Joachim group certainly did not spring from a lack of perception of the artistic quality of Liszt's compositions, but came from the impossibility of understanding their "exalted" nature from the standpoint of the Germanic soul.[9]

Stuff like this was not confined to Germans. It descends to Anglo-Saxons through Coleridge, Arnold and Carlyle, whose reverence for German "ethics" was only equalled by their certainty that the French did not know the meaning of the word. In this reckoning, which ignored the weight of contrary evidence from Pascal to Flaubert, the French were fundamentally frivolous, their national character an unsavory blend of rationalism and sensuality. (Carlyle on the cultivated Madame de Pompadour: "High rouged, unfortunate female of whom it is not proper to speak without necessity.") This shallow-minded race bowed and scraped its way through history right up to the revolution, which revealed a more sinister aspect: the French were also king-killers and anarchists.

In contrast was Germany, steeped in mystically perceived truths, devoted to *Kultur* and *Bildung*. A nation not founded on these qualities was "more fitly to be called a varnished than a polished people," said Coleridge, pointedly. And *Kultur* and *Bildung* (a kind of transcendental self-improvement) were in fact ennobling ideals in the old disunited Germany — half a century or more behind France and England economically and politically. "We Germans are of yesterday," said Goethe, not with pride. But to too many of his countrymen their backwardness was evidence of primitive virtues and racial superiority. Thus Herder's muddled attempt to equate the original noble savage with a Hunnish tribesman and Schiller's belief that the "world-spirit" had selected the German race to "work, during the conflict of time, at the eternal structure of human culture." Inoffensive in the eighteenth century, these and other determinations that Germans were ordained instructors paved the way for a cruder racism that allowed an otherwise respectable scholar like Wilhelm von Humboldt to announce that Germans were "destined to be the purest mirror of human potentialities."

Liszt ran headlong into these prejudices, which are responsible to this day for the common opinion that he was flashy and a fraud if not an outright charlatan.

Schumann to Clara: How extraordinarily he plays, boldly and wildly, and then again tenderly and ethereally! I have heard all this. But Clärchen, this world — his world I mean — is no longer mine. Art, as you practice it, and as I do when I compose at the piano, this tender intimacy I would not give for all his splendor — and indeed there is too much tinsel about it.[10]

Here in all its willfulness was the German position: innocence opposed to worldliness, sentiment to passion, in a way that recalls the national fondness for cuckoo clocks and chair-backs shaped like hearts. Schumann does not say why tender intimacy is superior to splendor — it just is.

Schumann made a special trip to Leipzig to meet Liszt in 1840. They had corresponded for several years, exchanged scores, and each had written a laudatory article on the other. With a fund of mutual admiration to draw on, it appeared their destiny to be friends. Schumann — like Chopin — said that to hear Liszt play him was the great artistic experience of his lifetime. But a veil was between them. Schumann seems to have suffered from delusions even then. He sat for hours in Liszt's hotel rooms, sunk in silence he broke once to say, "There now! We've been talking again with open hearts." Liszt thought Schumann "excessively reserved," adding in his ego-centric way that he imagined Schumann would be "much attached to me."

Schumann clearly found Liszt in the flesh an unsettling experience; he might not have turned into an open enemy if it hadn't been for Clara. A distinguished musician, a devoted wife, and — we are always told — a charming woman, she had an unassailable position in Germany. It was as unthinkable to criticize the Schumanns as in other circles to speak ill of the Brownings, whom they resembled in having married over the objections of a psychotic father, and in their union of genius with virtue. She was nevertheless odious to Liszt, inexcusably because no man did more for her adored husband's music; and her grounds were pitiful. When she first heard him in 1838 she sobbed aloud — "it overcame me so." She also appeared with him several times, once at Dresden in 1841 when they played four hands (to have heard that!). But she early decided that he was immoral, a libertine whose compositions, it followed, were disreputable. He was "not German." He was perhaps *anti*-German. His music anyway was unethical, and she became the founder of the cabal against him. Her disapproval did him infinite harm, but whether because he was used to disarming women or because he couldn't grasp the basis for her dislike, he couldn't get it through his head that she detested him. He thought she was wonderful, dedicated his Paganini studies to her, and when he was living in Weimar, was always asking her to visit him there. Years passed before the Schumanns' insolent ungraciousness sank in.

It was the same, more or less, with Mendelssohn, in 1840 the conductor of the Gewandhaus orchestra in Leipzig, which was the most prestigious in Germany. Liszt knew Mendelssohn from the winter of 1831–1832, which Mendelssohn spent in Paris. He didn't take to French life. His preferred foreign capital was London, where he was idolized. He suited exactly the Victorian ideal of the gentlemanly, domesticated artist — domesticated in every sense. So thoroughly had he submerged his Jewish background and assimilated himself into the national ethos that he perfectly represented the "good German." (He might have been Prince Albert over again as far as Queen Victoria was concerned; and so sluggishly do cultural matters move ahead in England that *Grove's Musical Dictionary*, in an edition printed as late as 1935, was still giving him more space than Mozart and Beethoven put together.) * The rowdy young French Romantics weren't his style at all. Of Liszt he said:

* If ever a composer was a darling of the gods, it was Mendelssohn. The adored son of a rich and gifted family, he never knew a moment's frustration but for his weak health. His childhood was a dream of happiness — the little Mendelssohns had their own theatre and orchestra, and the house was eternally filled with clever people of all ages. When the time came for his grand tour, Felix travelled like a young prince, loaded with money and letters of introduction. His career went without a hitch. And on top of

. . . You will find in him, when once you have penetrated beneath the surface of modern French polish, a good fellow and a true artist, whom you can't help liking even if you disagree with him. The only thing that he seems to me to want is true talent for composition. I mean really original ideas.[11]

With this he became an early promulgator of the *idée fixe* that Liszt had no originality, perhaps the one accusation against him that won't hold water. Even Moscheles knew better than that, and so advised Mendelssohn, who answered:

What you say about Liszt's harmonies is depressing . . . if that sort of stuff is noticed and admired, it is really provoking. But is that the case? I cannot believe that impartial people can take pleasure in discords or be in any way interested in them.[12]

That was in 1835. By 1842, Liszt's playing was giving Mendelssohn the purest pain: ". . . works by Beethoven, Bach, Handel, and Weber rendered in such pitiably imperfect style, so uncleanly, so ignorantly, that I could have listened to many a middling pianist with more pleasure," [13] a remark that can be usefully compared with what he said about Berlioz's orchestration — "so entirely slovenly — scrubbed up anyhow — that one has to wash one's hands after reading one of his scores." [14] Mendelssohn liked Berlioz personally much better than he liked Liszt, so the mention of uncleanliness in both cases is striking: it suggests that he suffered from a mild form of that mania that associates dirt with foreignness. He didn't, as it happened, appreciate Schumann either, didn't know what to say when Schumann dedicated the quartets to him; but he didn't call him unclean.

His manners, anyway, quite equalled those of the French man of the world. He went out of his way to be agreeable to Liszt in Leipzig, nursing him through a cold with the aid of syrups. Gossip attributed the cold to the Leipzigers' poor reception. Forced to pay double for Liszt's first concert, they decided he wasn't worth it. They were known to be the stuffiest audience in Germany — the city was called *die Tante* in musical circles — and they agreed with their concertmaster about modern music: Liszt gave them Schumann's *Carnaval* and it fell flat. Mendelssohn was distressed and to dispel the impression made by his parishioners, arranged a lavish fête in Liszt's honor. Liszt was mollified — and not destined to read Mendelssohn's private account of it:

350 people, orchestra, chorus, punch, pastry, *Meerstille*, *Psalm*, Bach's *Triple*

---

everything else, he was a charming man, universally beloved. It would be too much if he hadn't made the most of it and left us a mass of lovely music.

Concert (Liszt, Hiller and myself), choruses from *St. Paul, Fantasia on Lucia*, the *Erlkönig*, the devil and his grandmother. Everyone was so delighted, and they sang and played with such enthusiasm that all swore they had never had a gayer evening — and my purpose was consequently most happily achieved.[15]

What purpose exactly? If Liszt in Leipzig resembled a peacock strutting in a wool market, Mendelssohn, kind though his impulse may have been, had merely found a way of exposing his vanity further. God knows it was easy to do. He couldn't resist occasions that centered on his person, and was too seldom willing to abide by an honorable failure. Proud prophet of the new that he was, he hadn't the stamina to let the public lump it. There are many stories of his starting off a program with something "difficult" only to succumb in the end and give them what they wanted, usually the *Galop chromatique* or the fantasia on *Robert le Diable*. "I am the servant of the public, that goes without saying," he would mutter furiously. But who if not Liszt was in a position to educate his audiences?

Then there were the women. Dutiful husbands and fathers like Mendelssohn and Schumann found it difficult to condone a colleague who mixed himself up with a flaming whore like Lola Montez, especially when she all but broke up a solemn occasion. The celebrations for the Beethoven monument in Bonn in 1845 were the perfect example of this kind of mismanagement. Liszt had taken enormous trouble, collected most of the money, commissioned the monument, composed a cantata — and yet was treated with marked ill will. It may have been as Berlioz said:

Some had a grudge against him because of his extraordinary talent and success; others because he is witty, and yet others because he is generous, because he has written too fine a cantata . . . because he speaks French too well and knows German too thoroughly, because he has many friends, and doubtless because he has not enough enemies. . . .[16]

Certainly he aroused jealousy. Imagine, then, the delight of his critics when Lola turned up and, after making a scene at the hotel, forced her way into the all-male banquet and leaped on the table to dance a fandango. Probably the proceedings were much enlivened but it wouldn't do, it wouldn't do at all, not in Germany, where the episode rankled for years.

England, on the whole, took the same position, with the difference that it was the only country where he didn't achieve a large popular following either. English society was amused (there was Lady Blessington's inane remark that it was a pity to put such a handsome man at a piano); but one shudders to read his orders to Marie to send him his Hungarian redingotes and dressing gowns, his Turkish trousers and medallions, for use in a country where the most rampant conceit must wear the mask of modesty. (The Queen on the other hand was enchanted with him; but then she had a well-known weakness for good-looking foreigners in fancy dress.) His English tours of 1840 and 1841 had in any case to be written off as financial failures,* and he didn't go there again until the end of his life. His future, as he had sensed in Vienna, lay in the countries beyond the Rhine.

* The first, though, had its moments of disreputable comedy. He actually shared the program with one John Orlando Parry, whose specialty was vaudeville songs — "Wanted, a Governess" was a favorite. They travelled like mountebanks, going as far as Ireland, where ridiculous incidents multiplied. Parry's diary describes a concert near Cork where the piano had been forgotten. Liszt used the hotel instrument: "'Twas like a private Matinee — so funny to see Liszt firing away at Guillaume Tell on this little instrument." At Dublin "he played a piece, 'Sonata of Beethoven' twenty minutes long! — 'Twas dreadful."

Chapter 24

ROMANTICISM IN France was officially buried with the failure of Hugo's play *Les Burgraves* in 1843. Poor Hugo, trying for a repeat of *Hernani*, asked the painter Nanteuil for "three hundred Spartans ready to conquer or die," only to receive the melancholy answer that "youth is a thing of the past." Not true, of course, Romanticism didn't go out like a skirt length or its adherents drop dead in a single year. It remained the dominant impulse in European art for another hundred years. All that had happened was the passing of a name, and of a too-strict ideology that had begun to bore. In the simplest terms, *Les Burgraves* was a bad play, a "pre-Wagnerian monster" one critic has called it, which does not make it less influential than *Hernani* but only castigates it from another angle. Still, every Napoleon has his Waterloo, and Hugo saw the analogy. Pacing the Tuileries late one night, he was heard to say, "If Napoleon were there now there would be but one great event in France — *Les Burgraves* — and the Emperor would have come to our rehearsals!" And maybe he would have but the artist who must appeal to a dead ruler is in a bad way. Hugo, founder of the avant-garde, acknowledged with that statement a serious defeat.

Other bastions of Romanticism fell soon after. Berlioz's *Damnation of Faust*, performed in 1846, sank like a stone and this was a more ominous event because, unlike Hugo, Berlioz was not repeating himself. The *Damnation* was a great advance — too great. Said d'Ortigue:

Being wholly absorbed in his innovations . . . M. Berlioz loses sight of his audience and goes beyond the bounds where their perceptions stop. M. Berlioz is of the stature of a great master, and has gone further than Mozart, Beethoven and Weber, not because he is superior to them, but because in his hands art has taken a step forward . . . but there will always be a gulf between the way . . . the mass of the public conceives of art . . . and the way M. Berlioz conceives it.[1]

The same was said of the *Fantastique*, sixteen years before. Missing, this time, was the *succès de scandale* that at least assures attention. No more than Hugo could Berlioz count on the bolstering presence of the *cénacle*. Only Gautier was faithful. "With Hugo and Delacroix," he wrote, "Berlioz completes the Romantic trinity." He was right. Unfortunately, it sounded like ancient history.

Intellectual styles, like those in architecture and revolution, take time to reach their destinations. Romanticism, in the decade before 1848, retained its revolutionary prestige in the fossilized societies and decaying empires to the east. The farther Liszt travelled from Paris, the greater the honor attached to his associations with Sand, Hugo and Lamartine, with Lamennais and the Saint-Simonists. (The names of French writers were known in the remotest outposts. Balzac, in 1843, found an ardent admirer in the postmaster at Tilsit on the Niemen. Later, when Berlioz was going to Russia, Balzac told him to be sure to look up the good man. Berlioz did, and was regaled with Curaçao.) In those uneasy lands, where rebellions bubbled just under the surface, the Romantic artist was a symbol of freedom, and the crowds that hailed Liszt were venting feelings that didn't necessarily have anything to do with music, a fact known to local police. The populist passions that centered on his person could be dangerous. Describing his departure from Berlin in 1842, an observer wrote that "he marched out not *like* a king but *as* a king, a king in the imperishable kingdom of the spirit." Thus did he deny the reality of temporal rulers.

Sensing that he was getting a swelled head, Marie was always reminding him of the difference between France and other countries. Byronism has had its day, she informed him. Proudly he told her what he had inscribed on his portrait given to Prince Schwarzenberg: *Au grand seigneur–artiste Fritz Schwarzenberg, l'artiste–grand seigneur, F. Liszt.* The answer was prompt: "You can allow yourself that kind of thing in Germany but here you must be careful." *Ce n'est pas la mode ici.* He was told that often and it did not increase his desire to return to France. For it must be admitted that his conquest of the aristocracies in these countries (of which one manifestation was the power to call a prince "Fritz") was quite as intoxicating to him as the plaudits of the mob; and it isn't certain whether he understood that there was a connection, that the titled admirers who flocked to his standard were for the most part involved with liberal politics — or like his friend Prince Felix Lichnowsky, who had fought with the Carlists in Spain and was rather disreputable, had already chosen to be adventurers. What seems a contradiction is not, once it is realized that he became a symbolic personage. It wasn't uncommon for him to step from a table of grandees onto a balcony in order to make his bow to a crowd of torch-bearing students. And if it is asked how a pianist could become the focus for such demonstrations, there is always the case of Paderewski whom the newly liberated Polish nation made its prime minister in 1919.

There was a time in the 1840's when the Hungarians could almost have done the same for Liszt. His return to his native land in 1839–1840 was a political event of the first magnitude. He was a national hero before he had played a note, or opened his mouth. The crowds shouted "Long live Liszt" as they did not for Austrian royalty. The Diet proposed to ennoble him. A group of magnates presented him with a "sword of honor" on the stage of the National Theatre amid scenes of patriotic enthusiasm that threatened public order. His playing of the rabble-rousing *Rákóczy* March was banned for fear it would provoke an uprising.* The Magyars left no doubt about the role he was expected to play. The two most important leaders of the opposition, counts Batthyány and Széchenyi, called on him at once. The poet Vörösmarty addressed an ode to him:

Famous musician who belongs to the world,
True to this land wherever you go,
Have you a voice amidst the mighty swell and fervor of your piano,
For your sick country?

It made no odds that for a culture hero he had his limitations, that not knowing a word of the language and almost as little of Hungarian history, he was poorly qualified to speak for his country.

Most serious of all, the spiritual son of Lamennais and Saint-Simon did not know, or apparently care, how sick his country was. Blinded by the glory of his reception, he ignored the facts that the faultiest memory might have supplied — that Hungary was a miserable land, sunk in feudal sloth and frightful inequalities, ripe for rebellion against Austria if not yet against its own ruling class. He made the pilgrimage to Raiding because it was ex-

---

* Most people think Berlioz wrote this smashing march, which is in the *Damnation of Faust*. He didn't, or even make the first arrangement of it. It is an old Hungarian battle tune that had for long been the unofficial national anthem. Liszt first scored it for piano in 1840, later turned it into the fifteenth *Hungarian Rhapsody* (which exists in at least three piano versions) and finally arranged it for orchestra. Berlioz, who didn't reach Hungary until 1846, claims in his memoirs that he was introduced to the tune by "a Viennese amateur," who advised him to orchestrate it for Hungarian audiences, which is manifestly not true. Liszt said flatly that "one of my earliest transcriptions served as the chief basis for [Berlioz's] harmonization, which differs strikingly from the rudimentary chords generally used by the gypsies and other small orchestras playing this march." (Quoted by Haraszti, "Berlioz, Liszt and the Rákóczy March," *Musical Quarterly*, vol. 26 [1940].) But though he was obviously right, he still loses the argument. Berlioz's famous arrangement is better than any of his.

pected of him, hiding his distemper. It was a gala day for the village, which turned out to feast him and kiss his hand in spite of the snow on the ground. "I saw all this again without tenderness," he confessed to Marie — which is not surprising. Warm memories weren't to be expected. But a touch of sympathy, a suggestion that remedies might be called for, the want of these is as inexcusable as it is hard to understand in a man more than ordinarily generous. In some strange way he seems to have lost his faculties, not to have realized what his appearance signified. Thus, the famous sabre he accepted with the weird statement that it was a peace symbol, a sign that "Hungary having covered herself with glory on so many battlefields, now calls on the arts . . . partisans of peace to provide new examples." [2] Alas, it was nothing of the kind.

The native son who returns to claim his identity is one of the oldest stories in the world. Liszt's triumphant reunion with his countrymen was a curiosity, and a distressing one, because it brought out the worst of his "national" characteristics, in place of the courage the vanity, not the elegiac sadness that a mournful land once evoked in its best poets but the love for display and the snobbery that are the by-products of feudal societies. Here is his testimony, posted off in all its vehemence to Marie:

Liszt to Marie: I mentioned a splendid day. The word is no exaggeration. I won't write about it to anybody, and even to you I will write badly because these things can't be described. On January 4 [1840], I played at the Hungarian Theatre the Andante from *Lucia*, the *Galop*, and the applause not ceasing, the *Rákóczy March* (a sort of aristocratic *Marseillaise*). Just as I was going backstage, in comes Count Leo Festetics, Baron Banfy, Count Teleky (all magnates), Eckstein, Augusz and a sixth whose name I forget, all in full Hungarian costume, Festetics holding a magnificent sabre set with turquoises, rubies, etc. (worth 80 to 100 louis), in his hand. He addresses me with a little allocution in Hungarian before the public, which applauds with frenzy, and buckles on the sword in the name of the Nation. I ask through Augusz for permission to speak to the public in French. I pronounce in a grave and firm voice the discourse I will send you printed tomorrow. It is frequently interrupted with applause. . . .

You can't have an idea of the serious, grave and profound sensation of this scene, which anywhere else would have been ridiculous and which could easily have become so even here. . . . It was magnificent. It was unique. But that wasn't all. The performance over, we get into carriages. And behold an immense crowd blocking up the square and 200 young people carrying lighted torches, led by military music, crying Eljen! Eljen! Eljen! [Hungarian for Vivat; pronounced eh-yen.] And notice what admirable tact. Hardly had we gone fifty paces than a dozen young throw themselves forward to unhitch the horses. No, no, cry the others, they did that for some wretched dancers . . . this one must be feted in another way. . . .

Festetics' house where I am staying is a long way from the theatre. When we had gone about a third of the distance, I said . . . "I won't go on, let's get down, let's not play the aristocrat in your carriage." I open the door, the shouting that hadn't stopped for ten minutes redoubles with a sort of fury. We at once arrange ourselves and walk, Festetics, Augusz and I (in the middle), all three in Hungarian costume (mine, in parenthesis, cost me a full thousand francs though it is quite simple: it was a necessary expense).

Impossible to give you an idea of the enthusiasm, the respect, the love of this population! At eleven o'clock at night, the streets are full of people. In Pest, everybody, even the most elegant, is in bed by ten. . . . [Yet] the shouting never stopped. It was a triumphal march such as La Fayette and one or two men of the revolution have experienced.

At one of the turnings, I asked Augusz, who has a great habit of making speeches . . . to harangue these young people; he acquitted himself admirably. I gave him for a theme "that I hadn't in any way deserved . . . the welcome given me by my country. But I accepted these more than flattering proofs as imposing on me new duties etc."

The first words were answered by the most explicit, unanimous and burning contradiction. . . . Yes, yes, they cried, you do deserve it and more. . . .

P.S. (Wednesday morning)

After a similar demonstration (in which, without exaggeration, all society as ·well as the population took part), I had the desire to do something on my side for the town and the country. I have therefore prolonged by several days my stay in Pest . . . and propose next Saturday to give an immense concert . . . for the Pest Conservatory, for which funds will be voted by the Diet. . . . I will direct the orchestra and the choruses, that's to say the whole thing, and further play the *Grande Fantaisie* of Beethoven, with chorus, and Weber's *Concerto*, whatever they like. One can't bargain with a public of this sort. . . .[3]

In France, all this was considered in terrible taste, especially the *sabre d'honneur,* a strange gift to a man of peace, said Berlioz (who was to get into the same kind of trouble over an exchange of batons with Mendelssohn. His thanks, "Great chief! We have promised to exchange tomahawks," were likewise set down as unsuitably martial.) The *Revue des Deux Mondes* snarled: "We let Beethoven and Weber die of hunger to give a sword of honor to M. Liszt." For years, the unlucky sword figured prominently in caricatures of him; nor did Heine let him forget it: "This Orlando Furioso with the Hungarian *sabre d'honneur* . . ."

His excuse (not that he used it) must be that of all social climbers. The little Liszt had kissed the hands of the magnates and his father addressed them in a cringing third person. He used the democratic French *vous* or even the intimate *tu* to them and outdid them in hospitality — forty-five *couverts* and the best singers from the Opera for one bachelor dinner. That was understandable. His mindless repetitions of their titles were not. He seemed unable to distinguish between such men as Batthyány and Széchenyi and a lightweight like Festetics. Yet the first two were remarkable men, too rare for their day and class, and their fates were accordingly frightful. Batthyány, who became premier, was executed after the defeat in 1849 and Széchenyi went insane. It is infuriating to recall this while Liszt is chattering on about "Casimir Esterhazy with whom I rode on account of his excellent coupé, the Baron Venckheim, two counts Zychyi . . ." and incidentally getting all the names wrong. (He could no more spell Zichy than the French could spell Liszt.)

Most exasperating of all is it to listen to the man who had *Génie oblige* for his motto chanting about his ennoblement:

As it is a national matter which I have neither sought nor asked for nor coveted in any way, I admit it will give me pleasure. . . . But there is a little difficulty. . . . If they give me letters of nobility, they also give me arms. So I would like you [Marie] to invent some. Up till now, Festetics has found only the owl admissible, because the lyre and the roll of paper would be absurd. . . . It is possible all this will be a nine-day-wonder, but it is very much in question. . . .[4]

He went so far as to boast that "if I cared a lot about an aristocratic origin, I could easily claim it. The authentic documents exist and are in the hands of the Fiscal of Ofen [Buda]. I'll look into it (out of curiosity) one of these days. . . ."[5] If he did look into it and discovered proof of aristocratic blood, it can only have been via somebody's illegitimate issue. And he may have, because he did not return to the subject.

He was made aware of the attacks on him. Marie saw to that. "Brace yourself for the jokes about [your sword] and your *noblesse*. Prepare your answers. . . . For the rest, I repeat . . . try to put the damper on. . . ."[6] His defense was probably as good a one as could be made. There must be, he said, some understanding of the difference between mere money-making success and the kind of tribute he had received. The sabre was a civic award, from a nation famous for warriors and politicians, which now hoped to be represented by an artist; it was a form of recognition to one who had served the cause of *l'art national*. Undeniably, he *did* put Hungary on the map. Her poets were unread outside her borders; she had no painters. Then and for several generations his was the only artist's voice she had. All the more unfortunate then that his Hungarian music is, by and large, as glittering a parure of costume jewelry as exists, exactly what one would expect from one to whom *ma sauvage et lointaine patrie* was a sort of showpiece.

Liszt to Marie, October 8, 1846: I have collected a number of fragments with the help of which one might fairly well recompose the musical epic of this strange country, whose *rhapsode* I want to become. The six new volumes, about a hundred pages in all, which I have just published in Vienna under the collective title

Melodies hongroises . . . form an almost complete cycle of this fantastic epic: half Ossianic (for there pulses in these songs the feeling of a vanished race of heroes) and half gypsy.[7] *

In almost the same breath he announced to Festetics that he wished to be known as "the first gypsy in the kingdom of Hungary." Both statements, which are elaborated in his book on the subject, reflect his fundamental error — which was to confuse Hungarian folk music with the gypsy manner of playing it, all *fioritura* and improvisation. On top of that, most of the melodies he chose to transcribe were not traditional, hence anonymous, but simply popular compositions by well-known dilettantes who were not even tziganes. The results were brilliant enough in their way, *tours de force* in which the violin and the cymbalon were reproduced with uncanny accuracy — faithful echoes of a gypsy band. But in no sense do these pieces constitute the "musical epic of a vanished race." Like the music they imitate, they have the power to dazzle and seduce but they lack the authenticity that he persistently claimed for them. Does it matter?

Bartók for one is inclined to be lenient, pointing out that the scientific approach to folklore was unknown at the time (not quite true — there were the brothers Grimm), that it wasn't understood that folk expression is basically collective, and that its social role was undefined. He further excuses Liszt on the ground that to have heard the classical peasant melodies he would have had to venture into the villages armed with some knowledge of the language — and even then would have run into difficulties that Bartók was familiar with, having encountered them himself: the peasant, like all "natives," is not easily induced to play his own music, and will invariably begin with what he thinks the gentry or the tourist really wants — about as close to the real thing as *O sole mio* or *Never on Sunday*. Generally speaking, it was music of this order that Liszt heard played by gypsies summoned to the castle, and for this reason that Bartók blames "our grandfathers" for his mistakes. They, says Bartók, knew perfectly well that what they called gypsy music only meant music played by gypsies, not composed by them — and they were shocked by Liszt's book. If they didn't correct him it was because the matter wasn't of sufficient importance. Bartók is emphatic that it would have been useless for Liszt to try to unravel the facts through his grand friends — "the peasants don't know anything" being their usual attitude. He had either to do his own homework or get it wrong.[8]

---

* The history of the Hungarian works is, like that of everything else he wrote, confusing. Besides a *Heroic March* in the Magyar style, composed in 1840 and later expanded into the symphonic poem *Hungaria,* he published ten volumes of piano pieces on Hungarian themes between 1840 and 1847 under the titles *Magyar Dállok, Magyar Rhapsodiak* and — a separate collection — *Ungarische Melodien.* This mass of material became the basis for the first fifteen Rhapsodies. Four more Rhapsodies belong to his old age, along with a group of five Hungarian songs.

I think Bartók overstates Liszt's case. Liszt had made too much fuss about "the music of the people," *Vox populi, vox dei,* to get away with the superficiality of the Rhapsodies and the absurd theorizing in the gypsy book. If his social climbing hadn't made a prisoner of him, obstacles to knowledge weren't that impossible to overcome. Ignorance of the language was a handicap — yes, but not a fatal one. Interpreters could have been found. Research did exist. (Adám Horváth's collection of songs made in the eighteenth century was one source and amateurs of the subject were not wanting.) In short it wasn't beyond him to do a respectable job, as Berlioz, one feels, would have. The question even arises of how interested in folk "epics" he really was. Sitwell notes that he seems, while in Spain, to have paid no attention to flamenco though he spent the greater part of a winter (1844–1845) in Seville and Granada. Was that because those particular gypsies didn't enter into his scheme of publicity for *ma sauvage et lointaine patrie?*

There was perhaps no intrinsic harm in cultivating the aristocracy, if the object was no more than to get his own back. (Beethoven said that "it is good to be with the aristocracy; but one must be able to impress them.") But why identify himself with the gypsies? With his acute social sense, he must have known that to do so was to adopt a kind of white *négritude,* analogous to that of the European who made a cult of jazz in the 1920's. The gypsy violinist crouched before his noble listener and was paid with banknotes slapped to his sweating brow. (This was still true in the twentieth century when summoning the gypsies meant an old-fashioned orgy, with smashed china and priceless glassware demolished in exhibitions of marksmanship.) Reading his letter to Marie, you might surmise that he had discovered an early form of fashionable radicalism and you would be half right. His tziganes were less real than Delacroix's Moors because uncorrected by observed reality. They belonged, as he inadvertently exposed, to the same fictive race as James Macpherson's Gaelic bard. (Citing Ossian, Liszt did not know he was the victim of a famous literary hoax — which seems typical too. They could have told him in England, if he had asked, that "Ossian" did not exist.)

Other works in the Hungarian manner — Brahms's *Ungarische Tänze,* for example — were equally spurious, if one wants to be a purist about it. Only there is a world of difference between avowed adaptations and the researches of a self-appointed *rhapsode,* or the composer who calls himself "first gypsy." There is rough justice in the fact that Liszt's Hungarian Rhapsodies, in his lifetime his most acclaimed works, should be more responsible than anything else for his later disrepute.

Chapter 25

AFTER Hungary Liszt organized himself on a professional basis — that is, he hired in 1841 a secretary-manager and began to invest some of his earnings. The secretary was an Italian, Gaetano Belloni, and there is an unconfirmed rumor that he swindled Liszt over his concert receipts. If he did Liszt didn't know it. He trusted Belloni and made a friend of him over Marie's objections that he was encouraging familiarity in a servant. A surprisingly clear picture of Belloni emerges from the correspondence as the all-purpose impresario and fixer. "Voilà pour le moment," he would say, rubbing his hands over some elaborate arrangement. His job required a certain gusto. The logistics of getting Liszt from place to place, together with his trunks of clothes, music, press clippings, special cigars, gifts from crowned heads, not to mention the Érards, must have been appalling. Belloni coped with all this, as well as hotel rooms, the banquets Liszt was in the habit of giving, and the details of the concerts themselves, which were far from routine. Concert halls as such being few, he played in all sorts of places: opera houses, the public rooms of hotels, the halls of universities, embassies and palaces.

In a letter from Russia in 1847, Berlioz inquired wistfully, "Don't you think you and I go around a good deal? Just now, I am sad, sad enough to die of it. I am having one of my bouts of *isolation*. . . ." [1] It is the familiar plaint of the eternal traveller and although Liszt didn't suffer to the same degree, he too sickened of vagabondage and began to lose his sense of contact with places. His letters grow less vivid, more perfunctory and concerned with sordid details: rows with music publishers, critics made to eat their words, the box office. He skips the triumphs and writes of exhaustion and midnight tears.

Accordingly there are some sizable lacunae in his vast itineraries. Spain and Portugal, for instance, about which he had little of interest to say; Denmark; and regrettably, Turkey, of which he had once had voluptuous visions: "I want to breathe in perfume, exchange coal smoke for the gentle whiff of the narghile. In short, I long for the East. *O mein Morgenland!*" And he dreamed of taking with him Marie Duplessis, the *dame aux camélias*, already coughing blood into lace handkerchiefs. That was in 1845. In 1847 he went to Constantinople alone and it was the end of a tiring road. He admired the view up the Bosphorus and bought the trinkets that tourists buy. If he had any more exotic adventures we don't hear of them. (Nor is it recorded that he made any headway with the project, once propounded to Nourrit, of interesting the Sultan in "humanitarian music" — if he had the nerve to mention it.)

It follows that except for those (increasingly rare) letters to Marie in which he gave a fairly full account of himself, we know more about what happened to him during the *Glanzperiode* from other people than from the primary source. This was even true of his trips to Russia, where he made contacts that were important to him for the rest of his life, and where his influence was second only to Berlioz's.

The lure of Russia was, quite frankly, money. Artists were offered staggering sums and only later discovered that Russian audiences were a joy to deal with, mad for any foreign thing. Nobody looked forward to getting there, especially in winter. Berlioz, never funnier than when the disasters multiply, devotes one of his finest passages to the horrors of an iron sledge in which he rattled "like shot in a bottle" for four terrible days and nights over the icy waste between the frontier and Petersburg, undergoing "tortures the very existence of which I had never suspected," and marvelling at the stupidity of the Russian crows, who instead of feasting on frozen dung, might have flown to a warm climate in a few hours. He thought of 1812 and shuddered.

Liszt travelled first class to Berlioz's third. He had a coach specially constructed to carry himself, Belloni, and a servant. It was spring and he didn't observe the crows. Or would he have anyway? Already by 1842, the date of this first visit, his letters have lost the quality, gross but naïve, that gave to his Hungarian boastings the just endurable charm of a child's. From Petersburg, where his success was in a way more flattering because unconnected with his nationality, he wrote with the nervous petulance of the performer — or the politician — who is more concerned with his moods and his reception than with where he is. Petersburg didn't agree with him and it is astonishing to learn by omission what Romanticism's child did not know: that Pushkin and Lermontov (both killed in duels, Lermontov only the year before) were major poets, that a novel called *Dead Souls* had just been published and changed the course of Russian literature. (To be fair, Berlioz four years later was no wiser.) He must be excused because of what he did discover — the world of Russian music, then unknown to the west, and despised of many Russians.

His guide was Glinka, the founder of the nationalist school. Only five years older than Gogol, this proud, melancholy man was a victim of the time-lag between music and literature: *Dead Souls* was a best-seller; his opera *Ruslan and Ludmilla,* produced later that year, was received with an indifference so discouraging to the composer that he left Russia. But Liszt immediately grasped Glinka's importance. He studied the *Ruslan* score and transcribed portions of it which he played at his Petersburg concerts with success — another instance of public willingness to accept a piano transcription while refusing the original, this time for no better reason than that Liszt was an imported talent. *Ruslan* is of a magical loveliness; its failure was solely due to the Russian inferiority complex about native music (not to speak of Circassian and Tartar airs), which was considered unfit for the operatic stage dominated by Rossini and Meyerbeer. It was "coachman's music" — that it also made use of the whole-tone scale probably went unnoticed, though not by Liszt.*

In Russia, he had in fact a unique opportunity to study the difficulties of creating national music, like national literature a hybrid brought forth by the grafting of Romanticism to regional self-discovery. In the mid-forties, the war between the Slavophiles and western-oriented intellectuals already raged; the conclusion was foregone. In Herzen's words, "Only the mighty thought of the West, with which all its long history is united, is able to fertilize the seeds slumbering in the patriarchal mode of life of the Slavs." In Glinka that fertilization had taken place, though he believed otherwise. "Music is really made by the people," he said. "We composers only use it, work it up" — a half-truth out of Rousseau. In reality, the people do not compose symphonies, operas or ballets. Folk art is proto-art and has its own life. Once it is scrutinized, "worked up" and made the focus for modern nationalism, it is already in dissolution.

It has been the fate of modern art to devour its source material down to

*Tchaikowsky, the only Russian composer Liszt didn't admire and vice versa, said of him that "the old Jesuit speaks in terms of exaggerated praise of every work submitted to him. He is at heart a good man, one of the very few artists who have never known envy, but he is too much of a Jesuit to be frank and sincere" (cited, Sitwell: p. 309). This seems to mean that Liszt's enthusiasms were inauthentic, voiced to gain some end. Glinka is a good example of how futile such a policy would have been. Liszt gained nothing by championing his music. (Frankness and honesty might also have compelled Tchaikowsky to admit his own debts to the old Jesuit: cf. his *Francesca da Rimini* out of the *Dante* Symphony; his B-flat Minor Concerto out of Liszt's No. 2 in A Major.)

the bones, to dig over the sites of inspiration until there is little left to explore beyond the refinements of technique or the possibilities of accident.
The Romantics had no intimation of this. The perspective looked endless
and they did not realize that in art as in nature there is a kind of ecology
that can be disrupted by over-exploitation, which was what happened to
folklore as the scientist and the artist converged on it. If Liszt was more
pretentious and less accurate in his use of native idioms than the Russian
composers who grew up inside the whale and were therefore more intimate
with its workings, they were alike in helping to kill the thing they loved.
Applying the standards of modern scholarship doesn't change this. Bartók's,
or Kodály's, renderings of Hungarian folk themes are more authentic than
Liszt's but they aren't the real thing either, only a faithful representation
of it.

Nineteenth-century Russian music drew on the national heritage; the
operas told the story of a people, but not as the people would have told it.
Neither the form nor the musical technology was indigenous and the local
color was a matter of décor. These are Europeanized spectacles, "worked
up" stories of the past (nationalism in its pre-Maoist versions always had an
element of nostalgia) and historically — their artistic merits aren't here in
question — they actually stand at the end and not the beginning of ethnic
self-realization.

Entering Russia at this stage of her cultural development, Liszt had
again struck at a psychological moment. With his background and his new-
found "nationality" he was bound to get a different reception from, say,
Thalberg. His personality did the rest. It was Hungary over again only
more so, on a grander scale. I hesitate to quote one more time what has
been done to death in every book about Liszt — his concert at the Winter
Palace as witnessed by Vladimir Stassov. But I am afraid we can't do without Stassov, who was eighteen when he saw Liszt and who partly as a
result of the experience went on to become Russia's foremost critic and
champion of The Five. (His friend Serov, who was with him, turned into
Russia's leading Wagnerite.)

We are watching Liszt's entrance into the vast, white and gold Salle de
la Noblesse, a hall of ice hung with eight gigantic crystal lustres, jammed
with three thousand boyars. He leans on the arm of Count Bielgorsky, a
stout elderly dandy and musical amateur he had known in Rome, a striking
personage whom nobody sees. All eyes are rivetted to Liszt, in evening
clothes and a white cravat on which reposes the Order of the Golden Spur
— other orders are pinned to his lapels. But what strikes the Russians dumb
is his *chevelure,* the lion's mane that reaches almost to his shoulders. "Outside the priesthood," says Stassov, "no Russian would have ventured on
such a style of hairdressing. Such dishevelment had been sternly dis-
countenanced since the time of Peter the Great." Stassov began to have

doubts. The orders, the famous "Florentine" profile, were perhaps too much of a good thing:

Liszt mounted the platform, and pulling his dogskin gloves from his shapely white hands, tossed them carelessly to the floor. Then, after acknowledging the thunderous applause, such as had not been heard in Russia for over a century, he seated himself at the piano. There was a silence as though the whole hall had been turned to stone, and Liszt, without any prelude, began the opening bars of the overture to *William Tell*. Curiosity, speculation, criticism, all were forgotten in the wonderful enchantment of his performance.

His Fantasia on *Don Juan*, his arrangement of Beethoven's *Adelaïde*, the *Erl-King* of Schubert, and his own *Galop chromatique* followed upon this. After the concert, Serov and I were like madmen. We scarcely exchanged a word, but hurried home, each to write down his impressions, dreams and raptures. We both vowed to keep this anniversary sacred forever, and never, while life lasted, to forget a single instant of it.[2]

Liszt paid two more visits to Russia, one the following year and the last in 1847. That was the extent of his physical contact with the country. But he *was* remembered while life lasted and well beyond, the memory passing to the next couple of generations. No other western composer had quite the same rapport with the Russians that Liszt did — and that includes Berlioz, Barzun's claims for him notwithstanding. According to Barzun, it was Berlioz and Berlioz alone who was "the predestined mentor of these ultimate creators of the century . . . Russian ballets, suites, monodramas, and symphonic poems were the offspring of the dramatic symphony; their light, transparent orchestration was his. . . ." One might take it from this that Liszt never set foot in Russia, or composed a symphonic poem, and that his orchestration was not also notable for its thinness and transparency.

There is no need to tear down one in order to build up the other. Berlioz's importance to Russian music is not in dispute. (He was, for example, closer to Glinka than Liszt was. After the failure of *Ruslan and Ludmilla*, Glinka went to Paris, where he and Berlioz became good friends.) It is still the fact that Balakirev, who for practical purposes headed the Russian school after Glinka's death, was a devoted Lisztian. One must decide for oneself whether his symphonic poem *Tamara* owes more to Liszt or to Berlioz but it is dedicated to Liszt; his *Islamey* is almost blatantly modelled on Liszt's transcendental studies. Rimsky-Korsakov was surely more in Liszt's debt than in Berlioz's, particularly in the field of tonal relationships.

Liszt also kept in personal touch with the Russians much longer than Berlioz did, for the simple reason that Berlioz died in 1869, giving Liszt almost a twenty-year edge. Thus he was in correspondence with Moussorgsky in 1873, and quite possibly saw a copy of *Boris Godounov* before its publication. Fat packets of music regularly reached him from Russia.

(His Russian pupil Siloti tells of his eagerness to open them: "Let's be quick . . . there is sure to be something good.") Borodin actually made the pilgrimage to Weimar in 1877 in order to show the old man the score of *Prince Igor*. He found Liszt perfectly au courant with his works. Moments after he presented himself, Liszt was playing his first Symphony in E-flat and telling him how he had performed it only two days before for the Grand Duke. At this period of his life he is known to have believed that "Russia holds the key to the future."

Finally, there was his influence on Russian pianists. There, no one else came close. There are Russians who say it endures to this day, that only in Russia has an approximation of the Lisztian style endured, in the playing of Richter, for example. In his lifetime, at any rate, Russian pupils beat a path to his door, turning Weimar almost into a Slav preserve. So many and so close in fact were his ties with Russia that it is inexplicable that he seems never to have considered revisiting it, preferring to spend a third of each year in Germany where his music, by the 1870's, was regarded as a somewhat embarrassing joke.

Although he never tried to repeat his Russian triumphs, Liszt can all the same be said to have lived a large part of his life in an atmosphere we know from the Russian novelists — compounded of tobacco smoke, cushions, fur rugs, tea, irregular hours and that effluvium, new then to Europe, called the Slavic soul. He met what used to be called his fate in the Ukraine in 1847, in the person of Carolyne Wittgenstein — a Pole in spite of her name, which she got by marriage. She kept him for a record twelve years and never lost his respect or affection. Had he managed to die in Rome instead of Bayreuth, it would have been in her arms, though they had ceased to be lovers a quarter century earlier. They parted, in that sense, in 1861 and he was long in choosing a permanent replacement; when he did it was another Slav, the Baroness Olga Meyendorf, née Princess Gortschakova, a much younger (and much prettier) woman than poor Carolyne. Olga devoted herself to giving him a comfortable old age.

In between, and less seriously, there was the six-foot snow queen, Marie Mouchanoff-Kalergis, the "Cossack" Olga Janina — and innumerable others whose names lie forgotten in the dust of his Russian tours. (One whose name we do know was Balzac's Countess Hanska, to whom Balzac was rash enough to give him a letter of introduction in 1842. It is obvious that he made a pass at her and that she was desperately tempted. "He is the human reflection of what is splendid in nature — but also of what is terrible," she wrote in her diary. "There are sublime heights, but bottomless depths . . . which will bring more than one disaster on himself and others. . . ."[3] A stiff letter from Balzac pulled her together and she repulsed him — or so she said.)

Such a variety of women can't perhaps be lumped together and called a type. Yet for purposes of social history there is such a thing as the wealthy, aristocratic, bluestocking Slav, and she plays such a notable role in the amorous life of the French Romantics that Liszt's addiction becomes part of a pattern. Every student of the period runs across these women who whether ugly or beautiful (and all but Carolyne were acknowledged seductresses) exercised a remarkable power over French artists and writers. Balzac and Dumas *fils* married theirs. Marie Kalergis was loved by numbers of literary men including Musset and Gautier, who wrote a famous poem to her, the *Symphonie en blanc majeur*. The fastidious Delacroix was ravished by Delphine Potocka and Marcelline Czartoryska, "charming Princess Marcelline," whose good fortune it was to inhabit the Hôtel Lambert on the Île St. Louis.*

Something of their allure can be gauged from Dumas *père*'s goggle-eyed description of one of them (not the one his son married). She received him lying on a divan:

> [She] was wearing a dressing gown of embroidered muslin with pink silk stockings on her legs, and slippers from Kazan on her feet. Her wonderful black hair hung loose to her knees. . . . It was easy to see from her sinuous movements that she was innocent of stays. . . . Round her neck was a triple row of pearls. There were pearls on her arms and in her hair. . . .[4]

This odalisque, who sounds like the whore of Babylon, was the Russian chancellor's daughter-in-law, Lydia Nesselrode, and like her cousin Marie Kalergis of the highest possible birth. With their friend Nadejda Naryschkine (eventually Madame Dumas), a green-eyed, tawny-haired tigress, they devastated Paris but they were not remotely to be thought of as courtesans. They were *femmes fatales,* a very different thing.

Europeans didn't know what to make of "these Russian ladies . . . endowed with a fineness of sensibility and an intuition far above the average, which they owe to their double inheritance as Asiatics and Europeans, to

---

* The historian with time on his hands might one day try to sort out the various countesses Potocka (pronounced Pototska). There were at least three. Sitwell, with typical adroitness, refers to "the inevitable Countess Potocka" and does not try for first names. Nor can this inevitable countess be identified by calling her "Chopin's friend." That could be Delphine — or Marie. Both were Chopin's friends, and also Liszt's. La Mara, who edited a correspondence between Marie Potocka and Carolyne Wittgenstein, remarks cryptically that this Potocka was also known as Madame Jaroslas — if that is any help. Turn then to André Maurois's life of Balzac. In this, a Countess Potocka, once called Marie, is variously identified as Madame Hanska's aunt, cousin, and sister. Three different women? Carelessness? Pursuing the Potockas to infinity, one also finds another one: Hélène. She was Maupassant's mistress for a time. (I ought to confess that a kind Polish acquaintance once offered to unravel all this for me, and even supplied a handwritten genealogy. Prolonged study of it left me more baffled than ever.)

their cosmopolitan curiosity, and their indolent habits . . . these strange
creatures who speak every language, hunt the bear, live off sweets, and
laugh in the face of every man who cannot master them . . . these females
with voices at once musical and hoarse, superstitious and skeptical, fawning
and fierce, who bear the indelible mark of the country of their origin, who
defy all analysis, and every attempt to imitate them. . . ." [5]

Alexandre Dumas, whose description this is, had as much experience with
women as any man including Liszt. The Slavs baffled him because they
were immune to European standards of avarice, snobbery, or decorum.
Rich beyond dreams, they treated money as savages do, with no regard for
its arbitrary value. The class distinctions that were so important to a Marie
d'Agoult meant nothing to them and they got away with conduct that
would have ostracized a European woman of the same rank. Where they
loved, they gave, and Europe with its long tradition of coquetry, the consequence of a price set on virtue (woman's jewel), could hardly believe in
such simplicity. "She has given me," said Dumas of his princess, "proofs of
disinterested devotion for which she does not even expect me to be grateful," a sentiment echoed time and again by Liszt and Balzac in their dealings with their Polish mistresses. They were also as lawless as cats. Among
the men who could not master them was the Tsar of all the Russias, who
spent an inordinate amount of effort trying to discipline them — cancelling
their passports, sequestering their estates, recalling them to Russia. In the
middle of the nineteenth century they demanded the right to live and love
as they pleased, and this was recognized to be menacing if only because it
led them so persistently into the arms of artists.

It is easy to see why. Art and union with an artist meant freedom to
these Andromedas of the steppe, and it is remarkable how often they were
able to achieve it — and under what handicaps. Eva Hanska, walled away
on her Ukrainian estate, wrote a fan letter to Balzac: he longed to know the
identity of the woman who signed herself *l'Étrangère*. Carolyne Wittgenstein, from an even more isolated position, piqued Liszt's curiosity with a
note that must have been very similar. (It is lost but the ladies wrote in the
same style: "Your soul embraces centuries, Monsieur. . . .") The odds
against these wild shots were fantastic. Yet the quarry was bagged in both
cases. Neither woman was perhaps quite typical, in that both had stainless
reputations and had endured several years of captivity before their deliver-
ers appeared. The Paris set was giddier and chose its men more boldly. Of
Marie Kalergis and Lydia Nesselrode, one scandalmonger wrote:

They have conceived the idea of a small circle the members of which would
indulge in amorous orgies . . . [with] young men . . . recruited from among
the more free and easy writers. . . . The Nesselrode put herself under the

tutelage of Dumas *fils*: the Kalergis chose Alfred de Musset . . . and the end of the whole business was that an order came from Petersburg recalling the countess to Russia. . . .[6]

Nadejda Naryschkine, on the other hand, having succeeded Lydia in Dumas's affections, made his life a hell with her nerve-storms and jealousy but in perfect propriety.

Liszt was on the whole fortunate in his Slav alliances, more fortunate than Dumas. Far from making him scenes, Carolyne asserted blandly that his "soul is too tender, too artistic, too impressionable for him to live without the company of women. He must have a number of them around him, just as in his orchestra he needs many instruments with rich, varied timbres." [7] The social slights inflicted on her in Weimar, analogous to those endured by Marie d'Agoult in Geneva, she was far too busy tending Liszt's flame to notice — an attitude also shown by the Baroness Meyendorf twenty years later. Most singular of all, given Marie's example, was Carolyne's capacity to see what he was trying to do.

Pious as a mujik and emancipated only to the extent that she was willing to live "in sin" with him — she never had another lover — she can't be called a modern woman. Furthermore she was musically coarse, untutored, and a not infrequent giver of bad advice. Yet she had a kind of sixth sense that told her what many more cultivated critics did not know, that Liszt stood in a special relation to his time. Some say she coined the phrase "music of the future," and she could have. She grasped, in an admittedly simplified way, that he was breaking new ground. "Generations will pass before he will be perfectly understood," she said. "He has hurled his lance much further into the future than Wagner." She was right about that, and if it is objected that she was only parroting what Liszt told her, there is evidence that she was not incapable of independent judgments: her championship of Berlioz at a moment when Liszt was at odds with him, and her obstinate insistence that *Les Troyens* was a masterpiece, an opinion that Liszt emphatically did not share. She stood up to him over Wagner too. To suppose she took everything he told her on blind faith and because she loved him is to make a mistake about the devotional type to which she belonged. She didn't think Liszt was a genius because she loved him; she loved him because she thought he was a genius.

*Liszt in his Polish fur coat. In English and in his own hand,
the Byron tag he was always quoting, "Here's a heart for
every fate." Photo by Zs. D. Erdökürti, National Museum of
Hungary*

Abbé Lamennais. Photo courtesy of Bibliothèque Nationale, Paris

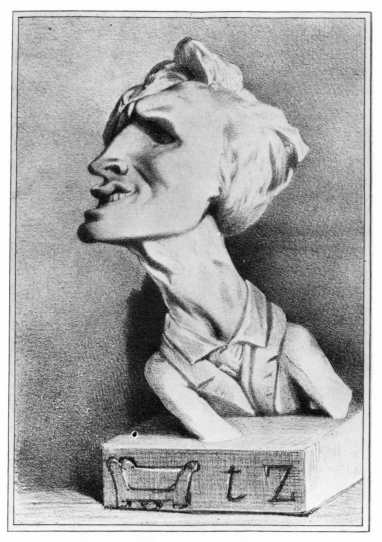

"M. Litz." Lithograph after caricature-sculpture by
Dantan. Photo courtesy of Bibliothèque Nationale, Paris

Liszt by Ingres. Collection of W. Wagner, Bayreuth. Photo by Lauros-Giraudon

Marie d'Agoult, 1840, painting by Henri Lehmann. Photo by Bulloz

Chopin, 1838, drawing by Delacroix

George Sand in Masculine Costume, by Delacroix. Musée Carnavalet, Paris. Photo: Collection Viollet

Berlioz, 1850, by Courbet. Photo courtesy of Jacques Barzun

Eduard Reményi, engraving by Marastoni. Photo by J. Karath, National Museum of Hungary

Paganini by Delacroix. Photo: The Phillips Collection, Washington, D.C.

"Galop Chromatique," 1843, *caricature by Grandville. Photo courtesy of Biblio-thèque Nationale, Paris*

A dolls' tableau, with George Sand at left. George Sand Historial de Montmartre.
Photo: Roger-Viollet

The Weimar Lohengrin. *Photo courtesy of Nationale Forschungs- und Gedenk-stätten der Klassischen Deutschen Literatur in Weimar*

Princess Carolyne Wittgenstein, circa 1848, in Rome. Photo: Collection Viollet

Richard Wagner in 1865. From Richard Wagner Photographische Bildnisse

Chapter 26

IN ONE OF HER MOMENTS of truth, Marie asked Liszt to "realize that our natures are diametrically opposed; you need the infinite, the illimitable, the unexpected; for me, regularity, the frame properly filled, the feeling of duty accomplished, the paths marked out. . . ." [1] Between 1840 and 1844, a precarious balance was achieved along these lines. For nine months of the year, he toured Europe while she lived in Paris. Three successive summers they vacationed together on the island of Nonnenwerth in the Rhine.

As he had foreseen, she was happier in Paris than she had been abroad. Though she moaned and groaned, comparing herself to Ariadne, a beautiful woman with plenty of money, just emerging from a famous love affair, is in no danger of pining away unless she wants to. Marie immediately set about furnishing an exquisite apartment that included a little *salon mauresque* with a tented ceiling, a Renaissance boudoir, a classical drawing room hung with old mirrors. Eugène Sue helped with the Moorish effects; Duban, an architect recommended by Ingres, worked on the smaller rooms. Lehmann sent lamps from Italy. Sainte-Beuve wrote fawning sonnets: *"Petit boudoir auguste, ô chapelle de la gloire!"*

Her setting arranged, she hired servants so well trained that *Figaro* described a footman putting on gloves to handle a calling card, and began to entertain. Not a name is missing from the bulletins posted off to Liszt: "De Vigny was here all evening; he has taken a lot of trouble and done me a thousand favors. He will read poetry here." [2] "I never stop thanking you for giving me Sainte-Beuve; he comes regularly . . . [and] when we are alone, tells me about his life." [3] Hugo reads from the *Feuilles d'automne* after dinner: "Not the least disenchantment. I found him of an adorable simplicity. . . ." [4] Undaunted by his part in the quarrel with Sand, she even tackled Lamennais: "I found a way to render a couple of small services to the Abbé which earned me a nice long letter; now he is obliged to come when I ask him. . . ." [5] Odder still, we find her at home to Balzac. How, after *Béatrix*, those two could look each other in the face is not explained but there he was, gobbling up her good food. And there too was Lamartine, the most prestigious figure of all. "I very much hope you'll make friends with him," Liszt wrote. He needn't have worried. Lamartine capitulated without a struggle: "I'm mad about her, the only woman a poet could love. If I were young! . . ." [6]

Liszt had advised her to reconcile herself with her family. This was done, on terms she found it easy to accept. The sole condition was that the little girls not live with her. (Daniel remained in Italy, for how long nobody seems quite certain; he was eventually returned to his Liszt grandmother.) Because she was later to tell everybody that Liszt had torn them from her arms, it should be noted that she herself suggested they board with Anna Liszt and that he agreed:

Necessarily you would direct all aspects of their education, physical and moral regime, getting up and going to bed, walks, diet, etc. . . . [But] don't delay about putting the *mouches* with my mother, because from what you say it is the principal point for your family, and it is good and just to give in to them on this matter. . . . [7]

Marie did not fail to tell him, a little later on, how vulgar his mother was: "In two years, she has lost whatever your presence gave her of dignity and intelligence. Perhaps I hurt you. If so, forgive me, I won't say anything more . . . [until] you have judged for yourself how it suits you to let them develop in that common atmosphere." [8] Fortunately, the children were unaware of their grandmother's shortcomings. Lavished with love for the first time in their lives, they throve in her care. When Blandine dined with Marie some months later she was unrecognizable — plump, rosy, and only "much afraid of not returning to her grandmama," wrote Marie sourly. But really she could not have cared less. To be surrounded with small children was no part of her plan.

That plan was simple, as far as the outward circumstances went. She intended to follow Liszt's advice to the letter, reestablish herself, begin to write, become a power. Unavowed, perhaps even in her private prayers, was the hope, the determination, that she would get him back somehow, someday live with him again. His hopes and desires are much less clear. He always had found it easier to love her at a distance and she was no sooner settled in Paris than he adopted the tone of the man whose metier necessarily takes him from home, a sailor perhaps, but who steers by his love and whose return is certain.

"Do you know that I have no other pleasure than that of writing you?" he would ask. And when her portrait arrived — Lehmann's where she leans with tragic eyes against a vine-clad pillar of the Villa Massimiliana — he burst into tears. How was he to endure his loneliness? "My life is so empty, so bare of all joys. . . . Sometimes I go back to those days we spent at Como, then in Florence, and I can hardly bear the memory. . . ." Declarations like these, which he made up to the very end, were pointless unless true. But in that case, did they really need to be apart for three-quarters of every year; and why above all did he deceive her so flagrantly?

He persistently laughed off, when he did not flatly deny, these affairs, and some of them were fantasy. Bettina von Arnim, for example. She was nearly sixty when he met her in Berlin, a still fetching relic of the little madcap who in youth had charmed Goethe. (Her *Briefwechsel mit einem Kind,* a largely invented correspondence between herself and the great man, was full of talent.) She was still extremely attractive and Liszt was fascinated by her but they cannot possibly have gone to bed together. Her affairs were in her head. Herzen, who was *not* fascinated, classed her with the German type he most disliked, whose passions were all contrived, spectral, bookish, "aesthetical hysterics which cost nothing but procure many tears, much joy and grief, many distractions and sensations, *Wonne.*" [9]

Marie however was infuriated by Bettina, though she must have known there was nothing in it.

I see a frightening affinity between you, this persistent moral surfeit that can produce nothing but a hangover [*Katzenjammer* is the German slang she used] of the soul, that is to say an aversion for all natural affections.[10]

In her anger, she sat down and wrote the first article she signed with her new pseudonym, Daniel Stern — a stinging attack on Bettina's writings. It appeared in the *Revue des Deux Mondes,* caused a great stir in Germany and was deeply embarrassing to Liszt, who had obviously supplied much of the factual material. He was furious in his turn: "Your abominable article on Madame von Arnim . . ."

There is something ridiculous about ungoverned lust and Marie, not herself driven by sensuality, clearly felt this about Liszt's infidelities, though the time inevitably came when she took a lover herself.* That, she believed,

* Vier is not absolutely certain that this only happened after her return to Paris. He calls the question "delicate" and indeed it is natural to wonder if all that string of admirers, going back to Ronchaud in Switzerland, sighed in vain. We will probably never know but my own instinct is that they did.

was different. She was not a *femme galante*. Her reasons were in fact repulsively rational. They are to be found in her essay *Sur la liberté:*

> In all civilized society, coquetry for women has become as profound a science as politics. In the idleness they are condemned to, they have learned to take advantage of masculine desires, to make [men] at least temporarily slaves, and all their finesse, intelligence, faculties of observation and calculation are applied to this unique goal: to inspire love without sharing it. Whence . . . a complicated art . . . calling on a hundred times more skill, perseverance, audacity, artifice, agility, deliberation and knowledge than would be needed to administer a kingdom, discipline a military camp, or rule an assembly.[11]

Ostensibly, *Sur la liberté* was a feminist document, deploring the conditions that made such calculations necessary. She nevertheless conducted herself precisely in the manner described. She took Émile de Girardin, the husband of Delphine who was supposed to be her friend, not because she was in love with him but because he was a powerful editor who presided over her nascent literary career.

But what were Liszt's affairs if anything more than demonstrations of conspicuous virility? The operatic flamboyance of the women he chose in the 1840's — with Marie Duplessis in particular we are in the third act of *Traviata* — seems to announce a deliberate use of sex for its own sake; and he was the first to say that it was a failure: ". . . the acclamations of the crowd . . . the banal and lying embraces of my mistresses . . . ," he told Marie, echoed the death-knell of their love. But was that quite true? These women also gave him something that Marie did not and it wasn't only sex. The self-educated *dame aux camélias* was not stupid and Lola Montez was bright enough to take in Lamennais's theories and brash enough to try to put them into practice when she graduated from Liszt to Bavaria's mad king. (Lamennais's ideas ripened in odd places but that was surely the oddest.) The musical and stage personalities with whom his name is linked were not imbeciles either: Camille Pleyel, in addition to being ravishingly pretty, was a first-class pianist. Ungher-Sabatier, Charlotte Hagn, had the intelligence that goes with reaching the top of one's profession. Physically, most of these women were attractive enough that no further explanation is needed for Liszt or any other man having gone to bed with them. But they shared another quality that may have been more important: they knew *who he was* — not a small thing when Marie d'Agoult's estimate is considered. One reads with stupor this, written in 1844:

> Liszt will be for some time yet a marvelous executant, probably a great composer, but never anything else. It is a good deal, undoubtedly, but it isn't enough when one has assumed such a responsibility and (allow me to say without too much arrogance) been loved as he has. . . .[12]

However lying or banal, any mistress must have been preferable to the woman who could say that. Marie couldn't see it and clung to her thesis, that "Liszt wanted to make an easy mistress of me, one more source of vanity in a life of vanities, a woman pleasant to show off, with whom he could relax between orgies. I wasn't right for the part; I tried it because I was so reluctant to separate from the only creature I have passionately and greatly loved." [13]

That was just untrue. It is impossible to read attentively their correspondence between 1834 and 1839, or her memoirs of the same period, and conclude that other women played any part in their gradual estrangement — of which they were rather the consequence than the cause. Not until he went to Vienna for the first time did she have anything to say on this subject. Nor did they part in 1839 on account of it. The issue was then and remained her conviction that he was a knave and a vulgarian if he played the piano in public. "Passionately and greatly loved" are fine words. They aren't worth much when esteem is missing.

"The need to dominate, to tyrannize even, isn't that the driving force most inherent in your nature?" he asked her in 1840. And at almost the same moment he warned her:

Tenderness being the least habitual of my defects, it is natural that men who please you . . . appear to be lakes of tenderness. [Since] in me energy often takes the form of harshness and violence, others necessarily seem to you frail reeds agitated by the breeze. This persistence of yours in finding supplements to my defects and qualities won't charm me forever.[14]

He was right. She rejoiced in her collection of tame cats, suitors who jumped when she cracked the whip, and boasted of her control over them. "In these matters," she assured him, "it is I who rule." That was apropos Girardin. When Sainte-Beuve tried to make love to her, he was instantly the buffoon, "singularly submissive and humble" and writing letters that were "unbelievably ridiculous." She outlines her management of Count Bernard Potocki, a passionate young Pole, in terms that will amaze any woman familiar with the type: "After two months of attentions, of more or less intimate conversations, he declared himself hopelessly smitten and I began the chemical operation; I separated the elements of love from those of friendship, to reject one and keep the other." [15]

These transparent attempts to make Liszt jealous would be pathetic if the men involved hadn't been sacrificed to her ridicule. And that naturally guaranteed their failure. Admiring Sainte-Beuve, and Girardin too, Liszt asked her to treat them gently. As for her frequent threats to take on this or that one, she must decide for herself: "Love me and do as you like." This may have been maddening; it was not unfair, and at the time, she accepted it. After all, it was she who filled her letters with the names of men who were crazy about her; he never dropped the least hint — until 1847 — that he was about to fall in love with another woman, or that she did not reign supreme in his heart.

Their letters written before and after their yearly meetings bear out that what she called "the cruel struggle" between them only incidentally involved his infidelities. Mostly, she couldn't restrain herself from tearing him down. His return to Paris in 1840 was prefaced by a typical series of admonitions from her: He must be "a good child" lest he be thought too "swollen with your success." She was surprised he intended to give a concert immediately. He ought to let himself be sought after, or better yet, not appear. He disregarded this advice, did give concerts, did score the usual triumphs; and once more, they were on the rocks. Ronchaud spoke of their "state of crisis" and for once had a word of censure for Marie, who he said was too severe, while Liszt was "ferociously irritable and domineering" — bored, it seems, with lectures and the Potockis underfoot.

A month later, he was off to London, and the argument continued by mail. "Abandon that savage pride that rears itself between us like a mountain," she wrote. ". . . It is my enemy in you, it is what makes you say, 'I have gained ground,' to which I answer softly, 'Yes, in a graveyard.'" Alas, she never knew when to stop. She ended:

Keep my love if you can. I am a little afraid that the trouble is you can no longer stand the truth or any restraint. Surrounded by Puzzis of various degrees, the language of the most absolute flattery is all you can listen to. . . .[16]

Nevertheless, she followed him to England. Though disliked by the English critics, he was acclaimed in London society. She stayed at Richmond and was miserable. "I can do nothing else now, and probably in the future, but be absolutely alone," she wrote. For some reason this stung him to the quick:

This is what you say to me! Six years of the most absolute devotion have only brought you to this. . . . And so it is with most of what you say. Yesterday (to recall only one occasion), the whole of the way from Ascot to Richmond, you didn't utter a word that didn't wound me, that wasn't an outrage. But what is the good of . . . counting over all these injuries? . . . Love is not justice. Love is not duty; it isn't pleasure either, and yet it contains mysteriously all these things. There are a thousand ways to feel it, to practice it, but for those whose souls thirst for the absolute and the infinite, it is one, with neither beginning nor end. . . . Let us not quarrel over words . . . or haggle or try our strength. . . . If we still have love in our hearts, all is said; if it has vanished, there is nothing to say.[17]

Lovers' quarrels grow tedious unless they lead to reconciliation or the final rupture. Four years is too long for the unresolved conflict. Marie is more and more the wounded heroine: "My life, away from you, is no better than a lie. . . . I long for you with all the strength of my soul and yet I sense a destructive element that does its work blindly and drives us to opposite poles. . . ." [18] But because we know she isn't going to throw herself under a train — she lived to a ripe old age — we simply wish she would manage better; and that Liszt, instead of telling her that "if we aren't happy, it may be because we deserve better," that "there is too much energy, too much passion, too much fire in our vitals for us to settle in a bourgeois way for the possible," would exchange his Romantic hubris for a little common sense. Instead they continue to court destiny, and in sensationally appropriate settings.

"Nonnenwerth will be the sanctuary or the tomb of our love," he said on the eve of their final summer.[19] It was the latter, in her words, "the tomb of my illusions, of my ideal life, the spoliation of my hopes." [20] Nonnenwerth is a beautiful wooded island lying between Remagen and Bonn, where German legend has it that Roland died of love. On it was a half-ruined convent that had been converted to a smart and secluded hostelry of a type we don't quite associate with the nineteenth century — not yet "discovered," she told Sainte-Beuve, as one might say of an unadvertised, expensive resort in the Lipari Islands today.

Her arrival made a commotion among the other guests, partly because she was at first believed to be George Sand. She appears to have been in a sort of disguise and signed the register with a false name. All this was breathlessly observed by the adolescent daughter of a German general staying in the hotel and it is thanks to this source that we get a glimpse of Marie's feminine presence which explains why, in spite of everything, Liszt was still in love with her. The young spy, who followed them everywhere, thought her beauty on the wane (she was thirty-six, the edge of middle age to a child) but her face and figure still unforgettable, and her personal arrangements the last word in elegance. She put perfume in her bathwater, her linen was exquisitely done up, her lingerie, secretly displayed by the laundress, perfection. Above all, there were her clothes — puffed silk skirts and those long gauzy scarves she wound around her neck as at Nohant; her magnificent fair hair confined in a net. She was surrounded with men: Liszt, but also Lichnowsky, Girardin, Thiers. . . .

Marie to Lehmann, August 21, 1843: The life we lead, would, I think, be infinitely agreeable to you. There is at once habit and diversity, the sweetness of outdoors and the refinements of elegant life, good nature, wit and imagination. Yesterday, for example, some Hungarian dancers, found for me at Cologne, executed national dances; after that Saphir (the Viennese humorist) gave us a lecture on witticisms and puns. We have as a regular reader a translator of Shakespeare who puts all the amusing little incidents of our days into verse. Ronchaud is always here; Potocki comes and goes; many others, Count Teleki, Count Lubinski, all this makes a little court of love of which I am the unworthy sovereign.[21]

What was the serpent in this paradise? A letter from the summer of 1842 says she can't get her folly out of her head:

I would be better as a friend than as a lover. I know I have nothing to reproach you with but I also know — I know nothing except that I suffer and would make you suffer eternally by staying. Goodbye, then. . . . Goodbye, Franz, this isn't a rupture but an adjournment. In five or six years, we will laugh at my tortures of today.[22]

It wasn't good-bye. She stayed six more weeks on the island. But another quarrel is memorialized, and since "I have nothing to reproach you with," it must have had to do with the old subject. The course of events isn't too difficult to follow:

Liszt to Marie, November 11, 1842: Perhaps I haven't understood the letter I have just received. I have reread it, and excuse me if I am mistaken, but it seems to me . . . that a complete and immediate rupture would give you pleasure. . . . Only, if you want [one], try to put me on the positive track of some perfidy . . . send me a letter or something that authorizes me to quarrel. Otherwise, it will be more reasonable (but I am very weary of reasonableness in the face of so many stupidities and follies) if I make a break before the end of the year. . . . Tell me simply what I am to do. It would be difficult to come to Paris but if you wish it, I leave tomorrow.[23]

Liszt to Marie, December 8, 1842: . . . It seems to me I have forgotten how to live. . . . I can attach myself to nothing; I would throw up the whole thing if you could be happy living with me again. But whether from perversity, hardness of heart, blindness of the spirit and the heart at once, I could no longer believe I was enough in your life, and as an alternative I preferred this life of vagabondage to a sickly stagnation which would have killed me without making you live. I am not deceiving myself. My life for the last three years has been nothing but a series of excitements . . . leading to disgust and remorse. I must spend, and spend again, life, strength, money and time, without joy in the present or hope in the future. . . . My health is iron. My moral force hasn't weakened, my character is perhaps more tempered. Are these the conditions for happiness? Is it still possible? I can't answer. It is for you to determine.[24]

Liszt to Marie, January 22, 1843: I am entirely of the opinion that I must soon end my virtuoso career. Hungary . . . is the natural and necessary conclusion. I imagine you would like that country, and cherish the idea of living with you there for a while. . . .[25]

The last was the only letter in this sequence to provoke a reply:

Marie to Liszt, January 30, 1843: Obviously you don't think of me at all. . . . I can't answer about Hungary. We must talk it over next summer, as you say, and since I won't be changed and you won't either, as you will yield to your fancy and I will never understand why your whims will not give way to my most reasonable and legitimate desires, you will break my heart again with no profit to anybody. But that seems your destiny, and I will serve you to the end in the exercise of your destructiveness. It isn't easy. Love and goodwill have always appeared preferable to fantasies I admit, but I don't know anything about life. Why didn't you let me die? [26]

At some point along the line, letters like this began to lose their efficacy. Her alternation of threats and pleas lost its power to move him, or turned into an evil apéritif taken, and regretted, before a concert or a grand foreign dinner. Yet he continued to trust her, and that was his mistake.

Chapter 27

LACKING THE DIARY or the memoir that he didn't write, we don't know when Liszt first thought of abandoning the piano for the orchestra and a broader range of composition. He knew, at any rate, from Berlioz's sad example, that to live by the orchestra in France was heartbreaking work. Germany with its multiplicity of courts and musical establishments, its symphonic tradition, was the logical place. Hence his ready acceptance of the offer made him in 1842 by the duchy of Weimar to be its honorary *Kapell-meister*. It was an attractive proposition, requiring his presence for no more than three months out of every year, and though the salary was laughably small, he signed a contract. How seriously he took it at the time is open to question. It was an anchor to windward. In 1842, he was a long way from seeing what it would lead to, and he still thought of himself as French — or at least an inhabitant of Paris, to which he returned each spring as faithfully as the migrating salmon in the Seine. He liked to say that it was impossible to consider living there except as a journalist, that sort of thing. In fact he never considered living anywhere else on a permanent basis, until Marie poisoned its wells for him.

How she did this has generally escaped notice. No one has called attention to the fact that her social rehabilitation was accomplished by a systematic trading on Liszt's old friendships. (In Vier's admiring assessment, she "dreamed of reconstituting her salon . . . regrouping around her some of the visitors to the rue de Baune or the château de Croissy." [1] There was no regrouping. Alfred de Vigny was the only important survivor of her pre-Liszt past to present himself.) Her memoirs paint a desperate plight: "Young, beautiful . . . proud . . . What to do? . . . I belonged to no milieu. . . . Men would be in love with me." [2] Having cut her ties with the Faubourg long since, she was entirely dependent on those who befriended her for Liszt's sake: Balzac, Hugo, Lamartine, Sainte-Beuve, d'Eckstein, Béranger, Berlioz, Girardin.

She was too skilled at social maneuvers to bore or antagonize this circle with recitals of Liszt's delinquencies — at first. As the tide of her grievances rose against him, the world was invited to take her side. That her miseries were broadcast is evident from a tactful warning given her by Lichnowsky six months after the final break:

> . . . As to you, my friend, I confess I can't think of the separation you tell me about as a disaster; you will remember perhaps what I said to you at the time; I must stick to my opinion; you musn't play the widow of Malabar, but go back to the world, taking Mlle d'Agoult by the hand, and like someone who has placed a large and insurmountable barrier between past and present, avoid going to meet danger, that is exonerating yourself for the past by talking about it. You are someone who has come back from a long voyage by land and sea and who has the good taste not to tire her listeners with impressions of the trip.[3]

His advice was not taken, which may be why there were some prominent dropouts from her guest lists. Avidly pursued, Hugo showed a reserve that quite possibly sprang from affection for Liszt (as well as his devotion to Delphine Girardin), whose defects he shared: had fate made Hugo a musician, he would have been exactly like Liszt — which made him a poor audience for Marie's complaints. The same applied to Balzac, who was a temporary acquisition too. Closer inspection provided him with an experience that must be rare for a novelist. The character he had invented out of his imagination and Sand's gossip turned out to be all too lifelike. In 1843, Madame Hanska was informed that Marie was "intolerably pretentious" and that "I have fled her forever."

From Liszt's point of view it made little difference whether his old friends believed Marie's story or his — blamed her, or him for tolerating her. He left his fences unmended for too long, and was to the last unsuspicious of the extent to which she took advantage of his absence. He had told her to stand on her own feet, "show who you are." She did. Through Lamartine she had access to high politics. Girardin showed her how to throw her weight around in the press and thanks to his instructions she learned the value of the written word as destructive instrument. The results burst on the world with the publication of her novel *Nélida* in 1846.

This book did more to discredit Liszt than can readily be believed considering its quality. It is their love affair at the housemaid level, with Liszt a lowborn painter of small talent and herself an ineffably aristocratic lady who is obliged to leave him on account of his sleazy affairs and pursuit of cheap success. Her desertion deprives him of his little talent and he squalidly expires — in Weimar, of all places, and lest the point be missed. The style is beyond respectable analysis, as the plot suggests. It is also familiar:

> But when he saw Nélida's hollow cheeks, her listless eyes, her pale lips, saw that she was still of an incomparable majesty in her sorrow, his lower nature was vanquished. He fell at her feet, clasped her to him with more ardor than on the first day, and in the madness of his transports soon made her forget all she had suffered from his cruel absence.[4]

Guermann-Liszt is in fact so despicable that it isn't at all clear why any woman would suffer from his absence, but Ernest Newman, for one, is certain this picture "was painted directly from life," and that the book is "a genuinely historical document."[5] There is, to be sure, a little trouble about this interpretation, which Newman disposes of by saying that Marie "could not pierce the future," and that events "proved her to be wrong" about the man she depicted as an insignificant boor. It wasn't events that proved Marie wrong. It was her arrogant stupidity about the man she claimed to love. She was wrong about the future because she had misread the past: once rid of her, Liszt went from strength to strength.

It is incredible that *Nélida* should have had more than a *succès de scandale* but in spite of setbacks (Lamennais declined to sponsor it, the *Revue des Deux Mondes* to publish it, and Sainte-Beuve to review it) it was handled with a certain respect. Girardin's *Presse* gave it a glowing notice; Ronchaud praised it in the *Revue de Paris*. Another paper actually spoke of its "profound study of character and elevation of style." Marie had done her spadework well. Long before its publication, long before it was written, the right people were talked to and later the manuscript circulated privately. "Those who are talking about your book are all the heads of the party," a friend told her in 1842. "Berryer, Odilon Barrot, Thiers, Chateaubriand, Béranger . . ."[6]

Liszt was therefore, like the deceived husband, the last to know. He took it in the only way he could, as if it had nothing to do with him, had kind words for the style, and suggested that one or two minor characters didn't quite come off. Marie assured Lehmann that "his letter, in which he asked me to do some little services and joked without the least irony or bitterness, is not written in a tone that would make one suspect the serpent hidden under the flower." And undoubtedly he did not then foresee the torment in store for him, the rain of "questions, insinuations, compliments, condolences, malignities of every kind" that would descend on him. It is also possible that he didn't immediately recognize himself in the painter Guermann Régnier, whom he seems at first to have thought was a portrait of Lehmann

— a natural enough mistake in a book so badly written. Only in the circumstances (Nélida leaves her husband, flies to Geneva with Guermann) was there any resemblance to persons living or dead.

Nélida is unreadable today; but it remains a singular piece of feminine pathology and the date (around 1842) when she began to plot it out casts a sinister illumination on her last two or three years with Liszt. *Nélida's* hero-villain dies but in the meantime he has already suffered a symbolic castration in the loss of his artistic gift when his mistress leaves him. This is the punishment that his sins deserve and she dwells on it with pleasure — just as the servant's quarters to which he is finally relegated represent, in her terms, that rung of hell reserved for fornicators. It had always been obvious that she hated Liszt's music partly because she made the primitive association with his sexual potency. The loss of one would entail the loss of the other. *Nélida* (an anagram, incidentally, of her pen name Daniel) shows that she willed this to happen. There is no other way to interpret the fantasy of Guermann's impotence — though there is the secondary implication that his powers derived from her, hence the cutoff when she leaves him.

Without probing the deeper level of her unconscious, that last was also important to Marie: the world must believe that she had left Liszt and not the other way around. She later dated her "freedom" to November 1843 and tried to create the impression that she made up her mind to break with him when he returned to Paris in the spring of 1844. The letters don't support this.

Hers are bitter enough. When kind friends informed her of his involvement with the pretty German actress Charlotte Hagn, she was in a rage. It was in this connection that she made an often quoted pronouncement: "I will be your mistress but not one of your mistresses," which might have been more effective if she hadn't had a lover and perhaps two.* As Liszt probably knew when he made her his grandiloquent answer:

The distinction is charming and very just. But let me tell you that the alternative has never existed for you. My faults, my mistakes and follies are my own, whatever false resemblance they may have to those of others. And you too are mine, and very much mine. Why talk of the rest! [7]

I think he understood her better than posterity has. Her ultimatums never stood up to rebuttal, or indeed to acquiescence — which brought on

---

* Vier, who accepts Girardin on the basis of unpublished letters and documents, has also unearthed "a decisive avowal" in her unpublished diary for 1842 that she succumbed at last to Charles Didier. He further thinks this procured yet another garotting for her in Sand's novel *Horace*. In this, the Vicomtesse de Chailly, a horrible character who lacks even the beauty that Balzac gave to Béatrix, was an obvious representation of Marie. That was recognized at the time. Vier goes further, and sees in Horace himself, a provincial *arriviste*, the figure of Didier. All this presumably stemming from Sand's irritation at Didier's defection to Marie.

their collapse. They seem rather to have been based on the hope that a good scare would "bring him to his senses." The recurrent fantasy, present also in *Nélida,* of a repentant Liszt at her feet, did not desert her. She spoke of final partings. When he took her at her word, she went to pieces.

He arrived in Paris the first week in April 1844. On the eighth, he asked to dine alone with her. Marie now had a new confidant (lover?), the German poet in exile, Georg Herwegh, and he was told to come between four and six on the day: "I am so sad, so tired of life and I see nothing to change, nothing to hope for, to want, to do. . . . *In vain,* seems to be the dénouement of my life. . . . I hate music, having loved it for too long. . . ." She seems to have understood that this was her last chance for immortality. We don't know what happened at this "last" meeting, or the one after it, or the one after that. But on the eleventh, Liszt wrote her a note with a terminal look:

I am mortally sad and profoundly afflicted. I count one by one the sorrows I have put in your heart and nothing and nobody can save me from myself. I want neither to speak to you nor to see you, even less to write to you. . . .[8]

Obviously this was unacceptable. His next says, "I don't understand your uncertainty. You desired to see me no more. I obeyed." And a little later, "Why threats from you to me?" From this sequence it is possible to guess she was seeking any means to prolong and complicate the rituals of farewell. Third parties were now invoked. She asked him to see Lamartine ("who doesn't consider me a disaster in your life"); Ronchaud was mentioned. Herwegh hovered in the background.

The excuse for the ruckus was the one thing about which they had never had a shadow of disagreement — the children. Suddenly she writes to Herwegh: "I will fight like a lioness to get my children back." Fight whom? Liszt was amazed, though he need not have been; it was a most feminine maneuver. The future of the children did not seem to him a question they could decide "from one day to the next" or one requiring intermediaries. It could be discussed by letter. He had thought that "the education of the children would be a source of embarrassment to you" — he didn't remind her that their exclusion from her home had been one of the terms laid down by the Flavigny family — and "moreover if you take up the position of an enemy, it would be impossible for me to leave them in your hands." But he did not insist:

Persuaded that you better than anybody would know how to direct the education of my daughters, I can only be grateful for the desire you express to occupy yourself with it more than in the past. I see no difficulty on my mother's side, she having up till now acquitted herself well, to my way of thinking, in the painful task which she accepted. Allow me to hope that you will have fewer annoyances and also to pray that you will send me news of these children from time to time, their health, their studies, etc. . . . . I make only one reservation: that of intervening once more in this matter you have made so painful . . . if it happens that in consequence of this solution . . . you draw on yourself the family embarrassments and vexations I wish to spare you as much as I can. You can be perfectly reassured about the pecuniary arrangements I will undertake. The interest on the capital I will invest will be enough to keep my two daughters. . . .[9]

This was of course not in the least what Marie had in mind. She didn't want the children, only a series of scenes and meetings *about* the children — all else having failed. For he had accepted the blame: "I have told no lies to my intimate friends. I have said flatly that you disapprove and condemn my orgiastic life, that you have therefore told me that it would be better not to meet again, and therefore that we will see each other no more." [10] Too late, she saw the futility of being right and yet losing the game. Many of her letters from this period are missing or mutilated but from other sources it is clear that some days after she received his final word, printed above, she changed her tack and tried, by reminding him of his duty to her and the children, to push for a reconciliation. Her instrument was Herwegh.

Herwegh to Marie, May 17, 1844: Liszt remains entirely true to his nature. Just as it is impossible for him to shake himself free of the present and of the thousand good-for-nothings who fasten themselves on him . . . so he will never free himself of his past. . . . He will never have the courage to break with anything. In order to assimilate everything . . . a man must be a *character*. Liszt will never be that as long as he persists in his virtuosity: this . . . has made him a veritable "man-eater" who will never find enough people to devour. His unparalleled success, which has been won less by his genius, his soul, than by his mechanism, has led him astray to the point where he judges men . . . without considering their moral basis. . . . But I admire in Liszt the splendid force that unhappily projects itself too much to the outside and splits him up into a thousand rays. . . . If it were possible to steady him by a violent shock of some sort and decide him to go more deeply into things instead of skating on the surface, we could save him. But that is perhaps more your affair than mine.[11]

To which she answered, "How can you think that what I attempted in vain for five years of absolute devotion and ardent passion, I could accomplish now that I can only speak in the name of duty and maternal tenderness?" There follows a passage that points directly to Herwegh's active intervention: "No, if your example, your serious and inspired eloquence make no impression on him, there is nothing for me to do but change my life and assemble my forces so as not to be dragged into and swallowed by that abyss. . . ."

Herwegh may even have approached Liszt a second time. On May 28, Marie wrote again:

What you say about Liszt does not surprise me: it confirms my belief in the necessity of a separation that will be absolute and eternal. It would really be too naïve to cherish the shadow of a hope, and what have I to do with a parvenu Don Juan, half mountebank, half juggler, who makes ideas and feelings disappear up his sleeve and looks complacently at the dumbfounded public that applauds him? Ten years of illusion! . . .[12]

A word about Herwegh, deemed a worthy "example" to Liszt. He was a poet of rather slight talent, which evaporated after some years of soft living on a rich wife. He was a liberal and exile from Germany, and beyond that there was little to be said for his character. To Herzen, whose marriage he callously destroyed, he was the most contemptible of men. In short, the perfect person to preach morality to Liszt, with whom he was scarcely acquainted. His insufferable interference may easily have been decisive as far as Liszt was concerned.

Marie left town toward the end of May, going to stay with her mother. To Herwegh, having dragged him into it, she had to concede defeat. Not so to her women friends, one of whom received the following:

At midnight on the eve of my departure, his [Liszt's] servant came to tell me that he was in a horrible state . . . that he was about to die and asking for me. I was in bed, I got up in haste, thinking it wasn't absolutely impossible that he had poisoned himself. Still, I was calm and resolute. I found him with a high fever but not in danger. He seemed happy to see me, but . . . even in that solemn hour, he soon returned to his usual discourse and proved . . . for the thousandth time that he has forever lost the consciousness of what his life should be, of what he ought to do for me and his children, that in short his poor head has been turned by a torrent of vanities. . . . I left him with the hope of seeing me again, but I am determined to stay as far away as possible. . . . I'm not uneasy about myself. As you put it so well, my life can be what I want. . . . It is well that I am with my family just now or I would be afraid that Liszt might come with éclat to join me. . . .[13]

Is there a woman who would not recognize this as a face-saver? The hint that he had taken poison left delicately in air, the midnight summons, that ineffable "I left him with the hope of seeing me again," all stamp it a preliminary chapter for *Nélida*. He wasn't given to deathbed scenes or futile pursuits. She however was, and it may also be that this was one of her transpositions — *she* may have summoned *him*. Or she may have seized on the excuse of a slight illness to pay him an unwelcome call (not at midnight).

It is certain anyhow that he left Paris without seeing her again, and that she sent him tentatives on the road. These are lost but their nature evident from his answer:

. . . However moved I may be at the softening of your anger, I can nevertheless not at all condemn my past. That past, Madame, was full each day of a serious and passionate devotion to yourself. The impulses and mistakes to be found there were neither lasting nor serious. The hand you promise to hold out to me some day when all is forgotten, I would be happy to seize and hold forever, but I can't, no, I never could tell myself that it ought to have been withheld for a single instant.[14]

He was badly hurt all the same. Ten years, when they come between the ages of twenty-three and thirty-three, are a lifetime and he could hardly remember what is was like to be without her. "My rupture with the Countess d'Agoult has ripped the veil of youthful dreams," he wrote his friend Massart. Was it this that made him think of Caroline de Saint-Cricq? It was at this time, turning aside from his route to Madrid, that he made a little pilgrimage to visit her — evidence, surely, that he was in that despairing state when the griefs of the past are preferable to those in the present, and those of innocence more desirable than those of experience.

With Marie, things went from bad to worse. Liszt left Paris with the understanding that Blandine would be placed in a smart school for girls while the other two stayed with their grandmother. Massart was put in charge of their finances, an arrangement that infuriated Marie. She utterly refused to give Massart any accounting of the funds she claimed were insufficient. At one stage she announced she would take Blandine to live with her — this daughter had "a delicate and passionate tenderness for me"; Cosima, an inferior production, was not really wanted, though her removal too was threatened.

In the spring of 1845, Liszt lost patience. He wrote to Massart:

As the terms are fixed, I obviously cannot contest . . . Madame d'Agoult's right to occupy herself with her two daughters and to intervene in any number of ways. My only resource . . . is to refuse the money she can demand for the purpose, and that is why I asked you to get back her accounts. Now, it is as certain that I will refuse to give three thousand francs for Cosima as it is undoubted that I will send you this sum regularly for Blandine. In my opinion, Cosima and Daniel ought to stay with my mother and I hope Madame d'Agoult will agree. If . . . she tries to take Cosima by force, I will retaliate in full by taking the three children to Germany where she will have no hold over them.[15]

At this, Marie lost her head. "He has broken his word," she shrieked. She hired a lawyer, who gave her some erroneous advice. He believed it impossible for Liszt to legitimatize the children and that unless he did he hadn't a leg to stand on. The lawyer was wrong. The children were not French citizens and could have been granted Austrian nationality, thus cancelling Marie's rights altogether. Liszt passed this information along through his own lawyer though it is doubtful if he then contemplated so drastic a step. All he actually wanted was to keep them out of Marie's hands, and for the best of reasons. In her mania for consultation and publicity, her determination to vilify him, Marie, who had talked to everybody including Lamennais, overlooked an important point: Liszt was not going to have his children educated to think him a blackguard. He had told her this before. He now said it again:

Liszt to Marie, May 2, 1845: A year ago, Madame, I could believe that the incredible view of me you have conjured up and put forth in numerous letters, would be a secret between us. I even concluded from your ardent devotion in the past that you would maintain with other people the same reserve I have imposed on myself in regard to you: now this illusion is no longer possible because I cannot ignore your telling all comers the wildest and most abusive things about me. . . . [Can] you really think it would suit me to have Blandine brought up by you so long as you keep us on a footing of armed warfare? . . .[16]

Her answer was an incredible document, smeared as it were with Niobe's tears:

You are capable of the worst cowardice: that of threatening *from a distance* and by *virtue of legality* a mother who reclaims the fruit of her womb. . . . I see I am vanquished, Monsieur, in a hopeless struggle in which I can only invoke your heart, your reason and your conscience. But I protest before God and man, I protest before all mothers the violence done me. . . . Henceforth, Monsieur, your children have no mother. . . .[17]

This went on for pages and with anyone but Liszt and Marie would have brought the correspondence to a halt. They seemed unable to break themselves of the writing habit and soon were back to normal, more or less. Liszt knew that apart from their ghastly taste her denunciations were meaningless: she wasn't really dissatisfied with his decision.

The victims were the children themselves. Neither parent consulted their wishes, which were unanimously in favor of living with their grandmother. When Blandine was sent to her *pensionnat*, Cosima missed her so acutely that she had eventually to be allowed to join her. Daniel (whom Marie had called "a child confided to Providence and hazard, of whom I would do best to think as little as possible") was in turn so unhappy without his sisters that his grandmama was in despair. A characteristic letter to Liszt beseeches him to write to his son, "*le pauvre bel amour*." There isn't much hope that he obliged. He missed all the important happenings of their childhoods, first communions, prizes awarded at school. (So, for that matter, did Marie.) He was in France as seldom as possible, after 1846 not at all. The children worshipped him like someone dead, and didn't set eyes on him for eight years.

Chapter 28

WHEN LISZT reached Kiev in February 1847, he was on the frontier of what to him was the civilized world. There is a good deal about this city with its three hundred domes like jewelled poppy-heads, its exotic population and savage history, in *The Gypsies and Their Music* but as that is from the hand of Carolyne Wittgenstein, it is a doubtful reflection of his observations. His letters do not describe Kiev, or the Ukraine either — which for all its resemblance to the Hungarian plain was not his kind of landscape. "Give me," he once said, "the countryside around Pisa, the Roman campagna, Constantinople — Venice, the lake of the four cantons, Lisbon, or the forest of Fontainebleau. . . ." [1] If the steppes of Russia were endeared to him in later life, it was because he associated them with Carolyne. Their story, as peculiar as any that the history of love has to offer, begins in Kiev.

She was there because the Ukrainian landowners, taking advantage of frozen, hence passable, roads, always went to Kiev in winter to settle their business affairs and indulge in social life. But she was an eccentric even by Russian standards, and at twenty-eight virtually a recluse in her pinnacled mansion. (Liszt speaks of "*vos chères tourelles gothiques.*") She attended Liszt's concerts. The chances of her meeting the lion himself, swamped as he was with invitations to balls and dinners, surrounded with women, looked slight. Fate, however, was on her side. She wrote him a note — *the* note, which is lost — and enclosed a hundred rubles for his next charity concert. Liszt, so the story goes, had heard of her, her bizarre habits and her stinginess (contradicted by the hundred rubles), and called on her the following day. Here again, circumstances were against her. Within a week, he was to leave Russia. She invited him to stop off at her estate some hundred miles to the west. Already in love, he accepted, and the rest is . . . But of course it didn't happen that way at all. Like all the Liszt legends, this one is full of holes. The given dates are a scramble * and Liszt was long past the age of sudden passions, had Carolyne been the woman to inspire one. In fact, she was almost comically unattractive.

Small, dark, saturnine, with a cast of feature often (and wrongly) described as "Jewish" by those who disliked her and thought the description invidious, she was the last woman in the world to attract adulterous glances; and never was desired by another man in that way. Fond of dress but pitiably wanting in elegance, she was innocent as a schoolgirl. She drove most people crazy, and poor woman, she knew it. She even had a pretty good idea of why she did. A letter to her daughter, written on her fortieth birthday, says it all:

I was always happy, radiant. In the midst of my worst agonies, I have never wished . . . I hadn't been born. I have always had a beautiful feeling for life, the supreme gift. . . . But I have never felt that the Lord had reason to rejoice in me . . . since from my earliest infancy I have been aware of the contrast between my soul and my body, between the harmony of my aspirations and the absence of it in my person. . . . I know that I am good and that I am not lovable; my goodwill is really infinite . . . but my reason demands justice. . . . The result is that, wishing everyone well, I am powerless to bring it about. . . . I want to be agreeable to everybody, and I can only impose myself. . . . I have a mania for detail that does not fit with my large views of the whole; and thus I always appear to judge when I only mean to excuse. The incessant view of the Good . . . of the True and the Beautiful, constantly applied to practical life, makes me such a stranger to many things that I feel myself walking through life as if surrounded by an air that others do not breathe and that makes an emptiness around me. . . . Everything stays at a distance. . . . No one warms himself at the heat of my heart. My common sense gives me no influence over the minds of others; nor my goodwill over their souls. . . . I am forty today, and it is thirty years, more or less . . . that I have sensed . . . the circle traced

---

* Mostly owing to the time-lag between the old Russian calendar and our own. All her life Carolyne kept the program for his concert of February 2, presumably the one for which she sent the hundred rubles. This was February 14 by western reckoning. But Liszt wrote a letter to Marie d'Agoult from Carolyne's country estate which is dated February 10. So something is wrong. But suppose that both dates, the second and the tenth, were Russian. Carolyne still worked with unbelievable speed. The journey to Woronince, her estate, can't have taken less than two days — and she was waiting for him when he arrived. So she can't have left Kiev later than the sixth or seventh, giving her a bare four days to effect her conquest.

There are other mixups. La Mara says Liszt arrived in time to celebrate her daughter's tenth birthday. But according to Hugo (*The Letters of Franz Liszt to Marie zu Sayn-Wittgenstein*, 1953), her birthday was August 15. The discrepancies aren't of great importance, but they reinforce an incredulity derived from other sources.

around me, the constraint that differentiates respect from tenderness, the something that silently says, "You are someone but not one of us. . . ." [2]

Before this frightening piece of self-analysis, criticism must fall silent. It
is worthy, almost, of a real writer — one who understands the effects of
psychological disturbance: "The circle traced around me . . . everything
stays at a distance." These are afflictions against which the complaints of
Cornelius, of Bülow and others, about her tactless personal questions, her
philosophizings, the cigars and the rest — look puerile. There is, to be sure,
a certain spiritual smugness seeping around the edges; but there is, too, the
knowledge uncommon for the period, that her position in life is no cause
for rejoicing and may itself be at fault. She wasn't, contrary to the opinion
of the mostly middle-class musicians who surrounded Liszt in Weimar,
proud of being a princess. It was their class-consciousness rather than hers
which made the position difficult.

Carolyne Iwanowska was the only child of a Polish nobleman so rich that
on his death he left her a property barbarously reckoned at thirty thousand
"souls," a cruel inheritance. The Polish landlords of the Ukraine were descended from the sixteenth-century conquerors of the province (which
reverted to Russia in the third partition of Poland) and were Roman Catholics; their serfs were Little Russians, and Orthodox. Thus were created all
the conditions for mutual hatred only slightly mitigated by the hatred of
both for the Russian government — to which the Ukrainians have never
been devoted and which the Polish aristocracy endured because it had no
choice.

The Ukraine was not a cheerful land to live in. A fantastic inefficiency
marked every phase of existence. House serfs given no quarters of their
own slept in the corridors of the great houses like animals. There was no
wood for the porcelain stoves, which had to be heated into petrifying blazes
with straw. The estates were so huge that there were no neighbors and
since public services were unknown the simplest communication was difficult. Countess Marie Potocka, living quite near Carolyne as distances were
calculated, noted "the positively Ottoman sang-froid" required "to conduct
a conversation in which our mujiks, mounted on their flayed rats, are
charged with transmitting our thoughts." This countess took her sons to
Switzerland to be educated under Sismondi, but it never occurred to her to
buy the mujik a decent horse, and her petulance was typical of a doomed
society.

Carolyne's parents contrived to give her an upbringing that was abnormal
even by these criteria. Her mother was a beautiful woman who preferred
to live abroad unencumbered, with the result that her daughter, Daddy's
girl, was a tomboy who rode her horses till they dropped, ate when she was

hungry, sat up half the night if she felt like it, and acquired her cigar habit at an early age. When she was seventeen, they married her off.

Like Marie d'Agoult's, this marriage had something odd about it, and was an instant failure. Prince Nicholas Wittgenstein, in spite of his resounding name, was penniless and without distinction of any kind, a bad *parti*. Queer as she was, with her colossal fortune she could have done better; but their relations were amiable. After the birth of their daughter Marie, he pursued his army career. Carolyne retired to her estate.

Woronince was a one-story villa of the type built all over Russia in the early nineteenth century — a blurred reminiscence of Palladio set in a mournful *jardin anglais*. Around it was an incalculable expanse of land so badly farmed that no more than a third of it was under cultivation at any one time. "It is emptiness," wrote Balzac, "the kingdom of wheat, the rolling plains of Cooper and their silence. This is where the humus of the Ukraine begins, dark, rich soil, fifty feet deep and often more, which is never dunged. . . ." [3] It might have been uninhabited for all Carolyne saw of her people. Having given up riding, she scarcely left the house, a curious refuge loaded with what La Mara (who often writes about Liszt and Carolyne as if Tristan and Isolde had somehow got crossed with Hänsel and Gretel) calls "the romantic symbolism." [4] Every room expressed a state of mind: in the drawing room, flowers represented "social life blossoming in monotony"; Carolyne's workroom, done up with the busts of poets, "the cheerful seriousness of study." In her bedroom symbolism really runs rampant. Gray-papered walls, crimson divans, a wooden crucifix espaliered from floor to ceiling — what does this tell us? "That in the midst of life's grayness is the disappointed and bleeding heart of the mistress."

These may be La Mara's interpretations: she never saw the rooms. But one feels they weren't inventions. The imagery is of a piece with Carolyne's outlook and vocabulary, and with that of an age that habitually dressed up its ideas of sex, death and art in a kind of domestic exhibitionism. Wagner's décors at Wahnfried (the name means freedom from illusion) would make a psychiatrist swoon: they included a sofa on which he and Cosima were to give up the ghost together, a *Liebestod* on pink plush. In that language, Carolyne's bedroom probably did advertise her starved emotions.

She had, when Liszt met her, only her little girl to love, and that was in a distracted way that left the child mostly to a Scotch governess, a Miss Anderson, who accompanied her charge to Weimar and was always known as "Scotch" or "Scotchy." For Carolyne was one of those women who, with nothing whatever to do, have no time to give to household affairs. All her life she was engrossed in projects whose size was only equalled by their futility, and like many untalented people she didn't know the meaning of laziness or discouragement. Continuously inspired, she wrote and read for hours on end. How she read! Hegel, Fichte, Bossuet, Goethe, the Talmud, Tacitus, Villani, Dante — she plowed through them all and might have saved herself the trouble. In the world of ideas, she was like someone who blunders into a dark closet and comes out wearing the wrong suit. A Byzantine monk was better equipped to make sense of western civilization.

Her religious mania ought, one might think, to have been a bar to adultery. But the religion of art was not unknown to bluestockings in the depths of Russia, where it may have combined itself more easily than elsewhere with the cult for holy men. To the rest of the world Liszt may have looked weak or evil — to her he was surrounded with the nimbus of genius; nor did she have any trouble attributing his advent in her life to divine intervention. Yet her virtue was so far beyond doubt that there existed a minority opinion that the affair might after all have been platonic, a theory that gained ground when they had no children.

We know surprisingly little about nineteenth-century birth control. "N'est-ce pas immoral?" Her sister-in-law puts this question to Anna Karenina when told that a woman may decide for herself whether or not to bear children. Tolstoy, grimly not on Anna's side, gives no hint of her method. I have assumed that Marie d'Agoult's pregnancies were deliberate on account of their timing. In any case, we don't know whether Liszt and Carolyne were childless accidentally or on purpose; whether Carolyne would have thought it more sinful to produce a bastard, or to do something to prevent it. At a guess, she would have welcomed Liszt's child as a gift from God and all but canonized it. So I think it can safely be assumed that heaven failed her.* She was a peculiar woman but not peculiar enough to have wanted — or achieved — a platonic relationship with Liszt. One writes of her as if she had been middle-aged, perhaps because her plainness and her pedantry suggest it. She was eight years younger than he and unless her

---

* There is however a report to the contrary. Peter Cornelius, who knew Liszt and Carolyne intimately, evidently told his son (who put the information in his biography) that Carolyne gave birth to three children "in towns other than Weimar" and had them brought up elsewhere. (Carl Maria Cornelius: Peter Cornelius [Regensburg, 1925], I, 158.) No proof is offered and there isn't the remotest hint in other sources that any such children existed. I simply don't believe the story — mostly for the reason given above: she would never have parted from any child of Liszt's. But even supposing that she did, that it was decided to conceal these births at the time, it is quite impossible that they could have been hidden forever. Somebody, somewhere, would have known who the children were and the truth come out.

As might be expected, Liszt was credited with numerous bastards. But as these were always sons and always musicians, their authenticity is open to doubt. It is too obvious how helpful such a claim would have been to a young man embarking on a musical career. A good example of what happens when innuendo is put to the test is Franz Servais. Newman is certain that this pianist was Liszt's and Carolyne's son, the proof being that he was born in Petersburg in 1847. Carolyne was in Petersburg in 1847, and, says Newman archly, "the reader must be left to draw his own conclusions" (The Man Liszt: p. 182). The reader would do better to look up the dates. Liszt met Carolyne in February 1847. She was in Petersburg in March-April. A miraculous gestation.

letters are exercises in hyperbole, of ardent temperament: "Dear master-piece of God . . . so good, so beautiful, so perfect, so made to be cher-ished, adored and loved to death and madness"[5] is a fair sample of her style, and blood-curdling it is but not more so than that employed by, say, Juliette Drouet to Victor Hugo: "There is not a hair of your head, not a hair of your beard, that I do not know by name — but that does not prevent me from being always surprised and ravished by so much beauty."[6] That was how one captured, and kept (more or less) the male of the species to which Hugo and Liszt belonged.

Cynics naturally believed there was more to it than that. Carolyne had money and she was a princess. From the outset she loaded him with expen-sive presents: a gold ingot inscribed with the Midas legend — a heavy-handed pun on his "golden touch" — an emerald-studded baton he managed to use only once, a large opal. He may have been impressed with this largesse, up to a point, but far less than Balzac was with the outward signs of Madame Hanska's fortune, and not as much as he would have been a few years ear-lier, before he had acquired trunkfuls of such stuff from royal and other admirers. And it wasn't true, as Newman puts it, that her wealth "promised to be at his service for the realization of his artistic plans."[7] The reference may be to the 20,000 thalers she offered for the construction of a diorama to serve as a setting for a Dante symphony not yet composed, an idea he certainly didn't take seriously. His only other "plans" concerned Weimar, and she couldn't help him there. Weimar's orchestra and theatre were fi-nanced from the royal treasury and her millions could have nothing to do with it. Nor did he need an income for himself. The sums amassed during the *Glanzperiode* yielded him 25,000 francs a year, quite enough for a man who had outgrown the urge to own three hundred cravats. Money anyhow is not a universal aphrodisiac. It wasn't, I think, to Liszt, who never spoke of people's wealth and whose period of greatest devotion to Carolyne was after she had lost a substantial portion of hers.

Her title, to such a snob, would have had more allure, had not ten years with Marie and innumerable affairs with titled women given him a certain detachment.* And if it hadn't, he was too experienced to see her as a social asset. In the world he lived in it wasn't enough to be a princess if one was also gauche, badly dressed and a religious fanatic. Socially, he would have been a hundred times better off without her disturbing presence, which was a burden he carried for years. To those who knew them, it wasn't a *mésal-liance* on her side but on his. The open question was, how could he?

* To illustrate his "grotesque reverence for titles," Newman tumbles into one of his howlers, saying Liszt couldn't bring himself to address Carolyne by the familiar *Du* instead of the more respectful *Sie*. (Newman: *Man Liszt*, p. 162, n. 6.) Of course they used neither, since they wrote only in French, and in French it was decidedly middle-class to *tutoyer* a mistress or a lover. He and Marie did not use this form either. Only when under exceptional stress did he employ the *tu* with any woman.

The answer must be more imbedded in the human heart than snobbery or avarice. Carolyne's love was as selfless as love ever is; and that was a quality most rare in his life, unless he also recognized it in his mother. Then again, he admired her. We hardly know the meaning of this word any more; it seems at once mawkish and vague, because it has become preposterous that love should be connected with spiritual attributes. But unless he lied to her with incredible consistency, Liszt really believed that Carolyne was a kind of saint, and he looked up to her. It upset him dreadfully when people called her ugly. "I, who claim to be a connoisseur in such matters, maintain that she *is* beautiful . . . because her soul lends her face the transfiguration of the highest beauty." [8] That is a feeling hard if not impossible to dislodge in a man — as many a woman more attractive than Carolyne has discovered.

Finally, there was the conspiracy of circumstances when they met. After eight years on the road, he had no home, and no friends — if by that we mean those whose lives we know intimately, with whom we are in constant touch. The women since Marie (with the exception of Marie Duplessis, for whom he confessed "a sombre and elegiac" sentiment) had meant less than nothing to him. With the passage of time, almost the only human being whose abiding interest in him he could be certain of was — and it is the final irony — Marie herself. The long letter he wrote her from Woronince has to be read in this light. It doesn't announce a new love, because he wasn't then *in* love with Carolyne, though the idea that he might be hovers somewhere on the horizon. What chiefly comes through is his mortal loneliness and his longing, though he denies it, for Paris and old friends:

Is the rupture between Sand and Chopin definite? And what caused it? If you have any details, tell me. For my part, I live outside a society that is itself outside these things. . . . Do you remember that we once talked of the Ukraine and Mme. Potocka's country as an impossible place? Well, here I am, very close to her estate, and yet I doubt if I will take it on myself to go and see her. Not, to be sure, that I don't remember her with affectionate gratitude, but constant travelling makes me lazy, and then, what use to renew relations when one has, like me, acquired the conviction that one is no good to anybody? . . . Do you know a piece of news? It is that I met at Kiev, by accident, a very extraordinary woman, but very extraordinary and distinguished . . . to a point that I decided . . . to make a detour of twenty leagues to talk a few hours with her. Her husband's name: Prince Nicholas Sayn-Wittgenstein, and her maiden name Iwanowska. It is from their place that I write. . . . In about a month I will be in Odessa, where I will wait for the fine weather to embark for Constantinople. Don't forget, please, to forward Lamartine's letter to Odessa, as I want to know Reschid by other means than . . . through the Embassy. Toward mid-July, I will be back in Weimar. . . . Paris doesn't tempt me in any way, though I may send for the children to come somewhere. . . . You ask for details of my personal life. This is a singularly embarrassing question. To make a jugged hare, you must have a hare, they say. Now I must frankly admit that since our quarrel I haven't for an instant thought of one. I try to observe, to understand and to feel, in order to get hold of certain real and valuable ideas. This seems to be a duty. The rest of the time I play the piano, scribble, dine and sup etc. . . . Need I tell you that there isn't a syllable of truth to this fantastic bourgeois tale about my proposed marriage? Three millions under those conditions would only embarrass me, and if ever I take the plunge I will do it, I hope, with more grace. Till the end of May address Odessa and . . . sign yourself rather Nélida than Daniel. You know I never cared for the latter name.[9]

Shortly before she got this, Marie wrote in her journal, "I persuade myself that he loves me," and there was little here to disabuse her. She certainly did not conclude that "my proposed marriage" meant Carolyne, who was not free to marry and was richer by many millions than the unknown referred to — some mercantile heiress by the sound of that pejorative "bourgeois." The dates alone would make it impossible that rumors about him and Carolyne, supposing there were any, could have reached Paris from Kiev in so short a time.

Carolyne's name cropped up again in May, when he was en route to Constantinople. At Jassy he found a batch of mail that included "a big (and illegible) letter from Berlioz in Petersburg, by the hand of Princess Wittgenstein (who is my new discovery in princesses, as Mme. Allart would say, with the difference that we don't dream of being in love with each other.)" [10] And the rest was about Berlioz's success in Russia, which did not prevent his being in despair, "poor great genius struggling with three-quarters of the impossible!" Nothing there to raise the alarm in Marie. And his letters to Carolyne herself were models of discretion. He addressed her as Madame, and asked her to write, "if you have leisure." They had a rather indefinite plan to meet in Odessa that summer, and that was all.*

Hopes Carolyne must have had — it would have been inhuman not to; she didn't advertise them. Marie Potocka was wild with curiosity to know what was going on between her old-maidish neighbor and Europe's most notorious libertine, and she was quite unable to find out. "So you've had Liszt at Woronince," she cooed. "I'm happy for him and for you. He is a

---

* One marvels accordingly at statements like the following in Sitwell: "By the time that Liszt left her [at Woronince], after a few weeks of this life, their plans for the future were all settled. He had only the very last of his public engagements to fulfil. The ultimate concert of all took place in October, at Elizabetgrad . . . now rechristened Stalingrad by the Soviet" (Sitwell: p. 157). Every word is wrong. He stayed a few days, not a few weeks; nothing was settled; he had seven months of engagements to fulfil, including Turkey (where Sitwell incorrectly places him in 1843–1844); his ultimate concert was in September and Elisabetgrad was not "rechristened" Stalingrad — it is the present Kirovgrad, if anyone cares. This sort of thing abounds in Sitwell's biography published in 1934. More shocking is the perpetuation of every error, and the addition of some new ones, in the chapter and chronology he contributed to *Franz Liszt: The Man and His Music,* published in 1970.

man to know and one can't say he isn't distinguished to his fingertips." [11] That was in February. In March, she tried again: "Something tells me you are still there and that our dear Liszt is enjoying the puffs of your cigars and the powerful lucubrations of your spirit. If so, a thousand and a thousand *tendresses* to dear, marvelous Liszt. . . ." [12] By June she was desperate: "Have you fixed on a house in Odessa? The hope of seeing dear Liszt has left not a vacant corner in the town." [13] The gloves are now removed: she has been reading *Nélida:* "What verve and elegance in the thought and sentiment!" On July 13, she loses her self-control altogether: "Polish women's virtue is no more to be counted on than rose petals in a storm. But you, my dear Princess, be firm . . . you are made the more conspicuous by your intelligence and the brilliance of your friendships." [14]

Had Carolyne not been one of the pure in heart, these communications must have given the keenest pleasure. The ugly duckling had succeeded where the swans had failed. For after a period of uncertainty, Liszt did come to Odessa, and was publicly seen to be all devotion. The details are unclear. Carolyne solved the housing problem by staying in her mother's villa; and Liszt may have done the same. He was anyhow a constant guest — and Mme Iwanowska the most tactful of chaperones. If startled by her daughter's spectacular conquest, she was all for love and encouraged them to spend the beautiful evenings pounding away at Bossuet, the Cimbrians, Hegel. "Try, Madame," said Liszt, "to keep your daughter from being *too* brilliant!" How they made the transition from these discourses to the bed isn't a matter of record.

One only supposes they must have because now came a change of plan. In the spring, Liszt had told Marie he might go to Athens, then back to Constantinople, thence to Weimar in December. That was now scrapped. It was from Odessa that he made the last journey of his virtuoso career, to Elisabetgrad; and it was understood that he would proceed from there to Woronince, to spend about three months. Carolyne cannot have been firm.

Chapter 29

HE WAS AT Woronince from early October until about the middle of January 1848, and if we knew more about what happened during those months, the emotional history of the following twelve years would be more intelligible than it is. The earth might have swallowed him. One of his few correspondents was the Austrian consul at Odessa. Their topics — a strayed Érard, Turkish knickknacks lost in transit — are mundane and the tone, on Liszt's side, unromantically cross: "I am enraged every morning when I get up and re-enraged every night when I go to bed." Not quite the bulletins of the happy lover, and a letter to his Viennese publisher doesn't add much: "I have worked pretty well these last two months, between two cigars in the morning, at several things that don't displease me," he wrote negligently,[1] and very possibly in reaction to the solicitude that surrounded him — because it was essential to Carolyne that he compose a masterpiece while under her roof. Here he will have experienced for the first time the pressure, the anxious midwifery to genius applied to him for the rest of their lives together, that for all its effectiveness was still a scourge to the nerves, often driving him to doses of coffee and too much cognac. But it isn't known what exactly he composed during the two months following his retirement.

The *Glanes de Woronince* perhaps, piano arrangements of Polish folksongs of no particular importance. One or another of the pieces in the collection called *Harmonies poétiques et religieuses* (not to be confused with the single piece of the same name), dedicated to her and played so often at

257

Weimar that the dog-eared copies fell apart. Only one, the *Bénédiction de Dieu dans la solitude,* can be called the masterpiece she was waiting for, except that he sketched it first in 1845 and its unadorned mysticism is the reverse of her fussy religiosity. Searle speaks of the "rather stifling atmosphere which has somehow turned sour most of this set," and they do seem stale and unspontaneous, as if composed with somebody looking over his shoulder.

Woronince also supplied some of the raw material for the gypsy book, one of the better chapters in fact:

Once, in Podolia, a fête was offered to us which took place in the woods. . . . It was the month of October, the sun having still some strength. . . . A great banquet had been prepared for some hundreds of peasants; gathered together from surrounding villages, and all belonging to the same landlord, who had selected this day to make good to them a year's taxes. The occasion being so suitable for dancing, the young people gave us the Casaque in a way that reminds us forcibly of Hungarian dances. The orchestra was set up under the branches of an enormous oak, upon wagons, the oxen being meanwhile at pasture. Two *szlachcice* (of the noble class) were scraping the violin between two gypsies and a blind Ukrainian peasant . . . [who] intoned . . . a ballad in honor of St. Nicholas and a hymn to the Virgin that in their nasal delivery and the monotony of their forlorn sentiment were enough to break the heart of a stone. The two gypsies who completed the group had one a pair of drums and the other a *balalaika.* . . . Their dance tunes . . . were of the simple square rhythm and lively character . . . [but] the Bohemians of Little Russia seem to have become infected by the profound grief of the Ukrainian serfs, which shows itself in their loss of hope and pride. Their voices vibrate plaintively and their speech drags like a funeral oration; and their songs are the same. One of the pathetic symptoms of this resignation (outwardly complete but to which their hearts cannot possibly assent) is their habit of calling everything they own "little" — "little hut," "little tree," and so on. This arises from their fear of arousing their masters' cupidity by allusions to anything that might seem of sufficient value to seize. . . . The women . . . extend this custom . . . to the beings nearest and dearest to them. Thus in their love songs . . . they are careful to add "poor" to any term of endearment . . . "Oh you poor little darling," etc. This melancholy shade of expression is particularly evident in the gypsy women because it is allied to the allegorical style of speech . . . so strongly impressed on the character of Oriental peoples. . . .[2]

Here the verbal chaos that makes *The Gypsies and Their Music* nearly unreadable takes over. The description, which I assume to be Carolyne's, has value because I take it for a confirmation of her alienation from the world that produced her. Liszt's own awareness of the gypsies' and the peasants' lot as adduced, say, from his comments on his return to his native village, was minimal. She, in other circumstances, might have become a nun or joined the "dark people" at Yasnaya. In other words, she was not insensitive to what was happening around her or to the human cost of her support; and I think this may explain the stoicism with which she faced her loss of status and descent into comparative poverty. Her love for Liszt wasn't the whole story. Her urge was for sacrifice, whether he had entered her life or not. She never expressed a regret at the loss of Woronince and its chattels, and I imagine felt none.

Neither did Liszt. No doubt it amused him to live like a feudal lord for a few months — in afterlife he was fond 'of visiting his magnate friends in Hungary. He mourned in perfunctory terms the loss of Woronince after its confiscation. He wasn't personally attached to it and it excited none of the acquisitiveness displayed by his neighbor all that autumn and winter.

For some reason nobody has noticed the coincidence that placed Balzac and Liszt within a few versts of one another in that remote corner of Russia, and in nearly identical situations. I can't discover whether they knew of it themselves. (There may be a mention in Balzac's letters; there isn't in Liszt's.) Carolyne and Eva were not friends. Balzac, still resenting Liszt's advances to Eva in 1842, may have wished to avoid him; Liszt may have decided that one *Béatrix* was enough and not cared to subject his new love to Balzac's scrutiny. They failed, anyway, to meet — even at Berdichev, the nearest posting station to both estates, whence they started for the West at almost the same hour — Balzac in a fox coat given him by Eva, with her draft for 90,000 francs in his pocket; Liszt with the emerald-studded baton and the opal in his trunk but certainly no money from the Woronince cashbox.

The contrast should be studied by anyone who thinks Liszt loved Carolyne for her millions. Eva's Wierzchownia, Woronince's twin in size and appearance, was to Balzac a fairy tale, a veritable Louvre in extent, "a Greek temple gilded by the setting sun," and the surrounding property alive with commercial possibilities. The waste shocked him deeply. The oak woods, for example: it was scandalous that they weren't harvested to meet the demand for railway sleepers abroad. He saw 120,000 francs right there. His questing eye also observed the corn harvest, its exact dimensions and the pilferings of the bailiff. He itched to get his paws on it and make it pay. Not that he could have. In practical affairs the fat, avaricious little man was a child. That, and the fact that the novelist can tell us more in five minutes than the composer did in five years, is why we forgive him. Charm is still absent from his eager survey of Eva's estate when it is seen as the culmination of fifteen years' putative devotion to her. All that time she was a married woman. Now she was a widow and Balzac — who loved her, no doubt about that — saw the consummation of several passions simultaneously within his grasp. He was intoxicated. Liszt on the other hand saw nothing at Woronince that he desired unless it was Carolyne herself.

The other difference was more serious. Eva Hanska was to Balzac a voluptuous object, who satisfied his every ambition including the sexual. Yet they never dreamed of marriage until her old husband died. They met when they could, usually at some foreign watering place, and for the rest kept their affair on the boil in correspondence. Without Balzac for a principal, it would have been an ordinary situation, even to Count Hanski, who knew all about it — so usual that it might have been the model for what Liszt thought would happen with Carolyne. But Eva was not Carolyne, and when the myth is set aside, it is obvious that Liszt miscalculated.

In Weimar, where they knew Liszt well and long before he introduced her into the picture, it was always assumed that Carolyne was the aggressor: the gossipy old ladies of the court said so to anybody who would listen. One who listened avidly was Theodor von Bernhardi, the Prussian historian, who spent the winter of 1851–1852 in Weimar, and wrote it all up. One of his informants told him this:

Liszt has treated the princess very badly. In Poland she lived a very original, isolated kind of life, never going into society. The originality, the intellect, the millions and the title of the princess attracted him, and he made love to her, *toute bonnement*, but all he had in mind was a liaison of the usual kind, each party knowing from the start what it all meant. She, however, took it seriously, though at first he didn't notice this. He had probably forgotten the matter and was living here in Weimar in a hotel with another woman — the usual Parisian kept woman. Suddenly, to his horror, he gets a letter from Carolyne, telling him she has made the sacrifice, and all that remains for him is to meet her at the frontier. He had to fetch her, because he couldn't get out of it. He did everything in his power to try to persuade her to terminate the relation, for without her millions — and at that time it looked as though she would lose them — Carolyne did not suit him.[3]

Like all gossip, this patches fact with fancy. Liszt had not "forgotten the matter" when he went back to Weimar — the old lady hadn't read his letters. Carolyne, we will see, didn't proceed without encouragement or what a woman of her inexperience could reasonably interpret as encouragement. But substantially the Weimar grapevine had it right. Marriage never entered his mind. He dreamed away an autumn in the Russian country, wrote irritable letters about this and that, which I think can be interpreted as withdrawal symptoms. It is all very well to assume his relief at the breaking of what he once called "the chrysalis of my virtuosity." Racehorses, we know, cannot simply be put out to pasture but must be carefully reconditioned not to leap the first fence they see and make for the track. Carolyne helped him accomplish this transition. Lying on her polar-bear rug, smoking her *tchibuk*, she listened to him play *Du bist die Ruh'*. She reminded him of his vocation and quoted Milton: "He for God only, she for God in him." Soothed and made proud, he luxuriated in the atmosphere of adoration that surrounded him. What he felt or desired beyond that must be conjectured from the letter he finally got around to writing Marie — a difficult one, to judge from the length of time it took to produce (it is dated December 10/22), and strangely inconclusive, for the announcement that seems imminent is in the end not forthcoming:

Instead of writing from Athens I am in the same room as last February. If I remember rightly, I told you then (because I can't lose the habit, good or bad, of telling you truthfully what is in my heart) of the deep liking I felt at first sight for a great character united with a great spirit. This liking has strengthened to a point where Mme. Allart's old prophecy seems on its way to becoming a real prediction. . . . Attribute then the change in my route to a very real change in my life, which against all expectation, is at least acquiring an objective once more, and if I was late in answering your last letter and thus deprived of the pleasure of a more active correspondence with you, put my silence down only to the need I felt of establishing a silence between my past and my future. What is happening to you, you will ask. What extraordinary discovery have you suddenly made? And what end do you hope to find to the nameless and pointless agitations that have thrown your best years to the winds? To that I will have no trouble replying; but for you to understand my answer, you must not mistake the sense of my heart. . . . We haven't seen each other for a long while, and I don't know that you ever found my simplicities so simple. Our last explanations have also contributed to this result. . . . How can I tell you more today without fear of talking out of turn and provoking comments as little flattering as deserved? [4]

And indeed he didn't tell her more, whether because he shrank from saying what he never had, that he was in love with another woman, or because he wasn't really announcing any such thing but simply telling her that another — and superior — woman loved *him*. That was a conundrum to puzzle Marie. The letter came at a bad moment; 1847 had been for her a year of melancholia, "I persuade myself that he loves me" given way to notes like these in her diary: "Where to go? What to do to cheat this miserable solitude? Whom to love? . . . Deep feeling of great things squandered in pure loss. What have I done?" [5] But she had courage:

Marie to Liszt: ". . . Nothing surprises me less than your plans. I always thought it would be easy . . . for you to change your life. . . . If I had seen you like so many others, at ease in your second-rate pleasures, I would have had no hope; but your feverish and extravagant disquiet were in my eyes the very sign of your superiority. I ought also to have understood that I was the last person in the world who could recall you to the peace of higher things. Your pride was on guard against me, and besides I had nothing to promise, having given everything. Your heart is engrossed in a new vision? All the better. That woman of great character, as you call her, would surely not consent to sharing you. She would not wish to be *one of your mistresses*; and as you must have, in these four years, arrived at more than satiety, at a mortal disgust of pleasure without love, you should seize with joy the thread offered you to get out of the labyrinth. I have only one regret . . . that Podolia should be so far from Paris, and that the Hungarian should turn Russian, because my . . . greatest joy will always be to see you in possession of yourself and reconciled with truth.[6]

She always did know how to get under his skin and it was clever of her to blow up what he hadn't said into a commitment to live in Russia with a woman who wouldn't stand for his philandering. It could have pulled him up and made him think twice about what he was getting into, and perhaps it did; because it is certain that when he left Woronince for Weimar he had no intention of returning. Still less did any plan exist for Carolyne to uproot herself permanently, try for a divorce, or settle in Weimar — the last place he would have thought of.

Certain things are so often repeated about Liszt and Carolyne they acquire the fixity of furniture that anyone can see is wrongly placed but that is too heavy to move. One of them is that Carolyne came to Weimar in the expectation that the Grand Duchess Maria Pavlovna, who was the Tsar's sister, would help with her divorce. The fact is that Maria Pavlovna was a strait-laced old lady who didn't consider interceding with her brother on behalf of a runaway subject living in adultery — and Liszt didn't dream of asking her to. She was among other things his particular patron at court, personally responsible for his appointment. He knew her views: far from her providing an excuse for Carolyne to settle in the town, the reverse was true. Maria Pavlovna's disapproval, which promptly made itself felt, was the best of reasons for Carolyne to seek residence elsewhere.

But had the old autocrat thought differently, had she tried to help instead of snubbing Carolyne, they still can't have believed in her ability to move the Vatican, and everything depended on that. A civil divorce such as could be (and eventually was) granted by the Russian government wasn't enough. For a marriage to take place, Carolyne's former marriage must be dissolved by Rome, a process that could take years if not forever. And in the meantime, what? It was to be expected that Wittgenstein would fight any action that threatened to deprive him of his wife's fortune, and he did; that the Tsar would support a loyal subject against a wife who deserted him and tried to take her money out of Russia — and he did.

Is it conceivable that Liszt would have encouraged Carolyne to step into this legal and ecclesiastic morass? And for what? He detested marriage as a bourgeois institution, unsuited to an artist's life. For him, domesticity was as ridiculous as it was impossible. If with Marie the subject had never arisen, even after the birth of three children, why should it with Carolyne after only a few months — or ever?

Naturally it didn't, as we immediately see when we turn from the story-books to his letters. They show a man in love — after a fashion: ". . . you are my angel of heavenly mercy — ineffable secrets are revealed to me in you — and hereafter I will die in peace, blessing your name," and so on. They say nothing whatever about marriage, divorce, annulments, or her coming to live in Weimar. (Hers, of which he saved only a very few, are entirely missing from this period.) Instead, they speak of an expedition abroad in the spring. There was no difficulty about this. She suffered from some form of arthritis that often obliged her to take the waters and with that excuse she could easily get the necessary permission to travel outside Russia. Her husband was not a problem, having no objection to her living her own life provided he was not inconvenienced.

Liszt to Carolyne, Weimar, February 22, 1848: You must count on me at any time, from the soles of my feet to the roots of my hair, my mane included. For the rest, I hope we can dispense, for a long while because I expect to make old bones, with other errand boys, it being understood that I myself count on doing all your commissions *in saecula saeculorum.* I beg you to have no scruples about putting me to any kind of job, and to be a little pleased in advance at the pleasure I will always have in attending to anything that has . . . a connection with you. If Holy Week in Venice tempts you? . . . After the 24th of March, I can leave Weymar [sic: always his spelling] ad libitum. Once again, neither Paris nor London nor Stockholm means anything to me. . . . See what it suits you to do. In any case, I will have the honor to escort you from Lemberg to Krakow, and from Krakow to Vienna and Venice. The carriage will be ready on April 5th. . . . Belloni at your feet and at your orders . . .[7]

There is a ghastly attempt at jocularity to this that makes one wonder if it could have been the answer to the letter, consecrated in Weimar gossip, that announced her "sacrifice." There is no way to know. He did go to meet her, though not at Lemberg. He waited for her at Krzyzanowitz, the smaller of his friend Lichnowsky's two Silesian properties, a little hunting castle on the inside of the Austrian frontier, a house he knew well from former visits. He had stayed there first in the summer of 1843, when there had been falcon meets, balloon ascensions and balls. In March 1848 it was deserted, his host away on what turned into a fatal errand. Lichnowsky was deputy to the Frankfort parliament convened to discuss the unification of Germany as a result of the disturbances in the spring of 1848, and in this capacity was murdered by a mob in obscure circumstances the following autumn. (It has never been clearly stated whether the bullets were aimed at him or struck him accidentally.)

Liszt wasn't cursed with second sight but the outbreak of revolution all over Europe threw him into a terrible state:

Liszt to Marie, Krzyzanowitz, March 30, 1848: My heart is in my mouth every time the courier brings the newspapers. Since I heard the first news of the provisional government with Lamartine as Foreign Minister, I have said that no matter how long it lasts it will strike at every European government except the English. [And] for that reason alone, the French Republic would be once more the century's most providential happening. Lamartine's manifesto has given me the most intense satisfaction of my life. Though my wretched percents won't be paid and my insignificant person have the honor of government persecutions, what does it matter? God protect France! And Christ deliver the world by love and liberty! [8]

The loss of his investments wasn't imaginary. From Belloni in Paris he had learned that the Rothschilds were suspending interest payments on the bonds that represented nearly the whole of his small fortune. If the suspension had persisted, he would have had to abandon his retirement, and go back to the concert stage. A year later he was poor enough to consider this. He actually thought of an American tour. (Berlioz was horrified. "I know how energetic and decided you can be at such moments," he wrote. "Still, your project seems to me *violent* — to cross the Atlantic to make music for Yankees who just now think only of California gold!") [9] It proved unnecessary but it does show that he hadn't any idea of letting Carolyne support him.

Meanwhile, at Krzyzanowitz, he was cutting an abject figure — dangling after an errant princess who, for reasons unknown except that she was the kind of woman who is chronically dilatory, kept him waiting for some three weeks. To Marie he did not mention her name. The rest of his letter is taken up with his plans to go to Hungary, where "my compatriots are doing great things," and after that — yes, to Paris, where he will give her further details, "of which the interest is lessened by events."

The disasters of 1848–1849 need not be gone into here except as they relate to Hungary and therefore to Liszt, the professional Hungarian who now found himself representing an actual country instead of the kingdom that nobody had quite believed in, a country with a leader as capable of capturing the public imagination as Garibaldi, Mazzini or Lamartine. This was Lajos Kossuth, who on March 3, 1848, denounced the "charnel house of the Vienna cabinet," demanded a modern constitution for Hungary and — the stroke of revolutionary genius — for Austria as well.

It almost worked. A popular uprising in Vienna quickly disposed of Metternich and the way was open to a parliamentary government that would accept the Hungarian terms: a free press, taxation that stripped the nobles of their age-old exemptions, partial suffrage, financial autonomy. The terrified Emperor Ferdinand actually signed the necessary legislation. This bloodless solution was much too good to be true. The diehards, smelling secession before the word was uttered, understood if the emperor did not that Kossuth's reforms meant the end of the Austrian empire. After reforms would come independence, and not only for the Hungarians. In this fact the counter-revolution also saw its chance. Hungary had her own minorities, Slavs and Rumanians whose resentment of Magyar hegemony far outweighed their dislike for the Austrian imperium. Vienna's strategy of fomenting rebellion among the Croats and Rumanians looked like lunacy to Western diplomats: it successfully postponed the inevitable until the next century. *Divide et impera* is a shopworn formula that seldom fails with the Danubian peoples. It doomed the Hungarian bid for independence. With her subject races arrayed against her, Hungary stood alone. In September 1848, a Croatian army, openly abetted by the Austrians, opened the attack. The Austrians followed in December.*

So began the real revolution, whose history is desolatingly familiar. For at first all went well. The Hungarians fought with their usual flair and in April 1849 signed a declaration of independence at Debrecen. The cause seemed to be won, but the patient died. The political instinct of the Magyars is for downfalls partly self-induced, and most of them end the same way. Sooner or later a Russian army crosses the Carpathians (unless as in 1956 it happens to be there already). Acting on the logical premise that a rebellion threatening one empire is a threat to all, Tsar Nicholas dispatched 200,000 men to deliver the coup de grâce. By the end of the year the country was in ruins, its armies surrendered, its leaders dead or in exile.

And where, as this cataclysm approached, was Liszt and what did he propose to do about it? He knew, even before he left Weimar for Lichnowsky's, that the most famous living Hungarian couldn't avoid making a statement, a gesture to equal or surpass the dash to Vienna at the time of the Danube floods.

Liszt to Carolyne, March 24, 1848: I who have always detested politics admit that I no longer know how to defend myself. My compatriots have been making me overtures so decisive, so Hungarian and so unanimous that it is impossible to refuse them a tribute of legitimate sympathy. As I write these words my glance falls on Goethe's statuette on my table, and that plaster smile cuts me short.[10]

---

* The inability to recognize one's real enemies was universal in 1848. When the Austrian armies crushed the revolt in Piedmont that year, there were Viennese democrats who cheered the victory over their fellow revolutionaries simply because they were Italian. Furthermore, Batthyány, the Hungarian premier, obligated under the Pragmatic Sanction to assist Austria against the Piedmontese, did not repudiate the agreement. He promised help, and would have given it if Hungary hadn't been attacked shortly thereafter.

He did nothing. Here if ever was the test — of his patriotism, his republican principles, of simple courage. He failed it. Because of Carolyne? Such an abdication must have many causes, but she was surely one of them.

She joined him on April 18, having nearly left her departure until too late. Russia was closing her frontiers against the revolutionary tide and Carolyne passed the barriers only moments before the order was given. Or so the story was told and it sounded well. People got the picture of a troika fleeing the Siberian wolves. In reality, her exit was stately and she was accompanied by an official outrider. She travelled in a carriage, or several carriages, since her party consisted of the child Marie, the Scotch governess, several servants, possibly a dog or two (there were dogs with Polish names at Weimar later), and a mountain of luggage.*

They were guests in Lichnowsky's castles for at least two weeks; and it is my belief that it was during this period that Liszt learned the full consequences of making love to a woman who had a ten-foot crucifix nailed to the wall of her bedroom. Carolyne had acted with the inspired canniness often found in the person supposed to have no practical know-how. In total secrecy she liquidated enough of her property to realize some three million rubles, which had been spirited abroad. Her petition for an annulment of her marriage with Wittgenstein was on file with the consistory of Zytomir; and a letter, surely in the hallowed tradition, on its way to her husband to tell him it was all over. (Also in the tradition, and in case he decided to ignore it, were other letters to her relatives affirming her intention to live with Liszt as his wife.) In short, all concerned knew what to expect with the probable exception of Liszt himself. It is really out of the question that so many arrangements and decisions could be made *with* his knowledge yet never discussed in the correspondence.

All sorts of sequences suggest themselves: her surprise that *he* was surprised — did he then wish her to undo what was done? No gentleman could have urged it. On the other hand, he wasn't quite a gentleman or he wouldn't have told Fanny Lewald six months later that it was "a hard decision for the Princess to follow me. *I hadn't expected her.*" (Italics mine.) [11] He could be pitied if it hadn't all happened before and in much the same way. Marie had "thirsted for martyrdom." Could Carolyne do less? How to have coped with that saintly obstinacy? Their erratic travels in the next few weeks are shrouded in an obscurity not lightened by the only

---

* There are the usual conflicting stories about who met her and where. La Mara says Liszt's "shrewd chamberlain" was at the frontier. That would be Belloni, except that he was in Paris serving in the National Guard. Lichnowsky is also mentioned. But Liszt's letters state categorically that Lichnowsky had left for Germany. A recent East German publication, a sort of chronology of Liszt's life, says the Viennese half-uncle was involved. Nobody is prepared to explain why Liszt didn't go himself; nor why, since he had been staying at Krzyzanowitz, the party presently moved to another Lichnowsky property, Schloss Grätz, not far away.

letter he wrote to an outside person. It was to Franz von Schober, an old friend serving at the Austrian legation in Weimar:

Regardless of the blocking of the Russian frontier, the Princess Wittgenstein passed safely through Radziwillov and Brody with a special official outrider, and established herself at Schloss Grätz four days ago with her very charming and interesting daughter. As it is still somewhat early for the German bath season, I should like to persuade her to spend a couple of weeks in Weimar before her Carlsbad cure (which alas! is very necessary to her). If I am successful I will arrive in Weimar between the 10th and 15th of May in order to prepare a suitable house or suite of apartments for the Princess. I should be so pleased if you could get to know her. She is . . . an uncommonly brilliant example of soul and mind and understanding . . . [and] it won't take you long to realize that henceforth I can dream very little of personal ambition and a future wrapped up in myself. . . .[12]

What was Schober supposed to make of this? It has the sound of something intended for public circulation, a formal awkwardness that Schober may have known how to interpret. He knew Liszt as well as anyone did, and it would be useful to learn whether he took it at face value or whether he heard the thrashing of a man in a trap. For Carolyne didn't go to Carlsbad or — yet — to Weimar either. In early May we unexpectedly find them in Vienna.

Guy de Pourtalès has no difficulty with this odd development: ". . . Carolyne, who had intimidated the chamberlains of Petersburg, the Diana of the steppes, the Catholic at once Byzantine and Nordic, had found her master. . . . Blushing with a shame that filled Franz with pride, she demanded that her lover not leave for Weimar without their visiting Raiding and Eisenstadt. And it was only after their pilgrimage to Franz's paternal lares that they finally arrived in the little town where they planned to live out the poem of their tenderness [Weimar]." [13] Sitwell picks up the theme: Raiding and Eisenstadt were places "to which he had not dared bring his former love, the Comtesse d'Agoult. But their own situation was very different . . . for no doubt can have existed in their minds that they would very shortly be married." [14]

Liszt had however no sentiment about Raiding and no desire to show it to anyone. Nor was it a moment for pilgrimages. Vienna was in a state of insurrection, Austria practically without a central government. Order, such as it was, was kept by committees of students and citizens. Barricades blocked the streets, and there were three serious outbreaks during the month they spent in the city. If Liszt had not later said that he *was* in Eisenstadt in 1848, though not that Carolyne was with him, one would dismiss the visit as fiction. Certainly it was not what impelled him to Vienna.

The weeks in Austria were either a delaying tactic or they were an attempt to come to terms with the revolution — probably both. He may have toyed with the idea of some *coup de théâtre,* may actually have intended to join his compatriots in Pressburg, as he had told Marie he would — and been dissuaded by Carolyne. The Viennese insurgents anyway were in no doubt that his presence signified his sympathy. As of old, crowds of students turned out to serenade him, and he made them speeches. One such is preserved and it is surprisingly bloodthirsty. "Even when all the instruments are in place," he told them, "a capable conductor is needed . . . and capable conductors are wanting. Discordances won't do in this case — the right leaders will have to use the bayonet!" [15] The other recorded episode is more in character. He visited a barricade commanded by the well-known basso, Karl Formes. Dressed in a frock coat, a *cockarde* of the Hungarian colors in his buttonhole, he dispensed cigars and money all around. We aren't told how these were received by the men on the barricade.

And there it ended. He didn't go to Hungary, didn't establish contact with Kossuth or the other leaders, or even risk a benefit for the Hungarian cause. In early June he went quietly back to Weimar to prepare for Carolyne's arrival. In a mild way he was compromised but had scarcely exposed himself to "government persecutions," and some years later he was given a decoration, showing there were no hard feelings.

Among Hungarians the inclination was, and still is, to play down this chapter. A small and defeated country cannot afford recriminations, and it is said that he did what he could — in effect, two or three compositions, the best of which, *Funérailles, October 1849* and *Heroïde funèbre,* are moving threnodies for the lost. The first is a huge, shattering piano piece, the second a sort of monument to his twenty-year struggle to compose a "revolutionary symphony," some of its material having been quarried from the work begun in 1830.* His compatriots were perhaps right not to expect more from an artist, though having lost their finest poet, Petöfi, on the battlefield, they might have.

Liszt didn't pretend to be a soldier. His dedication to *Heroïde funèbre* is a handsome denial of martial values:

In these successive wars and carnages, sinister sports, whatever the colors of the flags that rise proudly and boldly against one another, they are on both sides soaked with heroic blood and endless tears. It is for Art to throw her ennobling veil over the tombs of the brave. . . .[16]

---

* Other works with revolutionary associations include the *Ungaria-Kantate,* composed in 1848 (never played in his lifetime); the *Arbeiterchor,* reworked into the *Mazeppa* March; and much later in time the curious sketches called *Hungarian Historical Portraits,* which can be tied to the revolution because six of the personalities were heroes in the struggle. These were not published until 1956 and are "almost totally unplayed" according to Louis Kentner (*Liszt: The Man and His Music:* p. 162), who regrets the omission, praising them highly. I myself have never heard them.

Admirable — if he had done less dramatizing of his Magyar heritage, had not clanked his *sabre d'honneur* across so many stages. His noble detachment when his country dangled at the rope's end rang false in the light of that recent memory; and there were many who felt he deserved Heine's vicious indictment in 1849:

> Liszt again appears on the scene. He lives, did not fall, red with blood, on a Hungarian field of battle. Neither Russian nor Croatian killed him. A last boulevard of liberty has fallen. And Hungary is bled to death. But the Chevalier Franz remains untouched — his sword as well — it is in the closet. . . .[17]

Few of his friends dared attack him so directly. One who did ask awkward questions was Princess Belgiojoso. "Your country at this hour has succumbed like my own," she wrote him January 1849, "and like mine it was betrayed. But why, my dear Liszt, didn't you take part in the struggle? Isn't Hungary your country in fact and by choice? Have you not declared yourself Hungarian? I thought you were there by the Danube, and I was disturbed not to hear your name. . . ."[18] Even Berlioz, no friend to rebellions, was moved to inquire: "They said you were in Vienna; did the Austrian storm pull a few feathers? . . . They often asked me your news in London, but I absolutely didn't know which European barricade you were on. . . ."[19]

Such queries show the special expectations he had aroused. But in his defense one can only say that he wasn't alone. The history of 1848 is not simple but the Romantics as a whole come out of it badly. Among Liszt's old associates, only Lamennais, Sand and Lamartine stuck to their principles. The rest emerged ingloriously.

Lamartine ruled France for a brief moment after Louis Philippe's abdication; a republic presided over by a poet ought to have been made to order for Romantic imaginations. Not a bit of it. No banker, no skinflint landlord or merchant could have upheld law and order more tenaciously than these former champions of liberty. "Make no mistake about it," said Balzac. "The King was the symbol of property. I'm afraid that before long property itself will be attacked."[20] (But when the mob sacked the Tuileries, the property-lover went along and filched a few mementoes from the throne room.) Sainte-Beuve was less candid. He called himself a republican until he was surrounded by a crowd of excited workers outside the Hôtel de Ville. He panicked, and in a scene notable for cowardly indecorum, had to be "rescued" by Lamartine in a carriage. He retired muttering that he was "in mourning for a civilization which I feel to be perishing."

Sainte-Beuve was a born librarian. Hugo, like Liszt, was a culture hero of major proportions, of whom heroic gestures were expected. Again like

Liszt, he was in debt to privilege. Louis-Philippe had made him a peer of France, and financially he was comfortably fixed. Paris in revolt was a stage on which he readily saw himself playing a star part. He couldn't summon the resolution. Lamartine offered him a ministry. He held back. "I am a man of thought," he kept saying, as if thought were sophistry. He was for "the little man against the big" but order must prevail. Ideas, he wrote, were "everything, facts nothing," and to prove it he invented two republics:

One . . . will set the tricolor beneath the red flag . . . will remove the statue of Napoleon . . . will destroy the Institute, the École Polytechnique, the Legion of Honor, and will add to the noble motto, *Liberté, Egalité, Fraternité,* the sinister alternative — *or Death.* . . . The other will be the sacred participation of all Frenchmen now living and, one day, by all peoples, in the principles of Democracy. It will found liberty without usurpation, and without violence, a liberty that will give free play to each man's natural bent. . . . Of these two republics, the second goes by the name of Civilization, the first of the Terror. I am prepared to devote my life to the establishment of the one and the checking of the other.[21]

With which specious apologia, he joined the conservatives.

Berlioz, with less to lose, might have done better. He did worse. Cowering in London, he had a kind of nervous breakdown:

Republicanism is at this moment passing like a vast roller over the face of the Continent. Musical art, which has long been dying, is now dead. . . . With the first shock of the earthquake which has overturned so many thrones, England becomes the center for streams of terrified artists. . . . How long . . . will Great Britain be able to maintain so many refugees? Will not their mourning voices be drowned by the acclamations of the neighboring nations, as each sovereign people is crowned? [22]

On the state of Paris, to which he returned in July, he writes like one demented — and entirely deprived of logic, as when he misses his own point about the poverty of musicians *before* the upheaval:

What a sight! What hideous ruins! . . . the fallen trees, the crumbling houses, the squares, the streets, the quays, seem still quivering with the murderous struggle! [This is the Faubourg St. Antoine, a small part of the whole.] . . . Fancy thinking of Art at such a period of wild folly and bloody orgies! . . . All the theatres are closed; all the artists are ruined; all the teachers are idle . . . poor pianists play sonatas in the squares; historical painters sweep the streets; architects are mixing mortar on the public works. . . . The Assembly has just voted fairly considerable sums toward the opening of the theatres, and in addition has granted some slight relief to the more unfortunate among the artists. But how inadequate to meet the wants especially of musicians! Some of the first violins at the Opera only had thirty-six pounds a year, and were hard put to it to live even by giving lessons as well . . . what is to become of the poor creatures? They will not be transported . . . for it would cost the government too dear; to get free passage one must have deserved it, and all our artists fought against the insurgents, and charged the barricades [which was untrue].[23]

It is hardly credible that Berlioz and so many others could have believed that a republic was such a threat — that they imagined a Europe laid waste not by royal folly, military savagery, or mercantile greed, but at the hands of the baker and the candlestick-maker; that the villain was parliamentary government. "Policy must be ruthless in maintaining social order," said Balzac. ". . . After what I have seen . . . I approve of the Austrian *carcero duro,* of Siberia and the methods of absolute power." [24] Was he serious? Whence the terrified conviction that civilization could hold together only if kings ruled, that (the phrase is Stendhal's) "government by the two chambers will spread over the world and deal the final blow to the arts?"

Politics as such had of course very little to do with it; nor yet the trauma, though it was real enough, dealt to their parents by the Terror. Obviously too, the Romantics were self-styled aristos to a man — hence, as Berlioz implies, too good to mix mortar. *Génie oblige* isn't an effective motto in a republic; and to have made money is a well-known deterrent to wanting others to be equally fortunate. Finally, the Romantics were now middle-aged and desirous of keeping what they had. But it wasn't any of these things that ultimately decided the point of view. The confusion was of republicanism (by which they meant democracy) with the consequences of industrialism. Berlioz, for example, did not foresee the mangling of ancient Paris carried out under Louis Napoleon. He equated mechanical destruction with rule by the rabble. Stendhal put the connection even more closely. Still mourning Italy (and how right he was), he said that "whether this country exists with or without the chambers [that is, a parliament], everything foreshadows the downfall of the arts during the nineteenth century. But, by means of an ingenious application of the steam engine, some American will be able, for six louis, to deliver to us quite a pleasing copy of a painting by Raphael." [25] Thus was popular government associated with the loss of human values and the degradation of taste and workmanship that were the outcome of industrialization — in itself a cause and not the consequence of spreading democracy, and inevitable in any case. That was not seen. America was an example at one end of the scale, Italy at the other: to the artist, a republic, which was hideous, must be inferior to a rundown papal state filled with beautiful monuments.

This is the wire on which the liberal conscience trips today, when it is clearer than it was to Stendhal that the more backward the country the more agreeable it is for the aesthete to live in. Landscapes beautified by human labor, the poor peasant walking the empty road cannot but be preferable to the slatternly industrial suburb. This seems elementary, but we have not found a way to solve the aesthetic of poverty. It is shameful that the poor and despotically governed country should have so much to recommend it to the refugee from the industrial state with money in his pocket. He can console himself only with the reflection that it won't last. The country will in a few years be liberated, improved, the peasant acquire his Sears Roebuck suit and the fishing village be "ruined." Conscience may be appeased by this outcome; the dilemma remains.

The parallel between the Romantic attitude and our own is not exact. But they were nearer to ours than to that of their fathers. The year 1848 was the watershed. Optimism about the future was gone; the past a lost cause. And so, like Hugo and Liszt and a host of others, they equivocated, saying they were for the revolution's aims but not its methods; distrusted the timing or the leadership, whatever objection was most pertinent at the moment — as if better men than Garibaldi, Lamartine, Kossuth, Mazzini could be conjured up if they waited and reforms acquire more validity with the passage of time.*

So we find Liszt, in an unconscious paraphrase of Hugo, telling Fanny Lewald in 1849 that "I would be the first to answer the call to arms, to give my blood and not tremble before the guillotine, if it were the guillotine that could give the world peace and mankind happiness. But who believes that? We are concerned with bringing peace to the world in which the individual is justly treated by society. We are concerned with the triumph of ideas, a triumph that is certain . . . with economics, the deep study of which must begin . . ." and more to the same effect. This speech finished with a description of conduct he deplored: the actress Rachel singing the *Marseillaise,* a "bloodthirsty hymn," on the stage of the Frankfort theatre: an "atrocity," so he said. [26]

The mention of the guillotine gives the lie. It was not a feature in 1848, not a risk he faced. To drag it up was pure *grand guignol* and this wasn't the only time he did so. In 1852 he told Bernhardi, "the guillotine will be everywhere introduced as a permanent instrument in the political orchestra," and gave this as the reason for his decision "to throw himself strongly into the Catholic system." (*Se rejeter fortement dans le système catho-*

---

* Luigi Barzini makes an astute point about the widespread failure of nerve in 1848, though his province happens to be Italy. Cavour, he suggests, brought off in 1859 what couldn't be done in 1848 because "he avoided the most serious mistake . . . always made and never noticed by revolutionaries. . . . In 1859 . . . he made sure that respectable people were not afraid of what was about to happen. He prepared a revolution that might seem desirable to patriots . . . but that also seemed acceptable or inevitable or at any rate not harmful to the rest. . . ." (*From Caesar to the Mafia,* 1971: p. 140.) And this has of course been true ever since.

lique.) [27] It wasn't his main reason, and Bernhardi saw through it at once. "This religiosity," he wrote in his diary, "that springs from fear is . . . nothing but the wish that others (especially the lower classes) may have faith so that we may be left undisturbed."

The sympathies on this occasion are with Bernhardi. One grows weary of Liszt's reiterations that Christ will save the world — a formula for which Carolyne must also be held responsible — and wearier still of his clinging to *le système catholique* as the century progresses, Pio Nono denounces "modernism," promulgates papal infallibility, and tries to rule Rome with bayonets. But it wasn't really based on fear of "the lower classes." Say, rather, on the fear of the complicated syndrome of modern ugliness. One is still entitled to resent the preachy sententiousness of one who refused the risks. *"Mon byronisme"* deserved a better burial.

PART FIVE

Weimar and the
Music of the Future
(1848-1858)

Chapter 30

FROM VIENNA to Weimar was no great distance in space. In time, it was a leap backward, almost into the eighteenth century. With no public transport, streetlights that didn't work, a town crier, it was preposterously old-fashioned – and still is, in spite of the presence of some fifty thousand Russian troops in the neighborhood, a legacy of World War II and a divided Germany. But for these, and under a light snowfall unmarked by traffic, it has the look of a town imprisoned within a paperweight, where all the clocks have stopped. And apparently it always has seemed like that.

The traveller stops either at the Elephant or the Erbprinz, two hostelries famous out of proportion to their size, or to Weimar's. Liszt's was the Erbprinz, on the principal square, and it is still there, exactly as he knew it, filled with swan-necked Biedermeier furniture, a Liszt piano in his former salon, a fussy little German garden out back – "for all the world like one you may see in many an English village at the back of a farm house," wrote George Eliot, who stayed there in 1855. The rusticity surprised everybody: "One's first feeling is: how could Goethe live here, in this dull, lifeless village?"

A second look improved matters. Weimar had its charms – a cultivated society, a theatre, a Gymnasium, the nearby University of Jena. It was crude. Sheep were driven through its streets and ducks floundered in the puddles – Thuringia has a rainy climate. But in a thoroughly German way it was adorable. Its aspect, medieval-rococo with here and there a classic façade, belongs to the fairy story. Hans Andersen who spent the winter of

1846 there might have been describing it in the tale of the princess and the swineherd, the one that ends, "And then he went into his kingdom and shut the door in her face. . . ." It was in the eighteenth century just a miniature realm, with a wall and a gate and a clerk who wrote down the names of those who passed in and out; and except for the clerk was pretty much the same in the nineteenth. Everything was within easy walking distance of the immense onion-domed castle (Madame de Staël said Weimar wasn't a town but an overgrown château). Goethe in his espaliered garden house on the Ilm, a toy river, enjoyed the fiction of a country retreat when a short stroll upstream through the park he designed, the haunt of nightingales and cuckoos, carried him to his patron's doorstep.

To foreigners, it was always the ideal representation of classical Germany, the reverse of brutal Prussia. Thackeray, a student there in 1830, remembered it as demi-paradise:

> Though [Goethe's] sun was setting, the sky around was calm and bright and that little Weimar illumined by it. In every one of those kind salons the talk was of Art and letters. The theatre, though possessing no very extraordinary actors, was still conducted with noble intelligence and order. The actors read books, and were men of letters and gentlemen. . . . At court, the conversation was friendly, simple and polished. . . . With a five-and-twenty years' experience since those happy days of which I write, and an acquaintance with an immense variety of human kind, I think I have never seen a society more simple, charitable, courteous, gentlemanlike than that of the dear little Saxon city, where the good Schiller and the great Goethe lived and lie buried.[1]

Germany in general and Weimar in particular were the last places in Europe to contest the thesis that culture is a metropolitan product. When Madame de Staël descended on it in 1803 she expected an Athens and was amazed to find that Goethe, that *esprit prodigieux*, never read a newspaper and took no interest whatever in European affairs. She concluded that nowhere on earth was theory so little tempered by experience. She wasn't quite right about this. In youth Goethe was "in love with the real" and fascinated with the practical details of running a state. Herder reformed the schools with realistic success. She was substantially correct that its character was at once utopian and provincial, its overriding desire to evade world-historical events. The Weimarers managed to stay out of history until Napoleonic times, when Bonaparte, whom they had rather admired, upset them by fighting the battle of Jena just down the road. They conceived themselves as above that sort of scuffle, an illusion the more easily sustained on account of the backwardness of the country, the bad roads and inferior public services. In this context, the broad, tree-lined *chaussées* designed by Goethe to connect Weimar with Jena and Erfurt were like ornamental avenues in a park, leading nowhere in particular. The Goethe-

Schiller correspondence travelled them in the baskets of market women, tucked in with the radishes and onions. The town acquired street lanterns in 1786 but they proved too expensive to operate and the streets remained unlighted until 1855, when gaslight came in. There was no industry, unless you count the Ilmenau mines that Goethe took such an interest in.

As might be expected, the dynasty who ruled this Arcadia was noted for its charm and cultivation. The original tone of the court, art-loving, free-and-easy about etiquette, was set by Grand Duchess Amalie, Frederick the Great's talented niece, who wrote, composed, painted, acted, and had her uncle's passion for brilliant men. Her "court of the Muses" must have been the only one in Europe where people had a good time, wit and not rank being the price of admission. The intellectual level had declined by Liszt's day but that wasn't the fault of the court, which retained its respect for brains and its delightful manners. (The Weimar princesses were trained to *cercler* — that is, move around a circle of guests, a dreary royal custom beloved of Queen Victoria — in the royal gardens, where they practiced polite conversation with rose bushes.) The court theatre continued to operate at a high standard, and if it couldn't quite live up to its past, the twenty-six years of Goethe's management when it was the nearest thing to a national theatre in Germany, that wasn't the fault of the dynasty either. They would have welcomed another Goethe, another Schiller.

Entrancing as Weimar was, it will be seen that it had its weakness. It suffered from the very qualities that made it idyllic. Amateurism first. We are so accustomed to praise Goethe's universality, we forget that two-thirds of his extra-curricular activity falls into the category of inspired dabbling. His studies in botany, optics, mineralogy were games played by a genius with scientific toys, and of no intrinsic value. His mind was not methodical; his observations and experiments were an artist's attempt to construct systems, "Nature's friendly game," and were entirely lacking in the provisional character of scientific study. He was in short a poet in a position to indulge his curiosity about the natural world, in the operations of government, and a hundred other things, without wetting his feet; and the same was true of all Weimar's sages working within that cozy vacuum. It has been pointed out that modern historians and sociologists will learn little from Herder's theorizing in these fields, the student of aesthetics and educational theory little from Schiller, and so, in a way, it was intended to be. It was their very imprecision, their rich and all-embracing vagueness that Hegel admired, seeing in them a peculiarly German "sense of natural totality."

This, with its humanism, defined the Weimar style. Different as they were, its great men were distinguished by a metaphysical squint that marked them members of the same tribe. Their contempt for politics, their other-worldliness and collective superiority complex, their sense of belonging to Lessing's "invisible church of us all," remind one of other secular congregations. There is something here of Brook Farm, but there is something missing too. On the side of the angels, Weimar lacked devils: war, capitalism, the industrial revolution. Its philosophers found no issue comparable to, say, slavery. In its heydey, Weimar journalism might have emanated from the moon; its little magazines, Schiller's *Die Horen* for example, were idealistic to a fault; they achieved a monumental irrelevance.

Goethe, to be fair, realized the drawbacks to Weimar's seclusion, especially after he began to travel. He saw the limitations of the small audience and the feebleness of courtly approval as opposed to the bracing give-and-take of great cities, and came to understand that his liberty was an illusion. The French revolution scarcely registered on Weimar's insensitive social seismograph. Democratic as its rulers were, they were still absolute monarchs, a situation that didn't change until 1848. If Goethe was treated like an equal by his Grand Duke, as Liszt was by his grandson, that didn't mean they *were* equal. They lived on royal favor and the rulers themselves couldn't devise a way out of this. Ennoblement for Goethe, *Kammerherr* status for Liszt were the best they could do and a poor best because in effect the receiver of such favors signed a contract, an agreement not to rock the boat. Hence the failure of the Weimar experiment with an aristocracy of brains and ideals — an experiment that if successful might have propelled Germany into the modern world by another route. As it was, the Weimar *Geist*, whose influence was once deemed incalculable (and it was for this reason that the name Weimar Republic was chosen after World War I, in conscious rejection of Prussianism), proved to be almost wholly ineffective.

Today's visitor to the little town sees a palimpsest of German history, Cranach's great altarpiece in the church, the organ in the court chapel on which nearly all Bach's masterpieces for that instrument were played for the first time. (He was *Hof*-organist for ten years.) Every other house has its illustrious ghost: Goethe, Schiller, Wieland, Liszt and many more. It is only when he approaches modern times that the visitor becomes aware of malaise, an uneasiness not exclusively generated by the Russian soldiers in the streets. Surely there is something newer to look at than all the pretty Gothic and rococo? There is, and the local tourist office will oblige with a ticket for the short bus ride to the wood where Goethe and his Grand Duke used to picnic with their friends, cleared now for a variety of modern structures.

This is Buchenwald, and it too belongs to Weimar history. Because it turns out that mass murder can be committed in surroundings as pleasingly rustic as those of any simple-hearted little resort — in low wooden buildings that could have been designed as steam baths, in a room with six little brick ovens for all the world like those in a village bakery. French used to be the old, civilized Weimar's second language. For some reason lost in the

Final Solution, French is also the language on most of the fading memorial wreaths in this room: À *Paul Dérou, hommages des anciens élèves du collège . . . À mon mari regretté . . .*

The East German government has not been blind to the horrible lesson. Blown-up portraits of all Weimar's great men, ending with Liszt, have been affixed in the best contemporary museum style to the entrance of the exhibits: the lampshades, the hair, the small shoes. A moral is clearly intended. But what exactly is it? These portraits can neither explain nor refute what happened, nor tell us which was the real Weimar, theirs or ours. Yet the time-span between the two is not long, in Liszt's case terribly short. Buchenwald was in operation only forty-seven years after his death — a hundred after Goethe's.

When Goethe wrote to his beloved city-state, "*O Weimar! dir fiel besonder los! Wie Bethlehem in Juda, klein und gross . . .*" * he was invoking a spirit that ought to have made the Final Solution impossible but was not proof against it.

---

* Oh, Weimar! You were chosen for an exceptional fate, like Bethlehem in Judah, small and great . . .

Chapter 31

SCHILLER SOMEWHERE SAYS that "the artist is indeed the son of his time, but woe to him who is also its pupil, or, still worse, its darling." Liszt, woe to him, was all three, which makes it the more extraordinary that he should have chosen to settle in Weimar. The author of *De la situation des artistes* in the pay of a petty prince? His very title, *Kapellmeister*, had an antiquated sound, suggestive of knee-britches. Obviously, he had something more in mind than serving up the usual musical fare to a Grand Duke and giving music lessons to his daughters (though he actually performed this last duty, and with apparent pleasure).

The first explanation is the simplest. He wanted to master the orchestra and no better way could be devised than to have one at command. At Weimar, like Haydn at Eszterháza, he could "make experiments, observe what made an effect and what weakened it," in relative privacy. He could teach himself the art of conducting, at which he was then a novice. But this presupposes that he had the symphonic poems in his mind as early as 1842, when he signed his original Weimar contract — which would also mean that he thought of the job primarily as giving him a sounding board for his personal use. And that isn't in the least what happened: far from converting Weimar into an exclusive forum for his own music, a Bayreuth in embryo, he turned it, for a space of about ten years, into a workshop of a unique kind, the only place in Europe where new music, neglected music, "difficult" music, could regularly be heard. There was nothing like it then.

There haven't been many such experiments since. It was a sensational move. In Saint-Saëns' words:

> After having been the incarnation at his instrument of all the panache of the Romantic era . . . [he] vanished behind the curtain of cloud that hid the Germany of that day. . . . We knew that at the court of Weimar, disdaining all his former principles, Liszt occupied himself with the highest forms of composition, dreaming of a rebirth of the art of music, and being, for that reason, the subject of the most disquieting rumors, as is always the case with those whose intention it is to explore a new world and break with accepted traditions.[1]

Hans von Bülow, the pupil who became his son-in-law, laid more stress on his "radical rejuvenation of opera," by which Bülow meant the Weimar productions of Wagner executed at a time when no other German house would touch them; and it was Bülow's estimate that carried the day in Germany, where even those closest to Liszt had little faith in his music. It was one of the crueler paradoxes of his career that the little city's second spring of fame should have owed more to his entrepreneurial than to his creative talents, that he found himself hitched to Wagner's star in the public mind.

He did give *Tannhäuser* its first performance outside Dresden, in 1849, and *Lohengrin* its first anywhere. He would have produced *Tristan and Isolde* several years before it finally saw the light in Munich, if Wagner and the Grand Duke of Weimar between them hadn't hamstrung his efforts. But he did as much for other composers. Schumann's ill will notwithstanding, his non-symphonic works were more consistently presented in Weimar than anywhere else — his opera *Genoveva* for example was in no other repertory; his hybrids for voice and orchestra, mostly slighted in other cities, were given in Weimar with particular care: *Faust* in 1849; *Manfred* in 1852, the première; *Paradise and the Peri* in 1857. Russia loved Berlioz but Weimar was his stronghold in the 1850's. Liszt gave *Benvenuto Cellini* its first (and for many years only) hearing after its disastrous Paris debut in 1838; and he did the unprecedented for a living composer, devoting two festive weeks to Berlioz's symphonic works in 1852 and 1855. At the same time, his revivals of older music showed that he wasn't nailed to the mast of modernism. Gluck, long in limbo, was strongly represented with a production of *Orfeo* in 1854, of *Iphigénie* in 1856. Beethoven's *Fidelio*, still a subversive opera for political reasons, he put on in 1854, the same year he produced Schubert's *Alfonso and Estrella* — a labor of pure love on account of a cumbersome libretto that had to be drastically revised.

Necessarily, there was a certain amount of stuffing. Raff's *King Alfred*, Lassen's *Landgraf Ludwigs Brautfahrt*, Rubinstein's *Siberian Hunters* would not detain modern audiences, and probably wouldn't have detained him if the composers hadn't been his friends and associates. On the other hand, these operas were also hits with his public and although Weimar had no choice but to take what he gave it or stay away, he didn't expect it to tolerate a steady diet of *Lohengrin* — for which the house usually had to be papered. For the same reason, he didn't try to cut out old favorites — Rossini, Donizetti, Bellini — who for that matter were his favorites too. He never learned to despise Italian opera, as was the fashion in *echt* musical circles. (Though unaccountably he wasn't much attracted to Verdi, he did give *Ernani* and *I due Foscari* in 1852 and 1856 respectively.) At times, he would go out of his way to flaunt the pleasure principle: because Rossini's *Il Conte Ory* "bubbled like champagne" he once ordered magnums of it served during the second act.

The management of all this, the rehearsals, the engaging of the singers, the mise-en-scène, the long analytic articles for the papers that coincided with every important production, should have been full-time work. They accounted for less than half of Liszt's. In these years, he composed twelve of the symphonic poems, the *Harmonies poétiques et religieuses*, the *Faust* and *Dante* symphonies, the revised *Transcendental* and *Paganini* studies, the Hungarian Rhapsodies, the *Graner* Mass, the Sonata in B Minor, not to speak of songs, transcriptions, and a number of minor but interesting works like the Two Episodes from Lenau's *Faust* — even an aborted opera: *Sardanapale*. These were also the years when his genius for teaching began to be realized, bringing the earliest of the "Lisztianer" to Weimar — Bülow, Tausig, Rubinstein, Mason — not in the floods that later descended on him, but because fewer, more exigent: Bülow alone would have eaten up the vitality of any teacher; Tausig was a holy terror of a child who lived in the house with him and required tireless supervision.

Not a glimmer of these activities appeared in his original contract, which simply called for him to spend three months a year in Weimar, and specified that "for the concerts he arranges, he desires to have the direction of the chapel orchestra, without, however, superseding M. Chélard, who will direct on all other occasions." The second and third clauses quaintly observed that "Herr Liszt wishes to remain Herr Liszt for life, without accepting any other title," and that "Herr Liszt will be satisfied with whatever sum may be thought suitable for his services." In practice, he appeared only on special occasions and didn't stay the full three months until 1848. He didn't conduct an opera there until February of that year, on his arrival from Woronince. It was Flotow's *Martha*, an item in the regular repertory.

Dreams of glory for Weimar nevertheless pursued him from the beginning. In 1844, he outlined a vast scheme to Marie:

Weimar under the Grand Duke August was a new Athens; let us think today of constructing a new Weimar. Let us renew . . . [those] traditions. Let us allow talent to function freely in its sphere . . . and arrive little by little at the triple result that should constitute the whole politics, the whole government, the Alpha and Omega of all Weimar: a Court as charming, brilliant and attractive as possible; a theatre and a literature that neither rots in the attic nor drowns in the cellar; and finally a university [Jena]. Court, theatre, university, that is the grand trilogy for a state like Weimar that can never have anything important in the way of commerce, an army or a navy. There it is, my principal theme that I will sound every note of in the distant hope that some good may come of it. . . .[2]

Ernest Newman, swatting away at his thesis that Liszt never did anything right except by accident and determined to show that he didn't think of turning Weimar into a musical center until Wagner's "idealism" showed him the way, makes much of this manifesto. It doesn't mention music; therefore Liszt "must have shared the general opinion . . . that a town so tiny as Weimar could neither afford the financial expenditure or supply the audience necessary to make it of any more account than twenty other similar pillbox German capitals were; it was only later when the name of Weimar suddenly went ringing through Germany as a result of Liszt's audacious production of *Tannhäuser* and *Lohengrin* that this new ambition took root in him." [3]

The contradictions declare themselves: if Liszt shared the general opinion of Weimar, how did he happen to choose it for his audacious productions? Why, for that matter, did it occur to him to mount these same productions in the first place? Anyone who has followed his career this far will know that the answer to the second goes back to the early 1830's and his concerts in Berlioz's behalf. His crusade for modern music long antedated the start of his friendship with Wagner in 1848–1849; and his letters to Carl Alexander, Weimar's young crown prince, express, throughout the 1840's, an increasing determination to make Weimar his venue — Weimar "where it is my ambition one day to acquire the freedom of the city . . . [which] has given me such a serene and serious consciousness of my future." That was in 1846. The following year came a stream of plans for the reorganization of the opera, the hiring of young singers and the creation of adequate choruses, winding up with this Lisztian flourish: ". . . above all, no censorship, freedom of ideas, the new talents, the strong conceptions that make our present 'big with the future,' to avail myself of a profound phrase from Liebniz." [4]

Newman also misses the Saint-Simonish overtones in the letter to Marie with its proposals for a state dominated by scholarship and the arts in general, not music alone. That apart, there was another reason for Liszt not to harp too exclusively on a musical theme. The Grand Duchess Maria

Pavlovna, who paid his salary from her own purse (her colossal *apanage*, brought from Russia, made Weimar much richer than its size would suggest), was devoutly musical. Her son Carl Alexander, who would one day rule, was not. Liszt's money troubles date from his succession in 1853.

Carl Alexander grew up in his grandfather's shade and longed to emulate him, to attract to Weimar such latter-day Goethes and Schillers as came his way. None did and he had to make do with such substitutes as Franz Dingelstedt, a third-rate dramatist though a fine theatrical producer, and poets of the calibre of Hoffmann von Fallersleben. Moreover he was inclined to be stingy, too often short-changing projects like Liszt's Goethe Foundation that would have brought lustre to his little state. He was perfectly willing for Liszt to revamp his musical establishment, if it could be done at bargain prices. Large expenditures for operas he neither liked nor understood put him off. "Music tickles my ear pleasantly," he said. "It doesn't go to my heart," and if there was a choice, his money went to the theatre. Hebbel's *Nibelungen* drama was lavishly staged under Dingelstedt's direction in 1861 — the same subject as Wagner's *Ring*, for which he wouldn't advance a penny.

Liszt's relations with him were cordial, even affectionate; but Carl Alexander was no Ludwig of Bavaria; nor did Liszt have Wagner's talent for shaking the money-tree. He didn't write letters beginning, "Oh my King! You are divine!" or gaze deep into the young man's eyes, and it would have done no good if he had. Carl Alexander was rather in awe of Liszt's celebrity but he could never quite make up his mind whether it was worth it to the exchequer to maintain him as artist-in-residence.

It took a long while for Liszt to realize his patron's limitations, and longer still for him to accept the paradoxes in his own position. For if Carl Alexander was a pale copy of his ancestor, Liszt bore even less resemblance to Goethe in his attitude to the duchy of Weimar, which as a practical proposition didn't remotely interest him. If Goethe was given more rope, it was because he asked for it. The supreme fixer, he meddled in everything from fire insurance to the budget, and made himself indispensable. To Liszt, the little duchy was an anachronistic absurdity. He rather fancied politics on an international scale — he could have seen himself like Lamartine or Chateaubriand, playing a certain role, and there is an unsubstantiated rumor that he did just that at the time of the Franco-Prussian War, that he acted as a French agent in Weimar during that period.*

---

* Liszt had important connections in France. His son-in-law was Émile Ollivier (who married Blandine), premier in 1869–1870. His sometime mistress Marie Kalergis was close to Napoleon III — whom Liszt greatly admired. According to Haraszti, who explored this subject in an article (*Musical Quarterly,* July 1949), she was also a Russian agent (I must insert that I don't believe this) whom Liszt may have used as go-between to communicate well-founded fears to the Emperor: that in the event of war, Austria-Hungary and the south German states would not remain neutral, and particularly not

He remained in any case very much the foreigner. He had no love for the German ethos and little tenderness for Weimar itself, whose citizens he regularly denounced as philistines. Now it happens that philistinism was a German conception long before Matthew Arnold introduced it to England and Gautier to France. The word is first recorded at the University of Jena in the seventeenth century, meaning outsider, ignoramus with a touch of the grind. Only later did it acquire its sense of anti-art and become linked to the frock-coated bourgeois who knows what he likes — the sense in which Schumann used it when he cast much of his musical criticism in the form of dialogues between the *Davidsbündler*, literally the David bunch, attackers of Goliath.

Liszt was of course right that Weimar had its philistines — what place has not? He was wrong to lump the whole population under that category, as in later years he did. The New Weimar League, for instance, a club he organized in the mid-fifties, provided in its by-laws that no local could belong unless he was an artist. All clubs exist to keep somebody out but this was a gratuitous insult to a town full of cultivated people. Goethe, the improver and enlightener, who invited everybody to lectures on subjects ranging from tattooing among the ancients to chemistry, wouldn't have made that mistake. It may have been beyond Liszt's power to create in Weimar the kind of audience he wanted. Perhaps he had no choice but to rely, as he did, on out-of-towners to fill the theatre for his important productions. We will never know because he didn't make the effort; and he didn't make the effort because, unlikely as it sounds, he was in spirit still fighting the battle of *Hernani*. His exemplar wasn't Goethe but Victor Hugo. In Haraszti's good phrase, "he remained in the midst of a German principality the last French Romantic, the lion . . . of yesteryear."

Not consciously, I imagine. (Though Peter Cornelius for one noted with irritation that Hugo and Lamartine and others alien to "us poor Germans" were a constant frame of reference in literary matters.) But his methods were those he learned at Hugo's knee and employed for the same purpose. The manipulation of the press for example, and his skillful build-up of *Lohengrin*, which achieved what a famous opera house like Dresden operating with ten times the budget couldn't do — overnight it made Wagner the most talked-about composer in Europe. He had help: Franz Brendel, who succeeded Schumann to the editorship of the *Neue Zeitschrift für Musik*,

---

Ludwig of Bavaria, whose mind had been poisoned against the French by Wagner. Haraszti concedes that a careful scrutiny of Quai d'Orsay archives has yielded no specific evidence, which — such as it is — rests on confidences that Liszt made in old age to one Abrányi, secretary to the Hungarian Academy of Music. But Haraszti is undoubtedly right that Liszt was always on the most intimate terms with whoever happened to be French ambassador to Weimar and that he sent his letters to France in the diplomatic pouch where they couldn't be censored. He was in a position to inform his son-in-law of many things that wouldn't necessarily appear in official archives.

was an early convert to the "music of the future," and his *Anregungen für Kunst, Leben und Wissenschaft*, founded in 1856, was even more partisan. Berlioz, still on the *Débats*, regularly received news and contributions, reviews, etc., from Weimar. Most significant of all was the resurrection of that Romantic refinement on the claque, the honor guard of pupils and admirers who accompanied the master everywhere, after the fashion of Hugo's Spartans: Hans von Bülow, Peter Cornelius, Joachim Raff, Dionys Pruckner, Carl Tausig, Karl Klindworth, Joseph Joachim, Eduard Reményi.

In Weimar parlance, they were known as the Murls (a word said to mean Moors though *Cassell's German Dictionary* hasn't heard of it) and Murlship was defined, roughly, as adherence to the modern school. "Murlship is wanting in him still," Liszt once remarked of Anton Rubinstein, and all was said. The Murls lived and studied in Weimar, but Liszt usually travelled with one or another of them, and sometimes with the whole crowd. They went *en bande* to Switzerland in 1853 to salute Wagner; and in the same year to Leipzig, to show the flag at Berlioz's concerts in that hostile city.

This militancy naturally raised hackles. "The music of the future" was a slogan quite as fight-provoking as any of Gautier's or Hugo's, and to conservative Germans doubly offensive when they considered the source. Wagner at least talked with a thick Saxon accent. That Liszt, the Frenchified Hungarian, the interloper, should undertake to chart the course of contemporary music aroused an animosity out of all proportion to the cause. The Brahms-Joachim manifesto of 1860, denouncing the revolutionary tendencies of the Weimar school, was in consequence not a coherent ideological document. Its burden was the personal dislike of men who were unworldly, conservative and provincial for a foreigner who was none of these things.

Wagner, it is true, was included in the attack; but Joachim had long since made clear to Liszt where the trouble lay. He was an early defector from the Murls, quitting Weimar but without telling Liszt why. He therefore continued to receive cordial invitations to visit until he unburdened himself as follows:

The continued goodness and confidence which you show me, great and courageous spirit, in including me in that community of friends who are dominated by your power, gives me a sense of shame for the lack of candor I have shown up to the present – a feeling . . . which would deeply humiliate me . . . if I were not at the same time consoled by the knowledge that this lack of candor, which contrasts so badly with my life at Weimar and your unchanging kindness, is not cowardice but has its root . . . in my best feelings. . . . What is the good of hesitating any longer to tell you plainly . . . [that] your music is entirely antagonistic to me; it contradicts everything with which the spirits of our great ones have nourished my mind from my earliest youth. If it were thinkable that I could ever be deprived of . . . all I . . . love and honor in their creations, all that I feel music to be, your strains would not fill one corner of that vast . . .

nothingness. How, then, can I feel myself . . . one with those who under the banner of your name and in the belief . . . that they must join forces . . . for the justification of their contemporaries, make it their life task to propagate your works? [5]

I quote this at some length because, as will be seen, it turned out to speak for the majority in Germany. The odor of sanctity betrays the grievance. The offense is to "our great ones," and will therefore justify an assault on an old teacher and patron that is really astounding in its cruelty.

It was futile for Liszt to defend himself — by pointing out, for a start, that nobody propagated his works; he propagated theirs. He had explained so often the function he believed Weimar should perform. ". . . Although Dresden and a hundred other cities may 'stop at Beethoven' (to whom, while he lived, they much preferred Haydn and Mozart), that is no reason for Weimar to do so," he wrote in 1855. "There is no doubt nothing better than to respect, admire and study the illustrious dead; but why not also sometimes live with the living? . . . The significance of the musical movement of which Weimar is the real center lies precisely in this initiative, of which the public doesn't understand much but which is none the less important in the development of contemporary art." [6]

The rancor that such statements aroused is still remarkable. For Liszt was not a wrecker. The conservative in every age deludes himself that art is best served when it "stops" with the revolutionaries of the previous one — now mellowed into respectability. It is equally a delusion that modern art in the hundred years after 1830 was out to sack the fortress of the past. Liszt was not, and those of us now in middle age can look back and see that the great iconoclasts of our youth, Picasso, Eliot, Stravinsky, Joyce, were not either. On the contrary: in the light of Pop, accidental sound and other developments, they look like the last of the traditionists, and the temptation is to ask whether the "modernist" syndrome is not itself a thing of the past. What was it if not a gigantic rescue operation, an effort not to sink two thousand years of cultural heritage but to save it by recycling it before the barbarians reached the gates? Like those Byzantine churches built in another terminal age, that incorporated in their walls everything from megalithic shards to metopes torn from crumbling temples, modern art so-called has most of the treasures of European history imbedded in its structure. Liszt's music, with its multiple quotations from Gregorian chant, folksong, Italian opera (not to speak of its literary and pictorial references), in this sense anticipates Stravinsky's — and it is the reverse of destructive. That he reached the twelve-tone scale half a century before Schönberg is no indication that he denied traditional values. The *Czárdás macabre*, for example, of which August Göllerich asked, "Is it allowed to write such a thing? Is it allowed to listen to it?" on account of its bare consecutive fifths, is still a native dance tune. But no matter. It was true that he invited attack from the likes of Joachim when he chose provincial Germany for his battle-ground.

Berlioz once outlined for Liszt the difference between the travelling virtuoso's lot and that of the conductor: "You, my dear Liszt, know nothing of the uncertainties. . . . With a slight modification of the famous *mot* of Louis XIV, you can say with confidence: 'I am myself orchestra, chorus and conductor. . . . Give me a large room and a grand piano and I am at once the master of a great audience. . . .'" In contrast, he then described what it was like to conduct at a small court theatre in Germany, giving what must have been exactly Liszt's experience when he took up his duties a few years later in Weimar:

Who can imagine the torture of the rehearsals? First [the conductor] has to submit to the cold glances of the musicians, who are anything but pleased at all this unexpected upset on his account. "What does this Frenchman want? Why doesn't he stay at home?" Each takes his place, but at the very first glance . . . the [conductor-composer] sees important gaps. He requests an explanation. . . . "The first clarinet is ill, the wife of the oboe has just been confined, the child of the first violin has the croup, the trombones are on parade — they forgot to ask for exemption from military duty today; the kettledrum has sprained his wrist, the harp will not come to rehearsal because he needs time to study his part," etc., etc. Still we begin. . . .

Disaster. The musicians play wrong notes and cannot keep up with the tempo. The winds produce weird discords. Berlioz, always wonderfully present on the page, now positively leaps from it:

"Let me hear the trumpets alone. What are you doing? . . . The first has a C which sounds F: give me your C. Fie! Horrible! You are playing E flat. . . ." Or again I say, "What the devil are you making that noise over there for, you kettledrum?" "Sir, I have a fortissimo." "Not a bit of it, it is mezzo forte. . . . Besides you are using wooden sticks, and you ought to have them with sponge-heads. It is all the difference between black and white." But this group has never seen sponge-heads. "I guessed as much, so I brought some from Paris with me. . . . Now then, where were we? Good heavens . . . you have forgotten the mutes." After three or four hours of such anti-harmonious skirmishes, not one single piece has been made intelligible. Everything is broken, inarticulate, out of tune, commonplace, maddeningly discordant, hideous! and you have to send away sixty or eighty tired and discontented musicians under this impression, saying everywhere that they don't understand what it is all about, that it is "an infernal, chaotic sort of music," and that they never tried anything of the sort before. . . . Only on the third day does . . . the poor composer begin to breathe . . . the orchestra walks, talks, becomes man! Acquaintance with the music restores courage to the astonished artists . . . taking them all around they are the best people in the world. . . . This time, *fiat lux.* . . . *Via!* And light dawns, art appears, the thought flashes out, the work is understood, and the orchestra rises, applauding and saluting. . . .[7]

Just such a jerry-built orchestra came into Liszt's hands in Weimar in 1848, except that it was smaller, thirty-seven men, with a chorus of twenty-three and a ballet of four to complete his resources. And he lacked entirely either Berlioz's authority or his experience, while his demands were more complicated. Berlioz had only to teach his musicians to play Berlioz. Liszt's men had to play a whole repertory of unfamiliar music. The technical problems were enormous and there were plenty of people to say that Liszt did not master them, that he was an incompetent with the baton.

The charge had a single, flimsy basis in fact — the breakdown of the Carlsruhe festival orchestra in 1853 while he was conducting it. For this, his old chum Ferdinand Hiller fell on him like an outraged schoolmaster. "It is not merely that . . . he does not mark the beat (in the simplest sense of the term, the way established by the greatest masters), but that by his baroque animation he continually, and sometimes dangerously, causes the orchestra to vacillate. . . . Is it any wonder that *not a single work* went with real precision?" [8] There was a lot more to this and it makes no odds that Hiller himself was an inferior conductor, famed for his sluggish tempos; nor that the musicians, recruited from scattered sources, were under-rehearsed and unaccustomed to Liszt. He was as responsible for the muddle as the captain whose vessel goes aground. That said, the charges were idiotic.

There was, to begin with, no way established by the greatest masters. Conducting, as such, was too new an art to have the fixed rules that that implies. The orchestra before 1800 relied for its beat on a cembalist, sometimes supplemented with a man whacking a stick or stamping his feet on the floor; or a little later on the first violin waving his bow at intervals. The conductor who faced his troops, baton in hand, was first seen around 1820 — and he was the invention of necessity as ensembles increased in size and scores in complexity. He was also likely to be inadequate to the task that modern music imposed. Berlioz took to the podium in self-defense for this reason; he was tired of the mangling his compositions got in the hands of old-fashioned directors.

He inaugurated a new age, and he was the first and greatest of modern conductors because at that time only the composer could interpret avant-garde music to players trained in the classical tradition, to whom the bar line was sacred and tempos immutable, who had to be indoctrinated to phrasing as we now know it, what Wagner, who wrote interminably on the subject, called the *melos* or song, the starting point — he thought and future conductors generally agreed — for decisions about tempo.[*]

That Liszt should have been a conductor of the new school was inevitable for temperamental reasons — but there was another that he may not have been conscious of himself: he conducted in phrases because he played the piano in phrases. The rhythmic flexibility and subtle accenting he insisted on, at the expense of the bar line, were a carry-over from his keyboard experience. In his playing, tempo was modified for expressive reasons, for the achievement of drama, nuance, poetry. It was a heretical approach to conducting, a pioneering step. Berlioz, for instance, was a much stricter adherent to the canon as then understood. Wagner, on the other hand, with strong leanings in the same direction, was a close student of Liszt's methods, and here, as elsewhere, not above borrowing from them.

Never loath to accept battle in those days, Liszt fired off a famous reply to Hiller's criticism — in effect one more paragraph in an interminable self-defensive brief:

The works for which I profess my admiration and predilection are mostly those which conductors more or less renowned (and especially the so-called solid *Kapellmeister*) have honored little or not at all with their personal sympathies . . . and rarely performed. These works demand *progress* in the style of execution itself. They establish between the musicians at the desks and their musical chief . . . a link other than that cemented by an imperturbable beating of the time. In many cases, even the rough, literal maintainance of the time . . . clashes with the sense and the expression. There, as elsewhere, *the letter killeth the spirit*, a thing to which I will never subscribe. . . . I think I have already said to you that the real task of the conductor, in my opinion, consists in making himself *ostensibly quasi*-useless. We are steersmen, not oarsmen.[†]

---

[*] Not that the classicists, so-called, could be counted on for accurate readings either. Liszt, Berlioz and Wagner often had occasion to complain about the slipshod handling of scores by those who professed to follow "our great ones." Berlioz dwelt on this point when he praised Liszt's direction of Beethoven's Fifth at the Bonn Festival in 1845, especially the third movement, which Liszt "gave just as Beethoven wrote it — not cutting out the double basses at the beginning, as was done for so long at the Paris Conservatory, and playing the finale with the repeat indicated by Beethoven." The reference is to Habeneck, founder of the Conservatory orchestra, who introduced Beethoven to France. He was a fine conductor, whom Berlioz nevertheless accused of terrible misdemeanors, notably his having paused in the midst of Berlioz's own *Requiem* to take a pinch of snuff. It is unlikely that Habeneck did anything so unprofessional, but Berlioz — who saw plots everywhere — remained convinced that Habeneck had been out to ruin him, and never missed a chance to scold the old man.

[†] The last sentence became historic, which makes it all the more annoying that we don't know exactly what the original (in French, translated into the German which is the only surviving version) may have been. I use Newman's translation from the *Gesammelte Schriften*, V, 232.

He sounded like an anarchist and was punished accordingly for the smallest slips. The same thing happened to Wagner, said to have conducted the London Philharmonic in performances "unparalleled for inefficiency" in 1855. Obviously, both men did better with groups familiar with their approach. The accusation of incompetence was ridiculous. Liszt at Weimar, Wagner at Bayreuth twenty years later, were the founders of the German school that endured into the twentieth century — and for that matter is with us still. Above all, they were interpreters, who did more than merely present the score as written, though as usual only Liszt interpreted his contemporaries, while Wagner's efforts, like Berlioz's, were confined to himself. Both were loud in Liszt's praise. Wagner heard "my second self" when Liszt conducted *Tannhäuser*. Berlioz would allow no one else to keep manuscript copies of his scores. Neither man ever conducted a work by Liszt.

The results he got from the Weimar orchestra are still a matter of wonder. There could be no better proof of his powers than the quality of the musicians he was able recruit at minimal pay. Joachim, whatever he felt later, leaped at the chance to be concertmaster in 1850 and occupied the position for three years. Ferdinand Laub, who succeeded him, Bernhard Cossmann, Leopold Damrosch, Alexander Ritter: all were first-class performers who went on to make distinguished careers.

He took risks. These were very young men and the difficulties they faced were impressive. His own compositions were not easy. A passage like the second subject in the *Dante* Symphony — possibly the first to be written in 7/4 time — needs meticulous rehearsal today, and Wagner's scores were "impossible" for the average orchestra. The Weimarers could also, it seems, do poorly when not under Liszt's command. Bülow has a story of a wretched performance during one of Liszt's absences, and the effect of his unexpected return in the middle of it.

He appeared suddenly . . . a few yards from me in the stalls, as though he had sprung from the earth by magic; a whisper ran through the whole house and reached the orchestra, which during his absence had run wild. . . . In their terror they played twice as badly, and Liszt got into a rage, and would have liked to seize the scepter from his humdrum deputy.[9]

But when the cat was in charge the mice played marvelously. He at any rate didn't feel there were grounds for apology. His constant invitations to composers to come and hear their works performed, his bulletins when they couldn't, radiate confidence. *To Berlioz:* "Hail the Master-Goldsmiths! . . . *Benvenuto Cellini*, which was performed here yesterday . . . revealed its full stature as a work of art." *To Schumann:* "The whole impression [of *Manfred*] was a thoroughly noble, deep and elevating one." *To Wagner:* "I don't know whether the sublimity of [*Lohengrin*] blinds me to the imperfection of the execution, but I fancy that if you could be present at one of our next representations you wouldn't be too hard on us."

Would *we?* So few of the practical details have come down to us that it simply isn't known how many of his productions were managed. Schumann's *Manfred,* for example. This is unhelpfully described (in *Grove*) as "hovering between stage and concert room" though we are also told that Schumann made a special adaptation of it for the Weimar stage. But what kind? Spoken words to a musical accompaniment? And what about the Wagnerian productions? *Lohengrin* certainly had its demerits — not enough strings, a middling tenor. Wagner was horror-struck to learn that the first night went on for four mortal hours. (Hadn't Liszt let the recitatives drag? No, he hadn't.) But *Tannhäuser* and *Flying Dutchman* seem to have satisfied everybody. Stranger still, neither Wagner nor Liszt expressed doubts about Weimar's capacity to mount the *Ring* cycle. For years, Wagner's line was "only for you, only for Weimar."

It didn't work out that way but it is interesting to note that when *Tristan* was at last produced in Munich, both Wagner and Bülow clamored to be allowed to do it in the tiny Residenz, smaller than Weimar's house, where they were rehearsing.

Wagner to Ludwig: Dear Exalted One. Please, *please* let us stay in the cosy Residenz! . . . You can't imagine how happy we feel in it. . . . Music sounds wonderfully beautiful here . . . the singers are delighted . . . everything is easier for them. . . . What takes place on the stage is all of a tender and intimate nature. . . . Only in such conditions and in such a theatre could *Tristan — Tristan* of all works! — be possible. . . ." [10]

He changed his mind, and it was the Court Theatre after all. With increasing megalomania, nothing was large enough, or too large, to house his conceptions. Yet that earlier, tenderer *Tristan* may indeed have been wonderfully beautiful, and so may Weimar's *Lohengrin* and *Tannhäuser.* (What, after all, would we now make of *Dido and Aeneas* sung by the schoolgirl cast for which Purcell composed it?)

The point for Liszt was anyway never the perfectly finished production. Weimar was a workshop, an experimental halfway station between the old world of hermetic little kingdoms manufacturing their own music and the coming, international one of symphonies and opera houses subsidized by nation-states. It wasn't the last word but the first in the music it explored, which is one reason it was antipathetic to those for whom art was literally dead — a *fait accompli* handed down by the immortals.

We are back to why Liszt undertook this vast and in the end unrewarding labor. The mysterious man left behind him only the most elliptic clues. In the will, for instance, that he wrote in a mood of savage bitterness in 1860, there is this sentence:

At a certain moment (about twelve years ago) I had dreamed of a new period for Weimar, comparable to that of Charles Augustus, in which Wagner and I would have been the leaders, as once Goethe and Schiller. The wickedness, not to say villainy, of certain local circumstances, jealousies and ineptitudes both within and without, have prevented the realization of this vision.[11]

But his dreams for Weimar's "new period, comparable to that of Charles Augustus" long antedated his acquaintance with Wagner or his works; and I believe they had an entirely different source.

Think what he might have done. In 1849, Berlioz pined for "orchestras to lead . . . rehearsals to go through," begged to "stay eight or ten hours on my feet, practicing with the chorus, singing their parts when they miss . . . let me carry music desks, double basses and harps." A little later, Wagner was bewailing his "silent scores." Notice that neither man is thinking of anyone but himself. Then consider the Berlioz solution, the Philharmonic Society he tried to launch in 1849 and the eloquent contrast between its activities and Liszt's. It *was* inadequately financed, and it failed partly for that reason. The fatal obstacle, according to Barzun, was Berlioz's inability to locate modern music other than his own to fill the programs: "There was, in 1850, no one else on whom to draw." Schumann was "entering his last decade in ill-health and mental darkness." Liszt was out of the running, because "given over to conducting and virtuoso work and was so far only planning his symphonic poems." Wagner was eliminated because "as far as anyone knew [he] was still far from his true path." [12]

Berlioz may have reasoned it that way. That is perhaps why he called on his friend Auguste Morel to write an overture; allowed a rich amateur called Cohn to pay for the performance of one of his compositions; permitted a prima donna named Frezzolini to be hauled onstage loaded with jewels to sing something or other; and discovered in consequence that there was "no one else" the public wanted to hear. The facts are otherwise. Schumann in 1850 had a mass of compositions available to interested parties — and to be accurate, was in good health in 1849–1850 and for another three years. Liszt was not engaged in "virtuoso work" and hadn't been since 1847; and if Berlioz had displayed the smallest interest in them, he had on hand *Prometheus*, the first version of *Ce qu'on entend sur la montagne, Tasso*, and part of *Les Préludes*. What Wagner's "true path" was is a good question, but Berlioz knew all about *Tannhäuser* because he printed in 1849 Liszt's long article about it, together with the urgent suggestion that the overture be played in France at the earliest opportunity. It is needless to say that Berlioz did not take this up. Like his biographer, he preferred to believe that he was alone in the world.

This was also Wagner's view. Though in the 1850's he was in no position to do anything for a fellow-artist, his apotheosis at Bayreuth doesn't suggest that it might have been otherwise. There, the mere mention of another composer's name was enough to throw the master into a tantrum. Who on earth was Verdi? Liszt, he had always imagined, wrote "finger exercises." And so on.

That left Liszt, and a lonely job he had of it. No one thanked him. Because the consciousness of obligation sits more heavily on the human spirit than any other, it was those most indebted to him who impugned his motives. Thus Cornelius: "With Liszt one is always uneasily conscious of the mask he puts on for the world. Yet he wants *himself, himself,* and again *himself;* no doubt about that . . . God preserve us from having genius!" [13] God preserve us from hangers-on like Cornelius, who got all he could from Liszt and switched to Wagner when he saw how the wind was blowing — the kind of friend whose treacheries make you long for an enemy. And Cornelius was a pinprick by the side of Wagner, Schumann, who wouldn't even let him keep the autographed score of *Manfred,* Joachim, Raff, Bülow, who turned on him in the end, and — yes, Berlioz too.

Why did he endure it, devote years of his life to helping people who held him in such low esteem or whose jealousy was such that they were incapable of observing the decencies toward him? I believe that to his inner eye, the punishment just may have fitted the crime, in other words that he felt he must pay for the indulgences and extravagances of the *Glanzperiode* in the disrespect they had engendered. It would be melodramatic to call the Weimar years his act of contrition. But something of the kind was certainly present in his handsomer gestures, his refusal to take umbrage at Schumann's treatment for instance. He came close to saying as much in a long letter to Schumann's biographer Wasielewski. In this he described how Schlesinger had sent him in Italy a selection of Schumann's scores, how "I felt at once what musical mettle was in them," and the critique he thereupon wrote for the *Gazette Musicale.* But he acknowledged that although he played Schumann's compositions everywhere, "the public did not care for them and the majority of pianists did not understand them," and this, he allows, discouraged him:

> The frequent ill-success of my performance of Schumann's compositions, both in private circles and in public, disheartened me from keeping them in the programs of my concerts — programs which, partly from lack of time and partly from the carelessness and satiety of the "Glanz-Periode" . . . I seldom . . . planned myself. . . . That was a mistake, as I discovered later and deeply regretted. . . . [But] however my faint-heartedness may be excused, it was a bad example I set, one for which I can hardly make amends.[14]

To make amends: well, he did that, over and over again.

Chapter 32

CAROLYNE REACHED WEIMAR sometime in the early summer of 1848 and moved into a large villa on the edge of town called the Altenburg.* Liszt continued in his regular apartments at the Erbprinz for more than a year — an arrangement always attributed to discretion. But as nothing happened in 1849 to make his living at the Altenburg more discreet than it would have been in 1848 and the palace for twelve long years pretended that he was still at the hotel (all official communications were sent to the Erbprinz; one thinks of the frog footman in *Alice's Adventures in Wonderland*, idiotically delivering an outsize envelope to the wrong door), discretion can't have had much to do with it.

Fanny Lewald offers a revealing vignette of this period. Lewald was a novelist considered advanced because she introduced social issues into her long, rather dull books, and because she lived openly with a married man, Adolph Stahr, a minor literary figure who later did some work on the Goethe Foundation. Liszt had known them both for some years and when

---

* It belonged to the Seebach family, royal riding masters, who rented her, originally, the two lower floors. At some later date it was bought by Maria Pavlovna, who rented her the whole of it. So says Adelheid von Schorn, an old Weimar resident who ought to know. It is not true as Alan Walker says (*Liszt: The Man and His Music:* p. 66) that Liszt's job "carried with it a free residence in the favor of the Duchy of Weimar, the Villa Altenburg." Nor do I know Howard Hugo's authority for saying that Carolyne purchased it in 1851 from a Herr Stock. This Stock appears in letters as a landlord or caretaker who wanted to cut down some trees. I don't think he can have owned it, or that Carolyne ever purchased it.

Lewald came to Weimar in the autumn of 1848 she was eager to see him and to meet his *amie*. He took her to call at the Altenburg, a disconcerting experience.

The big house was bleak, "like an abandoned Italian castle," full of rented furniture with an orphaned look, and the discomfort not limited to the surroundings. Carolyne talked without cease, asking the personal questions she was renowned for, wandering into metaphysical mazes. Lewald found the conversation impossible to follow. If only, she thought, they could drop philosophy and speak about what was uppermost in every mind, "the bizarre and inexplicable circumstances of the *ménage*." What on earth had Liszt got himself into?

Obviously he trusted Lewald because when they got back to the hotel he talked to her with rare frankness. He enlarged on Carolyne's noble qualities – he always did that. Then he described the situation as "complicated." "We'll have to see how it works out. The Princess is bound on all sides in Russia, and they always forget here in Weimar that we are not Protestants, and we wouldn't dream, either of us, of a conversion" (that is, to facilitate a divorce). He delivered a lecture against matrimony: "Who can swear he will stay the same forever? I know I am easiest to get on with when I keep my freedom, and that it's risky to tie me down, to a person or a place." And he added the sentence already quoted, about not having expected Carolyne "to follow me here." [1]

Lewald felt that she understood and an expedition they all made together the following summer did nothing to change her mind. This was to Heligoland, and it reads like a mournful reprise of the voyage to Chamonix, North Sea sand dunes substituting for the Alps, Lewald in a minor Teutonic key for Sand; and in place of Marie d'Agoult, Carolyne, humorless and unadjustable too but devoid of the beauty and elegance that awed the Princess Mirabella's companions. They were a jolly band of bohemians, who included Stahr, Franz Dingelstedt, and some painters – and Liszt, according to Lewald, was at his wildest, ordering champagne, banging on warped seaside pianos, cracking bad jokes, rolling down the dunes. Carolyne, who had never seen her lover's fun-loving side, must have been horrified. By coincidence or not, it was his last outing of the kind. When they returned to Weimar she had him firmly in hand. He moved to the Altenburg shortly afterward.

His residence at the Altenburg had no discernible effect on Carolyne's tangled case. Nicholas Wittgenstein wasn't interested in his wife's conduct – only in her money. Her difficulties with a civil divorce revolved solely around that point. That was why she was ordered to return to Russia and when she refused, her property confiscated. But Wittgenstein was willing to be reasonable, according to his lights. He wanted in fact to marry again himself, if he could get his hands on enough capital, and Carolyne seems to have offered him a property settlement. At this point, 1852–1853, Bernhardi enters the picture, and it is thanks to his ungentlemanly curiosity and interference in an affair that was no business of his that we have some knowledge otherwise lacking.

Wittgenstein, says Bernhardi, came to Weimar that winter. He had learned from his lawyers that a divorce decree with a property settlement written into it was invalid. He therefore proposed that Carolyne make him a gift of a seventh part of her lands, including Woronince, after which he would obtain a Protestant divorce, marry again, and Carolyne petition a Catholic tribunal for an annulment — on the ground that he was a bigamist. Even Baron Maltitz, the Russian ambassador to Weimar, whose life was blighted by this case and who cordially disliked Carolyne, could see that this ingenious scheme was pure blackmail. Wittgenstein would have his freedom, and the money besides, but what would Carolyne get out of it? The bigamy charge would not hold, he thought, and he was right.

Bernhardi has caustic things to say about Liszt's behavior during Wittgenstein's stay — how he refused to let him set foot in the Altenburg, threatened to box his ears, and referred to him simply as "Nicholas," which Bernhardi regarded as an impertinence from a social inferior, a "poltroon" to use his word. But he insists that some arrangement was made, that Wittgenstein visited Carolyne in her box at the theatre, "gave her his hand in *conspectu omnium* . . . [did] everything in fact to smooth out difficulties." [2] And it looks as though poor Carolyne went through with some part of his plan. He did get his cut, the rest of the property going to their daughter with the dividends paid to Carolyne until the girl married. He did marry again, and expressed the hope to Bernhardi that Carolyne would: "I don't want her to go on bearing my name." But she was no nearer a Catholic divorce than before — no nearer, that is, to being able to marry Liszt.

These legal complications were infinitely distasteful to Liszt, who contrived to grasp or to seem to grasp so little about them that it is impossible to get out of his letters what *was* going on. They must however have been a large part of the reason why he had eventually to drop the fiction that Carolyne was just a good and dear friend who happened to have taken up residence in Weimar. Not received at court, cold-shouldered by many of the townspeople, she was in a pitiable position and he could hardly tell the world that he hadn't asked her to get into it. There was something else. With Marie d'Agoult there had never been any subterfuge: they lived together without disguise. Why not with Carolyne, who was prepared to put up with almost anything but the humiliation of being less ruined in love than her predecessor?

Finally, there was an inducement that may have been the trump card — her daughter Marie. Liszt's adoration for this child verged on the morbid and was in unpleasant contrast to his feelings for his own daughters. There is no doubt that much of Carolyne's power over him was in Marie's hands. When they were separated he wrote to her almost as often as to her mother — charming, tender letters about her dogs, her rose bushes, and when she was older, more serious matters, treating her like a wise woman while she was in her teens. She had that quality. Wagner always called her The Child in tribute to her dignity and aplomb. "Her dark and pensive eyes gazed at us so calmly . . . we . . . felt that in her innocence she unwittingly understood the cause of our gaiety," he wrote once — a mistake.[3] She wasn't very intelligent — contemptuous, it developed, of the gifted people she grew up with — and not at all nice. On her marriage to Prince Hohenlohe-Schillingfurst she washed her hands of her mother, Liszt, and artists in general. Clearly she had suffered from her unconventional upbringing more than they knew: she longed simply to be "correct." Yet at one time she appeared to return Liszt's affection. In Weimar it was the fashion to say she worshipped him. Guests were often treated to touching scenes like one recorded by Hebbel:

. . . At the piano Liszt is heroic; behind him stands the young princess, dressed in Polish-Russian national costume . . . turning the pages, and then running her fingers through his long hair that in the heat of the performance flutters wildly. A dream-like fantasy . . .[4]

Was Hebbel trying to tell us something? I don't think so. Liszt's terrible reputation didn't extend to young girls, and anyway it wasn't that kind of relationship. Magnolet, Farfadet, Magne — he had a dozen loving nicknames for her — composed with her mother a sacred tableau, Saint Anne and the Virgin, whose charm for him isn't hard to analyze. It wasn't sexual. Inferior by any standard of beauty or elegance to Marie d'Agoult, it was essential to Liszt's *amour propre* that Carolyne be judged by a loftier standard: the spirituality, the beauty that only he could see, her motherhood.

His beastliness to his own children knew no bounds at this time. Still lodged with old Anna, they were forbidden to speak Marie d'Agoult's name or to know her whereabouts. The strategy failed, probably with Anna's connivance. The girls soon found out where their mother lived and began to visit her. Liszt's rage when he discovered this gives the show away. The girls were, with real brutality, removed from Anna's charge and placed with an ancient governess of Carolyne's, a Mme Patersi who was summoned from Russia to Paris to serve as a kind of high-class jailor. They were in despair but submitted because they had no choice and because inexplicably they adored their father. "Dear Papa," wrote Cosima, "I hope you will not be dissatisfied with this letter. I am very depressed [at leaving her grandmother]. All my life long I will always do everything to give you pleasure. . . ." They pined to visit him in Germany: "In spite of the charms of Paris, the Altenburg seems more beautiful and enviable to me, and often we find ourselves transported there in our wishes." [5]

Their letters were to break the heart but they left Liszt unmoved. His answer was as often as not a pompous lecture:

As precious as your affection for me is, I tell you in all sincerity that I value it only in so far as you are truly daughters after my own heart, whose upright will, sound judgment, cultivated talents, noble and firm characters are such as to bring honor to my name and some consolation to my old age. [6]

That to a bastard daughter. This to Carolyne's little girl: "I can never stop saying to you, dearest Magnolette, that you are grace, kindness, *wisdom,* and even *perfection.*" [7]

His ugly attitude to his children is, with Carolyne's advent, usually blamed on her. It is said that she dictated his letters to and about them and supervised the unfeeling arrangements made for them. I am afraid it isn't true. His callousness long antedates her ascendancy and in her clumsy way she may even have been trying to do the right thing: Mme Patersi, much as the girls hated her, was a cultivated woman and good teacher. Prod the wound, remind him of Marie's false evaluation of him, Carolyne did by her mere presence, and perhaps in words. It was beyond her power to create resentments not already there. The children weren't her victims; they were the sacrifice to his outraged pride. (As in a dim way, they themselves understood — especially Daniel, as we will see.) I think Carolyne knew this, and that that was why she didn't mistake — as she might well have — the nature of his feeling for her own daughter, which she correctly interpreted to be a reflection of his attitude to herself. Because it isn't every woman who can tolerate her lover kissing her female child's "dear little braids," or the child hugging and calling him her "fiancé" even in fun. These things happened, and Carolyne was wise enough to take them as demonstrations in her own favor. She also knew that as long as Magnolet lived in it, the Altenburg was an attractive place to him.

That wasn't all there was to it, naturally. A part of him was not averse to the idea of a home, and as his plans for Weimar expanded, even an establishment. Liking to have people around him, he enjoyed being able to make the lavish gesture — invite five or a dozen people to his table without ceremony, offer a room or a whole apartment to an impecunious student. Though he probably thought of it as a waste of time, he liked, and surprisingly, knew how to organize an elaborate and enjoyable daily routine.

His arrival transformed the Altenburg from the dreary caravansary that Lewald saw in 1848, with Carolyne huddled in it like a displaced person. Sending for his possessions in Paris, he soon filled it with books, pictures, a variety of musical instruments, potted plants, crystal and silver. He once called the building's exterior *mesquin et vulgaire*. It wasn't, only rather ponderous, a typical central European villa in yellow stucco, solid as an ark, with double windows against the cold, a Palladian doorway, a gravel sweep. In summer the family ate outdoors. There were rose trees in the garden and peacocks shrieked on the lawn. (His last act when he closed the place in 1861 was to leave money for the feeding of these creatures of whom he was fond.)

One expects graphic records of so famous a house, which is still standing though a derelict, the garden shorn away — but there is no telling what the interior looked like in Liszt's time. For some reason, the sketches and watercolors that normally took the place of photographs are missing from the archives. All we have is a rigid little engraving of a room hung with scalloped muslin curtains, lined with carved bookcases, the furnishings consisting almost entirely of two enormous pianos, broad and flat as gaming tables, though we are told that in life they were always piled high with music. On the floor is a polar-bear rug. This is labelled *"Der Musiksalon,"* which is no help because the music room is supposed to have contained four and not two instruments: the Alexandre organ, Mozart's spinet, a pair of Érards. Beethoven's Broadwood, which one of the pianos in the engraving may be, is usually placed in the library.

Accurate reconstruction is impossible. The house had, according to Liszt, some thirty rooms and it may be that no one person saw them all. Descriptions are hopelessly at variance. Carolyne and her daughter had a separate suite of apartments (on the first or the second floor, depending on which book you read); Liszt lived in a wing over the garden; such of his students who stayed in the house, and other guests, were lodged on the top floor; two large rooms were set aside on the street level for the students' use, lessons, and every Sunday morning, the Weimar string quartet's informal sessions. So far there is general agreement. For the rest, La Mara and others conduct us through suites of confusingly situated salons, with low armchairs, "beautiful pictures" on the walls (those will be the Ary Scheffer portraits of Liszt, one showing him as the youngest of the Magi; and Preller's Homeric studies in sticky marzipan colors), and a wealth of "the symbolism" — conscious and otherwise.

There was for example the muniment room where reposed in vitrines the costly detritus of the *Glanzperiode:* the sword of honor, the jewelled batons and snuffboxes, programs and laurel wreaths dipped in silver to preserve them, gold and malachite objects, all the titivating memorials of his wicked past. At the other end of the spectrum — and the house — was a little oratory where the outrageous lovers knelt together at critical moments and always before Liszt's journeys; and next to that was the holiest of holies, Liszt's workroom. Here the nineteenth-century religion of art was consecrated, with no doubt in anyone's mind that it was the terrain for the bringing forth of masterpieces. It had a name, the *chambre bleue,* and a patron saint (Liszt's), who was Francis de Paola, the Calabrian who crossed the Straits of Messina dryshod, avoiding Scylla and Charybdis, his cloak spread like a sail.

This Francis was the subject of one of Liszt's finest piano pieces. (The other, of Assisi, inspired its twin in the set: *St. François prédicant aux oiseaux,* no less fine but less exciting.) In principle, one wants to avoid comparisons between music and painting but Sitwell has got the atmosphere of *St. François de Paule marchant sur les flots* exactly right when he evokes the Seicento, Longhena and Magnasco. From which we only derive another lesson in the Romantic fallacy: one masterpiece does not beget another. Liszt's picture was *not* a Magnasco but the work of one Steinle, which he horridly described as follows: "He stands on heaving ocean waves . . . his right hand extended in the act of blessing . . . his gaze turned upwards, where the word CARITAS glows, surrounded by an aureole." Charity notwithstanding, the significance of this picture is clear: the artist too works miracles.

The Altenburg belongs to a lost world of feeling about art, society — and love; a lost Europe too, since like all of Weimar today it is under a grubby communist shroud. But a sort of mist hung over it at its apogee, and we soon see why. Its attitudes like its furnishings needed a Balzac to describe them, and there was none. The 1850's were a fallow literary period in Germany. The giants were either dead, moribund like Heine, in exile, or both. No German novelist could be spoken of in the same breath with Flaubert, Dickens or Turgenev; no poet with Baudelaire or Hugo. Accustomed to the top levels of literary society, Liszt must often have felt that he had fetched up with a road company.

He did his best. He needed writers, if only to satisfy Carl Alexander's desire to found a new court of the Muses. He looked in particular for dramatists — and found one or two. He couldn't conjure up what wasn't there, which was for him a minor frustration only. For the biographer, it is a major one. The young Liszt lives in the pages of journals, *romans-à-clef,* satires. The middle-aged one, lacking a literary reflection, is curiously muffled. Though he was fighting an ideological war, you wouldn't know it from the writers who came to Weimar.

Hoffmann von Fallersleben was one, and typical of the period. A poet, he wrote the words to *Deutschland über Alles,* which isn't what most people think. It refers to the unification of Germany, a liberal aim in those days because it meant the end of Germany's antique little kingdoms, and Hoffmann was in respectable exile when he wrote it in 1841. (Doubters should know that it was made the national anthem during the Weimar Republic and not by Hitler. The tune of course is Haydn's, out of the old Austrian

Gott erhalte.) He was also a distinguished scholar. His *Horae belgicae,* a collection of early Germanic song, was a pioneer work in the field first explored by the brothers Grimm; the *Zeitschrift für deutsche Sprache,* which he edited with Oskar Schade for Liszt's Goethe Foundation, did valuable work. He was prominent in Altenburg social life. His *vers d'occasion* were the mainstay of every party. But it isn't difficult to conjecture that "our good Hoffmann" ("Father Hoffmann" to Berlioz) was a crashing bore. His toasts wore thin even on Cornelius, who starts out quoting them and ends in agreement with George Lewes that "in England, Shakespeare himself wouldn't do this unending reading of toasts before dinner."

His Weimar diary might have been written by a schoolboy instructed to note every visit paid, birthday celebrated, album presented. Of a dinner at the Altenburg, he records that "the discussion was lively." Carolyne was intelligent, good to the poor; her daughter "like a budding rose"; Liszt was "always the witty, important artist . . . sympathetic friend" — with never a hint of the controversy surrounding him. Hoffmann wanted a safe berth and was not looking for trouble.

He wasn't alone. Heine had spotted the problem long since: too many German writers who derided the philistines because it was fashionable were themselves philistine at heart, "secure behind . . . high mud walls," victims of "the lack of temperament which poses as moral superiority, the pedantry which would like to set up as school teacher to the nation, the belief in being able to rule the world with ideas while one grovelled before petty despots . . ." Talents easily went rotten in this climate, as the careers of Dingelstedt and Freitag show. Both pretended to intellectual independence; neither practiced it. Freitag's novels, mildly critical of nobility and court, openly anti-Semitic, were in no way calculated to offend his patron, the Grand Duke of Saxe-Coburg. Dingelstedt, like Hoffmann, had his fling at radicalism in 1841 when he mingled with the German *émigrés* in Paris (where Liszt first met him). Returning to Germany, he soon made grovelling before petty despots the business of his life. When Freiligrath, a fellow writer, decided for political reasons to surrender his Prussian pension, he received these lines from Dingelstedt: "To fling away a royal pension so that the liberal rabble . . . may bring you its public offering with peasant pride? Good heavens, Freiligrath, not that!"

Liszt was responsible for Dingelstedt's coming to Weimar, where he was made Intendent in 1857. Seldom had Liszt judged worse. There was trouble between them almost immediately. Old friends though they were, their aims were totally opposed. Dingelstedt knew exactly what Carl Alexander wanted and how to give it to him without fuss. He was a model civil servant and he outlasted Liszt by ten years. (Following his own prudent advice, he stayed the exact length of time needed to collect a pension.) Whether he was or was not actually behind, as alleged, the notorious episode that brought on Liszt's resignation — the booing of Cornelius's opera *The Barber of Bagdad* — will be discussed later. The point here is that he was not a man with whom Liszt could have worked productively. Yet he wasn't the worst available; he may have been the best.

He, for example, introduced Friedrich Hebbel, who was rated Germany's most distinguished dramatist — a title there was no one to dispute unless it was Wagner, who loathed Hebbel for his appropriation of the Nibelungen material which ought to have been Wagner's private property. What Liszt really thought of Hebbel we don't know but he backed him strongly in the theatre (*Agnes Bernauer* in 1852, the première; *Judith* in 1857) and often had him to stay at the Altenburg. Hebbel was ecstatic. "I cannot as a lay-man pass judgment on Liszt's music but he has gathered around him a cir-cle such as I have never seen on this earth," he burbled.[8] His descriptions of evening parties are of a piece with Hoffmann's: "The conversation was woven of gold, because harmony was in the air."[9] He too spreads a smoke screen of indiscriminate praise. Liszt, Carolyne, the Grand Duke, Dingel-stedt are uniformly charming and charming to *him*. Not a whiff of trouble anywhere. He does mention that prevailing conservatism of the town but rather as one might call attention to the damp climate. He saw no threat to the theatre, or to Liszt.

In this bland sea it is a relief to strike the rock of Bernhardi. Queen Vic-toria, who couldn't stand him, said he was "steeped in Prussian conceit," which was true, and he was a fool about music, solemnly relaying Raff's opinion that "Liszt is so poor a general-bassist that he is no good at compo-sition" and other absurdities. But at least he saw the Altenburg from a cer-tain perspective, and his disapproval is a useful demonstration of what Liszt and Carolyne were up against. He had all the prejudices of his class and country. Thus he described Carolyne as a "small, dark, ugly, sickly, very clever Polish woman with a slightly Jewish nuance" — using two stones to kill his bird. If anything was worse than a Pole, it was a Polish Jew. (The villain in Freitag's *Soll und Haben* for instance is a sly Polish-Jewish dealer — expectable typecasting for the period.) He knew she was not Jewish (neither was she very clever and one trembles for Bernhardi's brains if he thought so); but he would use any weapon against her because she had be-trayed her class when she took up with a musician. Not that he believed she would go through with it: "She will lift up her voice loudly enough when it is really a question of her becoming Madame Liszt."

Bernhardi, with these views, might have accused Liszt of trying to better himself socially through Carolyne. He was too sophisticated to fall into that trap, and furthermore, was convinced that Liszt was a closet radical:

Franz Liszt comes to see us. . . . He is not a man of great intelligence, but he has a certain worldly wisdom, and . . . in a high degree the tact that goes with this. It is a settled system with him never to express an opinion . . . so as not to compromise himself or offend anyone. He, the favorite of the prince, has spent the evening in the taproom of a club where the musicians of the orchestra meet . . . to smoke and drink beer. He smelt horribly of tobacco. He also acts as a sort of intermediary between the prince on one side and Fanny Lewald and Adolph Stahr on the other. He is thus clever enough to have a foot in both camps. Liszt and Carolyne are the sort of people who conduct their lives not in obedience to a conviction but solely for personal interest. . . . The prince may rest assured that his friend Liszt will prove unfaithful to him when the wind blows from the other quarter.[10]

He was comically off the mark in several ways, not least his unawareness that Carl Alexander and Fanny Lewald were close friends, corresponded for years and didn't need an "intermediary." But his worst blunder was not to see that Liszt and Carolyne were models of persons who conduct their lives in obedience to a principle. They believed that they lived for art and were therefore beyond the conventions. If there was a touch of absurdity about them as a couple, they also inspired a certain awe, that prevented Bernhardi himself from taking liberties with them. They didn't think of themselves as ordinary lovers and most people shared this view. (Berlioz refused an invitation to stay at the Altenburg in 1852 because he was travelling with his mistress, Maria Recio; it simply didn't occur to him that Liszt and Carolyne's connection resembled his own.) They weren't respectable; but they were grand, and their household was ruled by a kind of transcendental etiquette that the most impertinent found it difficult to breach.

The very confusion that surrounds the arrangements seemed designed to create a distance. When they entertained, some had the impression that she was the hostess and Liszt the honored guest, others that it was his house placed at her disposal. The practical side was managed with such hauteur that, to put it crudely, we still don't know who paid for what. The Polish servants were surely Carolyne's responsibility if not actually her property, since the serfs were not emancipated until 1861. (We don't know how many "souls" she brought from Russia.) On the other hand, the champagne from abroad and the delicacies for the table frequently mentioned in Liszt's letters seem to have been his province. "Ah," he once said, "if I had written only *Faust* and *Dante* symphonies, I wouldn't be able to give my friends trout with iced champagne!" He was incapable of economy; she was rather stingy, and a canny investor. His will, drawn up in 1860, thanks her for "the conservation, augmenting and regular placement of the funds which constitute my heritage," amounting to 220,000 francs. But money ran short on both sides, when her dividends failed to arrive or they overspent.

Liszt to Wagner, 1856: I have more than once explained to you my difficult pecuniary situation, which simply amounts to this, that my mother and my three children are decently maintained with my former savings, and that I have to manage on my salary as Kapellmeister of 1,000 thalers, and 300 more by way of a present for court concerts. For many years, since I became resolved to live up to my artistic vocation, I have not been able to count on any additional money from music publishers. My symphonic works . . . do not bring in a shilling, but on the contrary, cost me a considerable sum which I have to spend on the purchase of copies for distribution among my friends. . . .[11]

Characteristically, this letter accompanied a loan of a thousand francs, loan being a euphemism, because Wagner was never known to repay and must be counted one of Liszt's regular expenses during the Weimar years. There were others who lived more or less on his and/or Carolyne's bounty. "I'm not a banker," he said to Cornelius, "but if you ever need a hundred thaler or so . . ." and the impecunious Cornelius did need. Unknown amounts were dispensed in this way, often to his pupils, so-called — he never accepted a penny for his teaching. It was part of his system — *Génie oblige* — to donate his services, and to treat like guests those students who boarded with him. Bülow, whose family was well off, expected at least to be charged for his breakfast. He was given a suite and a grand piano; Liszt's valet, he discovered, was assigned to take care of his boots and clothes. The subject of money did not arise.

The Altenburg was undoubtedly a potent weapon for a musician to possess. Though inferior in artistic and social brilliance, not to say *haute cuisine*, to Rossini's villa in Passy, and in fashion surpassed by Pauline Viardot's château in the Seine-et-Marne, there was nothing like it in Germany and it gave him unique advantages: a center, a place where the troops, so to speak, would be always on call. That he also lived there "in sin" and with a princess was a complication of sorts. It meant the waging of a social as well as an artistic war. But on that front, Bernhardi notwithstanding, he really could not lose, nor could Carolyne as long as she was under his protection. Did it really matter if Maria Pavlovna snubbed her and a few old ladies followed suit? Memoirs of the Altenburg revolve around dinners, soirées, musicales attended by as many as fifty guests; the spare rooms were perpetually occupied. To balance the picture, one should know how enviable, how impregnable these two looked to the less fortunate — not only to Berlioz and his mistress but to such a pair as Marian Evans and George Lewes, who came to Weimar in 1854 on their illicit honeymoon, escapees from Victorian England.

Marian (not yet calling herself George Eliot) and Lewes had in addition to poverty far more to endure of hypocritical cant, even from their old friends, than Carolyne and Liszt ever did. Harriet Martineau, Carlyle, Joseph Parkes lifted their hands in pious shock at their liaison; whereas in Weimar, wrote Marian, "no one seems to find it at all scandalous that we should be together." Lewes, doing research for his life of Goethe, was welcomed by the local scholars. At the Altenburg, they were introduced to a representative group of fellow guests: Anton Rubinstein, Clara Schumann ("a melancholy, interesting creature. Her husband went mad a year ago and she has to support eight children"), the French ambassador, the Marquis de Ferrière, Gustav Schöll, director of the Art Institute. . . . Marian may have missed some of the overtones but her impression was of ease and worldliness, a couple who could afford to be indifferent to public opinion.

On arriving at the Altenburg we were shewn into the garden, where in a saloon formed by overarching trees, the déjeuner was set out. We found Hoffmann von Fallersleben, the lyric poet, Dr. Schade, a Gelehrter who has distinguished himself by a critical work on the 11,000 virgins (!) and a Herr Cornelius. . . . Presently came a Herr or Doctor Raff, a musician who has recently published a volume called Wagnerfrage. Soon after we were joined by Liszt and the Princess Marie, an elegant, gentle-looking girl of 17, and last, by the Princess Wittgenstein with her nephew Prince Eugène and a young French (or Swiss?) artist, a pupil of Scheffer.

The appearance of the Princess rather startled me at first. I had expected to see a tall distinguished looking woman, if not a beautiful one. But she is short and unbecomingly endowed with embonpoint; at first glance the face is not pleasing, and the profile especially is harsh and barbarian, but the dark, bright hair and eyes give the idea of vivacity and strength. . . . She was tastefully dressed in a morning robe of some semi-transparent material lined with orange-color, a black lace jacket, and a piquant cap set on the summit of her comb. . . . The breakfast was not sumptuous. . . . When the cigars came, Hoffmann was requested to read some of his poetry, and he gave us a bacchanalian poem with great spirit. I sat between Liszt and Miss Anderson, the Princess Marie's governess. . . . G. sat next the Princess and talked with her about Goethe, whom she pronounced to have been an egotist. My great delight was to watch Liszt and observe the sweetness of his expression. Genius, benevolence and tenderness beam from his whole countenance, and his manners are in perfect harmony. . . . A little rain sent us into the house, and when we were seated in an elegant little drawing room, opening into a large music-salon, we had more reading from Hoffmann. . . . Then came the thing I had longed for — Liszt's playing. I sat near him so that I could see both his hands and face. For the first time in my life I beheld real inspiration — for the first time I heard the true tones of the piano. He played one of his own compositions — one of a series of religious *fantaisies*. There was nothing strange or excessive about his manner. His manipulation of the instrument was quiet and easy, and his face was simply grand. . . . There was nothing petty or egoistic to mar the picture. Why did not Scheffer paint him thus instead of representing him as one of the Magi? [12]

In passing, it is interesting to note that Marian's view of Liszt was in the tradition of sacred monstrosity — her eyes fastened to his hands and face as if the secret of his music were to be found there. She didn't seem to know what he was doing in Weimar — or doesn't say. Neither she nor Lewes could sit through *Lohengrin*. She liked *Flying Dutchman*, was mildly taken with *Tannhäuser*, thought *Freischütz* completely spoiled "by the terrible *lapsus* from melody to ordinary speech." If she heard any of Liszt's symphonic works, she omitted to mention them; nor did the phrase "music of the future" register. Yet she undertook to translate an article by Liszt into English. It appeared in the *Leader* under the title "The Romantic School of Music" and not having read it, I confess to bafflement. What article can it have been? Her biographer says it was "on Meyerbeer and Wagner" but Liszt never lumped these unwilling bedfellows together in any article and if she somehow combined one on Meyerbeer and one on *Flying Dutchman*, which he did write that year, it must make peculiar reading. It is of no importance. Her memories of Weimar are valuable documents to the Lisztian because they show him, for once, through non-German lenses — and because she is George Eliot.

She leaves us with two vivid little glimpses:

Dear Weimar! We were sorry to say good bye to it, with its pleasant group of friends — the grand, fascinating Liszt, the bright, kind Princess, the Marquis de Ferrière . . . the hearty animated Schöll. . . . We breakfasted twice, by way of farewell with Liszt and the Princess — the first time without any other visitors. The Princess Marie showed me a remarkable series of sketches from Dante, while Liszt went to rest and George talked with the Princess. After this, we all sat down together in the Princess Marie's room, Liszt, the Princess and her daughter on the sofa, G and I opposite to them, and Miss Anderson a little in the rear. I like to recall this moment, and Liszt's face with its serious expression, as we talked about his coming to London. . . . The next time we breakfasted with them the Marquis . . . and young Cornelius were there, and I had a long theological seance with the Princess on the sofa. She parted from us very prettily, with earnest wishes for my happiness in particular. G was so grateful for this that he couldn't help saying "God bless you" to her, and she repeated it, calling after me too. "God bless you" . . .[13]

Chapter 33

THE YOUNG PIANISTS at the Altenburg were the first generation of authentic Lisztians. Puzzi Cohen excepted, he gave no regular lessons to anyone between 1836 and 1851, when Bülow arrived in Weimar; while the hundreds, maybe thousands, who claimed to have "studied with Liszt" belong to a later date. In the 1870's and 1880's, anyone could attend his classes — held three times a week and free of charge — and everybody did: they were a regular tourist attraction. (Like Goethe, Liszt lived long enough to turn into a national monument, and Weimar had to adjust, as before, to being overrun. The "Lisztianer" were reckoned such a nuisance that anybody practicing the piano before an open window risked a fine of three marks.) Of these later hordes, perhaps two or three dozen really were the old sorcerer's apprentices, and many of them were famous names well into the twentieth century: Joseffy, Siloti, Rosenthal, d'Albert, Friedheim, Lamond, Aus der Ohe, Stavenhagen. . . . There was no doubt about Liszt's genius as a teacher. But the lack of discrimination, the willingness to be victimized in those last years were outward signs of something that too few acknowledged. He was a profoundly disillusioned man, resigned to being recognized only as a pianist, a failure at everything else. Bülow in 1882 raged at the "Abbé's stable." He didn't ask himself how far he, and the opinion he represented, had contributed to Liszt's indifference.

Bülow was first, and first favorite, at the Altenburg — "my Hans . . . the artist . . . who is dearest to me, and has . . . grown out of my musical heart." Only Liszt could have said that. Bülow was an outstandingly unlovable man, even in youth. His witty remarks were all at somebody's expense: "A tenor is not a man but a disease." To a trombone player: "Your tone sounds like gravy running through a sewer." To someone who ventured that Bülow didn't remember him: "You win." (He got some of this back. Cui said to him, "You don't shave but you have a razor in your mouth.")

From a noble family, Bülow had a mental apparatus designed for military service or the law and his parents would have preferred either to a musical career. He was also a musician, blood and bone. Hearing Liszt conduct *Lohengrin* in 1850 gave him courage to make the break. He fled first to Zurich and Wagner, with whom he worked a season at conducting. He then returned to Weimar. To his dictatorial mother Liszt was by many degrees less unappetizing a mentor to her son than Wagner and she accepted his assurance that "Hans is evidently gifted with a musical organization of the rarest kind. His executive talent will easily place him in the front rank of the greatest pianists." [1]

Liszt was right on both counts. Bülow's was by far the finest musical intellect to pass through his hands, and in some ways the most interesting because it belonged to a new order — a hateful one be it said. Not a creative personality, he was the model of the serious, slave-driving interpreter, the first great modern conductor who was not also a composer. We must also believe that he was a great pianist, though conflicting accounts make it sound as though he had been a disconcerting mixture of scholarship and a kind of forced romanticism, as if he had tried to graft Lisztian bravura onto a style naturally arid. (One of his Weimar letters announces solemnly: "My piano playing has latterly made substantial progress. I have gained in virtuosity and a certain virtuoso chic. . . .") [2] Above all, he personified German music's superiority complex. Though like many Prussians of his class he spoke perfect French, and in his youth he admired Berlioz, he had most of the Teutonic vices: arrogant chauvinism, anti-Semitism, the drill sergeant's mania for precision. Whole scores were imbedded in his memory as in a block of ice, and he expected the same skills from the musicians who worked under him. The Meiningen orchestra which he conducted in the 1880's was the most disciplined on earth. Its members played without notes and standing up, like a military band. Audiences respected him to the point of terror: he didn't hesitate to hector and insult them.

He had his virtues. In spite of his chauvinism he was in politics an unreconstructed "red republican," and when the Kaiser announced that "anybody who doesn't like the way things are going in this country can shake the dust from his shoes," Bülow complied. Ostentatiously wiping his boots with a handkerchief at the conclusion of a concert, he went off and died in Cairo (1894). He was by then certifiably a little crazy but there was a downrightness about him that was always attractive. A diminutive, goateed mandarin but for his bulging, fanatic's eye, he was to those who knew him an abyss of sensibility beneath the Prussian veneer; and he was subject to violent crushes, the first on Liszt – "a sympathy, which is quite involuntary, for the mere sight of his noble and expressive features" – the second on Cosima (a predictable consequence of the first); the last and fatal one on Wagner. That way madness lay and it destroyed Bülow's life.

He was twenty-one when he came to Weimar and a fiend for work. Hours of practice were interspersed with any task Liszt cared to set him. He conducted, played in concert with the Weimar quartet, revised scores, and like every Altenburg inhabitant who could hold a pen, he waded into the journalistic maelstrom. "He has on the one hand an incredible self-command, certainty and aplomb, then again a boundless imprudence, which may drag him into the worst of quarrels," said his mother, from whom he inherited both tendencies; they combined to make him a savagely effective polemicist, and a doubtful recruiter for the cause. His articles enraged some who might have been inclined to agree with him, and often accomplished the opposite of what he intended: to enlist Berlioz for example. Berlioz would never have played the part assigned to him; without Bülow's prodding he might have been less testy about it:

> The young man [he wrote] is one of the most fervent disciples of the extravagant school known in Germany as the music of the future. They will not give up their determination that I should be at their head as standard bearer. I say nothing, write nothing, and let them have their way. Sensible people will know what to make of it all.[3]

Berlioz misstated the case. Bülow wasn't asking him to be the standard bearer, a position he had long since assigned to Wagner. And sensible people did *not* know what to make of it all. They were divided as over no other issue in nineteenth-century music; and that was where Bülow might have come in. He alone perhaps had the brains, or call it the mental organization, to formulate the position without fear or favor. Had he also had the detachment, he might have succeeded where Liszt himself failed because suspect, for a thousand reasons, to all concerned. Bülow's emotions got in the way. He was too bound up in the personalities involved – and ultimately in the nationalities as well. When he fell for the Wagnerian mystique, he lost his grip on the issue of modernity, which had to exist independently: the true music of the future could not be German, French, or Russian; it was outside nationality. Bülow, lost among the Nibelungs, couldn't see that. Music for him became German or nothing.

The wild little Tausig probably came next in Liszt's affections. "My dear and extraordinary budding genius" was too young to take part in ideological battles but Liszt is known to have thought his career at the piano might parallel his own. He was brought to the Altenburg in 1855 at age thirteen, by his father; and he was refused a hearing. "I have no time for these artists *die werden sollen* [who are to be]," said Liszt. But somebody smuggled the child to the piano while the wine and cigars were being passed, and he dashed into Chopin's A-flat Polonaise, "knocking us over with the octaves," according to Cornelius.

He was accepted and stayed two years, a constant source of agitation. He stole, once, the only copy of the *Faust* Symphony and sold it to a servant, who put it in the dustbin. A friend managed to trace it. "Carolina, Carolina, we are saved!" cried Liszt, while the friend wondered what punishment would be meted out.[4] None was. Liszt's indulgence, boundless with children not his own, verged on the extravagant with Tausig, in whom he perhaps detected the nervous disorder that brought his career to a halt well before his early death. (Typhoid killed him at thirty.) Tausig had an urge to smash things. Once when a piece of music fell on the keys, he went on playing through the paper, jabbing it to tatters. Wagner, whom he visited in 1858, found him "a terrible youth . . . with his fearfully excessive cigar-smoking and tea-drinking . . . a rich catastrophe . . ."[5] In fact he hadn't it in him to be a successor to Liszt. While he lasted, he was the most exciting pianist around. "Hear Tausig! Hear Tausig!" cried Seroff. But for all his *mains de bronze* — Liszt's phrase — and an intelligence more broadly based than that of most executants, he was more eccentric than original and he was no composer.

Liszt enjoyed human variousness, which may be why he took on the young William Mason, a decided oddity in that atmosphere. His father was Lowell Mason, composer of "From Greenland's Icy Mountains" and other hymns, and he was not unlike a staid Jamesian hero in his encounters with foreigners. He was himself not sure what had recommended him to Liszt, whose earliest American pupil he was. At a guess, his prim New England ways amused the master. Whatever the reason, he is a boon to biographers, his memoirs being the only ones to describe this period from the student's angle, and with some distinction.[*]

Mason arrived in Weimar in 1849, having crossed the Atlantic in a sidewheeler; but he found Liszt preoccupied with the Goethe Festival and didn't try again for four years. In 1853, he again presented himself. A butler admitted him. These servants intimidated the applicant who was poor or flustered (Cornelius was so put out by a chambermaid who made him wait that he hysterically counted every step of the staircase to the

[*] It is an odd coincidence that the two best accounts of Liszt in Weimar should be by Americans. The other is Amy Fay's *Music Study in Germany,* much superior to Mason, really a small classic. Unfortunately for my purposes, Fay belongs to the last years. She never knew the Altenburg. In her time, Liszt lived in another part of Weimar, in a small garden house presented to him by the Grand Duke, called the Hofgärtnerei, now the Liszt Museum. Those who were little more than boys in Altenburg days — Bülow, Tausig, Joachim, Rubinstein — were giants on the musical scene in hers.

bel étage: twenty-nine) and the butler took Mason for a wine merchant. He stood his ground and was taken upstairs to the dining room where Liszt was having a favorite tipple, coffee with cognac. "*Nun,* Mason," he said coolly. "*Sie lassen lange auf Sich warten* — I've been waiting for you for four years." [6] They went to the drawing room. "I have a new Érard piano from Paris," said Liszt. "Try it and see how you like it." He was moving about collecting papers to take to the castle: "As it's on the way to the hotel, we can walk as far as that together." He seemed not to know what the young man was there for and Mason was in agonies. He sat down and played, as quietly as he could, one of his own compositions. "That's one of your own?" Liszt asked. "Well, it's a charming little piece." They were halfway down the hill before he spoke the words Mason died to hear: "You say you're going to Leipzig . . . ? While you're there you had better choose your piano and have it sent here. Meanwhile I'll tell Klindworth to look up rooms for you. . . ."

Mason you feel was a scrupulous witness. He was bowled over by Liszt, the personal elegance, the "fascination impossible to describe." But he doesn't pretend to have known him better than he did. Much of the Altenburg remained terra incognita to him; he wasn't sure which part of it Carolyne lived in:

We boys saw little of the Wittgensteins, and I remember dining with them only once. I sat next to the Princess Marie, who spoke English very well, and it may have been due to her desire to exercise in that language that I was honored. . . . Rubinstein met her when he was in Weimar . . . and composed a nocturne which he dedicated to her. When he came to this country in 1873 he told me that he met her again some years later at the palace in Vienna but that she had become very haughty and had not been inclined to pay much attention to him. There are many Wittgensteins in Russia. . . . There was but one Rubinstein.[7]

Mason's colleagues, "we boys," were at this time Karl Klindworth, Dionys Pruckner, Joachim Raff (Liszt's secretary and copyist), Bülow when he wasn't on tour; and they were like a family, most of them with their own apartments in town, all of them coming and going as they liked in the Altenburg's lower rooms. One reads of the charms of student life in nineteenth-century Germany with a certain scepticism, wondering about the sombre side, the duelling and the anti-Semitism. But there was none of that in Weimar, and when Mason, no sentimentalist, tells us that to the young men around Liszt, this was *Die goldene Zeit,* he can be believed.

The lessons were irregular. "Tell the boys to come up tonight between six and eight," Liszt would say. He didn't supervise their practice — that was their business. Nor like old Wieck, or the later Leschetizky, did he have a "method," the hands held this way or that, the arm firm or relaxed, all the tricks that make piano study later in the century sound like calisthenics.

Technique as such didn't interest him, or what he called "finger-virtuosi." He told the boys that the completion of the *Transcendental* Études had finished his interest in that direction. So what did he teach? Mason, like everybody else, finds it hard to say. He quotes Liszt:

> You are to learn all you can from my playing, relating to conception, style, phrasing, etc., but do not imitate my touch, which I am aware is not a good model to follow. In the early years I was not patient enough to make haste slowly — to develop in an orderly, logical and progressive way. I was impatient for immediate results, and took short cuts, so to speak, and jumped through sheer force of will to the goal of my ambition. It is true that I was successful, but I do not advise you to follow my way, for you lack my personality.[8]

That struck Mason not as vanity but the simple truth. Of course they were not there to be turned into copies of Liszt, and his actual instructions were modest, low-key. The pupil played his piece. He might finish, or he might find himself gently pushed aside and Liszt sitting down himself to render a phrase in amplification of a spoken comment.* It was all very casual and easy but Mason got so worked up at his first session that he had stiff muscles all the next day, as if he'd been taking violent exercise.

There were other lessons. The boys were to acquire social polish and learn to present a brave face to the world. Once when Mason and the others were to play at the castle, an Altenburg servant delivered white ties to their rooms — which Mason sensibly didn't take amiss: he thought it showed attention. "Liszt liked to have us about him," he says. "He wished us to meet great men. He would send word when he expected visitors, and sometimes he would bring them down to our lodging to see us." When Wieniawski the violinist and some other guests were staying at the Altenburg, Liszt asked Mason to lay on a breakfast for them. Rather aghast, Mason asked what should be served. "Oh," Liszt replied carelessly, "some rolls, caviar, herring and so on." That went off all right but it was a wet day, pouring as it often did in Weimar. Liszt nevertheless proposed "a stroll in the garden," and the garden "was only about four times as large as the back yard of a New York house, unflagged and muddy from the rain. Never shall I forget the sight of Liszt, Joachim, Wieniawski and our other distinguished guests 'strolling' through this garden . . . in mud two inches deep."

Mason's rather proper sense of humor alerted him to the absurdities in Liszt but made him a not unsympathetic observer. He agreed that appear-

---

* In amusing contrast is Amy Fay's description of Tausig's teaching. His way was to stand over a pupil, shouting at him not to "make Spektakel," and uttering exclamations of horror: "Terrible! Shocking! Oh God!" He would then sit down to play the passage himself, with the request that it be rendered just so. "I used to feel," writes Fay, "as if someone wished me to copy a streak of forked lightning with the end of a wetted match." (Fay, p. 83.)

ances mattered and didn't mind when the master's Napoleonic attention to detail focused on his eyeglasses. (I take Mason to mean pince-nez here. A later photograph shows him wearing these and closely resembling Grover Cleveland.) "I don't like to see you wearing those," Liszt said. "I will send my optician to fit you with spectacles." This was done and Mason received two pairs. But presently Liszt went to Paris, and returned with a different opinion: "I find that gentlemen are wearing eyeglasses now. In fact, they are considered quite *comme il faut,* so I have no objection to you wearing yours." Mason treasured his Weimar spectacles for many years.

In a more sober vein, he was an eye-witness to a scene famous in musical annals, which occurred at the Altenburg in 1853. He and the others were summoned to meet a young man "said to have great talent" and his travelling companion. The young man was Brahms, then twenty years old, and his friend the "gypsy" violinist Reményi. (His real name was Hoffmann.) Mason draws a blank on Brahms's personality and appearance. What he noticed was a pile of music in all but illegible manuscript lying on a table, on top Brahms's Scherzo from Opus 4 – which he notes because it was presently to show Liszt's legendary capacity to sight-read. Entreated to play, Brahms, who was shy or surly or both, refused, and Liszt, picking up the Scherzo at random, played it himself, deciphering the scribble without trouble. Brahms was "amazed and delighted" – which makes him the third composer after Chopin and Schumann to have heard his music turned to gold in Liszt's hands, and to have repaid him in lead.

Liszt was then asked to play his B Minor Sonata, an undoubted masterpiece, a kind of cosmic self-portrait that is sometimes called his *Wanderer* Fantasy on account of its emotional affinity with Schubert's work but also because the ideas of thematic metamorphosis and unbroken sequence (in this sonata the traditional movements are dissolved) partly derive from Schubert's single, revolutionary use of them in the *Wanderer.* There the resemblance ends. Liszt's treatment is at once more sophisticated and more profound. The B Minor recasts the familiar sonata form into a single unit in which the motifs are twisted, unwound, rewoven like a serpent's coils.* It moves like some extraordinary, iridescent object through space, now grandiose, now threatening, now heavenly, until it explodes into one of the great climaxes in piano literature, dying away to an exquisite epilogue. In Liszt's hands it must have been miraculous.

At the close of the Andante, Liszt was seen to glance at Brahms and observe that he was dozing in his chair. He finished the piece, rose quietly

---

* For the importance of this technique to the music of future generations, see Searle: ". . . The serial technique of Schoenberg, for instance, uses precisely the methods of Liszt's thematic transformation within the framework of an entirely different language. . . ." (*The Music of Liszt:* p. 61.)

and left the room. Seldom can he have been offered such an insult and it remains inexplicable. Brahms had arrived with a letter of introduction from Joachim, who may have poisoned his mind in advance. He need not have presented the letter. His animus toward Liszt must be more deeply rooted than we know. The Brahms-Joachim manifesto of 1860 took aim at theories of composition "strongly to be deplored and condemned," "contrary to the innermost spirit of music," etc., and one of these was surely the technique of metamorphosis embodied in the B Minor. Alan Walker points out that it was also one of several borrowings from Liszt that Brahms made without apology or acknowledgment: there is more than one way to cancel a debt. Or was it simply that he resented Liszt's failure to hail him as a genius on sight — as Schumann presently did?

Mason wasn't sure how far Brahms's boorishness influenced Liszt. He is positive that Liszt wasn't enthusiastic about the compositions shown him — and it would have been strange if the Scherzo had impressed him. No doubt he recognized the classicist, and that to him spelled a cul-de-sac. Or it may have been one of those antagonisms that defy explanation.

At least one classicist did make his way into the Altenburg, though Liszt did not immediately recognize him as such and had other reasons for receiving him. This was Anton Rubinstein, whose dynamic personality and pianism at one time raised Liszt's hopes for something more. These hopes were dashed. Rubinstein's reflections on music, set down in 1894, make discouraging reading. "With the death of Schumann and Chopin, *finis musicae*," he intoned. Berlioz was "subtilized, neither beautiful nor great," Wagner "in comparison with the great ones of the past . . . of a very questionable art." [9] Into the dustbin go the Russian Five, and needless to say, Liszt: "His desire for novelty (*à tout prix*) gave him the idea of forming whole compositions of one and the same theme. Sonata, Concerto, Symphonic Poem, all with one theme only — an absolutely unmusical proceeding." (Hanslick: "A monstrous, antimusical procedure." Variations on this phrase were used ad nauseum by Liszt's critics.) Nor were these opinions the desiccated fruit of old age. Very probably they had their genesis in the Altenburg in 1854–1855.

Liszt knew Rubinstein from a child. He arrived from Poland in Paris in 1840, a ten-year-old curlilocks as beautiful as *le petit Litz* had been, but looks were deceptive. He was a savage and soon grew a lion's head to match his personality. (He strikingly resembled Beethoven, hence Liszt's nickname for him: Van II.) Liszt was never his teacher. He had no time for teaching in the 1840's, as Rubinstein ought to have known. Rubinstein nevertheless contrived a grievance about it, and his autobiography makes much of some fancied slights. They didn't stop him from turning up at the Altenburg, staggering under a load of valises that contained several tons of his own music. He spent weeks in Weimar, occupying the best room in the house, and the next we hear is that Liszt is producing his opera, *The Siberian Hunters*.

It is unknown what Liszt saw in this work, which surely did not belong with the music of the future. I would guess that the production represented more of his hopes for Russian music than confidence in the opera itself.

Liszt to Brendel: I don't want to preach to [Rubinstein] — he may sow his wild oats and fish deeper in the Mendelssohn waters, and even swim away if he likes. But sooner or later I am certain he will give up the apparent and the formalistic for the organically real. . . .[10]

He was forced to change his mind during the Berlioz week of February 1855. Berlioz's visits to Weimar were always high holidays. Even Carl Alexander was ready to honor the man, whatever he thought of the music, bestowing decorations and giving ducal dinners with appropriate toasts from Fallersleben. "We boys" vied to play the lesser percussion instruments in the orchestra and were joined on this occasion by Liszt, who managed the Chinese gong in *Lélio* as well as playing the piano part. With this particular week, which introduced the *Enfance du Christ* along with more familiar works, Liszt took rather more pains than usual. The wretched Harriet Smithson had lately died and he knew Berlioz to be suffering from the remorseful grief of one relieved of a nearly intolerable burden. ("She inspired you, you loved her and sang your love . . . her mission was fulfilled," he wrote, in a rare burst of chauvinism, which consoled Berlioz and will enrage feminists.)

Rubinstein was Berlioz's fellow guest at the Altenburg, and Liszt may have counted on this to effect a conversion. We learn what happened from a note: "Your *fugue* this morning, my dear Rubinstein, is very little to my taste, and I much prefer the preludes you wrote at an earlier date in this same room, which to my surprise I found empty when I came to fetch you for the Berlioz rehearsal. Is it a fact that this music works on your nerves?"[11]

The flight was forgiven but as his want of Murlship grew more irksome the Altenburg lost interest in Rubinstein, whose career Liszt observed with a certain there-but-for-the-grace-of-God cynicism. He never acknowledged Rubinstein to be his successor at the piano. "Have you heard Tausig?" he would ask. And naturally this was ascribed to the old king's envy. I don't believe it. He wasn't in competition with Rubinstein, and when it came down to it knew he could stand any comparison. Siloti has a story about that. When he was a student at Weimar in the 1880's he went once to Leipzig to hear Rubinstein and returned in a glow: the "Moonlight" had been especially marvelous, and it happened to be a piece he had never

heard Liszt play. Like many others, it was also forbidden the pupils "because when I was young it was my specialty." But praise of Rubinstein
roused him up and he sat down to the piano. Siloti held his breath:

Rubinstein had played on a beautiful Bechstein in a hall with very good
acoustics. Liszt was playing in a little carpetted room, in which small space
thirty-five or forty people were sitting, and the piano was worn-out, unequal
and discordant. He had only played the opening triplets however when I felt
as if the room no longer held me and when, after the first four bars, the G sharp
came in in the right hand, I was completely carried away. Not that he accented
this G sharp; it was simply that he gave it an entirely new sound, which even
now, after twenty-seven years, I can hear distinctly. . . .[12]

Siloti idolized Liszt. He had as little faith in the compositions as the
rest. It is characteristic that he should tell us how Liszt played Beethoven
and say not a word about the interpretation of the late piano works being
composed under his nose. (He wasn't alone: Amy Fay seems never to have
heard these either, and perhaps Liszt, out of weariness or tact, just did not
play them.) Indeed he hasn't much to say about any of Liszt's music,
which he handles sparingly, as one who would minimize a loved one's
weakness.

We are back at the beginning. From Bülow onward, Liszt never trained
a successor — Bülow least of all. Rarely has there been a more cruel turn-
around. Bülow married Cosima in 1857; in 1864 he lost her to Wagner.
When this scandal broke, Liszt was entirely on Bülow's side and on his
account severed relations with the adulterous pair for some years. Yet
somehow Bülow was able to forgive Cosima, and even Wagner. He had
been, he said masochistically, "too small a personality" for so great a
woman, who deserved "a colossal genius." To Liszt on the other hand he
became increasingly inimical and he developed a pathological hatred for
his music, "un-music, quack music, anti-music," "an unexampled scar on the
face." He spat these judgments like nails, culminating in his refusal of
Liszt's invitation to teach at the Budapest Conservatory in 1875 — "the very
dubious temple of a people that is half-barbarian, half-Israelitish or Israel-
ized." [13] Thus did the Wagnerian virus work in people's veins.

No other Altenburger went that far but none did him much honor either.
Mason introduced Beethoven, Chopin and Schumann to America but not
Liszt. Klindworth hitched his wagon to the Wagner star. Fears of a poor
reception may have influenced some of them. Pruckner took a terrible
drubbing when he attempted the E-flat Concerto in Vienna. Alternatively
described (this is typical of Liszt criticism) as the vulgarest concerto ever
written and by Bartók as "the first perfect realization of the cyclic sonata
form," it was so mauled by the critics that Pruckner might well have felt
there wasn't much future in Liszt interpretation.

Sadly, Liszt never met the only nineteenth-century pianist who was at once his equal at the keyboard and his most devoted and intelligent interpreter. Busoni could just have made it to Weimar before Liszt's death but did not and heard Liszt play only once, when he had hurt his hand and wasn't at his best. Nevertheless, Busoni could see inside Liszt's head, and around him too. "We are all descended from Liszt radically," he said, "without excepting Wagner, and we owe him the lesser things that we can do. César Franck, Debussy, the penultimate Russians, are all branches of his tree." [14]

Busoni was virtually the discoverer of the late piano music, and perhaps for this reason did not adopt the familiar mannerisms of the so-called Lisztian style. As tremendous a pianist as ever lived — they spoke of his "chords like cast bronze, glittering runs, the mighty roaring of the arpeggios" — Busoni was also an intellectual who shaped his conceptions with a control quite foreign to belaborers of the piano like Moritz Rosenthal, eccentrics like Joseph Weiss, head-tossers like Friedheim, performers who with the best will in the world may have done Liszt more harm than his worst enemies, for they not only distorted his keyboard style but chose their Liszt from the second or third drawer down, flailing away at the Rhapsodies, the operatic paraphrases and, yes — the E-flat. These men, one ventures to say, did not understand Liszt's music, hence could not play the best of it. In this he was the victim of copyists like those in European museums, who with frightful fidelity reproduce the least worthy pictures in the collection.*

Louis Kentner observes that the good Liszt player "must be a good Beethoven player, Mozart, Schubert and Bach player, he must see how far Liszt looked into the future and make Debussy and Bartók integral parts of his musical diet. . . . In this, as in many other respects, Busoni is still a model worth following: his omnivorous catholicity of taste covered all music, from Bach to Schoenberg, with Liszt as a sort of musical lodestar." [15] Nobody did this in Liszt's lifetime. Again and again we get the feeling that time is running the wrong way. It is the pupils who seem to be drinking

---

* But how good was any nineteenth-century pianist who lived long enough to be recorded? Harold Schonberg's researches into this question (*The Great Pianists*, 1963) are extremely disconcerting. Even allowing for extenuating circumstances — age or decrepitude in the artist, technical shortcomings in the apparatus — pianist after pianist sounds like a catastrophe. To stick to Liszt's pupils, take these examples. Eugène d'Albert, of whom it was said that "the mantle of Liszt has fallen [on him] in our generation." His recordings, says Schonberg, "cause nothing but embarrassment . . . his playing is eccentric, sloppy and undisciplined . . . full of wrong notes, memory lapses and distorted rhythms." Or here is Weiss, admired by Mahler. According to Schonberg, his recording of Liszt's Twelfth Rhapsody is "the Liszt school at its worst — eccentric, inaccurate. . . ." Frederic Lamond: "Whenever he had anything difficult to play . . . he failed quite devastatingly." These are random choices. The list is long and by no means confined to Liszt's followers.

the exhausted dregs of his Romanticism — the old man modern, the young ones old-fashioned, *démodé*.

There are many signs that the homage paid to him on the wrong grounds exasperated him: the shortness of his temper, the lengthening list of works taboo'd in his atelier, not only the "Moonlight" but Chopin's B-flat Minor Sonata and most of his own Rhapsodies. His penultimate years breathe a kind of fury wrapped up in a deadly politeness; and in the end he trusted nobody.

What, for example, happened to the *Sketches for a Harmony of the Future?* It has been hoped that this treatise might be located among the unpublished pieces buried in the Weimar archive, bequeathed like them to posterity. If found, it might open a new chapter in musical history — disclosing his thoughts on the suspension of tonality, the restructuring of chords (dispensing with the triad and building in fourths, hailed as Schönberg's achievement at the beginning of this century), and other experiments carried out in the last piano pieces. (But he was interested in an *ordre omnitonique* as early as 1832 and actually composed a *Prélude omnitonique* that was seen in manuscript in London in 1904 and has since vanished.)

Friedheim saw a notebook or a manuscript answering to the description in 1885 when he was Liszt's secretary and helping to put his papers in order. His comment was, "This will make you responsible for a lot of nonsense which is bound to be written someday" — which I don't quite know how to interpret. Did Friedheim mean the book would be misunderstood, or that its contents were nonsense? He says he expected a rebuke, and Liszt's grave answer, "That may be. I have not published it because the time is not yet ripe," suggests that he deserved it. (And of course, maddeningly, he doesn't tell us a single thing we want to know about the book itself.) That is the last that has been heard of it. Did Liszt destroy it in despair? Turn it over to someone who thought it not worth keeping? He didn't anyway entrust it to any of his pupils, which may in the end define his attitude to them. Like Diaghilev to Cocteau, he seemed always to be saying, "Astonish me!" And not one of them did.

Chapter 34

IN 1868, Peter Cornelius was asked by a German publisher to write a biography of Liszt. He declined on a number of significant grounds, the first that "my own artistic development has brought me to a point where I can no longer take the tone of a panegyrist toward the majority of his works." [1] Then there is the moral difficulty — "the ethical conflict, about which I ask myself, without being able to answer, whether Liszt has succeeded in emerging victoriously from it." Lastly there is the matter of his resignation from Weimar: Liszt "ought to have remained at his post in spite of every misunderstanding: self-renunciation in this sense was the touchstone by which the gold of his labors proved itself, to the outer world, not to have been free from alloy." Liszt in fact resigned out of pique "at not being accepted by the Germans during his lifetime as a demigod after he had boldly and adroitly soared to distinction on Wagner's shoulders."

Since these objections represented a large body of opinion both within and without Liszt's own circle, they need examining along with the "ethics" of those who opposed Liszt on moral grounds. Bülow's views and behavior we know. Here is Joachim, writing in 1855 to Clara Schumann:

I have much to tell you, dear sympathetic friend, about Liszt. . . . I have not been so bitterly disillusioned for a long time as by [his] compositions; I have to admit that a more vulgar use of sacred forms, a more repulsive coquetting with the noblest feelings for the sake of effect, has never been attempted at the conductor's desk. . . . Meyerbeer, Wagner, the morbid side of Chopin's muse, not his proud patriotism but his sugary tenderness, Berlioz, all this is combined in one *sample*, without the disorder due to the richness of material. I shall never be able to meet Liszt again, because I should want to tell him that instead of taking him for a mighty . . . spirit striving to return to God, I have suddenly realized that he is a cunning contriver of effects. . . . You were right, dear Frau Schumann. . . .[2]

Dear Frau Schumann, heavily in Liszt's debt for his productions of her husband's compositions and not averse to accepting Altenburg hospitality, did her work well. She found it child's play to alienate Liszt's followers — Cornelius fell for her too — but she couldn't make an honest man out of Joachim, who continued to visit Weimar and to present a loyal face to Liszt while writing this kind of thing to their mutual friends:

Joachim to Gisela von Arnim, March 1857: Stern wishes to produce my overture at a concert at which compositions by Liszt and Berlioz are to be performed. I have no objection, for what I am most interested in is that *you* should hear it. The unhealthy neighborhood of Liszt's music will not endanger mine in your ears, so I shall not worry Stern with trifling objections from motives of artistic prudery. Whenever I declare myself to be opposed to participation in Liszt's musical endeavors, it must be in a more dignified manner than by a feeble protest which would make me seem afraid of the conductor with whom I was associated for so many years.[3]

The dignified means he found was the letter already quoted, which burst upon Liszt later in the year, and three years after that, the Manifesto, about which there is this further point to be made. Joseph Joachim was a Hungarian Jew. Wagner's tract, *Jewry in Music,* must have caused him the deepest offense. But when he became director of the Berlin Hochschule he refused admittance to former Liszt pupils who would not repudiate Liszt's "doctrines" — while rising sufficiently above his hostility toward Wagner to conduct his music at the Hochschule concerts.

Joachim's final stroke was delivered after Liszt's death. This was his testimony in a case cooked up by the widow of Joachim Raff. Raff always claimed to have taught the ignorant Liszt all he knew about orchestration. He was Liszt's secretary from 1849 to 1854, and in that period made his pretensions known to everyone. At a rehearsal of *Prometheus,* he said to Cossmann: "Listen to the orchestration. It's mine." A letter from December 1849 announces with ineffable brass: "I have cleaned up Liszt's first *Concerto symphonique* for him. . . . Now comes the scoring and copying of an overture called *Ce qu'on entend sur la montagne.*"[4] *Tasso* was largely his, and so on.

Joachim upheld these claims. To Helena Raff he wrote:

> . . . I was the intimate friend of Raff, as of Liszt, and I had many occasions to know exactly the kind of work done by Raff for Liszt. This work consisted in completely orchestrating the outlines [*esquisses*] written for piano, then in work of a completely independent character.[5]

Peter Raabe and others who have ransacked the Weimar archives have discovered no such *esquisses*. What they have found are rough drafts, in Liszt's hand, of orchestral scores, which can be followed through as many as six revisions made as rehearsals progressed, until the final version was readied for the printer — always by Liszt himself. The dates further falsify Joachim's testimony. He left Weimar in 1853. The first six of the symphonic poems were published in 1856. How and when did he have the occasion to compare the final texts with the various revisions that led up to them? It would also be interesting to know why he wanted Raff to get the credit for compositions so despicable. Hatred has its own logic.

"Impure harmony," "gratuitous ugliness," "a room reeking with fumes." "Were you to teach temperance at a ginshop door, and let your congregation taste the poison sold therein that they might know its vileness, they would come out drunkards." "No originality, only glitter." Criticism as irresponsible as it was scurrilous poured in on Liszt for more than thirty years.[6] The list of his failures is long: *Mazeppa* greeted with catcalls in Leipzig; the *Dante* Symphony such a flop in Dresden as to put that city off-limits to him for many years. A man endures these things if he has a circle of devoted admirers, but we have seen what Liszt's largely consisted of. I don't want to imply that there were no exceptions. Leopold Damrosch gave *Le Triomphe funèbre de Tasse* its first performance — in New York of all places — in 1877, with all the pomp and polish that the composer could desire. Alexander Ritter, one of his instrumentalists in the Weimar orchestra who went on to become conductor at Stettin, often put Liszt on his programs. But those who worried about Liszt's ethics overlooked his reaction to the treatment he was subjected to. He had, owing to his position in Weimar, a certain amount of weight and he might have used it. He could have reminded Bülow and others of their IOU's to him. He did the opposite. "On my advice, von Bülow will not play my A major Concerto, nor any other compositions of mine," he wrote the conductor Herbeck,[7] and again to Herbeck: "It seems to me high time that I should be somewhat forgotten, or at least placed very much in the background. My name has been frequently put forward; many have taken umbrage at this, and been needlessly annoyed by it."

Ritter was discouraged from an all-Liszt concert in these terms:

Have you considered that Orpheus has no proper *working out section*, and hovers quite simply between bliss and woe? . . . Pray do not forget that Tasso celebrates no *psychic triumph*, and has already been denounced by an ingenious critic (who was probably mindful of the "inner camel" that Heine calls indispensable to German aesthetics). . . . Should you be of another opinion, allow me to keep you at least from too greatly compromising yourself, so near as you are to the doors of the spotless Berlin critics. . . .[8]

Jessie Laussot received an illuminating *vale:*

Knowing by experience how little favor my works meet with, I have had to force on myself a sort of compulsory disregard of them and a passive resignation. Thus during the *years of my foreign activity in Germany* [my italics] I constantly observed the rule of never asking anyone whatsoever to have any of my works performed; more than that, I really dissuaded many persons from doing so. . . .[9]

Jessie Laussot was an Englishwoman married to a Frenchman, and that "years of foreign activity" (together with the swipe at Heine's "inner camel") confirms the nature of many of the complaints against him — the Teutonic chauvinism of which he was aware and in a milder way reciprocated with his refusal to alter the infamous "French salon tone," the "fatal habit of posing and pontifying he had picked up in Paris." (The phrases are from Carl Maria Cornelius's biography of his father, and must be hand-me-downs from Cornelius the elder.)

Such was the man Cornelius called a monster of egotism, who had adroitly climbed to fame on Wagner's shoulders. Let us examine *their* relations: Cornelius came to Weimar poor as a churchmouse — and if the mouse were dipped in water, had its hair slicked back and granny glasses placed on its nose, he exactly resembled one. Liszt put him on his feet, gave him money, work, and encouragement to compose. There was a price, and Cornelius found it high. He took the line that Carolyne was "a great and unfortunate soul," horribly wronged by Liszt: "I pity this poor woman from the bottom of my heart: all the world is against her, and she has to bear her sorrow in silence and alone." He was certain that Liszt would never marry her if there was an honorable exit. Their daily lives were another matter. She drove Cornelius mad.

It was Cornelius's task to translate Liszt's Weimar articles into German, which meant interminable sessions with Carolyne. Whoever wrote the original drafts, and it seems to have been much the same story as with Marie d'Agoult — that is, Liszt supplied the ideas and an outline, and Carolyne did the rest — Cornelius wound up her victim. He describes his tortures with the article on *Rhinegold,* read and approved by Liszt. Then Carolyne took over, and "every little word was twisted and questioned." Undeterred by her poor command of German, she pressed for the perfect nuance:

Then it seemed to me that I was losing my mind, as for the word *vergangenes* she tried to find another and was not satisfied with *durchlebtes, dagewesenes* and several more. I said, "Why don't you write *passiertes*" — and she wrote it! She told me later, however, with her sweetest little laugh, "Oh, perhaps you'll find a still better word. It does sound rather prosaic." . . . If only there *was* a right word. But this is idiocy. When I said to her simply that it would be more fitting if Liszt expressed himself on the score (for the entire article is a construction of monumental phrases — "The Rhinegold develops its strict majestic lines under the blue sky of Germany" — what would a wild Indian think if he read that sentence?), she answered me, "Well, Liszt can't do that because he can't praise it." [10]

The sympathies of anyone who has ever worked with a blockheaded editor must be with Cornelius. He had a lot to put up with including Carolyne's manners: "It upset me on several occasions that the Princess in her rapid and vehement manner asked for me as if I were a servant. I couldn't control myself sufficiently not to show my agitation. . . ." [11] He saw it all: "It isn't wholesome for the Princess . . . only to have discussions with people who are invited to dinner. If she saw more people from the outside, or who were more like herself (which, of course, is saying a good deal!), she wouldn't always want to hear the echo of her own opinion."

He had in short a hundred understandable grievances — all but the major one, Liszt's resignation over the *Barber of Bagdad*, Cornelius's own opera. This has an interest not directly related to what follows. Those who have heard it in modern times, Bernard Shaw among them, say it is an entrancing work, a sparkler (Shaw wanted d'Oyly Carte to revive it) — to which Wagner's latest biographer appends the fascinating information that the Barber himself is a spoof on the *Gesamtgenie* or "total genius" who is simultaneously actor, poet, dramatist, musician, and that Cornelius makes him speak "a jargon that is a delicious, highly polished mockery of Wagner's." [12] I can't imagine a more inspired idea than to make Wagner a comic character, Figaro with a touch of Münchausen. This adds a new dimension to the production. Did Liszt notice the parody? Did Dingelstedt, who disliked Wagner and to whom this ought to have recommended the opera? * The questions must go unanswered. The whole incident is full of uncertainties.

The story is that Dingelstedt, determined to get rid of Liszt, hired a claque to whistle the opera out of the theatre on the opening night, that

---

* Did Wagner? He took a tremendous fancy to Cornelius and in 1862 suggested to him that they live together and belong to one another "like a married couple." Wagner didn't see the Weimar *Barber* but surely if it was generally known that it parodied him, he wouldn't have forgiven the composer? In short, I have some doubts about the parody, which seems a little too good to be true.

fights broke out which the Grand Duke for reasons of his own did not order quelled, and that Liszt, quitting the theatre, snarled at Dingelstedt, "After what has happened this evening, I will never again set foot in your *den!*" This took place in 1858 and he didn't conduct another opera in Weimar, though the Grand Duke wouldn't accept his resignation and he stayed in the town for another three years.

Whether Dingelstedt was or wasn't the instigator of the affair, unprecedented in Weimar's well-behaved little theatre, will probably never be known. I would rather doubt it. He was a thorough professional and unlikely to stoop to such means. All agree that the demonstration was directed against Liszt, not Cornelius or his pretty opera, and there may have been enough feeling against him (and Carolyne) to manifest itself without benefit of claques or plots. The fact remains that Liszt made a tough stand on Cornelius's behalf — insisting that the Grand Duke in effect apologize to the man (which he did), and trying in every way he could to make it up to him. If he had further reasons for his resignation, they weren't exactly Cornelius's business, and for Cornelius to criticize him for that action, and on the basis he chose, really passes all bounds. Who was he to counsel self-renunciation?

Cornelius, Joachim, the Schumanns, Bülow would seem enough for any man not bent on self-immolation, on "making amends," to endure. But you could say they were mere finger exercises, tuneups to put Liszt in condition for his dealings with the master ingrate of them all, that devourer of other men's talent, energy, time and money, the egotist who brings new meaning to the word: Richard Wagner. Wagner was a disaster to everyone whose life he touched closely but Liszt's subjugation to him was entirely voluntary. He expected no gratitude, which was just as well. In Wagner's view, Weimar existed to serve him personally, and on the whole Liszt agreed. His need for atonement matched Wagner's urge to exploit. They fitted like lock and key.

That was the calamity — for Liszt. For Wagner, no relationship, however degrading his part in it, was without comic relief. Cornelius's parody (if it was one) won't surprise readers of *Mein Leben,* a confession as screamingly funny as it is unconsciously cruel. The flight from Wagner's creditors in Riga, horribly impeded by the Newfoundland dog Robber, to whom the Wagners were devoted, is pure slapstick. And who could improve on the dialogue with Bakunin at the time of the Dresden uprising? *Wagner:* I have just been inspired by a study of the Gospels to conceive the plan for a tragedy for the ideal stage of the future, entitled *Jesus of Nazareth. Bakunin:* Spare me the details. Wagner knew that was comic. Time and again, he shows himself executing the inspired pratfall, and *Mein Leben* is, among other things, a survival kit for the aspiring con man: the shell game, the fake sale, all the tricks of the trade are there, related with such irresistible panache that you would love him if he weren't, humanly speaking, a criminal of impressive dimensions, and a case made to order to confirm the average man's distrust of genius. He *was* a genius — and also a monster virtually without a redeeming feature. His moral values anticipated those of Hitler's Reich, which mitigates the comedy. His behavior to his friends was such that Liszt's involvement with him (whatever the artistic rewards) came to personify the disillusions of a lifetime.

Chapter 35

THE ALTENBURG'S DISPENSATIONS to Wagner begin with a famous little note sent up to Carolyne in May 1849: "Can you give the porter 60 thalers? Wagner must fly and I can't help him at the moment." The trouble was serious. Wagner was a political fugitive with a warrant about to be issued for his arrest. It shows where imagination can land a man, because as he kept saying, he wasn't a bona fide rebel; he was a loyal son of Saxony seduced by the *idea* of revolution: clandestine activity, barricades, placards. The tocsin of revolt tolling over Dresden sent him into an hallucination in which it appeared that the light changed to a coppery glow, like that of an eclipse. "I felt a sudden strange longing to play with something hitherto regarded as dangerous. . . ." He was not without his collection of injustices: the Dresden opera, which was trying to humble its bellicose young *Kapellmeister* by keeping his operas out of the repertory; his insensitive creditors and all the other representatives of oppression — Jews, courtiers, intendants, publishers. Nor was he quite the innocent bystander that he pretended after the collapse of the insurrection.

Though he was technically correct in saying he hadn't belonged to the provisional government, he was on intimate terms with its leaders: Röckel, Bakunin and Huebner. Where they went, he went. He had helped print seditious articles and made at least two hellfire speeches. When Huebner and Bakunin threw in their hands and fled to Chemnitz, he fled too and was saved from arrest when they were taken only because he happened to alight at another inn.

At Chemnitz he woke from his trance, saw the game was over and that he must get out of Saxony, leaving his household to bankruptcy and the police. This household consisted of his wife, the unfortunate Minna; the little dog Peps, successor to Robber, a highly strung animal that burst into sobs whenever it heard *Rienzi;* a parrot; Wagner's books, scores and a grand piano that wasn't paid for. He abandoned this little ménage and set off for Weimar, where he arrived penniless, passportless, his future in Liszt's hands.

Mein Leben: The dreamy unreality of my state of mind at this time is best explained by the apparent seriousness with which, on meeting Liszt again, I at once began to discuss what seemed to be the sole topic of any real interest to him in connection with me — the forthcoming revival of Tannhäuser at Weimar.[1]

Wagner was a man of sudden intimacies, dictated by his wants. In his reckoning, Liszt was an old friend by virtue of demands already made on him. The reality was that they didn't know each other well. Liszt could never remember their first meeting, which was in Paris in 1840. (Wagner on the contrary remembered perfectly the disagreeable sensation of being one of a crowd of suppliants in Liszt's suite, all of them gabbling in the detested French.) They were next introduced by Schröder-Devrient in Berlin in 1842. Liszt now grasped who Wagner was and promised to make a point of hearing *Rienzi* as soon as he could. That was better: "I now realized for the first time the almost magic power exerted by Liszt over all who came in close contact with him." Two years later, Liszt was in Dresden where he exercised his semi-royal prerogatives to request a special performance of *Rienzi,* which Wagner conducted for him. The opera made a powerful impression.

Liszt to Wagner, November 1857, from the Hôtel de Saxe, Dresden: How could I think of you otherwise than with constant love and sincerest devotion in this city, in this room where we first came near to each other, when your genius shone before me? *Rienzi* resounds from every wall, and when I enter the theatre I can't help bowing to you before everyone as you stand at your desk.[2]

We skip to 1848. Wagner, whose salary at the Dresden opera is fifteen hundred thalers a year, is nevertheless broke as usual:

The very next thing I must do was to attempt to establish my hopes for a larger income. . . . In this respect, it occurred to me that I might consult my friend Liszt . . . [when] lo and behold, shortly after those fateful March days, and not long before the completion of my Lohengrin score, to my great delight and astonishment the very man I wanted walked into my room. He had come from

Vienna, where he had lived through the "Barricade Days," and he was going on to Weimar, where he intended to settle permanently. We spent an evening together at the Schumanns' and had a little music, and finally began a discussion of Mendelssohn and Meyerbeer, in which Liszt and Schumann differed so fundamentally that the latter, completely losing his temper, retired in a fury to his bedroom for quite a long time. This incident did indeed place us in a somewhat awkward position toward our host, but it furnished us with a most amusing topic of conversation on the way home. I have seldom seen Liszt so extravagantly cheerful as on that night, when, in spite of the cold and the fact that he was clad only in ordinary evening-dress, he accompanied first the music director Schubert, and then myself, to our respective homes. Subsequently I took advantage of a few days holiday in August to make an excursion to Weimar, where I found Liszt permanently installed and . . . enjoying a life of the most intimate intercourse with the Grand Duke. Even though he was unable to help me . . . his reception of me on this short visit was so hearty and so exceedingly stimulating, that it left me profoundly cheered and encouraged.[3] *

Thus does Wagner inadvertently give away the nature of his friendship with Liszt from the very beginning. His letters are balder still.

Wagner to Liszt, June 23, 1848: You told me recently that you had closed your piano for some time, and I presume that you have turned banker. I am in a bad state, and like lightning the thought comes that you might help me. I need 5,000

---

* Ramann makes this evening at the Schumanns' the prelude to Liszt's hearing *Rienzi:* "The music could not lift him . . . above the impressions of that disagreeable evening. And so he left the opera house with no particular opinion either for or against Wagner . . . but with the impression that *Rienzi* had not wholly escaped the influence of Meyerbeer" (Ramann: p. 52). Aside from the jumbling of events that were four years apart, this makes no sense: why should the quarrel with Schumann have influenced Liszt's opinion of *Rienzi?* And since the inference is that he *defended* Meyerbeer, why was it a bad thing for *Rienzi* to show traces of Meyerbeer (as indeed it does)? The conclusion is still more baffling: "From that evening," writes Ramann, "dated Wagner's illwill against Liszt, to which he gave free and angry expression to others. In his [letters to Liszt], there is indeed no hint of this. . . . But on Wagner's own testimony it existed; and Liszt knew it. It estranged him, though it did not affect his willingness to help Wagner" (*ibid.*: pp. 53–54). Does this mean that Liszt told Wagner that his opera "had not wholly escaped the influence of Meyerbeer"? Surely not. Or that Wagner took umbrage at Liszt's defense of Meyerbeer at the Schumanns'? In that case, his story in *Mein Leben* is a lie. Newman too gets into trouble here. He believes the Ramann version (except for the dates) is correct and important as throwing "new light" on Liszt's relations with Wagner before 1849: they were in fact inimical. Or so he surmises on pp. 199–200, volume II, of his Wagner biography — having forgotten that in volume I, p. 494, he said something quite different: "After this meeting [at the Schumanns'], Wagner was so sure of Liszt's affection that it was not long before he began to look hopefully in his direction for assistance in his financial troubles." *Mein Leben* is a thoroughly untrustworthy book to be sure. But so is the Ramann biography. On this occasion I would be inclined to trust Wagner. The Ramann account is a little too obviously Carolyne's attempt to rewrite the past and prove that Liszt always did see through Wagner, knew he wasn't to be trusted, etc. — which alas was not true.

thalers to cover my debts incurred in the publication of my three operas. Can you get me such a sum? Have you got it yourself, or has someone else who would pay it for love of you? Wouldn't it be interesting if you were to become owner of the coypright to my operas? [4]

The insolence of the suggestion that Liszt has "turned banker" and has a rich woman behind him is only matched by the offer of the copyrights — a typical ploy. The copyrights had already been given as collateral for loans to one Pusanelli — who was later asked to repurchase what was already his by default. (Otto Wesendonk after buying the rights to *Rhinegold* quickly discovered that they had earlier been sold to Schott of Mainz. He managed to hang on to the autographed score; in 1865 he had to surrender that too, to Ludwig of Bavaria, the biggest dupe of all. Having sold him the rights to the *Ring* for a colossal sum, Wagner turned around and auctioned them off to individual theatres.)

Luckily for him, Liszt couldn't use the copyrights and he passed over the suggestion that Carolyne cough up five thousand thalers. His answer, not quite direct, was to produce *Tannhäuser* seven months later; and it is at this point that his entanglement with Wagner properly begins, with an opera he hadn't heard. Wagner had urged him to come to Dresden for a performance. For inscrutable reasons, he sent Carolyne instead, and wonderfully helpful her comments must have been if they were anything like her letter to Wagner after the Weimar premiere: "Allow me, dear sir, to add another voice to the chorus of admiration which sings 'Gloria' to the author of the double poem of *Tannhäuser* . . . the wonderful moments when I listened to your melodies . . . those elegies which one whispers only to the evening star, those prayers which bear the soul away. . . ." This was all Liszt had to go on. He didn't know *Flying Dutchman;* nor had he yet seen the *Lohengrin* score. No doubt Wagner had talked to him, as he talked to Bakunin and anybody who would listen, of the titanic dramas swelling in his head: he had sketched the Nibelungen cycle, outlined *Meistersinger,* even felt the first stirrings of *Tristan.* Liszt was still acting on faith and Wagner's power to convince.

For his part, Wagner believed he had struck gold.

To Liszt: No theatre in the world has so far thought it advisable to perform my *Tannhäuser* for years . . . it was left to *you* to settle down for a time from your worldwide travels at a small court theatre and at once set to work so that your much-tried friend might get on a little . . . you yourself undertook the unaccustomed task of teaching my work to the people . . . [of] making it understood and received with applause. . . . It isn't to complain, but merely to convince you of the force of that impression, when I tell you that just now, in the very week [February 1, 1849] when you gave my *Tannhäuser* . . . our manager insulted me in so gross a manner that for several days I was asking myself whether I should endure any longer being exposed to such infamous treatment. . . .[5]

It was on this basis that with the collapse of the Saxon revolution he headed for Weimar, confident that Liszt would fix everything, and by chance found *Tannhäuser* in rehearsal once more. He was smuggled into a box, where he could hear if not see. "I was filled," he says, "for the first time with the flattering warmth of emotion aroused by the consciousness of being understood by another mind in full sympathy with my own." [6] He was euphoric and informed the distracted Minna that in Weimar he was safe "as in Abraham's bosom."

He may have had a reason other than Liszt's protection to think so. His family history, teeming with irregularities, has also this one. His mother is believed to have been the illegitimate child of Prince Constantine of Saxe-Weimar — which would have made him the reigning Grand Duke's first cousin once removed. He probably knew this. *Mein Leben* speaks of "an exalted fatherly friend" who looked after his mother's education. But did the Grand Duke? If so, it would explain the royal family's unusual lenience. Weimar had an extradition treaty with Saxony and by rights Wagner should have been turned over to the Saxon authorities as soon as the warrant for his arrest was published — three days after his arrival at the Erbprinz. He wasn't and neither was *Tannhäuser* cancelled. A month or two later, Liszt sent Minna a hundred thalers, which he told Wagner came from "an admirer of *Tannhäuser*, whom you do not know and who has specially asked me not to name him. . . ." Surely the Grand Duke, or possibly Maria Pavlovna. It has so far gone unnoticed that although Wagner's proscription interfered with the production of his operas elsewhere in Germany for another eight or ten years, the issue was never raised in Weimar, where the objections were financial not political. Weimar's liberal tradition does not quite answer here. Carl Alexander wasn't that liberal and Maria Pavlovna was imbued with the autocratic principles of the Romanovs. Yet her behavior was oddest of all. She demanded to meet the refugee and asked Liszt to convey him secretly to nearby Eisenach for the purpose.

The locale was flatteringly chosen. Eisenach, some miles to the west of Weimar at the edge of the Thuringian forest, is the setting for the *Tannhäuser* legend. One of the low surrounding mountains is the Venusberg. Landgrave Hermann's castle looms on a precipice over the town. Wagner happened never to have seen it, except for a glimpse from a train, and it filled him with "strange musings," a premonitory nostalgia for the Germany where his days were numbered. He tells us about that but not about the interview, which must have given him food for thought. Harbor him indefinitely, the royal house of Weimar could not. Some assurance of a safe-conduct he must have obtained. His subsequent "escape," recklessly delayed and courting exposure at every turn, couldn't have been managed without their turning the blind eye. A letter to Liszt a year later seems to say that he knew this, and that what had been done once could be done again:

> Tell me, my dear Liszt, how we could make it possible for me to attend the first performance [of *Lohengrin*] in Weimar incognito. . . . Listen: I hold the Grand Duchess in high regard; would not this lady . . . at your suggestion be inclined for the stroke of genius of duping the police of united Germany, and of getting me a safe-conduct under an assumed name from Switzerland to Weimar and back to Zurich? I promise faithfully to preserve my incognito . . . to lie *perdu* in Weimar . . . and to go straight back.[7]

The snag was to picture Wagner lying *perdu* and Liszt said no. He had by then some experience with handling Wagner.

When he dropped Wagner off at Eisenach he was himself on his way to Carlsruhe where business detained him for several days. Minna's letters to her husband were being sent for safety's sake to the Erbprinz in his name. Wagner therefore did not know what was happening in Dresden and he spent happy hours roaming the countryside, telling himself it was all a passing nightmare and composing huge *pièces justificatives* to everybody from the King of Saxony on down. Röckel meanwhile was captured with the other leaders of the provisional government and was found to be carrying an incriminating letter in Wagner's handwriting. In Dresden, they were saying that Wagner had been in a plot to burn down the opera house.

With Liszt's return from Carlsruhe and the opening of Minna's letters, Wagner's confidence collapsed. Minna wasn't certain of the details but she knew enough to be panic-stricken. The police had searched their apartment and she urged him to flee without delay. She was furious too. Poor Minna. Plebeian, uncultured, her once pretty face beginning to sag, she was a burden he would gladly have dispensed with, and she, with her hard-won respectability lost through what she considered an imbecile action, was very ready to part with him. When it came down to it, neither could face the prospect. She had the habit of steadfastness under stress. He valued her more than he knew. Whatever her intellectual deficiencies she was a good wife. His life's work was mapped while he was married to her and his grosser tendencies under some restraint. She treated him like a mortal man, not the demiurge that Cosima made of him, and when he went too far, screamed home truths at him. This made her unsuitable for the role of goddess-companion he envisioned in later years. In 1849 he was still human enough to be devoted to her and to tell Liszt that he couldn't consider leaving Germany without seeing her. Liszt proceeded with the Chinese rescue that would make him indefinitely responsible not only for the injured one but for his wife.

On the morning of May 19, Wagner set out for Magdala, a village some three hours away on the Jena road. He carried the sixty thalers donated by Carolyne and a false identity provided him, with unconscious humor, by a professor friend of Liszt: he was to be a financial expert sent to administer the affairs of an estate near Magdala. The steward of this estate, in the plot, sequestered him for three days during which, by way of lying *perdu,* he attended a meeting of revolutionaries in the neighborhood.

Minna arrived on the twenty-second, with plenty to say to him; and whether for this reason or some other, to continue the quarrel or in hopes of ending it, a further farewell was then scheduled at Jena, a lunatic arrangement. From no motive that logic suggests, Wagner made the six-hour journey on foot. Minna, passing through Weimar for the second time in as many days, followed a route not elucidated by the map. She was accompanied by Liszt and a Professor Widmann; the rendezvous was the house of a Professor Wolff, all these academics being friends of Liszt and Widmann having brought along his passport for Wagner's use.

The final arrangements were to Wagner thoroughly distasteful. Liszt, he says, "insisted on my going to Paris," and he hated Paris, always an unlucky city for him. But Liszt, whom we may imagine at the pitch of exasperation by this time, carried his point, with an emendation contributed by Widmann that Wagner travel the longer but safer route via Switzerland. They got him off at last and Minna returned sadly to Dresden. Under the illusion that he was in a fair way to safety and independence, Liszt went back to the Altenburg.

Sighs of relief were premature. Wagner's star guided him to Zurich, where the scheme fell apart. He was enchanted with the city and at once determined, as he put it, "to do nothing to prevent" his settling there. There was in fact nothing to prevent it, except the desirability of supporting himself and Minna, and for that Zurich was not a tenable venue. Paris was: all he had to do was to make certain that it rejected him.

Liszt had worked hard to prepare the ground. Belloni was alerted, and put Wagner up at his country house for some weeks. Berlioz was asked to print the laudatory article on *Tannhäuser.* It appeared on the day (May 18) that Wagner was crouching in the box at Weimar and created a great stir. Who was Wagner that Liszt should be so enthusiastic about him? Berlioz knew. He had given Wagner some journalistic chores in 1841 and witnessed the humiliating rehearsal of a juvenile overture called *Columbus.* He had heard *Rienzi* and *Flying Dutchman* in Dresden, without enthusiasm. He was accordingly unmoved to learn from Liszt that Wagner had written an opera marvelously instrumented, "the various colors so felicitously applied to the movements of the drama," and of course ignored the suggestion that the overture be played without delay.

Others were more impressed and something might have come of it if

Wagner had been less determined to be rude to everybody, starting with the all-powerful Meyerbeer, who had the Opera in his pocket. Wagner gives the following dialogue, which took place in Schlesinger's music shop — Schlesinger being another Jew, another *bête noire*. *Wagner:* Really I am not at all anxious to find work. The idea is odious. *Meyerbeer:* But Liszt published such a brilliant article about you in the *Journal des Débats*. *Wagner:* Ah, it hadn't occurred to me that the enthusiastic devotion of a friend could be regarded as mutual speculation. *Meyerbeer:* But the article made a sensation. It is incredible that you shouldn't seek any profit from it. . . . What do you expect to get out of the revolution? Are you going to write scores for the barricades? *Wagner:* I am not thinking of writing any scores at all.[8]

This interchange, bone-chilling to Liszt if he had heard it, Wagner naturally did not relay. He complained instead that "artistic affairs here are in so vile a condition, so rotten, so fit for decay . . . [that] apart from all political speculation, I am compelled to say openly that in the soil of the anti-Revolution, no art can grow." (It is interesting to remember that Berlioz was blaming the revolution itself at the same moment for the same conditions.) Liszt's advice — "not to neglect Janin, who will surely lend a helping hand," "to pay a little court to Madame Viardot," "to take a position in the musical press that would avoid socialist stuff and personal hatreds [i.e., Meyerbeer]" — might as well not have been written. Later, Wagner told him the truth:

> Listen, my dear friend: the reason why for a long time I could not warm to the idea of writing an opera for Paris was a certain artistic dislike of the French language. . . . You won't understand this, being at home in all Europe, while I came into the world in a specifically Teutonic manner.[9]

Zurich was the place where he could most congenially get to work on the specifically Teutonic opera he wanted to compose and Liszt had to acquiesce. He sent the money to cover the journey and promised a small sum before autumn to keep Wagner afloat.

The opera was *Siegfried's Tod*, conceived as "theatre for the revolution." As originally planned, in anticipation of the Dresden uprising, it was an optimistic allegory of current events in which a corrupted society was redeemed by the hero's deed, the flames of Siegfried's funeral pyre marked the beginning of a new order, and the father-king was saved. (Those who accused Wagner of conspiring to burn down the Dresden opera were wrong — he didn't but he could have: he was an incendiary of the imagination and obsessed with the purifying properties of fire.) That poem was discarded. The guilt of the gods wasn't so easily disposed of and in the final version, reworked into the chaos that became *Götterdämmerung*, Siegfried is the agent of their destruction. Unworthy, the gods go under.*

Wagner spared Liszt the details of *Siegfried's Tod*, because he didn't get down to writing it; and the opera he promised to prepare "for Paris" — largely as a sop — didn't make much progress either. This was *Wieland the Smith*, a fascinating sketch to Wagnerians because so many themes — swans, magic rings, fire — are prefigured in it. For Paris it was, designedly, hopeless; and the libretto died on the vine. Meanwhile, there was no money, and Wagner wanted his wife: "Give me my poor wife, make it possible for her to come quickly to me."

Liszt sent a hundred thaler to Minna, who packed up the dog, the parrot and the Breitkopf piano (not Wagner's library, which was confiscated by a creditor) and set off for Zurich. She was an expert at tricking out dreary lodgings and she soon had a habitable apartment arranged. It was her understanding, as it was also Liszt's, that Wagner was seriously at work on the Paris project. They were both fooled, and Liszt should have been warned by several documents already received. While still in Paris, Wagner had proposed a kind of consortium:

> Your friends must get me some yearly allowance, just sufficient to secure for me and my wife a quiet existence in Zurich. . . . I talked to you in Weimar about a salary of three hundred thalers which I should wish to ask of the Grand Duchess. . . . If the Duke of Coburg and the Princess of Prussia [Augusta of Weimar] were to add something, I would willingly surrender my whole artistic activity to these three protectors.[10]

Presently it dawned on him that "my sufficiently public participation in the Dresden rising has placed me in a position that must make these royal personages think of me as one opposed to them on principle," and Liszt agreed. There was still no question but that Wagner must be supported by somebody:

Wagner to Liszt, October 1849: Think what you can do for me, dear, princely man! Let someone buy my *Lohengrin*, skin and bones; let someone commission my Siegfried! . . . If nothing else will answer, you might perhaps give a concert

---

* Bernard Shaw thought Bakunin the model for the original Siegfried. To me, Siegfried looks too like a projection of his creator, the self-appointed savior of German culture. Bakunin, for what it is worth, was contemptuous of Wagner's political theories as expressed in Eddic gods and heroes, and was surely wrong to be so. In Germany, such expressions can come to terrifying life. As Edmund Wilson has noted, the Hegelian triad is just such a myth — and he remarks in parenthesis that it is a wonder Wagner didn't compose a music-drama on the Dialectic: "Indeed, there does seem to be something of the kind implied in the Nibelungen cycle by the relations between Wotan, Brunhilde and Siegfried." (*To the Finland Station:* p. 223.)

"for an artist in distress." Consider everything, dear Liszt, and before all manage to send me soon — some money.[11]

Liszt considered. Could not Wagner arrange to give concerts in Zurich? "Your personal dignity, it seems to me, would not in the least suffer by it." Publish a book of lieder? (Liszt was himself short of cash at this moment.) Wagner could not, and Minna was urging him back to France. In January 1850 he went, financed by Liszt's draft of five hundred francs on the Rothschilds. Liszt and Minna awaited the results with some anxiety.

Once in France, Wagner devoted the better part of five months to an outstandingly messy and pointless affair with Jessie Laussot, whose family had up till then been prepared to back him.* Indeed it was Wagner's marvelous thought that they still would, after he and Jessie had eloped to the isles of Greece, or wherever fate wafted them. There was however the sticky question of what to do with Minna, and it was probably with this in mind that at the height of the Laussot affair, Wagner issued his ultimatum to Liszt:

Perform my *Lohengrin!* . . . To none but you would I entrust the creation of this opera. . . . Perform it where you like, even if only in Weimar. . . . Perform *Lohengrin* and let its existence be your work. . . .[12]

---

* Co-sponsor in this plan was Frau Julie Ritter, the mother of Alexander and Karl. When the Laussot side of it collapsed, the Ritters stuck by their promise and gave Wagner an allowance he consistently overspent but that lasted until the wealthy Otto Wesendonk took on his support.

Chapter 36

LISZT FIRST SAW the *Lohengrin* score in June 1849, when Minna sent it with the rest of Wagner's manuscripts to Weimar for safe-keeping, and he read it with misgivings. "The super-ideal tone you have maintained throughout will, I fear, go against it in performance," he wrote, which wasn't out of place.[1] With its fluid structure, the unedited stretches where nothing seems to be happening, it isn't without *longueurs*, perhaps what Liszt means by "ideal." Wagner's phrase, "even if only in Weimar," is puzzling (where else would Liszt have produced it?) but may mean they had discussed it and agreed that it required a more sumptuous *mise-en-scène* than Weimar could provide.*

The decision to produce it was, anyway, somewhat sudden, and Newman believes it was taken largely to oblige Wagner in his "spiritual crisis" over Jessie Laussot.[2] But does one really produce an opera merely to oblige a philandering friend? Newman's alternate explanation is more interesting: Wagner's appeal arrived in the midst of plans for the Goethe celebrations

---

* Why *Lohengrin* was not the "opera for Paris" is a mystery. Liszt in a letter to Belloni dated May 1849 mentioned "a grand, heroic and enchanting musical work" it was "imperative" to get produced. The hitch is that the letter is said to be a forgery — though nobody seems to know what the object of such a forgery would have been. Authenticated letters do not, at all events, speak of *Lohengrin* for Paris. Liszt keeps harping on *Rienzi*, perhaps because it was in the Meyerbeer tradition, and suggesting that Wagner rework it. Wagner hated this idea, but why *he* didn't suggest *Lohengrin* instead of the unsuitable *Wieland the Smith* is beyond fathoming. If nothing else, it was complete when *Wieland* wasn't even a sketch.

the following August, to which Liszt had summoned delegates from all over Germany to discuss the Goethe Foundation. "For this purely Germanic gathering, called together for a purely Germanic ideal, nothing, Liszt may have reasoned, could be more appropriate than the most purely Germanic opera that had yet been written."

They celebrated Goethe's birthday every August in Weimar (and the previous year, the centenary, had put on a big show) but the centerpiece of that particular week in 1850 was the unveiling of a monument to Herder. The delegates summoned from all over Germany are imaginary — there were none and Liszt didn't get around to the Goethe Foundation until the following year, when he published his brochure on it. Finally, it wasn't intended to further a purely Germanic ideal. In essence the Foundation was simply a plan to help artists and scholars in various categories, to publish their writings and exhibit their work, with no special emphasis on Teutonic content. Wagner, when the time came, opposed it on exactly that ground. Why, he asked, set up an "art lottery," when what was wanted was a national theatre that would shape the minds and hearts of the German people?

Liszt's invitations make clear that he had no such jingo scheme in mind. To Simon Löwy:

Arrive Weymar the 23rd of August and stay until the 30th at least. You will find several of your friends here — Dingelstedt, Jules Janin, Meyerbeer, etc., — and you will hear, first . . . a good hour and a half of music I have just composed . . . for the *Prometheus* of Herder, which will be given as a festal introduction to the inauguration of his statue in bronze . . . second, on the evening of the 25th, Händel's *Messiah*; third, on the 28th . . . a remarkably successful Prologue, made ad hoc for the day by Dingelstedt, followed by the first performance of Wagner's *Lohengrin*. This work, which you certainly will not have the opportunity of hearing so soon anywhere else, on account of the composer's special situation, and the many difficulties of its performance, is my idea of a *chef d'oeuvre* of the highest and most ideal kind.[3]

Liszt's purpose was achieved in the flood of articles on Wagner that followed: Gérard de Nerval's in *La Presse* (Nerval came all the way from Paris), Stahr's in the Berlin *Nationalzeitung*, and many more.

The mention of "German ideals" still cannot be passed over. Liszt, according to Newman, was unable to seize the significance of Wagner's "profoundly German art." In spite of his correspondence with his friend, his presumed reading of his prose works, he continued in the obstinate delusion that "Wagner was simply one of an international body of composers who . . . were . . . contributing to the 'progress of music.'"[4] And this time Newman hits the nail on the head. Enamored of the music, Liszt did turn aside from the mind that produced it. He said so himself, to Halévy in 1861:

I have proclaimed without reserve my high admiration for Wagner's genius . . . while always distinguishing between . . . the theoretician, the poet and the musician. Nowhere have I said or written that I adhered to any troublesome theory whatever. . . . Wagner is the [foremost] poet and dramatic composer in Germany today — enough reason for me to pay him homage. The rest will settle itself or be forgotten. . . .[5]

In the long run, he may have been right. In the short, the music of the future wrecked itself on the rock of Wagner's theories, and it might have been better to pay closer attention to them for that reason alone. (Liszt, after all, couldn't be expected to know that Buchenwald would be founded on them too.)

Art and Revolution (1849), *The Art-Work of the Future* (1849), *Jewry in Music* (1850), *Opera and Drama* (1851), the fruits of Wagner's early years in Switzerland, are a hodgepodge of phoney history, inflated aesthetics and spurious paganism, under little or no intellectual control. The first two are the least objectionable, being little more than Romantic hand-me-downs. The "total artwork" that combined music, dance, poetry wasn't exactly a new idea; nor was it a startling thought that it should express the collective life of a people, like Athenian drama. If there was news here it was in the implied advent of a Teutonic Aeschylus, who would revitalize the dreams of *das Volk*. Lip service was also paid to the function of revolution in freeing society from materialism and on this point alone Wagner was to change his mind, when it turned out that only a wealthy king could bear the expense of the *Gesamtkunstwerk*.

The third essay unveiled an important condition for the anticipated renaissance: the expulsion of the Jews from German life. The history of German-Jewish culture is that of a love-hate relationship that may only be unravelled by the discovery of hitherto unknown viruses like those now believed to cause cancer. *Jewry in Music* is the work of a man with a terminal disease, who doesn't know he has it, and if read before *Opera and Drama* has a nullifying effect: knowing the man is sick, one is wary of his nostrums. In fact the Wagnerian prescription for opera — that it contain no arias, duets or ensembles, that the orchestra take over the role of the chorus, that the melodic line be unified by motifs representing persons, places, and so on — is so much systematic nonsense, which he himself disregarded. Its perniciousness consists in the pretense that art is pseudo-science. Armed with Wagner's portentous terminology, thematic recall and the rest, captivated by myths whose nationalist tendencies were easy to grasp, the German philistine could tell himself that he was at last on terms with high art. Add to this that the Wagnerian gods and goddesses are (as Nietzsche pointed out) bourgeois characters with "modern" problems, and you see why apotheosis was inevitable. "Wagner knows what our age likes," said Nietzsche again, "idealizes our age, and thinks too highly of it," and he saw that Bayreuth was "an example of the spirit on which the Reich was founded." [6]

Unfortunately it can't be left at that. Nietszche, like Liszt, also knew that in certain areas Wagner stood alone: "Nobody can approach him in the colors of late autumn . . . he knows of a chord which expresses those secret and weird midnight hours of the soul, when cause and effect seem to have fallen asunder." No tragedy in music equals the crippling of this enormous genius by an intelligence so crankily inhumane and out of date, so dominated by instincts that after 1848 never led him right. In 1870, crowing over the French defeat, he turns the stomach. *Capitulation,* a farce, ridiculed the hunger of the Parisians during the siege and included a satire on *Les Misérables* that had Victor Hugo popping out of sewers while Gambetta proclaimed "the rat's republic."

For a long while Liszt went out of his way not to fathom what Wagner was determined to tell the world. Of *Art and Revolution* he said he couldn't follow the reasoning. When *Jewry in Music* was published pseudonymously, he inquired mildly whether the "famous article in Brendel's paper is by you?" and ignored the tongue-lashing he got in reply — "You must know the article is by me. Why do you ask? . . . I felt a long repressed hatred for this Jewry. . . ." [7] Wagner's anti-Semitism he seemed to put in the same class with a propensity to scatalogical humor, not to be taken too seriously. Describing his visit to Zurich in 1853, he told Carolyne that "when there is a question of anything to do with his reputation . . . [Wagner] jumps on my neck or rolls on the floor, caressing his dog Peps and talking nonsense to it, spitting on the Jews, which to him is a generic term, with a meaning *très entendu*. . . ." [8]

Not so *entendu* were the attacks on Berlioz that were early warnings against the hope of a tripartite alliance with Weimar for its capital. *Opera and Drama* took a gratuitous swipe at Berlioz's creations of "gigantic machines" devoid of "human feeling." (Very funny, said Saint-Saëns, when you remember the *Ring*.) That was nothing however to the eruption when he heard that Liszt was going to revive *Cellini*, an eruption not in the least qualified by the fact that he had neither seen nor heard the opera, nor the *Damnation of Faust* either.

Wagner to Liszt: Candidly speaking, I am sorry to hear that Berlioz thinks of recasting his *Cellini*. . . . To me there is something horrible in witnessing this attempt at galvanizing and resuscitating. . . . Believe me, I *love* Berlioz, although he keeps apart from me in his distrust and obstinacy; he does not know me, but I know *him*. If I have expectations of anyone it is of Berlioz . . . but not in the direction he has arrived at in the absurdities of his *Faust*.[9]

Bülow got the story in cruder, less mendacious form:

The means that Liszt is now employing must of necessity lead to quite another end than the one he has in view: by productions of Berlioz, he can only confuse public opinion still further with regard to myself. . . . Liszt could be of service to me by productions of Berlioz and so on only if he said to people, "See, this is what Wagner does *not* want. . . ." But this Liszt will *not* do, for he is too unclear within himself as to the vast difference between Berlioz and people such as myself. . . . If he cannot see what the point really is, but is simply bent on pushing Berlioz, in God's name let him go on doing so. But if he imagines he is cutting a path for *me* . . . you should do everything in your power to convince him how utterly wrong he is. . . . What is of service to me is not money but the spirit in which the material is shaped. On this point I have already written to Liszt in full, in connection with the Goethe Foundation. Has that letter had no effect on him? Have you people not read *Opera and Drama*? [10]

There was more to this than professional jealousy. Wagner had as much trouble acknowledging his musical as his financial debts. *Romeo and Juliet,* the *Fantastique,* as later the *Damnation,* the *Requiem* and *Cellini* itself, were to him mines of thematic material and orchestral effect.* Art on his scale need not fear such disclosures. Yet he lived in dread of them. Richard Pohl's not ill-intentioned comment that the *Tristan* prelude showed traces of Lisztian harmonics drew a famous blast. Some truths were unutterable: "For instance, that since my acquaintance with Liszt's compositions, I have become quite another being harmonically from what I was before . . . when friend Pohl blurts this secret out before the whole world . . . that is, to say the least, indiscreet; and am I not to assume that he was authorized to commit such an indiscretion?" [11]

---

* I can't however share Barzun's contention that this has had a destructive effect on Berlioz — that, for example, "the precision and connotations of the original are spoiled when a fine passage of the *Symphonie fantastique* comes up as the "Thought Motif" in *Siegfried* . . . when the Prologue of *Romeo and Juliet* is distended into the plan for making *Rheingold* the prologue and thematic catalogue of the *Ring* . . . when the Sylphs in the *Damnation of Faust* re-enchant us in *Parsifal*" and so on. (*Romantic Century:* II, 185.) Who, in fact, is going to confuse the one with the other? I agree that "we cannot play fast and loose with the value of originality . . . say that priority is trivial when Wagner borrows, and then credit him with 'innovations of genius' " — but not that "the acceptability" of rehandled themes or materials "is no test of its artistic rightness." Surely it is the only test? Wagner's grabbings from other people (who must include Liszt, Meyerbeer, Schumann and even Mendelssohn as well as Berlioz) make him rather like a chemist, who having stolen his formulas, goes on to win the prize for a new compound. It is maddening, it is perhaps unfair; but Wagner is greater than the sum of his parts, and he created a musical world like no other.

Of course he was *not* authorized: that was just the way Wagner's mind worked. Notice that he doesn't deny the truth of Pohl's assertion; the point is that no one should know it. This habit of repudiation grew on him until he was saying, in effect, that he couldn't have borrowed from Liszt because there was nothing to borrow. The *Christus* Oratorio was dismissed as "thoroughly un-German" and reflective of "belief without faith," a fascinating observation, as his latest biographer notes, from one about to embark on *Parsifal* — that piece of religious *art nouveau*. Lilli Lehmann, singing *Mignon's Lied* one day at Wahnfried, provoked the remark that he hadn't realized Liszt composed "such pretty songs," having thought his contribution to music consisted of piano fingerings. Lehmann was not amused.

Amateur psychoanalysis isn't needed to see that legitimacy was a *leitmotiv* in Wagner's life as in his dramas. A bastard, a Jew, a robber of other men's treasure, he obviously feared the revelation that he was any or all of these. To someone of this compulsive type, systems appeal as a prop to their fantasies. He was a phenomenon, even so. No other composer, let alone one of his gifts, has been driven to rear so vast and hideous a superstructure over his creations. "My musical creed," said Berlioz, "is in what I have done and what I have not done." [12] Liszt too was silent on the subject of his own compositions, strongly as he believed in promotional journalism. It was perhaps that very belief that prevented him from reading the small print in Wagner's texts.

Any student of Wagner's prose could have foreseen Bayreuth. It was implicit in his obsessions. Yet in a horrible way Liszt also contributed. Wagner, the big spender, had always craved to live better than he could afford by honest means, and the itch was aggravated after 1849 by the contrast between the Altenburg and his Swiss lodgings. That house and its rituals, Liszt's life "of the most intimate intercourse with the Grand Duke" gnawed at Wagner's vitals and induced a mendicant self-righteousness:

When I think of your sympathetic and nobly refined home, free as it is from the cares of common life . . . observe how your personality and your . . . art enchant and delight all around you, I find it difficult to understand what your sufferings really are.[13]

The Altenburg was a bad example to a man born without altruism, and with a lust for grandeur. Once he shed his revolutionary skin, which was quickly, Wagner was revealed as the perfect new-rich vulgarian. But excruciating taste was the least of Bayreuth's defects. In its bloated way, it parodied the Weimar ideal — down to Cosima's conscious modelling of herself on Carolyne. She had observed, if nobody else had, what it took to enslave her father, and she applied the lesson to Wagner. Abject devotion, imperious manners were her hallmarks. She only differed from Carolyne in the French elegance she had from her mother and couldn't discard. But for Wagner, the abiding attraction was of course that she was Liszt's daughter, ravished, as it were, not from Bülow, an obstacle more to be pitied than hated, but from the old king himself. His jealousy of Liszt as father-in-law, his hysterical scenes when father and daughter spoke French together, were those of a man unhinged. Raging at Cosima in coarse Saxon dialect, he revealed a paranoia that reached behind her to Liszt himself — the dear princely man who was his antithesis, as Weimar with its open door policy, its collaborative international spirit, was the polar opposite of Bayreuth.

The production of *Cellini* explained to Wagner that Weimar's theatre was not going to be his exclusive forum or going to concentrate on the development of *das Volk*. From that moment he felt free to practice a series of minor but detestable deceptions, to treat Liszt as his only friend and representative in Germany while other chums like Uhlig were getting very different information: that *Siegfried's Death,* for example, though he had accepted a commission and a contract for it from Weimar, would require a festival theatre all to itself; that it couldn't in fact be written until he had composed a *Young Siegfried* to precede it — which would likewise be wrong for Weimar.

Wagner to Uhlig, November 1851: Tell Frau Ritter that when she gave me the advice, through you, not to "break" unnecessarily with Weimar, the matter was quite unclear to her; that I am not inimical to Weimar through presumption, caprice or obstinacy, but that I have in hand something . . . which makes it impossible for me to consider Weimar any more.[14]

This would have been convenient for Liszt to know: it would have saved him a world of trouble. And Newman believes he ought to have read between the lines of Wagner's interminable screed of November 1851, in which he outlined his "entire myth in its deepest and widest significance," saying it would take three years to compose, after which, if Weimar was "still standing," they would see:

But let us cherish no illusions. . . . What you, and only you, have so far done for me in Weimar is wonderful . . . without you I would have completely disappeared by now; instead of which you have turned the public attention of the friends of art to me [with] all the powers at your disposal, with such energy and success that it is solely due to you that I am now able . . . to think of carrying out such plans as those I have outlined to you. . . . [Yet] I must tell you that, after all, I consider your trouble at Weimar to be fruitless. Your experience is that as soon as you turn your back the most perfect vulgarity springs luxuriantly from the soil in which you have labored to plant the noblest things. . . . On every side of you I see the stupidity, the narrowmindedness, the empty vanity of jealous courtiers.[15]

Liszt to Wagner: Your letter, my glorious friend, has given me great joy. . . . The task of developing a dramatic trilogy and setting to music the Niebelung epic is worthy of you, and I have not the slightest doubt about the monumental success of your work. Your [understandable] fears about my Weimar activity I pass without reply; they will be proved or disproved by events during the three years that you dwell among your Nibelungs. . . . In any case, I am prepared for better or worse, and hope to continue in my modest way.[16]

To Newman, this expresses relief that Weimar wasn't going to be asked the impossible. Liszt's more detailed promises in his next letter, "to obtain the necessary things and people" for what is not yet referred to as the *Ring* cycle, are called meaningless. Wagner's subsequent change of front is harder to get around. Having done a little scouting, he presently wrote that after all a large town, where the musical atmosphere would be abhorrent, would not do, only a beautiful quiet corner "far from the smoke and odor of industrialism — such a quiet corner I could behold in Weimar, but in no larger town." [17] (Newman leaves this alone.)

I cannot read Liszt's mind any more than Newman can. Perhaps he did know how to interpret Wagner's contradictory proposals, wasn't fooled when Wagner kept saying, "I will produce my *Siegfried*, but only for *you*, only for *Weimar*," [18] and was only going along with an admitted fiction when he wrote as late as 1858 that the Nibelungen production was "our ultimate goal." The point wouldn't be worth laboring except as it turns on the good faith of both men, and to me it seems indubitable that although Liszt ought to have had the good sense that Newman ascribes to him, he hoped and planned to the last hour of his tenure at Weimar that he could wangle it somehow; and that Wagner, in constant need of advances as well as the encouragement that only Liszt could give ("When I am composing and scoring, I think only of *you*, how this or the other will please you. . . ."),[19] did not want to disabuse him.

Yet flogging Wagner is poor work. As egotists go, he is so much without alloy, the perfect specimen, that one must rejoice to watch him in action, as one may feel pleasure in watching a leopard execute a kill: he was every bit as unconscious of evil intent. Only in later life did he break the rule not to kill what you can't eat. In the 1850's, his infantile disregard for others could still be classified as grimly quaint. To Röckel, his fellow conspirator at Dresden who was serving what was supposed to be a life sentence, he wrote this account of himself:

My nervous system is in a bad way . . . the necessary result of my abandoning myself to that passionate and hectic sensitivity that makes me the artist I am. . . .

I ought perhaps to congratulate myself on being secure from anxiety as to my immediate needs. But I am *very lonely:* I lack congenial company, and I feel more than ever that the exceptional nature of my position has become a veritable curse. . . . A prisoner would not be able to understand why I am mostly so depressed and longing for death. . . .[20]

What do you say to a man like that? Most people, and that included Liszt, couldn't quite believe him, or imagined that they were favored. "I regard myself," said Liszt, "as the complete and absolute exception to his habitual arrogance." Two incidents, neither related to Weimar, may be selected to prove how wrong he was.

In the autumn of 1855, Wagner once again toiled under his habitual mountain of debt * and Liszt was once again invited to find a solution. He was to offer Breitkopf and Härtel the rights to *Lohengrin,* those, that is, that weren't already disposed of, for a grand total of 15,000 francs. Doubting perhaps his ability to put this proposition on paper, he went personally to Leipzig — and was turned down. Leipzig was enemy territory for Wagner, *and* Liszt. There was however enough interest for a performance of *Lohengrin* to have been scheduled at the opera, which Liszt hoped might alter the position. According to Wagner, Liszt was to have had full charge of this, gone to Leipzig "as my alter ego, with the right even of veto." In fact, the local *Kapellmeister,* not unnaturally, wouldn't even let him attend the rehearsals, though he went twice to Leipzig, a tiring journey, for the purpose. And in the end, it was badly done. Liszt, breaking this to Wagner, tried to look on the bright side. All concerned had shown good will and "we can rejoice at that . . . the rest will come gradually of itself."

Wagner was in a rage, insanely so considering that he was ready to throw both *Lohengrin* and *Tannhäuser* to any little dog of a *Kapellmeister* so long as he was paid, and with no stipulations whatever about the quality of the performances. In 1857, he let a Viennese variety theatre do *Tannhäuser.* Over and over was Liszt told that the situation was desperate, that he couldn't "sleep on straw and drink bad whiskey," that his neck was "under the yoke of the Jews and Philistines." The imperfections of the Leipzig performance remained an insult — and Liszt's fault:

Wagner to Bülow: Liszt has behaved in . . . a way that is rather incomprehensible to me. He seems not to have understood rightly the conditions under which I granted *Lohengrin* to Leipzig. . . . The fatal thing in him is that only in the rarest cases can he bring himself to fall out with anyone. . . . He understood

* Which nobody can explain. Where did it all go? In the previous eighteen months he had earned 7,500 francs from the "hailstorm," his word, of *Tannhäuser* productions here and there. Frau Ritter gave him 3,000 francs a year. There ought to have been more than enough to maintain a childless household, with something left over for a rainy day. Wagner liked nice things but he wasn't investing in expensive works of art or keeping another woman and the sums he dispensed are in excess of any normal need.

my conditions perfectly . . . but why then did he not put an end at once to the whole affair? Did he look on the Leipzig production as a necessity, even if it turned out badly? Comic politics! [21]

The second incident was a direct outcome of the first. The opera was *Tannhäuser*, the city Berlin, and there was no doubt about Wagner's stipulation that Liszt be in charge of the production and the negotiations leading up to it. The Berlin management naturally resented his intrusion and did not want him to conduct. This time he was rebuked for sticking to his guns:

Wagner to Bülow: From every possible side, I am urged to desist from the "senseless" condition that *Tannhäuser* be given in Berlin only with the cooperation of Liszt: everywhere the cry goes up that they don't think much of him as a conductor; they assure me also that, as matters are, people see in Liszt's demand (for they all believe that it comes solely from him) nothing but boundless vanity. . . . How much philistinism there is behind all this I know . . . but I also know that . . . I am acting less for myself than for Liszt, for whom I would . . . gladly secure a triumph through me. It only surprises me that Liszt remains so completely impotent in this matter: I really thought he was more of a diplomat and had more influence than seems to be the case. But he knows the fix I am in: and that he has found no way by which I can get over the loss of the Berlin royalties rather lowers my faith in his shrewdness and solicitude.[22]

There was more to this than Liszt was aware. Reasoning that if Wagner could conduct the opera himself Liszt would have a face-saving excuse to step aside, Minna went off to Dresden to beg for an amnesty. It was refused. Meanwhile, Wagner had also tried to borrow from his niece Johanna against the expected royalties. (Johanna was to sing Elizabeth if the production came off.) This earned him a stinging letter from his brother Albert, her father, that it is a pity Liszt could not have seen: "You have no conception of thankfulness for what is past," said Albert. ". . . Much as I esteem and love your talent, it is anything but so as regards your character. . . . In Johanna's name and my own I give you this answer: as soon as your opera is put into rehearsal at Berlin, and I receive from you a fully valid assignment, confirmed by the management, of your royalties . . . I am willing to advance you a round sum against them. . . . [Johanna] is doing quite enough; as for you, I know that you have enough to live on in a becoming way, if you could regulate your affairs." [23] So much from one who had known Wagner from a child. Significantly, Albert concluded that he didn't think *Tannhäuser* had a chance that year in any case, "for other forces are secretly at work," undoubtedly political.

Liszt on his side maintained that "I have *all along* left it . . . to Wagner to leave me out of the game and to handle the affair directly, according to his way of thinking, *without me*. . . ." [24] He ought to have known that in a pinch Wagner always preferred to take the cash and let the artistic credit go. In the event, the opera *was* produced in January 1856, as a direct consequence of his continuing diplomacy with the Berlin management, which was glad to let him supervise several of the piano rehearsals. He did not conduct and musically the production left a lot to be desired. But this time Wagner held his peace.

Not again would he intervene actively in Wagner's haggles with theatres. Wagner nevertheless continued to try to drag him into his innumerable disputes over fees. The deterioration of his relations with Dingelstedt may even have begun when Dingelstedt was still Intendant at Munich and subject to Wagner's assaults. Wagner made himself intolerable over the Munich *Tannhäuser* and Liszt was forced to arbitrate a wrangle that boded ill for the future. Dingelstedt, shortly to move to Weimar, had every reason to distrust Wagner, and by extension Liszt as well.

Chapter 37

ONE DID NOT SERVE Wagner merely by arranging his business affairs, lending him money, and producing his operas. Spiritual aid and comfort were also needed.

Wagner to Liszt, March 30, 1853: . . . My impatience *to see you* grows into a most violent passion. Can you come in May? On May 22 I will be forty. Then I shall have myself rebaptized; would you not like to be my godfather? I wish *we two* could start straight from here to go into the wide world. I wish you, too, would leave these German Philistines and Jews. Have you anything else around you? [1]

Liszt couldn't go at the time proposed, and by May Wagner was lapsing into excessive language not uncommon with him:

I thirst for a long, long sleep, to wake only when my arms are around you. Write me very precisely whether you are inclined, after a little stay at Zurich, to go with me to the solitude of the Grisons; St. Moritz might, after all, do you good, dearest friend. . . . [2] *

---

* Letters like this (mild compared to the correspondence with Ludwig of Bavaria, which is really hair-raising), together with Wagner's propensity to get himself up in drag and furnish his bedrooms to resemble a whore's boudoir, the strong aroma of homosexuality in *Parsifal*, all combine to suggest that Wagner was queer. The Munich populace certainly thought he stood in that relation to their young King — they called him Lolotte in memory of Lola Montez and the earlier Ludwig. But in the simplest

Liszt at no time sought Wagner's company. As men, they had almost nothing in common. It was a strain on Wagner to talk French, a strain on Liszt to talk German. Wholly self-absorbed, Wagner was an asphyxiating conversationist. (On a certain occasion, he was so distraught to find his guests chatting to one another without regard for him that he uttered a piercing scream.) As a companion he was tiring as a child. Liszt nevertheless felt obligated to meet the demands for his physical presence — though whether their meetings did more to unite or to divide them would be hard to say.

The first, in July 1853, was the most successful. It was brief and Liszt was alone. Wagner was like one demented. He met Liszt at the quayside, screaming like an eagle, and he wept and laughed for half an hour afterward. When Liszt could look about him, he found Zurich by no means the howling wilderness that Wagner had increasingly depicted it. The family flat was full of little *élégances,* the cellar full of good wines. The meals, excellently cooked by Minna and served by Liszt's manservant, were offered to no fewer than a dozen people.

Wagner said he had broken with all the local political refugees. He meant the indigent ones. In his inner circle were several of the other sort: Georg Herwegh, Marie D'Agoult's former confidant, lived in a luxurious villa nearby and was an intimate friend. Another was François Wille, a newspaperman married to the daughter of a Hamburg shipowner. These were ex-lions whose teeth had been drawn by wealth and were no longer to be classed as radicals. To them were shortly to be added the Otto Wesendonks, a rich bourgeois couple of doubtful background.

Liszt got the picture at a glance. Huge sums were casually bandied in discussion of how the *Ring* was to be produced — a hundred thousand francs, Wagner thought, could easily be raised for an outdoor theatre in the neighborhood. "Many of his friends and protectors belong to the ultra-conservative faction," wrote Liszt. "He is afraid one of the spies who report to Berlin and Dresden is personally hostile to him because he once treated him *de haut en bas,* which indeed is his custom. . . ."[3] Wagner swore on the Nibelungs that he would never again mix in politics.

It was for the reading of this libretto — or poem, whatever at that stage it was to be called — that Liszt had come. Beautifully bound copies had been posted to Weimar earlier in the year and read aloud to select groups; but Wagner was very reasonably concerned about Liszt's, or anyone's, ability to visualize the operas that were to emerge from it. Musically, Wagner in 1853 was like a river suffering the effects of a six-year drought. The banks,

---

meaning of the term, a preference for one's own sex, he just was not a homosexual and any presumption that he was would be seriously misleading. Physically he loved women and not "masculine" women either.

the naked rocks were there; there was no water; and as he faced up to the dilemmas he had invented for himself in this colossal work, he contracted a massive case of composer's block. The deluge that would fill the arid channel was backed up in his brain. So far, the release mechanism remained stalled. Liszt was told it would all fall into place "once I can plunge head and ears into the fountain."

Liszt's faith was boundless but blind. The volumes sent to Weimar nonplussed the Altenburg and he could find nothing more helpful to say than that he "heartily shared the joy you must be feeling in the printed copies," which wasn't good enough. "Why do I go on living?" cried Wagner when no further comment was forthcoming. "I print my new poem: I send it to all my friends whom I might presume to be interested. . . . I indulge myself in the hope that now I have *compelled* people to show me a sign: Franz Muller . . . and Karl Ritter have written me about it, but not a single one of all the others has thought it worthwhile even to acknowledge receipt." [4]

Liszt to Wagner: Don't take it amiss that I haven't written you about the Nibelungen-Ring. My task is not the criticizing and analyzing of so extraordinary a work, for which I intend later to do all I can to win a proper place. . . . I am delighted with your poetic accomplishment. Almost every day the Princess greets me with *Nicht Gut, nicht Gold, noch göttliche Pracht.* . . .

Not for the world would he have said so but it is a safe guess that Liszt was not enthralled with the Nibelungen myth; and it is certain that Wagnerian stagecraft was not to his taste, his own bias being all in favor of allusive, oratorio-like techniques that dispensed with weighty connective tissue and left large areas to the imagination.* The Wagnerian dogma was "Nothing that lies within the possibility of representation on the stage should be thought or indicated; everything should be actually shown" [5] — thus paving the way for lovers armored like tanks, Rhine maidens entangled in gauze, and live Percherons. (On the other hand, I cannot do without the magic fire and I agree with Auden that the sooner Fafner and Lohengrin's swan are restored the better; and while we are at it, Hunding's hut.) Liszt's view was set forth in a review of a book by A. B. Marx — his oratorio

---

* The earliest *Ring* scenario (1848) moved rapidly and might have evolved into a filmlike series of scenes, the so-called Shakespearean approach. In the end décor got the better of him and he couldn't escape the ponderous Meyerbeer-style ground plan. "Right up to *Parsifal,*" Gutman writes, "Wagner's aesthetic remained that of the Rue Le Peletier, and it is really not surprising that the Opéra opened its gates to *Tannhäuser* and shut out Berlioz's *Trojans*" (*Richard Wagner:* p. 154). It is interesting also to note that the reforms made by Wieland Wagner at Bayreuth largely denied his grandfather Wagner's aesthetic in favor of his great-grandfather Liszt's, that he "on occasion attempted to convert [the] operas into staged oratorios in the manner of Liszt's *Legend of St. Elizabeth*" (*ibid.:* p. 143).

Moses was given at Weimar in 1853 — that complained of the limitations of the stage. Liszt agreed:

Marx is absolutely right in regarding the stage as too confined a field for the lofty passions . . . it lacks the indescribable magic of perspective, or mirage, or half-shade that the vision of marvelous pictures permits to the fancy. The inadequate reality of the stage can only hinder these as soon as it tries to replace the resplendent visions of the imagination by the visible scene. . . . There cannot be any question that in many cases art does not suffer in the least when it renounces the attempt to represent *everything*, realize *everything*, make *everything* clear to the senses.[6]

With these prejudices and in the absence of the music, it is doubtful if he got much out of the Nibelung readings at Zurich — delivered with "incredible energy" to an audience that included Herwegh. All the profit from this visit was Wagner's. Liszt had brought along manuscripts of the symphonic poems which were gone through at the piano. "My delight over everything I heard by Liszt was as deep as it was sincere, and, above all, extraordinarily stimulating," says *Mein Leben,* adding with disarming candor: "What could be more full of promise and more momentous to me than this long-desired meeting with the friend who had been engaged all his life in the masterly practice of music, and had also devoted himself so absolutely to my own works . . . ?"[7] Liszt's presence had such a galvanizing effect on him that he could hardly bear the parting.

Wagner to Liszt, July 15, 1853: Sadness! Sadness! After you had been taken from us I did not say a single word to Georg. Silently I returned home; silence reigned everywhere. Thus we celebrated your leave-taking, you dear man; all the splendor has departed. . . . Oh, come back soon, and stay with us a long time. If you only knew what divine traces you have left behind you! Everything has grown nobler and milder. . . . Farewell, my Franz, my holy Franz. . . .[8]

Shortly after this he plunged off alone into Italy, where in a squalid little hotel at Spezia he had a celebrated annunciation. It is so like him to tell us that he was suffering from dysentery at the time ("everything should be actually shown"), which had given him a slight fever. He was dozing on a sofa when he was seized with a sensation of drowning:

The rushing sound took musical shape in my brain as the chord of E flat major, which continually reechoed in broken chords; these seemed to be melodic passages of increasing motion, yet the pure triad of E flat major never changed but seemed . . . to impart infinite meaning to the element in which I was sinking. I awoke in sudden terror . . . [and] at once recognized that the orchestral overture to the *Rhinegold,* which must have lain dormant within me . . . had at last been revealed.[9]

The drought was over. He returned immediately to Switzerland, "to compose or die," in reality to subject himself to an inexplicable delay.

For no reason that their letters make clear, he had settled with Liszt to go to Paris that autumn — though neither had business there and Wagner dreaded it: "I'm afraid of Berlioz. With my bad French, I am simply lost." Liszt had perhaps a vague idea of seeing his children, but his behavior to them when he got there was too offhand to make them his main motive. It may simply have been one of those things that once proposed nobody knows quite how to get out of.

The Grand Duke Carl Friedrich of Weimar died that July. Liszt talked optimistically about the new reign but may have had qualms when he thought of Carl Alexander's parsimony. There was a money shortage at the Altenburg too — though not serious enough to keep Carolyne from a tour of German watering places, or to restrain Liszt from his usual lavish expenditures. In October he was in Carlsruhe for the music festival. Other conductors earned honorariums for their services but whether because he refused them or it somehow seemed out of place to offer him money, his appearances aren't spoken of as sources of income and must actually have cost him something. He told Carolyne it would take him two weeks to round up his musicians in various Rhine towns, which he did in person, always staying at the best hotels and entertaining everybody.

Too much to arrange in too short a time may in fact have contributed to the mishap already alluded to, when his under-rehearsed and miscellaneous orchestra broke down. But perhaps because he didn't yet realize how tirelessly the critics would worry this bone, the incident didn't disturb him unduly. He had introduced a lot of new music, the Murls were with him in force, and he was in a radiant temper when they all set off to meet Wagner in Basel.

Basel was chosen because it was the nearest point to the German frontier, which Wagner of course could not cross. (Did the name of the hotel where they were to rendezvous give Liszt a stab? It was the Drei Königen, where he had joined Marie d'Agoult in 1835.) Wagner describes the scene: he was sitting alone in the hotel dining room when he heard a chorus of male voices singing the trumpet fanfare from *Lohengrin*. "The door opened and Liszt entered at the head of his joyful little band, whom he introduced to me." They were Bülow (whom Wagner naturally knew already), Joachim (shy at being presented to the author of *Jewry in Music*), Cornelius, the critic Richard Pohl, Dionys Pruckner, and Reményi the "gypsy." The party lasted most of the night:

The bright and merry spirit which prevailed at that gathering (which like everything that Liszt promoted, in spite of its intimate nature, was characterized by a magnificent unconventionality) grew to a pitch of almost eccentric hilarity as the night wore on. In the midst of our wild mood, I suddenly missed Pohl. I knew him to be a champion of our cause through . . . his articles. . . . I stole away and found him in bed with a splitting headache. . . .[10]

The carouse at the Drei Königen was the end of what Liszt called his Valhalla days with Wagner. The next morning Carolyne arrived with her retinue and the whole atmosphere changed — to Wagner surely for the worse, though he puts a good face on it, so much so that I am inclined to think their supposed dislike for each other greatly exaggerated. Carolyne objected, as any woman would have, to Wagner's plundering of her lover and he was too crass and bumptious to have pleased her as a man. But I don't think she entertained a pathological hatred for him (which Newman sees in her smallest act) or that Wagner's estimate of her was different from most people's. He deplored her intervention, or what he took to be her intervention, in purely musical matters; and he included without directly blaming her in his rather hypocritical fears that Liszt's life was too hectic, too full of social and other obligations. But if he erred it was on the side of generosity. *Mein Leben* is not unkind. At Basel he says their happiness was complete when the ladies arrived.

In those days it was impossible for anyone coming in contact with the Princess Carolyne not to be fascinated by her brilliant manner and the charming way she entered into our little plans. She was as much interested in the more important questions that affected us as in the accidental details of our lives in relation to society, and she had the magnetic quality of extracting the very best out of those with whom she associated.[11]

Like Liszt, he fell for Magnolet, the Child — who reciprocated by falling in love with his Nibelungs. Wagner's readings did not give universal pleasure. His most fervent admirers found them only slightly less stunning than the yowls, brays and wrong notes of his musical auditions. The Child adored them. When it was found that there wouldn't be time to finish the cycle before Wagner and Liszt went off to Paris, she "persuaded" her mother that they must all go in order to continue the readings.

Wagner was unsuspicious that Magnolet might have been coached in this maneuver, though it is obvious that Carolyne, not included in the original plan, preferred not to have Liszt in Paris with only Wagner for a chaperone. Liszt never opposed the Child's caprices. It was therefore arranged, with the usual consequences of prolonging a party beyond its normal limits. On their arrival in Paris Wagner found himself sequestered in a hotel room reading to the ladies, while Liszt was absent on "private business" — which helped to put Wagner in his habitual Paris temper.

It was one thing, he discovered, to indulge in horseplay with Liszt in a Swiss hotel, another to watch him resume his French persona. Their first evening together, spent strolling the lamplit boulevards, wrenched from Wagner the reflection that their feelings "must be as diffierent as our circumstances." The raw recruit to civilized living didn't like it a bit and was, for once, even conscious of his financial dependence — for he was Liszt's guest, and in France itself only by Liszt's favor. There had been trouble over his French visa, which Liszt in his grand-seigneur way fixed up with a word to the French minister to Switzerland. Wagner sulked. Liszt, he said, either left him to his own devices or dragged him off to parties where he was miserable. Berlioz, whom they saw daily, endured his readings "with quite admirable patience," while letting it be seen that the Nibelungs bored him to tears. Jules Janin's slangy Parisian French was "unintelligible." Marie Kalergis affronted him with praise of Louis Napoleon. And to add insult to these injuries, Liszt forced him to the opera and a performance of Meyerbeer's *Robert le Diable,* after cautioning him with really insufferable patronage to wear evening dress because they would be sitting in a box.

In the midst of these activities, time was found for Liszt to pay a call on his children. Seemingly, there was no rush, though they were almost ill with excitement at the prospect of seeing their father after eight years. Only Daniel could behave naturally, leaping with simple animal frenzy on Liszt's neck. The girls were paralyzed with shyness complicated by Liszt's decision to make a party of it. Long afterward Cosima wrote:

> It was on the same day on which I saw my father again after eight years that there suddenly appeared in our quiet home my father, the Princess Carolyne, her daughter Marie, Berlioz and Wagner, who read us *The Death of Siegfried.* This was a great deal to happen all at once to three children who thought themselves cut off, not only from the world, but also from family life . . . on that occasion I did nothing but look at the floor, my weak eyes and shy disposition made me unable to do anything but snatch at everything by stealth as it were. . . .[12]

Sweet Magnolet remembered this meeting too in later years:

> I was older than the two girls who were still rather unpolished and looked out at the unfriendly world with timid doe eyes. The elder, Blandine, was prettier, plumper, more pleasing, though in no way heaven-storming, and she was already rather pleased with herself. Poor Cosima, however, was in the worst phase of adolescence, tall and angular, sallow, with a wide mouth and long nose, the image of her father. Only her long golden hair, of unusual sheen, was beautiful. In the poor child's heart a volcano raged . . . dark stirrings of love and overweening vanity. . . . Now and then her thin lips would curl with the inborn mockery of the Parisian. . . . After a simple meal . . . in the small, plain salon of the rue Casimir-Perier, Wagner read to us the end of the *Nibelungen.* The children scarcely knew enough German to understand the words. Still, even they were gripped by our emotions. Daniel's laurel wreaths, which according to French

custom he had received at school, were hanging on the wall. Half as a joke, I took one down to crown Wagner with it. I can still see Cosima's rapturous expression, with the tears running down her sharp nose. At that time, Wagner had no eyes for the ugly child. . . .[13]

Aside from its heartlessness, this tells us that Magnolet, in spite of her superior position, knew what it was to be envious. The Liszt girls made far better marriages than she did. Her princeling was an insignificant fellow, a mere courtier. Émile Ollivier, Blandine's husband, reached the summit of French politics; Bülow and Wagner were brilliant matches however you looked at it. Their long noses notwithstanding, the daughters of Liszt and Marie d'Agoult could hardly be unattractive. They were in fact fascinating creatures — and when she first knew them neither so awkward nor so young as she says. Cosima was exactly her age, sixteen; the voluptuous Blandine two years older and already receiving offers of marriage. She was right that Wagner had no eyes just then for his future wife. About Blandine we can't be so sure. Always drawn to Liszt's daughters, he is supposed to have had an affair with her in 1860–1861, and was at least sufficiently infatuated to arouse Minna's suspicions.

The girls, not in the secret of Marie Wittgenstein's character, tried hard to make friends with her and a correspondence was initiated that lasted for several years. She was all they longed to be — their father's favorite, permanent inhabitant of the Altenburg, with a mother who doted on her. For whatever their hopes may have been, Liszt's attitude to them didn't alter with this visit. They scarcely saw him. "We were taken nowhere with him," wrote Cosima, "and we found it quite natural that he went out with Carolyne and Marie." Carolyne may have been kinder to them than he was. When he was back in Weimar they wrote him to "tell the Princess that we already love her like a mother and that she said things to us which we will never forget . . . we pray that God will leave you nothing more to desire, and that we may be able to give the name of mother to her . . ." which may not have been quite what he wanted to hear either.[14]

Wagner to Liszt, October 26, 1853: Here I stand and stare after you. . . . I haven't much news for you from "the world." Tomorrow I start for home, but shall see your children before I go. . . . From Zurich I will write you again. Be thanked for your blissful love! Greet the Princess and the Child! . . . Farewell, farewell, you dear beloved ones.[15]

Wagner's *envois,* more suited to antique tragedy than a simple parting of friends, speak louder than any words in *Mein Leben* about the interior mechanism of those meetings in the 1850's. Wagner could never understand why anyone as necessary to him as Liszt should go on living his own life. But for his proscription they would have had Wagner in Weimar for good; failing that, he couldn't see why Liszt wouldn't settle in Zurich — as at later periods he expected Cornelius, Nietzsche and half a dozen others to attach themselves like tails to his kite. He did sometimes notice that there were strains between them — "If we had not loved, we might have terribly hated one another," he said once — but he attributed this to every cause but the right one.[16]

Liszt to Blandine, May 1858: A certain one (who is indeed someone) of our friends sometimes embarrasses me as to what I can do for him, seeing that he has a peculiar talent for managing his affairs badly. . . . With his immense genius, which becomes more incontestable in all the silly combats he has to engage in, he unfortunately doesn't manage to free himself from the most griev-ous domestic upsets, to say nothing of the evil consequences of his fantastic cal-culations. He resembles those high mountains that are radiant at the summit, but wrapped in mist up to the shoulder — with the difference that imaginary mists are more truly inconvenient than real ones.[17]

The equation of Wagner with a mountain was well-chosen. Like an Alp he was best viewed from a distance. Humanly speaking, he provided few footholds. But unless one knows the terms of the friendship as they actually were, on whose back the burden rested, Wagner's pleas are piteous, Liszt's responses repulsively cold. "My dearest, dearest, unique Franz . . . If I could live with you in beautiful retirement, or, which would be the same thing, if we could live here wholly for each other instead of frittering away our beings with so many insipid and indifferent people, how happy I would be." [18] Aside from the implication that Liszt is wasting his time in Weimar, letters like this, larded as they are with requests for money, pleas for amnesty and innumerable other matters requiring Liszt's immediate attention, are not as pathetic as quotes out of context can make them look. Wagner, like Berlioz, couldn't help observing that their correspondence was somewhat lopsided:

When we compare letters someday, I will look like a veritable babbler by the side of you, while you . . . will make a noble show as a man of deeds. But dearest Franz, a little confidential chat is not to be despised. Take note of this, you aristocratic benefactor.[19]

Wagner was a slow study. When he wrote this, he had been sitting for some two months on the scores of the symphonic poems. Had the circum-stances been reversed, he would have been out of his mind. He said he had a skin infection (variously described as herpes, eczema or erysipelas) that incapacitated him for work but the doctor thought it was nerves and it didn't make a very convincing excuse. The truth was he had highly ambiva-lent feelings about Liszt's music. Not unlike the scholar who both longs and dreads to examine a fresh source, knowing the revisions it will probably entail as well as the pleasure it will give, he shied from confronting these compositions. (At other times — while the second act of *Tristan* was germinating was one — he had a young pianist play Liszt to him for hours.) And when at last he did get down to them, his usual avalanche of words dried up, his bulletins were confusing. "Even in May, when I saw them only through dark clouds, I received the electric shock that only great things produce." [20] In July, "I read the *Symphonic Poems* every day, fluently and without stopping. I feel every time as if I had dived into a deep crystal flood, to be there quite by myself. . . ." Yet there is an impediment: "It is very well to read something of that kind but the real salt, that which decides and solves all doubts, can only be enjoyed by actual hearing." True, but could a transcription, even played by Liszt himself, really have given him a clearer idea than the orchestral scores?

Wagner often maintained that he couldn't grasp Liszt's music unless Liszt played it for him, and one's first thought is that this was a transparent and rather endearing device for getting his dearest Franz to Zurich. Reading his amplifications on the theme one can't be certain that he wasn't also toying with the less complimentary proposition that Liszt's orchestral works were no more than an extension of the virtuoso's art:

Marvelous as your playing was, it did not properly exist without your actual presence. Hearing you, one felt sad, because these marvels were to be irretrievably lost with your person. . . . But nature . . . showed you the way. You were led to perpetuate the miracle of your personal communication in a way that made it independent of your personal art, by the orchestra, that is, by compositions. . . . Your orchestral works represent to me, so to speak, your personal art.[21]

This is either gibberish, an attempt to be profound, or it conceals a knife, and I am not sure which. Neither probably was Liszt — who at best can only have felt that Wagner's blandishments were on the wrong track: the symphonic poems were not intended to perpetuate the miracle of his virtuosity. But by the summer of 1856 when these letters were written, he was feeling the wind of adverse opinion, soon to grow into a hurricane, and kind words were welcome.

At the end of August he conducted the first performance of his *Graner Mass*, commissioned for the dedication of the huge and hideous new basilica at Esztergom (called Gran in German) in Hungary. The Magyars gave it an ovation but there had been a lot of unpleasant politicking beforehand, including a cancellation of the commission by the Cardinal Primate of Hungary, and a personal betrayal of Liszt by his former friend Leo Festetics, who announced that he could not "see without comment the

Cardinal Primate of Hungary go down in history as the Maecenas of this musical nonsense known as 'music of the future. . . .'" With this venom injected beforehand, the Mass met with a rocky reception.

To the Hanslicks, it went without saying, almost without listening, that the virtuoso and famous voluptuary was play-acting when he wrote liturgical music. "We do not raise the slightest doubt about the religious feelings of the composer but . . ." the Mass was theatrical, a showy novelty. The killing quip was that Liszt had tried "to smuggle the Venusberg into church music." (It was for Nietzsche to utter the last word, to say of *Parsifal:* "First impression on reading it: there is more Liszt than Wagner. . . ." But to Nietzsche neither man had any right to call himself religious: "If Wagner was a Christian, then Liszt was perhaps a Church Father," he said, and there he erred. Liszt *was* a Christian and could have been a church father of the Baroque, Latin type that arouses the Martin Luther in Nordics.) The *Gran* is not perfect but if for the pejorative *theatrical* the mirror-words *dramatic* or *expressive* are substituted we get a fairer idea of its beauties. He himself said it had been more prayed than composed but what earthly difference does that make to the musical quality — did anybody worry about Verdi's spiritual condition when he wrote the *Requiem?*

Criticism on this basis, to which no reply was possible, made Wagner's praise, however equivocal, the more attractive. But it is improbable that Liszt would have journeyed all the way to Zurich to hear it if Wagner hadn't, for several months, been muttering darkly about a crisis "that will mean the end of my art," from which only Liszt could extricate him: "Try, best and dearest friend, to arrange another meeting of us two: my whole life depends on this. . . . I cannot keep my head up in my present situation." [22]

A love affair was to be inferred and this proved to be the case but with Wagner it was rarely that uncomplicated. As early as 1854 he had written Liszt:

Since I have never in life tasted the actual happiness of love, I must raise a monument to the fairest of all dreams, in which from beginning to end that love shall be thoroughly satiated. I have in my head *Tristan and Isolde*, the simplest but most full-blooded musical conception. . . . [23]

Over the next two years this conception grew on him until it began to displace the Nibelungen, and since he always identified himself with his heroes (Tristan, immersed in the death-wish, might, like his creator, have been reading Schopenhauer), this was distressing news for those around him. "My poetic conceptions have always been so far ahead of my experiences that I can only consider these conceptions as determining and ordering my moral development," he wrote once. In simpler terms, life followed art and for the duration of his opera a simulacrum of Isolde would be needed. He found her in Mathilde Wesendonk, the pretty wife of his benefactor Otto Wesendonk, the millionaire silk manufacturer, now to be cast as King Mark. Dressed like a doll in glossy rosettes and laces, the bird-brained Mathilde comes down to us as a charming image but the situation was squalid. Minna, her beauty gone and her ailing heart literally failing her, was to break down completely over it. The sight of "my ridiculously vain husband" taking Otto's money with one hand and his wife with the other was too much.

Liszt would have done anything to avoid being dragged into this business, the details of which were forced on him the moment he arrived in Zurich, October 18, 1856. This was his last and least satisfactory meeting with Wagner in that decade and Wagner as usual was at a loss to explain his friend's abrasive temper during most of the six weeks that it lasted. About Mathilde Liszt hadn't much sympathy to offer. Such a connoisseur of the passions will have seen that this was rather a domestic melodrama than a tragedy, and that as soon as it had served its purpose Wagner would want out. The *Liebestod* notwithstanding, it isn't absolutely certain that Mathilde was in fact ready to go through with a consummation. For all her finery she was a cautious little bourgeoise who had no intention of sacrificing a nice rich husband for Wagner — who for his part always insisted their relations were "pure," and maybe, technically, they were. Liszt wouldn't have understood that either. So we can assume that although he listened politely to "my sad tale," it soon palled.

Aside from the Wesendonks, there were others in Wagner's circle who were active irritants. Young Karl Ritter, the son of Frau Ritter, Wagner's other financial backer, got on his nerves. This cissy boy wore in his presence a satirical smile not warranted by any claim to musicianship, or sense; it was simply meant to show that he was acquainted with Liszt's frailties, above all his French bias. The latter brought on an explosion. "When in an attempt to make clear the important influence of France on European culture, Liszt mentioned as an instance the French Academy," says *Mein Leben*, "Karl indulged in his fatal smile. This exasperated Liszt beyond all bounds, and in his reply he included some such phrase as, 'If we aren't prepared to admit this, we prove ourselves to be — baboons!' " [24] Ritter rushed from the house, and next day demanded an apology. It developed that "baboon-face" was an epithet that had been hurled at him before and when this was explained, Liszt was very ready to apologize. Too late. Ritter ostentatiously withdrew from their gatherings, and what was far more serious, complained to his mama, who promptly cut off Wagner's allowance. (Temporarily — it was soon restored.)

Exhibitions of bad manners were so rare with Liszt, and Ritter so trivial a cause for rancor that the real one must be closer to home. It is, I think, to be found in the passage that immediately precedes the episode in *Mein Leben*. Liszt had brought with him the *Faust* and *Dante* symphonies in manuscript. After they were played to him, Wagner pounced: "As I was sure that Liszt must be convinced of the great impression his compositions made on me, I felt no scruples in persuading him to alter the mistaken ending of the Dante symphony." [25]

This was touchy ground. At issue was the sudden irruption of "a pompous plagal cadence" in the concluding *Magnificat* — a *fortissimo* that Liszt explained was to represent the Deity. "No," shouted Wagner, "not that! Away with it . . . no majestic Deity. Leave us with the fine soft shimmer." Liszt's answer horrified him. "You are right. I said that too; it was the Princess who persuaded me differently. But it shall be as you wish." (But as Wagner later discovered, it was allowed to stand, marked *ad libitum* perhaps as a sop, and that he says, in a rare outburst against Carolyne, "was exactly typical of my relations with Liszt and his friend Princess Carolyne Wittgenstein.")

We only have his word for it that the conversation took place. Whether it did or not, he was dead right about the coda, which is coarse and banal, a ruinous afterthought. He still wasn't telling the whole story. He was against the idea of this symphony from its inception and had said so at length — warning Liszt in particular away from the *Paradiso*: "The chorus of the [Beethoven] Ninth is the weakest part, and discloses to us in a very naïve way the difficulties of a real musician who does not know (after Hell and Purgatory) how he is to represent Paradise." He then lashed out at the poem itself: the *Paradiso* merely affirms "the Catholic doctrine of a God who for his own glorification has made a hell of my existence, with the most elaborate sophisms and childish inventions, quite unworthy of a great mind." He even took a swipe at Beatrice, "preaching keen-witted ecclesiastic scholasticism." He ended:

Dante in the Paradise has not succeeded in getting beyond a caricature of truth. . . . I faithfully record the impression which the *Divine Comedy* makes on me, which in the Paradise becomes to my mind "a divine comedy" in the literal sense of the word, and which I don't care to take part in, either as a comedian or as a spectator. [26]

What the Altenburg made of these silly ravings is not recorded. But it can't be, as always alleged, that they were responsible for Liszt's decision to drop the original plan of three movements corresponding to the divisions of the poem, substituting for the *Paradiso* the foreshortened glimpse of it in the ethereal chords of the *Magnificat*.* Had he followed Wagner's ad-

---

* Searle is perhaps being ironic when he says that "Unfortunately Wagner managed to persuade him that no human being could dare portray the joys of Paradise" —

vice, he wouldn't have composed the symphony at all; and the difficulties were not as Wagner represented them. The *Paradiso* is not the weakest part of the *Divine Comedy,* though it is the most taxing, "either incomprehensible or intensely exciting" as Eliot has said. It is also the least susceptible to musical interpretation for the very reason that makes it Dante's highest achievement — his power to seize the unseizable in one astounding verbal image after another: the passing of the centuries caught in *Nettuno ammirar l'ombra d'Argo:* the *più di mille splendori* compared to the fish in their crystal pond, *trarsi ver noi, ed in ciascun s'udia: Ecco che crescerà li nostri amori.* These and a score of others are lightning bolts that can't be made to strike twice; they are beyond music as they are almost beyond poetry, as Liszt will have seen when he came to grips with them. It wasn't the idea of heaven that eluded his grasp — the *Magnificat,* minus the coda, solves that rather well — but Dante's metaphysics rendered in some of the most breathtaking allegorical language ever written.

In the *Dante* he put Romantic theory to a test that might have shown him where its weakness lay. The *Divine Comedy* can no more be transmuted into another art form than a drawing by Leonardo. That he didn't immediately see this (and the *Dante* gave him immense trouble, taking much longer to compose than the *Faust* though it is a shorter work) may have been due to his previous success with a less congenial subject. The *Dante* for all its splendors is half a failure. The *Faust* is a triumph partly because the material is more adaptable to translation but also because he didn't make too many demands on it. Described as three character sketches after Goethe (Faust, Gretchen, Mephistopheles), it makes no attempt to cling to the original sequence. The treatment is impressionistic — in the Mephistopheles section with its parodying of the Faust themes, brilliantly so.* Moreover, this symphony, his *chef d'oeuvre,* proves that he wasn't always wrong or Wagner always right in the matter of endings. Three years

---

Wagner's point being that the joys of Paradise are a hoax. Newman too is misleading when he says that Wagner "set out in full his reasons for holding that the Paradise section, which is the weakest in the *Divina Commedia,* would not lend itself to musical treatment and that Liszt recognized the soundness of the argument" (*The Life of Richard Wagner:* II, 495). What Wagner set out in full was his detestation of Dante's theology — not a convincing argument to Liszt. Nowhere in his letter does he show any appreciation of the poem, which it is obvious he only read, and hastily at that, after he learned that Liszt was writing the symphony. Nietzsche observed that where Wagner lacked a faculty, he invented a principle outlawing it. This is a good example.

* It is interesting to note that both this and the *Dante* were originally thought of as operas — the *Dante* as early as 1845, with a text by Autran. In 1850 he had the idea of a collaboration with Dumas on *Faust,* and as late as 1854, with Gérard de Nerval. The Nerval is a tantalizing loss. Between them they might have given us that unorthodox, free-form opera later evolved by Maeterlinck and Debussy in *Pelléas.* It is implicit in Goethe's original, with its quick changes in time and space. Here if anywhere would have been Liszt's opportunity to compose the opera that did *not* "represent everything, realize everything, make everything clear to the senses."

after its completion he added a coda that, this time, worked perfectly. A choral setting for Goethe's Chorus Mysticus that closes Part II, it is at once summary and comment on a dazzling score. Wagner however opposed it just as vehemently as he had the *Dante* coda, bracketing them together indeed, which leads one to think he was less outraged over an artistic fault than at Liszt's failure to follow his prescriptions.

That doesn't excuse the *Dante* ending, or Liszt for letting Carolyne dictate it to him, if she did. Unfortunately, it is the kind of mistake he was quite capable of on his own. Deprived of the climax that the sensibilities have been trained to expect, the symphony hangs fire so to speak, and it wasn't unnatural that he should grope for something more, a final statement. He wasn't up to it, but he loved Dante too well to leave it alone. It is a truism that we kill the thing we love and Liszt was only following a well-known rule when he did better with material for which he felt some antipathy. Disliking Goethe and the character of Faust in particular ("decidedly bourgeois . . . lets himself be driven, hesitates, experiments, loses his way, considers, bargains, and is only interested in his own little happiness") he handled them more effectively.

The issues raised by these symphonies between Liszt and Wagner did not of course turn on anything so superficial as a coda. For each, the problem of the other's music was admiration in the abstract not infrequently coupled with distaste for the material, reflecting a cultural fissure impossible to close. Wagner's crude analysis of Dante had its counterpart in the attacks Liszt felt compelled to mount on writers sacred to Germans, beginning with Goethe. His remark to Bettina von Arnim that "the worst Jesuit is better than your Goethe" cost him her friendship. At Zurich he engaged in a ridiculous argument over the personal character of Egmont and according to Wagner, got so hot that though "we never came to blows . . . from that time onward there remained with me . . . a vague feeling that this might someday happen, and that the combat would be terrific." [27]

Neither would acknowledge this psychic incompatibility, which was so evidently the cause of Liszt's bad temper, and Wagner hit on the explanation that Liszt's "strange and exciting mode of life" was to blame. He wrote Bülow that he couldn't remain indifferent "when it is clear to anyone with eyes in his head that Liszt is due before very long for a breakdown unless he withdraws himself radically from *every* excitement and undertakes the most drastic and enduring cure."

These sinister hints turn out to be based on nothing more than his wildly distorted idea of Liszt's life with Carolyne, glimpsed when she joined them at Zurich, where she stayed some weeks at the best hotel:

The curious spell of excitement which this lady immediately threw over everyone she succeeded in drawing into her circle . . . amounted almost to intoxication. It was as if Zurich had suddenly become a metropolis. Carriages drove hither and thither, footmen rushed in and out, dinners and suppers poured in on us, and we found ourselves suddenly surrounded by an increasing number of interesting people whose existence in Zurich we had never suspected. . . . But a really refreshing sense of freedom and spontaneity pervaded everything and the unceremonious evenings at my house in particular were remarkably free and easy. . . . The Princess, with Polish patriarchal friendliness, would assist the mistress of the house with the serving. Once, after we had some music, I had to give the substance of my two newly conceived poems, *Tristan and Isolde* and *The Victors*, to a group which half sitting, half lying before me, was certainly not without charm.[28]

For Liszt's forty-fifth birthday Carolyne gave a large party. "Everybody who was anybody in Zurich was there," says Wagner, though it has been a slight letdown to learn that most of her acquisitions were professors from Zurich University, not exactly a giddy throng; and we smile when he tells us that a poem by Hoffmann von Fallersleben was telegraphed from Weimar, and "at the Princess's request was solemnly read aloud by Herwegh in a strangely altered voice." (But Herwegh wasn't much of a poet himself by this time. The *Dante* Symphony inspired these distressing lines: *La fleur lumineuse dans la sombre couronne/ Que tu as tressée de tragiques destins,/ C'est Francesca, ô maitre Franz!/ En elle, j'ai senti profondement ton être intime.*) A run-through of *Valkyrie's* first act came next — Liszt at the piano, an amateur soprano doing Sieglinde and Wagner undertaking both Siegmund and Hunding. Wille was heard to say rather enigmatically that he was too seduced by this glorious performance to give an opinion — he would have to hear it badly done. Next came the symphonic poems arranged for two pianos, and then they all went in to dinner. Liszt's demons were at him again. This time it was an argument with Mathilde Wesendonk about Heine. Whatever you think of him, said this nitwit, apparently unaware of the things Heine had written about Liszt, "his name will be forever inscribed in the temple of immortality." "Yes," said Liszt, "in mud."

Such were the diversions that Wagner called dangerous to Liszt's health and sanity. What he didn't say but might understandably have wondered about was Carolyne's effect on the nerves of anyone who lived with her. She clearly got on his, especially when she gave him a grilling on the Nibelungs. She couldn't get the plot straight. "In the end I felt as though I had explained a French society play to her," he says disgustedly — and not very fairly. To find the *Ring* impenetrable isn't to betray a preference for Sardou. But one can believe that her questions were tiresome.

It was in fact time to go home. "We were compelled to remain together in a state of nervous tension and aimlessness," says Wagner, because Carolyne was indisposed.[29] They all were; Liszt was in bed for a week with skin trouble. But as their parting brought about a miraculous cure, the origin of their illnesses can be surmised. Wagner supplies a weird tale of one of Carolyne's "attacks." The party had moved on to St. Gall where they were staying at a local inn. Here Wagner, who was Carolyne's neighbor, was kept awake half one night by the sound of the Child's high-pitched voice reading aloud to her mother. At 2 A.M. he was pumping his bell and demanding to be given another room. The next day they informed him calmly that she sometimes had "hallucinations" which the reading was to ward off. She isn't known to have suffered from hallucinations. Were they trying to tell him something else?

The epilogue at St. Gall was curious in itself. Wagner despised the place for its "wretched theatre, an abominable set of singers, and a ghastly orchestra." Yet in November, in response to an invitation from the music director, he and Liszt spent a whole week there (together with the Wesendonks, Herweghs, etc.) and on November 23 took turns at conducting the ghastly orchestra. Wagner did the *Eroica*, Liszt his own *Orpheus* and *Les Préludes;* and Newman thinks it was Wagner's desire to hear Liszt's works performed by an orchestra — this was one of the few times he did — that induced him to accept the invitation. He might of course have given himself that pleasure earlier, by the simple expedient of putting something by Liszt on one of his own programs in London or Zurich. But if that was doing Liszt too much honor, St. Gall, by virtue of its obscurity and the unannounced and impromptu character of the concert itself, was the ideal place.* And I would agree that he wanted to study Liszt's effects in performance, his technique on the podium. He says as much: "We watched each other . . . with a closeness and sympathy that was genuinely instructive," though he admits he made a hash of the *Eroica,* owing to the unfavorable conditions.

That was the end of the visit, about which his farewell letter perhaps tells us more than he does himself. "Though you are so dear to me," he wrote, "you are a continual sermon of repentance; I cannot think of you without being heartily ashamed of myself." [30]

---

* Newman cites the "letter" to Marie Wittgenstein, published in the *Neue Zeitschrift* in April 1857, "On Liszt's Symphonic Poems," as an example of Wagner's unobserved generosity to Liszt. And it might serve if it had had a noticeable connection with its putative subject. But in Newman's own words it deals with "the new musico-poetic forms rather than specifically with Liszt's musical achievement" (*Richard Wagner:* II, 501).

PART SIX

Death of an Ideal
(1858-1861)

Chapter 38

SERMONS OF REPENTANCE were notoriously wasted on Wagner, who over the following two years showed no signs of having attended to this one. In 1857 he moved into the pretty villa, archly called the Asyl, built for him by the Wesendonks on their property. (*Mein Leben* romantically tells us that he awoke on Good Friday in a delicious sun-filled room and instantly conceived the outline for *Parsifal:* a displaced memory it seems; from the dates, this must have happened the following year.) By the summer of 1858 a domestic inferno raged in this retreat. Minna had had enough, and so too had the long-suffering Otto. Wagner, seeing that he had lost control of the situation, solved it in his usual way: he fled, leaving Minna to cope with his swarming creditors, helped, it is believed, by Otto — somebody salvaged the big Érard and some bits of furniture from the forced sale of their household goods and he is the likeliest candidate. Wagner made for Venice, where he rented two large rooms in Palazzo Giustiniani, encased them in ruby velvet and got to work on *Tristan*. No qualms of conscience disturbed his peace. In September a comet blazed over the lagoons. "I chose it with a certain defiance as my star," he said. "Am I such a comet myself? Have I brought misfortune? Was that *my* fault?"

The news that the *Ring* was to be abandoned burst on Liszt with some abruptness in June of 1857. "I have led my young Siegfried into the beautiful forest solitude, where I have left him under a linden tree, and with tears from the depths of my heart said farewell to him," Wagner wrote.[1] He then announced that he would finish *Tristan* "on a moderate scale" that would make it feasible for ordinary theatres, possibly Strasburg or Carlsruhe: "And so I hope, by the Grace of God, once more to produce something in my own style and on my own account without the Grand Duke of Weimar, thus winning refreshment and consciousness for myself."

What did the truculent postscript mean? There were plenty of valid reasons for dropping the *Ring* cycle in favor of a produceable opera that would bring in something to live on. In spite of Liszt's promises to Breitkopf and Härtel on Wagner's behalf, and his reckless commitment of Weimar to a production, "by the grace of God," within a year of receiving the completed score, neither Breitkopf nor Carl Alexander was prepared to come through with an advance. But neither were Strasburg or Carlsruhe, names that Wagner seems to have chosen at random when he threatened to give away his first viable opera since *Lohengrin* to any theatre in Germany that wasn't Weimar.

Whether this was intended to punish or to blackmail Liszt is an unanswered question. His façade didn't crack: "We will all come to Strasburg and form a guard of honor for you," he wrote. But the injury wasn't unfelt and Wagner knew it. Liszt didn't go to Switzerland that summer, though Wagner begged him: "My dearest Franz, whatever there may have been in my conduct to make you angry with me, you must, I pray you, forgive me for the sake of our friendship, while I . . . am quite willing to forgive the person who may have set you against me. . . ." [2]

This feeble attempt to involve Carolyne (probably Carolyne, though Wagner, who saw enemies under every bush, may have meant Berlioz or any of several other people) got nowhere. Liszt, in the unnerving way he had, refused every gambit. He wouldn't quarrel; neither would he go to Wagner's rescue in the next and fatal summer of 1858 — which Wagner considered nothing less than an act of treachery. Only Liszt, says *Mein Leben*, could have brought "light and reconciliation" to the troubled Asyl. Liszt's diplomacy, his finesse — reviled in the matter of the *Tannhäuser* negotiations with Berlin and Leipzig — were now all that could save him. He overlooked a few details. Horrified at the prospect of playing mediator between Wagner and Minna, Minna and the Wesendonks, Liszt wouldn't set a definite date for a visit he obviously didn't intend to make; but somehow August lodged itself in Wagner's mind as his hour of deliverance. In August, Bülow and Cosima, married less than a year, took their summer holiday in Zurich, where they were joined by Marie d'Agoult. Wagner can have paid very little attention to Liszt's emotional life if he didn't know Liszt's dread of encountering Marie. And in September, which Liszt proposed instead, Wagner decamped for Venice, whence he informed Liszt that his excuses for not coming to Switzerland earlier "pardon me for saying so, appeared extremely trivial."

The holiday Liszt took instead was a happy one, the last that he and Carolyne were to spend in carefree wandering. They explored the Tyrolese Alps and went to Munich, a city they ought to have discovered earlier. It was full of artists, their favorite being Kaulbach, creator of that dreadful picture that is the subject of Liszt's eleventh symphonic poem, *The Battle of the Huns.* More cosmopolitan than Weimar, Bavarian court and society were also more cordial to Carolyne.

Back in Weimar, Liszt seemed to have no suspicion that the coming season would be his last. If Dingelstedt was busy concocting a plot to ruin him, he was not only unconscious of it, he was writing to Wagner about a *Rienzi* production the following year and beyond that even looking forward to *Tristan* and the *Ring:*

Liszt to Wagner, November 5, 1858: I very much wish to incline Dingelstedt a little more favorably towards the performance of your works and to cooperate with him in perfect sympathy. That cooperation is of importance to me not only as regards *Tristan,* which will meet with no difficulty, and, as I hope and longingly wish, will open your return to Germany, but chiefly with a view to the performance of the Nibelungen, which is our ultimate goal. The honorarium of 25 louis d'or [for *Rienzi*] which our theatrical exchequer can offer you is very small, but I advise you to accept it, and take it upon myself to get you a small *douceur* from the Grand Duke's privy purse later on.[3]

That Liszt should still be talking about *Tristan* was perhaps due to his prescience that Carlsruhe would back out — as it did. ("Now at last," said a Berlin paper, "the title 'music of the future' . . . is justified: the present cannot even perform this music! Ostensibly the shelving of the work was on the singers' account; but according to trustworthy reports the demands on the orchestra are equally exorbitant. . . .") The mention of the Nibelungen is more mysterious. With his now intimate knowledge of its scope he cannot have believed Weimar's pocket theatre capable of mounting it. If he was simply trying to cheer Wagner up, he failed. From Venice Wagner answered in the tough idiom that was growing on him that he had no desire to deal with Dingelstedt: "Good God, what Jacks-in-office you all are! None of you can put himself in the place of a poor devil like me who looks upon every source of income as a lucky draw in a lottery." Two weeks later he didn't want *Rienzi* done at all:

I do not desire you to force this juvenile production on Weimar. The reasons for keeping on good terms with this person or that do not exist for me, and my sincere wish is that they not exist for you either. In this matter we two should agree. Whether or not I perform my Nibelungen at some future time is at bottom a matter of indifference to me. . . . [Besides] would the Weimar receipts have allowed me to pay the 1,000 francs I owe you?[4]

The débâcle with the *Barber of Bagdad* followed immediately on the receipt of this letter. In the circumstances, Wagner's Christmas present — proofs of *Tristan's* first act — can't have arrived a moment too soon. Liszt was enchanted: "All the children in the world cannot be more delighted with their trees hung with golden apples and presents than I am . . . with your unique *Tristan.* . . . What blissful charm, what a wealth of beauty in this fiery love potion!" [5]

Not to mingle bad news with congratulations, he said nothing about the storm raging at Weimar, merely remarking that Wagner's refusal of *Rienzi* had come at the right moment: "It is only too true that my influence in local matters is small. I have declared that I won't enter the orchestra for some time to come." As well if the letter had ended there. Unfortunately, he thought it necessary to add that the Grand Duke of Saxe-Coburg wanted to dedicate his opera *Diane de Solange* to Wagner: "Accept it in a friendly spirit," he advised, "even though you will find yourself in the somewhat strange company of Meyerbeer. The composer — the brother-in-law of the Grand Duchess of Baden — is well disposed toward you. . . ."

Wagner went up in smoke. The courtier in Liszt always aroused him to a fury that would have been admirable if he had made less assiduous use of Liszt's talents in that direction:

Wagner to Liszt, December 31, 1858: In the name of God, what can I do with *Diane de Solange?* . . . You answer me too pathetically. . . . Dingelstedt! Grand Duke! *Rienzi!* All stuff and nonsense! All I want is money. . . . Tell them that Wagner does not care a curse for you all, your theatres, even his own operas; he needs money; that is all. . . . Send me your *Dante* and your *Mass.* . . . But don't write me again earnestly and pathetically! My God! I have told you all lately that you are tiresome. Hasn't that been any use? [6]

Overnight, he must have perceived that he had gone too far. He shot off a telegram (now lost) saying he was *"wunderbar miserabel"* and the next day posted what for him passed as an explanation of "the storm I let loose on you, no doubt to your sorrow." It went on for pages, a whining reiteration of demands that Liszt could have recited by heart: pardon from Saxony, a steady income that didn't involve service at a court, always understood to be all right for Liszt but not for him — to be supplied by a consortium of German princes. There was no nonsense this time about three hundred thalers a year being adequate; he would need two or three thousand to gratify "my somewhat refined and not altogether ordinary wants," and they must in no way be linked to amnesty. When no reply to this was forthcoming, he dashed off two frantic lines: "Have you *nothing* to say to me? What is to become of me, if *everyone* ignores me?"

Liszt did have something to say and had never said it so forcefully before:

Liszt to Wagner, January 4, 1859: In order not to expose myself again to the danger of boring you with pathetic or serious talk, I am sending back to Härtel the first act of *Tristan* and soliciting the favor of not making the acquaintance of the rest until it is published. Since the *Dante Symphony* and the *Mass* are not valid bank stock, it would be superfluous to send them to Venice. Not less so, in my view, is it to receive in future telegrams of distress or wounding letters from there.*

Liszt's weaponry wasn't of a calibre to pierce Wagner's hide. Wagner continued to excuse himself in terms that were anything but acceptable: he had only meant to frighten Dingelstedt into paying the 25 louis d'or at once; Liszt's intervention had resulted in no payment at all. He crowed that he had foreseen the difficulties that would arise with Dingelstedt, "making silent reproaches when he was called to Weimar through your agency." Yet he was willing to forgive:

It is you, my friend, whom I see to be suffering and needing comfort, for the extraordinary letter which you found it possible to send me must have sprung from a terrible inner irritation. . . . Let me assure you that you have in no way hurt me, for your arrows did not hit me; their barbs stuck in your own heart. May this letter free you of them.[7]

The Altenburg received this in silence. Nearly a month went by before Bülow managed to make Wagner see what he had done.

Wagner to Liszt: I have heard to my horror how great your annoyance must be, and B's account confirmed my impression that you were deeply annoyed and grieved by my ingratitude, faithlessness and even treachery. . . . I must also thank you for the alarming New Year's greeting you sent me. I believe it has been beneficial to me; I am aware that I have too little control over myself, and rely on the patience of others to an undue extent. I feel . . . that I must have cut a very ugly figure. That was proved to me by the effect I had on you, for we know little of how we look until we see ourselves in a mirror, and in your irritation I recognized my ugliness.[8]

---

* Newman calls this mild reproof a "missive of studied insult" caused by a misunderstanding. (Newman, *Wagner* II, 579.) Liszt was answering Wagner's *Diane de Solange* letter before the "explanation" of January 2 reached him, and he had misinterpreted that earlier letter, which he construed as "a rough rejection of his congratulations on *Tristan.*" I don't see that this helps at all. Liszt had quite enough to be furious about before the "explanation," which was simply another squeeze play, and could only have brought on another burst of rage when it arrived. In fact the mails seem to have been rather better than they are today and it is entirely possible that he *had* received Wagner's letter of January 2. But it makes little difference.

He was forgiven, but only just. Liszt was later to tell Carolyne that she must deal gently with Wagner because "he is ill, incurable. That is why one can only love him." He even dedicated the *Dante* Symphony to him "in unchangeably faithful love." But he delayed many weeks the sending of this copy to Wagner, giving the inscription something of the quality of an adieu. The link between them was in fact broken, the change in his feelings irretrievable. He evaded every offer to meet Wagner face to face and allowed longer and longer intervals to elapse between his letters. Though perhaps not fully conscious of it himself, he had renounced the man and practically speaking the composer as well, since he could be of no further service to him.

Chapter 39

IF LISZT HAD EVER TRIED to fix on the moment when the price of Wagner's friendship became exorbitant, he might have chosen the attempt to exclude Berlioz from Weimar, which foreclosed the kind of collaboration that alone would have given the enterprise some viability. Both Liszt and Bülow put pressure on Wagner to this end.

Liszt to Wagner, April 7, 1852: Let me just add this, that the reasons which decided me to give [*Cellini*] have proved completely right, and advantageous to the further success of my activity here. "Why *Cellini* in Weimar?" is a question to which I am not bound to provide anyone with a reply, but which will resolve itself practically in a way that may be satisfactory to us. Perhaps you haven't yet grasped the matter . . . as you will later. . . .[1]

Bülow said succinctly that sympathy must be shown and *Cellini* praised "because one must now support Liszt in everything he does."

These appeals were a waste of breath. Wagner's determination to make Weimar his personal arena had only this to recommend it: it was honestly stated. Berlioz wasn't less anxious to be first for all his above-the-battle stance, and he hated Wagner with an intensity just as doomful to Liszt's efforts as Wagner's aggression. Liszt's efforts to soothe these two egos, to juggle them into a favorable conjunction, are never written about from his point of view. Like one who intervenes in a domestic argument, he has gotten it from both sides — his motives impugned by Berlioz's and Wagner's partisans alike. No matter who writes the story, he is in the wrong. Forgotten in the scuffle is the absence of any obligation to expend his time and energy on either of them.

Berlioz took a haughty line from the start. "I am as convinced as you are that it won't be hard for me to mesh gears with Wagner," he wrote in 1853, "if only he will put a little oil in the wheels. As for the words to which you refer [the digs in *Opera and Drama*], I have never read them and hold no grudge on their account. I have too often fired into the marching throng myself to be anything like surprised at getting broadsides in return." [2]

The opportunity to mesh gears occurred two years later in London where both were conducting — Berlioz to applause, Wagner to brickbats from the press.

Berlioz to Liszt: We spoke a great deal about you with Wagner recently, and you may imagine with how much affection, since, on my word of honor, I believe he loves you as I do. He will no doubt tell you about his stay in London and of all he has had to endure from prejudiced hostility. He is superb in his ardor and stoutness of heart, and I confess even his violence pleases me. . . . If it is true that we both have asperities [they] will dovetail into each other. [He illustrated this with two lightning zigzags of his pen.][3]

Wagner too rushed the good news, just as characteristically:

One real gain I bring back from England — the cordial and genuine friendship which I feel for Berlioz and which we have mutually declared. I heard a concert of the new Philharmonic under his direction and was, it is true, little edified by his performance of Mozart's *G Minor Symphony*, while the very imperfect execution of his *Romeo and Juliet* made me pity him. A few days later, we two were the only guests at Sainton's table. He was lively, and the progress I have made in French . . . permitted me to discuss with him for five hours all the problems of art, philosophy and life in a most fascinating conversation. . . . He appeared to me quite differently from before. We discovered we were in reality fellow sufferers, and I thought that upon the whole I was happier than Berlioz. After my last concert he and other friends . . . called on me; his wife also came. We were together until 3 o'clock in the morning and took leave with the warmest embraces.[4]

The necessary footnotes to these joyous accounts were not of course supplied to the gratified Liszt. Of this same evening, Berlioz wrote another friend that "we went to drink punch with Wagner after his concert, he renews his expressions of friendship, embraces me passionately, saying he had entertained many prejudices against me; he weeps and stamps his foot and hardly has he left me when the *Musical World* publishes the passage in his book where he slates me in the most amusing and witty fashion,

Davison roaring with delight as he translates it for me — the world's a stage, as Shakespeare and Cervantes have said." [5]

Berlioz didn't tell Liszt either how much he had agreed with the London critics about Wagner's conducting — "sempre rubato, the way Klindworth [Liszt's pupil] plays the piano." Or how easy he found it to make Wagner look like a bumpkin, a very Gallic talent that not infrequently depends on the inability to master other languages, thus forcing foreigners to speak French. *Mein Leben* struggles to be good-tempered about this:

. . . I found it . . . difficult to talk serious stuff with the real Frenchman . . . fluent and glib of tongue, who was so sure of himself that it never occurred to him to doubt whether he had understood his companions aright. Once, in a pleasant glow of inspiration . . . I tried to express to him my idea of the "artistic conception." I endeavored to describe the powerful effect of vital impressions on the temperament, how they hold us captive, as it were, until we rid ourselves of them by the unique development of our . . . spiritual visions, which are not called for by these impressions, but only aroused by them from . . . slumber. The artistic structure, therefore, appears to us as in nowise a result of but on the contrary a liberation from vital impressions. At this point, Berlioz smiled in a patronizing, comprehensive way, and said: "*Nous appelons cela: digérer.*" [We call that digestion.][6]

One sees why Wagner remembered this conversation so precisely. Every foreigner has had the experience at one time or another and must love France and the French very much if he is to overlook it. For Wagner, it was just another piece of kindling thrown on the fire — and Berlioz had in fact *not* summarized his rambling point correctly. He did better by Berlioz, on the whole, than Berlioz by him.

For Wagner, it was quite simple. Would Berlioz but leave opera, *his* domain, alone, he was ready to acclaim him, to call him (it is true, after Berlioz's death) "the savior of our musical world." Berlioz, with an intelligence twice as acute, either turned his head from the spectacle of Wagner, or when that was impossible, damned him with the unworthy expedient of playing dumb. When Wagner arrived in Paris in 1860, almost his first act was to send Berlioz the score of *Tristan,* handsomely dedicated "*au grand et cher auteur de Romeo et Juliette, l'auteur reconnaissant de Tristan et Isolde.*" Berlioz waited three weeks to acknowledge receipt. When Wagner's concerts forced some discussion of it, he then wrote:

I have read and re-read this strange piece of music; I have listened to it with the profoundest attention and lively desire to discover the sense of it; well, I have to admit that I still haven't the least notion of what the composer is driving at.[7]

The 1860 concerts were Berlioz's chance to prove his vaunted disinterestedness. He told Carolyne that he could "no more help adoring a sublime work of art by my greatest enemy" than "execrating some horrible absurdity by my most intimate friend." He wasn't of course obliged to admire and still less to champion Wagner's music; some indication that he could distinguish him from Clapisson was imperative. He could, for example, have argued that excerpts (the *Flying Dutchman* Overture; the *Tristan* Prelude, selections from *Tannhäuser* and *Lohengrin*) aren't the way to judge compositions for the stage. That wasn't the ground he chose.

His now historic article in the *Débats* of February 9, moving from lukewarm praise to outright attack, closed with a diatribe at "the music of the future" itself. His method was to erect a thesis as flimsy as Wagner's own and then to demolish it. If the music of the future means one is tired of melody, that the ear is to be abused by bad harmony, bad modulations, conflicting tonalities, that the art of singing is to be abandoned in favor of declamation, "if it costs singers as much trouble to memorize and perform a work as to learn a page of Sanskrit . . . if the witches in *Macbeth* are right, and the beautiful is horrible and horrible beautiful . . . if this is the new religion, I am far from professing it; I have never professed it, I do not profess it now, and I never will profess it. . . . *Non credo.*" [8] *

Worse than foolish and uncharitable, this gave Wagner the perfect opening. His dignified reply deplored the obtuseness of "a critic so honest, a friend so sincerely valued as yourself," in dragging up a ten-year-old phrase to flog him with. The "music of the future," he said, was the coinage of a Professor Bischoff of Cologne and the result of a misreading of his *Art-Work of the Future.* "For myself, I heartily regret having ever made public the ideas set forth in that book, for when the artist is so little understood, even by the artist . . . when even the most cultivated critic is so much the victim of the prejudices of the half-educated amateur . . . how is the thinker on art ever to be understood by the public . . . ?" [9] He closed with the hope that Berlioz would not hinder the French from giving "sanctuary to my lyric dramas," and that he might soon be allowed to hear "the first, and let us hope, the thoroughly successful performance of your *Troyens.*"

That last was a cruel stab. Berlioz's stifled yawns at the Nibelung readings were more than equalled by Wagner's reaction to the *Troyens* libretto, portions of which Berlioz read to him in 1858: "In [his] dry and theatrical delivery, I fancied . . . I could see the character of the music to which he had set his words, and I sank into utter despair about it, as I could see that he regarded this as his masterpiece, and was looking forward to its production as the great object of his life." [10] Berlioz was indeed, and he now knew

---

* A brilliant defense of Berlioz vis-à-vis Wagner can be found in *The Romantic Century*: II, 176 et seq., the drawback being that it is Barzun's and not Berlioz's. Barzun avoids direct quotation from the *Non Credo*, which he describes as "light and fanciful," an extraordinary interpretation. As Berlioz's private letters show (see below), he would cheerfully have seen Wagner destroyed at this period.

that the chances of his ever launching his leviathan were poorer than ever. If the Paris Opera were to throw its weight behind a Wagner production, he was lost; for no house could bear the expense of mounting both.

Berlioz's chagrin was natural. It won't quite suffice to palliate his conduct when *Tannhäuser,* after a long and painful *accouchement,* was at last presented to the public amid scenes of unparalleled violence. The story is well known: how the aristocratic members of the Jockey Club organized themselves like a band of hoodlums and armed with hunting whistles and flageolets reduced the opera house to a shambles; the laughter and jeers of the audience; the mortification of Napoleon III and Eugénie, frozen in their box and fully conscious that they as well as Wagner were the targets. The demonstration was in fact more political than artistic. The Austrian faction at court, headed by Princess Pauline Metternich and Marie Kalergis, was unpopular, and known to have backed Wagner. The war against Austria of the preceding summer was not forgotten: it was a popular joke that although Austria had given up Lombardy, a secret clause in the Treaty of Villafranca had foisted *Tannhäuser* on France. But whatever the reasons behind it, the episode was degrading and so regarded by French artists: "What will Europe think of us?" cried Baudelaire. "A handful of rowdies have disgraced us *en masse.*" Berlioz was virtually alone in maintaining a conspicuous silence. He didn't even write a review, handing that chore over to d'Ortigue.

It was an abdication of principle that his most ardent partisans cannot paper over, and the publication of his letters has not helped:

What a performance! What outbursts of laughter! The Parisian showed himself yesterday in an entirely new aspect; he laughed at the bad musical style, he laughed at the absurd vulgarities of the orchestration, he laughed at the naïveté of an oboe; he now realizes that there is such a thing as style in music. As for the horrors, they were splendidly hissed.[11]

He even rejoiced at the personal insults offered to Wagner, who was treated "as a rogue, an insolent fellow, an idiot." "As for myself," he said, "I am cruelly avenged."

He was nothing of the sort. The revenge, if anyone's, was Wagner's when *Les Troyens,* in a mutilated version that broke Berlioz's heart, sank ingloriously two years later. As thirty years of corroding experience might have told him, *Tannhäuser's* fate in no way augured success for an opera with far less popular appeal and even greater production problems. The lesson that Liszt had tried to teach once again fell on deaf ears. Only an effective alliance could prevent these disasters. Had Berlioz stood by Wagner on principle, the *Tannhäuser* débâcle might not have happened. With the forces at his command, and they were considerable, the Jockey

Club's tactics might have been forestalled or counteracted, and the more honor to Berlioz if he had rallied what was left of the Romantic legions and gone to the defense of a fellow artist. Conversely, who can say that the prestige garnered in *Tannhäuser's* explosive failure would not have accrued to Berlioz's benefit — had Wagner seen his way to supporting *Les Troyens?* Wagner at least had moments when he glimpsed these truths. He complained to Liszt of Berlioz's unfriendliness, "it is always I who had to seek him out or invite him," yet "in the world of the present only we three belong to each other — you, he, and I. But that is what one must not say to him: he kicks up his heels when he hears it." [12] And of course, when it came to specifics like *Cellini,* so did Wagner himself. Liszt knew it. These mighty egos, whose claims were exacerbated by their nationalities and their temperaments, defeated him in the end. Unable to reconcile, he couldn't help them either.

The sorrow this knowledge cost him is only obliquely visible. Since his aim was to minimize their differences, his policy was least said, soonest mended; and he concealed from Berlioz his row with Wagner over *Cellini* as from Wagner his disputes with Berlioz over the music of the future. Whatever he may have said in private, he also avoided discussions by mail and that includes his letters to Carolyne. No word of his can be quoted that might have supplied ammunition to any of them, and it is partly for this reason that I entirely disbelieve in the intrigues that Carolyne is supposed to have set in motion on his behalf. They were the last thing he wanted or would have allowed, aside from the fact that strategically they make no sense.

We are told that she championed Berlioz in order to undermine Wagner, backed *Les Troyens* in hopes it would outdistance the *Ring,* and generally pursued a balance of power policy worthy of Metternich, all in order to benefit Liszt. But it is difficult to see how he would have been helped had such a strategy succeeded. Since he didn't write operas, he wasn't in direct competition with either man. Lacking control over a major opera house, she wasn't in a position to influence the outcome of the Wagner-Berlioz struggle, and it would have made no difference if she had. Win or lose, neither was going to raise a hand for Liszt, though the edge was in Wagner's favor. He at least showed a flattering interest in Liszt's compositions, which Berlioz never did. Wagner's failure to conduct Liszt was shabby but conducting wasn't really his profession and neither was criticism. Berlioz's avoidance of anything to do with Liszt's music was the more pointed in that he earned his living at both. The choice was between Wagner's rapacity and Berlioz's wounding indifference. The fact that Carolyne did undoubtedly choose Berlioz cannot be shown to have benefited Liszt any more than opting for Wagner would have done. And if her object was to move Liszt himself, drag him away from Wagner and orient him toward

Berlioz, her supposed ascendancy over him must go by the board, for his parting of the ways with Berlioz comes at precisely the point that her subtle intrigues, so-called, were set in motion.

Les Troyens was Carolyne's opera. Berlioz said so many times and described its birth, so to speak, in the Altenburg drawing room:

> Something led me to speak of my admiration for Virgil and of an idea I had formed of a grand opera on the Shakespearean model, to be founded on the second and fourth books of the *Aeneid*. I added that I was too well acquainted with the . . . difficulties of such an undertaking ever to attempt it. "Indeed," replied the Princess, "your passion for Shakespeare, combined with your love of the antique, ought to produce something grand and uncommon. You must write this opera, or lyric poem, or whatever you choose to call it. You must begin it, and you must finish it." I continued my objections, but she would hear none of them. "Listen," said she. "If you are shirking the inevitable difficulties of the piece, if you are so weak as to be afraid to brave everything for Dido and Cassandra, never come to see me again, for I will not receive you." This was quite enough to decide me. On my return to Paris I began the poem of *Les Troyens*. I next attacked the score, and after three and a half years . . . I finished it.[13]

Les Troyens was "*our* work" from then on — Carolyne may have made an otherwise unsatisfactorily explained visit to Paris in 1859 in order to encourage him and hear bits of it privately sung by Pauline Viardot-García — and it was the subject of innumerable letters.

Berlioz's correspondence with Carolyne is the source of some embarrassment to his admirers. They read, says Newman, "easily and beautifully, without any of those abrupt distortions and exaggerations that pull us up with a shock in the earlier ones. When he has to castigate, he does it like a gentleman, with a rapier, not a bludgeon. And how perfectly does he maintain the essential dignity of the artist against this well-meaning but inquisitive and slightly vulgar aristocrat; with what fine breeding . . . does he repel her interferences. . . ."[14] Barzun isn't that easily satisfied. ". . . We must not misread Berlioz when he stops working and tries to give an account of himself to the Princess. A born letter writer always adapts his epistle to its reader, and Berlioz being particularly adept at this adjustment, his letters enable us to infer what hers were like. Full of extravagant praise, of prying curiosity, and also of mystical moralizing about duties that he understood quite as well as she . . ."[15]

So what ought we to make of the following, very typical effusion? Berlioz is writing of *Les Troyens'* opening night:

> You were not there, nor Liszt either. . . . But let me now put myself at your feet, take both your hands in mine, and thank you with all my heart . . . for your sympathetic words, your unforgettable friendship, your flights of soul, and

your harmonic vibrating to the distant echoes of *our* work. Again my thanks, dear intelligence, believe in the deep and grateful feelings of your devoted Berlioz.[16]

One hopes that Berlioz was not here adjusting to his reader, for if the words are insincere then they are contemptible. Nor does maintaining his dignity against a slightly vulgar aristocrat seem to be the issue: Berlioz was the poorest judge in the world of women. His dependence on them for love and sympathy, his inability to detect coarseness exposed him to one degrading relationship after another. His second wife, worse than his first, did him incalculable harm with her fishwife tongue and if he hadn't disgraced himself over *Tannhäuser,* she would have done it for him. The sad fact is that the only woman of any respectability who ever gave him the affectionate encouragement he craved, who in her overheated fashion did uphold his artist's dignity, was Carolyne. And he responded by pouring out his heart to her. The Wittgenstein letters are the best and sometimes the only source for his intimate feelings in these years. Her praise may have been sickening. "You tell me things at such a pitch that you seem to be treating me like a vain and credulous child to whom one promises that the angels in heaven will come down and bring him toys and candy" is the nearest he came to a rebuke. He wasn't at all in love with her or she with him but I think it possible that if they had met at another junction her blandishments might have hooked him as effectively as they did Liszt, and that it was some consciousness of this that disposed her in his favor. Though no woman can have been less the coquette, she would have been inhuman if the atmosphere of devoted admiration with which Berlioz surrounded her had left her indifferent; the implication that she had mothered his masterpiece was impossible to withstand. (Even Liszt didn't quite do that for her.) Add to this her Polish preference for France and an antipathy to Germans, and her choice of Berlioz over Wagner needs no further elaboration.

Her inability to transfer this bias to Liszt remains something of an enigma, since his leanings ought to have been in the same direction. Not only was Berlioz his oldest friend, they had much more in common musically than was the case with Wagner. They shared a country of the imagination. *Faust, Hamlet, Tasso, Heroïde funèbre,* the *Christus* Oratorio, all have antecedents in Berlioz or touch his mind at some point; and while harmonically dissimilar, their orchestration is alike in its textural transparency as opposed to Wagner's steamy impasto. The symphonic poem is obviously more nearly related to Berlioz's *genre instrumental expressif* than to the *Gesamtkunstwerk.* One could go on: both are essentially aristocratic composers, Wagner a pleb; theirs is a Mediterranean mythology, his the forest-dweller's. Nevertheless, Liszt stood firm against Berlioz over Wagner. In later life he denied that it had even come to an outright dispute. "Without any silly personal quarrel, the burning question of Wagner's art led to coolness between Berlioz and myself," he said, and that was all he said. There must have been more than that. Berlioz remembered "appalling arguments" at Weimar in 1856, and that is the year when personal communication between them stopped, when Carolyne began to play Wall. "Tell Berlioz that I am still fondly attached to him. . . ." "Tell Liszt . . ." The messages are warm, but still messages conveyed through a third person.

Barzun sees it as an outright case of desertion. "Liszt abandoned Berlioz's side to support Wagner's opposite system." [17] Aside from the distressing implication that those are schoolboys choosing "sides," we know that Wagner's system struck Liszt as totally irrelevant. His view of Wagner was contained in a single sentence: "You are and remain *an immense musician*" (the italics are Liszt's), and that was all he asked that Berlioz acknowledge.* We have seen his refusal to convert Weimar into Wagner's exclusive forum. At no time could Berlioz with any justice claim to have been elbowed aside.

The exception was *Les Troyens*. This opera and its misfortunes surely had more to do with Berlioz's estrangement from Liszt than has been realized. Curiously, Liszt took only the most tepid interest in it. One could argue that because the Baths of Caracalla are not too overpowering a setting for it, there was no point in discussing it for Weimar. (Nor was it ready for production until several years after Liszt's resignation.) But the same objections applied to the *Ring* cycle. A pettier man might also have been revenging himself for Berlioz's lifetime of neglect with a calculated lassitude. But that doesn't fit Liszt's character. Barzun offers the explanation that although he read the libretto "with delight," he had to "trust his friend's genius for the musical richness of the whole" because unable to penetrate Berlioz's scores except in rehearsal and "by ear." [18] Wagner's scores on the other hand "had the great advantage of being readable and transcribable on the piano." This can't mean quite what it says. Liszt, the master reader, transcriber of Berlioz for more than thirty years, unable to make his way through an operatic score? No — it can only have been one of those instances where the sympathies for some reason fail: the long-awaited novel that abruptly disappoints, say. He simply didn't believe in this opera and we will never know exactly why. His only comment on it (made to Brendel) is a model of strangled restraint. "Berlioz," he wrote, "was so good as to send me the printed piano score of his opera *Les Troyens*. Although for Berlioz's works piano editions are plainly a decep-

---

* Equally mistaken is Barzun's statement that Wagner in 1859 was "a new companion-in-arms," that Berlioz knew "Liszt was bestirring himself on Wagner's behalf," but not that "for two decades to come it would be an exclusive apostolate." (*Romantic Century*: II, 167.) Liszt of course had been working for Wagner since 1849, and 1859 marks the end, not the beginning, of this apostolate.

tion, yet a cursory reading . . . has made an uncommonly powerful impression on me. One cannot deny that there is enormous power in it, and it certainly is not wanting in delicacy – I might also say subtlety – of feeling." [19] This "cursory reading" seems to have been his first glimpse of it – six years after the first discussion at the Altenburg. Clearly he hadn't seen, or asked to see, the work in progress.

It is impossible that his withdrawal of interest should have been taken as calmly as Berlioz appeared to take it – appeared, but I think did not. Far more than the quarrel over Wagner's merits, it was, I believe, the real basis for Berlioz's insensate opposition to the music of the future. Put another way, he might just have swallowed Wagner if Liszt had also made a cause of *Les Troyens*. When he didn't, Berlioz attacked – not only Wagner but Liszt as well. The *Non Credo* strikes at both, which was well understood at the time. (Joachim later confessed that it had incited his contribution to the *Manifesto*.) The review of the *Tristan* Prelude, for example, cannot be disentangled from an adverse opinion about Liszt: ". . . without any theme but a sort of chromatic moan, filled, however, with dissonances the cruelty of which is increased by long appoggiature that take the place of the real note of the harmony," etc., is either a direct reference to what everybody else has long since observed and that Wagner as good as admitted when he said, "my treatment of harmony has become very different from what it was before my acquaintance with Liszt's compositions," – or Berlioz was stone deaf. The so-called *Tristan* chord, the most famous in nineteenth-century music, occurred almost note for note in Liszt's song *Ich möchte hingehen*, composed ten years earlier, which is conceivably coincidence. If so, it is unimportant: the whole opera is so infused with a Lisztian presence that Wagner's latest and best biographer flatly calls it "an unrestrained Lisztian symphonic poem with vocal parts." * It is asking too much to believe that Berlioz's acute ear did not inform him of this, and much too much that Liszt did not interpret the criticism correctly. He might, and perhaps did, very reasonably assume that when Berlioz singled out *Tristan* for special disapprobation, he was belaboring his old benefactor with intentional force.

Nothing occurred after 1860 to dispel that impression. Berlioz's last chance to do something for Liszt came in 1866, when the *Graner* Mass, the first of Liszt's orchestral works to be done in France, was performed at St. Eustache. Though technically retired from the *Débats*, Berlioz had only to

---

* There are many parallels of this kind in their music – between *Valkyrie* and the *Faust* Symphony; between themes in Liszt's *Excelsior!* (1874) and *Parsifal* (1882), the latter noticed by the composers themselves and commemorated by another repeat in Liszt's threnody, *Am Grabe Richard Wagners* (1883). Searle feels that such "reminiscence-hunting is of little value" – and of course in a way it is: Liszt also learned from Wagner. The derivations seem pertinent here largely because they underline the impossibility of Berlioz's having overlooked Liszt's influence when he came down on *Tristan*.

raise his voice to be heard. He fell back on his well-worn device of letting d'Ortigue write the review he couldn't endure to put on paper. Meanwhile, he walked out of a gathering for whom Liszt was going through a transcription of the Mass, and he let it be known that here was "a negation of art." The similarity to the Brahms-Joachim phrasing, as to that of every other reactionary who had ever attacked a modern composer, is so startling that it is a wonder he didn't choke on it. Thirty years at hard labor, a thousand evenings of reviewing Boieldieu, Thomas, Adam, Limnander, Boisselot, Villebranche, Clapisson, Castinel, Déjazet, Grizet and other musical grocers too numerous to list — Berlioz's years in the galleys came down to this: he couldn't write a decent review, or any review at all, of his two greatest contemporaries.

Berlioz's relations with Wagner aren't hard to analyze, once you accept the envy of a proud and disappointed man, and their instinctive antagonisms. But what did he finally feel about Liszt, closer to him in every way than Wagner could ever be? A great deal of resentment certainly. Sold on the idea that Liszt had abandoned him for his worst enemy, ignorant of Liszt's sufferings at the hands of his German incubus, he nourished a grudge that suited his nature. We all have our defense against the misfortunes inflicted by life or our own mismanagement. Wagner's was a cold-blooded avarice: "All I want is money. . . ." Liszt's was a defiant worldliness and a retreat to Mother Church. Berlioz's was a titanic gloom — "I am surrounded by lunatics," he wrote in 1861 — all-is-lost. After fifty, his health declined at a terrifying rate; he became an old man, body and soul.

Yet he knew that Liszt when all was said had never really failed him, and that in any scale of justice the weight was all on Liszt's side. This made him hang his head. Their meetings after 1860 were shrouded in a kind of shame probably deepened by Liszt's compassion. They dined together in 1861 in Paris. Liszt reported to Carolyne that *Les Troyens* had little chance of being put on at the Opera — this was after *Tannhäuser* — because Berlioz had quarrelled with the director:

"*Voilà*," says Berlioz, "the grain of sand I must struggle with. All the press is for me, numberless friends push me forward and support me. . . . I have the honor of dining with H.M. the Emperor — but none of that is any good! M. Royer doesn't want me. . . .[20]

This bluster didn't deceive Liszt. Berlioz's article on Wagner had injured him as much as it had Wagner, he wrote, and "his home life weighs on him like a nightmare . . . [while] outside it, he meets with nothing but obstacles and mortifications . . . he now habitually speaks in a low voice — and all his being seems inclined toward the tomb. . . . In fact, he has neither friends nor partisans — neither the sun of public favor nor the sweet shade of intimacy." It could have been Berlioz's epitaph.

Chapter 40

IN 1860, Weimar celebrated Liszt's birthday with a torchlight procession and made him an honorary citizen. He was unmoved. "I am as *dépaysé* as ever," he wrote a friend. "If I have spent a dozen years here it is because I have been sustained by a feeling not wanting in nobility — the honor, dignity and great character of a woman to safeguard against infamous persecutions — and beyond that, a grand idea: that of the renewal of music . . . a development more free and . . . *more adequate* to the spirit of the times." [1] That seems clear, except for the circumstances. In 1860, his resignation was two years old, and while he had conducted a number of his own works with the orchestra, and the Grand Duke was personally cordial, his official duties were at an end: he had no professional reason for remaining in Weimar. Still less was he detained by duty to Carolyne for she was in Rome, the last stop on the *via dolorosa* of her divorce. If he was stalled in Weimar — and he was alone in the Altenburg for some eighteen months — it was because he had reached an impasse, one of life's waiting rooms. With Carolyne it was in fact all over; musically he was entering a new phase (there was of course a connection between the two); but as he knew neither of these things for certain, he couldn't act.

Carolyne always maintained that she lost him in those eighteen months. Adelheid von Schorn, who knew her as well as anyone in Weimar did, writes:

I feel it my duty to repeat what the Princess assured me and others in tones of the utmost sincerity and deepest sorrow, that during the period when they

386

were separated . . . Liszt became indifferent; the thought of a legal union with her no longer appealed to him as a necessity. . . . He was of course ready at any time to go to the altar with her; but her womanly feelings told her that if he did so, it would only be to fulfill a duty. And she never spoke to him of marriage again.[2]

But would it ever have been anything but a duty? References to marriage are so few and far between in his letters, so reluctant when they do occur that together with his known views on the subject they add up to a decided negative.

Yet there was a time, in 1850–1851, when he might have undertaken it with good grace. Carolyne's arthritis confined her for many months in a little spa called Eilsen, where Magnolet also fell ill with typhoid. Worried about both of them, he showered them with loving letters and one or two of these express the hope that there will be "a reversal of opinion in your regard . . . [if] they rob you a little more and [if] you marry a poor beggar like me." He visited often at Eilsen, where they seem to have been especially happy — pacing at leisure under *allées* of trees and discussing the Chopin book, happy too in love, in the physical sense that is generally absent from his letters to her. Four years later, he caught sight of Eilsen from a train window: "The valley was like a crater still smoking with our love," he wrote.[3] Alas, the scorched imagery was painfully apt. The train was carrying him to Düsseldorf where he had a rendezvous with another woman.

Marie d'Agoult, who watched the Altenburg with the frantic vigilance of a cat at a mousehole, also had information in the winter of 1850–1851 that made her think a marriage imminent. "Liszt's marriage certain, what a future for me!" says a note in her journal, news that can't of course have been based on the realities of Carolyne's situation, with which Marie was unfamiliar. The following summer, she breathed more easily: "The Weimar marriage won't come off." In 1853, she dispatched her own agent to see how the land lay. This was a young man called Carlos Davila, who purportedly wanted Liszt's consent to his marrying Blandine. He stayed long enough at the Altenburg to compile a report that may have been tailored to his audience but that is confirmed elsewhere: Carolyne's love was a visible burden on Liszt, who was going gray and looked emaciated. Others agree that he was bound hand and foot by her homage. We hear of her kneeling to light his cigars; Cornelius winced at her cry, "Is that you, my angel?" if he stirred in the next room.

How unfair it all is from a woman's point of view. Marie d'Agoult lost him because she denied the god within. Carolyne, worshipping the ground he trod on, fared better but not much. He deceived her too, if far more discreetly. Agnes Klindworth, his secret love all those years, came to

Weimar in 1853 and lived there until 1855, after which she moved to Brussels — where Liszt contrived to see her quite often as well as meeting her in various cities in Germany. She was a cousin of the pianist Karl Klindworth, was either widowed or divorced, with two small sons, and in her only published portrait is a handsome young woman with spaniel curls and huge, well-drawn eyes. That is really all we know about her beyond the volume of Liszt's letters to her — discreetly labelled "to a friend" though it is obvious she was more than that. She was as mute as Liszt about their relations, so much so that Wagner, introduced to her in Brussels in 1860, was confused about who she was, "the daughter, or some said the wife," of Councillor of State Klindworth, retired diplomat. He got that straightened out (she was the daughter) but seems not to have guessed her connection with Liszt.

The letters to Agnes are those of an older, infinitely harassed man indulging himself in the sympathies of a much younger woman in no position to make demands on him. Agnes, one can gather, had troubles of her own; she was poor and had to teach for a living (the move to Brussels apparently had something to do with this); frankly he didn't want to hear about it: "Don't lament too much the uncertainty of your fate; however painful it may be, your head will always have a place to rest in my heart." [4] More than once he counselled stoicism — "You know my motto. . . ." — which didn't prevent him from painting his own miseries in vivid colors though the cause is left indistinct: "Such a weight has pressed on me for the last eight days that it has seemed to me impossible to go on living" [5] is typical.

The consciousness of double-dealing makes some men cruel. In Liszt it manifested itself in a kind of emotional hypochondria. He flogged himself with Carolyne's virtues, with the magnitude of her sacrifice. If we are to believe him (and all the other self-proclaimed weepers of the nineteenth century: Wagner and Berlioz were always in floods), a book, a landscape, a new moon, almost anything could reduce him to tears, but especially anything connected with her.

Liszt to Carolyne, Pest, 1856: My heart began to weep at the [Hungarian] frontier, when I saw one of those simple tableaux of a shepherd grouped . . . with his sheep and cows. . . . My heart flew lovingly, like a wounded pigeon, toward you, my good angel — toward your peasants, your fields, your Podolia, your sunrises, your still days that burned your soul with so ardent a fire. Dear, adored, unique one, you abandoned all that for me . . . who am no more than a vacillating shadow, who can give you nothing, do nothing for you.[6]

The more he felt his bad faith, the more he idealized *ma bonne ange* while lamenting his own insufficiency. "This need to be *something* to *somebody* is a wound of my youth that has never healed," he wrote bitterly to Agnes.[7]

He had, he said, always known that he must keep clear of "family senti-ments, property, establishments," and he quoted Byron: "Whatever sky's above me . . ." but it was a feeble cry, like a message scribbled on a prison wall. He knew he was in for it.

Liszt to Wagner, March 1855: Whether the great political event, the death of the Tsar, will have a softening effect on my personal fate, remains questionable. In a few weeks, I will have direct news. Whatever it turns out to be, I cannot waver or hesitate.[8]

The death of Nicholas I perhaps did hasten Wittgenstein's civil divorce, which was granted that year. In Liszt's distractingly vague terminology, the "Catholic consistories in Russia" further issued an annulment in 1860, which if I read him rightly, the Vatican considered invalid. He quotes the Pope as saying: "It is an opinion, not a judgment."[9] Both he and Carolyne have given the impression that a malign cabal was at work against her, and this is supposed to have included the Hohenlohes, Magnolet's in-laws.* On the other hand, no one behaved more oddly than Liszt himself. In 1861, he was saying that for several months there had been no further religious obstacles to the marriage but that "reasons of propriety and foresight" might necessitate "an indefinite adjournment."[10] He noted with triumph his checking of the Grand Duke's inquiries. Why, Carl Alexander wanted to know, didn't they just get a priest and make an end of it "now that every-thing was settled"? *Liszt:* That would be very dangerous. *Carl Alexander:* But what will happen then? *Liszt:* We must wait! (And he actually refused an offer of one of the royal castles for the ceremony.)[11]

Meanwhile, it would surely have been kinder to state his feelings clearly, before Carolyne set so much noisy machinery in motion. He couldn't do it — mostly because he loved her in his odd way but also for the less honorable reason that his reputation was in her hands. She alone could give the lie to

* Cardinal Hohenlohe was her brother-in-law, and Carolyne certainly believed he had intervened in some way. A long and garbled letter she wrote him in 1877 forgives him on the ground that he thought he was acting for the best when "certain Poles, whose names and motives . . . I will not disclose," represented to him that her marriage to Liszt would be a scandal. "I found this out first from the Holy Father himself. . . . I heard it also from you, my dear Eminence. . . . Enough — although it looked as though your previous measures against me were taken with the intention of saving your brother from the misfortune of having a mother-in-law who was no longer a princess, I know for certain that this wasn't your dominant motive . . ." (*Zwei Menschenalter:* p. 84). Against that, Hohenlohe was Liszt's best friend for the last thirty years of his life. It was he who arranged for Liszt to occupy apartments in the Villa d'Este. This doesn't of course preclude his having tried to stop the marriage not for the reasons given above but because he knew Liszt did not want to marry — and the *mauvaises langues* said as much. I am inclined to doubt it. Hohenlohe and Liszt had only just gotten to know each other at the time of the divorce and Liszt wouldn't have confided in him to that extent. Let us say simply that Liszt didn't resent any steps that the Cardinal may have taken against the divorce.

the destructive stories that marred his good name: *she* would never write a *Nélida*. He exploited her perhaps but who would not prefer to be taken at his own valuation?

Liszt to Carolyne, February 1861: My life has been a long odyssey, if you will allow the comparison, in love. It has been my nature to love — and up to now, alas, I have loved badly but . . . I have never loved what was bad. . . . My danger is this need for I don't know what intensity of feeling, which leads me easily into paradox in matters of the intelligence and into intemperance in the use of strong drink. . . .[12]

Carolyne knew his vices, of which the worst to her were laziness and the inability to keep away from "the salons, the open pianos, and the thousand tasks imposed by large towns" — as he put it. In that respect but in no other she set up to be his conscience. She never censured his morals or questioned his sincerity, as Marie had. She was, and remained, a prop to his pride he couldn't well have dispensed with. If the price was a permanent legal tie, he would pay it but the effect on his nerves of the prolonged struggle over the divorce was worse than on hers. She had hope to sustain her.

By the summer of 1855 the strain was telling. He was working like one possessed. In a few months he composed the *Graner* Mass, the *Dante* Symphony, the settings for Psalm 13 and the Beatitudes, the organ Prelude and Fugue on B.A.C.H., a number of songs; he published half a dozen articles — all this in addition to his work in the theatre. (We hear, for example, of a five-hour rehearsal of *Tannhäuser*.) The Grand Duke was so worried at his haggard looks that he urged him to take time off in one of the many royal retreats. Liszt wouldn't hear of it. The "inner griefs and outer vexations" he complained of to Agnes if anything drove him to work still harder and it was Carolyne who took a holiday, in Berlin.

Liszt to Agnes, July 15, 1855: I have much urged this visit because Weimar offers very little at the moment. Happily the curiosity and passionate interest the Princess takes in works of art have lately reawakened in her. . . . This will do her more good than walks in our park and sterile correspondence.

Happily indeed, if it was so. She did fancy herself a connoisseur. She returned from Berlin with portfolios of sketches, Kaulbach's for *The Battle of the Huns,* Schwind's for the St. Elizabeth frescoes that were installed in the Wartburg at Eisenach that summer. Later she purchased a little Delacroix in Paris and commissioned Ary Scheffer to paint Magnolet. Like Marie, she was a tireless examiner of artifacts and no doubt enjoyed the little trips she was increasingly urged to take, though she would surely have enjoyed them more if Liszt had managed to accompany her, and there is a presentiment here of the Roman years when she spun her *Histoire de l'Église* into a Penelope's task (but that there were no suitors), Liszt always assuring everybody that she was perfectly happy and the Roman climate so good for her. She had fortitude and dutifully followed Liszt's suggestions that she make a detour through Belgium to see the Rubenses, visit Chartres, prolong her stays here or there. It can't have been cheerful work.

In this atmosphere of mounting tension the children re-entered his life. In May, Marie wrote to say that the ancient Mme Patersi was failing and some other arrangement desirable for the girls. She proposed that he come to Paris for forty-eight hours to discuss the question, assuring him he wouldn't regret the time given to "affections both lively and deep" and pathetically she sealed her letter with a device designed for her in Geneva — a rhododendron blossom circled with her motto: *In alta solitudine.* Far from touching his heart, this reminder of the past put him into a rage so out of proportion to the cause that it may tell us more than anything else about the state of affairs in the Altenburg. Even at this late date, his emotional temperature can to some extent be taken from his letters to Marie. When all is well he can write casually, collectedly. When it isn't, she is the first to suffer. To her suggestion that he come to Paris he replied icily that no such interview seemed necessary. However, if she thought it was, she was at liberty to come to Weimar: "You are freer of your time than I am . . . and will cause no inconvenience." The thirty-hour trip might even be agreeable. In any case, "I will be only too happy to contribute to the efficacy . . . of your maternal sentiments." [13]

This invitation was not of course accepted and it would have done no good if it had been because he had already made up his mind to remove Blandine and Cosima finally and forever from her vicinity. Once again, Carolyne gets the blame for the really bizarre decision to place them with Mme von Bülow, Hans's mother, in Berlin, and once again, she may not deserve it. If jealousy of Marie really drove her to the pitch we are told it did, the obvious move was to get them to the Altenburg and make the conquest of their affections that would have been so easy. They were ready to love her — to love anyone who would give them access to their father. As it was, they gave her the benefit of every doubt, and on the whole preferred her to their mother. For these children, though dazzled by Marie in her gorgeous Paris setting, never learned to respect her. *"Elle est trop digne pour être digne de nous,"* [14] said Daniel. (Roughly: She is too proud to be worthy of us.) "We are all three too good for her, we have that from Papa." Liszt's bastards must, after all, have read *Nélida* too. "You tell me," wrote Daniel to Blandine in 1859, "that you have completely detached yourself from the grandeurs of Mimi [their name for her]. There nature made a real copy of Goethe minus the genius and sooner or later you were bound to break with her. . . ." [15] Blandine in fact loathed her mother, "who was never a mother," and Cosima, though slower than the other two to make a case of it, did not like her either. None of them saw Carolyne as the villainess of the piece. Daniel, who spent the summer vacation of 1854 at the Altenburg without his sisters, didn't find her an enemy; and his reports, avidly read in rue Casimir-Perier, had weight. To the girls, Weimar remained the promised land. And the one who excluded them from it wasn't Carolyne but Liszt himself. "I neither can nor wish to have them under my roof," he told Agnes, and the first person singular has a convincing ring.

Children are supposed to know instinctively who loves them, which ought to have ruled out Liszt as well as Marie. Like Jove in a thundercloud he hurled anathemas at them, and like a god was worshipped in spite of his capricious cruelty. The only objections to the Berlin plan came from Anna, who was indignant.

Anna Liszt to Liszt, August 1855: I am so upset since hearing the latest decision about Blandine and Cosima ten days ago. The Princess told me about it with the greatest indifference, that they would be sent to Berlin under the charge of Madame de Bülow. . . . I could find nothing to say except that they are too big for another change. The Princess replied that otherwise there would never be an end to Madame d'Agoult's scribblings, as she has been impertinent to you for some time past. . . . The children are good, and must be guided by love, for they have proud, sensitive hearts. Madame de Bülow seems . . . a kindly disposed woman, but to send the children away to Prussia on account of their mother! [16]

Carolyne's "indifference" may have been in the eye of an angry beholder. No more than Anna would she have appreciated an action of Liszt's solely dictated by his feeling, whether of love or hatred, the two being dangerously close, for Marie. And if she and Liszt were in perfect accord on this matter, what was she doing in Paris? She left the day before Blandine and Cosima, still unconscious of their fate and imagining that they were only making the longed-for visit to the Altenburg, arrived in Weimar. Liszt's letters to her during the six weeks she stayed away are confused and irritable, implying a quarrel. Meticulously she looked up every last one of his French friends, and he wasn't pleased. Such a strange idea to call on Heine — "it wouldn't have occurred to me." (Neither of them can have known that Heine, all but blind and strung like a skeleton on ropes that were his only means of moving his ravaged body, was dying one of the most horrible deaths known to literature — Watch out for him, he's a bit of a Jew and a hack, said Liszt, one of his very few anti-Semitic remarks.) As for Sand: "I don't know what line she'll take with you. She gets on her high horse rather easily." *

---

* This strange circuit of Liszt's former Paris circle is poorly documented from the French end. Her only established conquest — aside from Berlioz, already an old friend

Bory, whose book *Liszt et ses enfants* is the authority on this subject, interprets Carolyne's abrupt exit from Weimar as a fit of conscience. Having engineered their exile, she couldn't face the girls. This doesn't square with her "indifference" to what happened to them, or with Liszt's often reiterated statement, which they seem to have agreed with, that she had a genuinely maternal feeling for them. I think it *could* have been conscience, but of another kind. She could just as well have disapproved of Liszt's arrangements, thought it wrong of him not to have told his daughters what was in store for them — and since she never opposed him outright, simply have removed herself from the scene.

Whatever led up to it, the visit was a kind of cataclysm, for Liszt, for everybody. It destroyed once and for all — and this was, of course, why he resisted it for so many years — the barrier he had painstakingly built between France and Germany, the past in whose name he had made them grow up without him and the precarious present. Long ago, he had mastered the art of dividing his life into compartments — that was one of the secrets of his survival: when one became untenable, he slammed the door. Now a door burst open.

French in language, manners and education, the children turned his drawing room into a suburb of Paris. Their mother's salon had accustomed them to the society of men like Renan and taught the girls how to dress; Mme Patersi had given them formidable educations; and with all this they were still young enough to romp like children. Liszt was beyond words charmed and exasperated. He couldn't look at them without acknowledging the chemistry of parenthood: "They are at once papa and mama." The reference was to *mes fillettes,* a much worse bother to him than the quiet, studious Daniel, about whom he never had much to say.* He was proud that they had already received offers of marriage, huffy that nobody suited them. "What they want for a husband is something like a Beethoven or a Raphael who is also a millionaire. . . . In the meantime I have sent them for a walk with Miss Anderson." [17] He complained of their racket: "They have invented a new form of government, the rule of noise," and he grumbled when they woke him at dawn. Such were the cavils of the man who a few weeks earlier had welcomed the unruly Tausig into his house without a qualm.

— was Delacroix. His journal for August 26 says: "Had a visit from that attractive woman the Princess of Wittgenstein and her daughter, the one for whom Liszt commissioned a drawing: I am to see them again, and dine with them on Tuesday" (*Journal:* p. 290).

* This excellent boy, who won every available scholastic prize at the Lycée Bonaparte and was the perfect son, who might have made a brilliant career at almost anything if he had lived, makes one wonder why anyone would have wanted to claim Liszt for a father. Much good it would have done them.

An unpleasant task remained to be performed. "*Les fillettes* don't care about settling in Berlin," he wrote, which was putting it mildly. "I hope that having sent them to the thirty thousand devils for their illogical arguments . . . they will end by being completely convinced of the sincerity and wisdom of my solicitude . . . for they have a great fund of tenderness for me." Tenderness or not, they were aghast to learn that they were to live in Prussia with Mme von Bülow, whom they thought an absolute fool — which she was.

In France, the repercussions were fearful. Marie did not know the Berlin plan. It was sufficient that the girls had been enticed to Weimar, where she very reasonably thought they were going to live, and which she took as the ultimate and insulting rebuff to overtures it must have shamed her to think of. In her frenzy she dashed off a set of letters to Blandine that were somehow left behind in the Paris apartment, where Mme Patersi found them. She gave them to Carolyne, who posted them to Liszt. With shocking indelicacy, all three of these unauthorized persons read them. Worse, Liszt undertook to answer them — not by writing direct to Marie but to his girls, as if they were responsible for their mother's words. The document he sent them was in that light inexcusable. It is also invaluable to the biographer because it reveals as nothing else does the subterranean link that always existed between his hatred of Marie and his submission to Carolyne, and the injured pride that played so large a part in both. He must have destroyed Marie's originals. But since he copied word for word the offending passages, and answered them as if in a courtroom, we know what she said. A sample is enough:

Marie: "They waited until I was out of the way to make you do something contrary to honor." *Liszt:* "Nobody dreamed of waiting until Mme d'A . . . was out of the way. . . . This trip was I think as much your [i.e., the children's] desire as mine. . . . I simply waited for Daniel's vacation . . . to reunite you three under the roof where I live. This house being, as you know, very spacious, has many floors and some thirty rooms. *Madame la Princesse* lives on the first floor, with her daughter. Up till now, the most distinguished persons have deemed it an *honor* to be admitted to it. . . ." *Marie:* "You will eat the bread of a *stranger* . . . who is not and never will be your father's wife. I would rather see you work for a living, or begging. . . ." *Liszt:* "From your birth until this day, your mother has never had the least concern in the *bread* you eat, the *place* you live, etc. Though she has always enjoyed a considerable income, she has thought fit to spend it on her personal pleasure, and to leave me, for nineteen years, the *entire* charge of providing for your needs and your education. . . . I note in passing that the expression *work for a living* is the supreme example of aristocratic democracy." *Marie:* "Tell your father that you don't want to live in luxury when you have no fortune. . . ." *Liszt:* "You must gather from your mother than I am preparing a series of ignominies that your conscience must oppose! . . . As to luxury, I dare say that the house in the Champs Elysées is far ahead of the Altenburg. . . ." *Marie:* "In heaven or hell, I am yours and you are mine." *Liszt:* "Allow me, dear children, not to accept this alternative in your behalf. As to the rights of possession that Mme d'A . . . claims, I can only repeat to you what I said in this room. . . . I would not undertake to dispute the affections of any of my children. . . . If you find, when it is all added up, that the share should be equal between one who has fulfilled his duties with conscience and devotion and one who forgot or betrayed them under a specious exterior, I will make no objection and when you attain your majority, you can freely make the choice that suits you. . . ." *Marie:* "Oh, my proud children, always keep your pride." *Liszt:* "This is a singularly imprudent apostrophe. . . . If you were only proud, you would have to blush at your mother's outbursts and ill feelings. Since she wishes me evil at all costs and on all occasions, and since she can strike neither at my position nor my conscience, she takes pleasure in injuring me in your affection, and in the respect and deep love that I hold, as the purest flame in my life, for a woman who ought also to be *sacred* to you on account of the devotion she has so nobly shown me in the afflictions, sacrifices and incessantly renewed griefs of the past nine years. . . ." [18] *

This savage dialogue reached the girls shortly after they arrived in Berlin and strangely enough had exactly the effect desired. The Patersi's odious espionage, their father's base action in reading their mail, were overlooked and they stopped communicating with Marie. Further to please their father, they even did their best to adjust to Berlin and the pretentious Mme von Bülow.

Berlin isn't an appealing city and certainly not to Parisians. Moreover, as they quickly discovered, it had never been friendly to Liszt's compositions. Mme von Bülow was intimate with the Arnims and through them with the Joachim circle, which Cosima perceived to be inimical — though Liszt didn't yet know it. She wrote a mocking description of Joachim trailed by sycophants enquiring after Clara Schumann: " '*Wie geht es Frau Schumann? Wie haben sie Frau Schumann verlassen?*' Schumann here, Schumann there, it's enough to give you nightmares." [19] They survived in fact by the strategy of private mockery. Blandine was an accomplished mimic of accents and mannerisms and both girls had a vivid dramatic sense. Discussing them with Mme von Bülow, Liszt spoke of their "bumptiousness and feverish vanity," and undoubtedly they had enough of both to make them unpopular. Blandine didn't care. She had no intention of living her life among

---

* This letter should serve to refute the frequently repeated idea that Carolyne supervised and/or dictated Liszt's letters to his children, and even to Marie. Except that it is harsher than usual, it is of a piece with his habitual tone, and it was written when she was out of the house.

Prussians and fled to Paris a year later. For Cosima it was different. Her scorn for Germany and all things German wore away when fate presented her with a German husband.

"*Ce poouvre Henns*" — thus Cosima reproduced Mme von Bülow's French accent and incidentally her hysterical attitude to her son, whose musical career still seemed to her a disgrace. (A cartoon in a Berlin paper depicting him as Sancho Panza to Liszt's Don Quixote upset her terribly: "What a dishonor!" "But, Madame," said Cosima, "my father is there too." "Oh, your father, that is something else," the good lady replied.) [20] Bülow was at this time twenty-five years old, battling enthusiastically for the music of the future, and making enemies right and left. He often seemed ripe for a nervous breakdown. When the audience hissed his conducting of the *Tannhäuser* Overture, he fainted away — an incident that precipitated his engagement to Cosima. Returning home at two in the morning, he found her waiting up for him and instantly proposed. But of course he had fallen in love with her on sight.

Bülow to Liszt: Till now it would have been impossible for me to write in view of the stupefaction, admiration and even exaltation to which they have reduced me, especially the younger. As to their musical dispositions, it is not talent but genius that they possess. They are certainly the daughters of my benefactor — completely exceptional beings. I busy myself rather consistently with their musical education in so far as they are not too superior to me in force of intelligence, delicacy of taste, etc. . . . How moved and touched I was to recognize you, *ipsissimum Lisztum,* in the playing of Mademoiselle Cosima for the first time! [21]

It has been said that Liszt had some such marriage in mind when he imported his daughters to Germany and he did tell Agnes Klindworth that they might do better there for husbands than in Paris. He also loved Bülow like a son, or in his case, better than a son. But about this particular marriage he had his doubts. Bülow's "migraines and rheumatisms," "inexplicable lack of confidence in your own superiority," worried him. He might have withheld his consent if the young people hadn't been so determined and if Marie hadn't unexpectedly opposed the marriage too. "Cosima, child of genius, is very like her father . . . she has the *inner demon* and will always make any sacrifice that it demands. Circumstances have pushed her into a marriage in which, I think, there will be happiness for no one." [22] She wanted Cosima to make a career at the piano, which Liszt was absolutely against, and this time she was right. Without having met Bülow, she guessed that Cosima wasn't in love with him. She wished to marry; Bülow was Liszt's favorite pupil; she was the master's daughter. It was all much too pat, as Liszt himself saw. He made Bülow wait two years for "*ma terrible fille*" but in the end he gave her away. They were married August 8, 1857, in his presence.

Bülow to Liszt: It is impossible for me to express fully the feelings of gratitude and devotion which I have in thinking of the further happiness I owe you, as I already owe all the happiness that has come to me . . . from Weimar.[23]

It was Bülow's idea that they spend their honeymoon with his other benefactor. He took his bride to Zurich, to the Asyl, where Wagner beat his leather wings at them. This was *poouvre Henns's* first mistake. He was to make others, but trusting Wagner was the worst.

Two months later, on October 22, her father's birthday, Blandine married Émile Ollivier in Florence.* Liszt became very fond of this son-in-law, a young southerner, "intelligent and *passionné*, with a rare and charming feeling for music, which is to say that he likes mine," who renewed his ties to France. It was a mutual esteem. Though originally Marie's friend, Ollivier turned against her after a nuptial visit paid to the Altenburg in 1858. Impressed with that household, moved by Liszt's person as well as his music, he responded coldly to the grilling Marie gave him after his return to Paris. Feigning concern about the attacks on Liszt in the German press and reports of instability in his relations with Carolyne, she prodded Ollivier for confirmation and did not get it. "Obviously," wrote Ollivier, "she would be enchanted if we were to side against him and take the view of a public that can't know what we know." [24] Thereafter the Olliviers were entirely in Liszt's camp and scarcely saw Marie though they lived in the same city with her. (It is interesting that Bülow's reaction should have been exactly the opposite. Meeting Marie for the first time, in Zurich in 1858, he was stunned by her beauty, "dignity and nobility of bearing . . . a fine, elegant, *laissez-aller.* . . . I must not think of it, lest I break out into a rage at the parodistic caricature which at the present moment acts as the shadow to his light at the Altenburg.") [25]

With these marriages, alliances that promised honor and respectability to his formerly almost clandestine family and to himself all the support that active and devoted sons-in-law can give, a new prospect seems to open on Liszt, with his fiftieth birthday approaching, a measure of stability to be within his grasp. A picture photographs itself on the mind: the drawing room at the Altenburg, Liszt seated, Carolyne standing with a doting hand on his shoulder; Blandine and Cosima share a sofa and gaze in his direction; Daniel and the sons-in-law (frock-coated) stand respectfully; grandchildren are disposed on the carpet. The time: circa 1870. The Altenburg has become a shrine and Liszt evolved into the artist-patriarch. He will grow old

* The circumstances are rather obscure. Blandine returned to Paris in 1856 and it isn't clear how or with whom she lived. Marie didn't offer her a home — they were on poor terms. But the following summer she suddenly took the girl to Italy, where they were joined by Ollivier. Marie had known him for several years; Blandine may or may not have met him before. The courtship anyway was rapid and ended in their marriage two months later. Liszt sent a hasty consent but wasn't present.

like this, as twilight descends on the nineteenth century. Almost, some such apotheosis seemed to be upon him. "How right it is," wrote Cosima in 1861, "to use the word grandiose for that personality which seems to have been made of love and inspiration. Every time I am here [Weimar] it seems to me that I am renewed, and that everything that life brings that is sad, burdensome . . . that all that vanishes and that I have come back to my homeland, to *the place* of my soul. I am consumed with incessant wishes for him; I want something great, vague, infinite. What can one wish for him that is positive? Earthly property? His great soul could only disdain it. The kingdom of heaven? But it is his." [26] But the Altenburg's days were already numbered. The photograph was never taken.

Chapter 41

NO SUCH PEACEABLE DECLINE was in store for the man who was to catch his death of cold in a train, and die in lodgings, in a strange bed. Ahead of him was another twenty-five years of travel, society, passion and disappointment, tragedy and occasional farce. It couldn't have been otherwise. If Daniel had not died of tuberculosis in 1859, Blandine of puerperal fever in 1862, if Cosima had eluded Wagner's clutches (or he hers), if, even, he had married Carolyne, Liszt wouldn't have achieved peace or stability. As for the Altenburg, the logical center for the orderly and productive life that to the very end he professed to desire, it lost whatever charm it had had for him the day Magnolet married her prince and drove away to Vienna, never to return.

No one seems to know how this marriage was arranged. It was unpopular with the Polish party in Vienna. Hohenlohe had fought with the Austrians in the Italian war of the previous summer — which did not put him in favor with irredentists. Carolyne surely wouldn't have chosen a son-in-law of his political stripe or meagre intellect; so it was probably Wittgenstein who was responsible. The wedding was still a curiously hole-in-corner affair, held in Weimar's Catholic church (October 15, 1859), with only the immediate family present — and for reasons unknown Liszt's friend, the Danish composer Lassen, the only one to tell us anything about the ceremony: Carolyne and Scotchy Anderson, the Child's governess, sobbed throughout — and when it was over, Carolyne left immediately for Paris. Lassen of course did not know why. He offered the opinion that the marriage might be a good thing because Carolyne could now concentrate on Liszt. Her flight rather suggests that she knew how desolating the Altenburg would be to him and didn't want to look the future in the face. A few weeks later, Liszt told Carl Alexander plainly that Marie's marriage had removed his last motive for remaining in Weimar:

Liszt to Carl Alexander: . . . The news from Petersburg about the divorce of Princess Wittgenstein demonstrates that a secret and evil power is at work. Because of this my position in Weimar becomes untenable. As long as it was a question of protecting a daughter not of age from this power, one could endure the unendurable. But now I foresee that, in spite of the pain that separation from you will cause, Monseigneur, I must as soon as possible look for a life away from Weimar.[1]

Setting aside the evil powers, and the mystery of how they could possibly render *his* position in Weimar untenable, the claim that he had protected Magnolet was fantastic: as her mother's lover he was a threat to her future and was so regarded by her Hohenlohe in-laws, whose earliest concern was to detach her from the Altenburg and everyone connected with it. And it was of course on this very account that the place had ceased to be desirable to him — as no doubt the Grand Duke, accustomed to Liszt's devious explanations, understood.

This letter was written December 5, 1859. Nine days later Daniel Liszt died in Berlin, aged twenty, of a galloping consumption. One supposes it was galloping. Liszt characteristically took no notice of it until it was terminal and the onset is not recorded. The boy had graduated, loaded with honors, from the Lycée Bonaparte in 1857, and had intended to study engineering at the Polytechnique. Probably because Marie d'Agoult approved this plan, Liszt vetoed it and ordered him to Vienna to read law instead. Though he shared, for a time, an attic with the lively Tausig, and could spend his holidays at the Altenburg or with the Bülows in Berlin, Daniel was not happy in *"ces maudits pays allemands,"* and who is to say that his disease was not partly attributable to the senseless thwarting of an ardent and affectionate nature?

He arrived in Berlin in August — to Cosima evidently and desperately ill. The Bülows nursed him devotedly for three months, but although it is impossible they didn't send alarming bulletins to Weimar, only Carolyne paid attention to them. Liszt's letter to her of December 12, the day before Daniel's death, makes it plain that it was she who was disturbed, she who insisted that he go to Berlin. "You were right to send me here," he wrote. "The doctor has no hope for him." [2] Daniel died quietly the following evening, while Liszt was napping in the next room.

Carolyne was shocked at Liszt's conduct, in particular that he had failed to get a priest to administer the sacraments; and indeed he had no adequate explanation to offer for this omission. Nor can he have been much help to Cosima, who performed the grisly last duties herself, making a sort of *chapelle ardente* and watching the body alone. "On reflection," Liszt decided not to watch with her but went back to his hotel, "recommending to Cosette not to wear out her strength." The funeral was desolating, only the three of them — Liszt, Cosima and Bülow — accompanying the coffin to a distant cemetery.

The Bülows were shattered. "Sometimes I feel my heart will burst," wrote Cosima, ". . . and then I think that he did not love life, that he suffered every moment and that he came only to touch it lightly, so to speak, and to fly to those regions which our hope makes us imagine. . . ." [3] Old Anna Liszt was brokenhearted. But Blandine noted with sarcastic despair that "Madame la Comtesse d'Agoult published at the moment of her son's death a letter on Brown in the papers. That was the only manifestation." [4] And Liszt, though shaken, certainly did not have the feelings that ordinary fathers would ascribe to him. Even the proposal for a requiem Mass had to come from Carolyne and the arrangements were made by the Vienna uncle, Edouard: the music was Terziani's *Requiem*. "When I have finished with some works that can't be postponed, Daniel shall have his requiem," wrote Liszt. [5]

Like many people who live to a ripe old age, and especially artists, Liszt was preoccupied with death in the abstract while remaining singularly immune to personal loss. I therefore rather doubt that the works always associated with the deaths of his children owe as much as we think to this source. Thus two of the three *Odes funèbres, Les Morts* and *La Notte,* are usually taken to refer to Daniel and Blandine respectively. But *Les Morts* with its quote from Lamennais ("They too have lived on this earth; they have passed down the river of time. . . .") could as well commemorate the Abbé as Daniel; and *La Notte* has no discernible connection with Blandine. If anything, it is yet another autobiographical fragment, whose main part is an orchestrated version of *Il Penseroso* (in the second *Année de pèlerinage*), and whose middle section is in Hungarian cadence. To this he affixed an epigraph from Virgil — *Dulces moriens reminiscitur Argos* — his way of saying that, like the Argive, he expected to die in Italy, far from his native land. I can see no evidence of parental anguish in either of these compositions — unless their dedication to Cosima proves something. His actions must, in any case, speak louder than his music. For the lovely Blandine he did seem to acquire a certain fondness, and her death at twenty-seven must have wrung a drop or two even from his stony heart. But poor Daniel never received a sign of affection; nor does his father's account of his end express more than a barely adequate grief — let alone the remorse that it ought to have excited.

In May 1860, Carolyne went off to Rome. Exactly what she hoped to achieve is anything but clear:

Liszt to Agnes Klindworth, May 28, 1860: The great business of [Carolyne's] life and heart has at last reached a favorable and legitimate solution . . . which would have happened *ten years* ago but for pitiful intrigues. It has been two months since the *nullity* of her marriage . . . was pronounced by the Catholic consistories in Russia . . . and countersigned by the Archbishop Metropolitan of Petersburg. . . .[6]

Presumably, as I have indicated, Rome did not agree and she wanted to press her case in person. Puzzled onlookers saw her departure with apprehension. "The Altenburg is an enigma to me," said Cornelius. "I believe the Princess will end her days where she is now," and for Liszt he feared the worst: "Liszt ought to put himself together and enter on the necessary final period of his creative work; if he does, I will follow him everywhere with love. . . . But to see him as he is now, among all these people . . ." [7]

Since all these people were musical friends and critics for the most part, they are unsatisfactory evidence for the moral collapse that Cornelius believed in progress. Liszt was perhaps drinking more than was good for him and staying up too late (Schorn confirms this), in short reverting to type. But whether this was a disaster or not depends on one's view of his mission and whether it agrees with that of middle-class Germans like Cornelius.

He entered Weimar convinced that it was his business to build big-scale masterpieces. And here it is useful to compare him with certain writers who tried to do the same thing and to whom very different standards are applied. Consider Balzac's huge, uneven output, much of it pot-boiling redeemed by genius. Balzac's repetitiousness and *grand-guignol* effects (Madame Marneff's death! Goriot's!) are flaws in a gigantic whole. Or take a more sacred subject: Flaubert. Who, since Gide took us aside and whispered that the first sixty pages of *Madame Bovary* are dull and ill-written, has been ready to refuse his valuation of himself? Dare say that *Salammbô*, for example, is on a par with Liszt's *Mazeppa* — an unconvincing costume drama? In literature, we take the rough with the smooth, or skip it altogether.

The average music-lover, and this includes your average critic, will not do this. He wants the oiled and running machine that has been fully tested for performance. This seems too obvious to stress. But what are we to make of a musical intellect like Bülow's (not average) when it decides that Liszt's symphonic poems are inferior to Mendelssohn's overtures, the *Hebrides*, etc.? There is no question here of right or wrong, or of quality. Mendelssohn is a ravishing composer. He is not superior to Liszt — who by the same token is not a Mendelssohn *manqué*, battling unsuccessfully with an identical medium. The symphonic poems break new ground, in which Mendelssohn was not interested. The trouble is that, unlike Mendelssohn, Liszt is not reliable. Faults abound, and though seldom guilty of Mendelssohn's sentimentality, he has his lapses, and it is fair to ask what part Carolyne's influence may have played in them.

The format for the orchestral works — big subjects splashed on a broad canvas: life, death, humanism — was his own choice. It is also true that she would have deplored a less schematic and ambitious approach. To her (and to him when he was under her sway), size was the first step to greatness; and she wasn't the one to foster or encourage the intellectual control that the big subject demanded. His failures, which have in common a loquacity, a mushy emotional undergrowth and a leaning toward the obvious in the material, have her atmosphere about them. Even his tendency to repetition seems, perhaps unfairly, to owe something to her presence. Like a bore who raises his voice, he had a way of saying the same thing twice — a semitone higher or in a changed key.* He defended this on the ground that it was part of his search for new forms and that it helped the uneducated public to follow what was going on. It also gave him a reputation for laziness that was undeserved. The tireless reviser of some seven hundred works can't be called lazy in the ordinary sense but he *was* too often unwilling or unable to muster the discipline needed to prune and refine — and Carolyne's uncritical adoration can't have helped.

It is anyway the fact that his least successful compositions are those most closely associated with her — the *Harmonies poétiques et religieuses;* above all, *Festklänge,* the seventh symphonic poem, written in 1853 in doubtful honor of their coming nuptials. In its final form it has an optional cut of no less than forty-five pages. As Searle says, Liszt in general saw no reason why a composer should not supply alternatives — a heritage, one could add, from his improvising past. But given the background, *Festklänge* looks like an almost perfect example of the "commissioned" work that goes dead for reasons inherent in its origins: the huge suggested cut actually follows on the Polonaise section that symbolizes Carolyne herself.

This isn't to patronize the large-scale creations of the Weimar period. It is to question whether Carolyne's murky mysticism, her inflated *pensées* did not interact, sometimes fatally, with a mind already oppressed by the Romantic heritage, magnetized by the heroic. The answer was, I think, given in 1860–1861 — and incidentally settles the point about his inability to work without her there to oversee him at his desk. Solitary in the Altenburg, indulging in whist and cognac in a way she would never have allowed, he quietly opened a new era for himself. He composed *Der traurige*

---

* Cf. the Ballade No. 2, in which the opening in B minor is repeated note for note in B-flat minor; the middle section of *Ce qu'on entend sur la montagne,* gone over twice, the second time a semitone higher; Mazeppa's ride, similarly repeated.

Mönch, a setting for voice and piano of words by Nicholas Lenau — the words being in fact declaimed, not sung, in anticipation of Schönberg's *Sprechstimme.* The poem itself is neo-Gothic. He completely transcended this material, in a manner he had never done before. Nor had anybody else: the music is almost entirely based on the whole-tone scale. He himself feared that its "keyless discords would prove impossible of performance," and with reason. The Brahms-Joachim manifesto had just been issued.

This document (to which, uncharacteristically, he did not reply) was a blow to his pride and personally wounding because it came from an old friend; it was not unexpected. Until 1857, he had never known the clamor of public failure — and the hisses that greeted *Mazeppa* at Leipzig, the *Dante* at Dresden, were more demoralizing than they perhaps need have been for that reason. They were portents all the same, and the demonstration over the *Barber of Bagdad* was another: it showed that Weimar, once his private preserve, was after all only a mirror of Germany. By 1859 he could see clearly the price he would have to pay for his inability to adjust to the German spirit, domesticate his genius and become a safe composer. The Manifesto merely ratified that observation, though psychologically it was the last straw and must have had more to do with his disturbed state in 1860 than the insensitive Cornelius, connecting everything with Carolyne, could realize. In fact an internal change was taking place that was to alter the course of his life no less than of his music.

He retired once and for all from the ideological struggle. His long labor of explication and propaganda ended even before his failure to answer the Manifesto. With the lone exception of an article on Robert Franz published in 1872, he ceased to write after 1859, when *The Gypsies and Their Music* came out. When he said, "It is high time I was somewhat forgotten," he had taken leave of the ambition that had driven his career like an engine since his early twenties, the need to "become somebody." The afterlife, as he called it, of his music was something else. He believed in it, but he also knew that he might not survive to see it.

Such a change, in a man like Liszt, is not simply a consequence of middle age. He had his fiftieth birthday in 1861. He lived to be seventy-five. The quantity of work he got through, his incessant travels, the demands of his teaching, his enthusiastic pursuit of love in the last twenty-five years do not suggest any diminution of his spiritual or physical strength. (His health was iron almost to the end.) But the Romantic fervor of his youth was gone, and he went his uncharted way without benefit of the convictions that had sustained it.

The Romantic did not cast his bread upon the waters. For him it was now or never, in art as in life; he wrote his name large for that reason. But Liszt after 1860 was in for the long haul, and the most immediately noticeable change was that he stopped composing his life in music and began simply to compose. Overboard went the big Romantic constructions and the symphonic treatment appropriate to them. (And it was of course this abandonment of a form distinctively German — had he not said himself that Germany was the land of symphonies? — that was to finish him there.) The *Trois odes funèbres* are the last of these tonal autobiographies. There are no straight lines in Liszt but from now on he moves steadily away from the glitter and the assertiveness of the middle years and toward a new restraint and austerity. The last piano pieces are almost surgical in their approach: melodies pruned to the bone — to four notes or fewer, a unit pure as a cube; rhythms compacted into a cellular refinement. This music wasn't less personal than what went before. It was perhaps more so, but in a radically different way. The sacred music excepted, one feels he was writing for himself alone — stark, Delphic utterances drained of dogma or rhetoric. Tonally and structurally ambiguous, the last works are light-years in mood from the Weimar masterpieces. They exist for their own sake and nothing more.

If, as I believe, Romanticism was the matrix of modern art, Liszt is the only composer who proves it within a single lifetime. No one else traversed the space between the Romanticism of the *Dante* Sonata, to choose a random example, and the instrumentally uncolored "purity" of *Am Grabe Richard Wagners* or the *Csárdás macabre*. The evolutionary process is in him speeded up — as if, had he been a painter, he had started out like Delacroix and ended like Juan Gris, with the proviso that his late music does not refute the earlier. It was a question of which strains came to predominate: the adventurousness, the iconoclasm were there in his adolescence. Of course he couldn't read the future, but you almost believe he could when you consider what happened to the traditions established in his time. To quote Searle: "The Wagnerian colossus blew itself up and finally exploded with Strauss and Mahler," [8] while the more classical approach of Schumann and Brahms led only to minor figures like Dohnányi. Of course I know that a composer's intrinsic worth is not identical with his historical importance — he isn't to be judged by the standard of who followed him. Brahms may well have been a greater composer than Liszt. It is also possible to argue that modern music as it descends from the experiments and inventions of Liszt has reached an end as dead as any other. What cannot be argued is the survival of Liszt's consciously avant-garde point of view. He is modern not only by virtue of certain discoveries in harmonics, chord structure, etc., but because his perpetual search for the new, unique in nineteenth-century music, has proved to be the cornerstone of modern aesthetics. As a prophet, he must have his place.

None of this happened overnight.* There is still every sign of a turning

---

* Even in his music, traces of the Weimar preoccupation with larger forms and Romantically flamboyant treatment linger for about three years. John Ogdon in his splendid essay on the solo piano music (*Franz Liszt: The Man and His Music*: pp. 134–

point in 1860–1861. The will he drew up in 1860 is not in the spirit of someone who suddenly fears death but of one who rearranges his life, turns
out the bureau drawers and determines what must go. A corroborative letter to Carolyne informs her that although he wouldn't mind living in Rome,
"my life must be quite different from the last dozen years, with more solitude, peace and independence." His sadness — and he was sad, desolate
sometimes to tears, he told Agnes Klindworth — was for the past, the shattering of his dream for Weimar, the cooled friendships. But he wasn't in
the least hopeless. When Berlioz finished *Beatrice and Benedict* in 1862, he
was only fifty-nine; yet he knew he had written the last notes of his life: "I
am eager to cut the bonds that attach me to art," he wrote, "so as to be able
to say to Death, 'At your service.' " [9] It is doubtful if Liszt in his last hour
would have shared that emotion. He treasured the bonds that attached him
to art. But he did resign himself to certain losses, or better to say, he cut
them.

"I wish I knew how to be something to Liszt," Wagner wrote to Bülow
in 1861. "But he has other and deeper norms for his ways and actions than
a poor plebeian like myself can fathom." By this he meant that Liszt seemingly took no further interest in him, which wasn't true. It was true that
the crusading days were over and that he utterly refused his former role
in Wagner's messy affairs. Where once he would have been available at
every stage of the *Tannhäuser* production in Paris, he was now aloof.

Liszt to Blandine: . . . To my thinking, the best thing he [Wagner] could do
would be to preserve a calm, dignified, and rather proud reserve. . . . I sincerely
wish him all imaginable success; at the same time, as I am convinced that the role
he is presently playing is not right for him, I will abstain completely from mixing
myself up in his procedure and pursuits. . . .[10]

He spoke of making it up to Wagner perhaps, with a production of *Tristan*
at Weimar but his musings were half-hearted. Wagner's financial demands,
he said, could never be met. He urged Carl Alexander to bestow a decoration on German music's stepchild, having in mind that it would look badly
if Wagner were to receive his only honors from the French emperor. But
he was running out of toys to offer his friend; and the laughable proposal
that Wagner maintain a dignified and proud reserve seems to apply rather
to himself, to be *his* future line: certainly it would not be Wagner's, under
any circumstances.

At the same time he did a curious thing. In the late spring of 1861, he

---

167) calls the two *Franciscan Legends*, the two Concert Studies, the *Weinen, Klagen*
variations and one or two other pieces "annotations of the Weimar period." They are
virtuoso works, the first four highly descriptive of physical effects — birdsong, waves.
The sheer pianism of *Weinen, Klagen* can be measured by its dedication to Anton
Rubinstein.

packed up and went off to Paris for a visit of more than three weeks. Carolyne, who evidently didn't like this and wanted an explanation, was told
that his appearance had "helped my position in Europe." In fact Napoleon
III gave him the Legion of Honor, and he lobbied for admission to the
Institute. Berlioz, who was to help in this endeavor, took a typically lofty
position. He was sorry Liszt "attached to the election an importance
which it has not for *him*. It was important for *us*, us alone." That was all
very well. Berlioz, while pretending disdain, had strained every nerve
toward his own election and might have understood why Liszt, smarting
from the wounds inflicted on him in Germany, set special store by this sign
of recognition. It wasn't given him — they elected Verdi instead. Would he
have stayed in France if it had been otherwise? I think it possible. His
course is from now on so erratic, his statements about what he intended to
do so contradictory (he had, for example, told Carolyne in January that he
would spend the winter at Fontainebleau or St. Tropez, where the Olliviers
had a property, "alone with my music paper and some books" — a plan he
abandoned without explanation) that he is like a man shaking a defective
compass, trying to make the needle come to rest.

Paris would have welcomed him home, that is certain. He boasted that
he was having "a kind of St. Martin's summer." Within a fortnight he had
lunched or dined with Lamartine, Sainte-Beuve, the Rothschilds, the Met-
ternichs, Michelet, Pauline Viardot-García, Gounod, Halévy, Rossini, Delacroix, half a dozen dukes and the French emperor. As it always did with
him — it was perhaps what saved him — the pleasure principle reasserted
itself. Little anecdotes pop from the page: his riposte to Napoleon III, who
said he felt a hundred — "Sire, you *are* the century." Rossini benevolently
stroking the still abundant mane: "All your own? . . . Look at me — nothing left up there, and I have no more teeth or legs either."

He saw little of Berlioz, and Wagner — whom he knew to be out of the
city when he rather suddenly decided to make the trip — he obviously
hoped not to see at all. Wagner however returned unexpectedly. *Mein
Leben* describes his outrage:

Liszt had already fallen back into his old current of life, even his own daughter
Blandine could only manage to get a word with him in his carriage, as he drove
from one visit to another. Nevertheless, impelled by his goodness of heart, he
found time once to accept an invitation to "beef-steaks" at my house. He even
managed to spare me a whole evening, for which he kindly placed himself at my
disposal for the settlement of my small obligations. . . .

Another day we met for lunch at Gounod's, where we had a very dull time
which was only enlivened by poor Baudelaire, who indulged in the most outrageous witticisms. This man, "*criblé de dettes*" as he told me, and daily compelled to adopt the most extravagant methods for a bare subsistence, had repeatedly approached me with adventurous schemes for the exploitation of my

notorious fiasco [*Tannhäuser*]. I could not . . . consent to adopt any of these, and was glad to find this really capable man safe under the eagle wing of Liszt's ascendancy. Liszt took him everywhere where there was the possibility of a fortune being found.[11]

There was the rub. Wagner was *not* taken everywhere. "[Liszt] was summoned to the Tuileries, to which however it was not thought necessary to invite me to accompany him." Nor was Liszt able to arrange a meeting with Lamartine. One could feel for Wagner — it is hateful to be left out — if it weren't for those "small obligations" (in reality he was in desperate straits) that Liszt was asked to settle, and the possibility that Wagner was conducting an affair with Blandine.* Try as one will to give him credit for a thwarted affection for Liszt, it is too evident that his main concern was the loss of Liszt's good offices and his inability to provoke a scene about it. Liszt had retreated behind his mask of politeness. He did not alter his opinion of Wagner's music but Wagner saw him vanishing into the distance and for a while it drove him distracted; he felt thoroughly ill-used.

Liszt saw one other person in Paris. His letters to Carolyne slid over Marie d'Agoult's name. Carolyne of course pressed him for details and when he was back in Weimar he was forced to be explicit. He had called on Marie, at her request, and then accepted an invitation to lunch — one of her perfect lunches with exquisite food, on which he commented. His fellow guests were a group of international journalists. "Nélida naturally announced that there was no more good taste or *bon ton* in France, that conversation had ceased to exist, that a great deal was built without its being architecture, etc." He didn't agree: "Our time is worth at least as much as others, there is still prodigious *esprit* in France, and the seven wonders of the ancient world together don't compare with the reconstruction of Paris under Napoleon." He left shortly after the coffee — having surely provided the journalists with some titivating material.

He called again eight days later. She was alone. They talked with some acidity of Sand, with whom Marie supposed he was still on friendly terms. No, he said, "Your quarrel made a little coldness between us — because though I thought you were wrong, I didn't on that account fail to take your part." "I imagined the contrary." "With no reason whatever, as in the past." That was dropped and they passed to other things — to George Eliot, who he nastily said was Sand's only real rival, and to Wagner and the music of the future. He launched on a familiar theme, how little he cared for friends

---

* Gutman takes this for an undoubted fact and says it was the reason for Liszt's avoidance of Wagner in Paris (*Richard Wagner:* p. 204). He may well be right but I don't know his evidence and am inclined to doubt an actual affair. Ollivier was far more attractive than Wagner and Blandine's letters suggest that she was very much in love with him. At a guess, she teased and flirted with Wagner, who would have been delighted to make her his mistress but ultimately took her sister instead.

or parties or newspapers; and, he says, she was struck with this program of voluntary isolation:

Listening to me talk this way of myself, of my egoism and my ambition, of the part I give to the public and that which is reserved to the artist, of the perfect identity between my endeavors and my ideas of today, of the permanence of that self she had found so "hateful" . . . her face was bathed in tears. I kissed her on the forehead for the first time in long years and said: "Come Marie, let me speak to you in peasant's language. God bless you. Wish me no evil." She couldn't answer but her tears fell faster. Ollivier had told me that when they were travelling in Italy, she often wept in places that recalled our youth. I told her I had been touched. She said, almost stammering, "I will always be faithful to Italy — and to Hungary!" On which I left her quietly. On my way downstairs, the image of Daniel came to me. There had been no mention of him in the three or four hours I had been talking to his mother.[12]

For seventeen years Marie had been the chief obstacle to his reestablishing himself in France. These interviews, whose tragic element he seems determined to present as cold-bloodedly as possible, may have been, on his side, an effort to normalize their relations — hence perhaps to remove that obstacle. Or his indifference may have been unfeigned — at long last. If we knew which, we would be nearer to reading his mind. There may even so be a clue in his conversation with Marie, his emphasis on the isolated road he had chosen to travel.

His St. Martin's summer showed him that whatever the fate of his music he would in France always dominate as a personality. Romanticism might be officially dead and many of its leaders (Lamennais, Heine, Musset, Balzac, Nerval) in their graves. One has only to read the Goncourt journals to see how powerful the survivors still were. Like the veterans of a great and glorious battle, they were revered by the younger generation. (Hugo, though in exile, was no more forgotten than Napoleon in the same circumstances, and his return was anticipated with the same emotions.) That, for Liszt, may have been just the trouble. Paris in a sense remembered him too well. There he would have been the aging Romantic living off the spoils of the past, the ex-virtuoso. His instinct was always to ring down the curtain, and though his renunciations of the world have a hollow sound, since he could never keep to them, it was true that he didn't want to bind himself to a particular society — figure, in this case, as our dear old Liszt at the Magny dinners. And so his rather melodramatic farewell to Marie, his declarations of independence, could be genuine. One only wonders whether Carolyne, toiling with the Vatican to bring about their union, understood that in his words to Marie there might be a message for her too.

He returned to Weimar in early June, by way of Brussels and Agnes

Klindworth. Tausig was with him. Tausig, says Wagner grudgingly, had originally taken refuge with *him* in Paris. "He now fell back into his natural dependence on Liszt," and went off with him to visit Mme Street in Brussels. Liszt told Agnes that Tausig would accompany him as far as Weimar and it is possible that Tausig was his only companion for the remainder of that dismal and puzzling summer.

Every day saw another section of the Altenburg sealed off. Edouard Liszt came from Vienna to take inventories of the silver and other valuables. Scotchy, Marie Wittgenstein's governess, who had remained with him as a sort of housekeeper, was sent back to England. Liszt sat alone in the *chambre bleue,* correcting the proofs of the next to last symphonic poems, *Hamlet* and *The Battle of the Huns.* But it wasn't quite over. They always said Liszt was an actor and it did look as though he couldn't leave without a *finale,* a last salute to the public. This time he had the collaboration of fate. It had long since been arranged that a congress of musicians would assemble in Weimar that August, in honor of the *Neue Zeitschrift's* twenty-fifth anniversary. Without premeditation, this turned into a celebration, half festival and half wake, of Weimar's achievements over the last dozen years. Everybody came: Cornelius, Bülow, Leopold Damrosch, Lassen, Tausig, Brendel, Draeseke and dozens more, including — the final *coup de théâtre* — Wagner himself, triumphantly amnestied. Only Berlioz was missing. Otherwise it was as if the whole cast had been most improbably assembled before the footlights. The young Olliviers came all the way from Paris. For the last time, the Altenburg was inhabited from top to bottom.

No one wanted to say that it was the end. Liszt's guests hovered uneasily over him, having no idea, says Lassen, what his future would be — "nor did he himself." Only Wagner was callously cheerful. He couldn't pretend to be concerned about Liszt's future, since it no longer involved his own:

And so I again crossed Thuringia, passing the Wartburg which, whether I visited it or merely saw it in the distance, seemed so strangely bound up with my departures from Germany, or my return thither. I reached Weimar at two in the morning, and was conducted later in the day to the rooms which Liszt had arranged for my use in the Altenburg. They were, as he took care to inform me, Princess Marie's rooms.[13]

The house party at the Altenburg was, in Wagner's words, "boisterously merry" with Bülow the "wildest of all," a perfect example of Wagner's blindness to other people. In addition to his distress on Liszt's account, Bülow was worried about Cosima, who had fallen ill nursing their first child and frightened them all with symptoms resembling Daniel's. She was now taking a cure and in fact recovering but Bülow's nerves, easily unsettled, were such that only Wagner could have confused them with gaiety. Cornelius too was trembling with agitation. Having said a good deal about preserving his principles by staying away from the Altenburg when Carolyne was not there, insisting that he would go only to "sing the praises of the old Liszt" — there he was, having allowed Liszt to pay his fare from Vienna. Nor did those who were genuinely devoted to Liszt see anything particularly joyful in the proceedings. To Lassen, "the last stone has fallen that began two years ago when [Princess] Marie went."

"Rather too many people . . . little talent but much inanity . . . music often very bad," was Wagner's private verdict to a friend. But Bülow conducting the *Faust* Symphony, Tausig playing Liszt's A Major Concerto, Emilie Genast singing a cycle of modern songs, Liszt's and Bülow's chamber concert, can't have been altogether tedious. Wagner however concentrates on an incident that was painful to Liszt because it recalled the *Barber of Bagdad* episode. The audience showed its ennui at Draeseke's *Germania Marsch*. Liszt, reacting to an old grievance, behaved badly. Red with rage, he leaned from the stage box, shouting "Bravo!" and waving his arms; it developed into "a battle between him and the audience." Wagner couldn't think why Liszt was so upset.

By August 10, all were gone — with tearful farewells according to Lassen, in a euphoric mood according to Wagner. *He* had been everywhere applauded; students came from Jena to serenade him; the final banquet "developed into a really hearty ovation for the composer of *Tannhäuser* and *Lohengrin,* whom they now welcomed back to Germany. . . ." He had attached himself to the Olliviers and was accompanying them to the spa where Cosima was making her cure:

As we were all saying good-bye to Liszt on the railway platform, we thought of Bülow, who had distinguished himself so remarkably in the last few days. He had started a day in advance, and we exhausted ourselves in singing his praises, though I added jestingly, "There was no necessity for him to marry Cosima." [14]

And Liszt added, bowing slightly, "That was a luxury." On that ominous note, Wagner disappeared from Liszt's life for three years. When they met again, Wagner was Cosima's lover.

If Liszt described any of these scenes to Carolyne, the letter is lost. There is a gap of nearly three weeks with no letters at all. Then on August 12, he wrote from the Erbprinz:

It is impossible for me to assemble on a single threshold all the emotions of my last hours at the Altenburg. Each room, each piece of furniture, down to the steps of the staircase and the green lawns . . . all was lighted by your love without which I should feel myself annihilated. . . . But after a last prayer at your prie-dieu, where we used to kneel before I set off on one of my journeys, I had a feeling of liberation that comforted me again.[15]

Carolyne's letters if we had them might help us to understand the inner history of the next two months. Why, for example, did he tell her he was "laying a false trail," giving out that he was going to St. Tropez (that again) and then to Athens, when he was doing nothing of the kind? Cornelius reports that his parting words at Weimar were, "Now I go to Rome for my marriage!" Lassen says they all knew he would go if Carolyne "asked him to." Tausig had no doubts, though like Cornelius he was sceptical of the outcome: "Liszt's whole journey to Rome was simply a *blague*," he said later.

Was it? Certainly he was in no hurry to consummate what in his language sounds more like a rite of absolution than a marriage. He was writing to Carolyne in his loftiest, and in the circumstances least attractive, vein: "Be then, and once again, my pardon — and forever my law, my mercy, my grace and my glory." [16] A little later: "May I give you serenity and peace in the approaching evening of your life." [17] (The poor woman was forty-one, not exactly decrepitude even in the nineteenth century.) Informed that October 22, his fiftieth birthday, was the date fixed, he was "deeply touched." Yet he took such a roundabout route — travelling via Löwenburg and Berlin — that he didn't reach Marseilles until October 12 and didn't embark for Civitavecchia until October 17, so late that the mildest of contrary winds would have delayed him beyond the day. He had in fact an excuse for lingering in Germany. Cosima, still recuperating, was in Löwenburg and wanted him with her; he escorted her home to Berlin. "*Elle me tyrannise*," he said, which wasn't likely, and may have meant she was his accomplice. She wasn't in favor of the marriage and can't have been unaware of the young woman who followed him to Löwenburg — in boy's clothing, it is said, to elude the vigilance of a jealous husband.

That touch of farce is so thoroughly Lisztian, it almost convinces one that Tausig was right: the journey was a *blague*. Almost but not quite, because it is impossible that Liszt meant to desert Carolyne at the altar — literally at the altar: when he arrived in Rome on October 21 the church, San Carlo al Corso, was already decked with flowers, the witnesses (who were they?) had been summoned. Other plans too must have been made — where they would live, how. He couldn't have backed out without disgrace to them both, even supposing that he was willing to inflict that kind of injury on a woman whom, after all, he loved. It won't do. He can only have hoped for a miracle, and preposterously enough, it happened. The event was unrealistic enough to have been fiction, and overdone fiction at that — like the *espagnolismes* in Stendhal.

Imagine, then, that the lovers are supping together in her apartment on the evening of October 21. Suddenly there comes a knock on the door. Bolts, chains, lights — a late visitor causes a commotion in Roman buildings. This is a messenger from Cardinal Antonelli, the Papal Secretary of State. Carolyne's relatives have learned at the last moment that the marriage will take place and declare it illegal; her divorce is invalid because she has perjured herself to obtain it; it is not true that she was forced into her marriage with Wittgenstein. This being the case, His Holiness has no choice but to re-examine the documents, reconsider the whole matter. The wedding must be cancelled. Next morning the sun rises on an empty church. The flowers are taken away, probably to be sold at half price in the Campo di Fiori. Liszt is free.

Countless books have described the moment when the traveller arriving from the port of Civitavecchia first saw Rome. On a certain rise in the campagna, the *vetturino* stopped his carriage, flicked his whip in the direction of an agate bubble on the horizon and pronounced the formula: *Ecco Roma!* Liszt, who didn't otherwise disdain the clichés ennobled by history, is almost the only traveller with Romantic antecedents *not* to have told us his feelings at that moment, though it was in some ways of greater significance to him than to any of them, and not only because Rome was his preferred place of residence in the last quarter of his life. His *vie trifurquée* as he called it — 1869–1886 — involved long periods in Weimar and Budapest. Yet Abbé Liszt is preeminently a Roman personage. He seemed to belong there as nowhere else, in that city where the costumed cleric is not out of place in smart society and worldliness is not incompatible with piety. The Romans never perceived the hypocrisy in Liszt that was taken for granted by non-Catholic Nordics. As for his music, they knew nothing about it, and this was not altogether a disadvantage either. The lack of interest in instrumental music that had irritated every foreign composer from Berlioz on down must often have seemed a blessing to one who was sick of controversy. Rome forgave him his musical sins because it did not know of their existence.

There were disappointments, profound ones. Though Pio Nono loved Liszt, loved to hear him "improvise," called him "my dear Palestrina," though he was given, through ecclesiastical grace and favor, one beautiful set of apartments after another to live in — on Monte Mario, in the Vatican, at Villa d'Este — the Church refused him his heart's desire: the music he wrote for it, more than sixty compositions, most of them for liturgical use. He may have minded this more than the failure of his symphonic poems in German cities. But Rome has consolations that Leipzig and Berlin do not possess. Delivered of his two enormous oratorios, the *St. Elizabeth* and the *Christus* (completed in 1867), he began for the first time to speak of his "*santa indifferenza*," a state he did not achieve to any degree that would qualify him as a contemplative but that was authentic as far as it went. Resignation would be a better word than indifference.

He was made an abbé on April 25, 1865. The following Sunday, writes Gregorovius, he received the tonsure in St. Peter's. "He now wears the Abbé's cassock . . . and looks well and contented. This is the end of the gifted virtuoso, a truly sovereign personality. . . ."[18] The gravity of his ordination should not be overestimated. He couldn't celebrate Mass or hear confession — he took no vows of chastity. He made a point of saying that he hadn't taken this step through "disgust of the world, and still less through lassitude for my art." There was simply no other way — or no other half as effective — in which he could have laid the ghosts of the past. He was free as he had never been, free to call on Carolyne (every day when he was in Rome) without any possibility of reproach; to go into retirement for weeks or months if he wanted to and no questions asked; above all, to go about his work in his own way. He was not unhappy. He was in the end even serene. Here is a description of him playing the *Angelus* (from the third *Année de pèlerinage*) to a visitor at the Villa d'Este, five years before his death, when his Romanticism had long since faded into history:

"You know," said Liszt, turning to me, "they ring the Angelus in Italy carelessly; the bells swing irregularly, and leave off, and the cadences are often broken up thus": and he began a little swaying passage in the treble — like bells tossing high up in the evening air: it ceased, but so softly that the half-bar of silence made itself felt, and the listening ear still carried the broken rhythm through the pause. The Abbate himself seemed to fall into a dream; his fingers fell again lightly on the keys, and the bells went on, leaving off in the middle of a phrase. Then rose from the bass the ring of the Angelus, or rather, it seemed like the vague emotion of one who, as he passes, hears, in the ruins of some wayside cloister, the ghosts of old monks humming their drowsy melodies, as the sun goes down rapidly, and the purple shadows of Italy steal over the land, out of the orange west!

We sat motionless. . . . [Liszt's] fingers seemed quite independent, chance ministers of his soul. The dream was broken by a pause; then came back the little swaying passage, of bells, tossing high up in the evening air, the half-bar of silence, the broken rhythm — and the Angelus was rung.[19]

There we may leave him.

Chronology of the Book

1811   October 22: Franz (Ferencz) Liszt born at Raiding (Doborján), in western Hungary, to Ádám Liszt, a steward in the service of Prince Nicholas Eszterházy, and his wife Anna Läger, a draper's daughter from lower Austria.

1820   Gives a concert for his own benefit in the palace of the Eszterházys in Pressburg (Pozsóny). A number of Hungarian nobles subscribe to a fund for his education.

1821   The Liszt family moves to Vienna. Czerny gives the child free lessons.

1823   He gives public concerts, visits Beethoven — who perhaps gives his blessing in the form of a kiss.
December 11: Arrives in Paris and is refused admission to the Conservatoire by Cherubini. Studies with Paer. Begins to be a fashionable prodigy in Paris salons.

1824   First visit to England.

1825   Tour of French provinces and second visit to England.
October 17: His opera *Don Sanche, ou Le Château d'amour* is performed at the Paris Opera and is a failure.

1826   Tours in France and Switzerland. Begins the *Études en douze exercices*.

1827   Third visit to England. Suffers from nervous exhaustion and talks of entering the Church.
August: Ádám Liszt dies at Boulogne.
Liszt returns to Paris and begins to support himself and his mother by giving piano lessons.

1828   He falls in love with Caroline de Saint-Cricq, whose father shows him the door. Nervous prostration. His death is reported in a Paris paper.

1829   He recovers and his name appears for the first time in association with Romantic writers: Mérimée, Hugo and perhaps Sainte-Beuve. Meets Lamartine and Vigny this year or the next.

1830   The July revolution completes his cure. He makes sketch for a *Revolutionary* Symphony.
October: Attends Saint-Simonist meetings at the Salle Taitbout and makes the acquaintance of Prosper Enfantin, the Saint-Simonist leader. Meets Émile Barrault.

December: Introduces himself to Berlioz and attends first performance of Berlioz's *Symphonie fantastique*.

1831 Paganini's first Paris concert, March 9, makes a tremendous impression.

Chopin arrives in Paris; he and Liszt meet shortly thereafter.

1832 February 26: Attends Chopin's first Paris concert.

Begins the *Grande Fantaisie sur La Clochette de Paganini*.

Visits his mistress, Countess Adèle Laprunarède, in the Savoie.

Introduction to Countess Marie d'Agoult at the house of their mutual friend, the Marquise de Vayer.

1833 Transcribes Berlioz's *Symphonie fantastique, Francs-Juges* Overture, *L'Idée fixe*.

Is witness at Berlioz's wedding to Harriet Smithson, October 3.

Plays in two Berlioz concerts.

First letters in his published correspondence with Marie d'Agoult date from Easter this year.

1834 April: Introduction to Abbé de Lamennais, whom he visits in September at his home in Brittany. Publication of the Abbé's book, *Paroles d'un croyant*, causes his final rupture with Rome. Liszt becomes his passionate partisan.

Publishes his first article, "On the Future of Church Music."

Composes *Harmonies poétiques et religieuses* (single piece), *Apparitions, De Profundis, Lyon*.

October: Meets George Sand, probably introduced by Alfred de Musset.

December: Marie d'Agoult's daughter Louise dies.

1835 Joins Marie d'Agoult in Switzerland. They settle in Geneva, where their daughter Blandine is born December 18.

First essay in the *De la situation des artistes* series published in *Gazette Musicale*. Begins *Album d'un voyageur*, earliest version of first *Année de pèlerinage*.

Writes the first of eleven *Lettres d'un bachelier-ès-musique*, which are published at intervals over the next five years.

1836 Summer: George Sand joins their party on expedition to Chamonix, writes words to his *Rondo fantastique, El Contrabandista*.

October: Liszt and Marie return to Paris. George Sand shares apartments with them at Hôtel de France. Liszt, Lamennais and Sand promulgate "humanitarian art."

Fantasies on *Les Huguenots* and *I Puritani, Soirées musicales* (from Rossini). Transcription of *Harold in Italy*.

1837 January–February: Chamber concerts with Urhan and Batta.

Spring: Marie d'Agoult goes alone to visit George Sand at Nohant. Liszt remains in Paris to duel with Thalberg.

Solo concert at the Opera March 19. He and Thalberg play in competition at house of Princess Belgiojoso March 31.

Final (solo) concert at Salon Érard April 9.

May–July: Liszt and Marie are Sand's guests at Nohant. He works on transcriptions of Beethoven Symphonies 5–7 and Schubert songs: *Erlkönig* is played at Nohant. They return to Switzerland to see their daughter Blandine.

September: They descend into Italy. Liszt gives concerts in Milan. They spend some time on Lake Como, where their daughter Cosima is born December 24.

1838   Spring months in Venice. Liszt goes to Vienna to give concerts for benefit of Danube flood victims.

They spend part of the summer in Genoa, then travel down Italian peninsula. Concerts at Milan, Florence, Bologna, etc. Liszt completes *Paganini* Studies, *Spozalizio, Il Penseroso, Petrarch Sonnets* (second *Année de pèlerinage*), *Grand Galop chromatique, 12 Grandes Études.*

1839   February–June: Liszt and Marie in Rome. Daniel Liszt born May 9.

Summer at Villa Massimiliana near Lucca.

November: Marie returns to Paris with Cosima and Blandine.

Liszt goes to Vienna and (end of December) to Hungary, where he is received like a national hero.

1840   Seven concerts in Pest. At the conclusion of January 4 concert, he is presented with sabre of honor. Revisits Raiding.

Spring: Concerts in Vienna, Prague, Dresden and Leipzig.

He meets Schumann.

April: Returns to Paris. First meeting with Wagner.

May–June: Concerts in London. Marie joins him.

Summer: Brussels and Rhineland towns.

August–November: Tour of England, Scotland and Ireland with John Orlando Parry.

1841   Concerts in Belgium, Germany, Denmark. Summer holiday on island of Nonnenwerth with Marie.

November: First visit to Weimar, then concerts in Dresden, Leipzig, Berlin, and other German cities. Composes fantasies on *Norma, Don Giovanni, Robert le Diable,* paraphrase on *God Save the King, Die Loreley* (song).

1842   Concerts in Berlin. Departs for Russia via Königsberg (where he is given honorary degree), Mitau, Dorpat, Riga.

April 20: First Petersburg concert.

Second summer holiday at Nonnenwerth.

Autumn: Second visit to Weimar, where he is appointed *Kapell-meister* in extraordinary service.

Tours Germany and Holland.

Many songs: *Mignons Lied, Comment, disaient-ils, Es war ein König in Thule,* etc.

1843   Second visit to Russia. Concerts in Warsaw, Cracow, Petersburg, Moscow. Meets Glinka and Dargomijsky. Transcribes *Tscherkes-senmarsch* from *Ruslan and Ludmilla.*

Last summer on Nonnenwerth.

Concerts in Germany, including Weimar.

1844   April: Concerts in Paris. Agrees on final separation from Marie.

Tours French provinces. Visits Caroline de Saint-Cricq at Pau, en route to Spain and Portugal.

1845   January–April: Concerts in Spain and Portugal.

August: Festival and dedication of Beethoven monument at Bonn. Liszt has given many concerts to raise money for the concert and composed *Beethoven* Cantata for the occasion but scandalous appearance of Lola Montez mars his credit.

Concerts in Freiburg and eastern France.

1846   Tours in France, Germany, Austria, Hungary and Rumania.

Marie publishes *Nélida.*

Composes Hungarian Rhapsody No. 1, transcribes Schubert songs and marches, Weber's *Freischütz* Overture, etc.

1847   Tour through Danube countries and south Russia. Meets Princess Carolyne Sayn-Wittgenstein at Kiev. Visits her estate, Woronince.

Goes to Turkey, where he plays for Sultan Abdul-Mejid.

Returns to Russia and spends July in Odessa with Carolyne.

September: Gives his final concert at Elisabetgrad.

Autumn and early winter at Woronince.

1848   January: Return to Weimar.

April: He goes to his friend Felix Lichnowsky's hunting castle in Silesia to await Carolyne, who joins him April 18. They journey together to Vienna.

June: Both are in Weimar but in separate residences, Liszt at Hotel Erbprinz, Carolyne in her rented villa, the Altenburg.

He composes first version of *Ce qu'on entend sur la montagne, Les Préludes, Arbeiterchor.*

1849   February: First performance of *Tannhäuser* at Weimar; also Schumann's *Faust,* Part II.

May: Wagner, now a political refugee, arrives in Weimar and is helped to escape to Switzerland.

Liszt composes first version of *Tasso, Consolations, Funérailles, Canzonetta del Salvator Rosa;* revises *Dante* Sonata.

He moves into the Altenburg, after holiday at Heligoland.

1850 Joachim comes to Weimar to lead orchestra.

August: First performance of Liszt's *Prometheus,* followed by *Lohengrin* première, August 28. This festival week attended by many celebrities, including Gérard de Nerval.

Works on *Harmonies poétiques et religieuses, Heroïde funèbre,* second version of *Ce qu'on entend sur la montagne.*

1851 Bülow comes to Weimar as Liszt's pupil.

Works performed during the year: Raff's *King Alfred,* Berlioz's *Harold in Italy,* Schumann's Overture to *The Bride of Messina,* Liszt's *Ce qu'on entend sur la montagne* and *Tasso.*

Compositions: *Mazeppa, Études d'exécution transcendante, Paganini* studies (second version), Schubert's *Wanderer* Fantasy (transcription).

1852 Berlioz's *Benvenuto Cellini* performed for the first time outside France, March 20. This is followed (November) by first "Berlioz Week," which the composer attends.

Other works given at Weimar include Schumann's *Manfred,* Verdi's *Ernani.* Life of Chopin published.

1853 Agnes Klindworth comes to Weimar.

Laub replaces Joachim as orchestra leader.

June: Brahms pays disastrous visit to Altenburg.

July: Liszt goes to Zurich to visit Wagner.

October: Music festival at Carlsruhe, where Liszt miscues the orchestra and is much criticized.

Accompanied by Bülow, Cornelius, Joachim, Reményi, Richard Pohl, he joins Wagner at Basel.

With Carolyne, her daughter and Wagner, he journeys to Paris, where he sees his children for the first time in eight years.

Works: *An die Künstler* (performed at Carlsruhe), B Minor Sonata, *Festklänge.* Hungarian Rhapsodies 3–15 are published.

1854 Rubinstein visits the Altenburg.

Hoffmann von Fallersleben settles in Weimar.

George Eliot and Lewes spend the summer, are often at the Altenburg.

Works performed include Dorn's *Nibelungen* (play), Schubert's *Alfonso and Estrella,* Rubinstein's *Siberian Hunters.*

With Carolyne's assistance, Liszt now doubles or triples his output of musical journalism: twelve articles (on *Fidelio,* on *Alfonso and Estrella,* etc., etc.) appear this year — nine the following.

He composes the *Faust* Symphony, *Hungaria,* transcribes portions of *Lohengrin.*

1855   February: Second "Berlioz Week" at Weimar. Berlioz conducts Liszt's E-flat Concerto with Liszt as soloist. Later in the year Schumann's *Genoveva* is given.

Liszt composes the *Dante* Symphony, the *Graner* Mass, *Psalm 13,* begins the *Beatitudes,* the Fantasy and Fugue on B.A.C.H. The first *Année de pèlerinage* is published.

Tsar Nicholas of Russia dies. Carolyne's husband obtains a civil divorce.

Agnes Klindworth moves away from Weimar to Brussels but meets Liszt at Düsseldorf music festival.

July: Tausig comes to live at Altenburg as Liszt's pupil.

August: Liszt's three children spend their summer holidays with him. Cosima and Blandine are then sent to Berlin to live with Mme von Bülow.

1856   February–March: Berlioz in Weimar. Quarrels about Wagner begin.

April: Bülow asks for Cosima's hand in marriage.

August: Liszt journeys to Hungary for first performance of *Graner* Mass.

With Carolyne and her daughter he pays long visit to Wagner in Zurich. They return via Munich to Weimar.

1857   The symphonic works begin to be performed outside Weimar, with several notable failures: the *Dante* at Dresden, *Mazeppa* at Leipzig, *Festklänge* at Aachen.

Bülow marries Cosima, August 18, Berlin.

Émile Ollivier marries Blandine, October 22, Florence.

Performed at Weimar: Schumann's *Paradise and the Peri,* Lassen's *Landgraf Ludwigs Brautfahrt,* Liszt's *Hunnenschlacht* (symphonic poem), *Faust* Symphony and *Die Ideale.*

Dingelstedt is made Intendant at Weimar.

1858   Visits to Prague and Budapest, where Liszt conducts some of his works.

December 15: First night of Cornelius's *Barber of Bagdad,* which is hissed in a demonstration that causes Liszt to resign his post.

He composes *Hamlet* (symphonic poem); the second *Année de pèlerinage* is published.

1859   Beginning of alienation from Wagner.

October: Marie Wittgenstein marries Prince Hohenlohe-Schilling-furst and is seen no more at the Altenburg.

December 13: Daniel Liszt dies in Berlin.

The Gypsies and Their Music in Hungary published.

1860   Brahms-Joachim Manifesto against the Music of the Future is published in *Das Echo*, March.

In May, Carolyne leaves Weimar for Rome in pursuit of her divorce. Liszt makes his will.

Compositions: *Les Morts, Psalm 18, Der traurige Mönch,* Two Episodes from Lenau's *Faust, Pater noster* from *Christus* Oratorio.

1861   Liszt goes to Paris, where he renews acquaintance with his old literary circle; also sees Halévy, Rossini, Gounod, Berlioz and, briefly, Wagner. Visits Marie d'Agoult. Dines with Napoleon III and Eugénie. His "St. Martin's summer."

August: Meeting of the Tonkünstlerverein at Weimar, which reassembles most of those associated with the Music of the Future: Wagner, Cornelius, Bülow, Pohl, Tausig, etc.

August 17: He closes the Altenburg for good and travels by circuitous route to Marseille, whence he sails for Italy October 17.

October 19 (?): He arrives in Rome. His marriage to Carolyne is to take place October 22. It is cancelled at the last moment. They remain in Rome but do not live together again.

[1865–1886:   Years of the Abbé Liszt; travels between Rome, Weimar and Budapest. He dies July 31, 1886, at Bayreuth.]

The above makes no attempt to provide anything like a catalogue of Liszt's works, of which there are more than seven hundred. Those interested will find the complete listing in *Franz Liszt: The Man and His Music,* ed. Alan Walker, New York, 1970, and in Humphrey Searle's *The Music of Liszt,* reprinted New York, 1966. Both these books also supply chronologies with which mine will be found to differ. I can only say that I believe mine to be correct.

Selected Bibliography

ORIGINAL SOURCES

LETTERS

Franz Liszts Briefe, ed. La Mara. 8 vols. Leipzig, 1893–1904.
I Band: *Von Paris bis Rom*
II Band: *Von Rom bis ans Ende*
III Band: *Briefe an eine Freundin*
IV, V, VI, VII Band: *Briefe an die Fürstin Sayn-Wittgenstein*
VIII Band: *Neue Folge zu Band I & II*

Liszt's Letters, ed. Constance Bache. 2 vols. London, 1894. (Translation of vols. I and II of *Franz Liszts Briefe*)

Briefe hervorragender Zeitgenossen an Franz Liszt, ed. La Mara. 3 vols. Leipzig, 1895–1904.

Briefwechsel zwischen Franz Liszt und Hans von Bülow, ed. La Mara. Leipzig, 1898.

Briefwechsel zwischen Franz Liszt und Carl Alexander Grossherzog von Sachsen, ed. La Mara. Leipzig, 1909.

Franz Liszts Briefe an seine Mutter, ed. La Mara. Leipzig, 1918.

A. Habets: *Letters of Liszt and Borodin*. Trans. Rosa Newmarch. London, 1895.

Correspondence of Wagner and Liszt, ed. Francis Hueffer. 2 vols. London, 1889.

Diverses letters inédites de Liszt, ed. Robert Bory. Basel, 1928.

Correspondance de Liszt et de La Comtesse d'Agoult, ed. Daniel Ollivier. 2 vols. Paris, 1933, 1934.

Correspondance de Liszt et de sa fille Mme Emile Ollivier, ed. Daniel Ollivier. Paris, 1936.

The Letters of Liszt to Marie zu Sayn-Wittgenstein, trans. and ed. Howard E. Hugo. Cambridge, Mass., 1953.

Aus der Glanzzeit der Weimarer Altenburg, ed. La Mara. Leipzig, 1906. (Letters to and from Carolyne Wittgenstein)

Briefe von Hector Berlioz an die Fürstin Carolyne Sayn-Wittgenstein, ed. La Mara. Leipzig, 1903.

AUTHOR'S NOTE: *Titles of the La Mara editions are misleading. Though her introductions, footnotes, etc., are in German, the letters themselves are in the original French.*

Les Années romantiques, 1819–1842. Correspondence of Hector Berlioz, ed. J. Tiersot. Paris, 1907.

Au milieu du chemin, 1852–1855. Correspondence of Hector Berlioz, ed. J. Tiersot. Paris, 1930.

Early Correspondence of Hans von Bülow, ed. C. Bache. New York, 1896.
Friedrich Hebbel. *Briefe*. Berlin, 1900.
Marcel Herwegh: *Au Printemps des dieux* (Marie d'Agoult–G. Herwegh). Paris, 1929.
Correspondence of Joachim, ed. N. Bickley. London, 1914.
Letters of Mendelssohn to Ignaz and Charlotte Moscheles. London, 1888.
Charles-Augustin Sainte-Beuve: *Correspondance générale*, ed. Bonnerot. Paris, 1935.
Correspondance de George Sand et d'Alfred de Musset, ed. Decori. Brussels, 1904.
George Sand: *Correspondance*, ed. Georges Lubin. 10 vols. Paris, 1967.
Solange Joubert: *Une Correspondance romantique* (Marie d'Agoult, Liszt, Henri Lehmann). Paris, 1947.

JOURNALS, MEMOIRS, RECOLLECTIONS

Juliette Adam: *Mes sentiments*. Paris, 1904.
Marie D'Agoult: *Souvenirs, 1806–1833*. Paris, 1877.
———. *Mémoires, 1833–1854*, ed. Daniel Ollivier. Paris, 1927.
Charles Baudelaire: *Intimate Journals*. Trans. Christopher Isherwood. Hollywood, 1947.
Hector Berlioz: *Memoirs* (1803–1865), ed. Ernest Newman. New York, 1966.
Theodor von Bernhardi: *Unter Nikolaus I und Friedrich Wilhelm IV: Briefe und Tagebuchblätter aus den Jahren 1834–1857*. Leipzig, 1893.
Mme August Boissier: *Liszt pédagogue*. Paris, 1927.
François-René-Auguste de Chateaubriand: *Mémoires d'Outre-Tombe*. 4 vols. Paris. Flammarion, 1948.
Peter Cornelius: *Literarische Werke: Ausgewählte Briefe, nebst Tagebuchblättern und Gelegenheitsgedichten*. 2 vols. Leipzig, 1904–1905.
Eugène Delacroix: *Journal*, trans. Lucy Norton. London, 1951.
Ferdinand Denis: *Journal*. Paris, 1932.
Amy Fay: *Music Study in Germany*. Chicago, McClurg & Co., 1891.
Arthur Friedheim: *Life and Liszt*. Taplinger, 1961.
Edmond et Jules de Goncourt: *Journal*, édition définitive, Paris. Fasquelle, 1935. 9 vols.
Ferdinand Gregorovius: *Römische Tagebücher*, ed. F. Althaus. Stuttgart, 1892.
N. de Gutmansthal: *Souvenirs de Franz Liszt*. Leipzig, 1913.
H. R. Haweis: *My Musical Life*. 2nd ed. London, 1886.
Alexander Herzen: *My Past and Thoughts*. 4 vols. New York, 1968.
Heinrich August Hoffmann von Fallersleben. *Mein Leben*. Hannover, 1868.
René Olga Janina: *Souvenirs d'une cosaque*. Paris, 1874.
Fanny Lewald: *Zwölf Bildern nach dem Leben*. Berlin, 1888.
William Mason: *Memories of a Musical Life*. New York, 1901.
Adolphe Pictet: *Une Course à Chamounix*, ed. Bory. Geneva, 1930.
Charles-Augustin Sainte-Beuve: *Carnet de voyage . . . Voyage en Italie*. Paris, 1922.

———. *Mes Poisons*. Paris, 1926.
Camille Saint-Saëns: *Portraits et Souvenirs*. Paris, 1900.
George Sand: *Journal intime*. Paris, 1926.
———. *Histoire de ma vie*. 4 vols. Paris, 1876.
Emil Sayn-Wittgenstein-Berleburg: *Souvenirs et correspondance*. Paris, 1888.
Adleheid von Schorn: *Das nachklassische Weimar*. Weimar, 1912.
———. *Zwei Menschenalter*. Berlin, 1901.
Alexander Siloti: *My Memories of Liszt*. Edinburgh, Methven Simpson, n.d.
Richard Wagner: *My Life*. 2 vols. New York, 1911.
Janka Wohl: *François Liszt, Recollections of a Compatriot*, trans. B. Ward. London, 1887. French edition, Ollendorf, 1887.

CONTEMPORARY LITERATURE

Franz Liszt: *Gesammelte Schriften*, ed. Lina Ramann. Leipzig, 1880–1883.
Vol. I   *F. Chopin* (1852).
Vol. II (1) Essays from the *Revue et Gazette Musicale:*
        "On the Position of Artists" (1835). "On the Future of Church Music" (1834). "On Popular Editions of Important Works" (1836). "On Meyerbeer's *Les Huguenots*" (1837). "Thalberg's *Grande Fantaisie* Op. 22, and Caprices, Op. 15 & 19" (1837). "To M. Fetis" (1837). "R. Schumann's Pianoforte Compositions, Op. 5, 11, 14" (1837). "Paganini: A Necrology" (1840).
     (2) *Letters of a Bachelor of Music* (1835–1840).
        1–3. "To George Sand." 4. "To Adolphe Pictet." 5. "To Louis de Ronchand." 6. "By Lake Como, to Ronchand." 7. "To M. Schlesinger, on La Scala." 8. "To Heinrich Heine." 9. "To Lambert Massart." 10. "To Schlesinger, on Music in Italy." 11. "To M d'Ortigue, on St. Cecilia." 12. "To Hector Berlioz."
Vol. III (1) "Gluck's *Orpheus*" (1854). "Beethoven's *Fidelio*" (1854). "Weber's *Euryanthe*" (1854). "On Beethoven's Music to *Egmont*" (1854). "On Mendelssohn's Music to *A Midsummer Night's Dream*" (1854). "Scribe and Meyerbeer's *Robert le Diable*" (1854). "Schubert's *Alfonse und Estrella*" (1854). "Auber's *Muette de Portici*" (1854). "Bellini's *Montecchi e Capuletti*" (1854). "Boieldieu's *Dame Blanche*" (1854). "Donizetti's *La Favorita*" (1854). "Pauline Viardot-García" (1859). "No Entr'acte Music!" (1855). "Mozart: On the Occasion of his Centenary in Vienna" (1856).
     (2) "Richard Wagner: *Tannhäuser* and the Song Contest on the Wartburg" (1849). "*Lohengrin* and Its First Performance at Weimar" (1850). "*The Flying Dutchman*" (1854). "*The Rhinegold*" (1855).
Vol. IV   "Berlioz and His *Harold* Symphony" (1855). "Robert Schumann" (1855). "Clara Schumann" (1855). "Robert Franz" (1855). "Sobolewski's *Vinvela*" (1855). "John Field and His Nocturnes" (1859).
Vol. V   "On the Goethe Foundation" (1850). "Weimar's September Festival in Honor of the Centenary of Karl August's Birth" (1857). "*Dorn-*

röschen; Genast's poem and Raff's Music" (1855). "Marx and his book, *The Music of the 19th Century*" (1855). "Criticism of Criticism; Ulibishev and Serov" (1858). "A Letter on Conducting; A Defense" (1853).

Vol. VI   *The Gypsies and Their Music in Hungary* (1859).

Published separately:

De la fondation Goethe à Weimar (1851).

Lohengrin et Tannhäuser de R. Wagner (1851).

F. Chopin (1852).

Des Bohémiens et de leur musique en Hongrie (1859).

Über John Fields Nocturne (1859).

R. Schumans Musikalische Haus- und Lebensregeln. French translation by F. L. Schuberth (1860).

Robert Franz (1872).

AUTHOR'S NOTE: *It seems appropriate in a book about Liszt to give his press publications in toto. For obvious reasons, I have not done the same with Berlioz, Schumann, etc., but confined myself to those of their works that I have read. For convenience, I have also given Liszt's titles in English, though none of the essays has been translated. Only the Chopin biography and the book on gypsy music exist in English, the first translated by E. Waters, the second by E. Evans. Many of the essays in Vol. II of the* Gesammelte Schriften *were collected and printed in a French edition,* Pages romantiques, *by Jean Chantavoine (Paris: Alcan, 1912).*

Marie d'Agoult (Daniel Stern): *Nélida,* ed. Lévy. 1846.

———. *Essai sur la liberté,* ed. Lévy. 1847.

AUTHOR'S NOTE: *I give here only those books by Marie mentioned in my text, but her bibliography is extensive — some seventeen books and many articles. A complete list will be found in Vier* (La Comtesse d'Agoult et son temps, *VI, 139 et seq.), who coolly lists all the* Bachelier ès musique *series as hers "sous le nom de Franz Liszt."*

Honoré de Balzac: *Béatrix.* Trans. R. and S. Harcourt-Smith. London, 1957.

———. *Lettres à l'étrangère,* ed. Lévy. 4 vols. Paris.

Charles Baudelaire: *L'Art romantique.* Paris. Pléiade ed. 1947.

Hector Berlioz: *Evenings in the Orchestra,* trans. C. E. Roche. New York, 1929.

———. *A travers chants,* ed. Lévy. Paris, 1898.

François-René-Auguste de Chateaubriand: *Le Génie du Christianisme,* ed. Calmann. 2 vols. 1885.

———. *Atala — René:* Vol. XVI of the *Oeuvres complètes.* Paris, 1816–1831.

George Eliot: *Essays and Leaves from a Notebook.* New York, 1884.

Theophile Gautier: *Histoire de Romantisme.* Paris, 1874.

Wolfgang von Goethe: *Conversations and Encounters,* ed. and trans. David Luke and Robert Pick. Chicago, 1966.

Heinrich Heine: *Lutèce: Lettres sur la vie politique, artistique et sociale de la France.* Paris, 1855.

Victor Hugo: *Oeuvres poetiques complètes.* Montreal, 1944.
Alphonse de Lamartine: *Oeuvres choisies,* ed. Levaillant. Paris, 1926.
Felicité de Lamennais: *Paroles d'un croyant.* Paris, 1874.
————. *Portefeuille de Lamennais,* ed. Goyau. Paris, 1930.
————. *De l'Art et du Beau.* Garnier, Paris, n.d.
George Lewes: *Life of Goethe.* Ungar, New York, 1965.
Alfred de Musset: *Confession d'un enfant du siècle.* Vols. VII & VIII of the *Oeuvres complètes.* 1866.
Gérard de Nerval: *Notes d'un amateur de musique.* Intro. by Coeuroy. Paris, 1926.
Alexander Pushkin: *Critical Prose,* ed. and trans. C. R. Proffer. Indiana, 1969.
Charles-Augustin Sainte-Beuve: *Vie, poésies et pensées de Joseph Delorme,* ed. Antoine. Paris, 1956.
————. *Port-Royal,* ed. Leroy. Paris, 1952.
George Sand: *Lettres d'un voyageur,* ed. Lévy. Paris, 1956 et seq.
————. *Elle et Lui,* ed. Lévy.
————. *Horace,* ed. Lévy.
————. *Lélia,* ed. Dupuy. 1833.
Robert Schumann: *On Music and Musicians,* trans. by Paul Rosenfeld. New York, 1946. An imperfectly organized but useful selection from the critical works originally published in the *Neue Zeitschrift für Musik.* Those at home in German will of course turn to the *Gesammelte Schriften.* (Leipzig, 1954. 4 vols.)
Étienne de Senancour: *Obermann.* Preface by G. Sand. Paris, 1840.
Mme de Staël: *De l'Allemagne,* ed. Garnier. Paris, n.d.
Stendhal: *A Roman Journal,* ed. and trans. H. Chevalier. New York, 1961.
————. *Vie de Rossini,* ed. Prunières. Paris, 1923.
Alfred de Vigny: *Chatterton,* ed. Lauvrière. Oxford, 1908.
Richard Wagner: *Prose Works,* trans. by W. A. Ellis. 8 vols. London, 1892–1899.

SECONDARY SOURCES

BIOGRAPHIES, STUDIES

Walter Beckett: *Liszt.* Farrar, Straus revised ed. New York, 1963.
Robert Bory: *Liszt et ses enfants.* Paris, 1936.
————. *Une Retraite romantique en Suisse.* Paris, 1930.
————. *La Vie de Liszt par l'image.* Geneva, 1936.
Jean Chantavoine: *Franz Liszt.* Paris, 1911.
August Gollerich: *Franz Liszt.* Berlin, 1908.
Marcel Herweigh: *Aux banquet des dieux: Franz Liszt, Richard Wagner et leurs amis.* Paris, 1931.
James Huneker: *Liszt.* London, 1911.
László-Máteká: *Franz Liszt. A Biography in Pictures.* London, 1968.
Ernest Newman: *The Man Liszt.* New York, 1970.
Guy de Pourtalès: *La Vie de Franz Liszt.* Paris, 1927.
Peter Raabe: *Liszts Leben.* Stuttgart, 1931.

Lina Ramann: *Franz Liszt als Künstler und Mensch.* Leipzig, 1880–1894. (One volume translated by C. Bache. London, 1898.)
Sacheverell Sitwell: *Liszt.* London, 1934.

Jacques Barzun: *Berlioz and the Romantic Century.* 2 vols. Boston, 1950.
Alexander Buckner: *Franz Liszt in Bohemia,* trans. R. F. Samsour. London, 1962.
Jean-René Derré: *Lamennais, ses amis et le Mouvement des Idées à l'Epoque Romantique.* Paris, 1962.
Richard du Moulin Eckhart: *Cosima Wagner.* 2 vols. Munich, 1929.
Robert W. Gutman: *Richard Wagner: The Man, His Mind and His Music.* New York, 1968.
Gordon Haight: *George Eliot.* New York and Oxford, 1968.
Berthold Litzmann: *Clara Schumann,* trans. G. E. Hadow. London, 1913.
David Magarshack: *Turgenev.* London, 1954.
Thérèse Marix-Spire: *Les Romantiques et la musique, le cas George Sand.* (1804–1838). Paris, 1954.
André Maurois: *Lélia.* New York, 1953.
———. *Olympio.* New York, 1956.
———. *Prometheus.* New York, 1965.
———. *The Titans.* New York, 1957.
Ernest Newman: *The Life of Richard Wagner.* 4 vols. New York, 1933–1945.
Harold Nicolson: *Sainte-Beuve.* London, 1957.
Arthur Phelps and E. J. Howard: *Bettina.* New York, n.d.
Joanna Richardson: *Princess Mathilde.* New York, 1969.
S. Rocheblave: *Une Amitié romanesque.* Imprimerie de Chaix. Paris, 1894.
Alice Sokoloff: *Cosima Wagner.* New York, 1969.
Jacques Vier: *La Comtesse d'Agoult et son temps.* 6 vols. Paris, 1955–1963.

GENERAL REFERENCES (MUSICAL, HISTORICAL, ETC.)

W. H. Auden: *The Dyer's Hand.* London, 1962.
Luigi Barzini, Jr.: *From Caesar to the Mafia.* New York, 1971.
Wilfred Blunt: *The Dream King.* New York, 1970.
E. K. Bramsted: *Aristocracy and the Middle-Classes in Germany: Social Types in German Literature, 1830–1900.* Chicago, 1964.
W. H. Bruford: *Culture and Society in Classical Weimar, 1775–1806.* Cambridge, 1962.
L. D. Coerne: *The Evolution of Modern Orchestration.* New York, 1908.
Claude Debussy: *Monsieur Croche.* Forward by L. Gilman. New York, 1928.
T. S. Eliot: *Selected Essays, 1917–1932.* New York, 1932.
Grove's Dictionary of Music and Musicians, ed. H. C. Colles. 3rd ed. 5 vols. New York, 1935.
Augustus Hare: *Walks in Rome.* 12th edition. 2 vols. London, n.d.
Harvard Dictionary of Music, ed. Willi Apel. 2nd ed. Cambridge, Mass., 1970.
Christopher Hibbert: *The Grand Tour.* London, 1969.
Dominic Kosáry: *A History of Hungary.* Cleveland, 1941.

Paul Henry Lang: *Music in Western Civilization*. New York, 1941.
Franz Liszt: The Man and His Music, ed. Alan Walker. New York, 1970.
André Malraux: *The Voices of Silence,* trans. Stuart Gilbert. New York, 1953.
José Ortega y Gasset: *The Dehumanization of Art.* New York, 1956.
Renato Poggioli: *The Theory of the Avant-Garde.* Cambridge, Mass., 1968.
Mario Praz: *The Romantic Agony.* Garden City, N.Y., 1967.
Herbert Read: *Surrealism,* ed. Herbert Read, and his essay in the book, "Surrealism and the Romantic Principle." London, 1936.
Harold Rosenberg: *The Tradition of the New.* New York, 1959.
Harold Schonberg: *The Great Pianists.* New York, 1963.
––––––. *The Great Conductors.* New York, 1967.
Humphrey Searle: *The Music of Liszt.* New York, 1966.
Igor Stravinsky–Robert Craft: *Retrospectives and Conclusions.* New York, 1969.
Paul Valéry: *Varieties,* II & III. Paris, 1930–1936.
Edmund Wilson: *To the Finland Station.* New edition. New York, 1972.
––––––. *The Wound and the Bow.* New York. Oxford Press. 1965.

ARTICLES

K. W. Bartlett: "Peter Cornelius and *The Barber of Baghdad,*" *Opera* (August 1956).
Béla Bartók: "Liszt Music and Today's Public." 1911, *Monthly Musical Record* (September 1948).
––––––. "The Liszt Problems." 1936 (address delivered to the Hungarian Academy), *Monthly Musical Record* (October 1948).
Jean Chantavoine: "Franz Liszt et Heinrich Heine," *Musical Observer,* vol. 12 (1915).
Arthur Friedheim: "Some Recollections of Liszt," *The Musician* (September 1915).
Emil Haraszti: "Berlioz, Liszt and the Rákóczy March," *Musical Quarterly* (April 1940).
––––––. "Franz Liszt and Richard Wagner in the Franco-German War of 1870" (with Bertita Paulard), *Musical Quarterly* (July 1949).
––––––. "Franz Liszt – Author despite Himself," *Musical Quarterly* (October 1947).
––––––. "Les Origines de l'orchestration Franz Liszt," *Revue de Musicologie* (December 1952).
Ernest Newman: "Berlioz: Romantic and Classic," *Musical Studies* (1905).
Rosa Newmarch: "Liszt in Russia," *Monthly Musical Record,* vol. 32 (1902).
Daniel Ollivier: "Lettres d'un père et de sa fille," *Revue des Deux Mondes,* December 15, 1935, and January 1, 1936.
J. G. Prod'homme: "Une Grande Dame cosmopolite et dilettante: La Comtesse Mouchanoff," *Le Ménestrel,* no. 31 (1930).
Carl Reinecke: "Recollections of Franz Liszt," *Monthly Musical Record,* vol. 26 (1896).
Edward Waters: "Liszt Treasures in Washington," *Étude* (October 1954).

Notes

CHAPTER ONE

1. When Monteverdi tried to add . . . Quoted by Jacques Barzun: *Berlioz and the Romantic Century* (Boston, 1950), I, 423, from *Traité d'instrumentation et d'orchestration.*
2. My prince was always satisfied . . . *Grove's Dictionary of Music and Musicians,* 3rd ed., II, 570: "Haydn," by Ferdinand Pohl.
3. It was this air he carried . . . Henry James: *The Art of Fiction* (Oxford, 1948), p. 105.
4. Yes, they had hair . . . Gautier: *Histoire de Romantisme,* p. 18.
5. *Elle paraissait* . . . Guy de Pourtalès: *Vie de Liszt,* p. 18.

CHAPTER TWO

1. *Si je n'avais pas perdu* . . . *Correspondance de Liszt et de Madame d'Agoult,* I, 59.
2. . . . completely irregular, careless and confused . . . Quoted by Harold Schonberg: *The Great Pianists* (New York, 1963), p. 153.
3. Little Liszt has urgently requested . . . Quoted by Sitwell: *Liszt,* p. 10.
4. There came over me a bitter disgust . . . "Lettre d'un bachelier ès musique," *Gazette Musicale* (January 1837), and Jean Chantavoine: *Pages Romantiques* (Paris, 1912), p. 102.
5. I leave you very much alone . . . Liszt: *Briefe an die Fürstin Sayn-Wittgenstein,* IV, 82.
6. It was all luminous, daring . . . Boissier: *Liszt pédagogue,* p. 54.

CHAPTER THREE

1. The classical I call healthy . . . Wolfgang von Goethe: *Conversations and Encounters* (Chicago, 1966), p. 106.
2. The essence of classicism . . . Paul Valéry: "La Situation de Baudelaire," *Variété,* 2 (1930):155–156.
3. I have no love for reasonable painting . . . Eugène Delacroix: *Journal* (London, 1951), p. 38.
4. The world is about to end . . . Charles Baudelaire: *Intimate Journals* (Hollywood, 1947), p. 56.
5. It is in his first youth . . . Alfred de Vigny, *Chatterton,* translated, condensed and reparagraphed by Barzun, I, 263.
6. For the artist — sufferings, debasements . . . "De la position des artistes," *Gazette Musicale* (May–October, 1935), *Gesammelte Schriften,* II (1), and *Pages romantiques,* p. 68.

7. As for you madmen . . . Berlioz: *Memoirs*, p. 480.
8. Today's generation have difficulty . . . Gautier, p. 2.

CHAPTER FOUR

1. About two hundred persons . . . Quoted by Barzun, I, 99, from Berlioz article in *Le Correspondant*.
2. Miserable newcomer . . . Quoted by André Maurois: *Prometheus* (New York, 1965), p. 149.

CHAPTER FIVE

1. Alfred de Musset talked a lot . . . Liszt-d'Agoult, I, 109.
2. I can't tell you how much this springtime . . . Tiersot: *Les Années romantiques*, pp. 260–261.
3. It is quite impossible . . . Quoted by André Maurois: *Olympio* (New York, 1956), p. 111, from unpublished letter.
4. I feel a strong need . . . Quoted *ibid.*, p. 12.
5. When one is in such a state . . . Sainte-Beuve: *Correspondance générale*, ed. Bonneret, I, 197–198.
6. Never was royalty more legitimate . . . Baudelaire: *L'Art romantique*, II, 519.
7. Decidedly it's the only world . . . Liszt-d'Agoult, I, 24.
8. When I've spent a few hours . . . *Ibid.*
9. Don't doubt that the future . . . George Sand: *Lettres d'un voyageur*, pp. 303–304.
10. The work of certain artists . . . "Lettre d'un bachelier ès musique à un poète voyageur," *Gazette Musicale*, February 12, 1837, and *Pages romantiques*, pp. 105–106.
11. It has been our aim . . . Quoted by Humphrey Searle: *The Music of Liszt* (New York, 1966), p. 70.
12. Hamlet, like every exceptional person . . . *Ibid.*, p. 74.
13. . . . the end of the *Bride of Abydos* . . . Delacroix, p. 39.
14. One has to realize what the poets . . . Quoted by Maurois, *Olympio*, p. 444. No source given.
15. . . . an ill-assorted and bizarre assembly . . . Quoted by Maurois, *Prometheus*, p. 336.
16. M. Beyle, who has written . . . Berlioz: *À travers chants*, p. 27.
17. . . . and the Beethoven sonata . . . Berlioz: Letter in *Gazette Musicale* of August 6, 1839, quoted by T. Marix-Spire: *Les Romantiques et la musique*, p. 553.
18. There are hearts broken with grief . . . Quoted by Searle, p. 11.
19. I adore the broken phrases . . . George Sand: *Journal intime*, pp. 46–47.
20. We can see Liszt . . . Searle, p. 11.
21. Imagine that, wearied . . . *Liszt's Letters*, ed. Constance Bache, I, 31.

CHAPTER SIX

1. Every composer . . . Béla Bartók: Address delivered to the Hungarian Academy, 1936, printed in *Monthly Musical Record* (September 1948). Trans. by Colin Mason.
2. For this fortnight . . . *Liszts Briefe*, I, 7.
3. Let the artist . . . Liszt: "Sur Paganini," *Gazette Musicale*, August 23, 1840. Quoted by Marix-Spire, p. 578.
4. . . . may be played upon . . . Quoted by Schonberg, *Great Pianists*, p. 19.
5. You see my piano is for me . . . "Lettre d'un bachelier ès musique à Adolphe Pictet," *Gazette Musicale*, February 11, 1838. *Pages romantiques*, p. 135.
6. . . . we cannot fail to observe . . . Robert Schumann: *On Music and Musicians*, pp. 146–147.
7. Such compositions must be heard . . . *Ibid.*, p. 150.

CHAPTER SEVEN

1. I write you without knowing . . . Chopin to Heller, quoted by Schonberg, *Great Pianists*, p. 141.
2. He may one day become a deputy . . . Chopin to Jules Fontana, quoted *ibid.*, p. 141.
3. Paganini had opened . . . *Ibid.*, p. 157.
4. . . . the effect of Chopin upon him . . . Sitwell, p. 27.
5. . . . what he chiefly showed Liszt . . . Searle, p. 5.
6. . . . all sunshine and dazzling splendor . . . Quoted by Schonberg, p. 159.
7. He protested . . . George Sand: *Histoire de ma vie*, IV, 440.
8. . . . stolen his prerogatives . . . *Franz Liszt: The Man and His Music:* "Liszt's Musical Background," by Alan Walker, p. 59.
9. . . . it does nicely . . . See pp. 58–67 in *The Man and His Music* for Walker's argument. Note also Walker's statement that "the two men were first introduced to one another by George Sand" (p. 59). Liszt, of course, introduced Chopin to Sand, and rather late in their own acquaintance.

CHAPTER EIGHT

1. The day before the concert . . . Berlioz: *Memoirs*, p. 114.
2. Neither significant in itself . . . Schumann, *On Music and Musicians*, p. 74.
3. . . . promotional aid . . . Barzun discusses this question, I, 152, et seq.
4. It is obvious . . . Liszt: "Compositions pour piano de M. Robert Schumann," *Gazette Musicale*, November 12, 1837. Quoted by Marix-Spire, p. 550.
5. People certainly err . . . Schumann, p. 181.
6. . . . Yet we shouldn't . . . *Ibid.*, p. 181.

7. Nothing was spared us . . . Quoted and translated by Ernest Newman in footnote to Berlioz: *Memoirs*, p. 103. From F. Hiller's *Künstlerleben*.
8. My enemies did not fail . . . Berlioz, p. 100.
9. Genius is grandeur in novelty . . . Liszt: *Le Monde*, December 11, 1836. Quoted by Marix-Spire, p. 529.

CHAPTER NINE

1. I would say an apparition . . . Marie d'Agoult: *Mémoires*, ed. Ollivier, p. 11.
2. Love for the world at large . . . Quoted by Maurois, *Olympio*, p. 66, from Victor Hugo: *Lettre à la fiancée*, p. 54.
3. I send you final farewell . . . *Correspondance de George Sand et d'Alfred de Musset*, ed. Félix Decori (Brussels, 1904), p. 136.
4. We look upon ourselves . . . Quoted by Maurois: *Lélia* (New York, 1953), p. 144. From unpublished letter in Spoelberch de Louvenjoul Collection.
5. Let us live . . . Liszt-d'Agoult, I, 178. Letter of July 23, 1836.
6. It is with a love full of respect . . . D'Agoult: *Mémoires*, p. 79.
7. . . . the ladies flocked around him . . . Alexander Herzen: *My Past and Thoughts* (New York, 1968), II, 114.
8. . . . it was impossible to count . . . Quoted by Jacques Vier: *La Comtesse d'Agoult et son temps* (Paris, 1955–1963), I, 416, n. 140, from *La Mode*, January 5, 1847.
9. These enthusiastic youths . . . Herzen, I, 149–150.

CHAPTER TEN

1. Béatrix is straight and slender . . . Balzac: *Béatrix* (London, 1957), pp. 93 et seq.
2. . . . exercised a sort of sovereignty . . . Marie d'Agoult: *Mes Souvenirs* (Paris, 1877), pp. 15 et seq.
3. . . . a German glance . . . Quoted by Vier, I, 324, n. 39, from unpublished manuscript in Charnacé Archives.
4. Six inches of snow . . . D'Agoult: *Souvenirs*, p. 349.
5. Here, for four months . . . Robert Bory: *Diverses Lettres inédites de Liszt*, p. 12.
6. You forget that I know thirty thousand people . . . Liszt-d'Agoult, I, 106.
7. What happened suddenly . . . D'Agoult: *Mémoires*, p. 29.
8. He whom I had seen . . . *Ibid.*, p. 30.
9. One day, under the cut . . . *Ibid.*, pp. 31 et seq.
10. I was only a child . . . Liszt-d'Agoult, I, 72.
11. A man false and vulgar . . . *Ibid.*, I, 88.
12. Another time, don't talk to me . . . *Ibid.*, I, 98.
13. Society, the world . . . *Ibid.*, I, 100.
14. As for my friend Chopin . . . *Ibid.*, I, 19.
15. It seems to me, Madame . . . *Ibid.*, I, 19.

CHAPTER ELEVEN

1. The undeniable beauty . . . Debussy: *Monsieur Croche* (New York, 1928), p. 108.
2. She said to me . . . D'Agoult: *Mémoires*, pp. 173–174.
3. . . . stick his nose . . . Heine: *Lettres confidentielles*, February 4, 1838. *Gazette Musicale*, p. 42. Quoted by Marix-Spire, p. 434.
4. I never had the honor . . . *Liszts Briefe*, I, 133. Letter of March 22, 1853, to Bockhaus.
5. At the risk of seeming still very naïve . . . Liszt: *Briefe an eine Freudin* (Leipzig, 1895), p. 169.
6. The artist isn't . . . Quoted by Marix-Spire, p. 429, from Emile Barrault: *Aux artists du passé et de l'avenir des Beaux Arts* (Paris, 1830).
7. I can't remember . . . Quoted by Marix-Spire, p. 434, from *Lettres de Montalembert à Lamennais*.
8. Catholicism . . . Quoted by J.-R. Derré: *Lamennais et ses amis* (Paris, 1962), p. 426, from *L'Avenir*, June 29, 1831.
9. Life is a gloomy mystery . . . Liszt-d'Agoult, I, 44.
10. My heart absorbs sadness . . . Quoted by Harold Nicolson: *Sainte-Beuve* (London, 1957), p. 45.
11. Art for art's sake . . . Lamennais: *De l'art et du Beau* (Paris, n.d.), p. 10.
12. Moved by a new spirit . . . Quoted by Derré, p. 430, from *L'Avenir*, December 22, 1830.
13. Oh how I loathe . . . Sainte-Beuve: *Correspondance*, p. 546.
14. What we look for . . . Quoted by Derré, p. 557, from *L'Avenir*, April 1831.
15. We will examine . . . Quoted by Derré, p. 534, from Guyon: *La Pensée politique et sociale de Balzac*.
16. . . . Whatever the imprudence . . . Georges Goyau: *Le Portefeuille de Lamennais* (Paris, 1930), p. 142.
17. Neither *le grand V* . . . Liszt-d'Agoult, I, 78.
18. You imagine perhaps that La Chênaie . . . Liszt-d'Agoult, I, 119 et seq.
19. Come hour of deliverance . . . Liszt: *Gazette Musicale*, August 1835, and *Pages romantiques*, p. 67.
20. The church composer . . . Quoted by Searle, p. 92.
21. Liszt came to interpret Catholic ritual . . . Dannreuther: *Oxford History of Music*, "Romantic Period," VI, 200.

CHAPTER TWELVE

1. *Vous n'êtes pas* . . . D'Agoult: *Mémoires*, p. 183.
2. Can I allow myself . . . George Sand: *Correspondance* (Paris, 1966), II, 760, n., quoted from Marix-Spire article in *Le Monde*, January 31, 1952.
3. I stayed until two . . . Liszt-d'Agoult, I, 131.
4. Monsieur Listz . . . Sand: *Correspondance*, II, 792.
5. What was it that Buloz . . . Sand: *Journal intime* (Paris, 1926), pp. 21–22.

6. Monday in bed . . . Sand: *Correspondance*, II, 813.

7. Do you take me for a conceited fool . . . *Ibid.*, p. 870.

8. I will make a feast . . . Quoted by Marix-Spire, p. 444, n. 105, from unpublished letter in Ollivier Archive.

9. Now then, didn't we . . . Sand: *Lettres d'un voyageur*, ed. Lévy (Paris, 1956–), p. 229, from *Revue des Deux Mondes*, August 31, 1835.

10. Imagine an assembly . . . "Une soirée chez Liszt," *Mercure de France*, June 15, 1835.

11. Even here, my heart . . . Liszt-d'Agoult, I, 125.

12. Form is the means . . . Lamennais: *L'Art et le beau*, p. 349.

13. It is you above all . . . Sand: "Lettre d'un voyageur sur Lavater," *Revue des Deux Mondes*, September 1, 1835. (This letter, addressed to Liszt, is No. V in *RDM*, No. VII in the Lévy edition.)

14. Do you remember . . . *Ibid.*

15. Franz invited us to dinner . . . D'Agoult: *Mémoires*, p. 207.

16. My beautiful countess . . . Sand: *Correspondance*, III, 43.

17. I saw you . . . *Ibid.*, p. 22.

CHAPTER THIRTEEN

1. The hours, the days . . . D'Agoult: *Mémoires*, p. 31.

2. I opened it at random . . . *Ibid.*, p. 37.

3. Monday midnight . . . Liszt-d'Agoult, I, 132.

4. My blood, so long congealed . . . D'Agoult: *Mémoires*, pp. 39 et seq.

5. God forbid . . . *Ibid.*, p. 202.

6. The illusory play . . . Ramann: *Franz Liszt als Künstler und Mensch* (Leipzig, 1880), I, 331. Given in English by Ernest Newman in *The Man Liszt*, p. 51. (I.e., this is not Miss Cowdrey's deplorable translation.)

7. The day you can tell me . . . Liszt-d'Agoult, I, 135.

8. From six to eight . . . *Ibid.*, p. 136.

CHAPTER FOURTEEN

1. Granite ramparts . . . D'Agoult: *Mémoires*, p. 42.

2. Book list in Vier, I, 190.

3. Liszt enters . . . Mme Boissier's journal, quoted by Robert Bory: *Une Retraite romantique en Suisse* (Paris, 1930), pp. 30–31.

4. He guessed nothing . . . D'Agoult: *Mémoires*, pp. 52–53.

5. Franz entered . . . *Ibid.*, p. 64.

6. Aversion for the virtuoso . . . Vier, I, 393, n. 33, passage omitted in published *Mémoires*.

7. How right you are . . . Quoted by Marix-Spire, p. 580, n. 199, from unpublished letter of July 4, 1838, in Ollivier Archive.

8. I ought to have been with you . . . Sand: *Correspondance*, III, 64.

9. Not a day passes . . . Quoted by Marix-Spire, p. 465, n. 29, from unpublished letter in Spoelberch de Louvenjoul collection.

CHAPTER FIFTEEN

1. Blandine Rachel . . . Quoted by Bory, *Retraite*, p. 41.
2. Her name is Blandine . . . *Liszt's Letters*, ed. Bache, I, 33–34.
3. The extraordinary position . . . Du Moulin Eckhardt: *Cosima Wagner* (Munich, 1929), I, 213–214.
4. . . . the cruel struggle . . . D'Agoult: *Mémoires*, p. 74.
5. I've allowed myself to be invaded . . . *Ibid.*, p. 69.
6. Now that the temptation . . . Liszt-d'Agoult, I, 147.
7. It is my only fortune . . . *Ibid.*, p. 156.
8. There has been only one event . . . Quoted by Marix-Spire, p. 466, from Spoelberch de Lovenjoul collection, unpublished letter.
9. *Grandissime succès* . . . Liszt-d'Agoult, I, 170.
10. He plays excellently . . . Quoted by Schonberg: *Great Pianists*, p. 177.
11. . . . the Sphinx's enigma of every pianist . . . Berlioz: *Gazette Musicale*, June 12, 1836.
12. M. Liszt, the pianist . . . Rodolphe Apponyi: *Vingt-cinq ans à Paris* (Paris, 1913–26), III, 265.
13. I came to Paris . . . Sand: *Correspondance*, II, 397, n. 2, quoted from Wladimir Karenine: *George Sand, sa vie et ses oeuvres* (Paris, 1899–1926).
14. If you aren't leaving until the end of June . . . Sand: *Correspondance*, III, 370 et seq.
15. Your letter, dear Father . . . Goyau: *Le Portefeuille de Lamennais* (Paris, 1930), p. 206.
16. To what a test . . . Liszt-d'Agoult, I, 174.
17. The Abbé de Lamennais has arrived . . . *Ibid.*

CHAPTER SIXTEEN

1. There are neither sun nor stars . . . Liszt-d'Agoult, I, 178.
2. I am disposed to enjoy myself . . . *Ibid.*, p. 176.
3. You should know . . . that among the bits of foolishness . . . S. Rocheblave: *Une Amitié romanesque* (Paris, 1894), p. 10.
4. If you want me to love you . . . Sand: *Correspondance*, III, 226.
5. Don't pity me . . . *Ibid.*, pp. 399–400.
6. George was not unaware . . . *Ibid.*, p. 400, n. 1.
7. I have forbidden . . . Quoted by Maurois: *Lélia*, p. 163.
8. Gentlemen, where are you stopping . . . Sand: "Lettre d'un voyageur à Charles Didier," *Revue des Deux Mondes*, November 1, 1836. *Lettres d'un voyageur*, pp. 288–289.
9. Monsieur has come to arrest . . . Adolphe Pictet: *Une Course à Chamounix*, ed. R. Bory (Geneva, 1930), p. 16.

10. Nature to you is a magic lantern . . . *Ibid.*, pp. 35–36.
11. Absolutely not, said Liszt . . . *Ibid.*, pp. 20 et seq.
12. George has absolutely nothing mysterious . . . *Ibid.*, p. 26.
13. Except for Liszt . . . Sand: *Correspondance*, III, 563.
14. Ah yes! I say to myself . . . Sand: "Lettre à Didier," *Lettres d'un voyageur*, p. 311.
15. One can't help but feel . . . Aloys Mooser, quoted by Marix-Spire, p. 497.

CHAPTER SEVENTEEN

1. One autumn evening . . . Jules Janin, *Gazette Musicale*, January 1, 1837. Quoted by Vier, I, 231.
2. . . . the most remarkable thing . . . Berlioz: "Première Soirée musicale de MM. Liszt, Batta et Urhan," *Gazette Musicale*, 1837.
3. I see a thousand inconveniences . . . Sand: *Correspondance*, III, 569.
4. I accept the proposal with joy . . . *Ibid.*, p. 570.
5. At the Hôtel de France . . . Sand: *Histoire de ma vie* (Paris, 1876), IV, 405.
6. Chopin received me very nicely . . . Quoted by Marix-Spire, p. 528, from letter in Warsaw Palace Archive.
7. I went to Chopin's . . . Ferdinand Denis: *Journal* (Paris, 1932), p. 69.
8. I like her better . . . Quoted by Maurois: *Lélia*, p. 228, from Didier's unpublished diary.
9. The coterie of George Sand . . . Sainte-Beuve: *Mes Poisons* (Paris, 1926), p. 106.
10. Lamennais has been odious . . . *Ibid.*, p. 93.
11. It was not without profound feeling . . . Liszt in *Le Monde*, January 8, 1837. Quoted by Marix-Spire, p. 532.
12. He has acquainted me . . . Quoted by Marix-Spire, p. 533, from Peyrat: *Béranger et Lamennais.*
13. It isn't Saint Peter . . . *Vert-Vert:* "Un Raoût des Dieux," quoted by Marix-Spire, pp. 530–531.
14. . . . in a mood of complete surrender . . . Quoted by Maurois: *Lélia*, p. 232.
15. He is so good . . . Quoted *ibid.*, p. 231.
16. To suppose that one has the right . . . V. Schoelcher in *Le Monde* of December 30, 1836. Quoted by Marix-Spire, p. 530.
17. What a man! . . . Berlioz: *Années romantiques*, ed. Tiersot (Paris, n.d.), p. 245.
18. One talked too much . . . Berlioz: Letter to Liszt printed in *Gazette Musicale* of August 11, 1839.

CHAPTER EIGHTEEN

1. She is leaving . . . Sand: *Correspondance*, III, 669n.
2. Good morning, dear Franz . . . *Ibid.*, p. 698.

3. An unheard-of thing . . . Ernest Legouvé: "Les Concerts de MM. Liszt, Batta et Urhan," *Gazette Musicale*, 1837. Quoted by Marix-Spire, p. 540.
4. Need I tell you . . . Liszt-d'Agoult, I, 191.
5. My God, my God . . . S. Rocheblave, *Une Amitié romanesque*, p. 30.
6. The keys seemed to bleed . . . Quoted by Jean Chantavoine: "Franz Liszt et Heinrich Heine," *Musical Observer*, 12 (1915):501–503. From *Lettres confidentielles*, February 4, 1838.

CHAPTER NINETEEN

1. [At Nohant] it is a life . . . René Bray: *Quelques lettres de Madame d'Agoult* (Lausanne, 1932). Quoted by Marix-Spire, p. 543.
2. Enclosed is a bit of paper . . . Quoted by Vier, I, 259, from unpublished letter.
3. Liszt made a fart . . . Quoted by Marix-Spire, p. 544, from unpublished letter in Spoelberch de Louvenjoul collection.
4. Her lack of dignity . . . Juliette Adam: *Mes sentiments* (Paris, 1904), p. 252.
5. A promenade along the Indre . . . D'Agoult: *Mémoires*, p. 94.
6. Dawn, my room . . . Sand: *Journal intime*, p. 55.
7. Magnificent weather . . . Sand: *Ibid.*, pp. 50–51.
8. Is he perhaps . . . *Ibid.*, pp. 45–47.
9. The moon went down . . . *Ibid.*, pp. 60–62.
10. He has two manias . . . Quoted by Marix-Spire, p. 544, from unpublished memoirs of Charles Duvernet.
11. Dear Mirabella . . . Sand: *Correspondance*, IV, 153.
12. I am convinced . . . D'Agoult: *Mémoires*, p. 97.
13. Madame Sand used . . . Janka Wohl: *François Liszt: Souvenirs d'une compatriote* (Ollendorf, 1887), p. 160.

CHAPTER TWENTY

1. One can still be in love . . . From Bory: *Retraite*, pp. 127–128.
2. The maestro is always charming . . . Liszt-d'Agoult, I, 203.
3. At an age when everything . . . D'Agoult: *Mémoires*, pp. 118–119.
4. . . . the luckiest of mortals . . . Letter of December 15, 1837 published in Marix-Spire, appendix, p. 618.
5. My heart was filled with poetry . . . Liszt-d'Agoult, I, 207.
6. Here is a beautiful day . . . *Ibid.*, p. 247.
7. Each day, reflection gives me . . . "Lettre d'un bachelier ès musique à Berlioz," *Gazette Musicale*, and *Pages romantiques*, p. 261.
8. We passed with respect . . . Letter of June 28, 1839, quoted in Bory: *Retraite*, p. 160.
9. I have dared to name . . . "Lettre d'un bachelier" to Schlesinger, *Gazette Musicale*, March 28, 1839, and *Pages romantiques*, p. 272.
10. I do not believe . . . W. H. Auden in *The New Yorker*, January 4, 1969.

11. The Italians want sweet sensations . . . Bory: *Retraite*, p. 124.
12. Well, there you are . . . *Ibid.*, p. 126.
13. The marquis is a vain fool . . . Quoted by Vier, I, 412, n. 84, from unpublished fragment of Marie's journal in Ollivier Archive.
14. Rossini has just . . . Liszt-d'Agoult, I, 251.
15. Crétin's tours . . . Letter to Sand of January 18, 1838, published in Marix-Spire, appendix, p. 620.
16. Crétin has become fantastically . . . Quoted by Marix-Spire, p. 620, from unpublished letter of July 4, 1838 in Ollivier Archive.
17. . . . the human soul needs . . . Stendhal: *Vie de Rossini* (Paris, 1923), p. 107.
18. From the aristocrat . . . Liszt: "Lettre d'un bachelier sur La Scala," *Gazette Musicale*, May 27, 1838, and *Pages romantiques*, p. 182.
19. Franz plays the Pacini . . . D'Agoult: *Mémoires*, p. 113.
20. Rossini has injured . . . *Ibid.*, p. 174.
21. I feel I lack the principle . . . D'Agoult: *Mémoires*, p. 140.
22. Love me . . . Liszt-d'Agoult, I, 203.

CHAPTER TWENTY-ONE

1. I can't get accustomed . . . D'Agoult: *Mémoires*, p. 255.
2. It's horrible . . . *Ibid.*, p. 143.
3. Treat this infantilism . . . Daniel Ollivier: *Autour de la Comtesse d'Agoult* (Paris, 1941), p. 159.
4. For me, everything is the future . . . Quoted by Vier, I, 423, n. 264, from unpublished letter to Lambert Massart.
5. The post is leaving . . . Liszt-D'Agoult, I, 218.
6. You ask me to join you . . . D'Agoult: *Mémoires*, p. 146.
7. Franz had abandoned me . . . D'Agoult: *Mémoires*, p. 147.
8. And anyway, yes, I love you . . . Liszt-d'Agoult, I, 231.
9. They had found . . . D'Agoult: *Mémoires*, p. 147.
10. You remember my words . . . *Ibid.*, p. 149.
11. The Fellows are more united . . . Quoted by Vier, I, 300, from unpublished letter of July 4, 1838, in Ollivier Archive.
12. Look, if I ever . . . Quoted by Vier, I, 422, n. 255, from F. de Langle: *Franz Liszt et Daniel Stern* (Paris, 1929).
13. I know that at present . . . D'Agoult: *Mémoires*, p. 154.
14. My place will be . . . *Ibid.*, p. 165.
15. I see him accepting an inferior . . . *Ibid.*, p. 184.
16. . . . the cruel struggle . . . Liszt-d'Agoult, I, 291.
17. Why despair . . . D'Agoult: *Mémoires*, p. 177.
18. I don't know why . . . *Ibid.*, p. 179.
19. I've heard the famous Liszt . . . Joanna Richardson: *Princess Mathilde* (New York, 1969), p. 334.

20. It will take all we have . . . Quoted by Vier; I, 423, n. 267, from unpublished letter of September 18, 1839, in Ollivier Archive.
21. I establish her . . . Quoted by Vier, I, 317, from unpublished portion of Marie's journal in Ollivier Archive.
22. Conversations with Franz . . . D'Agoult: *Mémoires*, p. 168.

CHAPTER TWENTY-TWO

1. I think you'll end by finding . . . Quoted by Vier, I, 306, from unpublished letter in Ollivier Archive.
2. Decidedly, I pride myself . . . Bory: *Retraite*, p. 147.
3. This trip to the Balearics . . . Sand: *Correspondance*, IV, 721, n. 1, and in Marix-Spire, p. 564, who originally published it in *Revue des Sciences Humaines* (April–September, 1951).
4. I can assure you . . . Sand: *Correspondance*, IV, 728, n. 1.
5. On what, if you please . . . Maurois: *Lélia*, p. 283, from unpublished letter of January 23, 1839, in Spoelberch de Louvenjoul collection.
6. You will perhaps be astonished . . . Sand: *Correspondance*, IV, 758n.
7. You saw how she accused . . . Sand: *Correspondance*, IV, 759, and Rocheblave: *Amitié romanesque*.
8. I don't understand your appeal . . . *Ibid.*, p. 799.
9. Certain serious and clearly defined . . . Maurois: *Lélia*, p. 251, from unpublished letter in Spoelberch de Louvenjoul collection.
10. From spite, I think . . . Quoted by Marix-Spire, p. 567, n. 139, from Ollivier Archive.
11. Forgive me . . . *Liszts Briefe*, I, 57–58.
12. Went with Liszt . . . Sainte-Beuve: *Carnet de voyage* (Paris, 1922).
13. My faculties are exhausted . . . D'Agoult: *Mémoires*, p. 166.
14. How to leave the soil . . . Liszt-d'Agoult, I, 262–263.
15. Goodbye, goodbye . . . *Ibid.*, I, 255.

CHAPTER TWENTY-THREE

1. I will work like a madman . . . Liszt-d'Agoult, I, 287.
2. We were like men in love . . . Vladimir Vassilievitch Stassov; quoted by Rosa Newmarch: "Liszt in Russia," *Monthly Musical Record*, vol. 32 (1902).
3. A pianist myself . . . Alexander Siloti: *My Memories of Liszt* (Edinburgh, n.d.), p. 35.
4. It does not seem as if it were music . . . Amy Fay: *Music Study in Germany* (Chicago, 1891), p. 214.
5. . . . root and branch . . . Quoted by Schonberg: *Great Pianists*, p. 165.
6. But since men of genius . . . Herzen, II, 860.
7. This Lisztomania . . . Quoted and translated by Arthur Friedheim: *Life and Liszt* (New York, 1960), p. 149.

8. Liszt's way in everything . . . B. Litzmann: *Clara Schumann* (London, 1913), II, 120.

9. Liszt certainly aimed . . . Arnold Schering: "Über Liszts Personlichkeit und Kunst," *Jahrbuch Musikbibliotek Peters*, 1926. Translated by Ernest Newman in *The Man Liszt*, p. 305.

10. How extraordinarily he plays . . . Litzmann, I, 285.

11. You will find in him . . . Mendelssohn: *Letters to Ignaz and Charlotte Moscheles* (Boston, 1888), p. 203.

12. What you say about Liszt's harmonics . . . *Ibid.*, p. 136.

13. . . . works by Beethoven, Bach . . . Quoted by Newman: *Man Liszt*, p. 10, from Du Moulin Eckhardt: *Ferdinand David und die Familie Mendelssohn-Bartoldy* (Leipzig, 1888).

14. . . . so entirely slovenly . . . Mendelssohn: *Letters*, p. 97.

15. 350 people, orchestra . . . Letter of March 30, 1840, quoted in "Mendelssohn," Grove, III, 399.

16. Some had a grudge . . . Quoted by Barzun, I, 471, from *Evenings in the Orchestra*, trans. Charles Roche.

CHAPTER TWENTY-FOUR

1. Being wholly absorbed in his innovations . . . Quoted by Barzun, I, 506, from Adolphe Boschot: *Le Crépuscule d'un romantique* (Paris, 1913).

2. Hungary having covered herself . . . Liszt-d'Agoult, II, 47.

3. I mentioned a splendid day . . . *Ibid.*, I, 350.

4. As it is a national matter . . . *Ibid.*, I, 331.

5. If I cared a lot about . . . *Ibid.*, I, 347.

6. Brace yourself . . . *Ibid.*, I, 390.

7. I have collected a number of . . . *Ibid.*, II, 368.

8. Bartók is emphatic . . . Bartók on Liszt: *Monthly Musical Record*, September 1948.

CHAPTER TWENTY-FIVE

1. Don't you think you and I . . . Berlioz: *Le Musicien errant*, ed. Julien Tiersot (Paris, 1919), pp. 178–180.

2. Liszt mounted the platform . . . Newmarch: "Liszt in Russia," from Stassov.

3. He is the human reflection . . . Quoted by Maurois: *Prometheus*, p. 448.

4. She was wearing . . . Quoted by Maurois: *The Titans* (New York, 1957), p. 252.

5. These Russian ladies . . . *Ibid.*, p. 314.

6. They have conceived the idea . . . *Ibid.*, p. 253, from Viel-Castel.

7. . . . soul is too tender . . . Adelheid von Schorn: *Zwei Menschenalter* (Berlin, 1901), p. 236.

CHAPTER TWENTY-SIX

1. . . . dreamed of reconstituting . . . Vier, II, 11.
2. . . . realize that our natures . . . Liszt-d'Agoult, I, 399.
3. De Vigny was here . . . *Ibid.*, II, 207.
4. I never stop thanking you . . . *Ibid.*, II, 234.
5. Not the least disenchantment . . . *Ibid.*, II, 127.
6. I found a way . . . *Ibid.*, I, 368.
7. I'm mad about her . . . Quoted by Vier, II, 41, from Ollivier Archive.
8. Necessarily, you would direct . . . Liszt-d'Agoult, I, 295.
9. In two years . . . *Ibid.*, I, 325.
10. . . . aesthetical hysterics . . . Herzen, II, 860.
11. I see a frightening affinity . . . Liszt-d'Agoult, II, 327.
12. In all civilized society . . . *Essai sur la liberté*, vol. IV, chap. 15.
13. Liszt will be for some time . . . Quoted by Vier, II, 288, n. 18, from letter of June 6, 1844, in Ollivier Archive.
14. Liszt wanted to make . . . Quoted *ibid.*, p. 284, n. 26, from letter of August 7, 1844, in Ollivier Archive.
15. Tenderness being the least habitual . . . Liszt-d'Agoult, II, 82.
16. After two months of attentions . . . *Ibid.*, I, 400.
17. Keep my love if you can . . . *Ibid.*, I, 425–426.
18. This is what you say to me . . . *Ibid.*, I, 450–451.
19. My life away from you . . . *Ibid.*, II, 118.
20. Nonnenwerth will be . . . Quoted by Vier, II, 269, n. 432, from letter of August 27, 1846, Marie to Madame Czettritz: *"Il me dit: Nonnewerth sera le sanctuaire,"* etc. Unpublished, in Ollivier Archive.
21. . . . tomb of my illusions . . . Quoted by Vier, II, 70, from Marie's unpublished memoirs, Ollivier Archive.
22. The life we lead . . . Solange Joubert: *Une Correspondance romantique* (Paris, 1947), p. 184.
23. I would be better as a friend . . . Liszt-d'Agoult, II, 175.
24. Perhaps I haven't understood . . . Liszt-d'Agoult, II, 299.
25. . . . It seems to me I have forgotten how to live . . . *Ibid.*, II, 242.
26. I am entirely of the opinion . . . *Ibid.*, II, 255.
27. Obviously, you don't think of me . . . *Ibid.*, II, 256.

CHAPTER TWENTY-SEVEN

1. Young, beautiful . . . D'Agoult: *Mémoires*, p. 183.
2. As to you, my friend . . . Quoted by Vier, II, 286, n. 55, from unpublished letter in Ollivier Archive.
3. But when he saw Nélida's hollow cheeks . . . Marie d'Agoult: *Nélida* (Brussels, 1846), II, 48 et seq.
4. . . . a genuinely historical document . . . Newman: *Man Liszt*, p. 125.

5. Those who are talking . . . Quoted by Vier, II, 287, n. 2, from letter of Hortense Allart, unpublished in Ollivier Archive.
6. The distinction is charming . . . Liszt-d'Agoult, II, 271.
7. I am mortally sad . . . *Ibid.*, II, 338.
8. Persuaded that you . . . *Ibid.*, II, 341.
9. I have told no lies . . . *Ibid.*, II, 339.
10. Liszt remains entirely true . . . Marcel Herwegh: *Au printemps des dieux* (Paris, 1929), pp. 71–72.
11. What you say about Liszt . . . *Ibid.*, p. 75.
12. At midnight on the eve . . . Quoted by Vier, II, 135, from unpublished letter in Ollivier Archive.
13. However moved I may be . . . Liszt-d'Agoult, II, 344.
14. As the terms are fixed . . . Vier: *Franz Liszt, l'artiste, le clerc* (Paris, 1950), pp. 73–74.
15. A year ago, Madame . . . *Ibid.*, p. 77.
16. You are capable . . . *Ibid.*, pp. 154–155.

CHAPTER TWENTY-EIGHT

1. Give me the countryside . . . Liszt-Wittgenstein, I, 197.
2. I was always happy . . . Bory: *Liszt et ses enfants*, pp. 220–223.
2. It is emptiness . . . Maurois: *Prometheus*, p. 509.
4. The romantic symbolism . . . La Mara: *Aus der Glanzzeit der Weimarer Altenburg* (Leipzig, 1906). Introduction, p. iii.
5. Dear masterpiece of God . . . Letter in Weimar Archive.
6. There is not a hair . . . Quoted by Maurois: *Olympio*, p. 193.
7. . . . promised to be at his service . . . Newman: *Man Liszt*, p. 160.
8. . . . I who claim to be . . . Liszt: *Briefe an seine Mutter*, p. 101.
9. Is the rupture . . . Liszt-d'Agoult, II, 375.
10. . . . a big (and illegible) . . . *Ibid.*, II, 379.
11. So you've had Liszt . . . La Mara: *Glanzzeit*, p. 33.
12. Something tells me . . . *Ibid.*
13. Have you fixed . . . *Ibid.*, p. 34.
14. Polish women's virtue . . . *Ibid.*, p. 35.

CHAPTER TWENTY-NINE

1. I have worked pretty well . . . *Liszt's Letters*, I, 82.
2. Once, in Podolia . . . Liszt: *The Gypsy in Music*. Trans. ed. Evans (London, 1926), pp. 161 et seq.
3. Liszt has treated the Princess . . . Theodor von Bernhardi: *Briefe und Tagebuchblätter aus den Jahren 1834–1857* (Leipzig, 1893), pp. 97 et seq., translated in *Man Liszt*, p. 180.
4. Instead of writing from Athens . . . Liszt-d'Agoult, II, 391.

5. Where to go . . . Quoted by Vier, II, 243, from unpublished journal in Ollivier Archive.
6. Nothing surprises me less . . . Liszt-d'Agoult, II, 417.
7. You must count on me . . . Liszt-Wittgenstein, I, 21.
8. My heart is in my mouth . . . Liszt-d'Agoult, II, 393.
9. I knew how energetic and decided . . . *Briefe hervorragender Zeitgenossen an Franz Liszt*, I, 107.
10. I who have always detested politics . . . Liszt-Wittgenstein, I, 29.
11. . . . a hard decision . . . Fanny Lewald: *Zwölf Bilder nach dem Leben* (Berlin, 1888), p. 350.
12. Regardless of the blocking . . . *Liszt's Letters*, I, 88.
13. Carolyne, who had intimidated . . . Pourtalès, p. 134.
14. . . . to which he had not dared . . . Sitwell, p. 159.
15. Even when all the instruments . . . János Hankiss: *Wenn Liszt ein Tagbuch gefürt hätte* (Budapest, 1966), p. 83.
16. In these successive wars . . . Quoted by Searle, p. 73.
17. Liszt again appears . . . Jean Chantavoine: "Franz Liszt et Heinrich Heine," *Musical Observer* 12 (1915):501–503.
18. Your country at this hour . . . *Briefe hervorragender Zeitgenossen an Franz Liszt* (Leipzig, 1895–1904), I, 104.
19. They said you were in Vienna . . . *Ibid.*, p. 100.
20. Make no mistake about it . . . Quoted by Maurois: *Prometheus*, p. 521.
21. One . . . will set the tricolor . . . Quoted by Maurois: *Olympio*, p. 263.
22. Republicanism is at this moment . . . Berlioz: *Memoirs*, p. ix.
23. What a sight! . . . *Ibid.*, p. 18.
24. Policy must be ruthless . . . Quoted by Maurois: *Prometheus*, p. 517.
25. . . . whether this country exists with or without . . . Stendhal: *A Roman Journal* (New York, 1961), p. 217.
26. I would be the first to answer . . . Lewald, p. 341.
27. The guillotine . . . Bernhardi: Translated in *Man Liszt*, p. 179.

CHAPTER THIRTY

1. Though Goethe's sun was setting . . . In George Lewes: *Life of Goethe* (New York, 1965), p. 558.

CHAPTER THIRTY-ONE

1. After having been the incarnation . . . Camille Saint-Saëns: *Portraits et souvenirs* (Paris, 1900). "Freely translated" by Sitwell, p. 162.
2. . . . Weimar under the Grand Duke . . . Liszt-d'Agoult, II, 323.
3. . . . must have shared the general opinion . . . Newman: *Man Liszt*, p. 106.
4. . . . above all, no censorship . . . *Briefwechsel zwischen Franz Liszt und Carl Alexander* (Leipzig, 1910), p. 17.

5. . . . The continued goodness . . . *Correspondence of Joachim*, trans. N. Bickley (London, 1914), p. 147.
6. . . . although Dresden and a hundred other cities . . . *Liszt's Letters*, I, 241.
7. Who can imagine the torture . . . Berlioz: *Memoirs*, pp. 267 et seq.
8. It is not merely that . . . Quoted by Ernest Newman: *The Life of Richard Wagner* (New York, 1965), II, 195n.
9. He appeared suddenly . . . *The Early Correspondence of Hans von Bülow* (New York, 1896), p. 91.
10. Dear Exalted One . . . Quoted by Newman: *Wagner*, III, 367.
11. At a certain moment . . . *Liszt's Letters*, I, 440.
12. There was, in 1850 . . . Barzun, I, 556.
13. With Liszt, one is . . . Peter Cornelius: *Ausgewählte Briefe, nebst Tagebuchblättern* . . . (Leipzig, 1904), II, 537–538.
14. The frequent ill-success . . . *Liszt's Letters*, I, 310.

CHAPTER THIRTY-TWO

1. . . . to follow me here . . . Lewald: *Zwölf Bilder nach dem Leben*, p. 350.
2. . . . gave her his hand . . . Bernhardi: *Briefe und Tagebuchblätter*, pp. 139–140. Trans. by Newman, *Man Liszt*, pp. 188–189.
3. Her dark and pensive eyes . . . Richard Wagner: *My Life* (New York, 1911), II, 606.
4. . . . at the piano Liszt . . . Adelheid von Schorn: *Das nachklassische Weimar* (Weimar, 1911, 1912), p. 100.
5. Dear Papa . . . Du Moulin Eckhardt: I, 53–54.
6. As precious as your affection . . . *Correspondance de Liszt et de sa fille Madame Émile Ollivier* (Paris, 1936), p. 45.
7. I can never stop . . . *The Letters of Franz Liszt to Marie zu Sayn-Wittgenstein*, trans. and ed. by Howard Hugo (Cambridge, Mass., 1953), p. 89.
8. I cannot as a layman . . . Friedrich Hebbel: *Briefe* (Berlin, 1900), VI, 175.
9. The conversation was woven of gold . . . Schorn: *Nachklassische*, p. 39.
10. Franz Liszt comes to see us . . . Bernhardi, pp. 97–108. Trans. by Newman, *Man Liszt*, pp. 184–185.
11. I have more than once explained . . . *Correspondence of Wagner and Liszt*, ed. and trans. by Francis Hueffer (London, 1889), II, 136.
12. On arriving at the Altenburg . . . Quoted in Gordon Haight: *George Eliot* (Oxford, 1968), p. 155, and George Eliot: *Leaves from a Notebook* (New York, 1884).
13. Dear Weimar . . . Haight, p. 168.

CHAPTER THIRTY-THREE

1. Hans is evidently gifted . . . Bülow: *Early Correspondence*, p. 52.
2. My piano playing . . . *Ibid.*, p. 116.

3. The young man . . . Quoted by Barzun, II, 128, from *Correspondance inédite*, ed. Daniel Bernard (Paris, 1879).

4. He stole once . . . Amy Fay: *Music Study in Germany* (Chicago, 1891), pp. 277–278.

5. . . . a terrible youth . . . Wagner-Liszt, II, 236.

6. Nun, Mason . . . William Mason: *Memories of a Musical Life* (New York, 1901), p. 87.

7. We boys saw little of the Wittgensteins . . . *Ibid.*, p. 95.

8. You are to learn all you can . . . *Ibid.*, p. 114.

9. With the death of Schumann . . . Anton Rubinstein: *A Conversation on Music* (New York, 1892), p. 90.

10. I don't want to preach . . . *Liszt's Letters*, I, 219.

11. Your *fugue* this morning . . . *Ibid.*, I, 232.

12. Rubinstein had played on a beautiful Bechstein . . . Siloti: *My Memories of Liszt*, p. 38.

13. . . . the very dubious temple . . . Hans von Bülow: *Neue Briefe*, ed. Du Moulin Eckhart (Munich, 1927), p. 507.

14. We are all descended from Liszt radically . . . Ferruccio Busoni: *Open Letter about Liszt*, 1916. Quoted in *Man and His Music*, p. 374. (Busoni's classic essay on Liszt is however not this but in *The Essence of Music*, reprinted London, 1956.)

15. Louis Kentner observes . . . *Man and His Music:* "The Interpretation of Liszt's Piano Music," p. 203.

CHAPTER THIRTY-FOUR

1. . . . my own artistic development . . . Carl Maria Cornelius: *Peter Cornelius*, II, 132–133.

2. I have much to tell you . . . Joachim, p. 113.

3. Stern wishes to produce my overture . . . *Ibid.*, p. 142.

4. I have cleaned up . . . Quoted by Newman: *Wagner*, II, 210, from *Die Musik*.

5. I was the intimate friend . . . Quoted by Emil Haraszti: "Les Origines de l'orchestration de Franz Liszt," *Revue de Musicologie* (December 1952).

6. . . . impure harmony . . . gratuitous ugliness . . . These phrases were all at one time or another applied to Liszt by the professors associated with the Leipzig Conservatory, Reitz, Hauptmann, David, etc. "Were you to teach temperance at the ginshop door," was said by Sir George Macfarren, Principal of the Royal Academy of Music (and a contributor to *Grove's Dictionary of Music and Musicians*), in explanation of his refusal to allow his pupils to hear Liszt's music.

7. On my advice, Bülow will not play . . . *Liszt's Letters*, I, 401.

8. Have you considered that *Orpheus* . . . *Ibid.*, I, 296.

9. Knowing by experience how little . . . *Ibid.*, II, 96.

10. Then it seemed to me . . . Cornelius, I, 187 et seq.

11. It upset me on several occasions . . . *Ibid.*, p. 170.

12. . . . a jargon that is a delicious . . . Robert Gutman: *Richard Wagner* (New York, 1968), p. 183.

CHAPTER THIRTY-FIVE

1. The dreamy unreality . . . Wagner: *Life*, I, 500.
2. How could I think of you otherwise . . . Wagner-Liszt, II, 213.
3. The very next thing I must do . . . Wagner: *Life*, I, 449.
4. You told me recently . . . Wagner-Liszt, I, 6.
5. No theatre in the world . . . *Ibid.*, I, 13.
6. I was filled . . . Wagner: *Life*, I, 501.
7. Tell me, my dear Liszt . . . Wagner-Liszt, I, 67.
8. Really I'm not at all anxious . . . Wagner: *Life*, I, 508. (Not in dialogue form as I give it, but the words are the same.)
9. Listen, my dear friend . . . Wagner-Liszt, I, 56.
10. Your friends must get me . . . *Ibid.*, I, 29.
11. Think what you can do for me . . . *Ibid.*, I, 50.
12. Perform my *Lohengrin* . . . *Ibid.*, I 63.

CHAPTER THIRTY-SIX

1. The super-ideal tone . . . Wagner-Liszt, I, 35.
2. . . . largely to oblige Wagner . . . Newman: *Wagner*, II, 201 et seq.
3. Arrive Weymar . . . *Liszt's Letters*, I, 108.
4. . . . . Wagner was simply one . . . Newman: *Wagner*, II, 193 and 300.
5. I have proclaimed without reserve . . . Liszt-Wittgenstein, II, 183.
6. Wagner knows what our age likes . . . See Robert Gutman's admirable study of Nietzsche's break with Wagner in the biography, pp. 352–361.
7. You must know the article is by me . . . Wagner-Liszt, I, 145.
8. . . . when there is a question . . . Liszt-Wittgenstein, I, 140–141.
9. Candidly speaking . . . Wagner-Liszt, I, 219.
10. The means that Liszt is now employing . . . Quoted and translated in Newman: *Wagner*, II, 299 et seq., from *Briefe an Hans von Bülow* (Jena, 1916).
11. For instance, that since my acquaintance with Liszt's harmonics . . . Quoted *ibid.*, II, 600.
12. My musical creed is what I have done . . . Quoted by Barzun, II, 73, from interview printed in *Ménestrel*, February 22, 1885.
13. When I think of your sympathetic . . . Wagner-Liszt, II, 291.
14. Tell Frau Ritter . . . Quoted by Newman: *Wagner*, II, 266.
15. But let us cherish no illusions . . . Wagner-Liszt, I, 175.
16. Your letter, my glorious friend . . . *Ibid.*, I, 179.
17. . . . far from the smoke and odor . . . *Ibid.*, I, 189.
18. I will produce my *Siegfried* . . . *Ibid.*, I, 77.
19. When I am composing and scoring . . . *Ibid.*, II, 29.

20. My nervous system is in a bad way . . . Quoted and translated in Newman: *Wagner*, II, 381.
21. Liszt has behaved . . . *Ibid.*, II, 402, from *Briefe an Bülow*.
22. From every possible side . . . *Ibid.*, II, 440n, from *Briefe an Bülow*.
23. You have no conception of thankfulness . . . *Ibid.*, II, 425.
24. I have all along left it . . . *Liszt's Letters*, I, 214.

CHAPTER THIRTY-SEVEN

1. My impatience to see you . . . Wagner-Liszt, I, 272.
2. I thirst for a long, long sleep . . . *Ibid.*, I, 289.
3. Many of his friends . . . Liszt-Wittgenstein, I, 144.
4. Why do I go on living . . . Wagner-Liszt, I, 270. (But here as occasionally elsewhere I have used Newman's translation, which is superior to Hueffer's, when available.)
5. Nothing that lies within the possibility . . . *Ibid.*, I, 191.
6. Marx is absolutely right . . . Liszt: Essay on Marx in the *Gesammelte Schriften*, vol. V. (Once again, the translation is Newman's.)
7. My delight as everything . . . Wagner: *Life*, II, 599.
8. Sadness, sadness! . . . Wagner-Liszt, I, 299.
9. The rushing sound . . . Wagner: *Life*, II, 603.
10. The bright and merry spirit . . . *Ibid.*, II, 605.
11. In those days it was impossible . . . *Ibid.*, II, 605.
12. It was on the same day . . . Du Moulin Eckhart: *Cosima*, I, 748–749.
13. I was older . . . Marie Fürstin zu Hohenlohe: *Erinnerungen an Richard Wagner* (Weimar, 1938). Translated in Alice Sokoloff: *Cosima Wagner* (New York, 1969), p. 61.
14. . . . tell the Princess . . . *Correspondance de Liszt et de sa fille*, p. 93.
15. Here I stand and stare . . . Wagner-Liszt, I, 333.
16. If we had not loved . . . *Ibid.*, I, 144.
17. A certain one . . . "Lettres d'un père et de sa fille," *Revue des Deux Mondes*, December 15, 1935, and January 1, 1936.
18. My dearest, dearest, unique Franz . . . Wagner-Liszt, II, 81.
19. When we compare letters . . . *Ibid.*, II, 154.
20. Even in May . . . *Ibid.*, II, 151 et seq.
21. Marvelous as your playing was . . . *Ibid.*, II, 152.
22. Try, best and dearest friend . . . Quoted by Newman: *Wagner*, II, 493, from Peter Raabe: *Franz Liszt: Leben und Schaffen* (Stuttgart, 1931), p. 175.
23. Since I have never in my life tasted . . . Wagner-Liszt, II, 54.
24. When in an attempt to make clear . . . Wagner: *Life*, II, 650.
25. As I was sure that Liszt . . . *Ibid.*, II, 649.
26. Dante in the Paradise has not succeeded . . . Wagner-Liszt, II, 92–99.
27. . . . though we never actually came to blows . . . Wagner: *Life*, II, 653.
28. The curious spell of excitement . . . *Ibid.*, II, 651 et seq.
29. We were compelled to remain . . . *Ibid.*, II, 655 et seq.
30. Though you are so dear to me . . . Wagner-Liszt, II, 166.

CHAPTER THIRTY-EIGHT

1. I have led my young Siegfried . . . Wagner-Liszt, II, 204.
2. My dearest Franz, whatever in my conduct . . . *Ibid.*, II, 213.
3. I very much wish to incline Dingelstedt . . . *Ibid.*, II, 258.
4. I do not desire you to force . . . *Ibid.*, II, 265.
5. All the children in the world . . . *Ibid.*, II, 266.
6. In the name of God, what can I do with *Diane de Solange* . . . Neither this letter of December 31, nor Liszt's reply to it — "In order not to expose myself again . . ." — was included in the first edition of the correspondence or the Hueffer translation. They are in Newman: *Wagner*, II, 577 and 579 respectively, without attribution.
7. It is you, my friend, whom I see to be suffering . . . Wagner-Liszt, II, 280.
8. I have heard to my horror . . . *Ibid.*, II, 283.

CHAPTER THIRTY-NINE

1. Let me just add this . . . *Liszt's Letters*, I, 196.
2. I am as convinced as you are . . . Berlioz: *Milieu du chemin*, p. 94.
3. We spoke a great deal about you with Wagner . . . *Briefe an Franz Liszt*, II, 30–31.
4. One real gain I bring back from England . . . Wagner-Liszt, II, 102.
5. . . . we went to drink punch . . . Quoted by Barzun, II, 111n, from letter published in *Le Temps*, December 20, 1894.
6. I found . . . it . . . difficult . . . Wagner: *Life*, II, 629.
7. I have read and re-read this strange piece . . . Berlioz: *Journal des Débats*, February 9, 1860. Printed in *À travers chants*, pp. 305–317.
8. If the music of the future means . . . *Ibid.*
9. For myself, I heartily regret . . . Wagner in the *Débats* of February 22, 1860; "A Letter to Hector Berlioz" in Wagner, *Gesammelte Schriften*, VII, 82–86.
10. In his dry and theatrical delivery . . . Wagner, *Life*, II, 676.
11. What a performance . . . Berlioz: *Correspondance inédite* (Paris, n.d.), pp. 278–280.
12. . . . in the world of the present . . . Quoted by Newman: *Wagner*, III, 21, without attribution. (This letter is not in the Hueffer translation.)
13. Something led me to speak . . . Berlioz: *Memoirs*, p. 494.
14. They read easily and beautifully . . . Newman: "Berlioz: Romantic and Classic," *Musical Studies*, 1905.
15. . . . we must not misread Berlioz . . . Barzun, II, 130.
16. You were not there, nor Liszt either . . . *Briefe an die Fürstin Sayn-Wittgenstein* (Leipzig, 1903), p. 132.
17. Liszt abandoned Berlioz's side . . . Barzun, II, 199.
18. . . . although he read the libretto with delight . . . *Ibid.*, II, 155.

19. Berlioz was so good . . . *Liszt's Letters*, II, 7.
20. Voilà, says Berlioz . . . Liszt-Wittgenstein, II, 172.

CHAPTER FORTY

1. If I have spent a dozen years . . . Liszt: *Briefe an eine Freundin* (Leipzig, 1893–1904), III, 135.
2. I feel it my duty . . . Schorn: *Menschenalter*, p. 107.
3. The valley was like a crater . . . Liszt-Wittgenstein, I, 214.
4. Don't lament too much . . . Liszt: *Freundin*, p. 28.
5. Such a weight . . . *Ibid.*, p. 9.
6. My heart began to weep . . . Liszt-Wittgenstein, I, 314.
7. This need to be something to somebody . . . Liszt: *Freundin*, p. 31.
8. Whether the great political event . . . Wagner-Liszt, II, 76.
9. It is an opinion . . . Liszt-Wittgenstein, II, 77.
10. No further religious obstacles . . . Liszt: *Freundin*, p. 155.
11. That would be very dangerous . . . Liszt-Wittgenstein, II, 192–193. (I have cast this in the form of a dialogue, which uses Liszt's words but which is not quite the way in which he presents them.)
12. My life has been a long odyssey . . . *Ibid.*, II, 129.
13. You are freer of your time . . . Liszt-d'Agoult, II, 410.
14. *Elle est trop digne* . . . Quoted by Vier, III, 137, from unpublished letter in Ollivier Archive.
15. You tell me . . . Quoted by Vier, III, 138, from unpublished letter in Ollivier Archive.
16. I am so upset . . . Du Moulin Eckhart: *Cosima*, I, 94–95.
17. What they want for a husband . . . Liszt: *Freundin*, p. 43.
18. They waited till I was out of the way . . . Bory: *Liszt et ses enfants*, pp. 104–110.
19. *Wie gehtes Frau Schumann* . . . *Ibid.*, p. 141.
20. What a dishonor! . . . *Ibid.*, pp. 132–133.
21. Till now it would have been . . . *Briefwechsel zwischen Franz Liszt und Hans von Bülow* (Leipzig, 1898), pp. 152–153.
22. Cosima, child of genius . . . Herwegh: *Au printemps des dieux*, p. 167.
23. It is impossible for me . . . Bory: *Liszt et ses enfants*, p. 212.
24. Obviously she would be enchanted . . . Quoted by Vier, III, 323, n. 111, from unpublished letter in Ollivier Archive.
25. . . . dignity and nobility . . . Quoted by Newman: *Man Liszt*, p. 151, from Bülow, *Briefe*.
26. How right it is . . . Herwegh: *Printemps des dieux*, p. 238.

CHAPTER FORTY-ONE

1. The news from Petersburg . . . Liszt–Carl Alexander, p. 84.
2. You were right to send me here . . . Liszt-Wittgenstein, I, 500–507.

3. Sometimes I feel my heart will burst . . . Bory: *Liszt et ses enfants*, p. 225.
4. Madame la Comtesse . . . Quoted by Vier, III, 323, n. 123, from unpublished letter in Ollivier Archive.
5. When I have finished . . . *Liszt's Letters*, I, 418.
6. The great business of her life . . . Liszt: *Freundin*, p. 122.
7. The Altenburg is an enigma . . . Cornelius, I, 474.
8. . . . The Wagnerian colossus . . . Searle, p. 122.
9. I am eager to cut the bonds . . . Quoted by Barzun, II, 228, from *Lettres intimes*.
10. . . . To my thinking, the best thing . . . "Lettres d'un père et de sa fille," January 1, 1936.
11. Liszt had already fallen back . . . Wagner: *Life*, II, 779–780.
12. Listening to me talk this way . . . Liszt-d'Agoult, II, 197, 198, 199.
13. And so I again crossed Thuringia . . . Wagner: *Life*, II, 787.
14. As we were all saying goodbye to Liszt . . . *Ibid.*, II, 790.
15. It is impossible for me to assemble on a single threshold . . . Liszt-Wittgenstein, II, 209.
16. Be then, and once again . . . *Ibid.*, II, 236.
17. May I give you serenity . . . *Ibid.*, II, 238.
18. He now wears the Abbé's cassock . . . Ferdinand Gregorovius: *Römische Tagebücher, herausgegeben von Friedrich Althaus* (Stuttgart, 1892), pp. 298–299.
19. You know, said Liszt . . . H. R. Haweis: *My Musical Life* (London, 1886).

Index

Photo: Rollie McKenna

Eleanor Perényi was born in Washington, D.C., the daughter of a captain in the United States Navy and the novelist Grace Zaring Stone. Married at an early age to the late Baron Zsigmond Perényi, she lived in Hungary for some years, and has described her life then in the memoir *More Was Lost*. In recent years she has written on the arts, travel, and people for *The Atlantic, Harper's, Esquire,* and other periodicals. The mother of a son, she now lives in Stonington, Connecticut.